AutoCAD® & AutoCAD
All-in-One Desk Refere
For Dummies®

T0281656

Commonly Used 2D and 3D AutoCAD Commands

2D Command	Purpose	3D Command	Purpose
LINE	Draws a line	DASHBOARD	Displays the Dashboard palette
CIRCLE	Draws a circle	BOX	Draws a 3D solid box
INSERT	Inserts a block or drawing file	UNION	Combines two or more 3D solids to form a single 3D solid
ERASE	Removes/deletes objects	3DORBIT	Rotates the camera of the current view around a drawing
MOVE	Moves objects	3DMOVE	Moves objects in 3D space
COPY	Copies objects from one place to another	3DROTATE	Rotates objects in 3D space
ROTATE	Rotates objects	LIGHTS	Adds user-defined lights
PAN	Pans a drawing	MATERIALS	Displays the Materials palette
ZOOM	Zooms in and out in a drawing	RENDER	Renders the current view of a drawing

Commonly Used AutoCAD Keyboard Shortcuts

Keyboard Shortcut	Command	Purpose
Ctrl+N	NEW	Creates a new drawing
Ctrl+O	OPEN	Displays the Select File dialog box
Ctrl+P	PLOT	Displays the Plot dialog box
F2	TEXTSCR	Toggles the AutoCAD Text Window on and off
F3	OSNAP	Toggles running object snap mode on and off
F8	ORTHO	Toggles ortho mode on and off
F9	SNAP	Toggles snap mode on and off
F10	POLAR	Toggles polar mode on and off

Drawing Scale and Limits Charts: Feet and Inches

Drawing Scale	81/2" x 11"	11" x 17"	24" x 36"	30" x 42"	36" x 48"
1/16" = 1'–0"	136' x 176'	176' x 272'	384' x 576'	480' x 672'	576' x 768'
1/8" = 1'–0"	68' x 88'	88' x 136'	192' x 288'	240' x 336'	288' x 384'
1/4" = 1'–0"	34' x 44'	44' x 68'	96' x 144'	120' x 168'	144' x 192'
1/2" = 1'–0"	17' x 22'	22' x 34'	48' x 72'	60' x 84'	72' x 96'
3/4" = 1'–0"	11'–4" x 14'–8"	14'–8" x 22'–8"	32' x 48'	40' x 56'	48' x 64'
1" = 1'–0"	8'–6" x 11'	11' x 17'	24' x 36'	30' x 42'	36' x 48'

For Dummies: Bestselling Book Series for Beginners

BESTSELLING BOOK SERIES

AutoCAD® & AutoCAD LT®
All-in-One Desk Reference
For Dummies®

Cheat Sheet

Drawing Scale and Limits Charts: Millimeters

Drawing Scale	210 x 297 mm	297 x 420 mm	420 x 594 mm	594 x 841 mm	841x 1,189 mm
1:200	42,000 x 59,400 mm	59,400 x 84,000 mm	84,000 x 118,800 mm	118,800 x 168,200 mm	168,200 x 237,800 mm
1:100	21,000 x 29,700 mm	29,700 x 42,000 mm	42,000 x 59,400 mm	59,400 x 84,100 mm	84,100 x 118,900 mm
1:50	10,500 x 14,850 mm	14,850 x 21,000 mm	21,000 x 29,700 mm	29,700 x 42,050 mm	42,050 x 59,450 mm
1:20	4,200 x 5,940 mm	5,940 x 8,400 mm	8400 x 11,880 mm	11,880 x 16,820 mm	16,820 x 23,780 mm
1:10	2,100 x 2,970 mm	2,970 x 4,200 mm	4,200 x 5,940 mm	5,940 x 8,410 mm	8,410 x 11,890 mm
1:5	1,050 x 1,485 mm	1,485 x 2,100 mm	2,100 x 2,970 mm	2,970 x 4,205 mm	4,205 x 5,945 mm

Drawing Scale and Text Height Chart: Feet and Inches

Drawing Scale	Drawing Scale Factor	1/8"Text Height	3/32" Text Height
1/16" = 1'–0"	192	24"	18"
1/8" = 1'–0"	96	12"	9"
1/4" = 1'–0"	48	6"	4 1/2"
1/2" = 1'–0"	24	3"	2 1/4"
3/4" = 1'–0"	16	2"	1 1/2"
1" = 1'–0"	12	1 1/2"	1 1/8"

Drawing Scale and Text Height Chart: Millimeters

Drawing Scale	Drawing Scale Factor	3 mm Text Height	2.5 mm Text Height
1:200	200	600 mm	500 mm
1:100	100	300 mm	250 mm
1:50	50	150 mm	125 mm
1:20	20	60 mm	50 mm
1:10	10	30 mm	25 mm
1:5	5	15 mm	12.5 mm

Wiley, the Wiley Publishing logo, For Dummies, the Dummies Man logo, the For Dummies Bestselling Book Series logo and all related trade dress are trademarks or registered trademarks of John Wiley & Sons, Inc. and/or its affiliates. All other trademarks are property of their respective owners.

Copyright © 2006 Wiley Publishing, Inc. All rights reserved. Item 5260-6. For more information about Wiley Publishing, call 1-800-762-2974.

For Dummies: Bestselling Book Series for Beginners

AutoCAD® & AutoCAD LT®

ALL-IN-ONE DESK REFERENCE

FOR

DUMMIES®

AutoCAD® & AutoCAD LT®

ALL-IN-ONE DESK REFERENCE

FOR

DUMMIES®

by Lee Ambrosius and David Byrnes

Wiley Publishing, Inc.

AutoCAD® & AutoCAD LT® All-in-One Desk Reference For Dummies®

Published by
Wiley Publishing, Inc.
111 River Street
Hoboken, NJ 07030-5774
www.wiley.com

Copyright © 2006 by Wiley Publishing, Inc., Indianapolis, Indiana

Published simultaneously in Canada

No part of this publication may be reproduced, stored in a retrieval system or transmitted in any form or by any means, electronic, mechanical, photocopying, recording, scanning or otherwise, except as permitted under Sections 107 or 108 of the 1976 United States Copyright Act, without either the prior written permission of the Publisher, or authorization through payment of the appropriate per-copy fee to the Copyright Clearance Center, 222 Rosewood Drive, Danvers, MA 01923, (978) 750-8400, fax (978) 646-8600. Requests to the Publisher for permission should be addressed to the Legal Department, Wiley Publishing, Inc., 10475 Crosspoint Blvd., Indianapolis, IN 46256, (317) 572-3447, fax (317) 572-4355, or online at http://www.wiley.com/go/permissions.

Trademarks: Wiley, the Wiley Publishing logo, For Dummies, the Dummies Man logo, A Reference for the Rest of Us!, The Dummies Way, Dummies Daily, The Fun and Easy Way, Dummies.com, and related trade dress are trademarks or registered trademarks of John Wiley & Sons, Inc. and/or its affiliates in the United States and other countries, and may not be used without written permission. AutoCAD and AutoCAD LT are registered trademarks of Autodesk, Inc. All other trademarks are the property of their respective owners. Wiley Publishing, Inc., is not associated with any product or vendor mentioned in this book.

LIMIT OF LIABILITY/DISCLAIMER OF WARRANTY: THE PUBLISHER AND THE AUTHOR MAKE NO REPRESENTATIONS OR WARRANTIES WITH RESPECT TO THE ACCURACY OR COMPLETENESS OF THE CONTENTS OF THIS WORK AND SPECIFICALLY DISCLAIM ALL WARRANTIES, INCLUDING WITHOUT LIMITATION WARRANTIES OF FITNESS FOR A PARTICULAR PURPOSE. NO WARRANTY MAY BE CREATED OR EXTENDED BY SALES OR PROMOTIONAL MATERIALS. THE ADVICE AND STRATEGIES CONTAINED HEREIN MAY NOT BE SUITABLE FOR EVERY SITUATION. THIS WORK IS SOLD WITH THE UNDERSTANDING THAT THE PUBLISHER IS NOT ENGAGED IN RENDERING LEGAL, ACCOUNTING, OR OTHER PROFESSIONAL SERVICES. IF PROFESSIONAL ASSISTANCE IS REQUIRED, THE SERVICES OF A COMPETENT PROFESSIONAL PERSON SHOULD BE SOUGHT. NEITHER THE PUBLISHER NOR THE AUTHOR SHALL BE LIABLE FOR DAMAGES ARISING HEREFROM. THE FACT THAT AN ORGANIZATION OR WEBSITE IS REFERRED TO IN THIS WORK AS A CITATION AND/OR A POTENTIAL SOURCE OF FURTHER INFORMATION DOES NOT MEAN THAT THE AUTHOR OR THE PUBLISHER ENDORSES THE INFORMATION THE ORGANIZATION OR WEBSITE MAY PROVIDE OR RECOMMENDATIONS IT MAY MAKE. FURTHER, READERS SHOULD BE AWARE THAT INTERNET WEBSITES LISTED IN THIS WORK MAY HAVE CHANGED OR DISAPPEARED BETWEEN WHEN THIS WORK WAS WRITTEN AND WHEN IT IS READ.

For general information on our other products and services, please contact our Customer Care Department within the U.S. at 800-762-2974, outside the U.S. at 317-572-3993, or fax 317-572-4002.

For technical support, please visit www.wiley.com/techsupport.

Wiley also publishes its books in a variety of electronic formats. Some content that appears in print may not be available in electronic books.

Library of Congress Control Number: 2006920621

ISBN-13: 978-0-471–75260-8

ISBN-10: 0-471-75260-6

10 9 8 7 6 5 4 3 2 1

1O/RY/QX/QW/IN

WILEY

About the Authors

Lee Ambrosius was a resident of a cubicle farm for about eight years. One day he decided that he wanted to do something different, so he went into business for himself. In 2005, Lee decided to venture off into the CAD industry as an independent consultant and programmer as the owner of HyperPics, LLC in De Pere, Wisconsin, and on the Web at www.hyperpics.com. He has been using AutoCAD since 1994, when he was first exposed to Release 12 for DOS, and has been customizing and programming AutoCAD since 1996. Lee has been an AutoCAD consultant and trainer for 10 years and is both an Autodesk Authorized Author and an Autodesk Authorized Developer.

During his past 10 years in the CAD industry, Lee has authored a variety of works that include articles for CAD magazines and white papers for Autodesk. He has also been a contributing author for a few AutoCAD books. Lee has done technical editing for the two most recent editions of *AutoCAD For Dummies* and the three most recent editions of *AutoCAD and AutoCAD LT Bible*. *AutoCAD & AutoCAD LT All-in-One Desk Reference For Dummies* is his first venture into coauthoring a book.

David Byrnes began his drafting career on the boards in 1979 and discovered computer-assisted doodling shortly thereafter. He first learned AutoCAD with version 1.4, around the time when personal computers switched from steam to diesel power. Dave is based in Vancouver, Canada, and has been an AutoCAD consultant and trainer for fifteen years. Dave is an AutoCAD Authorized Author, a contributing editor for *Cadalyst* magazine, and has been a contributing author to ten books on AutoCAD. Dave teaches AutoCAD and other computer graphics applications at Emily Carr Institute of Art + Design and British Columbia Institute of Technology in Vancouver. Dave has tech edited six editions of *AutoCAD For Dummies* and is coauthor of *AutoCAD 2007 For Dummies.*

Dedication

From Lee: To Kristina, Isaac, Amber, and Chloe; my wife and lovely kids for hanging in there during the long hours I was working on this book. I also can't forget everyone else who has had some influence on my career, through both the good and the bad.

From Dave: To Anna and Delia, the two women in my life, who remind me there are other things besides keyboards and mice (and sometimes they have to try REALLY hard).

Authors' Acknowledgments

Lee Ambrosius: I have to give a special thanks to the great folks at Wiley for being supportive through this entire project and giving me this opportunity. Next, I want to thank David for letting me be a coauthor on this project. Moving up from technical editor to coauthor was a big step — thanks for giving me the chance. The next two people were very inspirational on this project and helped keep things moving along: Colleen Totz Diamond and Tiffany Franklin. I think we made it.

Thanks to Shaan Hurley, Bud Schroeder, Kelly Miller, and the other great professionals at Autodesk for taking the time to answer questions as they came up during this project. Last, but not least, thanks to our technical editor, Mark Douglas. Mark is most definitely not a stranger to AutoCAD; he is blazing his own trail in the CAD community as a respected individual who is always willing to help out a fellow user in need.

David Byrnes: Thanks to Mark Middlebrook for bringing me aboard the Dummies train and for collaborating on the initial proposal and table of contents for this book. Thanks, also, to Lee Ambrosius for joining up in the book's darkest days and for picking up more and more of the project as time went on.

Thanks, too, to colleagues and friends at Autodesk — Shaan Hurley, Nate Bartley, and Bud Schroeder — who never seem to mind being asked even the dumbest questions.

At Wiley, thanks to Terri Varveris, who got the project off the ground, and Tiffany Ma, who shepherded it through with enthusiasm and an unbelievably awesome degree of patience. It was also a great pleasure to work with project editor, Colleen Totz Diamond, who deserves medals for patience and diplomacy!

And by no means last (someone has to bring up the rear), thanks to Mark Douglas for taking on the tech editing job. Mark's expertise and enthusiasm are well known and respected in the AutoCAD community, and we're delighted to have him with us.

Publisher's Acknowledgments

We're proud of this book; please send us your comments through our online registration form located at www.dummies.com/register/.

Some of the people who helped bring this book to market include the following:

Acquisitions, Editorial, and Media Development

Project Editors: Colleen Totz Diamond and Linda D. Morris

Acquisitions Editors: Tiffany Ma and Kyle Looper

Technical Editor: Mark Douglas

Editorial Manager: Jodi Jensen

Media Development Manager: Laura VanWinkle

Editorial Assistant: Amanda Foxworth

Sr. Editorial Assistant: Cherie Case

Cartoons: Rich Tennant (www.the5thwave.com)

Composition Services

Project Coordinator: Tera Knapp

Layout and Graphics: Carl Byers, Andrea Dahl, Denny Hager, Joyce Haughey, Stephanie D. Jumper, Alicia South

Proofreaders: Vickie Broyles, Melissa D. Buddendeck, Leeann Harney, Christine Pingleton, Dwight Ramsey

Indexer: Valerie Haynes Perry

Publishing and Editorial for Technology Dummies

    Richard Swadley, Vice President and Executive Group Publisher

    Andy Cummings, Vice President and Publisher

    Mary Bednarek, Executive Acquisitions Director

    Mary C. Corder, Editorial Director

Publishing for Consumer Dummies

    Diane Graves Steele, Vice President and Publisher

    Joyce Pepple, Acquisitions Director

Composition Services

    Gerry Fahey, Vice President of Production Services

    Debbie Stailey, Director of Composition Services

Contents at a Glance

Table of Contents

Introduction

For many reasons, AutoCAD is much different from most applications that you will ever use. The main reason goes back some 20 years to when AutoCAD was first introduced as a low-cost CAD solution on microcomputers. (CAD stands for *Computer-Aided Drafting* or *Computer-Aided Design,* depending on whom you ask.) Most CAD applications back then ran on very large and expensive mainframe computers, not something that you could take on-site with you.

With the introduction of AutoCAD, CAD wasn't as foreign of a topic as it once was, but it still had an uphill climb against the wide use and adoption of drafting boards. A drafting board, you might be asking yourself? Yes, prior to computers and CAD, all designs were done with pencil and paper; if you were really good, you used ink and paper. Today, paper still plays a role in distributing designs, but most designs are now done in a CAD application that allows you to do much more complex things that were not possible with board drafting.

As times and drafting practices have changed, AutoCAD has either led in setting the pace for change or has forced change with some things. Some of these changes have helped to usher in the era of improved design collaboration across the Internet and better electronic file sharing with non-CAD users. Since all objects in a drawing are electronic, AutoCAD allows you to quickly manipulate and mange them without the need to break out the eraser shield and eraser as you would on a board. Autodesk continues to improve the way you can visualize designs and concepts through improvements in 3D modeling and other features.

AutoCAD 2007 gives you the tools you need to create accurate 2D and 3D designs, but isn't very easy to just pick up and become productive right away. This book helps you get up to speed faster so that you can be productive in all main areas of the application — which include 2D and 3D drafting, printing and sharing designs, and customizing and programming.

About This Book

The *AutoCAD & AutoCAD LT All-in-One Desk Reference For Dummies* gives you an understanding of all the main features that you need to know in order to be productive with AutoCAD and AutoCAD LT. The *All-in-One Desk References For Dummies* are much different from other *For Dummies* books you may have read; more information is crammed between the two covers, and the content is more in-depth. This book is laid out to focus on individual topics and allows you the freedom of moving around between its minibooks. We recommend that if you are not familiar (or somewhat familiar) with AutoCAD that you read through Books I and II before moving on to the other minibooks.

After you read this book, don't let it run too far from your desk — you will find it helpful as a reference whenever you might need it.

Foolish Assumptions

We expect that you know how to use the Windows operating system and understand the basics of navigating folders and starting applications. To take advantage of everything that AutoCAD offers and what is contained in this book, we assume that you have at least an Internet connection — dial-up at least, but a high-speed cable or DSL connection would be best. As long as you have AutoCAD or AutoCAD LT installed on the computer in front of you and a connection to the Internet, you are ready to get started.

Conventions Used in This Book

Text that you would type at the command line or dynamic input tooltip, in a text box, or any other place you enter text appears in **bold typeface.** Examples of AutoCAD prompts appear in a `special typeface`.

At times, you may see something like the phrase "choose File⇨Save As." The small arrow (⇨) in this example indicates that you are to choose the File menu and then choose the Save As command.

How This Book Is Organized

The following sections describe the minibooks that this book is broken into.

Book 1: AutoCAD Basics

Book I familiarizes you with the AutoCAD interface and the basics of working with drawing files. It provides some background on AutoCAD and AutoCAD LT, and lists which versions are compatible with each other. It explains how to start the application and sends you on a guided tour of the interface. You also see how to interact with commands using dialog boxes and the command line, and how to get help when you need it from the application. You also get a brief rundown on creating and modifying some of the basic 2D objects, and using a few of the viewing commands. The last two chapters of the minibook show how to use some of the general object and drawing format properties and settings, as well as the different drafting aids that help you create accurate 2D and 3D drawings.

Book II: 2D Drafting

Book II covers many of the commands that are used for creating and working with 2D designs. The first part of the minibook focuses on creating 2D objects that range from lines, circles, and arcs to more complex objects, such as ellipses. Then you see how to select and modify objects that have been created in a drawing. Modifying objects is one of the main tasks that you perform in AutoCAD, next to viewing and creating new objects in a drawing.

Book III: Annotating Drawings

Book III covers how to create an annotation in a drawing that explains a feature or shows the measurement of an object. Annotation in AutoCAD includes text, dimensions, leaders, and hatch. For example, you see how to create single and multiline text objects and tables. The chapter also includes formatting specific characteristics of text and tables, performing spell checking, and doing a find-and-replace on text strings.

Book IV: LT Differences

Book IV focuses on AutoCAD LT and how it is different from AutoCAD, along with using it in the same environment as AutoCAD and expanding AutoCAD LT through customization and other means. This minibook also explains what to watch out for when you use both AutoCAD and AutoCAD LT in the same office.

Book V: 3D Modeling

Book V covers how to create, edit, view, and visualize 3D objects. You get the basics of working in 3D, and see how to specify coordinates and adjust the coordinate system to make it easier for you to create and modify objects above the x,y plane. This minibook also tells you how to navigate and view a 3D model in AutoCAD and AutoCAD LT.

Book VI: Advanced Drafting

Book VI covers the advanced drafting features that go beyond 2D drafting, which include working with blocks, external references, and raster images.

Book VII: Publishing Drawings

Book VII covers generating a hard copy (paper copy) or an electronic version of a drawing that can be viewed without AutoCAD or AutoCAD LT. You see how to use page setups to define how part of a drawing should be printed, and how to create floating viewports and layouts to help output a drawing. You also discover sheet sets, and how you can use them to manage and organize sets of drawings. Sheet sets provide ways to open drawings, keep data in sync through the use of fields and views, and output a number of drawings. This minibook also shows how to create plot configurations and plot styles, and how to plot and publish a drawing layout or layouts to create hard copies or electronic versions of drawings.

Book VIII: Collaboration

Book VIII covers some advanced topics that include CAD standards and file sharing, as well as how to use electronic files for project collaboration. You gain an understanding of the concepts behind CAD standards, as well as how to use the available CAD standards tools to help maintain and enforce CAD standards.

Book IX: Customizing AutoCAD

Book IX covers techniques that are used to customize AutoCAD and AutoCAD LT, which allows you to reduce the number of repetitive tasks and steps that you might have to do to complete a design.

Book X: Programming AutoCAD

Book X covers extending AutoCAD through some of the different programming languages that it supports. Programming AutoCAD is different from customizing it, but the goal of reducing repetitive tasks and steps that you have to do to complete a design are the same.

Icons Used in This Book

This book uses the following icons to denote paragraphs that may be of special interest:

This icon indicates information that may save some time or help you not to fall too far from the path to success. For the most part, Tip paragraphs are designed to help guide you through some of the overwhelming parts of AutoCAD and to give you at times what might not always be the most obvious way to get to the desired end result faster.

These paragraphs give insight into the inner workings of AutoCAD or something that you won't typically need to know to use the program, but may find interesting. As you read through the book the first time, you might want to think of the Technical Stuff paragraphs as bonus material and not as required reading, so feel free to skip over them.

This icon helps you to stay away from the deep-end of AutoCAD and helps you to keep out of trouble. Failure to adhere to the message may result in an undesired side effect to your design.

This icon helps to give the gray matter an extra nudge here and there for things that we talked about earlier in the book. AutoCAD is a large program, and it takes a bit of time to put all the pieces together, so we give you some friendly reminders along the way.

This icon helps those who are using AutoCAD LT to know what features are missing from AutoCAD LT that are in AutoCAD. At times, you may not know the differences between the two programs, and these paragraphs can help you determine whether you should be using AutoCAD instead of AutoCAD LT.

This icon highlights what's new in AutoCAD 2007.

Book I

AutoCAD Basics

The 5th Wave   By Rich Tennant

"You know kids – you can't buy them just <u>any</u> multi-dimensional drafting software."

Contents at a Glance

Chapter 1: Drawing on (and in) AutoCAD

Welcome to *AutoCAD & AutoCAD LT All-in-One Desk Reference For Dummies,* your one-stop shop for AutoCAD users of every skill level. If you've read this far, we assume you know a thing or two about the world's most popular computer-aided drafting program — enough, at least, to know that computer-aided drafting usually goes by the much friendlier acronym of CAD. (And if you're a brand-new user, you might also cast an eye at this book's companion volume, *AutoCAD 2007 For Dummies.*)

The *AutoCAD & AutoCAD LT All-in-One Desk Reference For Dummies* is aimed at AutoCAD users in every discipline — architecture, mechanical design, mapping and GIS, product design, survey and civil engineering, diagramming . . . whatever your field, you'll find useful information here. We cover the entire CAD workflow process, not forgetting that 90 percent of the time, what you need to produce at the far end of the workflow is a clear and well laid-out paper drawing.

Using CAD in the Drawing Office

Personal computers revolutionized the drafting trade in the 1980s. Before that, some drafting was computerized, but the computers were mainframes or minicomputers (equivalent to the Stanley Steamers and Baker Electrics of the early days of motoring), well beyond the price range of most small architectural or engineering firms.

As a result, even as recently as 30 years ago, virtually all drafting was done by grizzled veterans wearing green eye-shades in smoke-filled back rooms. And not on computers!

In the old days, apprentice drafters (who were called draftsmen — or even draughtsmen — for it was a male profession) started their careers on the boards as tracers. Hard to believe, but there was a time before mechanical reproduction when every copy of an engineering drawing had to be traced, by hand, from an original. If you're being forced to learn AutoCAD, you may grumble, but you should be thankful you don't have to go through a procedure like that!

Today, your job is much easier because of AutoCAD. Maybe your boss is making you use AutoCAD, or you have to pass a course. But there are other reasons to use it — some of which may help you pass that course or get home from the office a little earlier. Here are some CAD advantages:

✦ **Precision.** AutoCAD is capable of precision to 14 significant digits (ask your math prof or your counselor why one digit should be more significant than another). That's way more precise than the best manual drafter could ever be.

✦ **Appearance.** AutoCAD-produced drawings are cleaner, easier to read when reduced, and more consistent than manually drafted drawings.

✦ **Reuse.** It's easy to copy and paste parts of drawings into other drawings for use in new projects.

✦ **Scalability.** You draw things full-size in AutoCAD on an infinitely large drawing sheet. This not only eliminates the possibility of scaling errors as you draw, it also lets you print your drawings at any scale.

✦ **Sharing work.** Drawing files can be shared with consultants and contractors who can add their own information without having to redraft the whole drawing.

✦ **Distributing work.** No more running dozens of prints and having them couriered to clients — using AutoCAD you can electronically transmit drawings via e-mail or upload them to shared Web space.

✦ **3D benefits.** You're not limited to 2D space; AutoCAD's drawing space is three-dimensional so you can create models of your projects and generate drawings from them.

Understanding AutoCAD Files and Formats

Like every other computer program under the sun, AutoCAD has its own digital file format. Unlike a Paint program, where the image is created by series of dots, CAD programs store the locations of objects in a database format. Every object in a drawing file — every line, arc, circle, dimension, and so on — is located in the 2D or 3D drawing space using a Cartesian coordinate system. For more on coordinate systems in AutoCAD, see Book VI.

AutoCAD is a *backward-compatible program*. This doesn't mean you can open drawings backward or upside-down. It simply means that files created in any version of AutoCAD can be opened in a same or newer version of AutoCAD. For example, if you have AutoCAD 2007, you can open a file created in any version of AutoCAD since the very first one. If you are working with an older version — say, AutoCAD 2002 — you can open files created in that version and older, but you can't open files created in AutoCAD 2004 or newer.

Unless we indicate otherwise (for example, with an AutoCAD LT icon), when we say AutoCAD 2007, we include AutoCAD LT 2007 as well. There are some differences — but more similarities — between the two programs. In the next section, "Seeing the LT," we take a closer look at LT differences.

Table 1-1 lists AutoCAD and AutoCAD LT versions together with their file formats.

Table 1-1	AutoCAD & AutoCAD LT Versions & File Formats		
AutoCAD Version	*AutoCAD LT Version*	*Release Year*	*DWG File Format*
AutoCAD 2007	AutoCAD LT 2007	2006	AutoCAD 2007
AutoCAD 2006	AutoCAD LT 2006	2005	AutoCAD 2004
AutoCAD 2005	AutoCAD LT 2005	2004	AutoCAD 2004
AutoCAD 2004	AutoCAD LT 2004	2003	AutoCAD 2004
AutoCAD 2002	AutoCAD LT 2002	2001	AutoCAD 2000
AutoCAD 2000i	AutoCAD LT 2000i	2000	AutoCAD 2000
AutoCAD 2000	AutoCAD LT 2000	1999	AutoCAD 2000
AutoCAD Release 14	AutoCAD LT 98 & LT 97	1997	AutoCAD R14
AutoCAD Release 13	AutoCAD LT 95	1994	AutoCAD R13
AutoCAD Release 12	AutoCAD LT Release 2	1992	AutoCAD R12

Remember, newer versions can open older files, but older versions generally can't open newer files. However, all recent versions of AutoCAD give you the option of saving back two versions. For example, in AutoCAD 2007's File menu, you can use the Save Drawing As command to save the drawing file back to AutoCAD 2004 format (which is also used by AutoCAD 2005 and AutoCAD 2006) so that anyone with that version can open your drawing.

AutoCAD 2007 saves all the way back to the AutoCAD R14 file format used by AutoCAD Release 14 as well as AutoCAD LT 97 and LT 98.

If you're using AutoCAD 2007, you can save drawing files that were created by Release 14, as long ago as early 1997. If you're using AutoCAD 2006 or earlier, you're limited to two file formats back. On the off chance you need to go back farther than that, go to www.autodesk.com/dwgtrueconvert and download a copy of the Autodesk DWG TrueConvert — a batch-conversion program that does not need AutoCAD or AutoCAD LT to be installed — and use it to save back to AutoCAD R14 DWG format.

Seeing the LT

As most people learn quickly, AutoCAD is an expensive program. To soften the blow, several years ago Autodesk introduced a slightly reduced-function version of the program called AutoCAD LT. There used to be an old rule called the 80–20 rule. The deal was, you got 80 percent of the functionality of AutoCAD for 20 percent of the price. Nowadays, the 20 percent is more like 40 percent of the price of AutoCAD, but it's still a good deal if you're unlikely to use all the features of the full program.

Mostly, this means if you never do (or never plan to do) 3D work in AutoCAD, you may — emphasis on *may* — be able to get away with LT and save a bundle. In other parts of this book, we tell you more about AutoCAD LT. Watch for the icons in the margins and read the LT-specific notes to see whether you're in that category. From personal experience, we can safely say that if you've never used AutoCAD before, you'll never miss the features that aren't carried over from full AutoCAD to LT. However, if you're a proficient AutoCAD user, and you find yourself in a new office that has LT rather than the full program, there may be dozens of features that you'll sorely miss.

We tell you much more about working with AutoCAD LT in Book IV.

Using AutoCAD's Latest-and-Greatest Feature Set

When we say *using AutoCAD's feature set,* we mean *really* using the program's features. It's all too common for offices to introduce new versions of AutoCAD to the drawing office without giving training or even demonstrations of new features to the people who have to use it. As a result, many drafters continue using the latest version in exactly the same way they learned 5 or 10 years ago. Through lack of interest (and since you're reading this book, we're sure *you* don't fall into that category) or — more likely — lack of time, many AutoCAD users simply bypass features that can make them more efficient.

For example, it's very common to read the AutoCAD newsgroups and see questions from people asking how to turn off this or that feature — often features like the right-click shortcut menus that specifically relate to the command being run.

In this book we're going to focus on some of the major new and enhanced features of recent releases such as sheet sets (new in AutoCAD 2005) and dynamic blocks (which first appeared in AutoCAD 2006). We're also going to make a strong pitch for paper space dimensioning, which was introduced way back with AutoCAD Release 11, but which only became really useable with AutoCAD 2002.

AutoCAD 2007 is the version to gladden the hearts of 3D mavens. Although there are a few new features for 2D users, the bulk of the new feature set takes off up the *z*-axis. AutoCAD 2007 at last makes working in 3D a relatively straightforward — even enjoyable — prospect. Here's a brief rundown of what's new:

✦ Enhanced 3D object creation and editing options, including the Dynamic User Coordinate System (DUCS) and the ability to select subobjects such as one face of a solid for editing.

✦ Easier creation of sectioned 3D objects.

✦ Enhanced 3D grid and 3D support for traditional drafting modes like polar tracking, object snap tracking, and Ortho mode.

✦ Lighting and a library of materials for working in 3D.

✦ Saveable visual styles, including "realistic" and "conceptual" modes.

✦ "First Person Navigation" — interactive motion through your 3D models using the 3DWALK and 3DFLY commands.

✦ Animated drawings — you can define and save a motion path within a drawing viewport. (They haven't figured out how to make it work on a printed drawing, though!)

✦ Workspaces have been around for a release or two, but they're really central to the full version of AutoCAD 2007. New workspaces are custom-tailored for 3D modeling and 2D drafting. (The latter is called "AutoCAD Classic.")

✦ The Dashboard is a new interface feature that blends the functionality of toolbars and menus.

Alas, LT still doesn't do 3D, so all those nifty new features are not part of the package. There is a new LT-only feature, however (it's LT-only because the full version already had it): AutoCAD 2006's dynamic blocks feature has been ported to LT. Now you can create as well as manipulate dynamic blocks.

There are still some goodies available to both full AutoCAD and LT, however:

✦ LT users have lamented the lack of full AutoCAD's Express Tools for years. The Express Tools package still isn't an option in LT, but all of perhaps the most useful subset — the layer tools — have been incorporated into the core program. And that means they're available to LT as well as to the full version.

✦ Both AutoCAD and AutoCAD LT sport a new way of working with external references: There's a new External References palette where you attach, detach, and otherwise manage not only external reference (DWG) files, but image files and DWF underlays as well.

✦ DWF Underlay provides a third type of "external reference." You can load a DWF as a base drawing in much the same way that you use external reference drawings.

✦ Both AutoCAD 2007 and AutoCAD LT 2007 can output to Adobe PDF format.

You can find more details on all these features throughout the rest of the book.

Chapter 2: Navigating the AutoCAD Interface

In This Chapter

✔ Starting AutoCAD

✔ Taking a quick tour around the AutoCAD window

✔ Talking (and listening) to AutoCAD

✔ Taking command

✔ Exploring program options

✔ Calling for Help

"*H*ow do I start thee? Let me count the ways . . ." (with apologies to Elizabeth Barrett Browning).

So, let me count the ways. . . .

Starting the Application

As with all good Windows programs — and AutoCAD is a very good Windows program — you can make your drawings appear on-screen in numerous ways.

For a start, there's the . . . er, Start button, the one that Mick and the Rolling Stones sang about way back when Bill Gates launched Windows 95 on an unsuspecting world. To get to AutoCAD 2007 (or AutoCAD LT 2007), you click Start⇨Programs⇨Autodesk⇨AutoCAD 2007⇨AutoCAD 2007. (You can tell you're at the end of the line because the last *AutoCAD 2007* has a unique program icon rather than a generic folder icon beside it.) Figure 2-1 shows the Windows XP Classic Start menu gradually revealing AutoCAD's program icon.

The Start button works, but one thing that working in Windows has taught us is to be efficient, and click-click-click-click-clicking is not the most direct way to go about opening the drawing editor. Wouldn't you know it — Microsoft and Autodesk between them have come up with several alternatives called — what else — shortcuts.

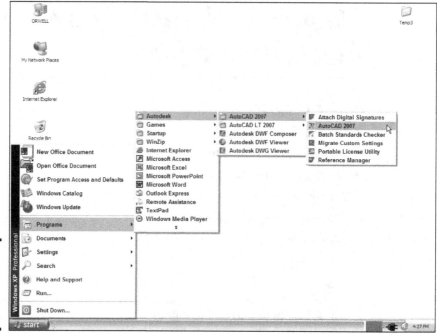

Figure 2-1:
Starting
AutoCAD
with the
Start button.

Creating Start menu shortcuts

If you're using Windows XP and the new XP-style Start menu (as opposed to the Windows NT/2000-style Classic Start menu), you may have a large AutoCAD 2007 button in the left column — the *top-level menu* in Windows XP parlance — that lets you click once to start the program (see Figure 2-2).

This section of the Start menu has room for six shortcuts. Supposedly, the programs you use the most inhabit these six slots, but somehow or other, most of them seem to be from Microsoft. You can remove these icons by right-clicking them and choosing Remove from This List.

To add an AutoCAD shortcut to the top-level Start menu, right-click an existing AutoCAD shortcut icon and choose Pin to Start Menu. If you're using the Windows 2000 or Windows XP Classic Start menu, you can still put a shortcut to AutoCAD on your Start menu by dragging a shortcut icon to your Start button (see Figure 2-3).

Figure 2-2:
Windows
XP's Start
menu.

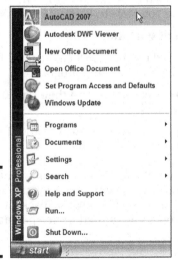

Figure 2-3:
The
Windows
XP Classic
Start menu.

Using desktop shortcuts

By default, AutoCAD creates a shortcut on your desktop when you install the
program. If you'd like more control over where AutoCAD opens — that is,

where it's going to save your files, or where it will look for files to open —
you can modify the desktop shortcut so that it directs AutoCAD to a specific
Start In folder. The following steps explain how:

1. **Right-click the AutoCAD icon on your desktop.**

   All recent versions of AutoCAD create a desktop icon by default. Unless
   you've renamed it, yours will say "AutoCAD 2007" (or earlier).

2. **Choose Properties from the shortcut menu.**

   A Properties window for the desktop icon appears, with the Properties
   tab current and a highlight in the Target field.

3. **Press Tab to place the highlight in the Start In field, and then type the
   path to your chosen folder.**

   By default, the Start In folder is identified as "UserDataCache," which
   actually points to your possibly overcrowded My Documents folder. If
   you're like us, a simple top-level folder (for example, C:\DRAWINGS)
   makes a lot more sense. Note that the folder must exist before you can
   modify the shortcut.

4. **Click OK to save the changes to the icon's properties.**

   The icon is now configured to open in — and save to — the specified
   folder, but there's another thing you have to do from inside AutoCAD.

5. **Double-click your new icon and start AutoCAD.**

   AutoCAD starts, but it's still wired for the My Documents folder. You
   need to modify a system variable to rewire the program.

6. **Type REMEMBERFOLDERS and press Enter, and then type 0 and press
   Enter to change the setting of 1 to 0.**

   When REMEMBERFOLDERS is set to 1 (the default), AutoCAD ignores the
   Start In folder specified in the desktop shortcut.

You can copy your desktop icon multiple times and set a different Start In
folder for each one. Using a *Start In* folder is helpful when you're working
on a couple of projects and you'd like to avoid switching back and forth
between the folders where your projects are stored while opening and
saving files.

Accessing files from Windows Explorer

If you need to work on drawings from multiple projects that may be in different folders all over your hard disk, sometimes it's easier to find the files in
Windows Explorer than in AutoCAD's Open Drawing dialog box. (Okay, we
find Windows Explorer handier than the My Computer window because you
can more easily move from folder to folder.) Simply double-clicking a drawing file will open that file in AutoCAD.

Touring the AutoCAD Interface

As far as Windows programs go, AutoCAD 2007 is about average in complexity. In fact, compared with its first Windows version (Release 12 for Windows), it's a marvel of simplicity. If you have a nodding familiarity with other Windows programs, you won't have difficulty navigating AutoCAD's interface.

Title bars

There are three levels of title bars in AutoCAD (and in most other programs as well). The program itself has a title bar, each drawing window has a title bar, and individual toolbars and palettes have their own title bars. Figure 2-4 gives you a sampling.

Toolbar handles

Program title bar   Drawing title bars

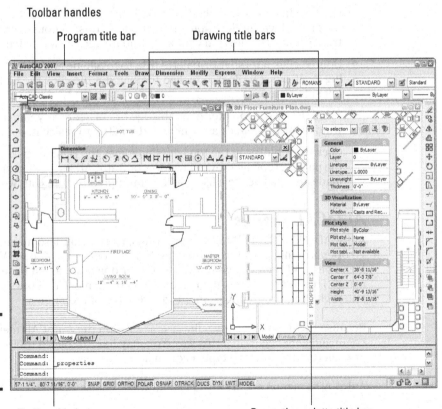

Figure 2-4:
A whole
mess of
title bars.

Toolbar title bar   Properties palette title bar

All three levels of title bar have more or less the same functions:

✦ The *program title bar* tells you the name of the program, which you know already

✦ The *drawing title bar* tells you the name of the drawing file you're working on and, optionally, its full path on your computer

✦ The *toolbar* or *palette* title bar tells you the name of a collection of tool buttons

Similarly, you can control all three elements — program, file, toolbar, or palette — through similar actions on the title bars. For example:

✦ Double-click the program title bar to toggle between a maximized or windowed application window

✦ Double-click the drawing title bar to switch a windowed drawing file to maximized within the application window (this, of course, is a one-way trip, as once the file is maximized, it no longer has a title bar)

✦ Double-click a toolbar or palette title to toggle between docked or floating locations. (To float a docked toolbar, double-click the handles at the left side or top.)

✦ Place the mouse pointer over an edge or corner of any unmaximized window or toolbar, or any undocked palette, to resize it.

✦ Click the X button at the top left (sometimes top right for palettes) to close the palette, toolbar, drawing window or AutoCAD itself. Of course, if you've made any changes to a file, you'll be prompted to save your work first.

AutoCAD menus

AutoCAD 2007, like all Windows programs, uses a standard menu interface. To open a menu, click the menu label (for example, File, Edit, or View) in the menu bar, and then run your mouse pointer down the menu to select a command. The first five or six menus are common to most Windows programs, although each program has unique as well as common items.

Because the menus occupy a finite space within the AutoCAD menu, not all commands are accessible this way. You may have to pick a toolbar button, or even (oh, the horror!) type a command.

AutoCAD's menus are arranged as follows:

✦ **File.** Create new or open existing files; print or publish drawings; add plotters or plot styles; access utility commands; close the program

✦ **Edit.** Undo/redo; cut/copy/paste; select objects; erase objects; find text in the drawing

Oddly enough, AutoCAD's editing commands are not located on the Edit menu — you'll find them on the Modify menu. Watch out especially for Copy, as there's one on each menu, and they do different things!

✦ **View.** Refresh the display; pan and zoom; create viewports; set viewpoints for 3D drawings; set render options

✦ **Insert.** Add blocks, raster images, and external references; insert objects from other programs; create hyperlinks

✦ **Format.** Establish layers, colors, linetypes, and lineweights; set appearance properties for text, dimensions, and tables; establish drawing limits

✦ **Tools.** Open dialog boxes or palettes to control system settings; edit blocks; use CAD standards; access customization tools

✦ **Draw.** Create primitive and complex objects; add text and hatching; define blocks and tables; create 3D surface and solid models (not in AutoCAD LT)

✦ **Dimension.** Add dimensions; format dimension styles

✦ **Modify.** Edit . . . er, modify existing drawing objects; check or match object properties

✦ **Express.** Additional tools and commands for creating and modifying all types of drawing objects

The Express menu is added as an option during program installation. We strongly recommend that you install the Express Tools when you install AutoCAD. Both Typical and Custom install options prompt you to install the Tools. If you blink and miss that option, you'll need to rerun AutoCAD 2007's Setup routine. The Express Tools are available in the full version of AutoCAD only — not in AutoCAD LT.

If you're using the full version of AutoCAD, we hope you've installed the Express Tools. We tell you more about the Express Tools in Book IX.

✦ **Window.** Cascade or tile open drawing windows; manage workspaces; lock down interface; select other open drawings

✦ **Help.** Access AutoCAD's built-in Help system; run Info Palette and New Features Workshop; access help on the Web

AutoCAD toolbars

AutoCAD 2007 has 39 toolbars (not including the Express Tools toolbars), most of which by default are closed. When you start AutoCAD for the first time and choose "AutoCAD Classic" as your workspace, you see the Standard, Styles, Layers, and Properties toolbars docked at the top of the screen, between the menu bar and the drawing area. Docked at the left is the Draw toolbar, and at the right, the Modify and Draw Order toolbars. Finally, the Workspaces toolbar is floating somewhere near the top of the drawing area. Assuming you installed the Express Tools, you also see the three Express Tools toolbars floating near the top of the drawing area (see Figure 2-5).

Docked toolbars   Floating toolbars

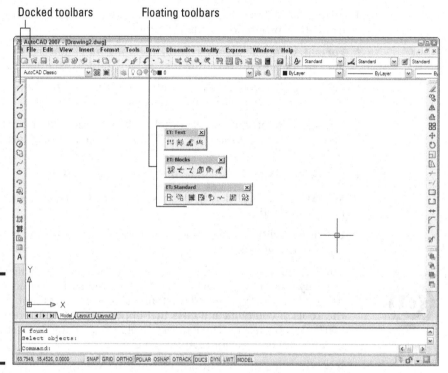

Figure 2-5:
The default
toolbar
arrange-
ment.

Unlike the menu system, the toolbars contain virtually all of AutoCAD's commands. Toolbars can easily be customized — we show you how in Book IX — and are a highly efficient way of working with the program.

You already know how to close toolbars. (*Hint:* It starts with an X.) The easiest way to open toolbars is to put your mouse pointer over any tool button and *right*-click. (Don't left-click or you'll run the command.) AutoCAD displays a menued list of all toolbars; just click the one you want to open.

To save constantly opening and closing toolbars, or having so many toolbars open that you can't see your drawing, you can open a bunch and then save them as a workspace. We tell you how in Book IX.

Palettes

AutoCAD 2004 introduced palettes, and they've become increasingly sophisticated with each release. Some dialog boxes from earlier releases, such as Object Properties, have been converted to palettes. Palettes have the advantage of staying open on-screen while you do other things (see Figure 2-6).

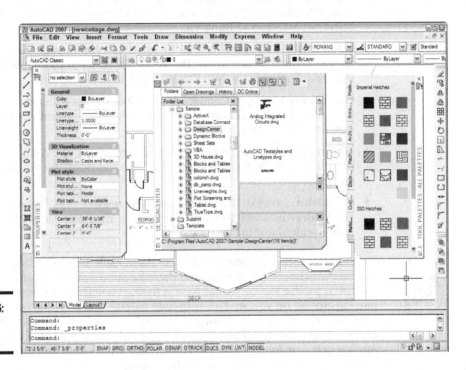

Figure 2-6:
A pile of
palettes.

You open and close palettes by clicking their tool buttons on the Standard toolbar, or use the Ctrl+key combination indicated in the following list. AutoCAD's tool palettes consist of the following:

- ✦ **Properties.** List all properties of selected objects, including layer, color, coordinates, style, and so on. (Ctrl+1). We fill you in on object properties in Chapter 5 of this minibook.

- ✦ **AutoCAD DesignCenter.** Use to copy objects from one drawing to another (Ctrl+2). We tell you more about DesignCenter in Book VI.

- ✦ **Tool palettes.** Use to access frequently used blocks, hatch patterns, and commands (Ctrl+3). For more on tool palettes, see Book VI.

✦ **External References.** The old Xref Manager and Image Manager dialog boxes have been combined into a new palette called, simply, External References. The new DWF Underlay feature is also managed from this palette. We give you the scoop on working with external reference drawings, raster images, and DWF underlays in Book VI.

✦ **Sheet Set Manager.** Set up drawing sets by project for printing and electronic distribution (Ctrl+4). We tell you all about sheet sets and the Sheet Set Manager in Book VII.

✦ **Info Palette.** Get Quick Help in the middle of commands; lock topics so they stay open as you follow the steps (Ctrl+5). For more info on the Info Palette, see "Using the Info Palette" later in this chapter.

✦ **DBConnect Manager.** Connect AutoCAD drawings with external database files (Ctrl+6). This is a pretty esoteric area of AutoCAD, and we don't cover it in this book.

✦ **Markup Set Manager.** Review electronic markups of DWF files and incorporate necessary changes (Ctrl+7). Check out Book VIII for more on this feature.

✦ **Calculator.** Just like the one in your desk drawer, only it works with stuff you've drawn as well as numbers (Ctrl+8). We cover AutoCAD's nifty built-in calculator in Book VI.

A great new feature in AutoCAD 2007 is anchorable palettes. (Docked palettes? Anchored palettes? Could there be some sailors at Autodesk?) An anchored palette is a combination of a docked palette that doesn't keep moving around on you, and an auto-hide palette that rolls out of the way when you're not using it. To anchor any palette, right-click its title bar and choose Allow Docking. Then right-click the title bar again and choose Anchor Left < or Anchor Right >. The palette scrolls shut and anchors its title bar at the left or right edge of the display.

Okay, at this point you're probably dying to know what Ctrl+9 and Ctrl+0 do, so go ahead and try them. And don't panic when parts of your screen disappear — remember, these are toggles, so just press Ctrl+9 again to bring back the command window, and Ctrl+0 to restore all your toolbars, title bars, and other screen components. We tell you about the command window a couple of paragraphs ahead.

Pressing Ctrl+0 issues a command called CLEANSCREENON, which maximizes the program window, and turns off the program title bar and all toolbars, and hides the Windows taskbar. This gives you the largest possible drawing area on-screen, but leaves you with only the menu system and the keyboard to work with. Press Ctrl+0 again to run the CLEANSCREENOFF command (aren't you glad you don't have to type command names?) to bring all those things back again.

If you've tried out AutoCAD 2007's 3D Modeling workspace, you'll have encountered a brand-new interface item called the Dashboard. The Dashboard is a combination tool palette and super-toolbar that's configured for working in 3D. We cover the Dashboard (and 3D in general) in Book V. There are several new palettes — Lights, Materials, Visual Styles, and Rendering — that we also cover in Book V rather than in this introductory section, which deals with 2D drafting.

Drawing area

That big black (or maybe white) area that occupies almost 90% of your AutoCAD window is the drawing area. Everything you draw goes here. There are actually two such drawing areas, and they're known as model space and paper space.

Keeping with the space theme, you can think of the model and paper spaces as parallel universes. We tell you a lot more about these two spaces in Chapter 5. At this time, you just need to recognize this part of the screen. The double-headed arrow figure at the lower-left corner of the screen (see Figure 2-7) is called the UCS icon. When it looks like this, you're in *model space*. And that's where you should be when you're drawing your buildings, valves, or bridges.

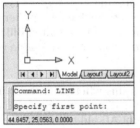

Figure 2-7:
The model
space
UCS icon.

If your UCS icon looks like the one in Figure 2-8, you're in the *other* space — *paper space*. This is where you put your drawing's title block and add notes and such. If your screen looks like Figure 2-8 instead of Figure 2-7, click the tab that says Model at the bottom left of the drawing area to switch to model space.

Crosshairs

The on-screen mouse pointer takes on at least two different appearances when you're working in AutoCAD. When you move the mouse outside the drawing area, it looks like the standard arrow pointer you see everywhere else in Windows. When you're inside the drawing area, it turns into a pair of lines that intersect at right angles, with a small square box (called the *pickbox*) where they cross. You can change the length of the crosshairs in the Options dialog box.

Figure 2-8:
The paper space UCS icon.

You also see the pickbox — without the crosshairs — when you're selecting objects. Many users find the default size (3 pixels square) too small, and we concur. To change the size of the pickbox, type **PICKBOX,** press Enter, and then set a new value. We find a 5-pixel-square pickbox a good compromise.

The floating command window

The *command line* — also known as the command *prompt* — is one of the things that makes AutoCAD *AutoCAD*. It's a throwback to earlier days, before dialog boxes, toolbars, and pull-down menus were a glint in Bill Gates's eye. The command line lives inside the *command window,* that area of text near the bottom of your screen.

AutoCAD is one of the few graphics programs where you still type. Not just numbers and distances, but actual command names and options. Unlikely as it may seem (but obvious to grizzled AutoCAD old-timers), communicating with AutoCAD through the keyboard is one of the more efficient ways of using the program.

When you're new to AutoCAD, though, it's not an obvious thing to remember. That's why most CAD classrooms have a sign in big red letters that says *Watch the command line!* AutoCAD 2006 made a slight lurch into the twenty-first century with something called *dynamic input.* When enabled, AutoCAD displays interactive tooltips near the cursor; these show you a lot — but not all — of the command line information. You may still need to look down at the bottom of the screen to get the whole story. And if you're using AutoCAD 2005 or an earlier version, WATCH THE COMMAND LINE!

In AutoCAD 2006 and later you can turn the command window off and on with the Ctrl+9 toggle. We've even seen books that recommend that you turn it off, but we think this is a bad idea. The dynamic input tooltips do not show you everything that the command window does, so even if you're using AutoCAD 2006 or later, and at the risk of repeating ourselves . . . *watch the command line!*

We tell you a bit more about the command window a couple of paragraphs from here. So you can stop watching it until then.

The status bar

At the bottom of the application window is the status bar. The status bar contains three elements. At the left side is the coordinates display, which shows the *x*-, *y*-, and *z*-values of wherever your crosshairs happen to be at a given moment. By default, the coordinates constantly update as you move your mouse around. Also by default, the coordinate values display as decimal numbers with four places of precision. If you change to a different type drawing unit (we describe units in Chapter 5 of this minibook), the format of the coordinates changes to match the new unit's type.

To the right of the coordinates readout is a set of buttons where you can easily toggle a range of drafting modes such as snap, grid, object snap, and so on. We tell you more about these modes in Chapter 6 of this minibook.

Finally, at the right end of the status bar, comes the status bar tray. You should see anywhere from three to eight icons here; their functions are listed in Table 2-1.

Table 2-1	Status Bar Tray Icons	
Button	*Function*	*Description*
	Communication Center	Connects to Autodesk's Web site and shows articles, tips, and software updates.
	Lock/Unlock toolbars/windows	Allows or prevents moving toolbars, palettes, and command window.
	Associated standards file	Visible if CAD standards checking is enabled; compare drawing properties (such as layer names, styles, and so on) with associated drawing standards file. We discuss standards checking in Book VIII.

(continued)

Table 2-1 *(continued)*

Button	Function	Description
	Manage xrefs	Visible if external reference drawings are attached to a current drawing, and indicates if xrefs need updating. We tell all about xrefs in Book VI.
	Plot/Publish	Signals the end of the plot or publish job and indicates errors (if any).
	Performance Tuning	Changes the way your computer performs when working in the 3D environment.
	Clean Screen	Toggles the Clean screen functionality as shown earlier.
	Trusted Autodesk DWG	Displays DWG files that were created by an Autodesk product or licensed real DWG.

You will see the Performance Tuning icon (the wrench) only from the time you first open AutoCAD 2007 until the first time you look at the Performance Tuning Log by clicking the icon. It will reappear if either Performance Tuning or the Communication Center needs to alert you of an update.

Communicating with Your Software

So now you know what everything is . . . but what do you do with it? You saw at the beginning of this chapter that there are a few ways to start AutoCAD. Now you're about to discover that you can do just about anything in multiple ways in AutoCAD, beginning with how you speak AutoCADese.

The command line

Not to be confused with the LINE command, the command line is the place where AutoCAD talks back to you (see Figure 2-9). Sometimes it just echoes what you type (it's easy to assume that it's not very bright), but more often it engages you in a helpful — if occasionally cryptic — dialog box.

Typically, you start your conversation with AutoCAD by issuing a command. If you want to draw something new, AutoCAD usually starts by asking where you'd like it to start. You pick a point, and then AutoCAD asks how big you want it. You tell AutoCAD, and the program draws the object.

Figure 2-9:
The LINE
command
on the
command
line in the
command
window.

```
Command: LINE
Specify first point:
```

If you want to edit something that's already there, you issue a command —
for example, MOVE. AutoCAD asks you to select the objects to move. You
select them and press Enter to confirm your selection. The command now
starts prompting — for example, the MOVE command prompts for a base
point (a from point) and a second point (a to point).

You can switch off the display of the command window, but we think that's a
bad idea. There's just not enough feedback from dynamic input on its own.

Dynamic input

Not that we're badmouthing dynamic input. In fact, it's a great addition to
AutoCAD, but it *is* one of those things that will probably be easier for the
newbies to adjust to than it will for the old-timers.

When dynamic input is enabled (by choosing the DYN button on the status
bar), AutoCAD displays tooltips near the crosshairs whenever a command is
active. When AutoCAD is expecting you to pick a point, the tooltip displays a
constantly updating coordinate readout (*x*- and *y*-coordinates only). If AutoCAD
needs more information, for example, the radius of a circle, you can type the
numbers into the tooltip.

Dynamic input mode is highly configurable. Right-click over the DYN button
and choose Settings to display the Dynamic Input tab of the Drafting Settings
dialog box. You can turn options off and on here and further refine them by
clicking the Settings buttons under Enable Pointer Input and Enable
Dimension Input.

Dialog boxes

AutoCAD has two different types of dialog boxes — *modal* and *modeless*.
Modal dialog boxes are the regular, old dialogs you see in every Windows
program. They pop up whenever you save an unnamed drawing, or want to
format your units, or make some drawing settings. Modal dialog boxes like
Save, Open, Plot, and so on, take command of AutoCAD. You can't do anything else while one of these dialog boxes is open.

Modeless dialogs *can* stay open while you do other things in AutoCAD. They're so unique, in fact, that they're not even called dialog boxes. They're called *palettes,* and you've already learned a thing or two about them. There are a half-dozen and more modeless dialog boxes — or palettes — in AutoCAD, and we'll highlight their importance at appropriate places in the text.

Running AutoCAD Commands

Even when you use the menus or toolbars to execute commands, there are still significant differences between AutoCAD and other Windows applications that you might be familiar with.

Grasping the AutoCAD Difference

The fundamental difference with AutoCAD is that AutoCAD expects you to take part in a conversation. When you tell the program you want to move something, AutoCAD asks what do you want to move, where do you want to move it from, and where do you want to move it to?

Most of this conversation takes place in dialog boxes and the dynamic input tooltip. We can't give you a standard format for this dialog. One of the delights of AutoCAD is the number of different ways the program has of doing what you ask it to do. All we can do at this point is refer you to the chapters to come (starting with the early chapters of Book II).

Repeating a command

Oftentimes in AutoCAD, you want to perform the same action on different objects. You might, for example, want to move a bunch of linework to a different layer, and then move a bunch of text to a third layer.

Pressing Enter or pressing the spacebar at a blank command prompt repeats the last command. You can also right-click and choose the last command from the top of the shortcut menu.

A nifty feature was added to AutoCAD 2004's Options dialog box, and you can use it in any 2004 or later version of AutoCAD or AutoCAD LT. On the User Preferences tab, Windows Standard Behavior area, click the Right-Click Customization button. In the dialog box, check the Turn on Time-Sensitive Right Click box. Click Apply and Close, and then click OK. Now, if you right-click within a quarter-second (the default value in the dialog box), you get a carriage return, just as if you'd hit the Enter key or spacebar. If you keep the right mouse button pressed down for longer than a quarter-second, then you get whatever Windows shortcut menu is appropriate to the current command.

Canceling a running command

To cancel a command, simply press Esc. If you're a long-time user of AutoCAD, and have been away for . . . well, a long time, you may be used to the Ctrl+C combination that issued a Cancel in all DOS versions of AutoCAD. If you're not one of those grizzled old-timers, you know very well that Ctrl+C copies selected objects to the Windows Clipboard. Whatever your origins, remember that Esc cancels whatever's going on at present.

Invoking transparent commands

Most AutoCAD commands are meant to be run without interruption. You wouldn't, for example, start drawing a line and then decide in the middle of the line sequence that you wanted to draw a circle. Well, maybe you would, but trust us, it's not very efficient.

There are other times, however, when it is efficient to run one command inside another. For example, you might be placing a very long linear dimension, and you'd like to be able to zoom in closely on one end of the object to be dimensioned, and then zoom in closely again on the other end.

You can do this with AutoCAD's display commands, as well as some of the drafting settings, because these commands can be run *transparently*. A transparent command is one that can be executed in the middle of another command.

You may, for example, be in the middle of creating a linear dimension. You realize you're zoomed too far out to be able to pick the defining points accurately, so you go to the Standard toolbar and pick one of the Zoom commands. You execute your zoom, and when you're done, AutoCAD takes you back to the command you were running. Same thing happens with toolbars — just click a tool button, and your top-level command is suspended while the secondary command executes.

You can mimic this behavior at the command prompt by typing an asterisk before the command. The asterisk is a sign to AutoCAD that what follows is to be executed transparently. Of course, not all commands can be run transparently, but many can, including most of the display commands. Go ahead and experiment: Just type an asterisk, and then a command, and see what happens.

AutoCAD system variables

Not everyone uses AutoCAD the same way. Despite its hundreds of commands, there are still specific ways that users want those commands to operate. AutoCAD accommodates with an array of system settings — called system variables — that cover nearly all the bases. Many system variables are toggles — they have a value of either 0 or 1, meaning they are either enabled or disabled. For example, the system variable MIRRTEXT controls what happens to text when a group of drawing objects is mirrored. If MIRRTEXT is enabled (that is, set to 1), then any text in the group is also mirrored — it reads backward on the screen. If MIRRTEXT is set to 0, the objects, including the text object, are all mirrored, but the text itself is not mirrored, so it reads right-way around.

Other system variables can have different settings (more than simply off and on), and still others can store values that remain intact until they're replaced with new values.

For a blow-by-blow of most of AutoCAD's system variables, go to the online help.

Reaching for AutoCAD Help

We hope that the *AutoCAD & AutoCAD LT All-in-One Desk Reference For Dummies* will answer most of your questions about using AutoCAD. Nevertheless, there are going to be times when you want to go to the horse's mouth. Here are some ways of accessing the AutoCAD Help System:

+ Enter a ? at a blank Command: prompt to display the AutoCAD Help System.

+ From the Help menu, choose Help.

+ Press the F1 function key at any time.

+ From the command line type **HELP**

Using built-in Help

Most of the time, AutoCAD's Help system is *context-sensitive*. If you're in the LINE command and press F1 (or choose Help⇨Help), the Help system will launch and take you to information about the LINE command.

You can get context-sensitive help at the command line, too, by entering an apostrophe and then a question mark (that is '?).

Using the Info Palette

This one is for newbies. If you turn on the Info Palette (click Info Palette on the Standard toolbar, choose Info Palette from the Tools menu, or use the Ctrl+5 key combination), you can see persistent help for whatever command you're working with. If it's a complicated sequence, you can click the padlock icon at the top of the palette. When it's "locked," the contents stay visible on-screen.

Finding online resources

Much as we'd like to think this book is all you'll ever need, we recognize that there are millions of one-off requirements that no book can possibly cover comprehensively. One of the best resources available is Autodesk's own discussion groups. Go to www.autodesk.com and click Discussion Groups to find your way to a shopping list of discussion groups based on AutoCAD (or AutoCAD LT version).

Chapter 3: All about Files

AutoCAD not only needs hundreds of files to keep itself going, it also generates more files than you can shake a stick at. All of these files are important, but none is more important than DWG — the drawing file itself.

In this chapter we cover all of the important files that you're likely to run into — and one or two that you're not very likely at all to run into, but just in case, you should know what they are.

It's also important that both AutoCAD and you be able to *find* the files you both need to work together. AutoCAD can usually take care of itself; after it's initially installed, all the files the program needs are in appropriate places. But *you* need to be able to find your drawing files too, and AutoCAD by itself isn't much help there. Left alone, it will save *all* your drawings in the Windows My Documents folder. It's up to you to organize your storage space, and we give you some ideas at the end of the chapter.

File Types in AutoCAD

AutoCAD's drawing (DWG) files contain everything that you draw, and a bit more besides. In addition to all those lines, arcs, circles, text, and dimensions, your DWG files also contain:

✦ Style definitions for things like your dimensions and text

✦ Properties associated with your drawing objects, such as color, layer, and linetype

✦ Layer definitions, each and every one of which includes such things as default color, linetype, plot style, whether the objects on the layer print or not, and so on

Not contained within the DWG file itself, but necessary for it to display properly, are associated files that define the fonts used by the text and dimension styles, hatch and linetype patterns, plot styles, and more. We cover those associated files in more detail a few paragraphs from now.

So obviously, there's a lot of file interaction going on when you work in AutoCAD. A very important aspect of drafting in AutoCAD — or any CAD system — is having a good version of your drawing to fall back on, just in case bad things happen to it. Luckily for us, AutoCAD by default creates backup versions of our drawing file every time we save the drawing. When you click the Save tool button (or whatever your preferred method of interacting with the program), AutoCAD makes a copy of your drawing (let's call it FOO.DWG) and renames the copy as FOO.BAK. After it's done that, it takes all the changes that you've made and stored in memory, and spoons them into the drawing file. When it's finished remembering everything, it saves a new version of FOO.DWG.

Not all programs will do this for you, but AutoCAD does, as long as you don't tell it not to. We cover that a bit more later on in the chapter.

One of the things that puzzles new users to AutoCAD is the fact that not all the data needed to generate a drawing is included in the drawing file. Problems don't arise if you only ever open your drawings on your own computer, but they can crop up if you ever have to send your drawings to someone else. If that someone else — a client, a contractor, your teacher, or boss — doesn't have all the same files on *her* computer that you did on *your* computer when you made the drawing, then the drawing is not going to look the same as it did for you when you drew it.

Here are some of the files that are external to your DWG file that must be available on every computer on which the drawing will be opened:

✦ **Fonts (SHX and/or TTF files).** AutoCAD comes with over 70 "vector" font files (SHX extension). These fonts are installed in AutoCAD's own subfolders within the Program Files folder (usually) on your C: drive. AutoCAD can also use TrueType (TTF) fonts, which are part of Windows itself, and which live in the Fonts folder of your operating system. We tell you lots more about fonts in Book III.

Be very careful about using non-standard fonts — either SHX fonts that didn't come with AutoCAD, or TTF fonts that didn't come with the Windows operating system. If you have to send your drawings to someone whose computer doesn't have the fonts you used, they won't see your drawing accurately.

✦ **Hatch patterns (PAT files).** Hatch pattern files (by default, AutoCAD uses a file named acad.pat; AutoCAD LT's version is named acadlt.pat, or aclt.pat in pre-2007 versions) are used to generate the cross-hatching that indicates objects cut in sections or specific areas on maps or plans. Hatching is also covered in depth in Book III.

✦ **Linetype patterns (LIN files).** AutoCAD's default linetype patterns are defined in a file named acad.lin (acadlt.lin or aclt.lin in AutoCAD LT). This file defines non-continuous linetypes such as center, dashed, and hidden used in standard drafting. We talk about linetypes in Chapter 5.

The acad and acadlt hatch pattern and linetype definition files are for use with imperial units. If you're working in metric, use the acadiso.pat (acadltiso.pat) and acadiso.lin (acadltiso.lin) files. If you start your drawings correctly, these files are available automatically.

✦ **Plot style tables (CTB or STB files).** Plot styles are collections of settings that tell your output device (a highfalutin way of saying printer) what color of drawing object corresponds to what thickness of printed line, or what printed properties are to be assigned to what drawing objects. (Don't worry about printing for now — we cover it in much greater depth in Book VII. You can worry about it then!) Plot style *tables* are the files where all the plot styles live, and AutoCAD needs to find them or your drawing won't print properly.

✦ **Image files.** AutoCAD can display and print raster images that are placed in drawing files, but the files do not become part of the drawing file itself. If AutoCAD can't find them (say, you forget to send them with the drawing file), then you get a rectangle showing the name of the missing file instead. We cover image files in Book VI.

✦ **Other DWG files.** You can attach drawings to other drawings so you don't have to keep redrawing the same things over and over again. Those attached drawings are called *external references* (or *xrefs* for short). The idea is that if you change something in a referenced drawing, it automatically changes in all drawings to which it's attached. It's a really useful feature, but it's complicated (don't worry — we tell all in Book VI!). The point here is that if AutoCAD can't find the referenced drawing file, you get another one of those missing file messages.

To sum up, if you're sharing drawings with others outside your office:

✦ You usually don't have to worry about the font, hatch pattern, or line-type files if you're using the standard fonts and patterns that come with AutoCAD.

✦ You *may* have to worry about plot style tables if you're using custom ones.

✦ You usually *do* have to worry about images and external references, since those are files that you create yourself, and are not part of AutoCAD.

Starting a New Drawing

If all that information seems a little daunting at this point, don't worry — all will be revealed within these pages. In the meantime, it's just possible that you want to actually get down and dirty and draw something. So let's look at a trio of ways to start a new drawing in AutoCAD.

If you're using AutoCAD 2005, 2006, or 2007 out of the box (AutoCAD veterans call this the "out-of-the-box experience"), when you click the QNew button on the Standard toolbar, you get a Select Template dialog box (see Figure 3-1).

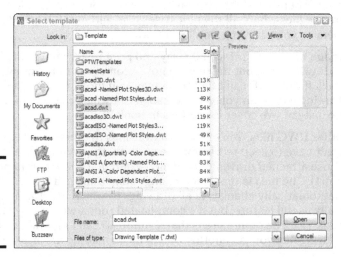

Figure 3-1:
Select a
template to
start a new
drawing.

It may look like a "New" button, but it actually runs a command called QNEW. Who knew? Here's what QNEW can do for you. If you don't change any settings in AutoCAD, clicking QNEW will always display the Select Template dialog box. Now, if you always start a drawing using the acad.dwt template (not the best idea, but read on), you have to click Acad.dwt, and then click OK. That can get a bit tedious. But if you go into the Options dialog box and click Files, you can identify a specific template file (maybe even Acad.dwt). Doing so will tell AutoCAD to start a new drawing using the specified template every time.

A further wrinkle in starting a new drawing occurs if a system variable called STARTUP is enabled. By default, STARTUP is disabled or set to 0; for more on system variables, see the sidebar "AutoCAD System Variables" in Chapter 2 of this minibook.

If STARTUP is enabled (or set to 1), the first time you start AutoCAD you see a Startup dialog box (see Figure 3-2).

Figure 3-2:
The Startup dialog box you see if STARTUP = 1.

From this dialog box, you can choose to open an existing drawing or start a new drawing in one of three different ways: starting from scratch, using a template, or employing a wizard. Once the first drawing in an AutoCAD session has been opened using any of these methods, subsequent clicks of the QNew button will display a Create New Drawing dialog box. This dialog box looks suspiciously like the Startup dialog box — it gives you the same three choices for starting a new drawing, but the icon for opening an existing drawing is grayed out.

The STARTUP system variable must be set to 1 in order for the Startup and Create New Drawing dialog boxes to appear when you start AutoCAD or when you click the QNew button. If you only ever see the Select Template dialog box on either starting AutoCAD or clicking QNew, then your STARTUP variable is disabled.

We suggest you leave STARTUP set to 0, as the other options for starting a new drawing — that is, from scratch or using a wizard — are much less efficient, as we explain now.

Starting from scratch

When you start a new drawing from scratch, you're starting AutoCAD with no preconfigured settings. There are no layers in the drawing other than Layer 0, nor are there any text styles, or dimension styles other than STANDARD. There are no table styles, and no predefined layouts. When you choose this option, you really do start from scratch, and you must spend a fair old whack of time making settings that you could easily make once and save in a template. For simple sketching, or working out design ideas, it's okay to start from scratch, but once you're into working drawing production, it's a lot more efficient to use a template. But even starting from scratch is better than using a wizard.

Using a Wizard

Wizard, schmizard — what do they know? Not much, when it comes to setting up drawings in AutoCAD. We don't mean to disparage all wizards — there are a few useful ones in AutoCAD — but the one that offers to start a new drawing for you is not one of them.

There are two kinds of wizard to choose from: You can run a Quick Wizard or an "Advanced" one (see Figure 3-3).

Figure 3-3:
Pick your
wizard.

The problem with the wizards — both of them — is that the settings that they make for you are not very useful. Both wizards will set these values:

✦ **Units.** Choose the format and precision for your linear drawing units (see Figure 3-4). Regardless of the format you choose, the units are based on inches if you live in the U.S.A, or millimeters if you live outside the U.S.A.

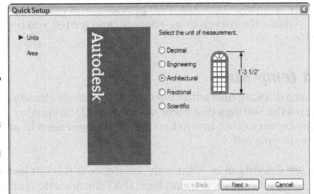

Figure 3-4:
Both
wizards (this
is the Quick
one) ask you
to select the
units type.

✦ **Area.** Specify the drawing area by its length and width. You arrive at the correct figures by multiplying the intended plot scale of the drawing by the dimensions of the paper on which it will be plotted.

In addition to units and area, the Advanced wizard also sets these values:

✦ **Angular Units.** Choose the format and precision for angular measure. The default type of angular measure (and the easiest by far for most people to work with) is decimal degrees.

✦ **Angle Measure.** Specify where in the circle 0 degrees lies. By default, 0 degrees lies due east. If you don't have a compass handy, you can also think of this direction as 3 o'clock, or to the right, in a dead horizontal alignment.

✦ **Angle Direction.** Specify whether angles are measured in a clockwise or counterclockwise direction. By default, angles are measured in a counter-clockwise direction, so if 0 degrees lies on an east-pointing horizontal axis, then 90 degrees is straight up, 180 degrees is horizontal pointing west (9 o'clock for you clock watchers), and 270 degrees is straight down.

Nearly all major industries go with the AutoCAD defaults for angular measure — that is, 0 degrees is on an easterly horizontal axis, and angles are measured in a counterclockwise direction. One exception to this rule is in surveying, where 0 degrees usually points north, and angles are measured in a clockwise direction. But if you're not a surveyor (and maybe even if you are), don't change the settings for angular measure from their defaults, as it can make editing the drawing a nightmare.

So why are we so down on the wizards? The settings they make are just not practical for most real-world drafting applications. By far your best bet is to use one of the templates that AutoCAD provides. You can modify any of those templates to make them even more efficient, and we tell you how to do that in Chapter 5.

Using a template

Templates are drawing files with collections of settings already made. You should regard the settings that come with AutoCAD as starting points; some of them may be very close to what you want, but you need to add the other 5 or 10 percent yourself.

Templates *are* drawing files — the only difference is the last letter of the file extension: DWG for regular drawing files, DWT for drawing templates. By default, AutoCAD is configured to place templates in a special Windows-generated folder under C:\Documents and Settings, although you can tell the program to look in another place.

AutoCAD comes with no fewer than 66 templates, but don't worry, you're not going to have to go through them all to find a useful one! Nearly all of them come in two versions, one configured for color-dependent plot styles, and one for named plot styles (we explain more about these two options in Book VII).

Unless you're told otherwise by your boss or teacher, you should probably choose the color-dependent plot-style versions of the template files. Color-dependent means the colors of the objects in the drawing determine how thick the linework will be plotted. Named plot styles, on the other hand, are independent of object color, and are specific properties applied to those objects. The reason we recommend you stick with color-dependent plot styles is that this is basically the system used by AutoCAD since the 1980s to plot drawings. But we have more to say about all of that in Book VII.

The templates break down as follows:

+ **ANSI templates.** (American National Standards Institute) Designed for drafting in Imperial units; templates for ANSI sheet sizes A, B, C, D, and E; if you work outside the United States or Canada, you can probably forget about these.

✦ **DIN templates.** (Deutsches Institut für Normung). Original European standards very similar to and slowly being replaced by ISO; designed for metric drafting; templates for metric sheet sizes A0, A1, A2, A3, and A4.

✦ **Gb templates.** Follow British Standards Institute criteria; templates for metric sheet sizes A0, A1, A2, A3, and A4.

✦ **ISO templates.** (International Organization for Standardization). International, European-based standard for metric system; templates for metric sheet sizes A0, A1, A2, A3, and A4.

✦ **JIS templates.** (Japanese Industrial Standards). Based on the ANSI system, adapted for metric drafting.

✦ **Miscellaneous templates.** These include Acad.dwt (imperial) and Acadiso.dwt (metric), as well as "architectural" and "generic" templates. Most are not based on specific sheet sizes. Unless these templates are specifically named otherwise, assume they're all set up for color-dependent plotting.

Which template should you use? If you're working in feet-and-inches in North America, the ANSI templates are a safe bet. If you're working in other parts of the world, figure out the metric templates that are closest to home (that is, European, British, or Japanese) and go with those. Remember that the supplied templates are just starting points, and you'll need to do some customizing of them to make them truly useful time-savers.

Saving a Drawing

We don't have to tell you that it's important to save often (at least, we hope we don't!). Everyone has their own little formulas for saving: every hour, every 15 minutes, on the solstices and equinoxes (and we *sincerely* hope you're not in the last category!).

Okay, let's get serious for just a moment. How often should you save your work? A really great mantra to keep in mind — or maybe even print out and pin to the wall over your desk — is, "How much work am I prepared to lose?" You may have just completed a complicated polar array of a kazillion objects, but it's still three minutes away from your quarter-hourly save. Forget the clock — hit that Save button right now! That's how often you should save.

Saving files in AutoCAD can be a little complicated. (By now, you were probably expecting that, right?) There are three different commands for saving files: SAVE, SAVEAS, and QSAVE, but they all fall naturally to hand (or to tool button, to be more accurate).

Save

AutoCAD does have a command called SAVE, and the Windows-standard Ctrl+S key combo works here too. But doing a Ctrl+S or hitting the Save button on the Standard toolbar doesn't run the SAVE command. It runs one of two other commands: SAVEAS, which displays the Save Drawing As dialog box, or the QSAVE command, which doesn't display anything.

Save As

If your drawing is unnamed (and if the title bar says [Drawing 15.dwg], it's unnamed), entering a Ctrl+S or clicking Save on the Standard toolbar runs the SAVEAS command. SAVEAS opens the Save Drawing As dialog box (see Figure 3-5), and here you can enter three different pieces of information:

✦ **Save in.** Use this drop-down list to navigate to the folder where you want to store the drawing. The list box below the Save in list shows all drawings stored in the current folder

✦ **File name.** Enter the drawing name. We'll have more to say about naming files at the end of the chapter.

✦ **Files of type.** You want to save a drawing, right? Well, there are drawings, and there are drawings. You can save your work as a DWG in the current format, or go back up to three DWG versions. If you have to go back farther than that, you can save in Release 12 DXF format. Finally, you can save your drawing as a template (DWT) file, or a Drawing Standards (DWS) file.

We're not talking about saving back two AutoCAD versions — you can save back up to three DWG versions. The current DWG version is AutoCAD 2007 DWG. The prior one was AutoCAD 2004 DWG, which was used by AutoCAD 2004, 2005, and 2006. The one before that was AutoCAD 2000 DWG, used by AutoCAD 2000, 2000i, and 2002. And before that came AutoCAD R14.dwg (used by that version only). So, if need be, you can save your work in a DWG format that can be read by a version of AutoCAD first released in 1997. For more on file formats and versions, see Table 1-1 in Chapter 1 of this minibook.

QSAVE

After all those Save and Save As options, QSAVE should come as a relief, because there are no options at all. As noted earlier, if a drawing is unnamed, clicking the Save button or issuing a Ctrl+S runs the SAVEAS command, displaying the Save Drawing As dialog box, and presenting a plethora of options.

Save In list

File list

File Name box

Files of Type box

Figure 3-5:
Name your
drawing and
give it a
home in
the Save
Drawing As
dialog box.

DXF: The Neutral Format

DXF, for *drawing interchange format*, is the officially sanctioned method for exporting AutoCAD drawing data to other CAD or graphics programs, or for importing vector graphics from other programs into AutoCAD. Autodesk publishes the DXF specification but keeps DWG proprietary. DXF should produce a very close representation of a DWG file, but some data types do not translate well; typically drawing geometry is translated better than some of that geometry's object properties. Since DXF is Autodesk's specification, it's up to other software developers to code their programs to support it properly. In other words, if your illustration program won't import a DXF file, the fault is likelier to be the illustration program's than Autodesk's.

Create DXF files through the Save Drawing As dialog box. In the Files of type drop-down list, there are four flavors of DXF to choose from: AutoCAD 2007, AutoCAD 2004, AutoCAD 2000/ LT 2000, and AutoCAD Release 12/LT 2. You can open DXF files through a similar Files of type drop-down list in the Select File dialog box.

For users of AutoCAD 2004, 2005, and 2006, DXF is one way (the only way, using plain AutoCAD) of converting a drawing back to Release 14 or earlier. AutoCAD 2007 *can* save back to Release 14 DWG format. If you're using one of those older versions, you can download a copy of Autodesk DWG TrueConvert from Autodesk's Web site that *will* let you save back to R14 DWG. If you need to go further back than that, then you really do need to use R12 DXF.

Once the drawing *is* named, clicking Save or doing a Ctrl+S runs the QSAVE command. QSAVE has no dialog box; in fact, it may look as if nothing happened. QSAVE simply resaves the named drawing file in the same location, with the same file name, and as the same type of file, all without any additional input from you. Any guesses what the *Q* in QSAVE stands for?

Opening an Existing Drawing

Opening an existing drawing doesn't present quite so many possible alternatives as creating a new one does. All you have to know is where the drawing is, and if you practice good file-management techniques, that shouldn't be a problem.

Open command

Clicking the Open button on the Standard toolbar, or using the Ctrl+O key combination displays the Select File dialog box, as seen in Figure 3-6.

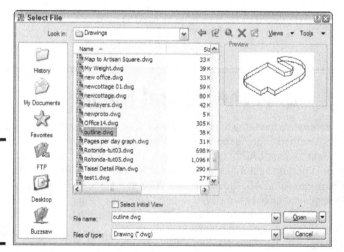

Figure 3-6:
Select files
to open in
the . . . er,
Select File
dialog box.

The default file type in the Files of type drop-down list is DWG. Unlike the Save As dialog box, which gives you a number of optional DWG versions, there's only one DWG listed in the Select File dialog box. This is because AutoCAD can open *any* current or older version DWG.

Your other choices of file types to open through the Select File dialog box are:

✦ **Standards (*.dws).** A DWS file is a regular drawing file that contains settings and properties that you want to use as a base standard for a project or for all your drawings. You can use the CAD Standards options on the Tools menu to configure a DWS file, and to review your current drawing to make sure it complies with the standards.

✦ **DXF (*.dxf).** Autodesk's neutral and non-proprietary version of the DWG format used for transferring drawing data into and out of AutoCAD. For more information, see the sidebar "DXF: The Neutral Format."

✦ **Drawing Template (*.dwt).** A DWT file is a regular drawing file that contains settings, properties, and drawing objects that you want to use in all the drawing files of a project. Using a template means you don't have to keep making these settings or drawing those objects over and over again.

Be careful when opening DWT files, as you may inadvertently make unwanted changes that will show up whenever you try to start a new drawing based on that DWT.

Can't find that drawing file? Funny . . . you knew where it was yesterday, right? Luckily, AutoCAD has a dandy, but well-concealed, utility hidden in the Select File dialog box. To find Find, click the Tools button on the Select File dialog box's toolbar, and choose Find from the menu; the Find dialog box opens. Enter a file name, or a partial file name, and lickety-split, AutoCAD will turn up files that meet your criteria (see Figure 3-7). (If lickety-split doesn't happen, try changing the Look in location to the root folder.) Highlight the file you're after in the list and click OK. The Select File dialog box reappears with the selected file in the File name box, ready to open.

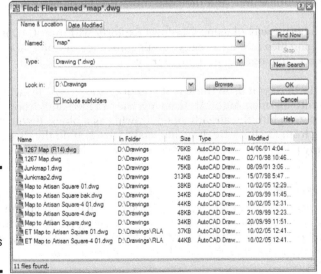

Figure 3-7:
Finding files through the Select Files dialog boxes Tools set.

Using Windows Explorer

When you can't quite remember where you put that danged drawing, the Find function in AutoCAD's Select File dialog box works well, but not many people know about it. *Everyone*, however, knows Windows Explorer, and the Search tool on the Windows Start menu. If the drawing was created in AutoCAD 2006 or later, you can even search on words that are part of drawing text. This is not the place to explain Windows XP's or 2000's Search function — if you don't know how to use it, click Help on the Start button.

Once you have searched and found, you can open your file and start AutoCAD at the same time.

And a double-click to open

You can always use Windows Explorer to open your drawings. Simply double-click to open them in AutoCAD.

One potential drawback of double-clicking in Explorer arises if you have more than one version of AutoCAD on your computer. If you're a one-person shop, that may sound unlikely, but lots of big organizations will have two versions of AutoCAD on their systems while they're transitioning from one release to the next. Such a company might have seats of both AutoCAD and AutoCAD LT, or "vanilla" AutoCAD alongside a Desktop product such as Architectural Desktop, Mechanical Desktop, or Land Desktop. When you double-click a drawing file in Explorer, the drawing opens with the last-used version of the software, and that may not be what you want at all. If you've only got one single version of AutoCAD, then no problem, but if you have access to several versions, don't do the double-click thing — start your AutoCAD of choice first, and then use the Open dialog box.

Perhaps a better way of using Windows Explorer with AutoCAD is dragging and dropping files into an already-running instance of AutoCAD (especially if you've more than one version on your system).

Be careful where you drop though. If you drag and drop a drawing from Explorer into an open AutoCAD drawing, the dragged-and-dropped drawing will be inserted into the already-open drawing as a block. If you want to open a drawing from Explorer by dragging, make sure you do the dropping in an empty gray part of the graphics area, as shown in Figure 3-8.

Partial opening

You can speed up the loading of very large drawings through the technique of *partial opening*. Doing a partial open of a drawing loads only the specified layers and/or view area. If you need to add more of the full drawing's data to a partially open drawing, you can do so using *partial loading*.

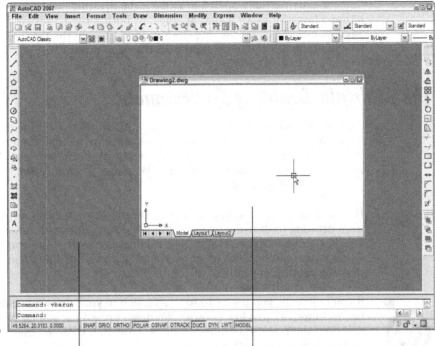

Figure 3-8:
To open a drawing from Explorer, be sure to drop it into an empty part of the graphics area.

Drop here to open drawing   Drop here to insert drawing as a block

You can access partial opening through the Select Files dialog box that appears when you use the Open tool button (see Figure 3-9). To add bits and pieces of the same drawing, choose Partial Load from the File menu, or enter PARTIALOAD at the command line.

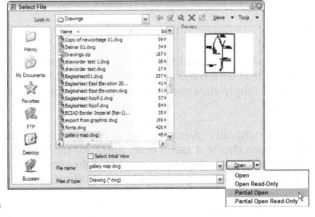

Figure 3-9:
Click the arrow beside the Open button to display the partial open options.

You can only partially open a drawing if the drawing has been saved with either a layer index, or a spatial index, or both. Create these indexes in the Save As dialog box by clicking Options, and then on the DWG options tab, selecting the desired index type from the drop-down list.

The Multiple-Drawing Environment

All twenty-first-century versions of AutoCAD support multiple documents. Big deal, you say — every Windows program can open multiple documents. Well, it *is* a big deal if you're a grizzled old-timer, because for several releases, AutoCAD was one of the few Windows programs that did *not* support multiple documents.

Having several drawings open at once means you can easily copy objects from drawing to drawing by using the Windows Clipboard. AutoCAD's Window menu lets you arrange several drawings within the graphics area, either by cascading them in an overlapping array, or tiling them so each drawing window is visible.

 If you're like us, you prefer to have as much of your drawing visible as possible. In AutoCAD, just like in other Windows programs, you can have several drawings open and maximized at once. To switch between them, use the Ctrl+Tab key combination.

 There are a few add-on programs for AutoCAD that can't handle multiple documents; they will only function if one and only one drawing is open at a time. AutoCAD has a system variable named SDI (Single Document Interface) that you can enable if you have one of these ornery add-ons. Set SDI to 1 to disable multiple drawings, or to 0 to allow multiple drawings. Note that it's highly unlikely that you'll need to change this variable, and if you do, the add-on's documentation should tell you so.

Closing Windows

Closing AutoCAD windows is just like closing files in other applications. All the window types that we looked at in Chapter 2 have Close buttons on their title bars. You can simply click the Close buttons to toolbars and palettes to shut them down.

 To *open* toolbars, right-click over a button — doesn't matter which — in any open toolbar to see a shortcut menu of all AutoCAD toolbars. If you're after one of the Express Tools toolbars, you need to right-click in an empty part of the docked toolbar areas to display a higher-level shortcut menu showing all loaded menus, not just the AutoCAD one. Click Express from this menu for a submenu of the Express toolbars. To open a palette, go to the Tools menu and select the one you want. After you've been working with the program a while, try to learn the Ctrl-key shortcuts; it's much more efficient toggling Ctrl+1 to open and close the Properties palette, for example, than to keep opening the Tools menu.

If you click the Close button on a drawing window, or the Close button on the AutoCAD title bar, and you've made unsaved changes, the program will display an alert box like the one in Figure 3-10. Click Cancel to go back and save your changes, click No to close the drawing without saving changes, or click Yes to save the changes and *then* close the drawing. If your drawing is unnamed, the Save Drawing As dialog box appears.

Figure 3-10:
Keep it or
toss it?
AutoCAD
asks
whether you
want to
save
changes
before
closing.

File Management for AutoCAD

Now that you know what all those files are, how to create new drawings, how to open existing ones, and how to close everything down, you need to think about effective file management. When you want to open an existing drawing file, the Find utility in the Select File dialog box is all very well, but it's not very efficient. It's much better if you *know* where you put those drawings, so you don't waste time looking for them. It's a lot like having all those papers that are neatly stored in file folders in your filing cabinet stacked up in piles on your desk.

The best approach here is to have a comprehensive organizational scheme that covers both naming and storage.

Naming drawing files

If you're working on your own, and you produce your own hard-copy versions of one-off drawing files, you can name your drawings pretty well anything you like. If you're an employee in a design or engineering firm, however, or are a student taking a course, you'll probably need to pay attention to the file-naming conventions in your organization.

Typically, drawings are seldom one-off — it's rare that something can be manufactured or constructed using a single drawing. When you start dealing with drawing sets, you really need to pay attention to a naming scheme that keeps all associated files together in your file folders. Individual companies may have their own system. In the United States, professional organizations, such as the American Institute of Architects and the Construction Specifications Institute, produce non-mandatory guidelines for naming CAD files. Following the AIA file naming specification may give you drawing names like A-FP01 or C-SP04, but even if you don't know the system, a quick check in the guidelines will tell you that you're looking at the first sheet of Architectural Floor Plans, or the fourth sheet of Civil Site Plans.

For more information on these and other file-naming protocols, visit these Web sites:

✦ American Institute of Architects. (www.aia.org)

✦ Construction Specifications Institute (www.csinet.org)

✦ National CAD Standard (www.nationalcadstandard.org)

Storing your files

Files go in folders, and it makes as much sense to name your folders sensibly as it does to name your files in a useful way. If you belong to an organization, then the file storage protocols will already be set up. You'll probably be saving to a network — in predefined folders that you may not be able to modify.

If you are on your own, then come up with a system that will help you find files quickly. Obviously, storing files by project is a sensible first step. If you're *really* busy (lucky you!) you might consider having the year as a top-level folder, and then individual projects down a level. Using a similar subfolder structure can really help you find those files, even if it does entail drilling down a bit. For example, if you design houses you might have a standard series of folders named SITE PLANS, FLOOR PLANS, ELEVATIONS, SECTIONS, and DETAILS residing under each project (see Figure 3-11).

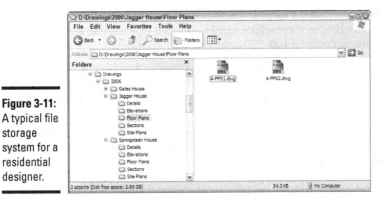

Figure 3-11:
A typical file storage system for a residential designer.

Backing Up Is Hard to Do . . .

. . . but losing a file you've spent two days working on is even harder. It's not a matter of *if* you ever need to call on your backups, it's a matter of *when*. Hardware is pretty reliable these days, but disks do fail. Remember that IBM, or Dell, or HP, or whomever it was that you bought your computer from, chose the lowest bidders as their suppliers.

We're not talking about your BAK files now, the ones we explained at the beginning of this chapter. AutoCAD's own backup files are all well and good, but they're not adequate for a backup system.

The likeliest thing to go is your hard disk, and luckily, that's what backup solutions are meant to protect. Invest in backup hardware; there's lots to choose from out there, so fire up your trusty search engine and see what you can find on the Web. Among your choices:

✦ **External hard drives.** Especially practical if you have more than one computer. Some drives are especially designed as backup units and come with software that lets you schedule and automate backups.

You can also use the built-in Backup utilities that come with Windows XP and Windows 2000. If you're using Windows NT (which means you're using AutoCAD 2005 or prior) or something even older, you'll need to invest in backup software.

✦ **Tape drives.** Tape is fairly obsolete now, and we don't recommend buying a new tape backup unit. But if it's all you have, it's better than nothing!

✦ **Removable disks.** The best known of these devices is Iomega's Zip Drive; the drives themselves can be internal or external, and the proprietary disks come in 100, 250, and 750 MB capacities.

✦ **CD-Rs and DVD-Rs.** Compact Disc-Recordable and Digital Versatile Disc-Recordable disks are cheap and efficient means to backing up data up to 700 or so MB. Most computers purchased in the last five years come with CD-RW drives, so the investment here is minimal.

✦ **USB memory keys.** A great idea, and now amazingly cheap: penknife-sized devices that plug into a spare USB port and are seen by Windows XP as just another drive.

How often should you back up your hard drive? It's worth revisiting that earlier question: "How much work do I want to lose?" Now, we're not suggesting that you run a full system backup every 15 minutes, but once a day, at the end of the day, is not excessive. If your hard drive does crash on you at your afternoon coffee break, you might have lost your day's work, but you can always use yesterday's backup.

If you have one.

Chapter 4: Basic Tools

*I*n this chapter, we look at some of AutoCAD's primitive drawing objects. That's not an insult; by *primitive* we mean *basic* drawing elements like lines, arcs, and circles. There are also complex drawing objects such as polylines, mtext objects, and dimensions, which we'll get to in good time.

The purpose of this chapter is to show you how to draw stuff as simply as possible. Remember that the purpose of a CAD drawing is to convey technical information accurately and precisely (and those two words don't mean the same thing!). This chapter shows you how to draw primitives, but don't get into the habit of drawing everything the way we show you here. In real drawing, you need to pay attention to object properties such as color, linetype, and layer, as well as precision.

Drawing Lines

Lines are the second most basic object you can have in AutoCAD. Lines are geometrically defined in any AutoCAD drawing by the coordinates of their endpoints. The only thing simpler than that is the point object, which is defined by a single set of coordinates. (Don't be too concerned about coordinates at this point — we tell all in Chapter 6 of this minibook.)

Lines are the fundamental building blocks of most types of drawing, especially if you work in architecture or general building design. If you do mechanical drafting, you may well draw as many circular shapes as straight ones (in that case, do we have a paragraph coming up for you — hang on tight!). If you do civil-engineering drawing or mapping, you're probably lucky if you see a straight line once every six months. But whatever kind of drafting you do, at some point you're going to need to draw lines.

You would think that a line is a line is a line, wouldn't you? But not much is as simple as that in AutoCAD. What looks like a line may or may not be a *line* — meaning a line object. Straight, linear-looking thingies on your drawing screen may also be *polyline* objects, or components of a *multiline* object. It may even be part of a *table* object. We cover all the various types of lines later in the book, but for now, what we're interested in is the primitive line object.

You draw primitive line objects with a command called . . . wait for it . . . LINE! You can start this command in a number of ways:

- ✦ **Draw menu.** Click Draw on the menu bar, and then move your mouse pointer down to Line and click.

- ✦ **Draw toolbar.** Click the Line tool on the Draw toolbar.

- ✦ **Keyboard input.** Type **LINE** (either uppercase or lowercase, it doesn't matter which; as we explain in the Introduction, we show proper command names in all upper case in this book). When you finish typing, press Enter.

- ✦ **Command alias.** More typing (actually, *less* typing). Press **L** and press Enter.

- ✦ **Tool palettes.** You'll find the LINE command (and a few others) on the Command Tools tab of the Tool palettes. If you don't see the tab, right-click the Tool palettes title bar and choose either Sample or All Palettes.

AutoCAD has several dozen command aliases that provide alternative short-cut keyboard methods for issuing commands. L is the alias for the LINE command, so typing either **LINE** (the full command name) or **L** (the command alias) and then pressing Enter both do the same thing: they run the LINE command. You can probably figure out a lot of aliases for yourself: C for CIRCLE, A for ARC, Z for ZOOM, and so on. For a complete list of AutoCAD's command aliases, choose Tools, Customize, Edit Program Parameters (acad.pgp) to open the program parameters file in Windows Notepad or your configured text editor.

The following procedure uses the Draw menu to start the command and draws a line from between two random points on the display.

1. **From the Draw menu, choose Line.**

AutoCAD starts the LINE command. The command line and the dynamic input tooltip (if DYN is enabled) prompt you this way:

```
Command: _line Specify first point:
```

2. **Specify the first point of the line by clicking a point on-screen.**

AutoCAD starts drawing a line from the point you pick. As you move the cursor, a *temporary line segment* (see Figure 4-1) joins the first point with the crosshairs. AutoCAD prompts:

```
Specify next point or [Undo]:
```

The second prompt displays a command option inside square brackets. Most AutoCAD commands have options, and the standard way of presenting them at the command line is to enclose them in square brackets.

To enter an option, type the uppercase letter of the option. In this case, typing **U** and pressing Enter runs the LINE command's Undo option; this command removes the previous line segment and backs up AutoCAD to the line's start point.

3. **Specify additional points by clicking them on-screen.**

Notice that AutoCAD does not end the LINE command after you've drawn a single line. You can keep clicking points on-screen, and AutoCAD will keep adding line segments to your drawing.

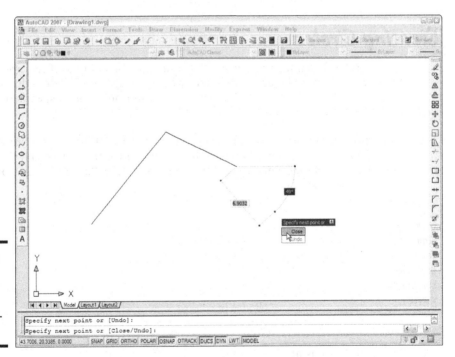

Figure 4-1:
Primitive lines (you have to start *some-where*).

After you click a third point, the command line changes slightly:

```
Specify next point or [Close/Undo]:
```

Two options appear inside the command line's square brackets. The Undo option is still available, but a Close option appears, as well.

4. Press C and then press Enter to close the shape.

AutoCAD locates the next point on the original start point, making a closed triangular or polygonal shape. AutoCAD ends the LINE command and returns you to a blank command line.

Figure 4-1 shows the command in process; notice the command line and the dynamic input tooltip, both showing command options.

When you enter **C** to close the group of lines and end the command, what you end up with is a series of separate line objects. If you click your mouse pointer on top of any line segment, you'll see that only that part of the shape highlights as being selected. In Book II, we look at another entity type called a *polyline,* where all the line segments are joined into a single AutoCAD object.

Creating Circles

Circles, like lines and every other drawing object in AutoCAD, are mathematically defined. Lines are defined by the coordinates of their endpoints. Circles are defined by the coordinates of the center point and a specified numeric value for the radius.

The default method of drawing circles in AutoCAD is by selecting a center point on-screen and then entering a number for the radius. But there are a half-dozen different ways to draw circles. Figure 4-2 shows these options on the Draw menu.

Figure 4-2:
You can
draw circles
six different
ways.

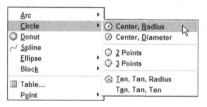

The options are

+ **Center, Radius.** Select a center point on-screen, and then either enter a value for the radius or drag a second point from the center point to indicate the radius. This is the default method for drawing circles.

In this case, *default* means what happens when you simply click the Circle tool button or enter **CIRCLE** at the command line, without specifying any options.

+ **Center, Diameter.** Select a center point on-screen, and then either enter a value for the diameter or drag a second point from the center point to indicate the diameter. Because it's a diameter distance that you're dragging, the second point is twice as far from the center as the circumference.

+ **2 Points.** Specify two points on-screen; the two points are treated as endpoints of the diameter of the circle.

+ **3 Points.** Specify three points on-screen; a circle is drawn through them.

+ **Tan, Tan, Radius.** Select two existing objects, and then enter a value for a radius. AutoCAD draws a circle tangent to the two selected objects with the specified radius (assuming such a circle is possible).

+ **Tan, Tan, Tan.** Select three existing objects and, geometry permitting, AutoCAD draws a circle tangent to all three of them. This one's not really an option of the CIRCLE command, but a special macro accessible only from the Draw menu. You can't do the tan, tan, tan at the command line.

Any of these options will get you a circle, but which one you would choose depends on the drawing geometry and the information you have. For example, if you're given the requirement for a circle of diameter 29.57137, it's easier to use the CIRCLE command's Diameter option than it is to dig out your calculator and divide 29.57137 by 2 to get the radius.

The following steps use the Circle tool button on the Draw toolbar to draw a circle using the Diameter option:

1. **Click the Circle button on the Draw toolbar.**

AutoCAD starts the CIRCLE command. The command line prompts you:

```
Command: _circle Specify center point for circle or
    [3P/2P/Ttr (tan tan radius)]:
```

If you want to use one of the available options, enter **3P** for 3 point circle, **2P** for a 2-point circle, or **T** to use the Tan, Tan, Radius option. You need to type the uppercase letters of the command option you want. For 2-point and 3-point, you press P after the 2 or 3, or AutoCAD thinks you are trying to enter a numeric coordinate location.

2. **Specify the center point.**

AutoCAD places the center of the circle and drags a rubber-band line between the center point and the crosshairs; AutoCAD prompts:

```
Specify radius of circle or [Diameter]:
```

If you simply pick a point or enter a value at this point, AutoCAD interprets the input as the radius. If you want to use the Diameter option, you must let AutoCAD know.

3. **Press D and then press Enter.**

   Entering D here lets AutoCAD know you want to use the Diameter option of the Circle command. AutoCAD prompts:

   ```
   Specify diameter of circle:
   ```

4. **Enter a numeric value for the diameter and press Enter, or drag the crosshairs out to indicate a length equivalent to the diameter and click.**

   AutoCAD draws the circle.

The steps in this and the preceding sections show how to draw two of the simplest object types in AutoCAD. The procedure for drawing most objects is basically similar. We look at drawing other kinds of objects in Chapter 1 of Book II.

Taking a Closer Look

One of the great advantages of AutoCAD is that you work on an infinitely large drawing sheet — so large, in fact, that you could design a solar system full size! With a drawing sheet that size, though, you need to be able to get up close to the drawing objects in order to add detail. Enter the display commands.

There are three broad categories of display command: ZOOM, PAN, and VIEW. We look at all of them in detail in Book II. Here, we're going to show you just enough of the basics so you can navigate around your drawing (or one of AutoCAD's sample drawings, in case you haven't actually drawn anything yourself yet).

We begin with the two so-called realtime commands, RTZOOM and RTPAN. They're called *realtime commands* because you can see the change in view in "real time" as you run the command.

Checking out Zoom Realtime

Zooming in a drawing increases or decreases the magnification of drawing objects. To make drawing objects appear larger, you zoom in; to make them appear smaller, you zoom out.

When you zoom in or out of a drawing, you make drawing objects look larger or smaller by moving your viewpoint farther away or closer. You are not changing the objects themselves. When we cover the Modify commands in Book II, you discover a SCALE command that really does make objects smaller or larger by changing their geometry.

There are a number of ways to initiate realtime zoom. Perhaps the easiest is to pick the Zoom Realtime button on the Standard toolbar.

When you start either Zoom Realtime or Pan Realtime, the crosshairs are replaced by a hand cursor or a magnifying glass cursor. Right-clicking displays a shortcut menu that lets you switch from Zoom to Pan and vice versa. There are also three Zoom options on the shortcut menu, as well as a link to the 3DORBIT command. For the time being, we're in a two-dimensional world, but we cover 3DORBIT in Book V.

Using Pan Realtime

Panning in a drawing changes the view without changing the magnification. To initiate realtime pan from a command prompt, click the Pan Realtime button on the Standard toolbar. A right-click in Pan Realtime displays the same shortcut menu as Zoom Realtime, although there are no specific panning options.

To zoom and pan in a drawing, follow these steps:

1. **Open one of your own drawings, or a sample drawing such as**
   `\Program Files\AutoCAD 2007\Sample\Blocks and Tables -`
   `Imperial.dwg`. **Click the Model tab at the lower-left corner of the graphics area.**

   Realtime panning and zooming work in layouts as well as the model tab, but to keep it simple for now, we'll stay on the model tab. (We cover model space and paper space differences in the next chapter.)

2. **Click the Zoom Realtime button on the Standard toolbar. (It's the button with the magnifying glass and the plus-minus sign.)**

   You can't use any other command during a realtime zoom or pan. The command line disappears and is replaced by this prompt:

   ```
   Press ESC or ENTER to exit, or right-click to display
       shortcut menu.
   ```

3. **Move the magnifying glass cursor to the middle of the screen and then hold the left mouse button and drag the cursor toward the bottom of the screen, and then toward the top of the screen.**

Dragging the magnifying-glass cursor upward zooms in closer to the drawing objects; dragging it downward zooms farther away.

4. **Click the right mouse button to display the shortcut menu shown in Figure 4-3. Choose Pan from the shortcut menu.**

   The magnifying-glass cursor changes to the hand cursor; you're now in realtime pan mode, just as if you'd started the Pan Realtime command from the Standard toolbar.

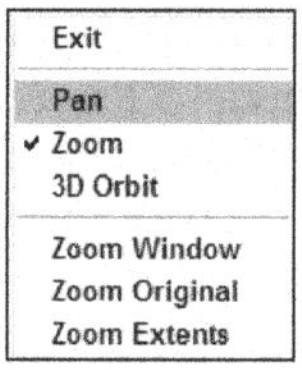

Figure 4-3:
The shortcut menu in real time.

Exit
Pan
✓ Zoom
3D Orbit
Zoom Window
Zoom Original
Zoom Extents

5. **Press and drag the left button across the screen to pan the drawing back and forth around the display.**

   You can toggle back and forth between realtime panning and zooming by right-clicking at any time and choosing the other mode.

6. **Right-click to display the shortcut menu. Click Zoom Original to return to the original view of the drawing.**

   This is a quick way to get back to where you started, in case you get lost with all the panning and zooming. We describe the other two Zoom options on the shortcut menu — Zoom Window and Zoom Extents — in Book II, Chapter 3.

7. **Right-click again to redisplay the shortcut menu. Click Exit.**

   The hand cursor or magnifying cursor is replaced by the standard AutoCAD crosshairs, and the command line looks like this:

   ```
   Press ESC or ENTER to exit, or right-click to display
       shortcut menu.

   Command:
   ```

In this chapter, we only cover very basic panning and zooming using one tool button. We cover the remaining zoom options — and there are several — in Book II.

Editing Objects

AutoCAD provides three ways to edit objects:

✦ Start the command first, and then select objects.

✦ Select objects first, and then start the command.

✦ Grip editing. When you select an object by clicking it, you see one or more little square blue boxes. These are called *grips*. You can click one of these blue boxes (it will turn red) and access a range of editing commands without ever needing to go to a menu or tool button. Book II is the place to go for more information on modifying objects with grips.

For now, we're going to stick with the traditional method of editing — choose the Edit command, and then select the objects. If you only ever learn one of these three methods, this is the one, because every Edit command is available this way. Not all commands will work in select-the-object-first mode, and even fewer work with grips.

Erasing and Unerasing Stuff

The vast majority of the work you do in any AutoCAD drawing consists of editing things that you've already drawn. Editing means copying, stretching, rotating — and getting rid of mistakes.

Using the digital eraser

There is a wide range of things you might want to do with objects in your drawing. You could move them, copy them, rotate them, scale them, mirror them . . . but maybe they're just bad objects, and more than anything you want to remove, delete, expunge, annihilate . . . erase them. Here's how:

1. **Open one of your own drawings, or a sample drawing such as**
   `\Program Files\AutoCAD 2007\Sample\Blocks and Tables - Imperial.dwg.`

   Again, this will go more easily if the Model tab is current.

2. **Click the Erase tool button on the Standard toolbar.**

   AutoCAD prompts:

   ```
   Command: e ERASE
   Select objects:
   ```

3. **Select two or three objects by clicking each one.**

4. **AutoCAD highlights the objects by displaying them in dashed linework and prompts as follows:**

```
Select objects: 1 found
Select objects: 1 found, 2 total
Select objects: 1 found, 3 total
Select objects:
```

AutoCAD continues adding objects that you select to its total.

5. **When you finish selecting objects to edit, press Enter.**

The selected objects are erased from the drawing.

These steps are typical for any editing operation in AutoCAD. The most important thing to remember is that you must press Enter when you finish selecting objects to complete any editing command.

Unerasing objects

Everyone makes mistakes, right? Including erasing objects in a drawing that *really* shouldn't have been erased. The real world doesn't have unerasers yet, but you're using AutoCAD now.

Like most Windows programs, AutoCAD has an UNDO command (covered in the next section). The problem with UNDO is that you can't selectively skip over a bunch of stuff to get back to the action that you really want to undo. Say, for example, you erased a wall and then drew a new wall in a different place, and then copied some bathroom fixtures, and then zoomed and panned — and then you realized you never should have erased that original wall in the first place. AutoCAD will let you undo back to just before that crucial erasure. Unfortunately, it will also undo the pan, the zoom, the copied bathroom fixtures, and the new wall in a different place that you really wanted to keep, all before it will undo that erasure.

There's a little-known command that's appropriately called OOPS. It's little known because it doesn't have a tool button, and it's not on any menu. You have to *know* it's there, and you have to type the command into the command line. OOPS has one single function: It unerases the last thing you erased. So, in the just mentioned scenario, if you'd entered OOPS instead of undoing back, you'd have maintained the view you got by panning and zooming, you'd have retained those copied bathroom fixtures as well as that new wall, and you'd restored that wall you never should have erased — because it was the last thing you erased, and that's exactly what OOPS is for. Remember OOPS. Write it down and pin it up over your desk. If anyone asks, you can tell them it's your mantra.

Undo. Redo. Undo. Redo . . .

Like all good Windows programs, AutoCAD has Undo and Redo functions. Typically for AutoCAD, the UNDO command is complex and has a number of options.

The simplest way to run UNDO is to use the Windows Ctrl+Z shortcut. Or type **U** at the command line and press Enter. Or click the Undo button on the Standard toolbar.

If you enter UNDO at the command line and press Enter, you get the full-blown AutoCAD UNDO command. The command line looks like this:

```
Command: UNDO
Current settings: Auto = On, Control = All, Combine = Yes
Enter the number of operations to undo or
    [Auto/Control/BEgin/End/Mark/Back]
```

We have more to say about UNDO in Book II.

Right next door to the Undo button on the Standard toolbar is a Redo button. In the latest versions of AutoCAD, you can redo multiple undos — great if you're one of those people who just *can't* make up your mind!

Chapter 5: Setting Up Drawings

In This Chapter

- Establishing drawing units
- Understanding systems of measure
- Establishing drawing limits
- Understanding scale and scale factors
- Choosing between model space or paper space
- Working with layers
- Understanding object properties
- Establishing standards
- Creating templates

AutoCAD is much more than an electronic sketch pad. Technical drawings — as we're sure you're aware — need to be accurate, precise, neat enough to be read easily, and standardized. The next chapter covers precision drawing techniques. This chapter explains how to set up drawings and introduces a number of ways to ensure standardization — ways that help you draw more efficiently.

Choosing Units of Measurement

In this book, when we discuss units of measurement in AutoCAD, we're not talking about *systems* of measurement, and it's important to keep those two separate.

Globally speaking, there are two main *systems* of measurement in use today. *Imperial* or *English* measure is based on inches, and metric measure is based on the meter (or metre, if you live outside the United States).

Several versions back, AutoCAD referred to *English* units and metric units. In AutoCAD 2000, the terminology switched — apparently incorrectly — to *Imperial* units and metric units. There are slight differences between English and Imperial liquid measure, although they're not likely to bother most

AutoCAD users who deal in linear and angular measure. For example, a U.S. pint has 16 ounces and a UK pint has 20 ounces, but a foot in both countries contains 12 inches. Come to think of it, maybe it *would* bother the AutoCAD user who's just ordered a pint of Guinness!

The metric system has been, or is being, adopted in virtually every country in the world, but some are taking longer than others to embrace it. The biggest holdout — wouldn't you know it — is the United States. Rumor has it, in fact, that the United States, Liberia, and Myanmar are the last countries in the world using English (or is that Imperial?) units.

Talking about units in AutoCAD can be confusing. It's worth establishing some definitions before we get to the nitty-gritty:

+ **Units:** *Units* is a generic term in AutoCAD, and it can cause a lot of confusion to both newbies and experienced users; it's best if you state specifically what *kind* of units you mean.

  • **Real-world units:** Real-world units are the units you measure things with every day. These units may be inches or miles, or millimeters or kilometers, or yards or nautical miles. Real-world units are established components of a uniform *system of measure* such as the metric system.

  • **AutoCAD units:** AutoCAD, like all CAD programs, works by crunching numbers, and numbers generally don't have real-world units attached to them — they're just numbers. AutoCAD units can be formatted so that they look like real-world units, but internally, they're just numbers.

+ **Unit types:** There are two types of AutoCAD unit: *linear* and *angular*.

+ **Unit formats:** Each of the two unit types can be formatted in one of five ways, as shown in Table 5-1.

+ **System of measure:** Globally, the most widely used system of measure is the metric system. Locally (if you're a North American, that is), the English (or Imperial) system of measure is much more widely used. These are the two systems of measure we focus on in this book, and we assume the vast majority of our readers are on the same pages.

Table 5-1		AutoCAD Unit Formats	
Linear	*Example*	*Angular*	*Example*
Architectural	1'-3 1/2"	Decimal degrees	90.000°
Decimal	15.5000	Deg/Min/Sec	90d'0"
Engineering	1'-3.5000"	Grads	100.000g
Fractional	15 1/2	Radians	1.571r
Scientific	1.5500E+01	Surveyor	N0d00'00.0"E

Regarding Table 5-1:

+ All linear examples are equivalent to one another, and all angular examples are equivalent to one another.

+ *Architectural units* in AutoCAD mean feet and fractional inches. Of course, architects outside the U.S.A. and Canada will have to configure decimal units if they want to work in metric units.

+ *Surveyor units* in AutoCAD mean quadrant bearings (for example, North 30 degrees West), but quadrant bearings are used only by American surveyors. Surveyors in other parts of the world work in whole circle bearings in either decimal degrees (for example, 120.000°) or Deg/Min/Sec (for example, 120d'00"00).

+ The default precision for Angular units is zero places; Table 5-1 shows the results of setting three places of precision.

Despite the large number of choices, chances are that you'll be working in either architectural (feet-and-fractional inches) or decimal linear units, and decimal degree, or possibly deg/min/sec angular units.

Don't be fooled by those foot-and-inch marks you see if you configure AutoCAD to display architectural or engineering units. It's just a clever program that sticks the inch mark on every unit, and whenever it reaches 12 of those, adds a foot value and foot mark. It may look like 1'–4 1/2" to you, but it's just 16.5000 to AutoCAD.

If you are working in architectural units, remember that the AutoCAD unit represents an inch. If you want to enter 6", entering **6** is enough. If you want to enter 6', then you need to include the foot mark. If you don't use a foot mark, AutoCAD assumes that you want to use inches.

AutoCAD units

AutoCAD ignores the differences between metric and English/Imperial units because it doesn't actually work in either. In AutoCAD, the fundamental unit is . . . the *unit*. It's up to you, the AutoCAD user, to determine what kind of real-world units AutoCAD *units* represent.

Unless specifically labeled otherwise, AutoCAD's drawing templates have their units *format* (not their units *type*) set to decimal units, with four places of precision. Those decimal units can represent any real-world unit you want; they could represent decimal inches, decimal meters, decimal miles — whatever real-world unit you decide to use.

When you set units format in the Drawing Units dialog box, you control the display of units in the coordinate display on the status bar, and in the Properties palette, command line, and dynamic input tooltip when you draw new objects or query existing ones. You are *not* affecting the display of dimension values. To see how to format dimension values, see Book III.

Imperial or metric

Despite the previous discussion on AutoCAD units versus real-world units, you still need to determine up front whether you're working in metric or Imperial (or is it English?) units. Remember, as far as AutoCAD is concerned, a unit is a unit is a unit.

Choosing a metric or Imperial default beforehand can make your drafting more efficient. Why? Because if you start a drawing with Imperial defaults, you're automatically configured to use the Imperial hatch pattern and line-type definition files, and if you start out with metric defaults, you're automatically configured for the metric equivalents.

AutoCAD uses external definition files for its hatch patterns and linetype patterns. For hatch patterns, AutoCAD has two files, acad.PAT and acadiso.PAT. Similarly for linetype pattern definitions, there are two files named acad.LIN and acadiso.LIN. (The equivalent files in AutoCAD LT are acadlt.PAT, acadltiso.PAT, acadlt.LIN, and acadltiso.LIN.) We discuss linetypes later in this chapter. See Book III, Chapter 3 for more on adding hatch patterns to drawings.

Here's how to determine whether to start with a metric-defaults drawing or an Imperial-defaults drawing:

✦ Starting with the template acad.DWT (acadlt.DWT in AutoCAD LT) sets Imperial defaults; starting with the template acadiso.DWT (acadltiso. DWT) sets metric defaults.

✦ Starting with any of the ISO templates (DIN, Gb, JIS, or ISO) sets metric defaults.

✦ Other templates that don't fall into either of these categories identify by their filenames whether they are set up for Imperial or metric.

System variables

You need to know about two system variables, especially if you work in both Imperial and metric systems of measure. If you work exclusively in one or the other, it still doesn't hurt to know about them, but you can file them in a dustier, less-visited part of your brain. (For more on system variables, see Chapter 2.)

✦ **MEASUREMENT:** This variable has a value of either 0 (Imperial units) or 1 (metric units). The MEASUREMENT variable is stored in each drawing, which means you can work with drawings based in either Imperial units or metric units.

✦ **MEASUREINIT:** This variable also has a value of either 0 (for Imperial units) or 1 (for metric units). MEASUREINIT is stored in the system registry and determines whether drawings started from scratch (without a template) call on the acad (acadlt) or acadiso (acadltiso) pattern and linetype files.

As long as you start your drawings from the appropriate template files (that is, acad.DWT or acadlt.DWT for Imperial units, or acadiso.DWT or acadltiso. DWT for metric units), the MEASUREMENT system variable is automatically set correctly. The value of the MEASUREINIT variable is set when you install AutoCAD; by default, it's set to 0 for Imperial units if you live in the United States, and 1 for metric units if you live anywhere else in the world.

Setting units in your drawing

The following steps show how to set architectural linear units and Deg/Min/Sec angular units for your current drawing:

1. **From the Format menu, choose Units.**

AutoCAD displays the Drawing Units dialog box (see Figure 5-1).

Figure 5-1: Format the display of drawing units in the Drawing Units dialog box.

2. **In the Length area, click the Type list box and then choose Architectural.**

The Precision list box and Sample Output display change to show feet and fractional inches.

3. **In the Length area, click the Precision list box and choose the desired precision format.**

The acceptable range of values is 0'0" to 0'–0 1/256".

You are not setting dimension format here. You'd never see a drawing dimensioned to the nearest 256th of an inch, but you might want to see more precision in the units on-screen as you're drawing.

For now, ignore the list box in the Insertion Scale area; we cover insert units in Book VI.

4. **In the Angle area, click the drop-down list box and choose Deg/Min/Sec.**

The Precision list box and Sample Output display change to show degrees-minutes-seconds format.

5. **In the Angle area, click the Precision list box and choose the desired precision format.**

Setting the maximum precision in the drop-down list formats angular units to degrees, minutes, and seconds to four decimal places.

Setting Limits for Your Drawings

Well, you don't want them staying out all night, do you? Or borrowing the car and leaving it in the impound lot?

Okay, different kind of limits. In AutoCAD, the limits of a drawing defines the drawing area. But you've already seen in Chapter 1 that in AutoCAD, you have an unlimited drawing area, so why does it now have limits?

It may not make a lot of sense to pay strict attention to limits when you can change those limits whenever you want. In fact, limits are a historical artifact in AutoCAD, and in our view, they're of . . . er, limited use on modern systems.

All the same, it's not a bad idea to know how big your drawing area is, even though it can be infinitely large and infinitely flexible. That's because sooner or later you're going to want to print that drawing, and that means you're going to have to fit it onto a piece of paper.

The theory behind limits is that you set your drawing limits according to the sheet size on which you'll ultimately plot your drawing. So if you're drawing a mouse pad, you might set your drawing limits to $11 \times 8\text{-}\frac{1}{2}$ inches so that the limits represent a letter-size sheet. If you're drawing a fax machine, you'd set the drawing limits to 36×24 inches, to represent a D-size sheet.

Here are some other reasons to set limits for your drawing:

✦ **Defining the grid:** AutoCAD can display a grid of horizontally and vertically aligned dots over your drawing area. This grid can help keep you aware of the relative sizes of what you're drawing and their size on the printed drawing. We cover the grid in detail in Chapter 6 of this mini-book, but for now, the key point is that the grid will be displayed over the area defined by the drawing limits.

✦ **Zooming:** An option of the ZOOM command is All. Issuing a Zoom and selecting the All option zooms the drawing out so that everything within the drawing limits is displayed. This can be useful if you want to see some white space (or black space, depending on your display configuration) around your drawing objects.

✦ **Plotting:** If you want to plot a drawing from the Model tab (we discuss the Model tab in the "Lost in Space: Model or Paper?" section later in this chapter, and we cover plotting drawings in Book VII), one of the options is Limits. Choosing Limits plots everything within the defined limits of the drawing.

Pay attention to the order of those values. In AutoCAD, the horizontal dimension always comes before the vertical, so a 24×36-inch sheet would be aligned in portrait (long side vertical) mode, and a 36×24-inch sheet would be aligned in landscape (long side horizontal) mode.

So far so good, but it gets a little more complicated when you start drawing things that *won't* fit on a sheet of paper at their full size — no matter how big the paper is. For more on scaling, see the "Understanding Drawing Scale" section a bit later on in this chapter.

You specify the drawing limits by entering coordinates for the lower-left and upper-right corners of the drawing area. The following procedure shows you how to set your drawing's limits:

1. **Choose Format⇨Drawing Limits, or type LIMITS and press Enter.**

AutoCAD does not provide a tool button for this command, nor is there a dialog box; you must use the menu or the keyboard. AutoCAD prompts you as follows:

```
Reset Model space limits:
Specify lower left corner or [ON/OFF] <0.0000,0.0000>:
```

2. **Press Enter to accept 0,0 as the lower-left corner.**

It's a good idea to accept the default value (0,0) for the lower-left limit. 0,0 is the origin of the coordinate system. Chapter 6 covers the coordinate system in detail.

AutoCAD then prompts:

```
Specify upper right corner <12.0000,9.0000>:
```

3. **Enter a new value in coordinates for the upper-right corner of the drawing limits, and then press Enter.**

Understanding Drawing Scale

Just now, we were talking about drawing mouse pads and fax machines, objects you can carry around easily, and which will fit on a letter-size or D-size drawing sheet. Most of the time however, you're going to be drawing things that won't fit very well, or won't fit at all, on a sheet of paper. In order to make your drawing objects fit on the sheet, you're going to have to use a scale factor.

You know that AutoCAD has an infinitely large sheet of virtual paper at its disposal. You've just learned that if your virtual drawing sheet isn't big enough, you can just make it bigger by altering the drawing limits. This is a great system — until you have to produce hard copy of your drawing.

Scaling on the drawing board

In manual drafting, you're given a sheet of paper on which to lay out a drawing. Assume that it's an ISO A1 sheet that measures 841 × 594 mm. By the time you've taken margins and room for a border and title block into account, you're left with a drawing area of, say, 550 × 475 mm.

Now suppose that you've been given a floor plan to draw. The building measures 45 meters by 70 meters. Obviously, you're not going to draw that building full size on an A1 sheet. You need to figure out a reduction factor that lets you draw your detailed plan of the building to an approved drafting scale and fit it on the sheet. You decide that the floor plan will fit on the sheet at a scale of 1:20. So you dig out your drafting scale, flip it around to the 1:20 scale, and start laying out your sheet.

When drawing manually, you scale everything down as you draw. Otherwise, things won't fit on the page.

Scaling in AutoCAD

You already know that in AutoCAD, you draw things full size, so that's how you've drawn your 45 × 70-meter floor plan. You're also given an A1 sheet on which to produce your drawing.

In AutoCAD, you have two ways to produce your drawing, which (you have calculated) needs to end up at a scale of 1:20 on the paper drawing:

✦ **Plot from model space.** When plotting from model space, you tell the PLOT command to print the drawing at a scale of 1:20. Most of the time you'll be plotting from a layout, so don't worry too much about this method.

✦ **Plot from a layout.** A layout represents a blank, physical sheet of paper on which you lay out your drawing sheet. You create a viewport — in effect, a hole in the drawing sheet through which you can view your floor plan in model space. You apply a scale of 1:20 *to the viewport.* You then tell the PLOT command to plot the drawing at 1:1.

Is your head hurting? We've just tossed you a bunch of terms you may not have come across before: *model space, layout,* and *viewport.*

Don't worry — we cover the differences between model space and layouts (paper space) in the next section of this chapter. All we wanted to get across here is the different methods of scaling between manual and AutoCAD drafting.

Scale factors

What both systems — manual drafting and CAD — have in common is *scale factor.* Whichever method you use to end up with a 1:20 scale plotted drawing, there's a scale factor involved. Now, prepare yourself for your head to hurt again, because we're going to do some math. To calculate the scale factor of any given scale, you take the inverse of the scale ratio itself.

Okay, this calls for some examples. The metric system is about as simple as it gets, because a drawing with a scale of 1:20 has a scale factor of 20. A scale of 1:50 has a scale factor of 50, and 1:100 has a scale factor of 100.

It gets a little more complicated with Imperial scales, because we're typically dealing with scales like 1/4"=1'-0" or 1"=20'. You'll notice that these scales have units, and here's what really messes things up: They have different units on each side of the equal sign. Before you can calculate the scale factor, you have to find the scale's ratio, and for that, you need to make both sides of the equation have the same units.

As an example, take the drawing scale 1/8"=1'-0". To find the ratio, first convert both sides of the equation to the same units; you arrive at 1/8"=12". Next, multiply both sides of the equation so that you're dealing with whole numbers; in this case, multiplying both sides by 8 gives you 1"=96". The scale can also be expressed as 1:96, and so the scale factor is 96. (The metric system is a lot easier, isn't it?)

Table 5-2 lists some common scales and their corresponding scale factors (*we* do the math!):

Table 5-2	Common Scales and Scale Factors	
Drawing Scale	*Ratio*	*Scale Factor*
1"=500'	1:6000	6000
1"=200'	1:2400	2400
1"=100'	1:1200	1200
1"=50'	1:600	600
1"=20'	1:240	240
1"=10'	1:120	120
1/16"=1'-0"	1:192	192
1/8"=1'-0"	1:96	96
1/4"=1'-0"	1:48	48
1/2"=1'-0"	1:24	24
1"=1'-0"	1:12	12
3"=1'-0"	1:4	4
12"=1'-0"	1:1	1
1:100	1:100	100
1:50	1:50	50
1:20	1:20	20
1:10	1:10	10
1:5	1:5	5
1:2	1:2	2
1:1	1:1	1

Using scale factors to establish drawing settings

You use the drawing scale factors that you've just worked out to establish a number of drawing settings. These include

+ **Drawing limits:** Multiply the scale factor by the dimensions of your plot sheet to arrive at the limits. For example, if you're going to print your drawing on a D-size sheet (36 × 24") at a scale of 1/4"=1'-0", multiply both sheet dimensions by the scale factor of 48. This gives you an area of 1728" by 1152", so you would set the upper-right corner of the limits to 1728,1152 (or 144',96').

+ **Dimension scale:** All dimension sizes and spaces are set to their actual plotted size. Text, for example, may be 2.5mm high. But 2.5mm text would be invisible next to a wall that is 70 meters long. If you're dimensioning in model space, you set the dimension scale factor equivalent to the drawing scale factor. We cover dimensions in Book III.

+ **Text height:** Some drawing text goes in model space — and once again, text that's specified as 1/8" high will be a speck beside a 200' wall. Multiply the desired text height times the drawing scale factor to arrive at a model-space text height that won't be a speck; in this case, you'd multiply 1/8" times the drawing scale factor of 48, and tell AutoCAD to make your text 6" high.

+ **Hatch pattern scale** and **linetype scale** are also based on the drawing scale factor.

Lost in Space: Model or Paper?

It's possible to print your drawing from the Model tab, but it's much more convenient to print from a layout. To do so, you must understand some of the differences between model space and paper space, where layouts live.

+ **Model space** is the drawing environment that corresponds to the Model tab. Model space can represent an infinitely large, three-dimensional area in which you create "real" objects. These objects are referred to as the "model," whether they are 2D or 3D. Every drawing entity that represents a real object is created in model space. Because only one model space exists, AutoCAD provides only one Model tab. On the Model tab, you can see only objects in model space.

+ **Paper space (also called a "paper space layout" or "layout space")** is the drawing environment that corresponds to the Layout tabs. Although model space represents the "real" 1:1 space where you create your models, paper space represents the 2D drawing sheet that you create to document them. Any objects you add to your model to document it — for example, border, notes, dimensions, section marks, and so on — are generally drawn in a paper space layout. (Notable exceptions are center lines and hatching.) Because you may want to create more than one drawing sheet from a model, you can have an infinite number of layouts in a drawing file.

✦ **Layout** is the tabbed environment where you create plottable drawing sheets. The layout represents what will be plotted to paper. In addition to borders, title blocks, text, and dimensions, layouts include *viewports* — windows cut through the paper so you can see the model. A layout can contain a single viewport, or several viewports that examine different areas of the model at the same or different scales. On the Layout tabs, you can see objects in model space and paper space, although you must select objects in one space or the other — never both at the same time.

Every AutoCAD drawing must have a Model tab and at least one Layout tab.

Create your object geometry on the Model tab. Create your sheet layouts on the Layout tabs. For more on layouts and viewports, see Book VII.

A Layered Approach

Layers are your principal tool for controlling information in an AutoCAD drawing. Layers are like transparent overlays in manual drafting, where you assemble different combinations of overlays to present different types of information.

On an architectural drawing, for example, one drawing can contain the walls, furniture layout, and ceiling grid with light fixtures and diffusers, as shown in Figure 5-2. If each type of information is on its own layer, you can generate a floor plan drawing by turning on the walls and furniture layers, and turning off the ceiling layer. Then you can turn off the furniture layer and turn on the ceiling layer to generate a new drawing, a reflected ceiling plan.

Figure 5-2:
Turn layers off and on to generate different sheets from the same drawing file.

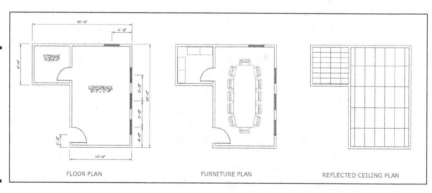

FLOOR PLAN   FURNITURE PLAN   REFLECTED CEILING PLAN

Layers are also used to segregate different drawing components. For example, dimensions usually go on their own layer, as does text, the drawing border, and any title-block information.

Layers must be created before they can be used. AutoCAD creates layer names automatically as you add layers, but it gives them names like Layer 1, Layer 2, Layer 3, and so on. It's a good idea to give your layers sensible names as you create them. Layer names can be up to 255 characters long (which is pretty impractical!), and you can have up to 65,000 layers in a drawing, which is also pretty impractical.

One process for setting up and using layers in a drawing is as follows:

1. **Create the layers you need.**

2. **Assign color and linetype properties as required.**

3. **Set the desired layer current.**

4. **Draw stuff.**

Anything you draw from this point on will be placed on the layer you made current, until such time as you make another layer current.

All AutoCAD drawings contain a layer called 0, which cannot be renamed or deleted. We recommend that you don't actually draw anything on Layer 0; instead, you should create layers specifically for the objects that you'll be adding to the drawing. Layer 0 has special properties when you create blocks, which we go into in Book VI. Another layer that can't be deleted is a special layer named DEFPOINTS; this layer is created the first time you add a dimension to a drawing. We explain dimensions in Book III.

Creating layers

The following steps explain how to use the Layer Properties Manager dialog box to create layers in any drawing file.

1. **Click the Layer Properties Manager tool button on the Standard toolbar.**

AutoCAD displays the Layer Properties Manager dialog box (see Figure 5-3).

2. **Click New Layer to add a new layer definition.**

AutoCAD adds a new layer named Layer 1 to the layer list. The layer name is highlighted, so you can type a new name to replace AutoCAD's generic label.

Delete Layer

Set Current

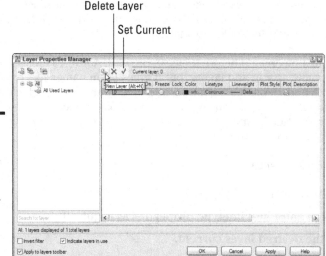

Figure 5-3:
Manage,
manipulate,
and modify
your layers
in the Layer
Properties
Manager
dialog box.

3. Type a new layer name (for example, WALL), and press Enter.

Give your layers sensible names. If you're doing very simple floor plans, it's enough to have layers named WALL, DOOR, WINDOW, APPLIANCE, and so on. Whatever you do, don't accept the default values of Layer 1, Layer 2, and so on, or you'll have no idea what objects are on which layer!

4. Continue adding layer names as required.

If you keep pressing Enter, you can keep adding (and renaming!) new layers.

5. Click Set Current to make a layer the current layer.

Only one layer at a time can be current, and anything you draw is created on the current layer.

Defining layer properties

Once layers are created, you can assign various modes and properties to them. Setting layer properties properly ensures that objects drawn on a given layer take on the color, linetype, lineweight, and plot style assigned to that layer.

Unless you have a really good reason to avoid doing so, it's advisable to use layers to control the appearance of objects. It's possible to set color and other properties of individual objects, but it's usually a bad idea unless you know what you're doing and have a good reason up your sleeve. Applying explicit colors and other properties to objects can make them difficult to edit when the need arises, because you can't tell on which layer the objects are located.

Layer properties include

✦ **Color:** When a color is assigned to a layer, objects drawn on that layer take on that color. Set layer color by accessing the Select Color dialog box through the Layer Properties Manager.

✦ **Linetype:** Most AutoCAD objects have the default linetype, which is a solid, continuous line. However, drafting conventions require the use of non-continuous linetypes (sometimes called *dash-dot* linetypes), such as center lines and hidden lines. You can assign a default linetype to a layer in the Layer Properties Manager dialog box.

✦ **Lineweight:** Lineweight refers to the visible width of lines on the drawing screen. When drawings are printed correctly, the hard copy always shows different line thicknesses — thin lines for dimensions, thick lines for borders, medium lines for object lines and text, and so on. But on-screen, objects usually appear with a single line thickness. You can assign default lineweights to layers in the Layer Properties Manager, so that everything drawn on specific layers will take on that lineweight property.

✦ **Plot style:** If your drawing is configured to use named plot styles, you can assign an already-existing plot style to a layer. If your drawing is set up to use color-dependent plot styles, the Plot Style column in the Layer Properties Manager is grayed out; the only way to change a plot style here is to change the layer color. Plot styles are a complex topic (especially named plot styles!), and we cover them in detail in Book VII.

You can also access the Select Color, Select Linetype, and Lineweight dialog boxes by entering their command names at the command line or by choosing Color, Linetype, or Lineweight from the Format menu. But doing those things does *not* set a layer property — it does something potentially more damaging. It sets the default color, linetype, or lineweight of *all* objects you draw, regardless of their layer settings, from that point forward.

When objects are allowed to take on the properties of the layers on which they are drawn, those properties are said to be *By Layer*.

Setting layer modes

In addition to layer properties, which have a wide range of possible settings, you can choose from a series of layer modes, which are toggles with only two possible settings (see Figure 5-4).

On/Off

Freeze/Thaw

Lock/Unlock   Plot/NoPlot

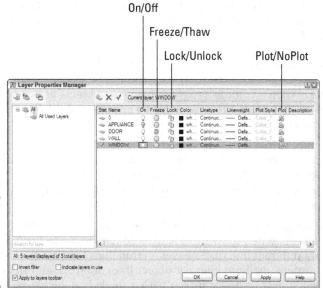

Figure 5-4:
Toggle layer
modes by
clicking
their icons.

The four layer modes are

✦ **On/Off:** Objects on the layer are visible if mode is on (the light bulb is switched on) and invisible if mode is off (light bulb is switched off).

Strangely enough, the current layer can be turned off; it's even possible to draw on a layer that's turned off, as long as it's current. So if you start drawing lines that don't appear on-screen, check the layer mode!

✦ **Freeze/Thaw:** Objects are visible if layer is thawed or invisible if layer is frozen. The difference between Off and Frozen is that frozen layers are not included when AutoCAD has to recalculate its numeric database. A glowing sun indicates thawed layers, and a snowflake means a layer is frozen. You can't set a frozen layer current.

✦ **Lock/Unlock:** When a layer is locked, you can see the objects on it, you can select them, and you can even draw on it. But you can't edit objects on a locked layer. A padlock icon indicates whether a layer is locked.

✦ **Plot/NoPlot:** You can set this layer mode so that objects on the selected layer are visible but will not appear on a plot or print preview.

Modifying layer settings

You can access the Layer Properties Manager dialog box at any time by clicking the Layer Property Manager button on the Layers toolbar, or by typing

LA and pressing Enter. You don't have to create all your layers when you start a new drawing; you can add (or remove) layers at any time in the drawing's life.

Nonetheless, the most efficient way of setting up and managing layers in any drawing is to create them all at once, and make the appropriate property and mode settings while you're creating them.

Setting layer color

The following steps explain how to modify layer properties and settings in the Layer Properties Manager:

1. **If the Layer Properties Manager dialog box is not already open, click the LPM button on the Layers toolbar.**

   AutoCAD displays the Layer Properties Manager.

2. **Select the layer whose color you want to change.**

   To select multiple layers, hold down the Ctrl key as you select them.

3. **Click the square color tile in the Color column.**

   AutoCAD displays the Select Color dialog box (see Figure 5-5).

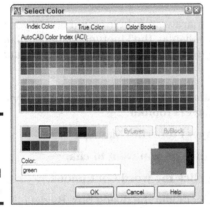

Figure 5-5:
AutoCAD's
standard
colors — all
255 of them.

4. **With the Index Color tab current, select one of the large color tiles near the bottom of the dialog box, and then click OK to close the dialog box.**

   AutoCAD closes the Select Color dialog box and returns focus to the Layer Properties Manager. The foreground color of the sample rectangles changes to the selected color, and the layer shows the new color and name under the Color column.

For more information on using color in AutoCAD, see the "Using AutoCAD's color systems" section later in the chapter.

Setting linetype

There's a wrinkle to setting linetypes in an AutoCAD drawing. Unlike colors, which are always available, non-continuous linetypes are defined in an external file that goes by one of these filenames:

✦ **acad.LIN:** The default linetype-definition file, designed for use with Imperial units drawings and based on inches.

✦ **acadiso.LIN:** The default linetype-definition file designed for use with metric units and based on millimeters.

✦ **acadlt.LIN:** The AutoCAD LT version of acad.LIN. (Prior to AutoCAD 2007, this file was named `aclt.LIN`.)

✦ **acadltiso.LIN:** The AutoCAD LT version of `acadiso.LIN`. (Prior to AutoCAD 2007, this file was named `acltiso.LIN`.)

For an explanation of the different linetype definitions, see the "Using linetypes" section later in the chapter.

You can load linetypes as a separate step, before you create your layers by choosing Format⇨Linetype to display the Linetype Manager dialog box. Alternatively, you can follow these steps to access Linetype Manager through the Layer Properties Manager:

1. **If the Layer Properties Manager dialog box is not already open, click the LPM button on the Layers toolbar.**

AutoCAD displays the Layer Properties Manager.

2. **Select the layer whose linetype you want to change.**

3. **In the Linetype column, click the word Continuous.**

AutoCAD displays the Select Linetype dialog box. By default, only the Continuous linetype is loaded.

4. **Click Load to display the Load or Reload Linetypes dialog box.**

Load or Reload Linetypes displays all linetypes defined in the current linetype definition file (see Figure 5-6).

Figure 5-6:
Linetypes
galore.

5. **Scroll through the list and select the linetypes to load, and then click OK.**

    Hold the Ctrl key to select more than one linetype. Load or Reload
    Linetypes closes, and the focus returns to the Select Linetype dialog box.

6. **Select the linetype you want to assign to the selected layer in the
    Layer Properties Manager, and then click OK.**

    The Select Linetype dialog box closes, and the selected linetype is
    assigned to the layer (see Figure 5-7).

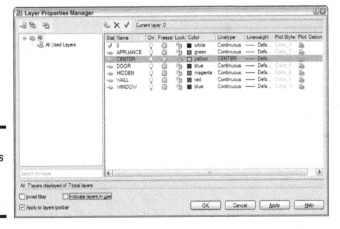

Figure 5-7:
Many clicks
later, a
linetype is
assigned.

Setting lineweight

Lineweights are like colors — they're always present and available, unlike linetypes which have to be loaded into the drawing before they can be assigned.

Lineweight is a display property that shows a representation of the relative thickness of different drawing objects. Lineweight works differently in model space and paper space:

✦ In model space, lineweight is based on a number of pixels, so that no matter how close you zoom in — or how far you zoom out — linework always appears to have the same visual thickness.

✦ In paper space, lineweight is part of the representation of the paper drawing. If you put linework on a paper drawing under a magnifying glass, the lines would appear thicker, and that's exactly how it works in paper space — as you zoom in, the lines appear thicker.

The following steps explain how to assign a lineweight to a layer:

1. **If the Layer Properties Manager dialog box is not already open, click the LPM button on the Layers toolbar.**

AutoCAD displays the Layer Properties Manager.

2. **Select the layer whose lineweight you want to change.**

3. **In the Linetype column, click the word *Default*.**

AutoCAD displays the Lineweight dialog box (see Figure 5-8).

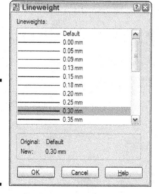

Figure 5-8:
Scroll to set a default lineweight for your layer.

4. **Scroll down the list to find the desired lineweight.**

Because plotter pens were traditionally sized in millimeters, AutoCAD's lineweights are also displayed in millimeters whether metric or English units are configured.

5. **Select the lineweight, and then click OK.**

The Lineweight dialog box closes and focus returns to the Layer Property Manager.

Assigning lineweights to layers is only half the story. You also need to press the LWT button on the status bar to display the lineweights. When the button is selected, lineweight display is enabled; when the button is not selected, all geometry appears in the default line width, which is one pixel.

The lineweight property can be applied to hard copy as well as to the visual representation of drawing objects. We tell you more about that in Book VII.

Setting layer modes

As already noted, the layer modes are toggles that let you control layer visibility, the amount of drawing data that's included in AutoCAD's math calculations, whether a visible layer's objects can be edited, and whether a visible layer's objects will be plotted.

The following procedure runs through the four layer modes in the Layer Properties Manager dialog box:

1. **If the Layer Properties Manager dialog box is not already open, click the LPM button on the Layers toolbar.**

AutoCAD displays the Layer Properties Manager.

2. **Select a layer whose mode you want to modify.**

3. **To toggle a layer's visibility on or off, click the lightbulb icon in the On column.**

4. **To freeze a layer's data from recalculation and turn off its visibility, click the Sun icon in the Freeze column. To thaw a layer, click the snowflake icon.**

5. **To lock or unlock a layer to prevent or allow its objects to be edited, click the padlock icon in the Lock column.**

6. **To prevent or allow objects on a layer to be printed, click the Printer icon in the Plot column.**

The Layer Control drop-down list

You have to use the Layer Properties Manager dialog box to modify layer properties, including color, linetype, lineweight, and plot style. You can also turn layer modes off and on in the Layer Properties Manager, but if the latter is all you need to do, there's a more efficient way than opening and closing a dialog box.

The Layers toolbar contains a drop-down list of all the layers in a drawing (see Figure 5-9).

Figure 5-9:
Switch layer modes in the Layer Control drop-down list.

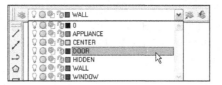

You can click the down arrow (or inside the list box) to expand the list, and then perform any of the following actions:

✦ Set a layer current by clicking the layer name.

✦ Turn layer visibility off or on by clicking the light bulb.

✦ Freeze or thaw a layer by clicking the sun or snowflake.

   You can't freeze the current layer.

✦ Lock or unlock a layer by clicking the padlock.

After you change the mode, click anywhere outside the Layer Control list to close the list and return focus to the drawing.

The third icon shows a sun or snowflake superimposed on a rectangle. This mode lets you freeze or thaw layers in a layout's viewport. We discuss this option in greater detail in Book VII.

Because the Layer Control drop-down shows a color tile for each layer, you might think you could click it to change a layer's color, but you'd be wrong. Color is a property, and properties can only be changed in the Layer Properties Manager.

Object Properties

In AutoCAD, all objects have properties. Every object in a drawing is created on a layer. Layers can have a number of properties assigned to them, and anything drawn on a specific layer takes on the color, linetype, lineweight and other "by layer" properties of that layer.

In addition to the properties that an object inherits from its layer, an object can have the following properties:

+ Color
+ Linetype
+ Lineweight
+ Plot Style

Object properties can be assigned directly (or *explicitly*) to objects, or they can be assigned to layers. For example, on a floor plan you might have a bunch of blue doors. The color blue may have been assigned to each individual door, in which case the color will be listed as *Blue*. Or the color blue may have been assigned to the layer on which the doors were drawn, in which case the color is listed as *BYLAYER*.

Is one method better than the other? We certainly think so. For example, you may draw a floor plan in which you make all the doors blue. Then you decide they should be green instead. If you changed the doors explicitly, you would have to go through the drawing and select each and every door, and then open the Properties palette and change their color to green. Alternatively, you could just open the Layer Properties Manager and change the color of the Door layer from blue to green. Obviously, one of these processes is easier than the other.

When objects do not have explicit colors or other properties set, they take on the properties of the layers.

 We strongly advise you not to change the properties of objects in a drawing, but instead to leave their color, linetype, lineweight, and other properties set to BYLAYER. Applying explicit changes to objects can make them difficult to edit because you can't tell on which layer the objects are located.

Using AutoCAD's color systems

In AutoCAD drafting, color has two main functions, neither of which is producing color drawings:

✦ Color helps you differentiate objects on-screen. When you assign colors to layers, you can tell immediately if something is on the wrong layer if it doesn't show up in the color you expect.

✦ Using the traditional color-dependent plotting system, the colors of objects determine the thickness of the printed linework.

Recent releases of AutoCAD support three color systems:

✦ **ACI Color Index:** The original and genuine 255 colors that have always been part of AutoCAD (see Figure 5-5).

✦ **True Color:** A range of over 16 million colors you can set by dragging sliders or entering RGB (Red Green Blue) or HSL (Hue Saturation Luminance) values.

✦ **Color Books:** Select colors using Pantone or RAL colors.

You may use True Color or Color Books colors if you were trying to match specific material colors. For most drafting purposes, the 255 standard colors on the ACI Color Index tab are adequate.

Don't get attached to the idea of using True Color or Color Books colors if you're using AutoCAD LT. AutoCAD's lower-cost sibling supports only the 255 ACI Color Index colors.

Using linetypes

The four linetype files (acad.LIN and acadiso.LIN, and their acadlt equivalents) include 45 different linetype definitions, broken down as follows:

✦ **Twenty-four AutoCAD standard linetypes:** 8 basic patterns (border, center, dashdot, dashed, divide, dot, hidden, and phantom) each in three spacing variants; for example, BORDER has normal spacing of its dash and dot elements; BORDER2's elements are half the size of BORDER's; BORDERX2's elements are twice the size of BORDER.

✦ **Fourteen ISO 128 linetypes conforming to ISO/DIS 12011 specification:** These are rarely used; we recommend you stick with the 24 standard linetypes, for Imperial or metric drafting.

✦ **Seven complex linetypes:** These include symbols or text as well as dash-dot line patterns. Linetypes include fence lines, railroad tracks, and batt insulation.

In addition to these 45 linetypes, the `acadiso.LIN` and `acadltiso.LIN` files include an additional 14 JIS linetypes. While all the above linetypes will work for either Imperial or metric drafting, the JIS linetypes are for metric work only. And we *still* recommend the 24 standard linetypes for most drafting in metric or Imperial.

Setting Up Standards

In this chapter, we discuss the many settings that you can use to enhance your AutoCAD drawings. You may have observed that AutoCAD provides a great deal of settings, and if you're like us, the last thing you want to do is go through those steps every time you want to create a new drawing.

The good news is, you don't have to!

In Chapter 2, we discuss the various file types available in AutoCAD, and we explain how to create a drawing using a template (DWT) file. We point out that templates are fine as far as they went, but that you probably want to add settings (and maybe even objects) in order to make them *really* useful.

Everything that we discuss in this chapter — from layers, to linetypes, to text and dimension styles — can be created and saved in a template drawing so that they're available to you in every drawing you start from that template. After going through this chapter, you know that you can add quite a few settings to a template to save yourself a great bit of effort for future drawings. In the chapters ahead, we look at annotation, inserting blocks, and other features that will enhance the usability of your template drawings as well.

Chapter 6: Precision Tools

In This Chapter

✓ Defining precision versus accuracy

✓ Understanding coordinate systems

✓ Entering coordinates

✓ Using Direct Distance Entry

✓ Using drawing modes, object snaps, and point filters

✓ Using object-snap tracking

The purpose of creating technical drawings, or *drafting,* is to convey enough information to a builder or fabricator so that she or he can construct or manufacture whatever it is that you've just technically drawn . . . er, drafted.

Manual drawings are as precise as the drafter can make them, which means as precise as a mechanical pencil dragged against a parallel rule or drafting machine. They're good enough to get the job done because the dimensions are going to confirm sizes and notes.

Dimensioning can be a major job in manual drafting, and luckily, you have an extra tool at your disposal with AutoCAD: You can add dimensions by clicking objects or selecting points. AutoCAD extracts the dimension value and adds the correct text to the dimension. Now, if you are precise in your drafting, the dimension values will be perfect, but if you are sloppy . . . you may be hearing from the builder whom you've asked to locate a wall 12'–6 29/256" from the corner!

This chapter tells you how to make use of AutoCAD's built-in aids to precision drafting.

Understanding Accuracy and Precision

You probably hear a lot of sloppy word usage in the technical-drawing field. One of the most common offenses is the idea that *accuracy* and *precision* mean the same thing. They're different, and here's how:

✦ *Precision* means the degree of fineness of measurement. AutoCAD is capable of extremely high levels of precision — and can create drawings much more precisely than, say, a building or a highway could ever be constructed.

✦ *Accuracy* refers to the relationship between what is being drafted and reality. You can create the most precise drawings of which AutoCAD is capable, but if the surveyor got the field measurements wrong, or you read her field notes incorrectly, your drawing is not going to be accurate to reality.

Although accuracy is important, precision is the order of the day when you work with AutoCAD. Here's the skinny on AutoCAD's precision tools:

✦ **Coordinate input:** Place drawing objects by specifying the *x*, *y*, and *z* coordinates that locate them in 3D space.

✦ **Direct Distance Entry:** Locate new points relative to a point you've just entered by dragging the mouse pointer to show direction and then entering a value for the distance.

✦ **Grid and snap:** Drafting modes you can toggle off and on; grid is a purely visual aid, but snap is a precision input method.

✦ **Ortho and polar:** More on/off drafting modes; when turned on, Ortho mode forces linework to be horizontal or vertical, and polar tracking guides linework along preset angles.

✦ **Object snaps:** Locate points that fall at precise locations on existing objects (such as endpoints and midpoints of lines, or centers and quadrant points of circles).

✦ **Object-snap tracking:** Use object snaps on existing objects to find new points to create new objects.

AutoCAD LT 2007 finally includes object-snap tracking! Earlier versions did not include this feature — it was part of the full version of AutoCAD only.

Through a combination of these different precision aids, you can create drawings far more precise than the most skillful manually drafted drawing. And what you'll quickly find as you gain experience is that drawing precisely is easier than drawing sloppily.

Understanding Coordinate Systems

In an AutoCAD drawing, everything is located in 2D (or 3D) space by a set of Cartesian, or *x,y* (*-z*), coordinates. Cartesian coordinates are named after the French philosopher Rene Descartes, who's probably better known for his saying, "I think, therefore I am."

Descartes believed that you could tease out the meaning of anything through a system of reasoning modeled on the certainty of mathematics. One of the side benefits of his mathematical thinking (arguably a more useful one than the system of reasoning) was the coordinate system named after him. Described simply, everything in 3D space can be located from a predefined origin by counting the number of units in each of the three directions between the object and the origin.

The 2D coordinate system — for the time being, we'll stick with 2D to keep things simple — is defined by a horizontal and a vertical axis. By convention, the horizontal axis is called the *x axis*, and the vertical axis is called the *y axis*. The *x* axis and *y* axis intersect at the *origin* of the coordinate system. The two axes define a plane called, naturally enough, the *xy plane*. The coordinates of any point are its distances from the origin along the *x* axis and the *y* axis, and the coordinates are expressed in the form *x,y*. For example, the coordinate pair 5,4 would indicate a point lying 3 units to the right of the origin along the *x* axis, and 2 units above the origin along the *y* axis.

The 3D coordinate system adds a third axis, the *z axis* (which is pronounced *zed-axis* outside the United States). The *z* axis also passes through the origin, and is perpendicular to the *xy* plane. We have more to say about the *z* axis in Book V.

The *x* and *y* axes divide the *xy* plane into four quadrants. Points located in the two quadrants to the right of the *y* axis have positive *x* coordinates; points to the left of the *y* axis have negative *x* coordinates. Points located in the two quadrants above the *x* axis have positive *y* coordinates, and points in the quadrants below the *x* axis have negative *y* coordinates. Figure 6-1 illustrates the 2D coordinate system.

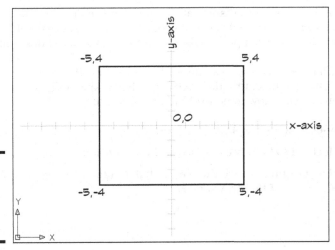

Figure 6-1:
The
Cartesian
coordinate
system.

UCS? We C U!

You can create multiple User Coordinate Systems in a drawing, and the WCS is always there, too. But only one coordinate system can be current, so there's only going to be one origin active at a time.

The Tools menu and UCS toolbar provide access to the many methods of creating your own User Coordinate Systems. Since these are more often associated with working in 3D, we'll cross that bridge when we come to it in Book V.

To keep coordinates simple, most drawings are created in the upper-right quadrant. This locates the origin (0,0) at the lower-left corner of the drawing area so that all coordinate values can be positive numbers.

The World Coordinate System

Everything you draw in AutoCAD is created in an infinitely large drawing space, and can be located by x and y coordinates. The default coordinate system in AutoCAD is called the *World Coordinate System*, or WCS. Many AutoCAD users spend their whole careers drafting in the WCS. Unless you're working in 3D, there's little reason to change the WCS to a user-defined coordinate system (or *UCS*), but it can be done if necessary. For more on working in 3D and user coordinate systems, see Book V.

The icon in the lower-left corner of the drawing area in Figure 6-1 is the UCS icon, and it's a handy device for recovering your bearings if you ever lose them. Figure 6-2 shows several variations in the icon's appearance. The box at the intersection of the two arrows means you're in the WCS.

If the UCS icon is set to display at the origin, it will move around the screen as the drawing is panned and zoomed. If the icon is set to display *off* the origin, it will always appear at the lower-left corner of the drawing area.

For the last several releases, AutoCAD has displayed the UCS icon at the origin. This can be distracting if you're only working in the WCS. The following steps explain how to control the UCS icon's display:

1. **Choose View⇨Display⇨UCS Icon.**

2. **Select On to turn the display of the icon off and on.**

3. **Select Origin to move the icon to 0,0,0 in the drawing, or to the lower-left corner of the drawing area.**

The third item on the UCS Icon menu is Properties. Selecting this option opens (surprise!) the Properties dialog box. Here you can control the appearance and size of the UCS icon. If you're a nostalgic type, you can even make the icon look the way it did in AutoCAD 2000 and earlier versions.

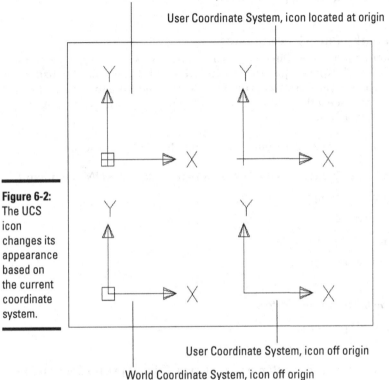

World Coordinate System, icon located at origin

User Coordinate System, icon located at origin

Figure 6-2:
The UCS icon changes its appearance based on the current coordinate system.

User Coordinate System, icon off origin

World Coordinate System, icon off origin

Entering coordinates

The standard way of feeding coordinates to AutoCAD is by typing them into the command line and pressing Enter. There are five types of coordinate entry commonly used in AutoCAD:

✦ Absolute *xy* coordinates

✦ Relative *xy* coordinates

✦ Relative polar coordinates

✦ Spherical coordinates

✦ Cylindrical coordinates

The first three types work in both 2D drafting and 3D modeling. The last two — spherical and cylindrical coordinates — are alternative ways of entering 3D coordinates and work in 3D only. These two coordinate-input methods are covered in Book V.

Entering absolute XY coordinates

You enter absolute coordinates as pairs of numbers separated by a comma, like this: *x,y*. No spaces, just the comma (this is AutoCAD, not English punctuation!). The *x* value is always expressed first, and then the *y* value is represented. If you see a third value — for example, *x,y,z* — the *z* coordinate is representing a 3D point.

To draw a square using absolute *xy* coordinates, follow these steps:

1. Click the Line tool on the Draw toolbar to start the LINE command.

AutoCAD prompts:

```
Command: _line Specify first point:
```

2. Type 3,3 **and press Enter.**

AutoCAD prompts:

```
Specify next point or [Undo]:
```

3. Type 6,3 **and press Enter.**

AutoCAD prompts:

```
Specify next point or [Undo]:
```

4. Type 6,6 **and press Enter, and then type** 3,6 **and press Enter, and then type** C **and press Enter.**

The command line appears as follows:

```
Specify next point or [Undo]: 6,6
Specify next point or [Close/Undo]: 3,6
Specify next point or [Close/Undo]: C
```

You might use absolute coordinates if you're working on a site plan, and the surveyor has supplied you with coordinates of parcel corners. Drawing this way satisfies the need for precision, but you'd have to do a lot of calculating to figure out the absolute coordinates of every point in the drawing. It's much handier to use relative coordinates.

Entering relative XY coordinates

Where absolute coordinates are always based on the origin of the drawing (that is, 0,0), relative coordinates are based on the last point entered. Input of the coordinates themselves is the same as for absolute *xy* coordinates, but you tell AutoCAD the location you're entering is based on the last point by typing an @ symbol before the coordinates — for example, entering **@5,4** makes a new point 5 units to the right and 4 units above the last point, not the origin.

To draw a square using relative *xy* coordinates, follow these steps:

1. **Click the Line tool on the Draw toolbar to start the LINE command.**

2. **At the Specify first point prompt, type** 5,5 **and press Enter.**

AutoCAD prompts:

```
Specify next point or [Undo]:
```

3. **Type @5,0 and press Enter.**

The @ symbol tells AutoCAD the next point is relative to the point you just entered rather than the origin. From this point, AutoCAD draws a line 5 units in the *x* direction and 0 units in the *y* direction.

AutoCAD prompts:

```
Specify next point or [Undo]:
```

4. **Type @0,5 and press Enter, and then type @-5,0 and press Enter, and then type** C **and press Enter.**

Create vertical or horizontal lines by specifying 0 as the relative *y* or *x* coordinate. Draw lines to the left of or below the last point by specifying negative coordinate values.

The command line appears as follows:

```
Specify next point or [Undo]: @0,5
Specify next point or [Close/Undo]: @-5,0
Specify next point or [Close/Undo]: C
```

In our experience, this method of coordinate input is rarely used. Luckily, there's another way of entering relative coordinates, one that makes much more sense than either of the preceding two: relative polar coordinates.

Entering relative polar coordinates

Relative polar coordinates are like relative *xy* coordinates in that both use the @ symbol to tell AutoCAD to draw that line from the last point, not from the origin. They're different from relative *xy* coordinates in that the two values are distance and angle, rather than offsets along the *x* and *y* axes. AutoCAD knows you're entering polar coordinates because instead of a comma, you type a left angle bracket (also known as the less than symbol). It's easy enough to remember because it's on the same key as the comma you use for *xy* coordinates; you just need to also remember to hold down the Shift key.

For example, entering @5,30 at a LINE command prompt tells AutoCAD to draw a line segment 5 units in the *x* direction and 30 units in the *y* direction from the last point. Entering @5<30 tells AutoCAD to draw a line 5 units long at an angle of 30 degrees. Obviously, the results are going to be very different, so if you want polar, don't forget to Shift!

To draw a square using relative polar coordinates, follow these steps:

1. **Click the Line tool on the Draw toolbar to start the LINE command.**

2. **At the Specify first point prompt, type 9,9 and press Enter.**

   AutoCAD prompts you as follows:

   ```
   Specify next point or [Undo]:
   ```

3. **Type @7<0 and press Enter.**

   Remember, the @ symbol means *relative to the last point*. Type the distance, and then — remember that Shift key! — the left angle bracket, the angle, and press Enter.

   AutoCAD draws a line 7 units long, at an angle of 0°.

   Chapter 3 explains that by convention in AutoCAD, 0° lies in the direction of the positive *x* axis, and angles are measured in a counterclockwise direction.

   AutoCAD prompts:

   ```
   Specify next point or [Undo]:
   ```

4. **Type @7<90 and press Enter, and then type @7<180 and press Enter, and then type C and press Enter.**

   With relative polar coordinates, you're always entering positive values.

   The command line appears as follows:

   ```
   Specify next point or [Undo]: @7<90
   Specify next point or [Close/Undo]: @7<180
   Specify next point or [Close/Undo]: C
   ```

Most users find that relative polar coordinates are the most logical method of coordinate entry in AutoCAD. You don't need to calculate displacements in the *x* and *y* directions; distances are actual distances.

So far so good, but AutoCAD has one more little trick up its sleeve that makes polar coordinates even easier. Read on . . .

Direct Distance Entry

An elaboration (actually a simplified method) of relative polar coordinates is called *Direct Distance Entry,* or DDE. When you enter relative polar coordinates, you specify distance and angle, typing no fewer than four keystrokes, two of which also require that you hold down the Shift key.

When using DDE, you enter the distance only. You specify the angle by dragging the mouse pointer on the screen. Not much hunting-and-pecking, and no holding down the Shift key.

"Waaaaait a minute," you say. "How *precise* can dragging the mouse pointer to specify an angle be?" The answer, of course, is not very precise at all, *if* you're simply dragging the mouse pointer without using the precision aids that AutoCAD provides. Ortho mode and polar tracking (both discussed shortly) help here: *Ortho* forces the mouse pointer to move at angles of 0°, 90°, 180°, and 270°. *Polar tracking* is like a loosened-up Ortho mode; you can specify any angle you like. Also, it doesn't force the crosshairs to follow those preset angles; it jumps to a specified angle and displays a tooltip to show you're tracking (see Figure 6-3).

Figure 6-3:
Now you're tracking! Polar tracking helps ensure precise angular input.

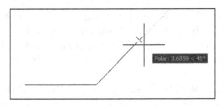

To draw a square using Direct Distance Entry, follow these steps:

1. **Click ORTHO on the status bar to turn on Ortho mode.**

Ortho mode forces any lines you draw to be precisely horizontal or vertical. We discuss Ortho mode in the following section.

2. **Start the LINE command as in step 1 above.**

3. At the Specify first point prompt, type 15,15 **and press Enter.**

AutoCAD prompts you:

```
Specify next point or [Undo]:
```

4. Drag the crosshairs to the right, then type 9 **and press Enter.**

It doesn't matter how far you drag the crosshairs — you're showing AutoCAD the angle, not the distance. AutoCAD draws a horizontal line to the right, 9 units long.

AutoCAD prompts:

```
Specify next point or [Undo]:
```

5. Drag the crosshairs toward the top of the screen, type 9, **and press Enter. Then drag to the left, type** 9, **and press Enter. Finally, type** C **and press Enter.**

With relative polar coordinates, you always enter positive values.

The command line appears as follows:

```
Specify next point or [Undo]: @7<90
Specify next point or [Close/Undo]: @7<180
Specify next point or [Close/Undo]: C
```

When you can use it, DDE is a terrific keystroke-saver.

Dynamic input and coordinate entry

We introduce dynamic input (DI) in Chapter 2 of this minibook. DI was new in AutoCAD 2006, and at this time, we're all getting used to it. For reasons best known to themselves, Autodesk's programmers decided to do away with the long-standard method of using the @ symbol as a prefix to indicate relative coordinates, and no prefix at all to indicate absolute coordinates.

If you turn off DYN mode, AutoCAD still accepts input the traditional way, but if you're using DI, the no prefix at all now indicates relative coordinates. And if you want to enter absolute coordinates using DI, you have to use the # symbol as the prefix.

Setting Grid and Snap

AutoCAD's grid, while sometimes helpful to get your bearings in the drawing, is not (strictly speaking) a precision aid. As we explain in Chapter 5 of this minibook, AutoCAD can display a non-plotting grid of horizontally and vertically aligned dots over your drawing area. This grid can help keep you aware of the relative sizes of what you're drawing — and their size on the printed drawing. It also gives you a visual cue when you're drawing outside your sheet limits.

If you're working in Isometric mode, the grid adjusts itself to a 30-60-90 angular alignment rather than horizontal and vertical. We do not cover isometric or other forms of 2D pictorial drafting in this book.

You can toggle the grid off and on with the GRID button on the status bar or by pressing the F7 function key. You can set grid spacing at the command line, but it's easier to use the Drafting Settings dialog box, as we describe in the next section.

If you're zoomed way out in a drawing and turn the grid on, you may see this message:

```
Grid too dense to display
```

This message is not an error — it just means the grid spacing is too small for AutoCAD to display at the current zoom ratio. Either zoom in closer (if you need to see the grid), or change the grid spacing (as we explain in the next section).

Snap constrains all crosshairs movement to specific increments; when snap is enabled, the crosshairs can no longer move freely about the graphics area but jumps to points on an invisible grid. Snap, like grid, is toggled off and on by clicking the SNAP button on the status bar, or pressing the F9 function key. Also like the grid, snap can be set to isometric mode. And finally, there's a polar snap that's available when you have polar tracking turned on. (We discuss polar tracking in the next section.)

The following steps explain how to specify settings and enable snap and grid in the Drafting Settings dialog box.

1. **Move the crosshairs around on the screen and look at the coordinates readout on the status bar.**

If the SNAP button on the status bar is not selected, the crosshairs move freely, and coordinate values show their location to four decimal places of random numbers.

2. **Click SNAP and GRID on the status bar so both buttons are pressed in.**

The grid turns on (it may be a little hard to see) and the crosshairs now jump from location to location. The coordinates readout shows that they move in constant increments.

3. **Right-click either the SNAP or GRID button and choose Settings.**

It doesn't matter which button you right-click; choosing Settings on either button's shortcut menu opens the Drafting Settings dialog box at the Snap and Grid tab (see Figure 6-4).

Figure 6-4:
Setting snap
and grid in
the Drafting
Settings
dialog box.

4. **In the Grid area, enter values for the *x* (horizontal) and *y* (vertical) spacing of the grid.**

Entering the *x* spacing first causes the same value to appear in the *y*-spacing box. For different *x* and *y* spacing, enter a new value in the *y*-spacing box.

5. **To configure rectangular snap, in the Snap area, enter values for the *x* and *y* spacing.**

As with setting grid spacing, entering a value for *x* spacing causes the same value to appear as the *y* spacing.

6. **To change the snap angle, or to move the snap origin from the default 0,0,0, enter the appropriate values in the Snap area.**

Snap can be rotated to any angle; doing so also rotates the grid to the same angle.

7. **To set up snap and grid for isometric drawing, select Isometric snap in the Snap type & style area.**

When isometric snap is enabled, both grid and snap adjust from horizontal and vertical to 30-60-90 angles.

8. **If you're using polar tracking, select PolarSnap in the Snap Type & Style area.**

   Selecting PolarSnap disables the settings in the Snap area and enables the Polar spacing area in which you can enter a polar distance.

9. **Click the Snap On or Grid On check boxes to enable snap or grid mode.**

   After you create all the appropriate settings, select the check boxes to enable the feature.

It's not actually necessary to open the Drafting Settings dialog box to toggle snap and grid off and on — just use the status bar buttons or F7/F9 function keys.

Understanding Ortho and Polar Tracking

Ortho mode and polar tracking are two precision drafting aids that force linework to specific angles. Ortho mode has been part of AutoCAD since the very beginning. When Ortho is on, you can draw lines or pick points horizontally or vertically *only*. This is handy as far as it goes, but most drawings could use some consistent angular guidance beyond 90° increments.

Using Ortho mode

Ortho mode could hardly be simpler. There are no settings to make; it's either on or it's off. If you find yourself drawing lots of horizontal and vertical lines, it's a boon to creating perfect right-angled linework. To toggle Ortho mode off and on, click the ORTHO button on the status bar or use the F8 function key.

Using polar tracking

It's a rule in AutoCAD (and in life!) that with flexibility comes complexity. Polar tracking is a lot more flexible than Ortho mode, and polar tracking has a ton more options than Ortho mode (hey, *one* more option would be a lot more!).

Sometimes AutoCAD makes things more complex and even confusing than necessary by using the same words for features that seem similar but are actually different from one another. *Tracking* is one of those words. In this section we're describing *polar* tracking, where AutoCAD displays "tracking vectors" to show you when you're on a preset polar tracking angle. At the end of this chapter we discuss *object-snap* tracking (after we've told you what object snaps are, of course!). With object-snap tracking, you use points on existing objects to find new points.

Simple stuff first: To enable polar tracking, click POLAR on the status bar or press the F10 function key.

Where Ortho mode forces you to draw horizontal and vertical lines and nothing else, polar tracking gently guides you along the right path by displaying a tooltip and a tracking vector to verify that you're heading the right way. All in all, polar is a kinder, gentler — and did we say more flexible? — version of Ortho mode.

The default angle setting for polar tracking is 90° which means you can use it instead of Ortho mode. Having polar turned on with the default setting means you can draw at any angle, but you'll see a tooltip when you're on a horizontal or vertical path.

Polar tracking and Ortho mode can't both be on at the same time; enabling one disables the other. If you're like many experienced drafters, you may consign Ortho mode to the virtual trash can.

The following steps explain how to configure and use polar tracking:

1. **In a blank drawing, click the POLAR button on the status bar until it's not pressed in.**

2. **Start the LINE command, pick a start point, and then move the crosshairs around the screen.**

   There's no restriction or input on where you pick the next point of the line.

3. **Right-click the POLAR button and choose Settings.**

   AutoCAD displays the Drafting Settings dialog box with the Polar Tracking tab current (see Figure 6-5).

4. **In the Polar Angle Settings area, select Increment angles (angles and their multiples that you want to track on screen) from the drop-down list.**

   Standard subdivisions of 90° appear in the drop-down list. AutoCAD also recognizes multiples of Increment angles; for example, if you select 45° from the list, AutoCAD also locks on 135°, 225°, and 315°.

5. **Check the Additional angles box, and then click New to add additional angles to polar tracking mode.**

Figure 6-5:
Configuring polar tracking in the Drafting Settings dialog box.

AutoCAD does *not* track multiples of Additional angles you enter; if you enter 16.87°, polar tracking will recognize that angle only, not 33.74° or other multiples of the original.

6. In the Object Snap Tracking Settings area, choose which tracking vectors you want to appear when using object snap tracking to find points.

Select Track Orthogonally Only to display only horizontal and vertical tracking vectors, or Track Using All Polar Angle Settings to display all the Increment and Additional angles you specified in the Polar Angle Settings area. Note that this only has an effect if the OTRACK button is pressed in. We cover OTRACK at the end of this chapter.

Although object-snap tracking settings appear on the same tab as polar tracking angles, they're actually independent of one another. Regardless of whether you choose track orthogonally only or track using all angles, when you're drawing stuff, all tracking angles show up. The object-snap-tracking settings only kick in if you're actually tracking from one object-snap point to another — that is, the OTRACK button on the status bar is selected. Are you lost yet? Don't worry; we discuss object snaps in the following section, and object-snap tracking at the end of the chapter.

7. In the Polar Angle measurement area, choose how the polar angles are to be measured.

Selecting Absolute is the least likely to get you lost, because the tracking angles are the same as the angular measure you set up in the Units dialog box; that is, 0° is to the right, 90° is straight up, and so on. Selecting Relative to last segment would display a vector at, say 45° to the last line, which will probably not be the same as the absolute angle of 45°.

When you're familiar with the system, of course, it's fine to temporarily set Polar Angle measurement relative to the last segment. But we think it's a Really Good Idea to remember to reset it to Absolute when you're finished.

8. Click the Polar Tracking On check box to enable polar tracking.

After you make all the appropriate settings, select the check box to enable the feature.

Clicking the Options button in the Drafting Settings dialog box takes you to the Drafting tab of AutoCAD's Options dialog box. For the time being, you don't need to change any settings here — the defaults all work fine. We cover the Options dialog box in detail in Book IX.

Working with Object Snaps

Up until now, you've been relying on AutoCAD's coordinate system to locate points and draw objects. That's fine, but if calculating and entering coordinates were the only way of drawing accurately, you'd probably run screaming back to your drawing board. After you use coordinates to get some objects drawn, you can start using another very important AutoCAD feature: object snaps.

Object snaps let you pick a precise point on an existing object; the point you pick depends on which Object Snap mode you select.

Object Snap modes are different from object to object, depending on the object type; for example, lines have endpoint and midpoint object snaps, circles have center and quadrant object snaps, and arcs have endpoints, midpoints, centers, *and* quadrants.

New users often get confused by snap and object snap. *Snap* is a status bar toggle that forces the crosshairs to jump from preset snap interval to interval. Snap is available whether there are objects in the drawing or not. *Object snap* is an aid to precision that lets you find exact points on existing objects; for example, the center of a circle or the insertion point of a piece of text. Snap doesn't need objects, but object snaps do.

There are two ways of using object snaps: They can be on and available all the time, in which case they're referred to as *running object snaps,* or you can select the ones you want from a toolbar, menu, or the command line, for one click only. Those ones are referred to as *single object snaps,* or object-snap *overrides.* Since there are some extra wrinkles involved in setting up running object snaps, we're going to deal with object-snap overrides first.

Table 6-1 lists the Object Snap modes and how they're used.

Table 6-1		Object Snap Modes
Button	*Function*	*Description*
	Temporary Track point	Sets temporary point using object snap tracking. (Object-snap tracking is covered at the end of this chapter)
	FROM	Sets temporary reference point from which you specify an offset
	ENDpoint	Locates precise endpoints of lines, arcs, elliptical arcs, splines, or polyline segments
	MIDpoint	Locates precise midpoints of lines, arcs, elliptical arcs, splines, or polyline segments
	INTersection	Locates precise intersection of two or more objects
	APParent INTersection	Locates visual intersection of two objects on different planes but appear to intersect on-screen
	EXTension	Projects a temporary vector from the end of a line, arc, elliptical arc, or polyline segment along which you can pick a point
	CENter	Locates the precise center of a circle, arc, elliptical arc, or polyline arc segment
	QUAdrant	Locates the precise quadrant points of a circle, arc, elliptical arc, or polyline arc segment
	TANgent	Locates the point of precise tangency on circles, arcs, elliptical arcs, splines, or polyline arc segments
	PERpendicular	Locates a point precisely perpendicular to an object

(continued)

Table 6-1 *(continued)*

Button	Function	Description
	PARallel	Lets you draw a line parallel to another line through any point
	INSertion	Locates the precision insertion point of text, block insertions, or external references
	NODe	Locates a point object
	NEArest	Locates the point precisely on an object closest to where you select the object
	NONe	Temporarily disables all running object snaps for one selection
	OSNAP settings	Displays Object Snap tab of Drawing Settings dialog box

Some Object Snap modes require two picks to set and therefore can't be used as running object snaps. For example, you can find a point midway between two unconnected points using Mid Between 2 Points (M2P or MID2) using the shortcut menu or keyboard, but you can't set it as a running object snap.

Hardcore typists can use the keyboard to set object-snap overrides by entering the capitalized letters in the table. To find the apparent intersection of two objects, for example, you could enter **APPINT.**

AutoCAD LT 2007 includes all the object snap modes listed here; however AutoCAD LT 2006 and earlier are missing some features, including Temporary Track Point and the Extension and Parallel object-snap modes. We cover AutoCAD LT in more detail in Book IV.

Using Point Filters

Sometimes it's useful to use part of a location's coordinates to locate a point in a drawing. You can find the center of a circle using object snaps. But, say you wanted to find the precise middle point of a square. Squares and rectangles don't have "centers" in the same way that circles do.

Using *point filters* (also known as *dot filters* or *xy filters*), you can locate a new point by combining the *x* coordinate from one point with the *y* coordinate from another (and, if you're working in 3D, the *z* coordinate from a third). It's a complicated system, and it takes some practice, but if you're feeling like taking The AutoCAD Challenge, follow these steps to draw a circle at the center of a rectangle:

1. **Open a drawing containing a rectangular area in which you want to draw a circle, or draw a rectangle in a blank area of the screen.**

2. **Right-click the OSNAP button on the status bar to display the Drafting Settings dialog box, and make sure that Midpoint object snap is selected.**

3. **Start the CIRCLE command.**

AutoCAD prompts:

```
_circle Specify center point for circle or [3P/2P/Ttr
     (tan tan radius)]:
```

4. **Hold down the Shift key and right-click. On the shortcut menu that appears, click Point Filters to open the point-filters list shown in Figure 6-6.**

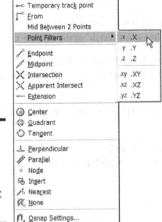

Figure 6-6:
Use the shortcut menu to select point filters.

5. **Click .X.**

AutoCAD prompts you as follows:

```
.X of
```

6. **Move the crosshairs over a horizontal side of the rectangle and click when you see the Midpoint object-snap marker.**

The prompt changes to

```
.X of (need yz):
```

7. **Move the crosshairs over a vertical side of the rectangle and click when you see the Midpoint object-snap marker.**

   AutoCAD locates the center point of the circle at a new point generated from the *x* coordinate of the first picked point, and the *y* coordinate of the second.

Working with Object Snap Tracking Mode

No, OTRACK is not the name of the Irish railway system. Sure and begorrah, OTRACK is much more useful than that. OTRACK is short for *object-snap tracking,* an AutoCAD feature that lets you locate new points based on object-snap points on existing objects.

Object snap tracking automates the point-filter process we described earlier. For example, here's how you'd use object-snap tracking to place a circle in the exact center of a rectangle:

1. **Open a drawing containing a rectangular area in which you want to draw a circle, or draw a rectangle in a blank area of the screen.**

2. **Right-click the OTRACK button on the status bar to display the Drafting Settings dialog box, and make sure that Midpoint object snap is selected.**

   You can also right-click the OSNAP button to display the Object Snap tab of the Drafting Settings dialog box.

3. **In the Drafting Settings dialog box, select the Object Snap On and Object Snap Tracking On checkboxes, and then click OK.**

4. **Start the CIRCLE command.**

   AutoCAD prompts:

   ```
   _circle Specify center point for circle or [3P/2P/Ttr
        (tan tan radius)]:
   ```

5. **Move the crosshairs to the middle of a horizontal side of the rectangle.**

   The Midpoint object-snap marker appears.

6. **Rest the crosshairs over the object-snap marker for a moment, but don't click yet.**

When you move the mouse, you should see a tracking vector passing through the object-snap marker.

7. **Without clicking, move the crosshairs to the middle of a vertical side of the rectangle.**

8. **When the object-snap marker appears, rest the crosshairs over it for a moment.**

Now when you move the mouse, you should see two tracking vectors, one running through each of the midpoints.

9. **Move the mouse until the two tracking vectors are aligned vertically and horizontally (see Figure 6-7), and then click to set the center point of the circle.**

If DYNamic mode is enabled, you also get confirmation that you're on the money in the dynamic input tooltip.

Figure 6-7:
Finding the "center" of a square using object-snap tracking.

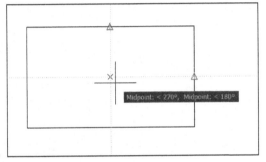

Midpoint: < 270°, Midpoint: < 180°

Although object-snap tracking has been part of the full version of AutoCAD for several releases now, it's just been introduced to AutoCAD LT 2007. It's not included in AutoCAD LT 2006 and earlier versions.

Book II

2D Drafting

The 5th Wave   By Rich Tennant

"Yes, I think it's an error message."

Contents at a Glance

Chapter 1: Drawing Objects

In This Chapter

✔ Input methods

✔ Using drawing tools

✔ Creating primitive objects

✔ Understanding construction objects

✔ Drawing complex objects

*W*elcome to Book II. It's time to get primitive! No, we're not asking you to move into a tree in the backyard and howl at the moon. In this chapter, we introduce AutoCAD's *primitive objects* and the drawing commands for creating them. Primitive objects include geometric entities like lines, arcs, circles, and points.

After we explore the primitive heart of AutoCAD, we look at some of its more complex object-creation tools. These include polylines, multilines (double lines if you're using AutoCAD LT), and some obscure entities like traces and 2D solids.

As we explain in Book I, you can interact with AutoCAD in several ways. You can start most drawing commands from the Draw toolbar or the Draw menu, or by typing the command name (or its short-form *alias*) at the keyboard. In nearly all cases, using any of these methods to start a command initiates a dialog with AutoCAD.

Locating and Using the Drawing Tools

Table 1-1 tells you where to find all the drawing commands AutoCAD provides, as well as what you can do with these commands. We don't cover the commands in this order; just think of this table as a handy reference chart. In the interests of fairness and democracy, Table 1-1 lists commands in alphabetical order by command name, not by popularity or frequency of use. LINE, ARC, and CIRCLE are the most frequently used commands.

Table 1-1			AutoCAD's 2D Drawing Tools		
Icon	*Draw Toolbar*	*Draw Menu*	*Command Name*	*Alias*	*Function*
	Arc	Arc	ARC	A	Draws circular arc objects.
	—	Block, Define Attributes	ATTDEF	ATT	Defines attributes to be included in block definition. Attributes are covered in Book VI.
	Make Block	Block, Make	BLOCK	B	Defines a block from drawing objects. Blocks are covered in Book VI.
	—	Boundary	BOUNDARY	BO	Creates polyline or region from edges of a closed area. For more on Boundary, see Book III.
	Circle	Circle	CIRCLE	C	Draws circle objects.
	—	Double Line	DLINE	DL	Draws double parallel lines (AutoCAD LT only).
	—	Donut	DONUT	DO	Draws circular polyline object specifying inside and outside diameter.
	Ellipse	Ellipse	ELLIPSE	EL	Draws ellipse objects.
	Gradient	Gradient	GRADIENT	GD	Applies gradient fill pattern to closed areas. Gradients are covered in Book III.
	Hatch	Hatch	HATCH	H	Applies solid or regular pattern to closed areas. Hatches are covered in Book III.
	Line	Line	LINE	L	Draws straight line objects between two points.
	—	Multiline	MLINE	ML	Draws multiple parallel lines (AutoCAD only).
	Multiline Text	Text, Multiline Text	MTEXT	MT	Draws multi-line annotation text objects. Text is covered in Book III.

(continued)

Icon	Draw Toolbar	Draw Menu	Command Name	Alias	Function
	Polyline	Polyline	PLINE	PL	Draws connected linear or arc segment objects.
	Point	Point	POINT	PO	Draws point objects.
	Polygon	Polygon	POLYGON	POL	Draws regular closed polygonal polylines.
	Ray	Ray	RAY	—	Draws infinite-length construction line starting from single point.
	Rectangle	Rectangle	RECTANG	REC	Draws closed rectangular polyline objects.
	Region	Region	REGION	REG	Creates a single closed object from nested objects.
	Revision Cloud	Revision Cloud	REVCLOUD	—	Draws revision clouds.
	—	—	SKETCH	—	Draws freehand sketches as polylines or multiple line objects.
	—	—	SOLID	SO	Draws 3- or 4-sided solid-filled shapes. Not related to 3D solids.
	Spline	Spline	SPLINE	SPL	Draws freeform spline curve objects.
	Table	Table	TABLE	TB	Draws table objects specifying rows and columns. Tables are covered in Book III.
	—	—	TRACE	—	Draws single-segment lines with width.
	Construction Line	Construction Line	XLINE	XL	Draws infinite-length construction line through specified points.

Book II Chapter 1

Drawing Objects

TIP

If a command can be executed only by typing its name (that is, it has no tool button or menu item), it's not going to be used that frequently; SKETCH, SOLID, and TRACE all fall into this category.

In this chapter, we're not going to cover every single drawing command in extensive detail — that's what the online Help system is for. The Command Reference has an alphabetical listing of every command and details about each command's options. To access the Command Reference, choose Help↪ Help or press the F1 key. Click the Contents tab, and then click the plus sign beside Command Reference.

Sometimes you have to dig pretty deep in the Help system for the last word on a command or feature. On many Help pages, there's an almost invisible little blue hyperlink that says, "Display all hidden text on this page." Remember it's there and look for it!

Let's Get Primitive

AutoCAD's primitive object types are lines, circles, arcs, and points. Each of these object types takes very little geometric data to define it in the drawing database. A line is defined geometrically by its two endpoints, arcs and circles by their center points and radii, and points by a single set of coordinates.

In this section, we look at the four commands that create these four primitive object types. The commands are (surprise!) LINE, CIRCLE, ARC, and POINT.

Keeping to the straight and narrow

The LINE command creates a line object. In AutoCAD, a line object is a single entity drawn between two endpoints. You use the LINE command to draw straight lines from point to point to point. The LINE command continues prompting for points until you explicitly end the sequence by pressing Enter or Esc. Whichever method you choose to start the command, AutoCAD prompts as follows:

```
Command: LINE
Specify first point:
```

Pick a point on-screen, or use an object snap (see Book I for more information on using object snaps) to find a precise point on an existing object, or type a pair of x,y coordinates to locate the starting point of your line sequence. After you pick the first point, AutoCAD prompts:

```
Specify next point or [Undo]:
```

Specify the second and third points using the methods just described. If you make a mistake, or change your mind after you pick the second point, press U (for *Undo*) and press Enter to undraw the previous line segment. As you continue to add line segments, you can press U at any time to undo the last segment you added.

Command options appear inside square brackets. To select a command option, type the uppercase letter in the option and press Enter.

Specify subsequent points in the same manner as the first points. After you pick the third point (that is, after you have two line segments), the command prompt changes once more:

```
Specify next point or [Close/Undo]:
```

There are now two options, Undo and Close. After you've drawn two line segments, you can create a closed shape by pressing C and pressing Enter. If you're using dynamic input, you can select Close from the dynamic display (see Figure 1-1). This will end the line sequence at the original starting point. To end the sequence, press Enter or Esc or the spacebar, or right-click and choose Enter from the shortcut menu.

**Book II
Chapter 1**

Drawing Objects

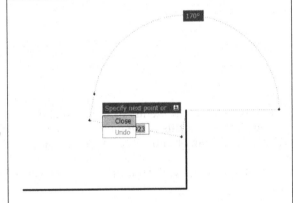

Figure 1-1:
Drawing
lines
dynamically.

In Book I, we talk about relative coordinates and how AutoCAD interprets the @ symbol as relative to the last point you picked. You can use the @ symbol by itself to tell AutoCAD you want to use the last point you picked on-screen or entered using coordinates. For example, if you enter @ at the Specify first point prompt, AutoCAD starts the line at the last point entered.

Going around in circles

Circles are pretty basic geometric elements, although you may not create them quite as often as you create arcs. We're going to talk about circles before we talk about arcs because circles are simpler to draw. Even so, there are five ways to create circles — six, if you use the pull-down menu. Figure 1-2 shows the pull-down menu with all six options.

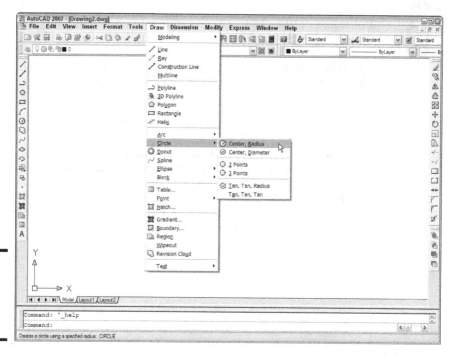

Figure 1-2:
How many
ways can
you draw
a circle?

The first Circle option on the Draw menu — Center, Radius — is the default method for drawing circles, and this is the method you get if you click the Circle tool on the Draw toolbar, or enter CIRCLE or its alias C at the keyboard.

If you start the command using the default option, AutoCAD prompts as follows:

```
Command: CIRCLE
Specify center point for circle or [3P/2P/Ttr (tan tan
    radius)]:
```

At this point, you can either locate the center point by picking a point on-screen or entering coordinates for the center point, or you can choose one of the three options inside the square brackets.

If you specify a center point, AutoCAD prompts:

```
Specify radius of circle or [Diameter]:
```

Another choice to make! You can either enter a value for the circle's radius or pick a point on-screen to specify the radius, or you can press D to choose the diameter option. If you enter a value or pick a point, AutoCAD draws the circle and returns you to the command prompt. If you press D, AutoCAD prompts:

```
Specify diameter of circle:
```

If this is the first circle you've drawn in this session, the command line is blank. If you've drawn a previous circle, a default value (the last-entered radius) is shown inside the angle brackets.

You can also draw circles by specifying two points that represent the endpoints of a line representing the diameter of the circle, or by specifying three points that lie on the circumference of the circle. You also can draw circles by selecting two objects your circle should be tangent to, and then entering a radius.

The Draw menu offers a sixth method that actually invokes a macro; instead of prompting you to enter a radius after you've selected the first two objects for tangency, AutoCAD asks you to select a third object.

Arcs of triumph

If you thought a half-dozen different ways of drawing circles was a lot, you ain't seen nuthin' yet! There are no fewer than 11 ways to draw arcs. Worse, the default method — 3 points — is the construction method for creating arcs that you're least likely to encounter. Figure 1-3 shows the Arc command's options available through the Draw menu.

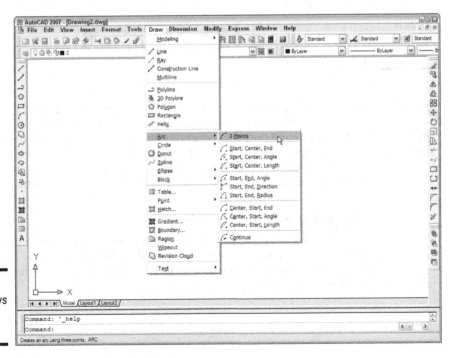

Figure 1-3:
Eleven ways
to draw
an arc.

While you're getting familiar with the program, it's easiest to use the Draw menu to choose the option you want. The nine central options on the Draw menu are all based on start points and center points, and then each has variations of end point, included angle, direction, length, or radius.

Choosing Draw⇨Arc⇨Start, Center, End, for example, presets the command options so that the three points you enter are indeed interpreted by AutoCAD as the start point, the center point, and the end point.

One little gotcha is that by default, AutoCAD draws arcs in a counter-clockwise direction. Figure 1-4 shows how you control the way your arcs are drawn.

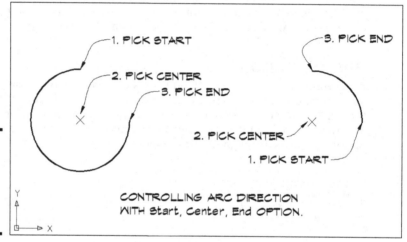

Figure 1-4:
Arc direction by default is counter-clockwise.

You're probably aware that pressing Enter or the space bar, or right-clicking and choosing Enter, repeats the last command. What it doesn't do is repeat the last command options you chose. Instead, it repeats the command with its default options. In the case of ARC, that will give you a 3-point arc, where the three points you pick are the start and end points and a random point somewhere along the arc itself. Most of the time this is not what you want.

The point of the exercise

After all that arcane arc knowledge, you're probably ready for something simple. You're in luck — the simplest of all AutoCAD objects is at hand. Points are geometrically defined in the drawing database by their x-, y-, z- coordinate location.

Although we've been talking about *x,y* coordinate pairs, in fact every object in an AutoCAD drawing is located by an *x-, y-, z*-coordinate triplet. In most cases for 2D drafting, the value of the *z* coordinate is 0.

Although we're dealing with 2D objects in this part of the book, your point object is pretty one-dimensional (kind of like some engineers we know). Since points have no length or width, they can be pretty small and hard to see. The default appearance for the point object is a single pixel, but you can change the appearance to something a little more visible by following these steps:

1. **Choose Format⇨Point Style.**

AutoCAD displays the Point Style dialog box (see Figure 1-5).

2. **Select one of the point styles by clicking its icon in the dialog box.**

The selected style will apply to all current and future point objects in the drawing.

3. **Specify the size of the point objects, and then click OK.**

Set the point size as either a percentage relative to the screen size or in absolute units. If you set point size in absolute units, the point objects appear larger or smaller as you zoom in or out; if you set point size relative to screen size, point objects stay the same size.

Book II
Chapter 1

Drawing Objects

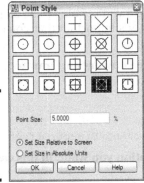

Figure 1-5:
Style your points in the Point Style dialog box.

As we mentioned earlier, the default point style is a single pixel. Click the top-left icon in the Point Style dialog box to select it. The next icon to the right is no display at all — that's right, you can create point objects that you can't see. Frankly, we don't see the point.

Creating Construction Geometry

In spite of snap, Ortho, polar, and object snaps, many AutoCAD drafters use the software the same way they drew things with pencils and t-squares — they draw temporary construction geometry to line things up and project drawing features from one view to another. AutoCAD has a couple of construction geometry tools that help with this process: *construction lines* and *rays*.

Xlines for X-men

Construction lines (commonly known as *xlines*) are created with the XLINE command, by default the second button down on the Draw toolbar. Xlines (and rays) are unlike any other object in AutoCAD in that they have infinite length.

Create a separate layer for your construction lines so you can easily turn them off and on when you want to see your drawing geometry without all the visual noise. Construction lines and rays will plot, so be sure to turn off the layer before you print your drawings.

Although xlines look a lot like lines, they don't have endpoints, so you have to construct your xlines accordingly. The following steps explain how to create a series of vertical xlines, as shown in Figure 1-6:

1. **Turn on appropriate object snaps.**

This is a very important step; because you're going to be aligning your xlines with existing drawing objects, it's important that you place them precisely.

2. **Start the XLINE command using the Draw menu, Draw toolbar, or the keyboard.**

AutoCAD prompts:

```
Command: XLINE
Specify a point or [Hor/Ver/Ang/Bisect/Offset]:
```

3. **Type the uppercase letter of the option you want. In this case, type V and press Enter.**

When you respond to the prompt, it doesn't matter whether you type an uppercase or lowercase letter. AutoCAD prompts:

```
Specify through point:
```

4. **Use the appropriate object snap mode and pick a point on the drawing geometry through which you want the xline to pass.**

AutoCAD continues to create xlines until you press Enter or Esc.

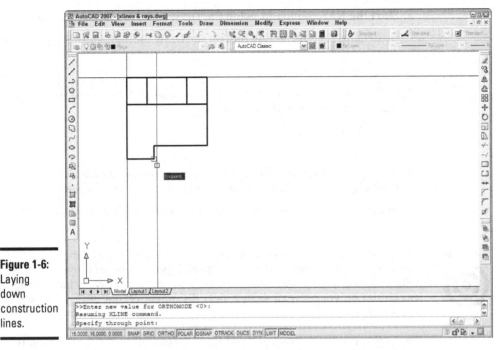

Figure 1-6:
Laying
down
construction
lines.

If you want to lay down a whole bunch of xlines at different angles, don't select a command option first. Your new xlines will pass through the point you pick but you'll be able to set the angle by picking on-screen. This is an especially efficient method of laying out construction lines for a drawing if you have polar mode turned on and the correct object snaps enabled.

A little ray of sunshine

The most significant difference between a ray and a construction line is that a ray has one endpoint and extends infinitely away from that endpoint. A construction line, on the other hand, has no endpoints and therefore extends infinitely in both directions.

The following steps explain how to create rays:

1. **Turn on the appropriate object snaps and enable Ortho or Polar modes as necessary.**

As noted already, construction lines and rays need to be created precisely to be of any use.

2. **Start the RAY command using the Draw menu or the keyboard.**

    By default, there is no Ray tool on the Draw toolbar. AutoCAD prompts:

    ```
    Command: RAY
    Specify start point:
    ```

3. **Use the appropriate object snap mode and pick the point in the drawing where you want the ray to start.**

    AutoCAD prompts:

    ```
    Specify through point:
    ```

4. **Again, use an appropriate object snap mode and pick a point on the drawing geometry through which you want the ray to pass.**

    AutoCAD will continue creating rays from the original start point until you press Enter or Esc.

When should you use rays and when should you use xlines? Xlines are easier to construct, since they only need a through point, whereas rays need a start point and a through point. Really, the only advantage of rays is having slightly less clutter on your screen — they only disappear off one side of the screen instead of two.

For more on construction lines and rays, check out the User's Guide in the Online Help system. Choose Help⇨Help⇨User's Guide, and then navigate to Create and Modify Objects⇨Draw Geometric Objects⇨Draw Construction and Reference Geometry⇨Draw Construction Lines (and Rays).

Without a Trace

Because the *AutoCAD & AutoCAD LT All-in-One Desk Reference For Dummies* is nothing if not comprehensive, we're going to cover the TRACE command. As Table 1-1 shows, TRACE has no tool button or alias, and is nowhere to be found in the menu system. The TRACE command, which creates trace objects (is that pattern settling in yet?) is a prime example of AutoCAD's attic. It's really hard to throw anything away, even though it's been 15 years since you last used it.

Traces had a function once. They were used in the preparation of printed circuit boards (or PCBs). Traces are more or less like lines with one significant difference: traces, like one or two other object types we'll get to shortly, can have width. As with the LINE command, you can keep picking points and AutoCAD will continue making traces, automatically cleaning up the intersections as it goes.

Traces offer no benefits over polylines (we'll get to polylines a bit later). Traces can't have curved segments (polylines can). The TRACE command lacks Close and Undo options like those in the LINE command. You can't even see traces as you draw them.

We're not going to tell you not to experiment with TRACE — who knows, you may find a unique use for that cast-off in AutoCAD's attic. For a very brief description of the command, look up TRACE in the index of the online Help system. Figure 1-7 shows you some sample traces.

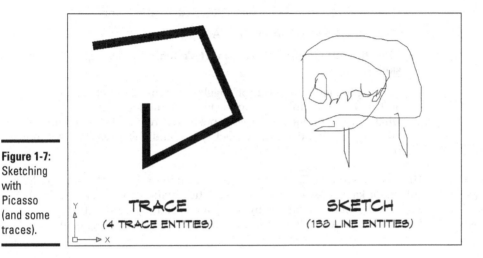

Figure 1-7:
Sketching with Picasso (and some traces).

TRACE
(4 TRACE ENTITIES)

SKETCH
(138 LINE ENTITIES)

A Bit Sketchy

Another antique tool from the attic is the SKETCH command. Like TRACE, you won't find an alias or a tool button or a menu item for SKETCH. You have to type out the whole command name to run it. The SKETCH command does not create its own entity type; the end product of a SKETCH sequence is either a polyline or a whole bunch of teeny lines.

In its earliest days, AutoCAD had no commands for freehand sketching. Enter the SKETCH command. Unless you use it every day (and we can't imagine many people do that), SKETCH takes some getting used to because it works unlike any other AutoCAD command. Follow these steps and you'll see what we mean:

1. **Type SKETCH and press Enter to start the command.**

The first cryptic message appears at the command line:

```
Command: SKETCH
Record increment <0.1000>:
```

Unlike with LINE, ARC, or CIRCLE, you don't have to select or enter points while you're sketching — simply moving the mouse creates the sketched entities. The prompt is telling you that any mouse movements greater than 0.1 units will be recorded. Change this value now if you want longer or shorter mouse motions to be turned into drawing entities.

2. **Press Enter to continue.**

   AutoCAD prompts (even more cryptically, if that's possible):

   ```
   Sketch.  Pen eXit Quit Record Erase Connect .
   ```

   "Sketch" is an order, from AutoCAD to you!

3. **Click the left mouse button to start sketching. Click again to stop sketching.**

   Clicking the left mouse button toggles Sketch mode between <Pen down> and <Pen up>. Simply moving the mouse a minimum of 0.1 units (or whatever record increment you specified) creates sketched entities. The SKETCH command ignores object snaps, and it ignores the right mouse button.

The system variable SKPOLY determines whether SKETCH creates polyline objects or kazillions of separate lines. The default value of SKPOLY is 0 which will generate many many many lines. Setting SKPOLY to 1 tells AutoCAD to create polylines from the connected sketch segments.

Drawing Parallel Lines

If you're drawing something like the floor plan of a house, you need parallel lines to represent the walls. The LINE command gives you a single line, which you then need to offset or copy to get a pair of lines that can represent a wall. Both AutoCAD and AutoCAD LT have commands for drawing parallel lines, but they're different in each program.

AutoCAD LT provides a command called *DLINE* that enables you to draw double lines. You specify a thickness, or separation distance, and then draw. The DLINE command creates pairs of line objects that can be edited or erased separately. The DLINE command is not included in the regular version of AutoCAD 2007. For more on using DLINE, see Book IV.

Multilines (which are not included in AutoCAD LT) are multiple parallel lines that can have different properties from one another. A multiline can have up to 16 elements. You create multiline objects with the MLINE command and edit them with a special set of tools. We cover editing multilines in the next chapter.

Multilines definitely belong in the ranks of AutoCAD's complex objects. To use multilines effectively, you'll need to be able to create and edit the multiple-line styles that format the multiline objects. And you'll need to be able to edit them in the unique way that they require. It has to be said that many AutoCAD users don't like using multilines because of their perceived inflexibility.

Making multilines

Figure 1-8 shows one example of a multiline object. Using the LINE command, it would take 24 separate lines (and a lot of editing) to get the same result.

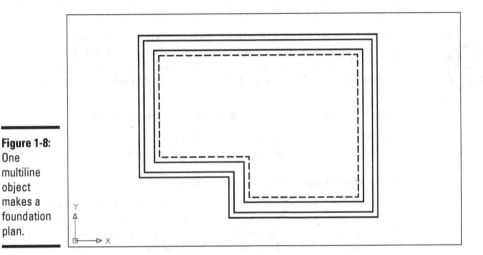

Figure 1-8:
One multiline object makes a foundation plan.

The following steps show you how to create a simple multiline shape.

1. **Choose Draw⇨Multiline or type ML to start the MLINE command.**

AutoCAD displays the MLINE options at the command prompt:

```
Command: MLINE
Current settings: Justification = Top, Scale = 1.00,
    Style = STANDARD
Specify start point or [Justification/Scale/STyle]:
```

2. **If you want to change justification from the current value, type J.**

Justification is either Top, Zero, or Bottom, and refers to where the multi-line elements are located relative to where you pick your locations. Zero justification centers the multiline elements on the points you pick. If Justification is Top, and you draw your multilines from left to right, the points you pick will be at the top element of the multiline. If you draw a closed shape with multilines, drawing clockwise with Top justification places the outermost element on the pick points. Logically, choosing Bottom justification does the reverse.

If you find the MLINE command's justification labeling as confusing as we do, you'll probably have better luck if you choose one justification (for example, Top) and one direction (for example, clockwise), and stick to it.

3. To change Scale from the current setting, type S.

The default value of 1.0 draws multilines exactly as specified. So if your multiline style has two lines with a 1-inch separation, that's how far apart they'll be in your drawing. If you wanted to use this multiline style to represent a 6-inch wide wall, you'd change the scale factor to 6.

Rather than try to do everything with a single multiline style, consider creating styles for real objects using real dimensions. For example, if you want a 6-inch wide wall, define the wall style so that the lines are 6 inches apart. That way you don't have to even think about the Style option.

4. Type ST to switch the current multiline style to another style.

The new style must already exist in the drawing; you can't create a new multiline style from the MLINE command prompt.

5. Pick a start point or enter coordinates.

The remaining prompts are identical to those for the LINE command. AutoCAD continues drawing multiline segments until you press Enter or Esc to terminate the command. After the second pick, there's an Undo option, and after the third pick, a Close option.

Because multilines are single objects, they must be created according to a defined multiline style. By default, every AutoCAD drawing contains a multiline style definition called *Standard.* The default Standard style is used to create pairs of continuous parallel lines.

That's how you create multilines and multilines. As for why you may want to use multilines, we leave that up to you but offer the following list of multiline shortcomings:

✦ A sequence of multilines, such as the foundation drawing example, is a single AutoCAD object, and therefore difficult to edit; frequently users create geometry with multilines and then explode them to individual lines (we discuss the EXPLODE command in the next chapter).

✦ Multilines can't have curved segments; if you're laying out a floor plan and need curved walls, you have to exit the command and draw the curved segments with regular lines and arcs.

✦ Multiline styles can't be modified if there are any multiline objects drawn with that style in the drawing. If you want a slightly different style, you have to create a similar-looking multiline style and then re-create the lines.

✦ You can't change the style of an existing multiline object in the Properties palette as you can with other object types defined by styles.

✦ Editing multilines requires a specialized set of tools and its own dialog box (although in AutoCAD 2005 and later you can use some regular editing commands on multilines).

✦ It can be non-intuitive — not to say, downright tricky — to define multiline styles.

Book II
Chapter 1

Drawing Objects

Complex Curves

Splines are smooth curves that pass near or through a series of control points. A spline object in AutoCAD can form either a closed or open shape. An *ellipse* is a symmetrical, oval shape that can be either closed or open (if it's open, technically it's an elliptical arc, but AutoCAD still classifies it as an ellipse). Ellipses are defined by a center point, a major axis, and a minor axis. In its early days, AutoCAD could only approximate spline curves and ellipses by creating polyline objects (we say more about polylines a little later). More recent versions have acquired the math skills to create what are known as Non-Uniform Rational B-Splines — or NURBS to their friends.

Lucy, you got some splining to do!

AutoCAD can create two different types of splines; one type is the spline-fit polyline, which we discuss in the next section. Industrial designers use splines to give form to organic shapes. Splines are created with the SPLINE command and are defined by an arbitrary number of control points. Depending on your needs, you can either eyeball your splines, or calculate the coordinates of their control points for absolute precision.

The following steps show you how to create splines and describe the options of the SPLINE command.

1. **Click the Spline tool on the Draw toolbar, or choose Draw⇨Spline, or type SPLine to start the SPLINE command.**

AutoCAD prompts as follows:

```
Specify first point or [Object]:
```

2. Pick a point on-screen, or enter coordinates to specify a precise start point for the spline.

If you type **O** at this prompt, you can select a spline-fit polyline to convert to a NURBS spline.

3. Pick another point on-screen, or enter coordinates for the second point.

After you pick the second point, AutoCAD prompts:

```
Specify next point or [Close/Fit tolerance] <start
    tangent>:
```

4. Type F to specify a Fit tolerance.

Fit tolerance determines how closely the spline object comes to the points used to define it (see Figure 1-9). The default value of 0 forces the spline to pass precisely through the control points. Values greater than 1 allow the curve to pass that point within that tolerance value.

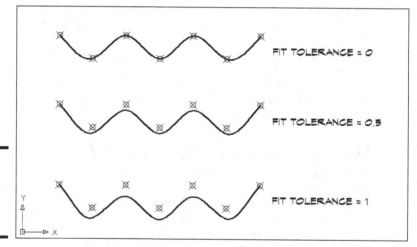

FIT TOLERANCE = 0

FIT TOLERANCE = 0.5

FIT TOLERANCE = 1

Figure 1-9:
A fit
tolerance
for your
splines.

5. To create a closed spline, type C and press Enter.

AutoCAD makes its best guess at closing the spline shape, but needs one more piece of information from you. The command prompt reads:

```
Specify next point or [Close/Fit tolerance] <start
    tangent>: C
Specify tangent:
```

You can either pick a point on screen to set the tangency direction, or simply press Enter to accept the default tangent direction.

6. **To create an open spline, press Enter to accept the default choice and specify a start tangent direction.**

AutoCAD prompts:

```
Specify start tangent:

Specify end tangent:
```

For each prompt, pick points on-screen, enter coordinates, or simply press Enter to accept the default tangency directions.

Solar Ellipses

Ellipses, like splines, are created as NURBS curves. Unlike splines, ellipses are closed, symmetrical shapes. Elliptical arcs are similar to ellipses, except that they're open.

Drawing ellipses

AutoCAD provides two methods for drawing ellipses. You can define the ellipse by locating the two endpoints of its first axis and one endpoint of its second. Or, you can locate the center of the ellipse, and then one endpoint on each of its axes. The following steps show you how to create an ellipse:

1. **Choose Ellipse from the Draw toolbar or Draw menu, or type EL to start the ELLIPSE command.**

AutoCAD prompts:

```
Specify axis endpoint of ellipse or [Arc/Center]:
```

2. **To draw an ellipse based on its center, pick a point or enter coordinates to specify the first endpoint of the first axis.**

AutoCAD prompts:

```
Specify other endpoint of axis:
```

3. **Pick a second point or enter coordinates for the second endpoint of the first axis.**

AutoCAD prompts:

```
Specify distance to other axis or [Rotation]:
```

You have three choices here: You can specify a point by picking or typing a coordinate pair (the default method); you can specify a distance (that is, the length of the second axis); or you can use the Rotation option to specify an angle between the two axes.

Acceptable angle values range between 0 and 89.4°. The higher the rotation angle, the flatter the ellipse, and a 0° rotation will generate a circular ellipse.

4. **To draw an ellipse using the default method, pick a third point above or below the first axis, or enter a coordinate pair.**

AutoCAD draws the ellipse.

Elliptical arcs

Drawing elliptical arcs is almost the same as drawing ellipses, except there are two additional inputs needed at the end of the process. The following steps explain how to draw an elliptical arc using the default construction method.

1. **On the Draw toolbar, click the Elliptical Arc tool.**

Use the toolbar button for the most direct route to this function, which is actually an option of the regular ELLIPSE command, as the command prompt shows:

```
Specify axis endpoint of ellipse or [Arc/Center]: _a
Specify axis endpoint of elliptical arc or [Center]:
```

The Elliptical Arc tool is actually a command macro that's programmed into the tool button to automatically choose the Arc option of the ELLIPSE command. The second line takes you to the first step of drawing a regular ellipse.

If you're really attached to the menu system, you can choose Draw➪ Ellipse➪Arc to run the same command macro (see Figure 1-10). But if you're a dedicated keyboarder, you must type the **A** (for Arc option) yourself. Sometimes AutoCAD makes you work *so* hard!

2. **Pick points on-screen to specify the first and second endpoints of the first axis, and the endpoint of the second axis.**

AutoCAD prompts as follows:

```
Specify other endpoint of axis:
Specify distance to other axis or [Rotation]:
```

The final prompts allow you to set the internal angle of the elliptical arc.

3. **Pick points on-screen to specify the start and end points of the elliptical arc.**

AutoCAD prompts:

```
Specify start angle or [Parameter]:
Specify end angle or [Parameter/Included angle]:
```

For information on the Parameter option (which doesn't do much that simply picking endpoints can't handle), refer to the ELLIPSE command on the Index tab of the online Help.

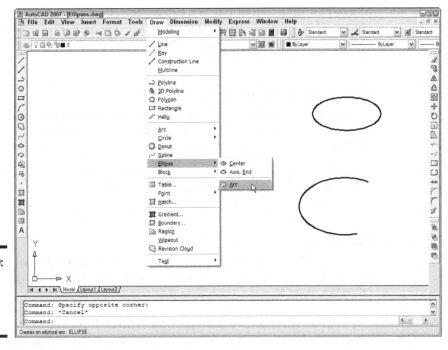

Figure 1-10:
Elliptical
arcs are
on today's
menu.

Complex Objects and Shapes

The last selection of commands and objects covered in this chapter are
somewhat more complex than most of those covered previously. Some, like
polylines, are extremely useful. Others, like 2D solids, are a lot less so.

2D Solids

The first thing to be said about 2D solids is that they're not three-dimensional
solid objects. We talk about working in 3D in Book V. Here we deal briefly
with another ancient AutoCAD entity type, the 2D solid. *Solid* here refers to a
solid-*filled* 2D outline.

A long, long time ago, AutoCAD was not able to solid-fill a closed area. If you
wanted the effect, you had to use the SOLID command. A big drawback is
that 2D solids can have only three or four sides — no more. So you might
have had to create dozens of 2D solids to fill a randomly shaped area. The
other problem with 2D solids is that their three or four sides are always
straight.

Ninety-nine times out of 100, you can get the effect you need with the HATCH command or a wide polyline. (We discuss hatching in Book III and polylines in the next sections.) If you still think you need 2D solids, check out the SOLID Command in the online Help.

Rectang, Polygon, Donut

No prizes for guessing what kinds of things that commands named REC-TANG, POLYGON, and DONUT make. (Actually you *may* have to guess, but we don't have any prizes for you!)

All three commands make polyline objects. A polyline is a very useful type of object, which can take almost any shape, as long as each part is connected to the other.

Rectangles

The RECTANG command creates four-sided closed polylines with horizontal and vertical sides. Command options allow you to draw rectangles in different ways. You can:

✦ Locate two diagonal corners

✦ Locate one corner, and then enter values for area and the length of one side

✦ Locate one corner, enter values for length and width, and then specify direction

✦ Locate one corner, specify a rotation angle, and then locate the other corner

In addition, before you pick the first point, you can

✦ Set chamfer or fillet values so that all four corners are automatically chamfered or filleted

In drafting, a *chamfer* is a straight line that forms the transition between two 2D objects that meet at an angle; one example is a beveled edge at a corner. A *fillet* is a curved transition between two 2D objects; an example is rounded edge at a corner.

✦ Set a width value so the sides of the rectangle have a 2D width

✦ Set elevation and thickness values for the rectangle if you're working in 3D.

Polygons

Polygons, like rectangles, are closed polyline objects. Unlike rectangles, by default polygons are regular: They have equal length sides and equal internal angles.

If you want to draw irregular polygons, use the PLINE command.

AutoCAD's POLYGON command draws regular polygons of a minimum of three and a maximum of 1,024 sides. After specifying the number of sides for your polygon, there are three options:

✦ **Edge:** Locate an endpoint of the first edge, and then pick or enter a value to locate the second endpoint.

✦ **Inscribed:** Locate the center of an imaginary circle, and then specify its radius. AutoCAD draws the polygon so that the corners touch the circumference of the circle (the circle is not actually drawn).

✦ **Circumscribed:** Locate the center of an imaginary circle, and then specify its radius. AutoCAD draws the polygon so that the sides are tangent to the imaginary circle.

Donuts

Now for the biggest disappointment of the whole chapter. No, AutoCAD does not generate snack food when you run the DONUT command. Trust us — it's better that way, anyway.

AutoCAD donuts are solid-filled polylines (as opposed to jelly-filled pastries). When you create donuts in AutoCAD, you specify an inside and an outside diameter, and then locate them by picking a center point.

A common use for donuts (the AutoCAD flavor, anyway) is in structural engineering drafting where you need to draw round reinforcing steel in a cross-section. You can specify an inside diameter of 0 to create a solid-filled donut. Just like asking for "Plain" at the coffee shop.

Polylines

A polyline is a single object that consists of one or (more usefully) multiple linear or curved segments. You create open or closed regular or irregular polylines with the PLINE command. Just like the LINE command, PLINE will continue adding line (or arc) segments until you terminate the command. Unlike the case with LINE, the objects you create with the PLINE command are single entities. Figure 1-11 shows geometry created with each command. The LINE command (on the left) created eight connected but separate line objects. The PLINE command (on the right) created one single object.

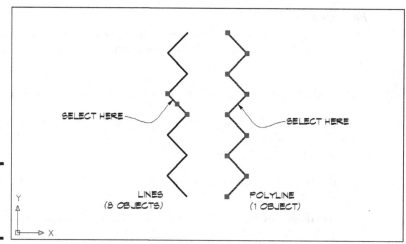

Figure 1-11:
Drawing
polylines
(and lines).

The following sequence from the command prompt shows how the polyline in Figure 1-12 was drawn:

```
Command: _pline
Specify start point: 40,20

Current line-width is 0.0000
Specify next point or [Arc/Halfwidth/Length/Undo/Width]: W

Specify starting width <0.0000>: 0

Specify ending width <0.0000>: 2

Specify next point or [Arc/Halfwidth/Length/Undo/Width]:
   @4<180

Specify next point or
   [Arc/Close/Halfwidth/Length/Undo/Width]: @4<180

Specify next point or
   [Arc/Close/Halfwidth/Length/Undo/Width]: W

Specify starting width <2.0000>: 2

Specify ending width <2.0000>: 4

Specify next point or
   [Arc/Close/Halfwidth/Length/Undo/Width]: @4<180

Specify next point or
   [Arc/Close/Halfwidth/Length/Undo/Width]: W
```

Specify starting width <4.0000>: **4**

Specify ending width <4.0000>: **0.5**

Specify next point or
    [Arc/Close/Halfwidth/Length/Undo/Width]: **@8<180**

Specify next point or
    [Arc/Close/Halfwidth/Length/Undo/Width]: **W**

Specify starting width <0.5000>: **0.5**

Specify ending width <0.5000>: **0**

Specify next point or
    [Arc/Close/Halfwidth/Length/Undo/Width]: **A**

Specify endpoint of arc or
[Angle/CEnter/CLose/Direction/Halfwidth/Line/Radius/Second
    pt/Undo/Width]: **@12<270**

Specify endpoint of arc or
[Angle/CEnter/CLose/Direction/Halfwidth/Line/Radius/Second
    pt/Undo/Width]: *<Press Enter to end the command>*

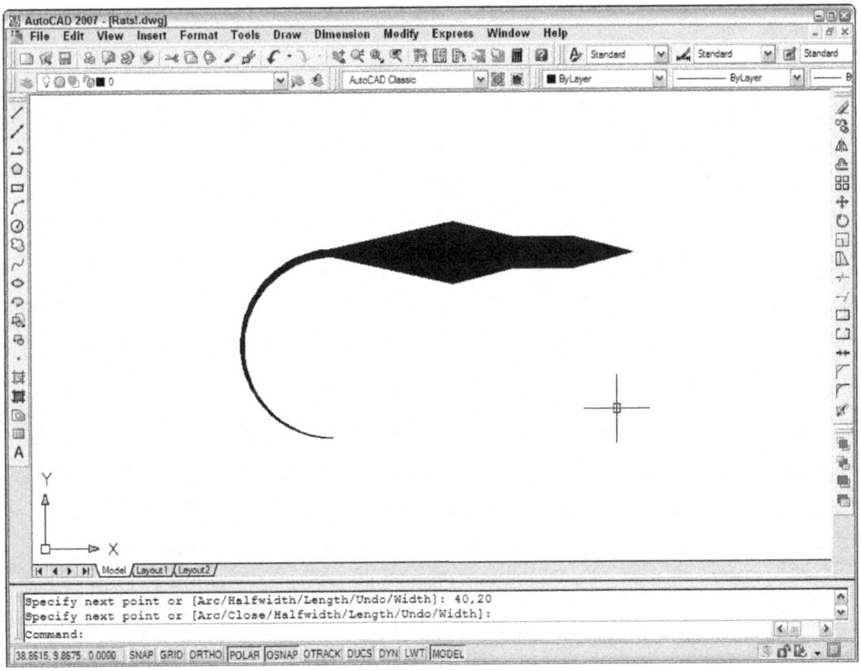

Figure 1-12:
Constructing
a polyline.

Chapter 2: Modifying Objects

In This Chapter

✔ Setting selection options

✔ Editing objects

✔ Using object groups

✔ Undoing and redoing

✔ Editing objects using grips

M ost of the work you do in any CAD drawing file involves modifying existing objects. You may need to move objects from one part of the drawing to another, or you may need to copy them from one part of a drawing to another, or even from one drawing to another. "Draw once, reuse as much as possible" should be your mantra when you work in AutoCAD.

Of course, before you can edit an object, you have to tell AutoCAD which object you want to work with. Sounds simple enough, but there's a bewildering number of methods you can choose from to select objects. AutoCAD's Options dialog box is the place to begin setting your choices for object selection, and that's where we're going to start with this chapter.

Setting Selection Options

Before we get to selecting and then editing, we need to briefly explore the Selection tab of the Options dialog box (see Figure 2-1).

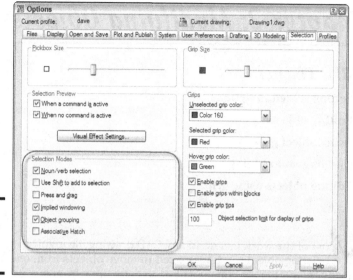

Figure 2-1:
Select your
selection
modes.

The six settings in the lower-left corner determine how you select objects:

✦ **Noun/verb selection.** Allows you to select objects for editing before you
start an editing command. Checked by default. See "Object selection
modes" later in this chapter for more information.

✦ **Use Shift to add to selection.** When unchecked (the default), selecting
items one after another adds them to the *selection set;* to remove items
from the selection set, hold down the Shift key and select them. When
checked, press the Shift key to add objects to the selection set; clicking
on a selected object removes it from the set.

Selection set refers to any selected objects that are ready to be edited.
There can be only one selection set active at a time, and when you make
a new selection, the old selection set is replaced. A selection set can
contain any number of objects, even including everything in the drawing.
It's also possible to save a selection set as a named group — see the
later section "Object groups."

✦ **Press and drag.** When unchecked (the default), you click once to set one
corner of a selection box, and then click again to set the other corner.
(For more on selection boxes, see "Selecting multiple objects" later in
this chapter.) When checked, you use Windows-standard pressing-and-
dragging with the left mouse button to set the selection box.

✦ **Implied windowing.** When checked (the default), picking a point away from any object starts an automatic selection box. Moving the mouse to the left creates a crossing box, and moving it to the right creates a window box. We explain the difference in the "Selecting multiple objects" section.

✦ **Object grouping.** When checked (the default), clicking one object that belongs to a defined object group selects every other object in that group. When unchecked, other group members are not selected when one member is selected. See "Object groups" for more information.

✦ **Associative hatch.** When unchecked (the default), selecting a hatch object selects only the hatch. When checked, selecting a hatch object also selects the boundary used to create it.

Figure 2-1 and this list point out the default selection settings. The following sections assume that these are the current system settings. If you get different results when you try some of these methods, open the Options dialog box and make sure that the settings jibe with ours.

Selecting Objects

You must decide two things when you see some drawing objects that need editing:

✦ How many objects do you want to modify? If there are several, are they adjacent to one another, or are they scattered all over the drawing?

✦ How do you want to modify the objects? Do you want to select them first, or start the command first? Or would you rather use another method altogether? (For the last, we're referring to object grips, which we discuss near the end of the chapter.)

The first thing you have to work out is whether you want to perform an action on one single object or modify a group of separate objects. Selecting a single object is (to use some technical language) a no-brainer — you just click it with the pickbox, and it's selected.

The little square box at the intersection of the crosshairs is called the pickbox, and whenever it's visible, you can use the crosshairs to select objects. The pickbox disappears from the crosshairs in any command in which you're being prompted to select a point. (And the crosshairs disappear from the pickbox when AutoCAD asks you to select an object.) By default, the pickbox measures 3 pixels square; you can alter the size by typing PICKBOX and specifying a new value.

Selecting multiple objects

If you start your editing process by selecting one of the Modify commands, AutoCAD prompts you to select objects. Use one of the following techniques to do so:

+ To select a single object, click it with the pickbox.

+ To invoke an automatic window selection box, pick a point above and to the left of the objects you want to select, and then move the crosshairs down and to the right to create a window box around the objects.

+ To invoke an automatic crossing selection box, pick a point above and to the right of the objects you want to select, and then move your crosshairs down and to the left to create a crossing box around the objects.

+ To invoke any other option, enter the capitalized parts of the option name as follows: Last, ALL, Fence, WPolygon, CPolygon, Add, Remove, and Previous.

Table 2-1 lists all the selection modes provided by AutoCAD. You can invoke any mode by typing the uppercase letters for the option (for example, F for Fence, ALL for All).

Table 2-1	AutoCAD's Selection Modes
Mode	*Description*
Window	Prompts for the first corner and then the other corner of a rectangular selection window. Only objects *completely within* the selection window will be selected. Window boxes are indicated by continuous border lines and blue shading.
Crossing	Prompts for the first corner and then the other corner of a rectangular selection window. Objects either *completely within or crossed by* the selection window will be selected. Crossing boxes are indicated by dashed border lines and green shading.
WPolygon	Prompts you to draw an irregular shape around the objects you want to select by picking points; once you've picked at least two points, the boundary becomes self-closing. Only objects completely within the WPolygon boundary polygon will be selected. WPolygon boundaries are indicated by continuous lines and blue shading.
CPolygon	Prompts you to draw an irregular shape around the objects you want to select by picking points; after you pick at least two points, the boundary becomes self-closing. Objects either entirely within or crossed by the CPolygon boundary are selected. CPolygon boundaries are indicated by dashed lines and green shading.
Fence	Prompts you to draw a series of line segments through the objects to select. All objects touched by the Fence line will be selected.

Mode	Description
ALL	Selects everything in the drawing except objects on frozen layers, and objects in paper space if you are in model space or objects in model space if you are in paper space. (Refer to Book I for more information on model and paper space.)
Last	Selects the last object created *that's visible in the current display.* (This may not necessarily be the last object added to the drawing.)
Previous	Reselects the last selection set. Any selection set can be recalled using the Previous option, until a new selection set is created.
Add	Lets you continue to add objects to a selection set. (You can also add to the selection set by simply picking more objects.)
Remove	Removes selected objects from a selection set. (You can also remove selected objects from the selection set by holding the <Shift> key and picking them.)

Figure 2-2 shows the results of selecting objects using Window, Crossing, WPolygon, CPolygon, and Fence modes.

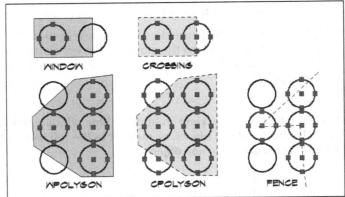

Figure 2-2:
Picking your way through AutoCAD objects.

Object selection modes

You can select objects for editing in two ways:

✦ **Verb-noun editing:** Start the desired edit command, and then select the objects you want to modify.

✦ **Noun-verb editing:** Select the objects you want to modify, and then start the specific edit command.

You're probably wondering if this is AutoCAD or Grade 6 English. Don't worry; this is just the terminology that the Autodesk programmers chose to distinguish the two methods.

The following steps show you how to use each mode. As an example, we've chosen the ERASE command, but the majority of commands work using either mode.

1. **In a new, blank drawing, draw some lines, circles, or other objects, or open a drawing containing a number of objects.**

2. **Start the ERASE command by clicking its icon in the Modify toolbar, or choosing Modify⇨Erase from the menus, or by typing E and pressing Enter.**

   To use verb-noun editing, select the command first. AutoCAD prompts:

   ```
   Select objects:
   ```

3. **Move the crosshairs so that they're on top of an object, and then click.**

   AutoCAD prompts

   ```
   Select objects: 1 found
   Select objects:
   ```

4. **Move the crosshairs until they're not on top of an object, and then click.**

   With Implied Windowing turned on (see the previous section, "Setting Selection Options"), moving the mouse to the left starts a crossing selection box, and moving it to the right starts a window selection box. AutoCAD prompts:

   ```
   Select objects: Specify opposite corner:
   ```

5. **Move the mouse to the right so that the blue window selection box entirely surrounds an object, or move it to the left so that the green selection box crosses some objects.**

   AutoCAD prompts:

   ```
   Select objects: Specify opposite corner: 2 found, 3
      total
   Select objects:
   ```

6. **Press Enter to finish selecting objects and complete the command.**

   AutoCAD continues prompting you to select more objects until the cows come home. Or until you press Enter to complete the command — which, we hope, you'll do first.

   Still got some objects left to erase? Good! (If not, click the Undo button on the Standard toolbar to get some of them back.)

7. **Make sure that no command is active, and then use any selection method you like to choose some objects.**

No command is active, but the objects are still added to a selection set. AutoCAD prompts:

```
Command:
Command: Specify opposite corner:
```

8. **Start the ERASE command by clicking its icon in the Modify toolbar, or choosing Modify⇨Erase, or typing E and pressing Enter.**

AutoCAD erases the drawing objects and prompts:

```
Command: e
ERASE 3 found
Command:
```

Object groups

The final object selection topic to mention is object groups. You know that selection sets can be recalled for subsequent edits, but only until you select a new object or bunch of objects — then the new bunch will overwrite the Previous set.

The *object groups* feature lets you save a selection set with a name so that you can recall it at any time. You can have as many object groups as you wish, and individual objects can belong to more than one group at a time. When object grouping is turned on, selecting one member of a group selects the entire group; when grouping is off, selecting a group member only selects the one you picked. You can turn object grouping off and on at the Selection tab of the Options dialog box (see the previous section, "Setting Selection Options" for details). An easier way exists, however; holding down the Ctrl and Shift keys and pressing A toggles object grouping off and on.

The following steps explain how to create an object group:

1. **Type GROUP and press Enter.**

The GROUP command is available only at the command line. The Object Grouping dialog box appears.

2. **In the Group Identification area, enter a name in the Group Name edit box, and optionally enter a description in the Description box.**

All groups must have a name so that you can select them. The description is optional.

3. In the Create Group area, check Selectable, and then click New.

AutoCAD prompts:

```
Select objects for grouping:
Select objects: Specify opposite corner: 2 found
Select objects:
```

4. When you're finished selecting objects, press Enter.

AutoCAD redisplays the Object Grouping dialog box (see Figure 2-3).

Figure 2-3: A newly-made object group.

5. Click OK to finish creating the group and close the dialog box.

AutoCAD LT does support groups, but it uses a different, and more limited, procedure from regular AutoCAD. Instead of the Object Grouping dialog box, AutoCAD LT does its group work with a Group Manager. For more on working with groups in AutoCAD LT, see Book IV.

AutoCAD's Editing Commands

Table 2-2 lists AutoCAD's most common editing commands and tells you where to find them and what they do. As with the drawing commands in the preceding chapter, we don't cover the commands in this order (which, in case you're wondering, is alphabetical by command name). You'll find most of these commands on the Modify toolbar and menu, as well as a few on the Standard toolbar and Edit menu. There's also a Modify II toolbar, which contains some of the more specialized editing commands.

To display closed toolbars, right-click on any tool button and choose a toolbar from the shortcut menu. If the toolbar shows a check beside its name, it's already open.

We cover an additional set of commands for editing text and dimensions in Book III. We also discuss 3D editing commands in Book V.

Table 2-2		AutoCAD's Editing Commands			
Icon	Toolbar (Modify U/N)	Menu (Modify U/N)	Command Name	Alias	Function
	Array	Array	ARRAY	AR	Duplicate objects in circular or rectangular pattern.
	Break at Point Break	Break	BREAK	BR	Break selected objects into separate objects at selected points.
	Chamfer	Chamfer	CHAMFER	CHA	Apply beveled corner to intersecting objects.
	Copy	Copy	COPY	CO	Duplicate selected objects.
	Standard, Copy	Edit⇨Copy	COPYCLIP	---	Copy objects to Windows Clipboard.
	Standard, Cut	Edit⇨Cut	CUTCLIP	---	Move objects from drawing to Windows Clipboard.
	Erase	Erase	ERASE	E	Remove selected objects.
	Explode	Explode	EXPLODE	X	Break complex objects into separate pieces.
	Extend	Extend	EXTEND	EX	Lengthen object by extending to other selected object.

(continued)

Table 2-2 *(continued)*

Icon	Toolbar (Modify U/N)	Menu (Modify U/N)	Command Name	Alias	Function
	Fillet	Fillet	FILLET	F	Apply rounded corner to intersecting objects.
---	---	---	GROUP	G	Create object groupings.
	Join	Join	JOIN	J	Connect selected discontinuous objects.
---	---	Lengthen	LENGTHEN	LEN	Change length of open objects.
	Standard, Match Properties	Match Properties	MATCHPROP	MA	Apply properties of one object to other objects.
	Mirror	Mirror	MIRROR	MI	Create mirrored original or copy.
	Move	Move	MOVE	M	Relocate selected objects.
	Offset	Offset	OFFSET	O	Create duplicate object specified distance.
---	---	---	OOPS	---	Unerase the last erased objects.
	Standard, Paste	Edit⇨Paste	PASTECLIP	---	Paste objects from Windows Clipboard.
	Modify II, Edit Polyline	Object⇨ Polyline	PEDIT	PE	Modify geometric properties of selected polyline.
	Standard, Properties	Properties	PROPERTIES	PR	List and change object properties.
	Standard, Redo	Edit⇨Redo	REDO	---	Reverse the last Undo.
	Rotate	Rotate	ROTATE	RO	Rotate selected object around base point.
	Scale	Scale	SCALE	SC	Resize objects from base point by a factor.

Icon	Toolbar (Modify U/N)	Menu (Modify U/N)	Command Name	Alias	Function
	Modify II, Edit Spline	Object⇨Spline	SPLINEDIT	SPE	Modify geometric properties of selected spline.
	Stretch	Stretch	STRETCH	S	Resize objects by dragging them.
	Trim	Trim	TRIM	TR	Shorten object by cutting with other selected object.
	Standard, Undo	Edit⇨Undo	U		Reverse the last single action.
	---	---	UNDO	---	Reverse a selectable series of actions.
---	---	---	XPLODE	XP	Break complex objects into separate pieces specifying properties after exploding.

Removing stuff

Everybody makes mistakes, and now it's time to clear away the evidence. We present the simplest-to-use of all of AutoCAD's editing commands: ERASE. We hope it's not your most frequently used command, but it doesn't really matter whether it is or not — you're not going to rub a hole in your screen by erasing AutoCAD objects.

Here are some ways to erase stuff from your drawing:

✦ Choose Modify⇨Erase, select the undesirables, and then press Enter.

✦ Choose Edit⇨Delete, select the undesirables, and then press Enter.

✦ Click the Erase tool in the Modify toolbar, select your objects, and then press Enter.

✦ Select the unwanted objects, choose Modify⇨Erase, or Edit⇨Delete, or click Erase in the Modify toolbar.

✦ Select the mistakes and then press Delete.

✦ Select the unwanted objects, right-click, and select Erase.

Relocating and replicating

Most commands require more direction than simply selecting objects and clicking a tool button. The first set of commands we look at enables you to relocate and duplicate already existing drawing objects.

MOVE

Moving objects requires three sets of input: the objects you want to move, a point to move them from, and another point to move them to.

Using noun-verb editing for simple commands like MOVE and COPY saves keystrokes. You don't want to overwork those pinkies, do you?

The following steps explain how to move objects using noun-verb editing:

1. Select a single object, or use one of the multiple selection methods described in the section "Selecting Multiple Objects" to select several objects.

AutoCAD highlights the objects and displays their grips. Don't worry about the grips (all those blue boxes and wedges) — we discuss them near the end of the chapter.

2. Click the Move button on the Modify toolbar, or choose Modify⇨ Move, or type M to start the MOVE command.

AutoCAD prompts:

```
Command: _move 4 found
Specify base point or [Displacement] <Displacement>:
```

AutoCAD shows you the number of objects that are going to be moved, and then tells you what to do next — it wants you to specify a *base point* ("take these things *from here*").

3. Pick a point on screen as the base point.

Sometimes you should pick a precise point for the base point, but if you're only moving or copying something a relative distance, it really doesn't matter where you pick. AutoCAD prompts:

```
Specify second point or
<use first point as displacement>:
```

4. Pick a second point or enter coordinates for the destination of the selected objects.

Remember, "second point" means "put it here." AutoCAD moves the objects and returns to the command line.

Even the simplest commands can throw you for a loop. You may get unexpected results if you press Enter in response to the Specify Second Point prompt. Pressing Enter tells AutoCAD to look at the *coordinates* of the first point and use those values as the *displacement* for the second point. We can pretty well guarantee this is not what you want.

COPY

When you use verb-noun editing, editing in AutoCAD is much more obviously a two-step process: you select the objects, press Enter, and carry on with the command. This is a good time to show you the difference, since the MOVE and COPY commands are pretty much the same.

Choosing Modify➪Copy runs the COPY command, which you use for duplicating existing objects within a drawing. Choosing Edit➪Copy runs the Windows Copy-to-the-Clipboard command, which AutoCAD calls COPYCLIP. Use COPYCLIP to copy objects from one drawing to another. Don't confuse the two.

Use the following steps to copy some objects using the COPY command and verb-noun editing.

1. Click the Copy button on the Modify toolbar, or choose Modify➪Copy, or type CO to start the Copy command.

AutoCAD prompts:

```
COPY
Select objects:
```

2. Select the objects to be copied using any object selection method.

If you choose a window or crossing, AutoCAD prompts:

```
Specify opposite corner: 4 found
Select objects:
```

3. Press Enter when you're finished selecting objects to copy.

The first prompts for COPY are exactly the same as for MOVE. What's different this time around is that we're copying using verb-noun selection, and we moved using noun-verb mode. After you press Enter to finish selecting, AutoCAD prompts:

```
Specify base point or [Displacement] <Displacement>:
```

4. Pick a point on-screen as the base point.

Again, use an object snap or other precision aid if you need to. If you're simply copying objects relative to their current location, it doesn't

Book II
Chapter 2

Modifying Objects

matter where you pick. Once you've picked the first point, AutoCAD prompts:

```
Specify second point or
<use first point as displacement>:
```

5. **Pick a second point or enter coordinates for the destination of the selected objects.**

You can enter relative coordinates, or use Direct Distance Entry (see Chapter 6) or any precision method (where appropriate), or eyeball a point. For example, typing **@2.85<0** makes a copy of the selected objects 2.85 units to the right of the originals.

AutoCAD prompts:

```
Specify second point or
<use first point as displacement>: @2.85<0
Specify second point or [Exit/Undo] <Exit>:
```

6. **Continue making additional copies or exit the command.**

By default, AutoCAD will continue offering to make copies until you tell it to stop. You can press Enter, the space bar, or the Esc key, or you can type **E** to exit the command.

MIRROR

MIRROR can create a single mirrored version of selected objects, or it can create a mirrored copy. Instead of picking a base and second point as you do with MOVE and COPY, with MIRROR you pick two points that are the end of an imaginary mirror. The selected object is "reflected" on the other side of the mirror line. The final MIRROR prompt asks if you want to retain or delete the original.

The following steps demonstrate the MIRROR command in verb-noun mode.

1. **Click the Mirror button on the Modify toolbar, or choose Modify⇨ Mirror, or type MI to start the MIRROR command.**

AutoCAD does its usual "Select objects" thing. By now you know the ropes — select some objects and press Enter. AutoCAD prompts:

```
Select objects: Specify opposite corner: 4 found
Select objects:  Specify first point of mirror line:
```

If it doesn't matter where your objects get mirrored to, just pick a random point on-screen. Do the same for the second point. More often than not, though, it *does* matter. If that's the case, make use of some of the precision drafting aids we discussed in Book I. In this example, the selected objects need to be mirrored precisely about the middle of a rectangle.

2. **Hold down the Shift key and right-click to display the object snap shortcut menu. Choose Midpoint and pick a horizontal edge of the rectangle when you see the triangular object snap marker.**

AutoCAD prompts:

```
Specify second point of mirror line:
```

3. **Hold the Shift key and click a second point directly above or below the first point.**

You need to be precise for your second point, too. Holding Shift invokes a temporary Ortho mode, when you move the crosshairs they will lock onto horizontal or vertical direction and remain that way until you release the Shift key (see Figure 2-4). AutoCAD prompts:

```
Erase source objects? [Yes/No] <N>:
```

4. **Type Y or N to erase or retain the source objects.**

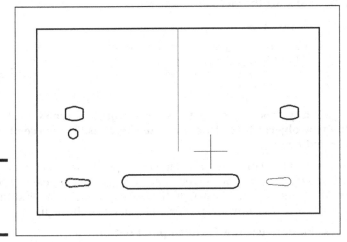

Figure 2-4:
Mirroring
objects
precisely.

OFFSET

OFFSET, like COPY, makes duplicates of selected objects, but it's more rigorous in where it lets you put those duplicates. It also doesn't make exact copies; different object types offset in different ways. Figure 2-5 shows the results of offsetting different entity types. You can OFFSET lines, arcs, circles, splines, ellipses, and polylines.

Figure 2-5:
Offsetting
different
object
types.

The following steps explain how to use OFFSET in verb-noun editing mode.

1. **Click Offset on the Modify toolbar, or choose Modify⇨Offset, or type O to start the OFFSET command.**

AutoCAD prompts

```
Current settings: Erase source=No  Layer=Source
   OFFSETGAPTYPE=0
Specify offset distance or [Through/Erase/Layer]
   <Through>:
```

2. **Optionally, type E to erase the source object, or type L to change the new object's layer from the same layer as the source object to the current layer.**

When offsetting objects, you can either specify an offset distance, or pick a *Through point* on-screen. Logically enough, choosing *Through point* offsets the object through the point you pick. The first time you run OFFSET in a drawing, the default value is <Through>.

3. **Press Enter to use the Through point option.**

AutoCAD prompts:

```
Select object to offset or [Exit/Undo] <Exit>:
```

If you simply pick a point, without pressing Enter to confirm the <Through> option, AutoCAD assumes you really want to enter an offset distance, will prompt you for a second point, and use the distance between the two points as the offset distance value.

4. **Select a single object to offset.**

You can specify only one object at a time; that is, you can't select a group of wall lines and offset them all in the same step. If you specified Through, AutoCAD prompts:

```
Specify through point or [Exit/Multiple/Undo] <Exit>:
```

For precise locations, use object snaps when picking through points. AutoCAD creates a new version of the selected object through the point you picked, and continues prompting for additional offsets and through points.

5. **When you finish offsetting, press Enter to return to the command line.**

If you enter a distance, you need to make an additional pick to show AutoCAD on which side of the source object you want the new object. The following steps show the process:

1. **Start the OFFSET command.**

The command prompts appear as follows:

```
Command: OFFSET
Current settings: Erase source=No   Layer=Source
    OFFSETGAPTYPE=0
Specify offset distance or [Through/Erase/Layer]
    <Through>:
```

2. **Type an offset distance value and press Enter.**

AutoCAD prompts:

```
Select object to offset or [Exit/Undo] <Exit>:
```

3. **Select the single object you want to offset.**

Because there are two possible directions that AutoCAD could offset the selected object, it wants you to show it which direction you want by prompting:

```
Specify point on side to offset or [Exit/Multiple/Undo]
    <Exit>:
```

It doesn't matter precisely where you pick, just so it's clearly on one side or the other of the source object.

4. **When you finish offsetting, press Enter to return to the command line.**

Figure 2-6 shows the effect of offsetting a set of joined linework. The closed shape on the left is a single polyline, and the shape on the right is drawn as separate lines with the LINE command. For this kind of result, it's obviously best to use a polyline rather than separate lines — you'll end up with no intersection cleanup.

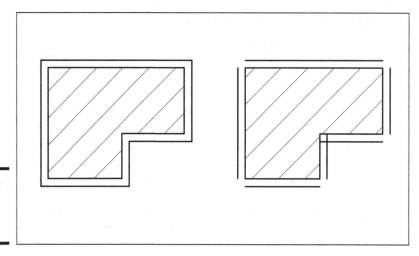

Figure 2-6:
Offsetting
polylines
and lines.

ARRAY

COPY makes multiple copies of objects by default. If it doesn't matter where the copies go, the COPY command is fine. However, if you need your ducks in rows (and columns, or even in a circle), the ARRAY command is for you.

ARRAY creates regular patterns of selected objects in either *Rectangular* (rows and columns) or *Polar* (circular) arrangements. The following steps explain how to create a rectangular array:

1. **Choose Modify⇨Array, click Array on the Modify toolbar, or type** AR **to start the ARRAY command.**

The Array dialog box appears. Figure 2-7 shows the dialog configured for rectangular arrays.

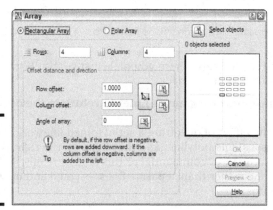

Figure 2-7:
Setting a
rectangular
array in a
dialog box.

2. **Make sure that the Rectangular Array radio button is selected, and then click the Select Objects button.**

   The dialog box closes, allowing you to select objects to array.

3. **Select one or more objects to array, and then press Enter to finish selecting.**

   The dialog box reappears.

4. **Specify the number of rows and/or columns, the row and column offsets, and (optionally) a rotation angle for the array.**

   If you want a single row or a single column, specify 1 in the appropriate box. Also, even though you're making copies of a source object, the number of rows and columns must include the number of copies you want *plus* the source object.

   You can also use the buttons beside the Row offset, Column offset, and Angle of array boxes to specify distances and angles. Clicking any of the buttons temporarily closes the dialog box and lets you pick points in the drawing.

5. **Click Preview to make sure your ducks are in a row.**

   The main Array dialog box disappears again, and AutoCAD previews the results of your settings together with a small dialog box with buttons to Accept, Modify, or Cancel.

6. **Click Accept to finish the command, or Modify to return to the dialog box, or Cancel to forget the whole business.**

Choosing a polar array changes the look of the Array dialog box (see Figure 2-8). To create a polar array, you specify objects to array, and then a center point, the number of items and angle to fill, and whether the selected objects should be rotated as they're arrayed.

**Book II
Chapter 2**

Modifying Objects

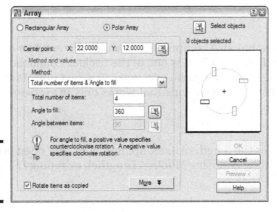

Figure 2-8:
Setting up a
polar array.

Rotating and resizing

The next set of commands modifies objects by changing their size or orientation in the drawing.

ROTATE

ROTATE spins objects around a base point, either rotating the original or making a copy and leaving the original in place. You specify the amount of rotation by entering an angle or using reference geometry. A typical ROTATE command sequence looks like this:

```
Command: ROTATE
Current positive angle in UCS:   ANGDIR=counterclockwise
   ANGBASE=0
Select objects: 3 found
Select objects:
Specify base point: 0,0
Specify rotation angle or [Copy/Reference] <0>: 32
```

After pressing Enter at the last prompt, the selected objects are rotated.

SCALE

SCALE proportionately resizes selected objects about a base point. You specify a numeric scale factor, or use reference geometry to specify the new size. The procedure is very similar to that for ROTATE: Select your objects, specify a base point, and then specify a scale factor.

Use the SCALE command if you need to convert a drawing done in millimeters so that you can work on it in inches, or vice versa. If you scale a drawing based in inches by a factor of 25.4, the distance values (including the dimensions) will be equivalent to true distances in millimeters. If you have to go the other way, scale the drawing by a factor of 0.03937.

STRETCH

STRETCH stretches but also compresses. Perhaps it should be called STRETCHANDSHRINK? STRETCH is one of the trickier commands to get a handle on because there's only one way you can select objects for stretching. It's also one of those commands that works only in verb-noun mode.

LENGTHEN

LENGTHEN changes the length of lines, splines, arcs, and open polylines. Start the command by choosing Modify⇨Lengthen or typing **LEN**. Lengthen (which can shorten, too) changes object length by the option you specify at the command line.

Breaking, mending, and blowing up real good

AutoCAD has let you break objects for years and years. And what's *really* great is that you never have to pay for the stuff you break. Recent versions have also let you fix things (well, a few things, under very particular conditions). But sometimes, there's just no alternative to blowing things up.

BREAK

BREAK is a tricky command to master because you really, really have to keep a watch on the command line. The normal function of BREAK is to remove a chunk of object — say a piece of a line to make two lines with a gap between, or a piece of a circle to turn it into an arc. The following steps describe how to use BREAK to create a gap in an object:

1. **Select Break (not Break at point) from the Modify toolbar, or choose Modify⇨Break, or type** BR **to start the BREAK command.**

You can use this command only in verb-noun mode. AutoCAD prompts you to select an object; once you've done so, the prompt reads:

```
Specify second break point or [First point]: F
```

BREAK's default behavior is to take the point where you selected the object as the first point of the break. The second point would be the other end of the break; after the second pick, AutoCAD would go ahead and break the object and then return to the command line. This is usually not a very precise way of working, so most of the time you should use the First point option.

2. **Type** F **to specify the First point option.**

AutoCAD prompts:

```
Specify first break point:
```

Use your favorite precision technique to pick the exact point where the break should start. AutoCAD then prompts:

```
Specify second break point:
```

Pick again to specify the second break point. AutoCAD removes the portion of the object between the first and second points.

Use the Break at Point button on the Modify toolbar to break an object into separate pieces without creating a gap between them — the objects would meet endpoint-to-endpoint. Break at Point is a command macro; you can achieve the same result by starting the BREAK command in other ways, but this way is the easiest.

JOIN

JOIN enables you to combine separate objects into single ones, as long as some fairly stringent criteria are met. For starters, all objects must lie on the same plane. Separated lines to be joined must be collinear. Arcs must be concentric. JOIN is another command that can be used only in verb-noun mode.

EXPLODE

That stick of dynamite down at the bottom of the Modify toolbar runs the EXPLODE command. EXPLODE breaks up complex objects into their primitive elements. You can explode polylines, as well as dimensions and blocks. (We discuss dimensions in Book III and blocks in Book VI.) If you use EXPLODE on a polyline, the separate entities (that is, lines and arcs) end up on the same layer as the original polyline.

A related command called XPLODE explodes complex entities and gives you a range of options you can set for the exploded objects.

Double-barrel commands

Love and Marriage. Horse and Carriage. Trim and Extend . . . Even though they don't rhyme, TRIM and EXTEND do work in similar fashion, so we're going to discuss them together here. And while we're at it, we'll talk about CHAMFER and FILLET, as well.

TRIM and EXTEND

TRIM and EXTEND use existing geometry to modify other geometry. The TRIM command lets you cut objects by selecting other objects that cross them. The EXTEND command lets you lengthen objects by selecting other objects that you want them to reach.

The following steps and Figure 2-9 describe how to use TRIM to shorten and extend objects:

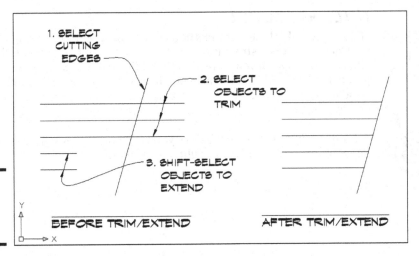

Figure 2-9:
The long
and short
of TRIM.

1. **Select the Trim button from the Modify toolbar, or choose Modify⇨
Trim, or type** TR **to start the TRIM command.**

In this two-part command, you first select the objects you want to trim
with — your temporary pair of scissors. AutoCAD prompts:

```
Current settings: Projection=UCS, Edge=None
Select cutting edges ...
Select objects or <select all>:
```

The first prompt line displays the current command settings. To change
the Projection or Edge settings, use the command options that display
after you've finished selecting your cutting edges. The second line tells
you that the objects you're going to select will be used as the cutting
edges.

2. **At the** Select objects: **prompt, use any object selection method to
select linework or other drawing objects as the cutting edges, or press
Enter to select everything visible as a cutting edge.**

After you finish selecting, AutoCAD prompts:

```
Select object to trim or shift-select to extend or
[Fence/Crossing/Project/Edge/eRase/Undo]:
```

3. **On the object that you want to trim, pick a point on the part you want
to get rid of, or choose one of the command options.**

TRIM and EXTEND are such close relatives that you can actually run
EXTEND from within Trim, and vice versa. To do so, simply hold down
the Shift key and select objects.

FILLET and CHAMFER

FILLET and CHAMFER offer methods of finishing off intersecting objects. CHAMFER creates a straight beveled edge between two non-parallel objects. FILLET creates a curved transition (actually an arc object) between two non-parallel objects. FILLET can also create a semicircular connection between parallel lines. Figure 2-10 shows a typical intersection after filleting and chamfering.

Setting the Fillet radius to 0 before you fillet lines or arcs creates a clean intersection, as shown at the right of Figure 2-10.

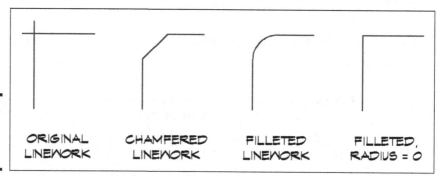

Figure 2-10:
Cornering your inter-sections.

ORIGINAL LINEWORK   CHAMFERED LINEWORK   FILLETED LINEWORK   FILLETED, RADIUS = 0

Specialized commands

Most of the commands we've discussed so far can work on any type of object; for example, you can trim or extend lines, arcs, or polylines. Some object types are sufficiently complex that they require unique edit tools. You'll find those tools on the Modify⇔Object submenu and the Modify II toolbar (see Figure 2-11). (To display the Modify II toolbar, right-click over any tool button and choose Modify II.)

Edit Hatch

Edit Spline

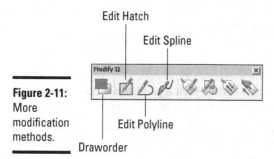

Figure 2-11:
More modification methods.

Edit Polyline

Draworder

The four tool buttons on the right side of the Modify II toolbar are for working with block attributes (we discuss those in Book VI). The four buttons at the left are for modifying graphic objects as follows:

+ **Draworder.** Invokes the DRAWORDER command; move objects in front of or behind other objects.

+ **Edit Hatch.** Invokes HATCHEDIT command; modify pattern, scale, and other properties of existing hatch objects.

+ **Edit Polyline.** Invokes PEDIT command; modify width, linetype generation, curve type, and other properties of existing polyline objects.

+ **Edit Spline.** Invokes SPLINEDIT command; modify curve type, vertexes, and other properties of existing spline objects.

For additional information on these commands, refer to the online Help.

Changing properties

All of the edit commands we've looked at so far have involved modifying or duplicating object geometry in some form or other. But sometimes you may just want to change an object's layer, or find out how long something is.

MATCH PROPERTIES

MATCHPROP is AutoCAD's magic wand. To use it to copy the properties (linetype, color, layer, text or dimension style, and so on) of one object to one or more other objects, simply click the source object, and then the objects you want to change.

PROPERTIES

PROPERTIES displays a window (or, palette) of its own (see Figure 2-12) in which you see listed every property (editable or not) of the selected object.

The Properties palette is a dockable window. Unlike dialog boxes, dockable windows can stay open while you're working in the drawing. And by double-clicking their title bars, you can *dock* them — that is, anchor them — at the left or right edges of the display.

Book II
Chapter 2

Modifying Objects

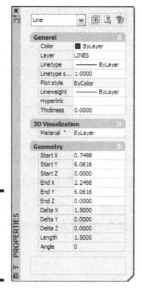

Figure 2-12:
Checking
out the
Properties
palette.

Changing your mind

We introduce you to UNDO in Book I and point out a little-known, but useful, AutoCAD command called OOPS. Remember: OOPS restores the last things you erased. UNDO undoes the last operation. Refer to Book I if you need a refresher on the difference.

Coming to Grips with Grips

When you select objects, not only do they highlight, they also sprout little blue boxes, called grips. You can perform a number of editing operations by clicking these grips and then following the command line (or the dynamic input tooltip if you're using it — and if you've forgotten what dynamic input is, have a look at Book I, Chapter 2).

By default, grips appear as solid blue squares at specific points on selected objects. Grip locations often correspond with object snap points, but they're not the same. To make a grip active, move the crosshairs over the grip and click. You'll know it's selected when its color changes from blue to red (see Figure 2-13).

Red grip   Blue grip

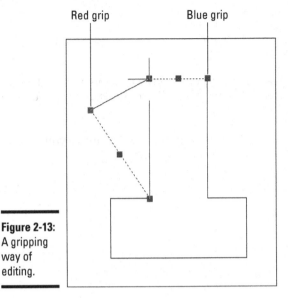

Figure 2-13:
A gripping
way of
editing.

Selecting a grip activates grip-editing mode. The grip turns red to show it is active. As soon as a grip becomes active, the command prompt is replaced by a series of five grip-edit commands. When a grip is active, you can choose the grip-edit commands and options in any of these ways:

✦ Press Enter or the space bar to cycle through the five commands. If you go past the one you want, keep hitting Enter until it reappears. To select an option, type its capitalized letter.

✦ Right-click and choose the command or option from the shortcut menu.

✦ If dynamic input is enabled, you can use the down arrow on your keyboard to choose an option, although you must choose the grip-edit command by right-clicking or pressing Enter or the space bar.

If you're using the keyboard, activating a grip replaces the command line with the grip-edit commands. They look like this:

```
** STRETCH ** <Stretch to point>/Base point/Copy/Undo/eXit:
** MOVE ** <Move to point>/Base point/Copy/Undo/eXit:
** ROTATE ** <Rotation angle>/Base
   point/Copy/Undo/Reference/eXit:
```

```
** SCALE ** <Scale factor>/Base
   point/Copy/Undo/Reference/eXit:
** MIRROR ** <Second point>/Base point/Copy/Undo/eXit:
** STRETCH ** ... and round and round you go.
```

Each grip edit command has options to change the base point or make multiple copies. The **ROTATE** and **SCALE** options also let you use reference options.

Grips also have an automatic object snap; as soon as you move your cursor close to a grip, it jumps to the precise control point.

Chapter 3: Managing Views

In This Chapter
↙ Zooming in and out of your drawings

↙ Panning around your drawings

↙ Going back to where you were with named views

*W*hen you draw things in AutoCAD, you draw them full size. If you're drawing the cross section of a 2 x 4 (or a 38 x 89 for our metrically inclined friends), you can look at it full size, so that the screen width is the same as the width of the actual piece of lumber. If your monitor is big enough, you could even view a 2 x 12 (38 x 286) on your screen at its real size. Sooner rather than later, though, it becomes uneconomical to keep getting a bigger monitor as you need to draw bigger things.

Luckily, the ZOOM command lets you increase or decrease the magnification of your drawing objects through a number of options, which we discuss in this chapter. In addition to zooming in and out of drawings, another couple of display commands will come in handy in your drawings: PAN and VIEW. PAN lets you move around in the drawing without changing the magnification. The VIEW command displays a dialog box in which you can save and restore named views.

Table 3-1 lists AutoCAD's 2D display commands in alphabetical order, together with locations for finding them and general descriptions of what they do.

Table 3-1			AutoCAD's 2D Display Commands		
Icon	Toolbar	View Menu	Command Name, Option	Alias	Function
		Aerial View	DSVIEWER	--	Displays the Aerial Viewer window. (See later in this chapter for details.)
	Standard, Pan	Pan	PAN	P	Moves around the drawing dynamically without changing magnification.
		Pan⇨Point	-PAN	-P	Moves around the drawing by clicking two points.
		Redraw	REDRAW	R	Refreshes the screen display.
		---	REDRAWALL	RA	Refreshes the screen display in all viewports.
		Regen	REGEN	RE	Recalculates the drawing database, and then redraws the graphics.
		Regen All	REGENALL	REA	Recalculates the drawing database, and then redraws graphics in all viewports.
		---	REGENAUTO	__	Enables or disables automatic regenerations.
	View, Named Views	Named Views	VIEW	V	Displays the View Manager dialog box to add or modify named views or set them current.
		---	VIEWRES	--	Controls visual smoothness of curved objects.
	Standard, Zoom Realtime	Zoom, Realtime	ZOOM, Realtime	Z	Starts Realtime option of ZOOM command.

Icon	Toolbar	View Menu	Command Name, Option	Alias	Function
	Standard (Zoom flyout)	Zoom	ZOOM	Z	Displays full Zoom flyout toolbar.
	Standard, Zoom Previous	Zoom, Previous	Zoom, Previous	Z	Replaces current drawing view with previous view.

As you see from the table, there aren't individual aliases for each option of the ZOOM command. Without custom programming (unavailable in AutoCAD LT), the quickest keyboarding options are to type **Z**, press Enter, and then type the key letter for the option and press Enter again.

As you can see in Figure 3-1, there are many more commands on the View menu. These others are 3D viewing commands, and we discuss them in Book V.

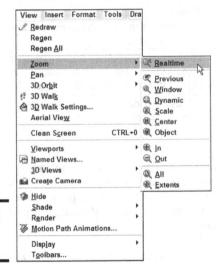

Figure 3-1:
A menu
to view.

A Zoom of One's Own

Zooming in closer and zooming out farther away should be simple enough, right? But this is AutoCAD, where little is as simple as it seems. There's a host of options for the ZOOM command (some simpler than others), and Table 3-2 sets them out for you.

Table 3-2		ZOOM Command Options
Icon	*Option*	*Description*
	Window	Pick two corners to define a rectangular view window. AutoCAD zooms in to the defined rectangular area.
	Dynamic	Combine both pans and zooms (like Realtime Pan & Zoom). Somewhat difficult to master, and probably made obsolete by the Realtime options.
	Scale	Specify zoom factor relative to current display, to entire drawing, or to paper space scale (usually 1:1).
	Center	Pick a point or enter coordinates for center of view, and then enter a magnification value.
	Object	Select an object; display zooms in so object fills screen.
	In	Zoom in closer on drawing by preset factor (default is 2x). Same as using ZOOM Scale and entering 2x as the scale factor.
	Out	Zoom farther out of drawing by preset factor (default is .5x). Same as using ZOOM Scale and entering 0.5x as the scale factor.
	All	Zooms out to predefined drawing limits. If drawing objects fall outside the limits, zooms to show those objects (that is, same as ZOOM Extents).
	Extents	Zooms out to display all drawing objects on non-frozen layers in current drawing space.

ZOOM Previous, another command option, has its own button on the Standard toolbar. Most ZOOM options are available from the Zoom flyout tool button on the Standard toolbar (see Figure 3-2). There's also a separate Zoom toolbar, but unless you've got acres and acres of screen real estate, it's probably more space-efficient to use the flyout.

In case you haven't encountered them before, flyout tool buttons are distinguished by tiny — and we do mean tiny — black arrows in their lower-right corner. Clicking any tool button that has one of those arrows displays a subset of tool buttons that run command options. Figure 3-2 shows the effect of holding down the Standard toolbar's Zoom button. To choose a command, run your mouse pointer down the tool buttons to the one you want, and then release the button.

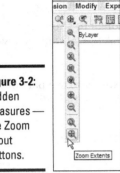

Figure 3-2:
Hidden
treasures —
the Zoom
flyout
buttons.

You can zoom in and out of your drawings by using one of three methods:

✦ **Wheel mouse.** The simplest method of all: Just scroll the mouse wheel forward or back to zoom in or out of your drawing. By default, scrolling the wheel away from you zooms in, and scrolling the wheel toward you zooms out.

✦ **Realtime zoom (and pan).** Start the command from a right-click menu or the Zoom Realtime or Pan Realtime button on the Standard toolbar. Press and drag to change the view visually on-screen.

✦ **Regular ZOOM command options.** Choose a specific command option from the View⇨Zoom submenu or the Zoom toolbar or flyout. The regular options do not zoom in real time — you have to complete the command before the view changes.

Wheeling through your drawing

Although there are lots of powerful options of the ZOOM command, both regular and realtime, sometimes simple is good. We honestly can't imagine anyone using AutoCAD without a wheel mouse. If you don't have one, drop what you're doing and go get one now!

Here are some of the reasons we like wheel mice:

✦ You can adjust the rate at which you zoom in and out as you scroll your mouse wheel with the ZOOMFACTOR system variable. The default value is 60, which means each detent you scroll through zooms you 60% closer in or farther out.

✦ Starting with AutoCAD 2007, you can reverse your wheel mouse's default scroll direction in the Options dialog box. On the 3D Modeling tab, check the box beside *Reverse mouse wheel zoom.* This works for 2D drafting as well as 3D modeling.

◆ Press down on the wheel and move the mouse to pan around the drawing.

◆ Double-click the scroll wheel to zoom out far enough to show everything in the drawing. (This is called a *ZOOM Extents* in AutoCAD and is covered later in this chapter.)

Before you start scrolling to zoom in, move the crosshairs to the part of the drawing you're most interested in seeing. As you scroll, that location will be the center of the zoomed-in view.

Realtime zooming

Realtime zooming and panning are two halves of the same command. (We cover PAN Realtime in the following section.)

The following steps explain how to move around a drawing using this command:

1. **Open a drawing that contains some objects that you might want to have a closer look at.**

   If you're really new at this and don't have any suitable drawings yet, you could open one of the sample drawings from the C:\Program Files\ AutoCAD 2007\Sample folder.

2. **Click Zoom Realtime on the Standard toolbar (it's the button with the magnifying glass and the plus/minus sign).**

   The crosshairs change to a magnifying glass cursor with plus/minus signs as shown in the middle of Figure 3-3.

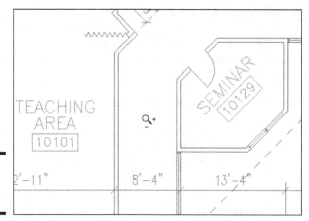

Figure 3-3:
Zooming in real time.

3. **Hold down the left mouse button and drag the magnifying glass cursor toward the top of the screen.**

   As you drag up-screen, you zoom closer into your drawing.

4. **Press and drag again, this time moving the cursor toward the bottom of the screen.**

   Your view of the drawing zooms back out.

   The command line reads:

   ```
   Press ESC or ENTER to exit, or right-click to display
         shortcut menu.
   ```

5. **Take the third choice: Right-click to display the shortcut (cursor) menu (see Figure 3-4).**

Figure 3-4:
Shortcut to
a new view.

6. **Choose one of the menu options or select Exit to end Realtime zooming and return to the command line.**

The shortcut menu (shown in Figure 3-4) presents the following options:

✦ **Exit.** Exit from the Realtime Pan & Zoom commands and return to the command prompt.

✦ **Pan.** Press the left mouse button and drag to move around the drawing without zooming in or out.

✦ **Zoom.** Press and drag to zoom into or out of the drawing.

✦ **3D Orbit.** As its name suggests, this one is for viewing a 3D model from different viewpoints. We talk about it more in Book V.

✦ **Zoom Window.** When you select Zoom Window from the Realtime shortcut menu shown in Figure 3-4, the cursor icon changes to an arrow and a box (see Figure 3-5). Press and drag to create a rectangular window; the display will zoom in to the area defined by the rectangle.

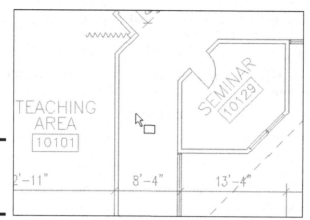

Figure 3-5:
Zoom me a
real-time
window.

♦ **Zoom Original.** If you change your mind about that Realtime Zoom Extents you just performed, Zoom Original will undo it for you, restoring the previous view.

♦ **Zoom Extents.** Zooms far enough out so you can see all of the objects in the drawing.

PAN and ZOOM can be run as *transparent* commands. A transparent command can execute in the middle of another command; for example, you might start drawing with the LINE command and realize the next point is off the screen. Without leaving the LINE command, you can click PAN or some of the ZOOM tool buttons and change your view. When you close the PAN or ZOOM command, the LINE command resumes where you left off. You can run PAN and ZOOM transparently from the command line by typing an apostrophe (') before the command name.

Pan in a Flash

The PAN command lets you change the view of your drawing without changing the magnification. PAN and ZOOM go hand in hand, but since PAN is the simpler, we talk about it first. There are four ways to pan around in your drawing — that is, to look at different parts of your drawing at the same magnification or elevation:

♦ **Realtime panning.** Pressing and dragging with the PAN Realtime command active lets you visually set your new viewing location.

♦ **Panning by displacement.** The old-style PAN command, where you pick a base point for your view change on-screen, and then pick a second point in the drawing that you want to see in the picked-point location. This one's as hard to use as it is to explain!

✦ **Scroll bars.** As in every Windows program; drag the slider bar, click either side of it, or click the arrows at the end of the scroll bars.

Realtime panning

There are a number of options (there are *always* a number of options, aren't there?) for starting real-time panning. The following steps explain them:

1. **Open a drawing that contains some objects that you might want to have a closer look at, and zoom in on them.**

Obviously, panning isn't going to achieve much if you're zoomed all the way out in a drawing!

2. **Click Pan Realtime on the Standard toolbar (it's the button with the disembodied hand in the blue sleeve and clean white cuff).**

The crosshairs change to the hand cursor, as shown in the middle of Figure 3-6.

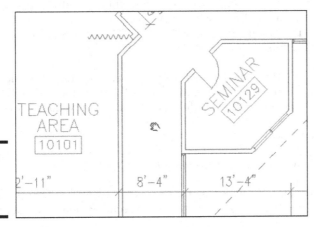

Figure 3-6:
Give us a
hand with
this pan.

3. **Press the left mouse button and drag the hand icon around the screen.**

The display pans in real time (meaning you can see it change as you move the mouse).

4. **Right-click to display the Realtime shortcut menu and choose Exit.**

AutoCAD returns to a blank command line. Note that you can also switch from real-time panning to real-time zooming with this menu.

Alternative ways to start real-time panning are

+ Type **P** and press Enter.

+ Press and drag with the mouse wheel (or, middle mouse button, if you have a three-button mouse).

+ With no command active and nothing selected, right-click anywhere in the drawing. Choose Pan from the default shortcut menu.

Be sure that no objects are selected and no command is active if you try this last method — otherwise the Zoom and Pan options will not appear on the menu.

Name That View

So if panning and zooming are that powerful and flexible, what more do you need? Why should you learn about named views, anyway?

Imagine you're on the phone to a subcontractor for your project, and you're discussing part of a drawing. You both have the same drawing open (you can tell that from the drawing title!) but you have to refer to a very specific area that you've spent a long time detailing. The conversation could go something like this:

"OK, zoom in to the room labeled *Seminar Area.* No, the one beside the office corridor. No, the other corridor, the one by the elevators. NO, NOT those elevators, the ones on the other side of the floor. OK, now zoom in on. . . ."

Or, it could go like this:

"OK, restore the view named *Seminar Room NE detail.*"

You can save a lot of frustration for yourself — as well as for others who need to use your drawings — if you set up some named views of important areas.

Creating views

The setup for saving named views has changed in recent versions of AutoCAD and AutoCAD LT. In AutoCAD 2007, the View dialog box has been promoted to a corner office and has a new title: View Manager (see Figure 3-7).

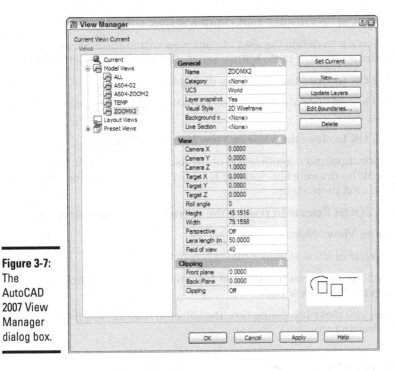

Book II
Chapter 3

Managing Views

Figure 3-7:
The
AutoCAD
2007 View
Manager
dialog box.

The following steps explain how to save, restore, and modify named views, beginning with steps that work in all recent versions of AutoCAD:

1. **Zoom into and pan around your drawing until you're looking at the area you want to save as a named view.**

You *can* define an area without displaying it exactly as you want to see it, but for now, do the zooming and panning.

2. **Choose View⇨Named views.**

In AutoCAD 2006 and earlier, the View dialog box appears. In AutoCAD 2007, the View Manager dialog box appears.

3. **Click New.**

In all versions, the New View dialog box appears on top of the View or View Manager dialog box.

4. **Type a name for the new view in the View Name list box.**

5. **Set the Current display radio button active.**

   If you want to define the area of your view within the current view, set the Define window radio button active. Ignore the other settings for now.

6. **Click OK to close the New View dialog box.**

   The View or View Manager dialog box shows the newly created view in its list box.

7. **Click OK to close the View or View Manager dialog box.**

   The location and magnification of the named view are now stored as part of the drawing file. You can restore the view at any time. Try it with these next three steps.

8. **Do a ZOOM Extents to restore the overall view of your drawing.**

9. **Choose View⇨Named views.**

   The View or View Manager dialog box opens.

10. **Select the view you just created from the list box and click Set Current. Then click OK.**

    When you close the dialog box, the selected named view is displayed in the drawing area.

Other view options

In AutoCAD 2005 and later, you can associate layer settings with a named view. For example, you may want to restore a view of part of a complex assembly, but only see the objects drawn on certain layers. The following steps explain how:

1. **Zoom in to the area you want to save as a named view.**

2. **Turn on (or thaw) the layers you want to see, and turn off (or freeze) the ones you don't.**

   Set the appropriate layer visibility states before you save the named view.

3. **Follow Steps 2 through 5 from the preceding section.**

   Open the View or View Manager dialog box, and then the New View dialog box. Give the view a name and make sure the Current display radio button is selected.

4. **Check the box beside Store Current Layer Settings with View (AutoCAD 2005 & 2006) or Save Layer Snapshot with View (AutoCAD 2007).**

   Checking this box means that when you restore this view, the current layer visibility states will also be restored.

Storing layer settings (2006 and earlier) or saving a layer snapshot (2007) are the default settings. Make sure you really want to save the layer settings before clicking OK, because your previous layer settings are not restored when you change views.

5. Click OK.

The New View dialog box closes and your newly created view shows in the View or View Manager list.

6. Click OK again.

View or View Manager closes and you return to the drawing.

You can easily change the boundaries of a view in the View Manager dialog box (or in the View dialog box in AutoCAD 2005 and 2006). Just select the view in the list and choose Edit Boundaries. AutoCAD shows you a grayed-out view of your drawing with the currently defined view highlighted in white. Then pick two corners to define a new view area.

AutoCAD 2007 replaces the two-tab version of the View dialog box with the Explorer-style View Manager (see Figure 3-7).

The View Manager lists *sheet views* as well as regular model views. Sheet views are named views associated with viewports in drawing layouts as part of AutoCAD's sheet set feature.

The third category of view, after model views and sheet views, is preset views. These are intended for 3D use and serve no purpose in 2D drafting. We'll have more to say about these preset views in Book V.

Book II
Chapter 3

Managing Views

Book III

Annotating Drawings

The 5th Wave   By Rich Tennant

©RICHTENNANT

"After Leroy sketched it out with CAD, Ronnie made the body from what he learned in Metal Shop, Sisy and Darlene's Home Ec. class helped them in fixing up the inside, and then all that anti-gravity stuff we picked up off the Web."

Contents at a Glance

Chapter 1: Text: When Pictures Just Won't Do

In This Chapter

✔ Types of text in AutoCAD

✔ Controlling text appearance

✔ Creating and using text styles

✔ Using single-line and multiline text

✔ Editing text

✔ Creating tables

You know the old saying about a picture being worth a thousand words? We've done some digging and discovered that with inflation and cost of living increases, a picture is now worth 3,712 words!

That's a roundabout way of saying that text is important, too. It's a lot simpler — and more precise — to specify a manufacturer and part number in numbers and letters than it is to try to draw the darned thing from every angle. And until you can teach your drawings to talk, adding text is a necessary part of drafting in AutoCAD.

In this chapter, we look at creating and editing text in AutoCAD drawings.

Text in AutoCAD

In AutoCAD, very little is as simple as it could be. Take drawing text, for instance. AutoCAD has not one but two different kinds. You use one if you want to enter single characters or short lines of text, and the other if you want to write a novel — or at least some general notes. The first type is called *single-line text,* and the second (wait for it . . .) is called *multiline text* (Autodesk also refers to the latter as *paragraph text.*)

Of course, there are other kinds of text in an AutoCAD drawing as well. These other kinds include

✦ **Leader notes:** Leaders are drawing notes that include a line with an arrow at one end that points to a drawing object. You create leaders with one of the Dimensioning commands.

✦ **Dimension text:** Dimension values appear as text and are formatted according to a text style, but they're not text objects — they're an integral part of dimension objects. (We cover text styles later in this chapter, and dimensions in the next chapter.)

✦ **Attributes:** Attributes are pieces of text attached to block insertions. What makes them different from regular text is that the text is variable and can be changed for each instance of the block insertion. We cover blocks and attributes in Book VI.

✦ **Tables:** Tables are another type of text-like object. Prior to AutoCAD 2005, you had to construct tables (for example, for bills of material, drawing lists, and so on) by drawing lines and then carefully filling in the spaces between them with regular drawing text. Table objects automate the process; the text part is defined with text styles, just like regular text.

✦ **Fields:** Fields are placeholders for textual data. You can place fields in tables or in multiline text objects. Fields contain changeable data such as filename, date last saved, drafter, and so forth.

We describe each of these different types of text or text-like objects in the sections that follow.

Getting familiar with text terminology

Before we go on, we need to define some terms:

✦ **Text:** *Text* usually refers to an AutoCAD object, either a single line of text (also called a text string) or a paragraph (called multiline text or mtext in AutoCAD). TEXT is also an alternate command name for DTEXT, the command used to enter single-line text.

✦ **Style:** *Style* refers to a named definition of the way your text appears when you place it on your drawing. Included in a style definition are the font, height, width factor, obliquing angle, and whether it will be drawn backwards, upside-down, or vertically. STYLE is also the name of the command used to create text styles. Text justification and rotation are not defined in a style; they are applied when you start the DTEXT or MTEXT command.

✦ **Justification:** *Justification* refers to the direction that text flows from the start point, and how subsequent lines of text align below the first line.

Left-aligned or left-justified text is the default in AutoCAD. We explain more about the many different justification options later in this chapter.

✦ **Font:** *Font* refers to the actual appearance of the letters, numbers, and symbols. AutoCAD supports two types of font:

- AutoCAD vector fonts
- Windows TrueType fonts

We go into more detail on both font types later in the chapter. For now, understand that you must use a font file to define a style, and you must have a style before you can create text objects.

If AutoCAD can't find the font files used to create text, the drawing won't load or display properly. A large number of add-on fonts are available for AutoCAD; however, you should use only the font files that come with AutoCAD or Windows, in case you ever need to send your drawings to other offices.

Will that be one line or two?

Every version of AutoCAD from the very first right up to (and hopefully, beyond) AutoCAD 2007 has provided single-line text. The idea is that you type a line of text and press Enter, and then press Enter again to end the command. You end up with a single object — the single line of text.

You can create multiple lines of text by simply typing another line after each press of the Enter key; you end the sequence by pressing Enter on a blank line.

But picture this scenario. You've carefully laid out your drawing sheet, and you've allowed a four-inch wide space along the right side of the sheet for your general notes. You add forty or fifty lines of general notes as single-line text, which means you have forty or fifty individual text objects.

Now your boss comes along and tells you you're going to have to squeeze those notes into a three-inch wide column so you can add some more details. Your mission — should you choose to accept it — is to edit each and every line, removing a word or two from the end of the first line and adding it to the second, and then removing two or three words from the second and adding them to the third . . . and on, and on, and on.

There ought to be a better way, and there is, although it didn't show up until the aptly numbered AutoCAD release 13. When you create multiline (or paragraph) text, you define a width for your text block by specifying a value or picking two points on screen. Multiline text wraps from one line to the next, just like your friendly word processor.

**Book III
Chapter 1**

**Text: When Pictures
Just Won't Do**

There are plenty of differences between single-line and multiline text:

✦ Single-line text has fewer formatting options, so it's simpler to create and edit.

✦ Multiline text has many, many formatting options, so it's much more complicated to create and edit.

✦ To place single-line text in a drawing, you simply pick a start point and type.

✦ To place multiline text, you specify two diagonal corners of a temporary bounding box; the lines of text are placed inside.

✦ Single-line text appears character-by-character as you type. To type a second line of text below the first, press Enter and continue typing. Press Enter on a blank line to exit the command.

✦ You enter multiline text in a special dialog box called the *in-place text editor.* AutoCAD automatically wraps lines of text based on the width of the bounding box you specify when you start the command.

✦ You create multiline text with the MTEXT command.

✦ You create single-line text with the DTEXT or TEXT commands.

Why are there two commands for creating single-line text? Remember that this is AutoCAD, where nothing is simple. By default, single-line text is created with the DTEXT command. "TEXT" is now an alias for the DTEXT command; typing either at the command line runs DTEXT. But the folks at Autodesk hate to throw anything away, so the old TEXT command is still there in the latest versions. To run it, put a hyphen in front: -TEXT. Go ahead and try it, and see why nobody uses it any more!

Single-line text is much more limited than multiline text in its formatting possibilities. You can define a few properties such as a single font or a preset height in a text style, but that's about it. You can go crazy in formatting multiline text, changing things like font, size, color, and numerous other properties. Later in this chapter, we explain how to add both types of text, and how to change the appearance of each.

So how do you choose which type to use? The usual advice is to use single-line text for things like letters or numbers inside grid bubbles or keynotes, and for short one-liners such as view titles and scales. Use multiline text for anything longer — certainly for anything longer than a couple of lines.

Justification

Justification (or alignment) refers to the look of a block of text on a drawing or page. If you're used to a word processor, you're probably pretty familiar with the standard text justification options. Most text is left justified, like in this book. You may prefer center-justified text for headings and titles. (Not us, we keep to the left!) Rarely, you even see right-justified text, which means the right margin of a block of text is neatly lined up, and the left margin is ragged. Many books (although very few drawings) use fully justified text, where both right and left margins line up tidily.

All of these word processor options have their counterpart in AutoCAD. But because AutoCAD is AutoCAD, it can't leave well enough alone. We have six justification options that you can apply to single-line text, and nine *different* options that you can use with multiline text. Figures 1-1 and 1-2 show you the choices.

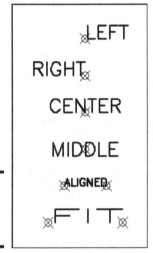

Figure 1-1: Justifying single-line text.

Justifying single-line text

The single-line justification options probably make more sense to most people because the line of text starts (or at least is based on) the insertion point you pick. Left- and right-justified are plain enough, but the other options need a bit of explanation:

✦ **Center:** The point you pick is the middle point of the text's baseline; the text flows equally to left and right from this point. Use this option for a title that you want centered under a drawing view.

✦ **Middle:** The text you enter is centered both horizontally and vertically about the point you pick. Use this option if you want to locate a letter or number in the center of a keynote or grid bubble.

✦ **Align:** You specify two points for this option, and the text you enter starts at the first point and ends at the second point. Aligned text maintains the height you enter, so characters are stretched or compressed to fill the space.

✦ **Fit:** Similar to Align in that you pick two points, but instead of maintaining height and changing proportions, fit text maintains the proportions of the font, but changes its height in order to fill the space.

If it's absolutely essential that you have fully justified text (that is, straight margins at both left and right ends), either Align or Fit is for you. Be aware, however, that they're pretty rare in AutoCAD drawings.

These six options are not the only justification choices for single-line text; it can also be justified to any of the additional nine options described in the next section, "Justifying multiline text." However, multiline text can't be justified using any of the six options described above.

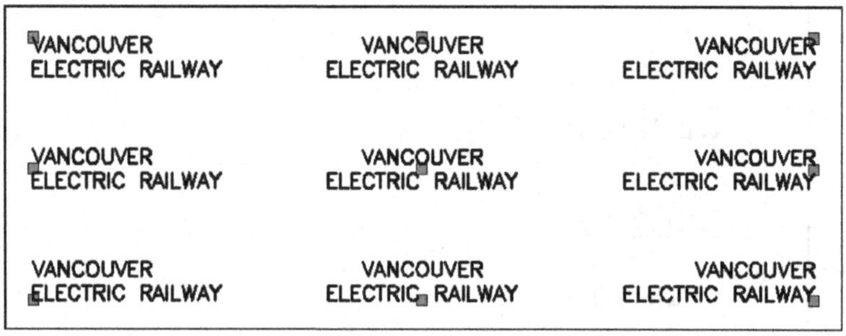

Figure 1-2:
Nine ways
to multiline.

Justifying multiline text

Multiline text is treated as a single object, and the insertion point is either a corner, or the midpoint of a side, or the absolute middle of the bounding box. Figure 1-2 shows the same block of text with the nine possible justification options. Oddly enough, given all the formatting possibilities with multiline text, it's not possible to fully justify a multiline text object.

Where should text go?

In Book I, we introduced the two spaces that exist in every AutoCAD drawing file. To recap:

✦ Model space is an infinitely large 3D environment where you create the "real stuff" that you're drawing. This is where you draw your house plans or highways full-size.

✦ Paper space, which is accessible in a layout, represents your drawing sheet, a 2D environment where you add the documentation that describes the "real stuff." This is where you place your border and title block, general notes, view titles, and symbols like section marks and north arrows.

These are just guidelines, of course. There are a kazillion drawings out there (we know because we've counted every single one of them) that are drawn entirely in model space, or that have dimensions and text in model space.

In our humble opinion, most text belongs in paper space. The single, arguable exception is leader notes because they often point directly to model space objects and have to move when the objects move.

Although many people like to place leader notes in model space, a potential for problems exists if you use external references (refer to Book VI for more on this advanced AutoCAD feature). If you reference an external drawing, you may want to see only the geometry, and not all the annotations. If you put your text (or your dimensions, or any other non-"real" stuff) in model space, you have to play around turning layers off and on before you get the picture you want. Life is a lot simpler if you keep these items in your layouts, in paper space.

Scaling text for model space

Another drawback to putting text in model space is the potentially messy business of scale factors. Say that you've drawn a floor plan, and you want to put a title under it, with the scale below that, as shown in Figure 1-3. Your office standard says that titles are 3/16" high, and the scale reference should be 3/32" high.

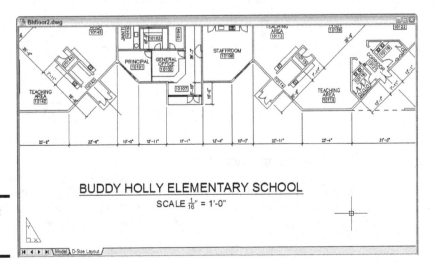

Figure 1-3:
A drawing
view title.

In order to make your floor plan fit on a drawing sheet, you're going to have to scale it — say, to 1/4"=1'-0". The scale factor here is 48 (refer to Book I, Chapter 5 for more on how to calculate scale factors). When you print your drawing, that 8" wall is going to measure a little over 1/8" wide on the page. So text that's 3/16" high is going to be a teeny speck. In order to make your text visible and in conformance with your office standard, you need to multiply 3/16" by the drawing scale factor. In this example, you'd multiply 3/16 by 48 for a result of 9. When entering the text for the view title, you need to make it 9" high. A similar calculation shows that the scale annotation needs to be 4-1/2" high.

If you do a lot of this sort of thing, you'll probably have a cheat sheet table (like Table 1-1, for example) with drawing scale factors applied to different printed text heights.

Table 1-1	Scale Factors for Model Space Text Height		
Drawing Scale	*Scale Factor*	*Large Text (3/16" / 5 mm)*	*Small Text (3/32" / 2.5 mm)*
1/16"=1'-0"	192	3'-0"	1'-6"
1/8"=1'-0"	96	1'-6"	9"
1/4"=1'-0"	48	9"	4-1/2"
1/2"=1'-0"	24	4-1/2"	2-1/4"
1"=1'-0"	12	2-1/4"	1-1/8"
3"=1'-0"	4	3/4"	3/8"
12"=1'-0"	1	3/16"	3/32"
1:100	100	500 mm	250 mm
1:50	50	250 mm	100 mm
1:20	20	100 mm	50 mm
1:10	10	50 mm	25 mm
1:5	5	25 mm	10 mm
1:2	2	10 mm	5 mm
1:1	1	5 mm	2.5 mm

Adding text to paper space

Did you say you wanted 3/16" text for your titles and 3/32" text for the scale annotations? If you put these on your layouts in paper space, the text heights will always be the same — 3/16" and 3/32" — regardless of the scale of any views in the layout. Still want to put that text in model space?

Fonts

A *font* is a character set that controls the look of the formatted text. AutoCAD uses fonts as part of a text style definition (we discuss text styles in the next section). You have literally thousands of fonts at your disposal. Some come with AutoCAD; some come as part of the Windows operating system; some come with different software programs that may also live on your computer. Remember, though, that you are drafting, not doing desktop publishing or authoring Web sites. (Or maybe you are doing desktop publishing or authoring Web sites, but, if so, you're using the wrong program!) In short, don't get carried away with ransom note- or medieval manuscript-style text. Your job is to present the text data on your drawing clearly.

Types used by AutoCAD

Modern versions of AutoCAD can use two different font types:

✦ **Vector (.SHX) fonts:** These are the fonts that come with AutoCAD and work with AutoCAD only. Vector fonts are made up of line segments (hence the name) and are more efficient than TrueType fonts.

✦ **TrueType fonts:** These are the fonts that come with Windows. They give you lots of fancy options but can slow down AutoCAD performance in common tasks like panning, zooming, and object selection.

Using fonts in drawings

You can go with the default font you get when you start entering text the first time you open AutoCAD, or you can configure the fanciest TrueType font on your system. We advocate a middle road, nearer the first option than the second. Our advice is to keep it simple and stick with AutoCAD's vector fonts — preferably the ones that come with the program.

There's a healthy aftermarket for .SHX fonts, but they nearly always come with a license that prevents you from distributing the font file to others. The same also applies to TrueType fonts that you purchase or obtain through installing other software programs. If your drawing is opened on a computer that doesn't have the fonts you've used, AutoCAD starts choosing alternates.

If someone sends you a drawing with text that uses a non-standard font, when you open the drawing, AutoCAD substitutes an alternate font and displays a message telling you this at the command prompt.

**Book III
Chapter 1**

Text: When Pictures
Just Won't Do

Two system variables control this font substitution process. FONTALT specifies a single font to use when AutoCAD can't find designated fonts. FONTMAP specifies the name of a mapping file that lists substitute specific local fonts for missing TrueType, Vector, and Postscript PFB fonts. (AutoCAD supported Postscript fonts for only one release, but there are probably hundreds of thousands of drawings out there that use them.) For more information on how to configure these two variables, see the online Help index.

Working with Text Styles

Before you can add text to a drawing, you have to have a text style — and luckily, every AutoCAD drawing contains at least one text style. The default templates include a basic text style named Standard. Text created with the Standard style uses a clunky looking font called txt.SHX. It's defined with a height of 0, which means you're prompted to specify a text height at the command line.

A *text style* is a collection of settings that's stored in the drawing file itself. Text style definitions include a designated font file, a height, and — depending on the chosen font — some options like width factor and obliquing angle.

Because text styles are created and saved inside drawing files, they're not necessarily available in all your drawing files. If you create your new text styles and save them in a template (.DWT) file, they become available in every new drawing you start from that template. If you've created a nifty text style and you want to use it in another existing drawing file, you can use DesignCenter to copy it from one file to the other.

Most people think the default font used by the Standard text style is pretty darned ugly. Seasoned users modify the Standard style or create new styles that use more pleasing fonts.

If you're sufficiently seasoned, feel free to modify the Standard style. If you're new to AutoCAD, we suggest you leave the Standard style alone, and instead create a new style of your own. That way, if you mess it up badly, you can always go back to the Standard style and start again.

The following steps explain the process.

1. Choose Format⇨Text Style to open the Text Style dialog box.

The Text Style dialog box displays the properties of the current text style (see Figure 1-4).

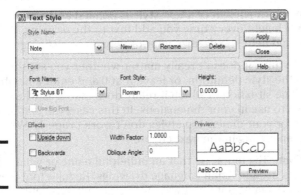

Figure 1-4:
Get stylin'.

2. **Click New and enter a style name (for example,** MyNewStandard) **in the New Text Style dialog box, and then click OK.**

   The New Text Style dialog box closes and you return to the Text Style dialog box. The new style starts off as a clone of whatever the current style is set to.

3. **In the Font area, click the Font Name drop-down list to display a list of all available fonts.**

   The list contains all TrueType fonts installed in your Windows Fonts folder, and all AutoCAD vector fonts.

4. **Select a font (that is, romans.SHX) from the list.**

   AutoCAD vector fonts are indicated by a teeny pair of dividers and display the file extension (.SHX). Windows TrueType fonts show a double-T icon and no file extension.

   The Roman Simplex font (romans.SHX) is probably the most popular font in AutoCAD because it combines efficiency with a much more pleasing appearance than the default txt.SHX font.

5. **Click Apply and then Close to save the new text style definition and set it current.**

   The Text Style dialog box closes. The new text style is now the current style and will be used for all text added to the drawing until it's changed to a different style.

The remaining options in the Text Style dialog box modify the style definition in the following ways:

✦ **Font Style:** If a TrueType font has style options (usually Bold, Italic, and Bold Italic), they appear in this list. Vector fonts don't have options, so the list is grayed out.

**Book III
Chapter 1**

**Text: When Pictures
Just Won't Do**

✦ **Height:** When the height of a text style is defined as 0, you are prompted to specify a height every time you add text to the drawing. You can save this step (and help standardize your drawings) by defining a height.

Most of the time, it doesn't really matter whether you set the text height as part of the style definition, or leave it at 0 and enter a height every time. But one situation in which it really does matter is when you define a text style to use in your dimensions. In this case, the text height *must* be set to 0 or your dimension styles don't work properly. We explain all about dimensioning in the next chapter.

✦ **Use Big Font:** "Big fonts" (is that an unhelpful name or what?) are special vector fonts used in Asian language drawings. Regular font files contain upper- and (usually, but not always) lowercase letters, numbers, and most of the symbols you see on your keyboard. Asian languages use many more characters than that, and big font files contain the definitions. For more information on big fonts, look up Big Font file in the online help system index.

✦ **Upside down** and **Backwards:** (What, no inside out?) These two text effects are self-explanatory. You might use Backwards if you were going to print on the back side of one-sided drafting film. We've bent over backwards to figure out when you might want upside down text, but we haven't come up with a reason yet.

✦ **Vertical:** The characters are horizontal, but the text string is vertical, like a movie marquee. Unless you're designing movie theaters, you're unlikely to use this option. It's not available with TrueType fonts, nor with many vector fonts either.

✦ **Width Factor:** You can modify the width of text characters by modifying this factor. Values of less than 1 compress the text, and values greater than 1 expand it.

If you set the width factor of the text style for dimensions to somewhere between 0.75 and 0.85, you'll be able to make dimension text fit between extension lines that might otherwise be forced outside them. For more on dimensioning, see the next chapter.

✦ **Oblique angle:** This is for do-it-yourself italics! You specify an angle to apply a slope to the characters. Positive angles slope the characters to the right, and negative angles slope characters to the left. If you do any isometric drafting, you'll want to use this effect.

✦ **Preview:** The Preview window shows you a sample of your text style that changes as you fiddle with the properties. You can highlight the sample text and replace it with a short text string of your own choosing.

You don't need to open the Text Style dialog box if you just want to change text styles. By default, AutoCAD displays the Styles toolbar, which contains drop-down listings of text styles, dimension styles, and table styles. Just open the list and select the style to make a different one current. The tool buttons adjacent to the drop-down lists open the respective style definition dialog boxes.

Creating Single Line Text

The following steps show you how to add multiple lines of single-line text to a drawing.

1. Choose Draw⇨Text⇨Single Line Text.

AutoCAD prompts as follows:

```
Command: _dtext
Current text style:  "Standard"  Text height:  0.2000
Specify start point of text or [Justify/Style]:
```

At this point, you can change the justification or style of your text input. To stay with the default justification (aligned left) and style (Standard), skip to Step 5.

2. To change the text justification, type J and press Enter.

AutoCAD displays this prompt:

```
Enter an option [Align/Fit/Center/Middle/
    Right/TL/TC/TR/ML/MC/MR/BL/BC/BR]:
```

To change justification from the default (left justified), enter the upper-cased letter of the option; for example, type **M** and press Enter to set your text input to middle-justified in the drawing. You have a lot of options here — we discuss text justification later in the chapter.

AutoCAD does not retain changes to text justification. If you want to place a number of middle-justified text objects, you need to specify the Middle option for each one.

3. To change the text style, type S and press Enter.

AutoCAD displays this prompt:

```
Enter style name or [?] <Standard>:
```

The current text style name is shown inside angle brackets. Just press Enter to keep using the current style. If you want to switch to a different style and you know its name, type it now and press Enter. The new text style must already be defined in the current drawing. (We cover text styles later in this chapter.)

4. For a list of text styles defined in the current drawing, type ? and press Enter.

AutoCAD displays this prompt:

```
Enter text style(s) to list <*>:
```

The default option is the asterisk wildcard. Press Enter and AutoCAD lists all text styles defined in the current drawing together with their style properties.

```
Text styles:
Style name: "Notes"        Font typeface: ArchStencil
   Height: 0.0000  Width factor: 1.0000  Obliquing
   angle: 0
   Generation: Normal
Style name: "Standard"     Font files: txt
   Height: 0.0000  Width factor: 1.0000  Obliquing
   angle: 0
   Generation: Normal
```

AutoCAD ends this command prompt sequence by redisplaying the current text style name and resuming the regular DTEXT command prompts:

```
Current text style: "Standard"
Specify height <0.2000>:
```

5. To specify the text height, either press Enter to accept the default height, or type a new value for the text height, and then press Enter.

You see the Specify height prompt only if your current text style is defined with a height of 0 (the default Standard text style is so defined). You can accept the default or enter a new text height here.

After you've entered the desired text height, AutoCAD displays this prompt:

```
Specify rotation angle of text <0>:
```

6. To specify the rotation angle, press Enter to accept the default value, or enter a new rotation angle.

Rotation angle refers to the angle of the whole text string, not to the slant of the individual characters, which is called the *obliquing* angle (see Figure 1-5). For horizontal text, leave the rotation angle at 0 degrees. Rotation angle is set when you're placing single-line or multiline text; obliquing angle is part of the text style definition.

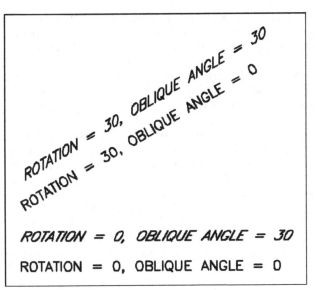

Figure 1-5:
Rotation
and
obliqueness.

After a whole lot of prompting, you're finally ready to start adding text to the drawing! The crosshairs change to a text box.

7. Type your text.

When you want to break a line and continue on the next line, press Enter and continue typing. When you're finished adding single line text, press Enter on a blank line to return to the command line.

Working with Multiline Text

As if single-line text wasn't bad enough, multiline text introduces even more levels of complexity! Many longtime users were slow to adopt multiline text because of the complexities, and really, you can get most annotation jobs done with single-line text. So why bother?

A few tasks that you need to do every so often are extremely difficult to achieve with single-line text. We've already talked about word-wrap in multi-line text, which lets you shift the space required by a block of notes by simply grabbing the grips of the mtext object and dragging them to a new location.

Nicely lined-up numbered or bulleted lists are pretty hard to create using single-line text because proportionally spaced fonts (and nearly all AutoCAD fonts are proportionally spaced) make lining things up virtually impossible.

Finally, a font's full character set (that is, non alphanumeric symbols) is readily accessible in multiline text. Single-line text offers just a very few special characters that have to be entered with special codes.

Hopefully the advantages of multiline text encourage you to hang in there with it. The final bit of advice is this: If you only learn one kind of text in AutoCAD, make it multiline text!

You create both single-line and multiline text in an *in-place text editor*. In-place means the text you create in the editor is going to appear in the drawing in exactly that place at exactly that size when you finish creating the text and close the editor. For single-line text, the in-place editor is simply a Windows-style text box, but for multiline text, it's much more elaborate, consisting of the two components shown in Figure 1-6:

✦ **Text formatting toolbar:** The toolbar contains a multitude of drop-down lists and tool buttons that would do a word processor proud. Set justification, color, or style; add symbols or fields; or fine-tune character or line spacing.

✦ **Bounding box with ruler:** The text you type appears within the bounding box. You can set margin and tab stops in the ruler by dragging the pointers, just like in a word processor. If you don't see a ruler atop the bounding box, click the Ruler button in the top row of the Text Formatting toolbar.

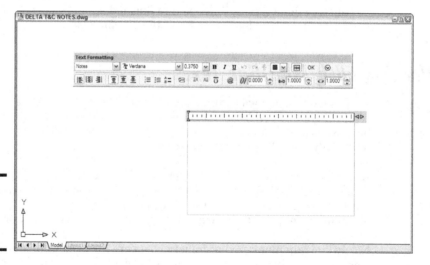

Figure 1-6:
The multiline text editor.

Creating Multiline Text

The following steps show you how to add a paragraph multiline text to a drawing:

1. **Choose Draw⇨Text⇨Multiline Text.**

The standard crosshairs change to a plain crosshairs and ghosted text in the current style and height. AutoCAD displays the current text style name and height at the command line and prompts as follows:

```
Command: _mtext Current text style:   "MyNewStandard"
     Text height:   2.6654
Specify first corner:
```

2. Pick the first corner of the bounding box.

The default multiline text justification is Top Left, so the first point you pick will be the upper-left corner of the text object. AutoCAD displays this prompt:

```
Specify opposite corner or [Height/Justify/Line
     spacing/Rotation/Style/Width]:
```

3. Enter a command option or pick the second corner.

Enter the uppercased letter of the option to change text height, justification, line spacing, rotation, style, or the overall width of the text box. To retain all the default settings, pick the diagonally opposite corner of the text box. The command prompt disappears, and the in-place text editor displays the Text Formatting toolbar and bounding box.

The bounding box sets only the width of the multiline text object. It doesn't matter how tall you make the box — it will expand as necessary to include all the text you enter.

4. Type your text.

The text you type flows across the bounding box. When it reaches the opposite side, it wraps automatically to the next line, just like your favorite word processor.

Formatting options

The two rows of buttons and drop-down lists in the Text Formatting toolbar (refer to Figure 1-6) enable you to perform many of the functions of a fully-featured word processor. You can change the style, font, height, and any number of other properties of your multiline text object. See the online Help system for a full description of each formatting option — on the Contents tab, choose Command Reference⇨MTEXT⇨In-Place Text Editor.

Book III
Chapter 1

Text: When Pictures
Just Won't Do

A multiline text object can be created using only one text style. If you type some text, change the style and type some more, the entire multiline text object changes to the new style. You can get the effect of different styles by highlighting some text and changing the font, height, color, and so on.

Numbered and bulleted lists

Another advantage of multiline text is that it supports bulleted and numbered lists. This feature is especially useful for creating general drawing notes, as shown in Figure 1-7. AutoCAD automates the process of creating numbered lists almost completely. Here's how:

1. **Follow Steps 1 through 3 in the previous section, "Creating Multiline Text."**

2. **Type a title; for example,** DESIGN CRITERIA.

   If you'd like to have your title underlined, click Underline on the Text Formatting toolbar before you type the title, and then click Underline again to turn it off.

3. **Press Enter to go to the next line and Enter again.**

   Leave a little more space between the title and the body of the text.

4. **Right-click inside the text editing window and choose Bullets and Lists⇨Numbered⇨Allow Auto-List⇨Use Tab Delimiter Only⇨ Allow Bullets and Lists.**

   The number 1 followed by a period appears on the current line, and the cursor jumps to the tab stop visible in the ruler at the top of the text editor's bounding box.

   Numbered places numerals followed by periods in front of items in a list. *Lettered* places uppercase or lowercase letters followed by periods in front of list items. (*Bulleted* places bullet characters in front of list items.) *Auto-list* enables automatic numbering — each time you press Enter to move to a new line, its number increments. *Use Tab Delimiter Only* means you must press the Tab key to move to the tab stop.

5. **Type the text corresponding to the current number or bullet.**

   As AutoCAD wraps the text, the second and subsequent lines align with the tab stop — that is, the text is automatically indented.

6. **Press Enter at the end of the paragraph to move to the next line.**

   Just like creating numbered lists in your favorite word processor, AutoCAD automatically inserts the next number at the beginning of the new paragraph, with everything perfectly aligned, as shown in Figure 1-7.

7. **Type the text corresponding to the next number or bullet, and then press Enter at the end of the paragraph to move to the next line.**

8. **Repeat Steps 5 through 7 for each subsequent numbered or bulleted item.**

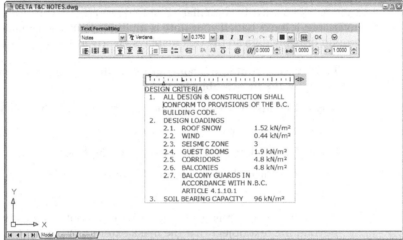

Figure 1-7:
Tabs,
indents, and
automatic
numbering
set to create
numbered
lists.

Fields, masks, and other multiline text delights

We haven't exhausted the features of the multiline text editor yet, and two especially useful ones are fields and background masks. The multiline text editor also offers a panoply of little functions and utilities that come in handy from time to time.

The convention in drafting is that text in a drawing is uppercased at all times. One way to avoid having to keep the Shift key pressed down is to use the Caps Lock key. But when you finish your texting and want to log in to your network, if you forget to turn off Caps Lock, you get an error message. The multiline text editor has a great solution for you. Right-click inside the editor and choose AutoCAPS. Everything you type in the text editor is uppercased, without benefit of Caps Lock.

Fields

Fields are placeholders for changeable data that updates automatically — for example, the author of a drawing and when it was created, last saved, or plotted. This data comes from drawing properties, or some system variables, or a sheet set (neither fields nor sheet sets are available in AutoCAD LT). To display the Field dialog box (see Figure 1-8), right-click inside the multiline text editor and choose Insert Field. For more information on inserting and updating fields, refer to the online Help system.

Background masks

Sometimes you just have to place a note on top of drawing objects, and invariably, it looks bad. If your note is multiline text, you can mask the background drawing data so the text displays clearly as follows:

1. **In a drawing containing some graphic objects, add some multiline text on top of the drawn objects.**

2. **Right-click inside the text editor and choose Background Mask.**

   The Background Mask dialog box appears.

3. **Check Use Background Mask to enable the feature.**

   The remaining dialog box options become accessible.

4. **Set a Border Offset factor.**

   This value, which must be between 1 and 5, controls the distance beyond the text object that the mask extends. When set to 1, the mask is tight to the text object.

5. **In the Fill Color area, either check Use Drawing Background Color or click the drop-down list to select a color for the mask.**

   If you don't want bright red rectangles all over your drawing, make sure you check the Use Drawing Background color box.

Figure 1-8:
Masking the
background
of your text.

Editing Text

After you've created either single-line or multiline text, editing it is a pretty straightforward exercise. As you might expect, there are two different editors for the two different types of text. So how do you know which editor to use? Easy — AutoCAD chooses for you if you double-click the text.

Editing single-line text

We've already pointed out all the formatting options available in multiline text, and if those are what you need, it's multiline text for you. Your editing options are fewer with single-line text, but for simple text, they should be more than ample.

Both types of text use an in-place text editor, where the text appears inside an edit box at the size and location it will appear in the drawing. Simply double-click a string of single-line text to display it in the in-place editor. All you can change here is the value of the text itself. If you need to change other properties such as style, justification, or height, select the text and make changes in the Properties palette.

If you're an old hand at AutoCAD and you absolutely hate the new single-line text editor, you can restore the pre-AutoCAD 2006 Edit Text dialog box by setting the system variable DTEXTED to 1.

Editing multiline text

Double-clicking a multiline text object also opens its in-place editor, but as you've already seen, it's an editor with a lot more bells and whistles. We've covered most of the options in the earlier sections on creating multiline text. To change all or parts of the text, select as you would in a word processor and apply your changes. Then click OK in the Text Formatting toolbar, or simply click outside the in-place editor.

Single-line text isn't allowed to have anything that paragraph text doesn't also have, so there is also an MTEXTED system variable that lets you revert to the previous editor. To do so, type **MTEXTED** and press Enter; then type **OldEditor** and press Enter. The old editor still has the same toolbar and ruler, but the bounding box does not display the selected text at its actual size or location.

Fiddling with text can be a tedious task, and lots of little-known commands and functions let you do your tweaking more efficiently. Two such commands let you adjust text height and justification in different ways:

+ **SCALETEXT:** Say you have a whole bunch of annotations in your drawing, and you want to reduce the size of all of them. The SCALE command would require a lot of selecting and moving, but SCALETEXT scales each text object about its own insertion point, so it stays where it ought to.

+ **JUSTIFYTEXT:** If you change the justification of text in the Properties palette or the multiline text editor, the insertion point stays put and the text moves. JUSTIFYTEXT lets you change the justification by keeping the position of the text where it is and moving the insertion point.

Turning the Tables

Table objects were introduced in AutoCAD 2005. Prior to that, if you needed to add a table — say a bill of materials, or a door schedule, or a drawing list, or any kind of data that can usefully be presented in rows and columns — you were in for several hours' work, drawing lines, adding text, moving lines, and lining everything up at the end. AutoCAD's tables can start at the top and flow downwards, as they would in most of the examples mentioned. They can also be anchored at the bottom of a sheet and flow upwards, which is the typical fashion for things like revision blocks. Tables can contain regular text, attributes, or fields.

Setting the table with styles

Tables, like text and dimensions, are defined according to styles. Every drawing has at least one table style waiting to be called on; the default templates contain a table style called (what else?) Standard. The following steps explain how to create a table style:

1. **Choose Format⇨Table Style.**

The Table Style dialog box appears, showing on the left a list of all table styles defined in the current drawing, and on the right a preview of the current style settings. You can select existing table styles to set current, modify, or delete; however, you can't delete the Standard style.

2. **Click New to create a new table style.**

The Create New Table Style dialog box appears.

3. **Enter a name for the new style; for example,** Door Schedule.

If you have more than one style defined, you can use the drop-down list to select an existing table style as the prototype for the new style.

4. **Click Continue.**

The New Table Style: Door Schedule dialog box opens, again with a preview of the current settings at the right (see Figure 1-9).

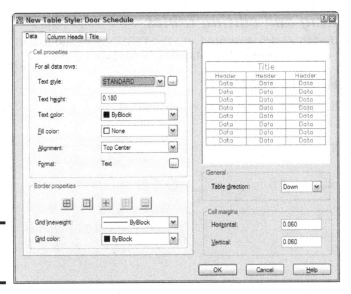

Book III
Chapter 1

Text: When Pictures
Just Won't Do

Figure 1-9:
Setting the
table.

A table style has up to three parts: the data, the column heads, and the title. Each of the three has a tabbed panel at the left side of the dialog box. The panels are identical, except there are check boxes in the latter two to turn off their display. In other words, your table can contain the data only; the data and column heads; the data and a table title; or the data, column heads, and a title.

5. **In the Data tab, configure the text options and fill color. To change the data format, click the button with the ellipses alongside the Format entry.**

   The Preview updates as you change settings in the left panel.

6. **Repeat Step 5 for the Column Headings and Title tabs, or clear the check boxes to turn off display of headings and title.**

7. **In the General area, specify whether the table direction should be Down (the default) or Up.**

8. **Modify the values in the Cell margins boxes to increase or decrease the space between the table text and the lines.**

   You don't specify row heights or column widths in the table style; specify these values when you create a table object.

9. **Click OK to close the New Table Style dialog box.**

   AutoCAD returns to the Table Style dialog box.

10. **Click Set Current, and then click Close.**

Creating and editing tables

After the table style is created, use the TABLE command to add a table
object to your drawing. The following steps show how:

***1.* Choose Draw⇨Table.**

The Insert Table dialog box appears (see Figure 1-10).

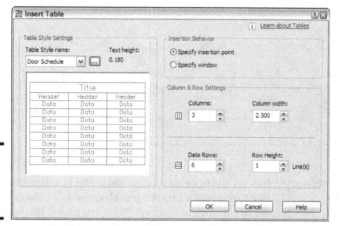

Figure 1-10:
Rows and
columns
for a table.

***2.* Select a table style from the Table Style Name drop-down list or click
Table Style dialog to create a new table style.**

The Table Style Settings area displays the current text height.

***3.* In the Insertion Behavior area, choose Specify Insertion Point or
Specify Window.**

Specify Insertion Point is the preferable option, as it maintains the
height and width settings you set in the table and text styles. Choosing
Specify Window squeezes or stretches the table into the rectangular
area you define. This option also disables the Data Rows value, which
generates as many rows as fit in the window you pick; however, you can
check the radio button to enable it again.

***4.* Specify the number of columns and data rows.**

"Data rows" excludes the rows for the title and column headings.

***5.* Adjust the column width and row height as required.**

One or the other pair of these options is grayed out if you choose
Specify Window in Step 3.

6. Click OK.

The empty table is placed in the drawing. The Text Formatting toolbar appears, and the first column cell is highlighted, ready for text input.

7. Enter the table title, column headings, and data.

It's now a matter of simply filling in the spaces. Now imagine creating a table like that with the TEXT and LINE commands!

If you just want to create the table frame and come back to input the text later, just click outside the highlighted cell.

To add table data, or to edit what's already there, double-click inside the table cell.

Combine tables and fields to automatically populate a drawing title block or revision block. Field data updates automatically when the data source changes.

Table cells can also contain blocks, so you could create a drawing legend with graphic symbols in one column and a description of what they stand for in another column.

Chapter 2: Dimensioning

In This Chapter

✔ Understanding what a dimension is made of

✔ Types of dimensions

✔ Using and creating dimension styles

✔ Creating dimensions

✔ Editing dimensions

✔ Leaders

✔ Geometric tolerances

Dimensions are a form of annotation that provides information about how a product should be created or assembled. Typically, dimensions provide information on how long a part is, the diameter of a hole, or a call-out in the form of a leader. In this chapter, you find out how to create and work with dimensions, leaders, and geometric tolerances.

AutoCAD and AutoCAD LT offer a number of dimension-related commands to help convey your design ideas to the people who are doing the construction (in the case of a building) or manufacturing (in the case of a machine part). Just as text styles manage the appearance of text in a drawing, dimension styles do the same thing for dimensions. Dimension styles allow you to define visually how dimensions appear in a drawing, but are much more complex than text styles.

Understanding What a Dimension Is Made Of

Dimensions are one of the most complex objects in AutoCAD and AutoCAD LT because of the many options that are available to control how they appear in a drawing. Dimensions are made up of several sub-objects or components that define what the dimension looks like. Some of the sub-objects that define a dimension are extension lines, dimension lines, arrowheads, dimension text, and origin points.

Before you begin creating dimensions, you should understand some of the common terminology for the different parts of a dimension (see Figure 2-1). Although each of the different dimension types has its own purpose, they do share some things in common.

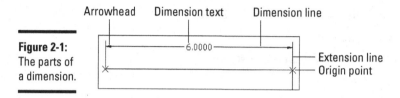

Figure 2-1:
The parts of
a dimension.

Here are the five main parts of a dimension:

✦ **Origin points:** Origin points are used to define the measurement value for the dimension text and are small non-printing points that are attached to the dimension. Origin points are typically placed on an object, which allows you to move or reposition a dimension that might need to be updated.

✦ **Extension lines:** Extension lines extend up and away from the object that is being dimensioned to the dimension line and arrowheads. Extension lines typically have a gap between them and the origin points of the dimension object and extend past the dimension line. A gap helps show that the dimension is not part of the actual object.

✦ **Arrowheads:** Arrowheads appear at the end of a dimension line and are used to indicate where a dimension starts and ends. Arrowheads can be displayed as open or closed arrows, architectural ticks, dots, or user-defined arrows, among other arrowhead styles.

✦ **Dimension line:** Dimension lines are displayed typically between the extension lines and go outward from the center of the dimension object towards the extension line. Based on where the dimension text is placed, the dimension line may appear broken or might appear on the outside of the extension lines.

✦ **Dimension text:** Dimension text provides the actual value of measurement that the dimension was created with and can be formatted in a variety of different ways. Some of the formatting options are the units the measurement is expressed in, the type of decimal separator that should be used, and how the value should be rounded.

Each of the parts of a dimension can be formatted globally using dimension styles, or individually using what are known as *dimension overrides*. We talk more about dimension styles and dimension overrides later in this chapter.

Types of Dimensions

Dimensions are a special type of block that AutoCAD treats differently from the blocks that you can create and insert into drawings; we cover blocks later in Chapter 1 of Book VI. Because dimensions are a special type of object, you interact with them differently. Dimensions can be created so that if the object that was dimensioned is changed, the dimension is updated automatically. Dimensions can also be created so that they are exploded after they have been created (which is not recommended because you won't be able to quickly update the dimension when the geometry in the drawing changes). They can also be created so that if the original object that is dimensioned is modified, the dimension doesn't update. No matter what type of dimension is created, they all look the same, but they are edited in much different ways.

Associative dimensions

Associative dimensions are created as a single object — so when you select any part of the dimension, the entire dimension is selected. An associative dimension is linked to the original object that was dimensioned, so when the original object is modified, the dimension is updated accordingly. Modifying the original dimensioned object by moving, rotating, stretching, or scaling it causes the dimension to update automatically. Fully associated dimensions were first introduced in AutoCAD 2002; prior to AutoCAD 2002, associated dimensions meant that the dimension was all one object and had no association with the dimensioned object.

Non-associative dimensions

Non-associative dimensions are created as a single object, just like associative dimensions are. Unlike associative dimensions however, non-associative dimensions are not linked to the original dimensioned object and therefore are not updated when the original dimensioned object is modified. If you select the dimension when modifying the original dimensioned object, it is still updated based on the type of modify command that is being used on both the object and dimension. Prior to AutoCAD 2002, non-associated dimensions were referred to as associative dimensions because they were a single object instead of individual objects.

Exploded dimensions

Exploded dimensions are created as individual 2D objects and are very hard to update because the original objects have to be deleted each time a change is made. We recommend that you don't create exploded dimensions because it can lead to inaccuracies to the dimensions if the text is not

Book III
Chapter 2

Dimensioning

updated. If you really need to create an exploded dimension, it is best to create associative dimensions and then use the EXPLODE command on a dimension.

Specifying the Type of Dimension to Create

To specify whether new dimensions are created as associative or non-associative dimensions, you can check or uncheck the Make New Dimensions Associative check box under the Associative Dimensioning section on the User Preferences tab (see Figure 2-2).

Figure 2-2:
Specifying whether new dimensions should be created as associative.

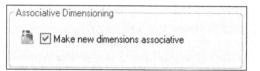

Follow these steps to determine whether new dimensions should be created as associative or non-associative.

1. **From the Tools menu, choose Options.**

   The Options dialog box is displayed.

2. **In the Options dialog box, click the User Preferences tab.**

3. **On the User Preferences tab under the Associative Dimensioning section, check or uncheck the Make New Dimensions Associative check box.**

   If the option Make New Dimensions Associative is checked, all new dimensions are created as associative.

   The setting to create new dimensions associative is saved in the drawing. When you get a drawing from a vendor or client, be sure that the setting is set to create new dimensions as associative.

4. **Click OK.**

   The changes are saved and the Options dialog box is closed.

Using and Creating Dimension Styles

Dimensions contain a large number of display options. Both AutoCAD and AutoCAD LT use dimension styles to contain groups of settings that control the appearance of dimensions. Dimension styles tell AutoCAD or AutoCAD LT how the dimension lines, extensions lines, dimension text, and arrowheads should be displayed for any dimension that is created in a drawing. Dimensions that reference a dimension style are updated when a change is made to the style, unless an override has been applied at the dimension object level.

Working with the Dimension Style Manager

Dimension styles are stored in a drawing file and are referenced by the dimensions that are created in the drawing. Each dimension that is created can reference a different dimension style. Dimension styles are created, modified, and managed through the Dimensions Style Manager dialog box (see Figure 2-3), which is displayed with the DDIM command.

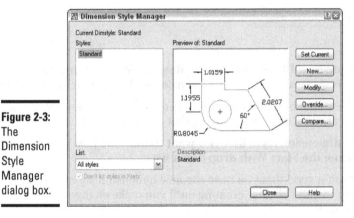

Figure 2-3:
The Dimension Style Manager dialog box.

**Book III
Chapter 2**

Dimensioning

To start the DDIM command and display the Dimensions Style Manager dialog box, follow one of the methods outlined below:

✦ **Format or Dimension menu:** Choose Format or Dimension⇨ Dimension Style.

✦ **Styles or Dimension toolbar:** Click the Dimension Style button on the Styles or Dimension toolbar.

✦ **Keyboard input:** Type **DDIM** and press Enter.

Creating a dimension style

Dimension styles can only be created from an existing style that already exists in the drawing; by default, each drawing contains either a dimensions style called Standard (imperial units) or ISO-25 (metric units). The Dimension Style Manager is used to create the new dimension style and then allows you to make any necessary property changes to the dimension style that was just created. The following procedure creates a new dimension style:

1. **Use one of the previously mentioned methods to open the Dimension Style Manager dialog box.**

2. **In the Dimension Style Manager dialog box, click New.**

The Create New Dimension Style dialog box (see Figure 2-4) is displayed.

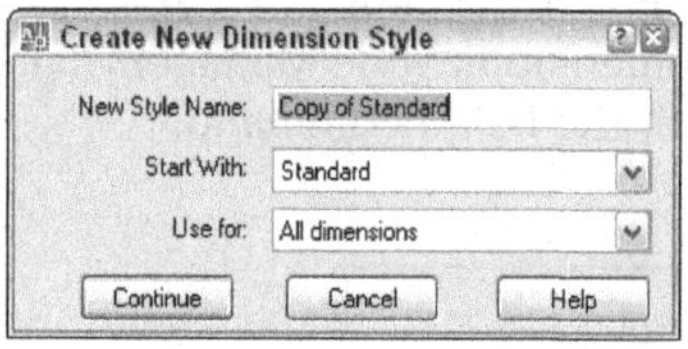

Figure 2-4:
Creating
a new
dimension
style.

3. **In the Create New Dimension Style dialog box, enter a name in the New Style Name text box for the dimension style that you are creating.**

The name entered is used to set the dimension style current when you want to create new dimensions using that dimension style.

4. **Select the dimension style that you want to base the new dimension style on from the Start With drop-down list.**

The dimension style that you base the new dimension style on will be identical to the one you are creating until you make changes to the new dimension style.

5. **Select All Dimensions from the Use For drop-down list.**

The Use For drop-down list allows you to create substyles for a dimension style. Substyles allow you to define specific characteristics for certain types of dimensions that can be created using a single dimension style. Substyles are used when the parent dimension style is used.

6. **Click Continue.**

The New Dimension Style dialog box is displayed and allows you to change the settings of the new dimension style.

7. **In the New Dimension Style dialog box, adjust the properties of the dimension style or the substyle as necessary.**

8. Click OK.

The New Dimension Style dialog box closes and the dimension style is saved in the drawing.

9. In the Dimension Style Manager dialog box, click Close.

The Dimension Style Manager dialog box closes.

The New Dimension Style dialog box

The New Dimension Style dialog box allows you to define how dimensions in a drawing look when they are created. The New Dimension Style dialog box is divided up into seven tabs, which help to organize the properties of a dimension style. As you change the properties for the dimension style, the preview of the dimension style in the upper-right corner of the dialog box is updated.

The Lines tab

The Lines tab (see Figure 2-5) allows you to define the display of dimension and extension lines. On the Lines tab, you can specify the color, linetype, lineweight, which extension and dimension lines are suppressed, and some spacing/offset values that help to define what a dimension should look like when assigned the dimension style.

**Book III
Chapter 2**

Dimensioning

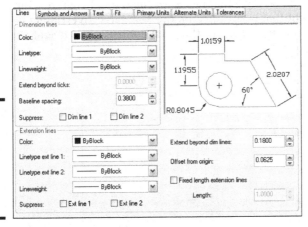

Figure 2-5:
The Lines tab of the New Dimension Style dialog box.

The Symbols and Arrows tab

The Symbols and Arrows tab (see Figure 2-6) allows you to define the characteristics of the terminators and symbols for dimensions. On the Symbols and Arrows tab, you can specify the type of arrowheads that are used, how center marks are drawn, the symbol that should be used for arc length dimensions, and the jog angle for jogged radial dimensions.

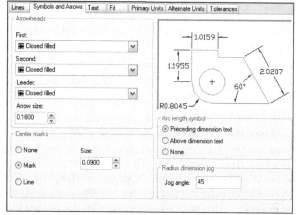

Figure 2-6:
The
Symbols
and Arrows
tab of
the New
Dimension
Style
dialog box.

The Text tab

The Text tab (see Figure 2-7) allows you to define how dimension text is placed along the dimension line and how it appears. On the Text tab, you can specify the color, text style, background fill color, height, and some other properties that affect how text is created, placed, and aligned with the dimension line.

If you assign a text style that has a specified text height to a dimension style, the text height that is specified on the Text tab is overridden by the value specified in the text style. For the most control, use a height of 0 (zero) when defining a text style.

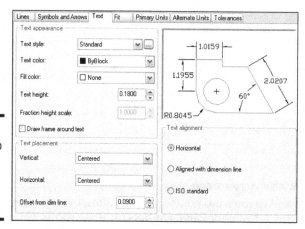

Figure 2-7:
The Text tab
of the New
Dimension
Style dialog
box.

The Fit tab

The Fit tab (see Figure 2-8) allows you to define how dimension text and arrowheads are placed between extension lines. You can specify how dimension text and arrowheads are placed in relation to the amount of space between the extension lines; the scale of dimension text in model space and on a layout tab; whether dimension text is placed with a leader; and whether a dimension line should be drawn between the extension lines.

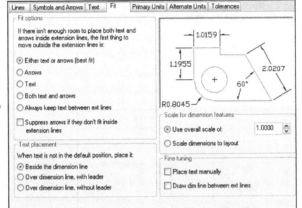

Figure 2-8:
The Fit tab of the New Dimension Style dialog box.

The Primary Units tab

The Primary Units tab (see Figure 2-9) allows you to define how dimension text should appear. On the Primary Units tab, you can specify how dimension text is formatted including decimal separators, rounding factor, measurement units, prefix and suffix for the dimension text, measurement scale factor, and how leading and trailing zeros are displayed. The settings affect both linear and angular measurement values for dimensions.

The Alternate Units tab

The Alternate Units tab (see Figure 2-10) allows you to define how alternate measurements appear as part of the dimension text. The Alternate Units tab allows you to control whether an alternate measurement value is placed with the primary measurement value. Typically, alternate units are used when you want to display dimensions with both imperial and metric values. The Alternate Units tab contains options that are used for the formatting of the alternate measurement text and its placement.

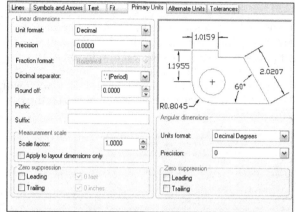

Figure 2-9:
The Primary
Units tab of
the New
Dimension
Style dialog
box.

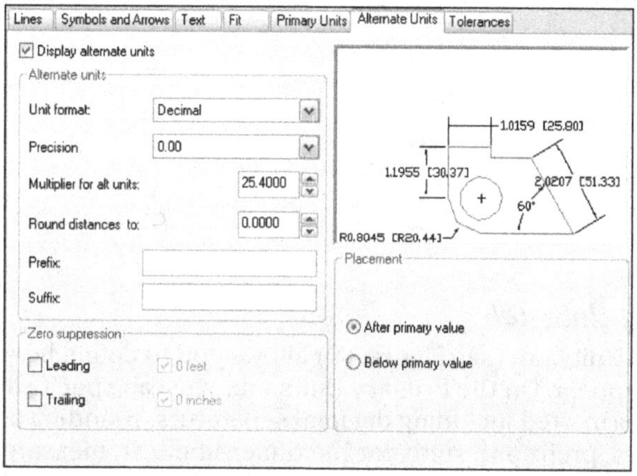

Figure 2-10:
The
Alternate
Units tab of
the New
Dimension
Style dialog
box.

The Tolerances tab

The Tolerances tab (see Figure 2-11) allows you to define how tolerances appear as part of the dimension text. Dimension text tolerances are much different from the geometric tolerance object, which we talk about later in this chapter. On the Tolerances tab, you can specify the type of tolerance that is displayed with dimension text, the format of the tolerance including precision, upper, and lower limits, and how leading and trailing zeroes are suppressed. The settings affect both linear and angular measurement values for dimensions.

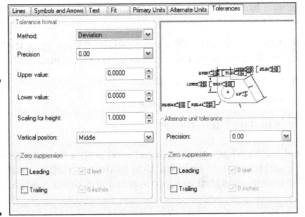

Figure 2-11:
The
Tolerances
tab of
the New
Dimension
Style dialog
box.

Dimension variables

AutoCAD and AutoCAD LT hide many of their complex workings from the user in the latest releases, but it has not always been this way. In earlier releases of AutoCAD, when dimensions were first introduced, you had to know a number of system variables that were specific to dimension styles. Even to this day, you can access the system variables that are specific to the current dimension style and make changes to them through script files as you are creating dimensions in a drawing. By changing the values of the dimension system variables in this way, you are creating an override for the current dimension style that is applied to each new dimension that is created in the drawing. You can get a list of the dimension system variables by doing the following:

1. **At the command line or dynamic input tooltip, enter SETVAR and press Enter. The following prompt is displayed:**

```
Enter variable name or [?]:
```

2. **At the prompt, type ? and press Enter. The following prompt is displayed:**

```
Enter variable(s) to list <*>:
```

3. **At the prompt, type DIM* and press Enter.**

The system variables that are specific to the current dimension style are displayed in the AutoCAD Text window or AutoCAD LT Text window.

4. **Press Enter to continue listing additional system variables that are related to dimensions.**

Keep pressing Enter until you see the dimension system variable that you want to change.

5. **Press ESC to end the SETVAR command, and then type the dimension system variable's name at the command line or dynamic input tooltip.**

You are prompted for the new value.

6. **Enter the new value and press Enter.**

The value is updated accordingly.

If you need help with what values can be used with a dimension system variable, press F1 and the online Help for that system variable opens. This also works well for commands that are in progress and other system variables.

Setting a dimension style current

Dimension styles need to be set current in order to be used to create new dimensions. AutoCAD and AutoCAD LT allow you to set a dimension style current in several different ways. The two most common ways of setting a dimension style current are

✦ **Styles or Dimension toolbar:** On the Styles or Dimension toolbar, select the dimension style that you want to set current from the Dimension Styles drop-down list.

✦ **Dimension Style Manager:** Double-click the dimension style under the Styles list box to set it current, or select the dimension style from the Styles list box. Select Set Current from the right-click menu or click the Set Current button.

Modifying a dimension style

At times, you may find that a dimension style needs to be updated. This could be due to changes to the current CAD standards or even requirements that dimensions be provided with specific arrowheads or formatting for a client. You are already familiar with creating a dimension style, so you will find modifying one isn't that much different.

Dimension styles are modified through the Dimension Style Manager dialog box. After the Dimension Style Manager dialog box is displayed, select the dimension style from the Styles list box and click the Modify button on the right side of the dialog box. The Modify Dimension Style dialog box is displayed, which is just like the New Dimension Style dialog box. Make the desired changes and then click OK to save the changes to the dimension style and to close the Modify Dimension Style dialog box.

Dimension style overrides

Dimension style overrides allow you to make small number of property changes to the current dimension style without creating a new dimension style altogether. Style overrides can cause some confusion in a drawing when creating new dimensions, unless you know that a style override is currently in use. To create a style override, you can change one of the dimension style variables, or click the Override button in the Dimension Style Manager dialog box and make the property changes that you want to be part of the style override.

Only new dimensions that are created with a style override current are affected, so you could draw dimensions using different text fit options, if necessary, to accommodate some dimensions in a drawing. Overrides are best done at the individual dimension object level using the Properties palette. Selecting a dimension in a drawing allows you to override any property of a dimension object through the Properties palette (see Figure 2-12). This makes it easier to get the correct override that you might want to use instead of setting it through the Dimension Style Manager dialog box.

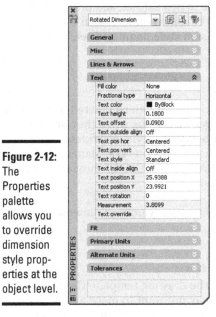

Figure 2-12:
The Properties palette allows you to override dimension style properties at the object level.

**Book III
Chapter 2**

Dimensioning

Dimension styles can be merged into the dimension style that they were created from by right-clicking over the text <Style Overrides> in the Dimension Style Manager dialog box, and selecting Save to Current Style. Only one dimension style override can exist in a drawing at a time, and switching to another dimension style discards the style overrides unless they are saved to the dimension style.

Dimension substyles

Dimension substyles are different from editing dimension styles and style overrides because the substyle limits which properties you can edit based on the substyle that is created. Dimension substyles are created just like a new dimension style is, with the exception that you select one of the types of dimensions from the Use For drop-down list in the Create New Dimension Style dialog box, and you don't need to specify a name for the dimension style. To modify a dimension substyle, select the substyle below the dimension style that the substyle is a part of and click the Modify button.

Renaming a dimension style

Only a dimension style can be renamed using the Dimension Style Manager dialog box or the Rename dialog box, but style overrides and substyles can't be. To rename a dimension style using the Dimension Style Manager dialog box, select the dimension style from the Styles list box and press F2. The in-place editor appears and allows you to change the dimension style's name. You can also right-click over the dimension style name and select Rename to replace the dimension style's name.

Deleting a dimension style

Dimension styles, substyles, and style overrides can be deleted from a drawing through the Dimension Style Manager dialog box when they are not being used. To delete a dimension style, a substyle, or style overrides, right-click over the item in the Styles list box of the Dimension Style Manager dialog box and select Delete. When the AutoCAD or AutoCAD LT message is displayed, click Yes to confirm the deletion.

The PURGE command can be used to remove any unused dimension styles from a drawing.

Importing a dimension style

Dimension styles should be created in the drawing template that you start your new drawing with. At times, you may not want to place a dimension style in the drawing template that you use, but that doesn't mean you have to go through and create the dimension style every time you need it either. You can use the DesignCenter palette to drag and drop dimension styles from one drawing to another. For more information on using DesignCenter, see Chapter 3 of Book VI.

Creating Dimensions

AutoCAD and AutoCAD LT allow you to create many different types of dimensions to communicate overall design concepts: dimensions in the form of lengths and widths, hole locations and depths, and others. The important thing to note about dimensions is which ones you need and how to create them. This section covers the different kinds of dimensions that you can create in AutoCAD and AutoCAD LT.

Linear and aligned dimensions

Linear dimensions are the most commonly used dimensions: They are used to measure an object or two points horizontally or vertically in a drawing. You use linear dimensions to dimension straight segments such as lines or polylines, the chord length of an arc, or the diameter of a circle, which can be created horizontally, vertically, or rotated (see Figure 2-13).

Figure 2-13:
Different linear dimensions that can be created with the DIMLINEAR command.

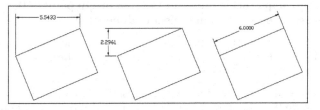

Linear dimensions are created using the DIMLINEAR command. To start the DIMLINEAR command, follow one of the methods outlined below:

✦ **Dimension menu:** Choose Dimension⇨Linear.

✦ **Dimension toolbar:** Click the Linear button on the Dimension toolbar.

✦ **Keyboard input:** Type **DIMLINEAR** and press Enter.

✦ **Command alias:** Type **DLI** and press Enter.

Aligned dimensions are similar to linear dimensions except they are not created orthogonally based on the origin points picked. The difference in the way aligned dimensions are created versus linear dimensions causes them to measure the actual distance between the origin points selected, instead of the horizontal or vertical distance. Aligned dimensions are created using the DIMALIGNED command, and its command prompts are for the most part identical to the DIMLINEAR command. To start the DIMALIGNED command, follow one of the methods outlined below:

+ **Dimension menu:** Choose Dimension⇨Aligned.

+ **Dimension toolbar:** Click the Aligned button on the Dimension toolbar.

+ **Keyboard input:** Type **DIMALIGNED** and press Enter.

+ **Command alias:** Type **DAL** and press Enter.

The following procedure starts the DIMLINEAR command and explains how to create a linear dimension:

1. **Use any of the four previously listed methods to initiate the DIMLINEAR command.**

The DIMLINEAR command starts and this prompt is displayed:

```
Specify first extension line origin or <select object>:
```

2. **At the prompt, pick a point for the first origin point of the dimension or press enter to select an object to dimension.**

If you select a point, the prompt `Specify second extension line origin:` is displayed. If you press Enter, the prompt `Select object to dimension:` is displayed.

When specifying points for the origins of dimensions, use object snaps to make sure that the dimensions are created with the correct measurement.

3. **At the `Specify second extension line origin` prompt, pick a point for the second origin point of the dimension. At the `Select object to dimension` prompt, select an object to dimension in the drawing.**

The prompt `Specify dimension line location or [Mtext/Text/ Angle/Horizontal/Vertical/Rotated]:` is displayed.

4. **At the prompt, pick a point to place the dimension or specify one of the command's options.**

The dimension is placed and the command ends. The options Mtext, Text, and Angle affect the value of the dimension text or how the dimension text is rotated. The options Horizontal, Vertical, and Rotated affect how the dimension is created in the drawing and the measurement value that is calculated.

Baseline and continued dimensions

Baseline dimensions allow you to create a string of dimensions (see Figure 2-14) that continue from the first origin point of the previous linear, aligned, angular, or ordinate dimension. Typically, you place the first dimension and then follow it up by creating baseline dimensions, but you have the option of creating baseline dimensions by selecting an existing dimension in a drawing.

Figure 2-14: Baseline and Continued dimensions based on a linear dimension.

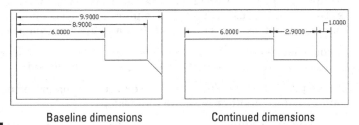

Baseline dimensions   Continued dimensions

Baseline dimensions are created using the DIMBASELINE command. To start the DIMBASELINE command, follow one of the methods outlined below:

+ **Dimension menu:** Choose Dimension⇨Baseline.
+ **Dimension toolbar:** Click the Baseline button on the Dimension toolbar.
+ **Keyboard input:** Type **DIMBASELINE** and press Enter.
+ **Command alias:** Type **DBA** and press Enter.

Book III
Chapter 2

Dimensioning

Continued dimensions allow you to create a string of dimensions that continue from the second origin point of the previous linear, aligned, angular, or ordinate dimension. As with baseline dimensions, you commonly place the first dimension and then follow it up by creating the continued dimensions, but you have the option of creating continued dimensions by selecting an existing dimension in a drawing. Continued dimensions are created using the DIMCONTINUE command, and its options are identical to the DIMBASELINE command. To start the DIMCONTINUE command, follow one of these methods:

+ **Dimension menu:** Choose Dimension⇨Continue.
+ **Dimension toolbar:** Click the Continue button on the Dimension toolbar.
+ **Keyboard input:** Type **DIMCONTINUE** and press Enter.
+ **Command alias:** Type **DCO** and press Enter.

The following procedure starts the DIMBASELINE command and explains how to create a baseline dimension:

1. **Use any of the four methods just listed to initiate the DIMBASELINE command.**

    The DIMBASELINE command starts and the prompt `Specify a second extension line origin or [Undo/Select] <Select>:` is displayed, or the prompt `Select base dimension:` is displayed.

2. **At the `Specify a second extension line origin or [Undo/ Select] <Select>` prompt, pick a point for the second origin point of the dimension or press enter to select an object to dimension.**

    If you select a point, the prompt `Specify a second extension line origin or [Undo/Select] <Select>:` is redisplayed.

3. **At the prompt, press Enter twice to exit the command or pick another point to place another baseline dimension.**

    After you press Enter once, the prompt `Select base dimension:` is displayed, which allows you to select another dimension to start creating baseline dimensions from.

Angular dimensions

Angular dimensions (see Figure 2-15) allow you to show the angular measurement in a drawing. The angular measurement might be based on the end points of an arc, the angular relationship between two straight segments, the center of a circle and another angle, or two vertexes that define an angle.

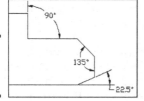

Figure 2-15:
Angular
dimensions.

Angular dimensions are created using the DIMANGLUAR command. To start the DIMANGLUAR command, use one of these methods:

✦ **Dimension menu:** Choose Dimension⇨Angular.

✦ **Dimension toolbar:** Click the Angular button on the Dimension toolbar.

✦ **Keyboard input:** Type **DIMANGULAR** and press Enter.

✦ **Command alias:** Type **DAN** and press Enter.

The following procedure starts the DIMANGULAR command and explains how to create an angular dimension based on two lines:

1. **Use any of the four methods just listed to initiate the DIMANGULAR command.**

The DIMANGULAR command starts and the prompt `Select arc, circle, line, or <specify vertex>:` is displayed.

2. **At the prompt, select a line segment.**

The prompt `Select second line:` is displayed.

3. **At the prompt, select another line segment.**

The prompt `Specify dimension arc line location or [Mtext/ Text/Angle]:` is displayed.

4. **At the prompt, pick a point to place the dimension or specify one of the command's options.**

The dimension is placed and the command ends.

Arc length dimensions

Arc length dimensions (see Figure 2-16) are similar to angular dimensions, except instead of measuring an angle, they measure the length of an arc or an arc segment of a polyline. Based on how an arc needs to dimensioned, you might use the arc length dimension over an angular or linear dimension.

Figure 2-16:
Arc length
dimensions.

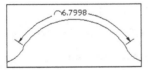

Arc length dimensions are created using the DIMARC command. To start the DIMARC command, follow one of the methods outlined below:

✦ **Dimension menu:** Choose Dimension⇨Arc Length.

✦ **Dimension toolbar:** Click the Arc Length button on the Dimension toolbar.

✦ **Keyboard input:** Type **DIMARC** and press Enter.

✦ **Command alias:** Type **DAR** and press Enter.

Radius, diameter, and jogged dimensions

AutoCAD offers four different types of dimensions that are used to dimension the radius or diameter of a circle or arc, or place a center mark at the center point of a circle or arc. Figure 2-17 shows the results of using the commands DIMRADIUS, DIMDIAMETER, DIMCENTER, and DIMJOGGED on a circle or arc.

Figure 2-17: Radius, diameter, and jogged dimensions along with center marks.

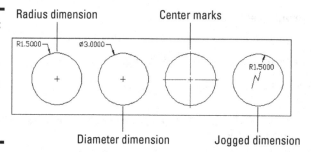

Radius dimensions

Radius dimensions display an uppercase R prefixed to the measurement value to designate that the measurement is for the radius and not the diameter of the arc or circle. When a radius dimension is placed, a center mark is also displayed so you know where the center of the object that is being dimensioned is. Radius dimensions are created using the DIMRADIUS command. To start the DIMRADIUS command, follow one of the methods outlined below:

✦ **Dimension menu:** Choose Dimension⇨Radius.

✦ **Dimension toolbar:** Click the Radius button on the Dimension toolbar.

✦ **Keyboard input:** Type **DIMRADIUS** and press Enter.

✦ **Command alias:** Type **DRA** and press Enter.

Diameter dimensions

Diameter dimensions are similar to radius dimensions except they are used to measure the diameter of an arc or circle. The two dimensions look almost identical, except the diameter dimension displays a diameter symbol in front of the measurement value. Diameter dimensions are created using the DIMDIAMETER command. To start the DIMDIAMETER command, follow one of the methods outlined below:

✦ **Dimension menu:** Choose Dimension⇨Diameter.

✦ **Dimension toolbar:** Click the Diameter button on the Dimension toolbar.

✦ **Keyboard input:** Type **DIMDIAMETER** and press Enter.

✦ **Command alias:** Type **DDI** and press Enter.

Jogged dimensions

Jogged dimensions allow you to show the radius of an arc or a circle like a radius dimension does, except instead of the dimension automatically indicating the center of the object, you specify a center override location. When a jogged dimension is placed, no center mark is displayed, but an angle on the dimension line is displayed to indicate that the radius isn't being measured from the center of the object. Jogged dimensions are created using the DIMJOGGED command. To start the DIMJOGGED command, follow one of the methods outlined below:

✦ **Dimension menu:** Choose Dimension⇨Jogged.

✦ **Dimension toolbar:** Click the Jogged button on the Dimension toolbar.

✦ **Keyboard input:** Type **DIMJOGGED** and press Enter.

✦ **Command alias:** Type **DJO** and press Enter.

Center marks

Center marks allow you to place a set of lines at the center of an arc or a circle. The lines that are created are not a single dimension object, but a bunch of separate line objects. The type of center mark created is based on the settings under the Center Mark section of the Symbols and Arrows tab of the New/Modify Dimension Style dialog box. Center marks are automatically created when you place radius and diameter dimensions, but you want to place center marks at the center of circles when placing linear dimensions to indicate that you are dimensioning to the center of the circle. Center marks are created using the DIMCENTER command. After the DIMCENTER command is started, select an arc or circle to create the center mark. To start the DIMCENTER command, follow one of the methods outlined below:

✦ **Dimension menu:** Choose Dimension⇨Center Mark.

✦ **Dimension toolbar:** Click the Center Mark button on the Dimension toolbar.

✦ **Keyboard input:** Type **DIMCENTER** and press Enter.

✦ **Command alias:** Type **DCE** and press Enter.

Book III
Chapter 2

Dimensioning

Ordinate dimensions

Ordinate dimensions (see Figure 2-18) allow you to place x and y coordinate values of features or specific points on a part. Each ordinate dimension represents an x or y value, but not both. Ordinate dimensions are not a commonly used type of dimension, but you might find them used on shop drawings used to manufacture parts.

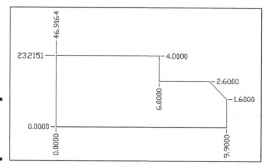

Figure 2-18:
Ordinate
dimensions.

Ordinate dimensions are created using the DIMORDINATE command. To start the DIMORDINATE command, follow one of the methods outlined below:

+ **Dimension menu:** Choose Dimension⇨Ordinate.

+ **Dimension toolbar:** Click the Ordinate button on the Dimension toolbar.

+ **Keyboard input:** Type **DIMORDINATE** and press Enter.

+ **Command alias:** Type **DOR** and press Enter.

When you create ordinate dimensions, they are based on the origin of the current user coordinate system (UCS). (For more information on the User Coordinate System, see Book V, Chapter 2.) Usually a point on the part is designated as 0,0. In order to do that, you need to specify a new origin for the current UCS. To specify a new origin, start the UCS command and then pick the point in the drawing you want to be the current 0,0 value. To undo the moving of the origin, use the World option of the UCS command.

The Quick Dimension command

The Quick Dimension (QDIM) command allows you to quickly place a number of dimensions in a drawing by selecting multiple objects at a time. The QDIM command allows you to create linear, continuous, staggered, baseline, ordinate, radius, and diameter dimensions. To start the QDIM command, follow one of the methods outlined below:

+ **Dimension menu:** Choose Dimension➪Quick Dimension.
+ **Dimension toolbar:** Click the Quick Dimension button on the Dimension toolbar.

+ **Keyboard input:** Type **QDIM** and press Enter.

The QDIM command is not available in AutoCAD LT.

Trans-spatial dimensions

Trans-spatial dimensions are not something you find in a science fiction novel, but instead a feature of AutoCAD that allows you to dimension objects that are in model space through a floating viewport. Trans-spatial dimensions allow you to place dimensions on layouts that measure accurately, but this brings up the question of where dimensions should be placed.

You should generally do dimensioning in model space (via the Model tab), but at times, you may find it beneficial to dimension objects that are in model space through a viewport. One of the main reasons that dimensions should be placed in model space is so they appear if the drawing is inserted or referenced into another drawing. In order to dimension objects correctly, the scale used for the dimension style should be set to a value of 1.

Before you attempt to take on dimensioning on a layout tab, we recommend you stick to dimensioning in model space for a while.

Editing Dimensions

Dimensions are edited in slightly different ways depending on what part of the dimension object you want to edit. In this section, we explain some of the common ways to edit dimensions.

Adding overrides to a dimension

At times, you may need to make adjustments to the location of an arrow-head, change the position and formatting of text, or change the dimension style of a dimension. The Properties palette allows you to override specific properties of a dimension object to supersede (or override) the properties defined by the dimension style that is assigned to the dimension object. Along with using the Properties palette, you can also select dimensions and then right-click to access some of the commonly used dimension overrides. From the right-click shortcut menu, you have the option to flip arrowheads individually so they are on the inside or outside of an extension line, change the precision formatting of dimension text, change the current dimension style for the dimension object, or even change the position of the dimension text.

Editing the dimension text

Dimension text can be edited to add a prefix or suffix to a measurement value to denote a typical dimension or quantity of holes. You can edit the text of a dimension using the DDEDIT command, or change the Text Override, Dim Prefix, and Dim Suffix properties with the Properties palette.

If you use the DDEDIT command, you should notice that the measurement value is displayed with a background fill color. If the measurement text doesn't display with a fill color, a text override has been applied. To add the true measurement value back into the dimension text, add the text <> to the In-Place Text Editor.

Two commands are specifically for editing dimension text: DIMEDIT and DIMTEDIT. DIMEDIT allows you to change the placement of dimension text and change the angle of extension lines. DIMTEDIT is used to move and rotate dimension text. If you need additional help with the commands, reference the online Help system.

Using grips to edit dimensions

Grips are a very powerful editing feature and can be used with dimensions. Using grips to edit dimensions allows you to reposition dimension text, change the placement of the dimension line along the extension lines, and move the origin points of a dimension. Moving the origin points can cause the dimension to become non-associative; however, you can make the dimension associative again using the DIMREASSOCIATE command which is mentioned under the section "Associating dimensions." If you use grips to stretch both the dimension and the object the dimension is associated to, the dimension remains associative to the object.

Associating dimensions

Dimensions, at times, can wander off and disassociate themselves from the original object that they were dimensioned to. Dimensions can become disassociated through the use of the DIMDISASSOCIATE command, or a dimension might break its associativity after being modified. If a dimension becomes disassociated, you can try counseling, but usually the DIMREASSOCIATE command is all that is really needed to correct the problem. The DIMREASSOCIATE command allows you to re-specify the origin points of selected dimension objects, making them once again associative to the objects in a drawing. The DIMREASSOCIATE command can be used to convert pre-AutoCAD 2002 dimensions to fully associative dimensions.

AutoCAD and AutoCAD LT for the most part do a pretty good job at watching for changes to objects in the drawing, and to make sure their associated dimensions are kept up-to-date. If a dimension seems to be confused after you update an object, you can kick-start it by using the DIMREGEN command. This forces the dimension object to update.

Leaders

Leaders are used to point to and call out features or draw attention to something in a design (see Figure 2-19). A leader typically has an arrowhead at one end pointing to something in the drawing, whereas the other end has text, an object, a block, or a tolerance object. The leader can contain any of the arrowheads that dimensions can, and the leader line can contain as many straight or spline segments that you want it to have.

Figure 2-19:
Examples of
leaders.

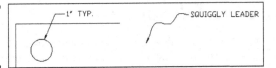

Leaders are created using the QLEADER command. To start the QLEADER command, follow one of the methods outlined below:

+ **Dimension menu:** Choose Dimension ⇨Leader.

+ **Dimension toolbar:** Click the Quick Leader button on the Dimension toolbar.

+ **Keyboard input:** Type **QLEADER** and press Enter.

As soon as the QLEADER command is started, it allows you to start creating a leader right away by selecting points. The number of points that you can pick are based on the settings of the QLEADER command. The Leader Settings dialog box (see Figure 2-20) is used to specify the options for the QLEADER command when creating a new leader. The leader line and arrowheads are created as a single object, but any text, block, object, or tolerance that is placed with the leader is treated as a single object.

Figure 2-20:
The Leader
Settings
dialog box.

When using the QLEADER command, follow the prompts at the command line or the dynamic input tooltip. Leaders can be edited using grips, the proper editing command based on the type of object inserted with the leader, and the common modify commands. If you need additional help, reference the online Help system.

Working with Geometric Tolerances

Geometric tolerances allow you to create a series of what are called *feature control frames*. Feature control frames can contain symbols, tolerance values, datum references, and projected tolerance zone values (see Figure 2-21). Geometric tolerances are used for mechanical drawings and vary based on the standards that you need to follow, such as ANSI (American National Standards Institute), ISO (International Standards Organization), or JIS (Japanese Industrial Standards).

Figure 2-21:
The
Geometric
tolerance.

Geometric tolerances are created using the TOLERANCE command. To start the TOLERANCE command, follow one of the methods outlined below:

✦ **Dimension menu:** Choose Dimension➪Tolerance.

✦ **Dimension toolbar:** Click the Tolerance button on the Dimension toolbar.

✦ **Keyboard input:** Click TOLERANCE on the Dimension toolbar.

✦ **Command alias:** Type **TOL** and press Enter.

When you start the TOLERANCE command, you are prompted for the insertion point of the geometric tolerance object and then the Geometric Tolerance dialog box (see Figure 2-22) is displayed. In the Geometric Tolerance dialog box you can specify the tolerances, datum references, symbols, and projected tolerance zone value. Geometric tolerances can be modified using grips, the DDEDIT command, and the common modifying commands. If you need help, reference the online Help system.

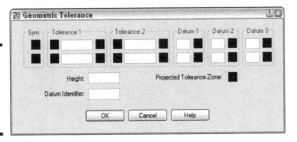

Figure 2-22:
The
Geometric
Tolerance
dialog box.

Book III
Chapter 2

Dimensioning

Chapter 3: Hatching Your Drawings

*I*n this chapter, you discover hatch patterns and fills and how to create and edit them. Hatch patterns and fills are used to communicate a design concept and help improve the way a flat 2D drawing looks. AutoCAD and AutoCAD LT offer two different types of hatches: hatch patterns and solid fills. Hatch patterns are made up of line segments that are stored in pattern files, whereas solid fills are a single color and are not made up of line segments. AutoCAD offers an additional hatch type called *gradient* fills.

Gradient fills are similar to solid fills except they are a blend of one color with a tint, or two colors, to give the illusion of depth and realism to a 2D drawing. Hatching allows you to quickly add a visual representation of floor tiles, shingles, or shakes on a roof for an architectural drawing. For a mechanical drawing, you might use a hatch pattern that creates diagonal lines to represent the part of a model that is shown cut through for a section view.

Hatch objects are created by default as a single object and are associative like dimensions. Hatch objects are created associative to the objects that form the closed boundary in which the hatch object is created. Keeping a hatch object associative allows it to be automatically updated when the boundary changes. Hatch objects can also be created non-associative, which keeps the hatch object from being updated when the boundary changes. Hatch objects can be exploded if they are created with a hatch pattern other than a solid or gradient fill. Figure 3-1 shows a drawing that uses hatch patterns and fills to indicate the materials used for the exterior of a building.

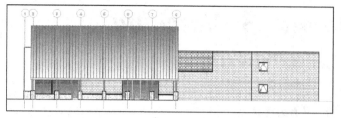

Figure 3-1:
Hatch
patterns and
fills.

Adding Hatch Patterns and Fills

Hatch objects are created using the Hatch and Gradient dialog box (see Figure 3-2), or, if you are using AutoCAD LT, the Hatch dialog box. The Hatch and Gradient dialog box allows you to specify which hatch pattern or fill should be used to hatch a closed boundary (or area). Based on the type of hatch you are creating, you might need to specify a pattern, scale, and angle.

Many different settings control how a hatch object looks after it is created. Most of the commonly used settings for creating and editing hatch objects are displayed by default, but if you want to access some of the more advanced settings, click the More Options button.

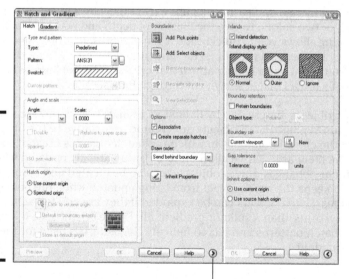

Figure 3-2:
The Hatch
and
Gradient
dialog box
with the
Hatch tab
active and
expanded.

More Options

Adding hatch to a drawing

Adding hatch to a drawing the first few times can be a little bit confusing, but that is to be expected because many elements in a drawing and the dialog box can affect how a hatch object is created. When you want to create a hatch object, make sure that the area you want to hatch is closed — meaning all lines, arcs, and so on define a boundary either by connecting at the end points of the objects or by overlapping each other. Hatch objects are created using the Hatch and Gradient dialog box, which is displayed with the HATCH command.

To start the HATCH command and display the Hatch and Gradient dialog box, follow one of these methods:

+ **Draw menu:** Choose Draw ⇨Hatch.

+ **Draw toolbar:** Click Hatch on the Draw toolbar.

+ **Keyboard input:** Type **HATCH** and press Enter.

+ **Command Alias:** Type **H** and press Enter.

The following procedure starts the Draw command and displays the Hatch and Gradient dialog box so you can create a hatch object using a predefined hatch pattern:

Book III
Chapter 3

1. **Use one of the methods just listed to start the Draw command.**

   The Hatch and Gradient dialog box is displayed.

2. **In the Hatch and Gradient dialog box under the Type and Pattern section, select Predefined from the Type drop-down list.**

   The controls that are used with a predefined hatch pattern are enabled.

3. **From the Pattern drop-down list, select one of the predefined hatch patterns.**

   A preview of the selected hatch pattern is displayed in the Swatch area below the Pattern drop-down list. You can click the ellipsis button to the right of the Pattern drop-down list to display the Hatch Pattern Palette dialog box (see Figure 3-3). The Hatch Pattern Palette dialog box allows you to select predefined and custom hatch patterns that come with the software.

4. **Under the Angle and Scale section, specify an angle for the hatch pattern by selecting a predefined value from the Angle drop-down list or entering a value in the text box.**

Hatching Your
Drawings

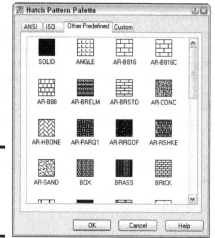

Figure 3-3:
The Hatch
Pattern
Palette
dialog box.

5. Specify a scale for the hatch pattern by selecting a predefined value from the Scale drop-down list or entering a value in the text box.

6. Under the Boundaries section, click Add: Pick Points.

You are returned to the drawing window to pick a point inside the closed boundary. The prompt `Pick internal point or [Select objects/remove Boundaries]:` is displayed.

7. At the prompt, click in the drawing window within a closed boundary to define the boundary for a hatch object.

The boundary is calculated, and you are prompted for additional closed areas. If the area is not closed or the boundary can't be calculated, a message box is displayed (see Figure 3-4).

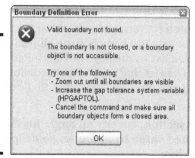

Figure 3-4:
The
Boundary
Definition
Error
message
box.

The system variable HPGAPTOL specifies if a tolerance value is used when calculating a closed boundary with objects that don't completely form a closed boundary. The value can also be specified under the Gap Tolerance section when the Hatch and Gradient dialog box is expanded.

8. **Press Enter to accept the selected boundaries and to return to the Hatch and Gradient dialog box.**

9. **In the Hatch and Gradient dialog box, click Preview.**

    The hatch object is displayed in the drawing.

10. **Press ESC to return to the Hatch and Gradient dialog box to make changes or press Enter to create the hatch object.**

    The hatch object is created and the command ends.

Hatching and tool palettes

You can create hatch tools on a tool palette that can be used to create new hatch objects in a drawing. A hatch tool can be created by dragging and dropping a hatch object from a drawing onto a tool palette. The hatch tool is created based on the properties of the hatch object. To use the hatch tool, click the tool and then click inside the closed boundary, or drag and drop the tool over the closed boundary. For more information on tool palettes, see Chapter 4 of Book VI.

Book III
Chapter 3

Hatching Your
Drawings

Hatching and DesignCenter

Hatch objects and hatch tools can be created from the DesignCenter. To create a hatch object or a hatch tool, browse to the location where the hatch pattern (.PAT) files are stored with DesignCenter. Double-click the hatch pattern file, and then drag and drop the hatch pattern over a closed boundary or over a tool palette.

Advanced settings for additional control

The Hatch and Gradient dialog box offers a number of options to control how a hatch object is created and how the boundary for a hatch object is generated. These options can be found under the Hatch Origin and Options sections and under the extended section of the Hatch and Gradient dialog box.

Specifying the origin for a hatch object

The Hatch Origin section allows you to define the base point in the drawing from which the hatch pattern is calculated. By default, the origin point of the drawing is used, instead of a point in the closed boundary. The Specified Origin option allows you to select the point that should be used for the origin that the hatch pattern of the hatch object should be calculated from.

Specifying an origin point allows you to make the appearance of hatch patterns predictable. This is important if you are using hatch patterns for creating tiles, bricks, and siding on a house; for example, you want to make sure you have a full run of bricks at the bottom of a house, and not just half of a run.

Island detection

Island detection is used when calculating the closed boundary for a hatch object. An *island* is defined as an interior boundary inside the outer boundary that is calculated. To access the island detection settings, you have to click the More Options button that is located in the lower-right corner of the Hatch and Gradient dialog box. Figure 3-5 shows examples of the three island detection options:

✦ **Normal:** The outer detected boundary is hatched, but hatch is turned off for any detected island until another island is detected.

✦ **Outer:** Only the outer detected boundary is hatched; no hatch is applied to islands inside the boundary calculated.

✦ **Ignore:** All islands are ignored and the hatch fills the entire area defined by the outer boundary.

Figure 3-5:
Island
detection
settings.

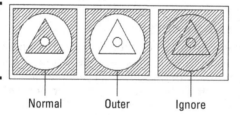

Normal   Outer   Ignore

The Remove Boundaries button allows you to remove and add islands to adjust the boundary of a hatch object when it is being edited.

Others settings available for defining a hatch object

Some additional settings allow you to specify a factor that should be used when defining a boundary that might not be completely closed. Another setting allows you to create separate hatch objects for each closed boundary that is defined when selecting objects or points to define boundaries. Another nice feature is to define the order in which the hatch object is displayed on-screen in respect to the objects that define its boundary. For additional information on the options of the Hatch and Gradient dialog box, see the online Help system.

A new system variable now controls whether object snaps can be used with hatch objects. If the system variable OSOPTIONS is set to a value of 1 or 3, object snaps are ignored for hatch objects.

Working with Hatch Patterns and Solid Fills

Hatch patterns and solid fills are the most commonly used types of hatches. AutoCAD and AutoCAD LT offer three different types of hatch patterns that you can use when adding hatch to a drawing: predefined, user-defined, and custom.

Predefined patterns

AutoCAD and AutoCAD LT come with a number of predefined patterns that are available in the files acad.PAT (acadiso.PAT for metric) and acadlt.PAT (acadltiso.PAT for metric). To use a predefined hatch pattern or solid fill, select Predefined from the Type drop-down list. The Pattern drop-down list is enabled, which allows you to select a pattern from the drop-down list. Alternatively, click the ellipsis button to the right of the Pattern drop-down list to select a pattern visually from the Hatch Pattern Palette dialog box.

The system variable MEASUREMENT is used to control which hatch pattern and linetype files are used for imperial or metric drawings. If MEASUREMENT is set to a value of 0, the imperial files are used; a value of 1 indicates that the metric files should be used.

Book III
Chapter 3

Hatching Your
Drawings

User-defined patterns

User-defined hatch patterns are not very common because they just don't offer much more than what the predefined hatch patterns offer. When defining a user-defined hatch pattern, you specify the spacing and angle of lines that run parallel or perpendicular to each other. One of the nice things about user-defined hatch patterns is that you specify the actual spacing of the lines in drawing units instead of a scale factor. To create a user-defined hatch pattern, select User Defined from the Type drop-down list. After User Defined is selected, set the angle and spacing values and specify whether double lines should be created.

Custom hatch patterns

Custom hatch patterns are typically supplemental patterns that offer something that is not available from the predefined hatch patterns that come with the application. Custom hatch patterns are usually much more complex than just a series of lines that can be generated as a user-defined pattern. Custom hatch pattern files must be placed in one of the support paths defined under the Files tab of the Options dialog box.

To use a custom hatch pattern, select Custom from the Type drop-down list and then click the ellipsis button next to the Custom drop-down list to display the Hatch Pattern Palette dialog box. The Custom tab is set current and displays the hatch patterns that AutoCAD or AutoCAD LT automatically found in the support paths. For more information on custom hatch patterns, see Chapter 4 of Book IX.

Using Gradient Fills

Gradient fills were added to AutoCAD 2004 to replace the fills that users had previously been creating with external paint applications. Gradient fills are created based on a choice of one color and a tint value or two colors, the direction of the color shift, whether the gradient is centered, and its angle. Gradient fills are created from the Gradient tab of the Hatch and Gradient dialog box (see Figure 3-6).

Creating a gradient fill isn't much different from creating a hatch object that uses a predefined, user-defined, or custom pattern. After the basic characteristics of the gradient fill have been defined, you define the boundary for the hatch in the same way you would for creating one of the hatch types from the Hatch tab.

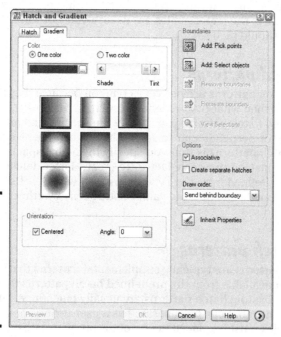

Figure 3-6: The Hatch and Gradient dialog box with the Gradient tab active.

Gradient fills can't be *applied* with AutoCAD LT, but are displayed in LT with no problem.

If a drawing is saved back to AutoCAD 2002 or earlier versions, gradient fills are displayed as a solid fill. The color of the solid fill is based on the closest ACI color to the first color of the gradient fill.

Editing Hatch Patterns and Fills

Editing a hatch object is very similar to editing a text object or other objects. Double-clicking a hatch object starts the HATCHEDIT command, which allows you to edit a hatch object. Alternatively, you can start the HATCHEDIT command by selecting and right-clicking a hatch object and choosing Hatch Edit from the shortcut menu. The HATCHEDIT command displays the Hatch Edit dialog box, which is identical to the Hatch and Gradient dialog box, except that some of the options used only for creating a hatch object are disabled. Make the necessary changes and click OK to apply the changes.

The MATCHPROP command is great for making one or more hatch objects look the same by copying the properties from one hatch object to another.

Book III
Chapter 3

Hatching Your Drawings

Book IV

LT Differences

The 5th Wave   By Rich Tennant

Contents at a Glance

Chapter 1: The LT Difference

In This Chapter

✔ Understanding the limitations of AutoCAD LT

✔ Determining whether AutoCAD LT is right for you

This minibook of the *AutoCAD & AutoCAD LT All-in-One Desk Reference For Dummies* takes a look at the differences between AutoCAD and AutoCAD LT. If you are considering purchasing AutoCAD or AutoCAD LT, you should understand what the strengths and weaknesses of the two programs are before making your final decision. Or maybe you already have AutoCAD LT and want to know what you might be missing out on by not having AutoCAD. In this minibook, we try to give you a good understanding of the differences between the two programs.

Understanding the Boundaries and Limitations of AutoCAD LT

AutoCAD LT is a scaled-down version of AutoCAD that is targeted at companies that create only 2D drawings and can't (or don't want to) afford the higher price of AutoCAD. AutoCAD LT is what Autodesk refers to as an AutoCAD OEM (Original Equipment Manufacturer) program: AutoCAD OEM is simply the AutoCAD platform or engine with some features removed and others added to make a new program without the need to reinvent the wheel — or recreate the program, in this case. Using AutoCAD as the basis for AutoCAD LT guarantees that the files that are created in AutoCAD can be read by AutoCAD LT.

AutoCAD LT contains roughly 80 percent of the functionality of AutoCAD for about 20 percent of the price. Most of the features that don't make it into AutoCAD LT are based on project collaboration, 3D, and the ability to create custom programs — add-ons. Autodesk removes these features from the program to justify the cost difference between the two programs. For the price, AutoCAD LT is an outstanding value and ensures that you will be able to communicate with others who use AutoCAD. However, because you can't create or use custom programs for AutoCAD LT, you can't do much to change or improve on any drafting workflow that doesn't already come with the program through custom add-on programs as you can with AutoCAD.

So what exactly are the differences between the two programs? The programs have a number of major and minor differences. Here is a list summarizing many of the differences between the two programs:

✦ **User interface:** For the most part, the user interfaces of AutoCAD and AutoCAD LT are identical (see Figure 1-1). Both programs take advantage of the Windows platform by using common user interface elements that can be found in most Windows-based applications. These common user interface elements are

Pull-down menus and shortcut menus

Toolbars

Status bar

Dialog boxes

Floating/dockable windows — palettes

Some of the common AutoCAD-related UI elements, such as the Text window, command line window, and dynamic input are present in both AutoCAD and AutoCAD LT. AutoCAD LT lacks some of the palettes that are found in AutoCAD only, such as the Dashboard, dbConnect Manager, Sheet Set Manager, and others.

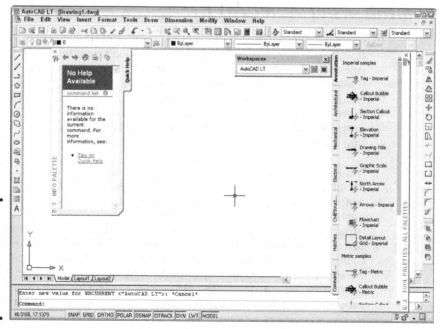

Figure 1-1:
The AutoCAD LT user interface out of the box.

For more information on the AutoCAD and AutoCAD LT user interfaces, see Chapter 2 of Book I.

✦ **2D drafting:** The foundation of both applications is 2D drafting, so both programs are very similar in the features and commands that are available for it. A few features do stand out as being different, however:

> AutoCAD supports the ability to create multilines with the MLINE command, whereas AutoCAD LT has a command called DLINE instead. Both commands allow you to create parallel lines, but the DLINE command is much easier to work with.

> AutoCAD LT doesn't support the use of True Colors or Color Book colors.

> Raster images can't be attached to a drawing as an external reference when using AutoCAD LT.

> The Reference Manager allows you to remap external references such as drawings, raster images, and .DWF underlays.

> Groups are created and managed differently in the two programs. AutoCAD LT offers a much easier-to-use interface and is dockable, versus the older dialog box interface that comes with AutoCAD.

For more information on 2D drafting, see Chapters 1 and 2 of Book II; for more information on external references, see Chapter 4 of Book VI.

✦ **Annotation/dimensioning:** The annotation and dimension features of the two programs are very similar, for the most part. A few notable differences are

> AutoCAD LT lacks the ability to create Gradient fills.

> The QDIM command is missing from AutoCAD LT, which helps to improve productivity by allowing you to place multiple dimensions at a time quickly in a drawing.

> You aren't able to insert fields in text, multiline text, or attributes when using AutoCAD LT.

For more information on annotating and dimensioning a drawing, see Book III.

✦ **3D modeling:** For the most part, 3D drawing in AutoCAD LT is nonexistent. You are able to create wireframe models, but you can't create surface or solid models. AutoCAD LT does offer some limited properties that do allow you to create pseudo-3D objects or objects that appear to be 3D, such as giving an object thickness or drawing objects at different Z elevations. The 3D modeling capability is one of the defining features that makes AutoCAD LT different from AutoCAD.

For more information on 3D modeling in AutoCAD and AutoCAD LT, see Book V.

Book IV
Chapter 1

The LT Difference

✦ **Viewing/navigation:** AutoCAD LT offers very basic ways to view a drawing compared to AutoCAD. Most of the available ways of viewing a drawing in AutoCAD LT are

Realtime zoom and pan, window, extents, previous, and others

Named and preset views

VPOINT and DDVPOINT commands

Toggling between Perspective and Parallel view

AutoCAD allows you to view and navigate a drawing the same way that AutoCAD LT does, with the added navigation features below:

3D Orbit to rotate the camera around objects in the model

Walk and fly through navigation features

Swivel and adjust the distance from the camera

Camera objects

For more information on viewing and navigating a drawing with AutoCAD and AutoCAD LT, see Chapter 3 of Book II and Chapter 4 of Book V.

✦ **Visualization/rendering:** Visualizing a 3D drawing is rather basic in AutoCAD LT compared to AutoCAD. AutoCAD LT allows you to display a drawing in 2D wireframe, shaded, or as a hidden line drawing. AutoCAD LT doesn't support rendering or the use of visual styles.

For more information on visualization and rendering of a drawing in both AutoCAD and AutoCAD LT, see Chapters 3 and 7 of Book V.

✦ **Collaboration/sharing:** Both AutoCAD and AutoCAD LT can be used to create drawings for a project, but AutoCAD offers features that allow better project collaborating or sharing of design ideas. Both support the ability to open and save files to FTP sites and the project collaboration site Buzzsaw. You can put drawings on the Web through the Publish to Web feature and send sets of drawings via eTransmit. Where the two differ is in the Sheet Set Manager, Publish, and Drawing Security features.

You can't create 3D .DWF files from AutoCAD LT, nor can you publish drawings to a named plotter with the PUBLISH command.

The Sheet Set Manager is not part of AutoCAD LT, so you can't share projects through this means with AutoCAD and AutoCAD LT users.

Drawings can't be secured with passwords when using AutoCAD LT.

For more information on publishing drawings and project collaboration with AutoCAD and AutoCAD LT, see Books VII and VIII.

✦ **Data exchange:** If you are working with vendors or clients that use different drafting packages other than AutoCAD or AutoCAD LT, you might run into exchange problems if you are using AutoCAD LT. AutoCAD LT doesn't offer as many file export and import options as AutoCAD does. If you are using AutoCAD LT, you can't import or export the following file formats:

> 3D .DWF file (export)
>
> ACIS file (import and export)
>
> Stereolithograph file (export)
>
> Encapsulated PS file (export)
>
> 3D Studio file (import)
>
> Drawing Exchange Binary file (import)

For more information on exchanging drawings in other file formats other than .DWG and .DXF from AutoCAD and AutoCAD LT, see Chapter 4 of Book VIII.

✦ **CAD standards:** Both AutoCAD and AutoCAD allow you to manage CAD standards through the use of drawing template files, layers, text styles, dimension styles, and blocks just to name a few. However, AutoCAD does supply a few additional tools that are not part of AutoCAD LT to make sure everyone is following the same standards. These additional CAD standards tools are

> CAD Standards Manager
>
> Batch CAD standards
>
> Layer Translator

For more information on using CAD standards with drawings created in AutoCAD and AutoCAD LT, see Chapters 1 through 3 of Book VIII.

✦ **Customization/programming:** Outside of 3D modeling, customization and programming is another key difference between AutoCAD and AutoCAD LT. Although AutoCAD LT does support customization to a certain extent, it doesn't support programming languages and platforms such as AutoLISP/Visual LISP, VB/VBA, and C++/ObjectARX. This makes it impossible to get the same level of productivity out of AutoCAD LT that you can with AutoCAD. Many third-party applications run inside of AutoCAD to help with things like block management, attribute extraction, modifying objects, and even programs that connect to external data sources.

For more information on customizing and programming AutoCAD and AutoCAD LT, see Books IX and X.

Book IV
Chapter 1

The LT Difference

✦ **Additional utilities:** AutoCAD offers many features that are improvements to older versions or features that are not available at all in AutoCAD LT. Some of these features are

dbConnect Manager, which allows you to link objects in a drawing to a table in a database.

Enhanced Attribute Editor, which is an improved version of the Edit Attribute dialog box.

Enhanced Attribute Extraction wizard, which is an improved version of the Attribute Extraction dialog box.

Express Tools, which contains additional tools that help with a variety of tasks in AutoCAD.

For more information on extracting and editing attributes in blocks, see Chapter 1 of Book VI; for more information on Express Tools, see Chapter 4 of Book IX.

✦ **Software deployment:** AutoCAD allows you to manage installation through a Network Deployment wizard and software licenses with a license manager. AutoCAD LT doesn't offer network deployment and license management, which can help to control the costs of the software. For example, if you have five drafters, but only three are typically in AutoCAD at a time, you could get away with buying only three network licenses. The license manager hands out licenses until there are no more to hand out. If no additional licenses are available, the fourth user gets a message that says all licenses have been checked out. The Network Deployment wizard allows you to streamline installing AutoCAD by allowing you to specify settings like user profile names, custom support paths, and files that should be used by default.

Determining Whether AutoCAD or AutoCAD LT Is Best for You

Now that you have an idea of what the differences are between AutoCAD and AutoCAD LT, you have to decide which one is right for you. It really depends on what you are doing: 2D drafting, 3D modeling, plotting drawings, or doing review comments. Here are six questions that should help you to determine whether AutoCAD or AutoCAD LT would work best for you. This list isn't comprehensive, but it should be enough to get you going in the right direction. Keep in mind that you have to consider what your current needs are versus what your future needs might be:

1. **Are the drawings you create or work with 2D only?**

   If so, you might think about using AutoCAD LT.

2. **Do some of the drawings that you create or work with contain 3D objects, or will you need to supply renderings to any of your clients?**

   If so, you might think about using AutoCAD: AutoCAD LT doesn't support rendering or the creation of 3D objects.

3. **Will you be doing nothing more than some light drafting, plotting, and reviewing of .DWG files?**

   If so, you might think about using AutoCAD LT unless you need to plot renderings.

4. **Do you need or want to run third-party applications to extend the functionality that comes with the program?**

   If so, you will need to use AutoCAD and not AutoCAD LT because AutoCAD LT doesn't support certain forms of customization and programming languages.

5. **Do you plan on working with a variety of different clients and vendors?**

   If so, you need to consider using AutoCAD and not AutoCAD LT. AutoCAD offers a number of features that make working with vendors and clients much easier due to the support of CAD standards and Sheet Sets. If you choose to use AutoCAD LT, you can still work with vendors and clients, but you might have some additional hurdles that you will need to plan for. Vendors have a tough time working with the lowest common denominator, AutoCAD LT in this case, if you are missing out on productivity features.

6. **What is your budget for software?**

   If you have a small budget and you do only 2D only drawings, the best choice is AutoCAD LT. Another solution you might consider is to buy a single seat of AutoCAD and the rest as AutoCAD LT if you are primarily doing 2D only drawings. This would allow you to at least see what those with AutoCAD created before they sent you the drawings, and it would also give you a way to work with vendors that use AutoCAD.

   If you have a medium or a large budget, you might consider buying AutoCAD and using the license manager to allow you to buy fewer licenses than you have staff. You can then add new licenses later as needed. If your budget is limitless, you could buy a license of AutoCAD for each user in your office and be done with it. (And hey, if you feel extremely generous, we could always use one too!)

Book IV
Chapter 1

The LT Difference

No matter whether you plan on using AutoCAD or AutoCAD LT, remember that you will be using the most popular CAD drafting package on the market, and will be able to communicate using the .DWG file format. Using the .DWG file is important because almost all the products that Autodesk develops can either create or read a .DWG file, and many other CAD-drafting packages on the market can at least read a .DWG file, which makes .DWG a popular exchange file format.

Chapter 2: Extending AutoCAD LT

In This Chapter

✓ **Customizing AutoCAD LT**

✓ **Object enabler technology**

✓ **Utilities available from Autodesk**

✓ **Companion products from Autodesk**

✓ **Third-party custom solutions**

his chapter takes a look at extending AutoCAD LT. Extending AutoCAD LT is similar to extending AutoCAD, but the choices you have are more limited. What exactly do we mean by extending AutoCAD LT? *Extending* means adding custom functionality beyond what comes out of the box. Extending could be creating a custom toolbar, or it could be a way to save drawing files to a different release without opening AutoCAD LT at all. In this chapter, we take a look at customizing AutoCAD LT, discover what object enablers are, and find out what utilities are available from Autodesk and third-party developers.

Customizing AutoCAD LT

Although it is true that AutoCAD LT lacks some methods of customization when compared to AutoCAD, it does offer some nice customizations. As previously mentioned in Chapter 1 of this minibook, AutoCAD LT doesn't support programming languages such as AutoLISP/Visual LISP, VB/VBA, VB .NET, C#, or C++ with ObjectARX. Even without the capability to use programming languages to extend AutoCAD LT, you can create script files, custom linetypes and hatch patterns, blocks, menu customization, and some other items.

It's in the script

Script files are ASCII or plain-text files that are created with a text editor like Notepad. Script files contain command and command option sequences and are used to reduce the number of repetitive or redundant steps in your workflow. Script files can be used to do some sort of drawing cleanup after a drawing is created, or it could be used to do initial drawing setup. Here is an example of a script file that creates a layer called Bolt, creates a hexagon with a radius of 1" at the coordinates 5,5, and then performs zoom extents:

```
-layer m bolt c 5


polygon 6 5,5  1
zoom e
```

For more information on creating and using script files, see Chapter 4 of Book IX.

Linetype and hatch patterns

AutoCAD LT comes out of the box with a variety of linetypes and hatch patterns that are used for architectural and mechanical drawings. Although quite a few patterns are available, chances are you might need others that don't come with the program. Linetype and hatch patterns are stored in ASCII or plain-text files and can be created or modified with the use of a text editor like Notepad. The CENTER linetype definition is shown here:

```
*CENTER,Center ____ _ ____ _ ____ _ ____ _ ____ _ ____
A,1.25,-.25,.25,-.25
```

For more information on creating custom linetypes and hatch patterns, see Chapter 4 of Book IX.

Blocks and DesignCenter

Blocks are one of the most powerful features in AutoCAD LT. Blocks allow you to create and define geometry once, and reuse it in as many drawings as you need. The DesignCenter palette (see Figure 2-1) allows you to access and place blocks in a drawing, as well as access other named objects in previously created drawings and add them to your current drawing. For more information on creating and using blocks, see Chapters 1 and 2 of Book VI, and for information on DesignCenter, see Chapter 3 of Book VI.

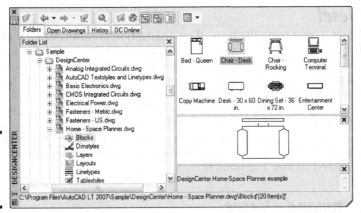

Figure 2-1:
The Design-
Center
palette.

Tool palettes

The Tool Palettes window (see Figure 2-2) allows you to organize reusable content so it can be accessed quickly. Tool palettes can contain blocks and external references, tools that allow you to create tables and hatch patterns, and commands. For more information on creating and using tool palettes, see Chapter 3 of Book VI.

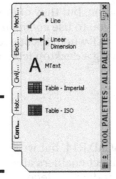

Figure 2-2:
The Tool
Palettes
window.

Changing the user interface with CUI

AutoCAD LT supports the Customize User Interface (CUI) editor, which allows you to create and modify toolbars, pull-down menus, shortcut keys, double-click actions, and other user interface elements. For more information on creating and modifying user interface elements, see Chapter 2 of Book IX.

**Book IV
Chapter 2**

Extending
AutoCAD LT

Diesel

Diesel is an interesting form of customization in AutoCAD LT. It allows you to display values in the status bar area, and it can be used to create conditional statements for commands when customizing the user interface with the CUI editor. AutoCAD LT uses Diesel in several of its own command macros to determine the current state before running a specific command. As an example, when you use the shortcut key CTRL+0, which toggles Clean Screen on and off, AutoCAD LT looks to see what the current state of Clean Screen is, on or off, and executes the correct command to change the current state. For more information on using Diesel with the status bar or menu customization, see Chapter 2 of Book IX.

Command aliases

Command aliases are frequently used to quickly execute a command from the command line. Instead of typing in the command's full name, you can type in a few letters to start it instead. Many of the popular commands have command aliases assigned to them right out of the box, but you can create or modify command aliases in the ACADLT.PGP file using a text editor such as Notepad. For more information on creating and modifying command aliases, see Chapter 1 of Book IX.

Desktop icons

Desktop icons are great for starting an application, but they offer so much more capability than that. AutoCAD LT allows you to use *command line switches* for changing the behavior of AutoCAD LT when it is started from a desktop icon. For more information on modifying a desktop icon with command line switches, see Chapter 1 of Book IX.

Object Enabler Technology

Object enablers have been around since AutoCAD R14, but were first supported in AutoCAD LT with AutoCAD 2000i. Object enablers allow you to view custom objects that are not part of the product by default. Often, you hear about object enablers when you work with drawings that are created in some of the AutoCAD-based vertical products such as Autodesk Building Systems (ABS) or Architectural Desktop (ADT). An object enabler is a series of files that AutoCAD LT loads on demand when it detects the use of custom objects; this allows for the objects to be displayed in their original form and be plotted correctly.

AutoCAD LT ships with a couple of the commonly used object enablers, but some need to be obtained and installed separately from Autodesk or a third-party developer. Autodesk posts its object enablers on its Web site at www.autodesk.com/enablers. If an object in a drawing requires an object enabler and one is not available for the object, it is still displayed in most cases, but as a *proxy graphic*. Proxy graphics are a graphical representation of the original object in a drawing that is displayed in an older release or when the object enabler is not installed. Proxy graphics were once called *zombies* back in AutoCAD R13. (How fitting for a release numbered 13!)

Additional Utilities Available from Autodesk

Even though AutoCAD LT doesn't allow for the loading of custom applications directly into the application, Autodesk provides some utilities that run outside of AutoCAD LT to help with some processes. Some examples are utilities that convert drawings from one drawing file format to another, and others give you the capability to view and mark up .DWF files that you can create with the PLOT or PUBLISH commands.

DWG TrueConvert

DWG TrueConvert allows you to convert an AutoCAD or AutoCAD-based drawing file so that it can be opened with AutoCAD R14 and later. DWG TrueConvert can be used to save drawing files to the latest release or even save them back to an older version (which comes in handy if you need to send drawings to a vendor who might still be using an older release). DWG TrueConvert doesn't require AutoCAD LT to be installed on the computer before it can be used because it is a completely standalone application. For more information on saving drawing files, see Chapter 3 of Book VIII.

Viewers

Autodesk supports two different viewers that allow you to view .DWF and .DWG files. If you are creating .DWF files, you should look them over before sending them out. To do this, AutoCAD LT provides a free .DWF viewer called Autodesk DWF Viewer, which allows you to view both 2D and 3D .DWF files. (Autodesk DWF Viewer doesn't support .DWF markups like its older brother Autodesk Design Review does, but then again, Autodesk Design Review isn't a free application.) Both of these viewers allow you to view the .DWF files that you can create with AutoCAD LT; typically, as an AutoCAD LT user, you won't be purchasing Autodesk Design Review, but someone in your office that reviews drawings might, though. For more information on creating .DWF files and the two different viewers, see Chapter 4 of Book VIII.

**Book IV
Chapter 2**

**Extending
AutoCAD LT**

Companion Products from Autodesk

Autodesk creates a huge portfolio of applications for the design community. Many of these applications are designed to be integrated solutions with other applications it sells. AutoCAD LT is no different, and the drawing files it creates can be used in other applications that Autodesk offers. Autodesk also offers many software packages that help to improve productivity. Most of these require the use of AutoCAD and not AutoCAD LT.

Autodesk Symbols 2000

Autodesk Symbols 2000 is a library of blocks that are ready to use in your drawings. The library contains blocks that are useful whether you do architectural, mechanical, or electrical drawings. More than 12,000 symbols are available for use through DesignCenter after the symbols have been installed. By using a precreated symbol library, you can save yourself a lot of time creating each symbol from scratch. To find out more information about Autodesk Symbols 2000, visit the Autodesk Web site at www.autodesk.com/symbols.

Autodesk VIZ 2007

Autodesk VIZ 2007 is a program that allows you to create complex 3D objects, apply materials to them, add lights, and then generate a rendered image or an animation. You can use the objects that you create in your 2D drawings from AutoCAD LT in Autodesk VIZ to create a 3D model for visualization purposes. If having the ability to create renderings and animations is important for your business, and you don't need the ability to create or use custom add-ons for AutoCAD, you might think about buying AutoCAD LT and Autodesk VIZ instead of a single copy of AutoCAD. Autodesk VIZ allows you to create stunning visual effects and photo-realistic renderings. Autodesk VIZ 2007 retails for about $1,900. To find out more information about Autodesk VIZ 2007, visit the Autodesk Web site at www.autodesk.com/viz.

Third-Party Custom Solutions

Although Autodesk's portfolio of applications is very large, one of the company's keys to success has been its large development community that builds even more applications on or around Autodesk products. Most of the applications that are developed by third-party developers are created to run on top of AutoCAD or one of the AutoCAD-based vertical products and not AutoCAD LT. Some companies create applications that run outside of AutoCAD LT that allow you to view .DWG and .DWF files online through Java-based applications, or to access block libraries. Many of these types of applications can be found using your Web browser and search engine.

Block utilities/libraries

One of the most time-consuming things about starting to use AutoCAD LT is that you have to create your own block libraries. To save time, you can download block libraries or symbols from the Internet. Many are available — it is just a matter of finding them.

Table 2-1 lists some of the different Web sites that contain block utilities or symbol libraries that can be used with AutoCAD LT. Some are free, others aren't.

Table 2-1	URLs to Block Utilities/Libraries
Web Site and URL	*Description*
AutoCAD Block	
`www.autocadblock.com`	Site lists symbol libraries and utilities that contain symbols for architectural, landscaping, and mechanical drawings. Some of the symbol libraries are free, while others start at about $515 up to about $1,125.
CADdepot	
`www.caddepot.com`	Site lists a wide range of 2D and 3D symbols for a variety of industries. Most of the symbols on the site are free for download after registering on the site; some symbols and utilities might need to be purchased, though. The symbols and utilities that are for purchase are available in a wide range of prices.
CADOPOLIS.COM	
`www.cadopolis.com`	Site lists symbols and utilities that contain a wide range of 2D and 3D symbols for a variety of industries. There are symbols and utilities that are available for free and for purchase. The symbols and utilities that are for purchase are available in a wide range of prices.
CADToolsOnline.com	
`www.cadtoolsonline.com`	Site lists symbol libraries for architectural and piping drawings. Some of the symbol libraries are free, while others have a price range that starts at about $60 and up based on the number of users and the type of library.

Viewers

A number of third-party applications allow you to view .DWG and .DWF files all in the same application; many allow you to view image and other file formats as well. Most of the third-party viewers aren't free, but if you shop around, you can find a reasonably-priced version. You can find viewers in all shapes and sizes: from desktop and server applications to even palmtop or PDA applications.

Table 2-2 lists some of the different viewers on the market that are available from third-party developers.

Table 2-2	URLs to Block Utilities/Libraries
Web Site and URL	*Description*
AutoVue	
`www.cimmetry.com`	AutoVue is one of the viewers on the market that supports the widest range of document and file formats. You can view AutoCAD drawings, .DXF, .DWF, .PDF, image files, Office files, and many others. Pricing is available by request only.
Brava! Viewer	
`www.bravaviewer.com`	Brava! comes in different styles and allows you to view Word, Excel, AutoCAD drawings, .PDF, and .DWF files plus many others in a single application. It also supports markups that can be saved in an XML file. Prices tange from about $30 to $350.
CADViewer	
`www.cadviewer.com`	CADViewer is a Java-based CAD viewing tool that supports AutoCAD drawings files, .DXF, .PDF, and some other file types. Pricing is available by request only.
PocketCAD DWFViewer	
`www.pocketcad.com`	PocketCAD DWFViewer is an application that runs on a device running Windows CE 3.0 or higher and allows you to view .DWF files on the go. Prices range from about $30 to $260.

Chapter 3: Mixed Environments

In This Chapter

✔ Using AutoCAD LT and AutoCAD in the same office

✔ Exchanging drawing files between AutoCAD LT and AutoCAD

*I*n this chapter, we take a look at issues that you encounter when you use AutoCAD LT and AutoCAD in the same environment, or when you open drawings created in AutoCAD with AutoCAD LT. Although AutoCAD LT and AutoCAD both create .DWG files and are both developed by Autodesk, that doesn't mean both see the same things in the same way. If you read the first two chapters of this minibook, you already know that AutoCAD LT and AutoCAD have differences. If you exchange drawings between the two programs, you discover even more differences.

Using AutoCAD LT and AutoCAD in the Same Office

AutoCAD and AutoCAD LT are developed with the needs of many different users in mind, which sometimes means that an office ends up using both programs. If you already use AutoCAD in your office and are considering purchasing copies of AutoCAD LT to control costs, you should pay close attention to this section.

Budgeting

When it comes to budgeting, the first thing you may think is, "That's not my job." But it is, when you think about it: You are the one who supports or uses the application. Everyone plays an intricate part in making the best decision for your department or the company that you work for. Three main things to consider during budgeting are hardware, software, and training for AutoCAD and AutoCAD LT. Being on the same release of AutoCAD and AutoCAD LT can make things run more smoothly than if everyone is on different releases, so you will want to keep in mind how much upgrades will cost and even new seats that you may need in the upcoming year.

To help make budgeting for upgrades easier, Autodesk offers an annual subscription program. As you upgrade your software, keep in mind that your hardware needs may change. Having the right hardware is key to ensuring that AutoCAD runs efficiently. Leasing computers on a two- to three-year cycle can help with budgeting and ensure that you are always on pretty current hardware.

The final piece of the puzzle is training, which is covered in the next section.

Training

Properly trained drafters help to ensure the creation of quality drawings. AutoCAD and AutoCAD LT by themselves are not enough to create a good drawing; it also takes time and a disciplined drafter committed to following company CAD standards. Training not only helps to ensure quality drawings, but it can also make sure that drawings are communicated properly to internal departments and external vendors. Training can be done by an external company or an internal member of the drafting department. You should not assume that everyone knows and understands the company's CAD standards, or how to communicate designs with internal or external resources.

Communication

Communication is important in every aspect of the drafting process: from getting the idea of the client on to a drawing to making sure the vendors have the right information that they need to make a proper bid on the project. Properly communicating company CAD standards is vital to making a mixed office run smoothly because a process that works on AutoCAD might not necessarily work on AutoCAD LT. Because AutoCAD LT lacks some of the features of AutoCAD, AutoCAD LT should be used as the basis for any company CAD standards. In the same way, those who use AutoCAD LT need to communicate what is not working for them back to those creating drawings with AutoCAD. A communication breakdown sometimes occurs when AutoCAD users don't realize that a certain function isn't supported by AutoCAD LT and users of AutoCAD LT don't report the problem.

Environment

Although AutoCAD and AutoCAD LT are very similar, they are slightly different in the interfaces and commands that they offer. Just because someone knows AutoCAD fairly well, don't automatically assume that they will be proficient on AutoCAD LT. Some features that they routinely use in AutoCAD might not be available in AutoCAD LT, which can lead to some frustration by the user.

Customization

AutoCAD and AutoCAD LT share some commonalities when it comes to customization. To make sure upgrading and supporting the two programs is as easy as possible, place all custom files in networked locations so they can be shared between the two programs. Files like scripts, custom linetypes, and hatch pattern files are easily shareable between the two programs because they are not product- or release-specific, whereas CUI files, standard linetype, and hatch pattern files are specific to each program. Blocks and drawing templates are program neutral, so you can safely create blocks and drawing templates that can be shared between both programs.

Deployment/installation

Installing and deploying AutoCAD and AutoCAD LT are somewhat different based on the type of licensing you have or plan on purchasing. AutoCAD can be deployed using a license manager to hand out software licenses, which makes it easy to manage the number of licenses in use. AutoCAD LT doesn't support this option. Both AutoCAD and AutoCAD LT support Stand-Alone and Multi-Seat Stand-Alone installation options. AutoCAD LT doesn't support the use of profiles, so you need to manually add or change any support paths that are necessary so that each one can locate company standard files such as templates and blocks.

Making the Trip from AutoCAD to AutoCAD LT

Exchanging drawings that are created in AutoCAD with those who use AutoCAD LT can be a challenge at times, based on which features you are using. If you use AutoCAD and are sharing drawings with someone who uses AutoCAD LT, you don't have to do anything special. However, you might need to show some restraint in using certain features if it is important for those on AutoCAD LT to be able to modify your drawings. In the next sections, we have gathered some of the key areas that you should know about if you are an AutoCAD LT user and work on drawings created in AutoCAD. We also cover issues for those of you who use AutoCAD and send out drawings to vendors that use AutoCAD LT.

2D drafting

AutoCAD allows you to create multilines. *Multilines* are a series of parallel lines that can have different colors and linetypes for each parallel line segments that the object is made up of. They are commonly used for streets showing the main part of the road and any offsets that the municipality or city requires from the road, and they can also be used for floor and basement plans of buildings. When a drawing with multilines is opened in AutoCAD LT, you don't have any control over the object other than changing its standard object properties and being able grip edit the object. If you need to make changes to the lines themselves, you have to explode the multiline object, which could be frustrating to the individual who originally sent you the drawing if you need to send it back to them.

Another issue that you have to deal with is raster images that are referenced externally. Raster images are displayed in the drawing with their previous values, but you can't alter their appearance like you can in AutoCAD. The raster images are listed in the External References palette (see Figure 3-1) and can be unloaded or reloaded as necessary, but can't actually be detached. For more information on multilines, see Chapter 1 of Book II; for more information on raster images, see Chapter 4 of Book VI.

Book IV
Chapter 3

Mixed
Environments

Figure 3-1:
The External
References
palette.

3D modeling

The ability to work with drawings that contain 3D solids and surfaces is very limited in AutoCAD LT. In AutoCAD, you have many different ways to modify 3D solids and surfaces, such as through the use of grips, the SOLIDEDIT command, and others; these are not available in AutoCAD LT. AutoCAD LT doesn't allow you to create and modify 3D solids and surfaces besides using basic modifying commands such as move, copy, and rotate. You are limited to changing only general properties of 3D solids and surfaces, such as their color, what layer they are on, and the other general properties that are available for the object. However, a 3D solid or surface can be exploded into wireframe models that are made up of regions or 2D objects.

If a drawing has a section plane and Live Section is enabled for the section plane, it won't look the same in AutoCAD LT as it does in AutoCAD (see Figure 3-2). The Live Section is not displayed, but the section plane will exist in AutoCAD LT, so if the drawing is saved and reopened in AutoCAD, it looks just like it did before it was opened in AutoCAD LT. For more information on 3D solids and surfaces, see Chapters 4 through 6 of Book V.

Figure 3-2:
Live Section
enabled in
AutoCAD,
and how it
looks in
AutoCAD LT.

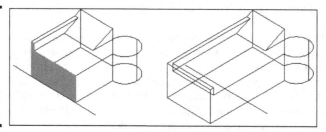

Annotation

AutoCAD and AutoCAD LT have very few differences in annotation. The two main differences that you have to be concerned about when exchanging drawing files between AutoCAD and AutoCAD LT are gradient fills and fields. Both gradient fills and fields are displayed in AutoCAD LT without any problems, but they can't be created or edited. If you use the HATCHEDIT command on a gradient fill, it turns into a solid fill. If you change the boundary associated to the gradient fill, it continues to exist as a gradient fill in the drawing.

Fields are used to associate properties of a drawing file or objects in the drawing with a text, multiline text, or an attribute. Fields can help make sure that information remains in sync when something is changed in the drawing or an object is modified. Based on the type of field, it either displays the last value or it updates based on changes in the drawing file. The expression that the field is created with can't be modified, but you can replace the field with plain text. That isn't recommended. If the field is replaced with plain text, however, it breaks the functionality that the field provided if the drawing is opened back in AutoCAD. For more information on hatch in a drawing, see Chapter 3 of Book III; for more information on Fields, see Chapter 1 of Book III.

Viewing

Cameras are displayed as glyphs in AutoCAD and are accessible from either the drawing window or the View Manager dialog box. AutoCAD LT doesn't display camera glyphs in the drawing, but it does list the camera in the View Manager dialog box. AutoCAD LT also is missing several properties that are available for a named view in AutoCAD. These properties are for things like backgrounds and live sections, which are not supported in AutoCAD LT.

Visualization

Drawings created with AutoCAD can contain a variety of additional objects and settings that really don't do anything in AutoCAD LT: One example is lights. Lights appear in the drawing and can be selected and modified via grips, but their properties can't be altered. Because AutoCAD LT lacks the ability to do renderings, you won't be able to use any material assignments that are on objects or be able to modify the materials that are stored in a drawing file. This can cause problems if a viewport on a layout tab is set up to use the Realistic visual style that AutoCAD offers. For the most part, all visual styles are supported by AutoCAD LT, with the exception of Realistic (see Figure 3-3). The visual styles can't be changed, but if they are assigned to a viewport on a layout tab, they will be displayed correctly.

Book IV
Chapter 3

Mixed
Environments

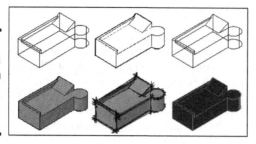

Figure 3-3:
Visual styles
saved with a
drawing are
displayed in
AutoCAD LT.

CAD Standards

The CAD Standards feature of AutoCAD uses Drawing Standards (DWS) files that are associated with the drawing file, but AutoCAD LT doesn't use or know about these files. This isn't a problem with AutoCAD LT because the feature doesn't exist in LT, but it can become a nightmare if you work on a set of drawings and use the eTransmit feature to repackage them up to send them off to someone else. Because AutoCAD LT doesn't know about these types of files, it doesn't know enough to inform you that they might be missing or are needed when sending off a set of drawings.

Collaboration/sharing

Collaboration plays a large role in designing a new building, creating a new machine, or engineering a new bridge. All these things and many more don't just happen by themselves: They require collaboration. AutoCAD allows you to create a Sheet Set of all the drawing files that are related to a project and maintain links from model views to drawing layouts. AutoCAD LT doesn't support the use of Sheet Set (DST) files because it doesn't have the Sheet Set Manager palette, so any values that reference part of the Sheet Set file through fields can't be updated. If a field value needs to be changed, it must be replaced with plain text, which causes problems if it is reopened later in AutoCAD.

Book V

3D Modeling

The 5th Wave   By Rich Tennant

©RICHTENNANT

"I used AutoCAD to create this 3D virtual-reality simulation of my own apartment."

"You need to dust."

Contents at a Glance

Chapter 1: Introducing the Third Dimension

In This Chapter

✔ **Understanding the different types of 3D models**

✔ **Entering coordinates above the *x,y* plane**

This book of the *AutoCAD & AutoCAD LT All-in-One Desk Reference For Dummies* takes you on a journey to a whole new dimension. No, we are not talking about space or time travelling to a different location, but rather giving your drawings some depth. AutoCAD is a very powerful 2D drafting tool, but it also sports a nice set of tools for 3D modeling. AutoCAD LT, unlike its older counterpart, has limited 3D drafting, visualization, and viewing capabilities. Most of what is discussed in the chapters of this book is geared toward AutoCAD only; but there are some things that apply to AutoCAD LT, and we point those out to you.

Most of us think best when drafting in 2D, but this is most likely due to a comfort level that we have from learning 2D drafting first and therefore, making 3D drafting seem somewhat foreign and difficult. In reality, 3D drafting is not all that difficult — much of what was covered in early chapters applies to 3D drafting.

AutoCAD allows you to create three types of 3D models: wireframe, solid, and surface. AutoCAD LT is only capable of creating and editing wireframe models, but you can use it to view solid and surface models.

Throughout the chapters in this book, you see how to select points above the *x,y* coordinate plane, and how to adjust and manipulate the coordinate system to more easily use drafting commands. After you have mastered selecting points in the drawing and working with the coordinate system, we take you on a tour of some of the navigation and viewing commands that AutoCAD and AutoCAD LT offer for viewing 3D models. After you have the basics under your belt, we show you how to use many of the different modeling and editing commands that are used with solids and surfaces. To close out the chapter, we touch on the concepts of creating renderings from AutoCAD.

Understanding the Different Types of 3D Models

AutoCAD and AutoCAD LT allow you to create and view drawings that are created as wireframe, surface, or solid models. These different types of models each have their own strengths and weaknesses.

✦ **Wireframe model:** Wireframe models are created with the use of 2D objects such as lines, arcs, polylines, and circles with no thickness. The 2D objects are drawings in 3D space using full *x, y,* and *z* coordinates, not just *x-* and *y*-coordinate values. Wireframe models are not intended to be used for visualization, as they do not have any surface area that allows them to hide objects beyond the geometry that they represent. Wireframe models provide for a great starting point when creating surface models. Figure 1-1 shows a cube with a hole drawn as a wireframe model and displayed with the HIDE command. You can think of a wireframe model as being much like a wire hanger.

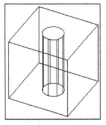

Figure 1-1:
Wireframe model of a cube with a hole in the center.

✦ **Surface model:** Surface models are created from 3D objects called faces. Faces can be made up of three or four points. Unlike wireframe models, surface models can be used for visualization. However, based on the type of visualization such as a hidden line drawing, some clean up might be necessary to hide the edges of faces that form a surface. AutoCAD offers several commands that allow you to create and manipulate surfaces. Figure 1-2 shows a cube with a hole drawn as a surface model and displayed with the HIDE command. The HIDE command shows the surfaces and edges of the surface model. You can think of a surface model as being much like a cardboard shipping box: It is hollow on the inside.

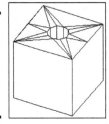

Figure 1-2:
Surface model of a cube with a hole in the center.

✦ **Solid model:** Solid models are created from 3D objects called *solids* ("primitives"). Solid objects are much more flexible than faces and 2D objects for creating wireframe and surface models. Solid objects can be created and modified through a number of commands in AutoCAD. These commands allow you to create primitive objects such as cubes, spheres, and cones, and then combine them to form compound objects. Unlike surfaces, solids do have mass and therefore are not hollow, which allows you to capture information about them. Solids are much easier to work with than surfaces. Figure 1-3 shows a cube with a hole drawn as a solid model and displayed with the HIDE command. The HIDE command shows the surfaces and edges of the solid model. You can think of a solid model as being much like a block of solid wood: It is not hollow on the inside unless you core it out.

Figure 1-3:
Solid model
of a cube
with a hole
in the
center.

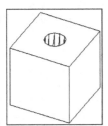

Entering Coordinates above the x,y Plane

Everything you have done up to this point has been with *x*- and *y*- coordinate values. This is all about to change as you step in a whole new direction with the *z* coordinate. Most of AutoCAD's commands are not true 2D commands; this means that commands like a PLINE for creating a Polyline can only be drawn at a single *z* height (or elevation). Out of what are known as the traditional 2D commands, only the LINE command allows you to specify two different *z* heights for the start and end points for the object that is being created with the command.

Orthographical (Ortho) mode has been improved for use with 3D drafting in AutoCAD 2007, and not AutoCAD LT 2007. You are now able to drag the crosshairs up or down after you specify the first point when orthomode is enabled, to specify the next point in the *z* direction. A tooltip is displayed to tell you which direction from the first point you are moving in.

Manually inputting coordinates

Chapter 6 of Book I explains how to input relative and absolute coordinates for 2D drafting. Both of these coordinate formats are great for both 2D and 3D drafting. The only difference that you will find when doing 3D drafting is the need to enter a z coordinate value. Along with those coordinate input formats, the relative polar coordinate input is expanded to include two additional formats called cylindrical and spherical designed for 3D drafting. Of course, you can use object snaps, point filters, and object snap tracking when creating and modifying 3D objects.

You can input coordinate values through the use of Direct Distance Entry and the using of Dynamic Input. Both of these are covered in Chapters 2 and 6 of Book I.

Absolute x, y, and z coordinates

Working with absolute coordinates in 3D drafting is just like you would input them for 2D drafting, except you add in the z coordinate. You supply the coordinate input in the format *x,y,z*. An example of using the LINE command to drawing a line in 3D space using absolute coordinate entry is shown below.

```
Command: line
Specify first point: 0,0,0
Specify next point or [Undo]: 2,3,7.25
```

Relative x, y, and z coordinates

Working with relative coordinates in 3D drafting is just like when inputting them for 2D drafting, except you add in the z coordinate. You supply the coordinate input in the format of *@x,y,z*. An example of using the LINE command to drawing a line in 3D space using relative coordinate entry is shown below.

```
Command: line
Specify first point: 2.125,7,-3
Specify next point or [Undo]: @0.5,0.125,7
```

Cylindrical coordinates

Cylindrical coordinates is the first of two coordinate entry formats based on relative polar coordinate entry for 3D drafting. You supply the coordinate input in the format of *@XYdistance<angle,Z*. An example of using the LINE command to draw a line in 3D space using cylindrical coordinate entry is shown below. Figure 1-4 shows the results in AutoCAD.

```
Command: line
Specify first point: 0,0,0
Specify next point or [Undo]: @5<45,2
```

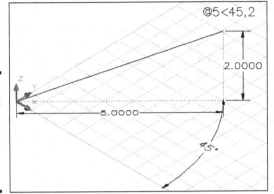

Figure 1-4:
Line created
in 3D space
using
cylindrical
coordinate
input.

Cylindrical coordinate input doesn't work very well when Dynamic Input is enabled. We recommend turning it off by clicking the DYN button on the status bar area or pressing F12 when wanting to use cylindrical coordinate input.

Spherical coordinates

Spherical coordinates is the second of the two coordinate entry formats that is based on relative polar coordinate entry for 3D drafting. You supply the coordinate input in the format of *@XYdistance<angle<anglefromXY*. An example of using the LINE command to draw a line in 3D space using spherical coordinate entry is shown below. Figure 1-5 shows the results in AutoCAD.

```
Command: line
Specify first point: 0,0,0
Specify next point or [Undo]: @5<30<30
```

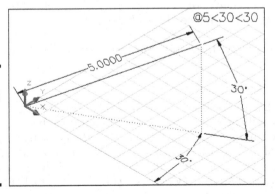

Figure 1-5:
Line created
in 3D space
using
spherical
coordinate
input.

Point filters

Point filters can be used for constructing coordinate values based on existing points on an object whether it is in 2D or 3D space. There are three point filters that are specific to 3D drafting. These point filters are *xy, xz,* and *zy.* Point filters can be typed in at the command line or dynamic input tooltip, selected from the Object Snap shortcut menu by pressing and holding down the Shift key while right-clicking, or right-clicking and choosing the Snap Overrides. Here is an example of using the LINE command to draw a line in 3D space using the *xy* point filter entry:

```
Command: line
Specify first point: specify a point or a coordinate value
Specify next point or [Undo]: type .xy and press enter
of specify a point or a coordinate value
(need Z): specify a point or a Z height value
```

Object snaps

Object snaps are a great way to ensure that you have the precise point in the drawing that you want. AutoCAD has a toggle that controls whether the *z* height of the point you select using an object snap or the current elevation value is used. (We cover changing the current elevation later in this chapter.) To switch between these two, follow these steps:

1. **Choose Tools⇨Options.**

   The Options dialog box appears.

2. **In the Options dialog box, click the Drafting tab.**

3. **Click the Replace Z Value with Current Elevation check box.**

   When you check the current elevation check box, AutoCAD substitutes the *z* height that was obtained with the object snap for the current elevation. When the check box is unchecked, the *z* height of the coordinate that is specified with the use of the object snap is used.

AutoCAD LT does not have the Replace Z Value with Current Elevation option.

Object snap tracking

Object snap tracking can be used above the current *x,y* plane. Object snap tracking has been enhanced in AutoCAD 2007 to improve the functionality of being able to track in the *z* direction. When using object snap tracking in the *z* direction, AutoCAD provides feedback in the form of tooltips when you are moving in the positive or negative *z* direction. Figure 1-6 shows an example of the tooltip displayed in AutoCAD when using object snap tracking in 3D space.

AutoCAD LT does support the use of object snap tracking in 3D space, but it doesn't provide the same level of feedback that AutoCAD does.

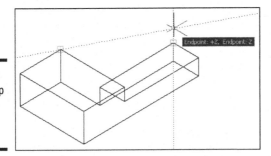

Figure 1-6:
Object snap
tracking in
the Z
direction.

Elevation . . . going up

Specifying a *z* height when entering coordinates is not the only way to draw objects above the *x,y* plane; you can specify a default *z* height for all new objects as they are created. If you are drawing a bunch of objects that need a specific *z* height, this can be a very efficient way to ensure they are placed at the correct height. You use the ELEV command to specify a new *z* height for new objects that are created. The value specified is used only if you don't use object snaps; if you use object snaps, the *z* height of the object snap is used by default. See the previous section "Object snaps" for more information.

To set a new elevation value, type **ELEV** at the command line or the dynamic input tooltip and then enter a new elevation value at the Specify new default elevation <0.0000>: command prompt. Then, at the Specify new default thickness <0.0000>: command prompt, press Enter.

Instead of changing the current elevation, you can use a custom UCS (user coordinate system) to create objects at a specific elevation. We cover using the user coordinate system and the world coordinate system in the next chapter.

Chapter 2: Using the 3D Environment

In This Chapter

✔ Setting up AutoCAD for 3D

✔ Understanding what the UCS icon is telling you

✔ Changing the coordinate system for 3D drawing

The preceding chapter covers the three types of 3D models you can create with AutoCAD and AutoCAD LT, as well as how to enter coordinates above the *xy* plane in the *z* direction. This chapter helps you get a grasp of the 3D environment in AutoCAD and AutoCAD LT. We take a look at some of the key settings and features that help you work efficiently with 3D models. Some of these settings are for getting the most out of your computer investment by enabling hardware acceleration if it is available, and some control the appearance of the grid, background color, and more in the drawing window.

One of the keys to becoming an efficient drafter with AutoCAD is understanding what the UCS icon is indicating, and in 3D drafting that is no different. The UCS icon provides you with information on which way is up or down in your model, and the direction of the *x*, *y*, and *z* axes. Not only can you get information from the UCS icon about the different directions that the axes are going in, but you can modify the coordinate system to draw 2D objects on a different plane. 2D objects are always drawn on the *xy* plane, so by changing the direction or elevation of the plane you can draw 2D objects on a new plane.

Setting Up AutoCAD for 3D

AutoCAD and AutoCAD LT offer various display, hardware, and drafting options that all play different roles when working with 3D. Properly configuring and understanding all these options can make things go more smoothly. Because AutoCAD LT doesn't support the creation of surface and solid models, many of these options are not available. We point out the differences as we go along.

Orienting yourself in the drawing window

The drawing window is where you create, modify, and view your 3D models. Based on how you are viewing your model, the background color, grid display, and the crosshairs change in the drawing window. You can customize the display settings for the drawing window through the Drawing Window Colors dialog box (see Figure 2-1). The Drawing Window Colors dialog box can be displayed by clicking the Colors button under the Window Elements section on the Display tab of the Options dialog box.

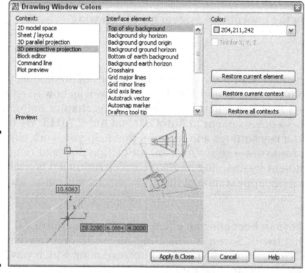

Figure 2-1: Customizing the appearance of the drawing window for 3D.

In AutoCAD, you have the contexts 3D parallel projection and 3D perspective projection that are related to 3D drafting. In AutoCAD LT, you have only one context called hidden that is related to 3D drafting.

The following procedure explains how to adjust the colors of the Crosshairs interface element under the 2D model space content:

1. **Choose Tools➪Options.**

The Options dialog box is displayed.

2. **In the Options dialog box, click the Display tab.**

The Display tab is set to current.

3. On the Display tab under the Window Elements section, click Colors.

The Drawing Window Colors dialog box is displayed.

4. From the Context list, select 2D Model Space.

The Preview at the bottom of the dialog box updates to show the current colors that the interface elements are set to, and which interface elements are available.

5. From the Interface element list, select Crosshairs.

The Color drop-down list displays the current color, and the Tint for X, Y, Z check box becomes enabled. The Tint for X, Y, Z option is used to give the crosshairs the colors of red, green, and blue to represent the different axes. The X axis is always represented by the color red, Y by green, and Z by blue. The tinting is by default enabled for the different 3D contexts.

6. Click Apply & Close.

The changes are saved and the Drawing Window Colors dialog box is closed.

7. Click OK.

The changes are saved and the Options dialog box is closed.

The Drawing Window Colors dialog box is an updated version of the Color Options dialog box.

Customizing crosshairs and dynamic input

You can customize the display of the crosshairs and dynamic input for working in 3D in AutoCAD only. These changes go beyond being able to change the size of the crosshairs or even color tinting of the different axes for the crosshairs. These options allow you to enable the display of labels on the crosshairs so you know which direction X, Y, and Z are without having to have the UCS icon displayed. You can also control whether the Z direction is indicated on the crosshairs as well. If you use Dynamic Input and manually enter points, you can control the display of a field for entering z-coordinate values. You can change these options under the 3D Crosshairs and Dynamic Input sections of the 3D Modeling tab in the Options dialog box.

The 3D Modeling tab of the Options dialog box is new and has a variety of options that affect the display of the crosshairs, dynamic input, UCS icon, creation and viewing of 3D objects, and the 3D navigation tools. The 3D Modeling tab is not available in AutoCAD LT.

Using workspaces to switch between 2D and 3D drafting

AutoCAD and AutoCAD LT come with a feature called *Workspaces.* Workspaces were introduced in AutoCAD 2006 and can play a role in efficiently switching between 2D and 3D drafting. You can create a workspace that displays the necessary tools that you need for a particular set of tasks. We talk about creating workspaces in Chapter 2 of Book IX.

A new workspace called 3D Modeling comes with AutoCAD 2007 but doesn't come with AutoCAD LT 2007. This workspace displays the Dashboard palette; Tool Palettes window; and the Workspaces, Standard, and Layers toolbars. The layout tabs at the bottom of the drawing window are hidden.

Introducing toolbars and palettes for 3D

AutoCAD comes with a number of toolbars and palettes that contain 3D-related tools for creating, editing, and navigating your drawings.

✦ The **Modeling toolbar** contains tools for creating 3D solid objects, and some of the more common editing tools.

✦ The **Solid Editing toolbar** contains tools that are used for editing individual faces and edges of a 3D solid.

✦ The **Dashboard palette,** shown in Figure 2-2, enables you to access many of the different commands for creating, editing, navigating, and visualizing 3D models.

Figure 2-2: Dashboard allows for quick access to a variety of different 3D-related tools.

AutoCAD provides other toolbars and palettes that are useful for working with various different aspects of 3D in AutoCAD. Many of these palettes and toolbars are discussed in later chapters.

The Dashboard palette is new in AutoCAD 2007 and allows you to access both 2D and 3D drafting commands, along with other 3D features. Dashboard is not part of AutoCAD LT 2007.

Accelerating your hardware

AutoCAD can use either software or hardware acceleration to display a drawing to the screen. AutoCAD LT, however, does not support hardware acceleration. By default, AutoCAD uses hardware acceleration (because some graphics cards are not designed for CAD applications).

When you first start AutoCAD, the program evaluates your graphics card and determines whether it can use hardware acceleration. If it can, it informs you that your hardware is capable of this. At times your graphics card might not support all features using hardware acceleration, so AutoCAD tweaks its display settings a little to help optimize regenerations and overall display quality of the drawing window. This process is called *adaptive degradation*.

The Adaptive Degradation and Performance Tuning dialog box (see Figure 2-3) allows you to change the display options and toggle the use of hardware acceleration. To open the Adaptive Degradation and Performance Tuning dialog box, open the Options dialog box and click the Performance Settings under the 3D Performance section of the System tab. Click Manual Tune to toggle the use of hardware acceleration and options that are related to using hardware acceleration, such as Full Shadow and Smooth Line display.

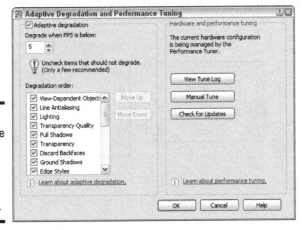

Figure 2-3: Performance tuning AutoCAD to get it to get rid of that extra regen.

Understanding What the UCS Icon Is Telling You

The UCS icon is similar to a tour guide and helps you to stay on track as to which path you should be following. The UCS icon doesn't tell you to stay with the tour and to keep up, but it does help you find the positive *x*, *y*, and *z* axes. It is important to know which direction these axes are going in for creating objects. It can get very frustrating when it doesn't look like your line is being created when it actually is and you just don't see it.

Orientating yourself with the UCS icon

The UCS icon can be strange at times depending on how you are viewing the drawing and whether you are in model or paper space. AutoCAD and AutoCAD LT display a different UCS icon for several situations; understanding these situations is necessary in order to help maximize the use of the user coordinate system, which we talk about later in this chapter. The UCS icon lets you know how the coordinates you type at the command line or dynamic input tooltip are affected. The appearance of the UCS icon is affected by the current visual style or whether the current view is displayed as hidden or shaded. We talk about visual styles, hide, and shade in Chapter 3 of this book.

Model space and 2D Wireframe visual style

When you are looking straight on at the *xy* plane, the UCS icon shows the positive direction for the *x* and *y* axes. If the current view of the *xy* plane is from an angle like one of the preset isometric views, you will see the *x*, *y*, and *z* axes called out. Figure 2-4 shows the UCS icon as it would appear when looking at the *xy* plane straight on and from an angle. If you don't see a box at the intersection of the *x* and *y* indicators, this informs you that you are not looking at the drawing from the world coordinate system.

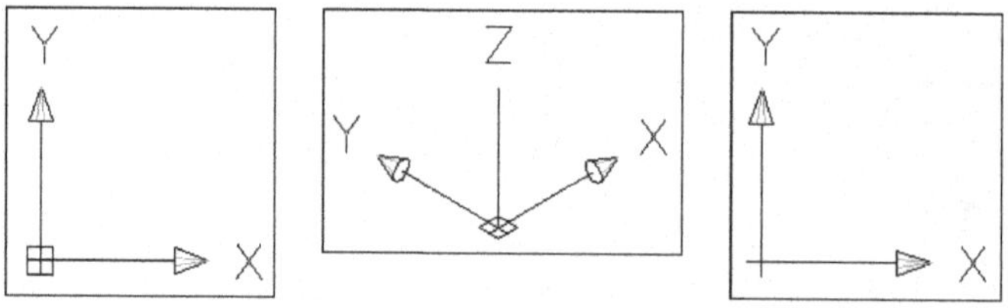

Figure 2-4:
UCS icon
displayed
in model
space
with 2D
Wireframe
visual style.

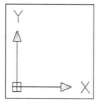 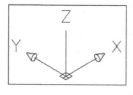

Model space and a 3D visual style

When you are looking straight on at the *xy* plane, the UCS icon shows the positive direction for the *x* and *y* axes, and the *z* direction coming toward or moving away from you. If the current view of the *xy* plane is from an angle like one of the preset isometric views, you will see the *x, y,* and *z* axes called out. Figure 2-5 shows the UCS icon as it would appear when looking at the *xy* plane straight on and from an angle.

Figure 2-5:
UCS icon displayed in model space with one of the 3D visual styles.

Paper space layout

Paper space layouts display a UCS icon that is a triangle and indicates the directions of the positive *x* and *y* axes only (see Figure 2-6). You cannot change the display angle of a paper space layout because the paper space layout is used to represent a virtual piece of paper.

Figure 2-6:
UCS icon displayed on a paper space layout.

Controlling the display of the UCS icon

The UCS icon by default has a 3D appearance to it and is displayed as a specific size, color, and location. You can tailor the display of the UCS icon with the UCS Icon dialog box (see Figure 2-7) and the 3D Modeling tab of the Options dialog box. To display the UCS Icon dialog box, choose View⇨ Display⇨UCS Icon⇨Properties.

Figure 2-7:
Changing the appearance of the UCS icon with the UCS Icon dialog box.

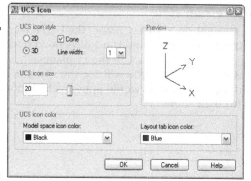

You can control where and if the UCS icon is displayed on-screen by using the following options.

✦ **Hide/Show the UCS icon:** You can toggle the display of the UCS icon by choosing View⇨Display⇨UCS Icon⇨On.

✦ **Display the UCS icon at the origin:** You can toggle the display of the UCS icon at the origin of the drawing by choosing View⇨Display⇨UCS Icon⇨Origin. If the UCS can't be displayed at the origin, AutoCAD places it in the lower-left corner of the drawing window.

✦ **Display the UCS icon in 2D or 3D visual styles:** You can control whether the UCS icon is displayed when the model is being viewed with a 2D or 3D visual style. This option is only available in AutoCAD, and not AutoCAD LT. To change the display of the UCS icon, display the Options dialog box, select the 3D Modeling tab, and uncheck the options as desired under the Display UCS Icon section.

Using the Coordinate System for 3D Drawing

The coordinate system in AutoCAD is very powerful and can be mysterious at times. When you are drawing in 2D, you don't worry too much about altering the coordinate system. When working in 3D, it becomes very important to know how to properly work with the coordinate system. By altering the coordinate system, you can draw objects going in different directions or on the sides of other objects. For example, you can draw an object on the xy plane and then move/rotate the object into place, but that would take some effort. By relocating the origin and direction of the coordinate system, you are able to draw the object as if you were on the xy plane.

Understanding the coordinate system

AutoCAD has two different coordinate systems called *world* and *user*. Both of these coordinate systems are used when creating new objects in a drawing.

World coordinate system (WCS)

The world coordinate system (or WCS) is a fixed coordinate system that all objects in the drawing are stored and defined to. By default in 2D views, the *x* axis runs horizontal (left and right) and the *y* axis runs vertical (up and down). Positive *x* is to the right and positive *y* is up. Unlike the user coordinate system, the WCS can't be moved or redefined.

User coordinate system (UCS)

The user coordinate system (or UCS) is a movable coordinate system and is much more flexible for creating and editing objects. The UCS affects coordinate entry, drafting aids (object snap tracking, dynamic input, grid, and others), and the orientation of dimensions and text.

Right-hand rule for left-brained people

When you first look at the coordinate system in 3D, you may feel a little overwhelmed. After all, the UCS can be moved and rotated. So at times you may not know which way you are heading in the *z* direction or which way is the positive rotation around an axis. AutoCAD provides a method called the *right-hand rule* that you can apply when you need to figure out the direction of positive *z* and the positive rotation.

To identify the positive *z* axis with the right-hand rule, you place the back side of your right hand towards the monitor so that your palm is facing you. Take your thumb and point it in the direction of the positive *x* axis, then take your index finger and extend it out so it forms a right angle with your thumb. Make sure your index finger points in the direction of the positive *y* axis. Bend your middle finger towards you so it makes a right angle with your index finger. Your middle finger now indicates the positive direction of the *z* axis.

To identify the direction of positive rotation around an axis in 3D space, point your thumb on your right-hand in the positive direction of the axis and then curl your fingers. The direction that your fingers curl in indicates the positive direction of rotation around that axis.

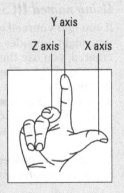

Y axis

Z axis   X axis

Adjusting the UCS

AutoCAD offers a variety of different ways to create and save custom UCSs for future use. When you want to create a new UCS, you have some options as to how you want to create it, such as by selecting three points in the drawing to indicate origin, positive *x*, and positive *y*, or selecting an object. After you specify a new UCS, you can decide to save it for future use by giving it a name.

Commanding the UCS

The user coordinate system can be changed through the use of the UCS command. To make it easy to create a new UCS, AutoCAD offers a number of options that can be selected from the Tools menu under the New UCS submenu. The New UCS submenu offers a total of 11 possible selections, but AutoCAD provides a few that are not available from the submenu and are only available at the command line. We have listed some of the most commonly used options of the UCS command to get you started. After the option is specified, follow the command prompts at the command line or the dynamic input tooltip. For more information on using the UCS options, refer to AutoCAD's online Help system.

+ **World:** Changes the UCS to match the world coordinate system.

+ **Face:** Allows you to align the UCS to the face of a 3D solid.

+ **View:** Creates a new UCS by rotating the *xy* plane to being perpendicular to your current viewing direction.

+ **3 Point:** Allows you to specify a new origin for the UCS and designate the positive direction for both the *x* and *y* axes.

Using named UCSs

If you find yourself going back to a particular UCS to create or edit objects, you might consider saving the UCS for future use. To save a UCS that you created, you use the UCSMAN command which displays the UCS dialog box (see Figure 2-8). The UCS dialog box lets you save and restore named UCSs on the Named UCSs tab, customize the distance between the *xy* plane of the six orthographic coordinate systems (top, bottom, front, back, left, and right) on the Orthographic UCSs tab, and control some of the save and display settings for UCSs on the Settings tab.

The following procedure uses the Tools menu to start the UCSMAN command and save a custom UCS.

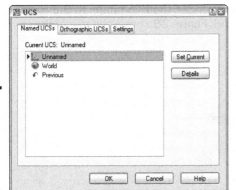

Figure 2-8:
Saving a
custom UCS
with the
UCS dialog
box.

1. **Choose Tools⊅Named UCS.**

The UCS dialog box is displayed.

2. **In the UCS dialog box, select Unnamed in the UCSs list.**

The Unnamed UCS is the current UCS in the drawing and is listed at the
very top of the list.

3. **Right-click Unnamed and select Rename from the shortcut menu.**

An in-place editor is displayed that allows you to change the UCSs name.

4. **Type a new name for the UCS and press Enter.**

The Unnamed UCS is renamed with the name entered.

5. **Click OK.**

The UCS dialog box closes and the UCS is saved in the drawing. To use a
saved UCS, open the UCS dialog box and then select the saved UCS from
the list and click Set Current.

Using the Dynamic UCS feature

Setting up a UCS takes a bit of effort and can be distracting if you need to
create one just to draw an object on the side of a 3D object. AutoCAD allows
you to create a UCS on the fly using the Dynamic UCS feature. This feature
can save you a great deal of time and is easy to toggle on and off. To toggle
Dynamic UCS on or off, click the DUCS button on the status bar area. For
example, when Dynamic UCS is turned on, you can start the CYLINDER command and position the crosshairs over one of the faces of a box to draw a
hole in the box. The face that is being tracked is highlighted and when you

click to start drawing the cylinder, the UCS jumps to the face until you are finished with the command. Figure 2-9 shows the use of the Dynamic UCS in action.

Figure 2-9: Dynamic UCS makes creating objects directly on solids easy.

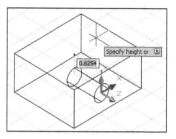

Dynamic UCS is a new feature in AutoCAD 2007. This feature is not available in AutoCAD LT 2007.

Chapter 3: Viewing in 3D

In This Chapter

✔ **Establishing a different view of a 3D model**

✔ **Orbiting around a 3D model**

✔ **Navigating a 3D model**

✔ **Adding a touch of visual style to a 3D model**

*I*n this chapter, we get immersed in 3D space as we explain how to navigate and view 3D models. AutoCAD and AutoCAD LT offer a number of ways to view 3D models in drawing files. These include basic preset views as well as much more sophisticated viewing tools, such as orbit and walk. After you have the model displayed the way you want, you can apply a visual style or a shade mode to make the objects appear shaded or hidden on-screen.

Establishing a Different Point of View

AutoCAD offers a number of ways to view a 3D model, but AutoCAD LT offers only a few. AutoCAD LT offers a very basic set of navigation tools for viewing a 3D model; we cover all of them in this section.

Using preset views

Both AutoCAD and AutoCAD LT offer some standard preset views that can help you view different sides of a 3D model quickly. The presets include being able to view the 3D model from the top, left, and southeast. If the presets don't offer what you need, you can use the Viewpoint Presets dialog box to get a little more control over the viewpoint.

Specifying a standard view preset

AutoCAD and AutoCAD LT have a total of 10 preset views. Six of these preset views are parallel to the current UCS — Top, Bottom, Left, Right, Front, and Back — and four of them are isometric views — SW Isometric, SE Isometric, NE Isometric, and SW Isometric. The presets are available from the 3D Views submenu under the View menu on the menu bar, from the View Manager dialog box, or from the View toolbar. Select one of the presets to start the VIEW command and use the option that matches the selected preset.

Changing with the Viewpoint Presets dialog box

The Viewpoint Presets dialog box (see Figure 3-1) gives you more control over the viewing angle than the preset views do. To display the Viewpoint Presets dialog box, choose View⇨3D Views⇨Viewpoint Presets. To change the angle, select either the Absolute to WCS or Relative to UCS option to set the viewing angle. Specify the angle from the x axis by entering a value in the From: X Axis text box or selecting the angle on the dial itself. After you set the x axis, specify the angle from the xy plane by entering a value in the From: XY Plane text box or from the dial on the right. Values above 0 allow you to look down on the model; values below 0 allow you to look up at the model as if you were below ground.

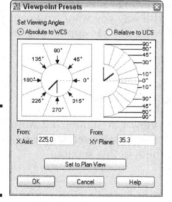

Figure 3-1:
The
Viewpoint
Presets
dialog box.

Finding your way with the compass and tripod

The preset views and the Viewpoint Presets dialog box are nice, but they do not provide a visual way to set a view. The VPOINT command allows you to see the current UCS via an axis tripod and a circular display known as the *compass* in the upper-right corner of the drawing window (see Figure 3-2). This allows you to specify the angle from the x axis and xy plane like the Viewport Presets dialog box does but is a little more visual and interactive. Although it is visually done on-screen rather than using a dialog box, it can still be a bit confusing. To select an angle above 0, keep the small crosshairs in the inner circle, which represents a positive z axis (the outer circle represents a negative z axis). Where the inner and outer circles meet is 0, or no change in the z axis direction.

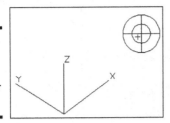

Figure 3-2:
Using the
tripod and
compass for
navigation.

Cameras

Cameras are similar to named views, with the exception that they have a graphical representation in a scene and can be updated via the Properties palette. Along with using the Properties palette, you can also edit a camera through the View Manager dialog box. The graphical representation is called a *glyph*, which allows you to manipulate the view of the camera with grips.

Cameras have been improved with AutoCAD 2007: They are now displayed and selectable in a drawing.

AutoCAD LT does not support the creation or use of cameras.

Creating a camera

To create a camera, you use the CAMERA command. To start the CAMERA command, select Create Camera from the View menu on the menu bar or on the View toolbar. As you create the camera, you specify a location for the camera and a target location. After the camera is created, you can change its name, location, height, target, lens, clipping, or switch to the cameras view. After the camera is created, the glyph is displayed in the drawing.

Adjusting the view of a camera

To adjust a camera, you select its glyph in the drawing and then adjust it using the grips that are displayed. Using grips, you can adjust the distance between the camera and target, along with the lens length of the camera. When a camera is selected, you should see the Camera Preview dialog box (see Figure 3-3) displayed on-screen, which lets you see what the camera is seeing without switching to the camera's view. The Camera Preview dialog box gives you an idea of what is being seen through the camera. If the Camera Preview dialog box isn't displayed when you select a camera in the drawing, right-click and select View Camera Preview on the shortcut menu.

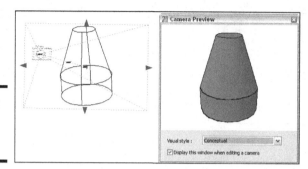

Figure 3-3:
Editing a
camera in
the scene.

Perspective versus parallel

AutoCAD and AutoCAD LT can display a 3D model in parallel view, which makes a 3D model appear flat and without depth, or in a perspective view, which makes a 3D model seem to disappear into the distance. Figure 3-4 shows a rectangle displayed in both parallel and perspective view. When you look at objects in real life, you see things in a perspective view. To enable perspective view in a drawing, type **PERSPECTIVE** at the command line or the dynamic ToolTip and enter a new value of 1. Perspective view is only available when a visual style or shade mode other than 2D wireframe is active. We talk about visual styles and shade mode later in this chapter.

Figure 3-4:
A rectangle
in both
parallel and
perspective
view.

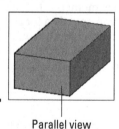
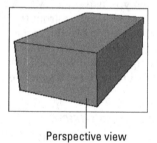

Parallel view   Perspective view

Orbiting around a 3D Model

AutoCAD comes with many different commands that allow you to zoom in and around a 3D model. Being able to rotate the view around a 3D model allows you to quickly see things from a different angle and make the necessary edits. The ability to rotate the view around the 3D model is called *orbiting,* like what planets do around the sun. Orbiting is done along a circular path; the rotation point is different based on the orbit command you choose to use. To access the 3D orbit commands, from the menu bar, choose View↪ Orbit and then one of the orbit commands.

AutoCAD LT does not support the 3D orbit commands.

Table 3-1 lists the three different 3D orbit commands available in AutoCAD.

Table 3-1		3D Orbit Commands
Icon	*Command*	*Description*
	3DORBIT	Constrained Orbit sets the target to a stationary point at the center of the objects that you are viewing when the 3DORBIT command is started. Dragging horizontally moves the camera along the current *xy* plane, and dragging vertically moves the camera along the *z* axis.
	3DFORBIT	Free Orbit sets the target of the view to the center of the arcball that is displayed. The arcball (see Figure 3-5) controls how the view is rotated around its center rather than the center of the objects you are viewing. Dragging inside the arcball allows you to freely rotate the model, whereas dragging on the outside of the arcball rolls the model perpendicular to the screen. Clicking and dragging in the left or right quadrants (smaller circles) causes the model to rotate around the vertical axis of the arcball, and clicking and dragging in the top or bottom quadrants (smaller circles) causes the model to rotate around the horizontal axis of the arcball.
	3DCORBIT	Continuous Orbit is similar to Constrained Orbit in the way it works, except you can send the model into a continuous spin on-screen that lasts until you stop it.

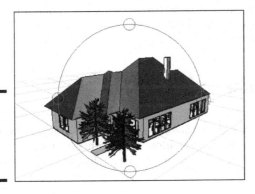

Figure 3-5: The Free Orbit command is active.

While one of the 3D orbit commands (or any of the other 3D navigation commands that we mention in the next section) is running, you can right-click and access the Navigation Modes menu (see Figure 3-6). This menu allows you to switch between Parallel and Perspective view, between different visual styles, or even to other navigation commands without having to exit one command in order to start another. You can also switch to a different navigation command by pressing the number next to it under the Other Navigation Modes submenu.

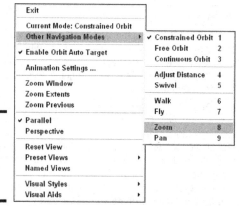

Figure 3-6:
The
Navigation
Modes
menu.

If you hold down the Shift key first and then press and hold down the middle mouse button, you can temporarily switch to 3DORBIT. Pressing and holding the middle mouse button and then pressing the Shift key temporarily places you in orthogonal pan mode.

If the drawing contains a lot of objects, you can select a small set of the objects before starting one of the 3D orbit commands. This can help with performance in larger drawings because only the selected objects appear while the 3D orbit command is in use.

Navigating a 3D Model

AutoCAD offers other 3D navigation commands besides just the 3D orbit commands. Both zoom and pan are offered in 3D versions, but you can still use other zoom options such as window and extents. However, a few additional commands are used specifically for 3D navigation. These commands make it feel like you are right in your drawing. The 3D navigation commands can be accessed from the View menu on the menu bar, under the submenus Camera⇨Walk and Fly, or on the 3D Navigation toolbar.

AutoCAD LT does not support the 3D navigation commands listed below.

AutoCAD 2007 offers two new 3D navigation commands called 3DWALK and 3DFLY.

Table 3-2 lists the other 3D navigation commands that are available in AutoCAD.

Table 3-2		3D Navigation Commands
Icon	Command	Description
	3DPAN	Allows you to interactively drag the view vertically, horizontally, and diagonally.
	3DZOOM	Allows you to move the camera closer to or farther away from the target, making objects appear closer or farther away.
	3DDISTANCE	Allows you to pull or push yourself in and out of the drawing by making objects come closer or go farther away from you.
	3DSWIVEL	Allows you to change the target of the view you are currently looking at in the drawing. Makes it feel like you are turning your head around in the drawing to view other objects while standing in a single spot.
	3DFLY	Allows you to interactively change the view of the drawing as you "fly" through it. You leave the *xy* plane to give you the feel that you are above the drawing.
	3DWALK	Allows you to interactively change the view of the drawing as you "walk" through it. You remain on the *xy* plane to give you the feel that you are walking through the drawing.

When using one of the 3D navigation commands, you can right-click and choose a different navigation mode from the shortcut menu.

Many of the 3D navigation commands and settings can be accessed directly from the 3D Navigation control panel (see Figure 3-7) of the Dashboard palette. Some of the settings are hidden at first; if you position the cursor over the control panel, an icon with double down arrows appears. Click the double down arrows icon to expand the control panel.

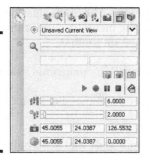

Figure 3-7:
The 3D
Navigation
control
panel of the
Dashboard
palette.

Adding Some Color and Style to a 3D Model

Looking at drawings that are displayed in 2D and 3D wireframe can make it rather difficult to visualize what is actually in there. AutoCAD and AutoCAD LT offer a few options to help you see what all of those lines actually mean. AutoCAD uses *visual styles* to display geometry so you only see the objects that are in front of others. AutoCAD LT doesn't support visual styles but instead has a feature called *shade modes*. Shade modes were available in previous releases of AutoCAD to hide faces that are not those closest to the current viewpoint.

Visual styles in AutoCAD

Visual styles allow you to see your drawing in a hidden, shaded, or semi-rendered state. Visual styles are available from the Visual Styles Manager palette or the Visual Style control panel on the Dashboard palette. To display the Visual Style Manager palette (see Figure 3-8) from the menu bar, choose Tools➪Palettes➪Visual Styles. Double-click one of the available visual styles to set it current. You can also make a custom visual style and make changes to it by changing its properties at the bottom of the palette. You can set a visual style current when drawing to give you a sense of what lines you might want to snap to.

Visual styles are new in AutoCAD 2007, and they make it much easier to get different looks to a 3D model for presentation purposes.

The Visual Style control panel (see Figure 3-9) on the Dashboard palette contains a variety of controls that allow you to change to a different visual style, enable *x*-ray mode to see through faces, control how faces and edges are displayed, and even the display of shadows in a scene.

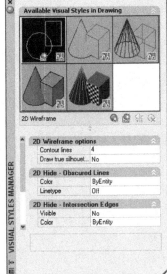

Figure 3-8:
Visual styles give a 3D model personality.

Figure 3-9:
The Visual Styles control panel of the Dashboard palette.

Shademode in AutoCAD LT

AutoCAD LT doesn't support the use of visual styles, but you can do a few things to get a similar effect when viewing a 3D model. AutoCAD LT offers a command called SHADEMODE, which allows you to view a model in 2D wireframe or hidden line view. SHADEMODE is similar to a visual style in most ways, with the exception that it cannot customize its appearance. AutoCAD LT also offers the SHADE command, which allows you to shade a 3D model based on the colors that the objects are assigned, and you can use the HIDE command to display a 3D model in a hidden line view. The SHADE and HIDE commands are available from the View menu on the menu bar. **SHADEMODE** must be typed in at the command line or the dynamic input ToolTip; next, select the option you want to use.

Chapter 4: Moving from 2D to 3D

In This Chapter

✔ Working with regions

✔ 3D polylines and helixes

✔ Creating 3D objects from 2D objects

✔ Creating 2D objects from 3D objects

✔ 3D modify commands

After you figure out how to get around a drawing, it's time to create some objects. First, you start off by creating 2D objects. (Yes, you read that correctly: 2D objects.) Although the result you want is a 3D model, you don't have to create everything using just 3D objects. Taking what you already know about creating 2D objects and applying that knowledge to 3D modeling helps you feel more comfortable with using and working in 3D. AutoCAD provides some tools that can help you create 2D views of the 3D model so you can generate the necessary shop drawings to get the model built.

At the end of this chapter, we cover some of the common 3D modify commands to help position 3D objects. Most of this chapter applies to AutoCAD only (not AutoCAD LT) and is designed to give you an overview of the different commands that allow you to go from 2D to 3D and back again. (An entire book could be written on just working with AutoCAD 3D alone.) For more information on the commands in this chapter, refer to the AutoCAD online Help.

Working with Regions

Regions are 2D objects that are created from closed shapes — or loops. A *loop* is a set of objects like lines and arcs that form a closed object but are not necessarily a closed object themselves, like a circle, polyline, or spline. You can create a region of polylines, lines, arcs, circles, elliptical arcs, ellipses, and splines. Regions can be great for creating complex areas to hatch, and can be used to create 3D objects. You can obtain centroid (the center point of the mass or volume of a region), moment of inertia (the value used to calculate distributed loads), and other information about a region using the MASSPROP command, like you can with 3D solids. For more information on the MASSPROP command, see the section "Getting more information about regions."

Creating regions

Because regions are created from existing objects in a drawing, you first must create the closed objects or loops and then use the REGION command to generate a region out of them. A region is created for each closed object or loop that is selected. To start the REGION command, you can select Region from either the Draw menu on the menu bar or the Draw toolbar. An example of the REGION command follows, along with the objects that were selected (see Figure 4-1):

```
Command: _region
Select objects: Select the closed objects or loops
Specify opposite corner: 8 found
Select objects: Press Enter
6 loops extracted.
6 Regions created.
```

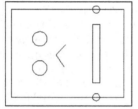

Figure 4-1: Closed objects converted to regions.

When you use the REGION command (and some of the other commands that are covered in this chapter), the original objects that you select to create the region or 3D object from are deleted automatically. To keep the original objects from being deleted, set the system variable DELOBJ to a value of 0.

Modifying regions

Regions are interesting objects because they are no longer 2D objects, nor are they 3D objects, so you modify them in a slightly different way. Although regions are not 3D objects, some of the 3D modify commands can be used on them. If you want to remove a portion of a region with another region, you wouldn't use the TRIM command; instead, you would use the SUBTRACT command. You can use the EXPLODE command to convert a region back to 2D objects.

Union

Union allows you to combine two or more regions into a single region. This allows you to create very complex 2D objects that can later be extruded to create a 3D object. A great example of this is a metal plate that is used to keep an object in place, or the side panel of a desk. The UNION command is available from the Solid Editing submenu under the Modify menu or the Solid Editing toolbar.

Subtract

Subtract allows you to remove a region from another region that it intersects or overlaps. This allows you to create holes, slots, or notches in regions before you extrude them to create a 3D object. The SUBTRACT command is available from the Solid Editing submenu under the Modify menu or the Solid Editing toolbar.

Intersect

Intersect allows you to keep only the part of two overlapping or intersecting regions that intersect. Using intersect is much more common when you are working with 3D solids. The INTERSECT command is available from the Solid Editing submenu under the Modify menu or the Solid Editing toolbar.

Getting more information about regions

Regions are complex objects that can be used to construct 3D solids or 2D objects that can be used to calculate additional information for the design, such as area and perimeter. The MASSPROP command allows you to obtain more information about a 2D region or 3D solid than what the LIST command displays. To start the MASSPROP command, choose Tools⇨Inquiry⇨Region/Mass Properties. An example of the MASSPROP command is

```
Command: _massprop
Select objects: Select a region(s)
Specify opposite corner: 1 found
Select objects: Press Enter
--------------    REGIONS    ---------------

Area:                   37.3681
Perimeter:              26.4645
Bounding box:       X:  15.9560  --  24.1580
                    Y:  6.3739   --  11.4041
Centroid:           X:  19.7700
                    Y:  9.0755
Moments of inertia: X:  3150.3487
                    Y:  14801.8030
Product of inertia: XY: 6725.9145
Radii of gyration:  X:  9.1818
                    Y:  19.9025
Principal moments and X-Y directions about centroid:
```

```
I: 68.9979 along [0.9864 0.1644]
J: 199.8441 along [-0.1644 0.9864]
```

Write analysis to a file? [Yes/No] <N>: *Press Enter*

3D Polylines and Helixes

Although a line object is not in one sense a 3D object, lines can have a different starting and ending *z* coordinate value, which makes it a 3D command. The 3DPOLY command allows you to draw 3D polylines, and the HELIX command allows you to create 2D and 3D spirals. These are not in one sense the same as a solid or a surface, but they can be created with varying different *z* coordinate values without the need to change the current user coordinate system (UCS). For more information on the UCS, see Book V, Chapter 2.

3D polyline

3D polylines are very similar to the 2D polylines that you are already familiar with, with the exception that they support only straight segments, and a different *z* coordinate value can be specified for the start and end point of a segment. You use the 3DPOLY command to create a 3D polyline, which can be started by choosing Draw⇨3D Polyline, or entering 3DPOLY at the command line or dynamic input tooltip.

Helix

Helixes can be used to create 2D and 3D spirals, shown in Figure 4-2, that might be used to represent springs, coils, or even door stops. To create a 2D helix, use a height value of 0. Use the HELIX command to create a helix. The HELIX command is started by selecting Helix from the Draw menu on the menu bar, or entering HELIX at the command line or dynamic input tooltip.

The HELIX command is new in AutoCAD 2007and is not supported in AutoCAD LT.

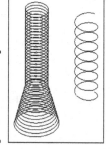

Figure 4-2:
Helixes can
be used to
create
springs.

Creating 3D Objects from 2D Objects

AutoCAD's roots started with 2D drafting. That continues to be the primary focus of the program, but Autodesk has shifted to making sure that 3D is a key part of the program. Because AutoCAD started off being a 2D drafting package, you can take your knowledge of 2D drafting to create 3D objects with it. This section discusses many of the different commands that allow you to take existing 2D objects and convert them into 3D objects. Some work with 2D profiles, whereas others might require you to create a region first or some sort of closed object. Everything in this section applies to AutoCAD only, with the exception of the Thickness section.

Thickness

Thickness is a property of most 2D objects, such as lines and circles. When you change the thickness of a 2D object, you are creating a surface out of the object, or a set of surfaces. These surfaces hide objects behind them, unlike wireframe models. If you add thickness to a circle, a cylinder is created that is capped on the top and bottom. Changing the thickness of a pline that has a width is a quick way to create a 3D wall. Thickness is also a system variable that can be set by typing **THICKNESS** at the command line or dynamic input ToolTip and entering a new value. New objects will be given the new thickness value.

Extrude

Extrude allows you to take an open or closed 2D object and create a solid or surface out of it. When you extrude a closed 2D object such as a polyline, spline, ellipse, circle, or region, you create a solid. If you extrude an open 2D object such as a polyline, spline, line, arc, or elliptical arc, you create a surface. Figure 4-3 shows the results of extruding an open and a closed object. You can extrude a face on a solid by holding down the Ctrl key and selecting the face when asked to select objects to extrude.

After you select the objects or faces you want to extrude, you specify a distance and direction to create the extrusion in. During the extrusion, you can select a path to extrude along which can be a 2D object or an edge of a solid or surface. To start the EXTRUDE command, choose Draw⇨Modeling⇨Extrude.

AutoCAD 2007 allows you to extrude open objects and generate surfaces from them.

If you want to keep the original object that is used to create the extruded object, set the system variable DELOBJ to 0.

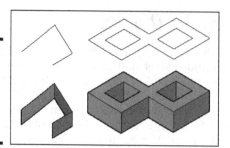

Figure 4-3:
The results of extruding open and closed objects.

Loft

Loft allows you to create a solid or a surface based on a series of specified cross-sections. The cross-sections are used to define the profile that is generated, and you must use a minimum of two cross-sections for the loft. If you use open objects for the cross-sections, the resulting loft is a surface; if you use closed objects for the cross-sections, the resulting loft is a solid. You can loft objects along a path by using guides or just the selected cross sections (see Figure 4-4). To start the LOFT command, select the Draw menu on the menu bar, and then choose Modeling⇨Loft.

The LOFT command is new in AutoCAD 2007.

Figure 4-4:
The results of lofting objects using cross-sections only.

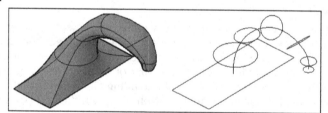

Sweep

Sweep is very similar to Loft except you use a single cross-section instead of two or more. The cross-section is used to define the profile that is generated. If you use an open object for the cross-section, the resulting sweep is a surface; if you use a closed object for the cross-section, the resulting sweep is a solid. You sweep the selected objects along a path (see Figure 4-5). To start the SWEEP command, select the Draw menu on the menu bar, and then choose Modeling⇨Sweep.

The SWEEP command is new in AutoCAD 2007.

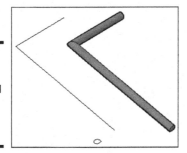

Figure 4-5:
The results
of sweeping
objects
along a
path.

Revolve

Revolve allows you to create a solid or a surface based on selected objects
and a specified axis that they should revolve around. If you use open objects,
the resulting revolve is a surface; if you use closed objects, the resulting
revolve is a solid. You revolve the selected objects around an axis and specify the angle at which you want the objects to be revolved (see Figure 4-6).
To start the REVOLVE command, select the Draw menu on the menu bar, and
then choose Modeling⇨Revolve.

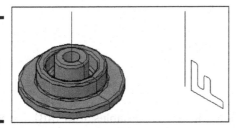

Figure 4-6:
The results
of revolving
objects
along an
axis.

Tabulated Mesh

Tabulated Mesh allows you to create a mesh based on a profile (path curve)
and a direction vector. Unlike some of the previously mentioned commands
in this section, such as extrude and loft, a closed profile doesn't create a
solid. You extrude the selected object (path curve) along a selected path
(see Figure 4-7). To start the TABSURF command, choose Draw⇨Modeling⇨
Meshes⇨Tabulated Mesh.

TABSURF uses the value of the system variable SURFTAB1 to control the
number of segments that the mesh is created with. The higher the number,
the smoother the mesh looks, and the better it follows the selected object
(path curve). By default, SURFTAB1 is set to a value of 6.

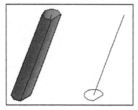

Figure 4-7:
The results of using TABSURF on a closed object.

Revolved Mesh

Revolved Mesh is similar to Revolve, except you are only able to select a single object with Revolved Mesh, and a mesh is created even when a closed object is selected. After you select the object you want to revolve, you specify the axis by selecting an object, and then you specify the start and include angles to revolve the object around the axis (see Figure 4-8). To start the REVSURF command, choose Draw➪Modeling➪Meshes➪Revolved Mesh.

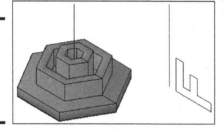

Figure 4-8:
The results of using REVSURF on a closed object.

REVSURF uses the values of the system variables SURFTAB1 and SURFTAB2 to control the number of segments that the mesh is created with. The higher the number, the smoother the mesh looks and the better it follows the selected object. By default, SURFTAB1 and SURFTAB2 are set to a value of 6.

Ruled Mesh

Ruled Mesh allows you to create a mesh between two selected objects. You can use both open and closed objects with the command, but if you use a closed object, the other object must also be a closed object. Ruled Mesh is similar to the way loft works because a new object is created based on the selection of two profiles (see Figure 4-9). To start the RULESURF command, choose Draw➪Modeling➪Meshes➪Ruled Mesh.

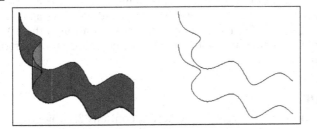

Figure 4-9: The results of using RULESURF on two splines at different elevations.

RULESURF uses the value of the system variable SURFTAB1 to control the number of segments that the mesh is created with. The higher the number, the smoother the mesh looks and the better it follows the selected object. By default, SURFTAB1 is set to a value of 6.

Edge Mesh

Edge Mesh allows you to create a three-dimensional mesh that follows the edges of four objects. The objects must be open objects, but their end points must match up with each other. The edges must be selected in a specific order to properly generate the mesh (see Figure 4-10). To start the EDGESURF command, choose Draw⇨Modeling⇨Meshes⇨Edge Mesh.

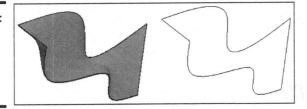

Figure 4-10: The results of using EDGESURF on four objects.

EDGESURF uses the values of the system variables SURFTAB1 and SURFTAB2 to control the number of segments that the mesh is created with. The higher the number, the smoother the mesh looks and the better it follows the selected object. By default, SURFTAB1 and SURFTAB2 are set to a value of 6.

Creating 2D Objects from 3D Objects

AutoCAD allows you to make the transition from 2D to 3D without having to completely abandon what you already know about 2D drafting. Wouldn't it be nice to be able to create a 2D representation of the 3D model that you spent numerous hours creating? You're in luck: AutoCAD comes with commands that allow you to take your 3D model and generate a 2D representation of a given view. After you have a 2D representation of the 3D model, you can then add any dimensions and notes necessary for construction or manufacturing.

Flatshot

Flatshot allows you to create a block that contains 2D objects based on the current view of a 3D model. By creating the 3D model first, you can create a block that contains only the objects that are visible in that view, or include the obscured lines in a different color or linetype (see Figure 4-11). Flatshot looks for all 3D objects that are in the current view and ignores all 2D objects. To start the FLATSHOT command, select Flatshot from the 3D Make control panel on the Dashboard palette.

The FLATSHOT command is new in AutoCAD 2007.

Figure 4-11: The results of creating three different views from one model with Flatshot.

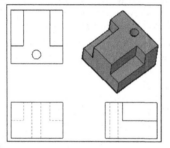

Section Plane

Section Plane allows you to cut a 3D solid without actually altering the object itself to generate a 2D or 3D object based on the geometry along the defined plane (see Figure 4-12). This allows you to quickly create different views of a model to help manufacture it, or even assemble it. Unlike Flatshot, a Section Plane can go through an object and be able to generate a 2D representation of the objects that are along the Section Plane. To create a 2D or 3D representation of the objects along a plane, you first start the SECTIONPLANE command, and then choose Draw⇨Modeling⇨Section Plane. After the Section Plane has been created, you have various different options of how you want to display the objects around the Section Plane. The options can be accessed from the right-click shortcut menu or the Properties palette.

The SECTIONPLANE command is new in AutoCAD 2007.

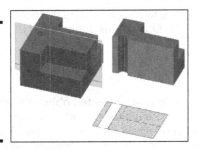

Figure 4-12:
The results of creating a 2D and 3D object from a Section Plane.

Solid Draw, Solid View, and Solid Profile

Three older commands called Solid Draw (SOLDRAW), Solid View (SOLVIEW), and Solid Profile (SOLPROF) work very similar to the Flatshot and Section Plane commands. These commands allow you to generate views of 3D models, but only work in a layout with viewports. Solid Profile allows you to create a profile of a 3D object out of 2D objects, which can be helpful if you want to create an exploded view of a part for an illustration guide.

Solid View and Solid Draw are used with each other. Solid View is used to create a viewport with specific layers frozen; after the viewport is created, you display the 3D objects in the viewport that you want to convert to 2D objects with the Solid Draw command. Start the Solid Draw command and select the viewport. All hidden objects are placed on a specific layer along with other objects and layers that are created from the command (see Figure 4-13). The SOLDRAW, SOLVIEW, and SOLPROF commands can be found under the Draw menu on the menu bar. Choose Modeling➪Setup and then Drawing, View, or Profile.

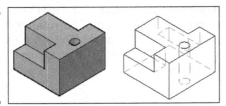

Figure 4-13:
The results of using SOLPROF on a 3D object.

3D Modify Commands

Surfaces and solids that make up 3D models can be modified using all of the modify commands that you already know, such as ERASE, MOVE, ROTATE, and more. However, AutoCAD also offers some special modify commands that are designed specifically for working in 3D. These specialized 3D commands can be used on solids, surfaces, and even 2D objects. All of these commands are located under the 3D Operations submenu of the Modify menu on the menu bar.

3D Move

The 3D Move command allows you to move selected objects along the *xy* plane and in the *z* direction. This command uses what is called a *grip tool* to allow you to restrict or constrain movement along an axis (see Figure 4-14). The command prompts are identical to the MOVE command, so using the 3D Move command should be familiar. The 3DMOVE command can be started by selecting 3D Move from the 3D Operations submenu under the Modify menu on the menu bar.

The 3DMOVE command is new in AutoCAD 2007.

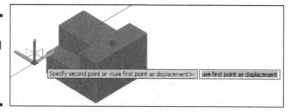

Figure 4-14: The grip tool for the 3DMOVE command.

3D Rotate

The 3D Rotate command allows you to rotate selected objects along the *x, y,* or *z* axis. Like the 3D Move command, the 3D Rotate command uses a grip tool to allow you to restrict or constrain the rotation along an axis (see Figure 4-15). The command prompts are similar to the ROTATE command, with one slight difference: You need to pick an axis for rotation, and then a start and end angle instead of just a rotation angle. The 3DROTATE command can be started by selecting 3D Rotate from the 3D Operations submenu under the Modify menu on the menu bar.

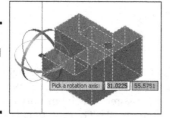

Figure 4-15: The grip tool for the 3DROTATE command.

The 3DROTATE command is new in AutoCAD 2007.

Align

The Align command can be used to align 2D and 3D objects based on one, two, or three pairs of points. Based on the number of pairs of points that you select and how they are selected, the Align command might move or rotate the selected objects into place.

3D Align

The 3D Align command is an improved version of the ALIGN command that includes some additional options, including the ability to copy the selected objects instead of just moving or rotating them, and the ability to use Dynamic UCS with the command.

The 3DALIGN command is new in AutoCAD 2007.

Mirror 3D

The Mirror 3D command allows you to mirror objects along the *xy* plane like the standard MIRROR command does, but it also allows you to specify the mirror plane using a number of additional methods to define it. The additional methods that you can define the mirror plane are by three points, an existing object in the drawing, a previously defined mirror plane, *z* axis, the current view, *xy* plane, *yz* plane, and *zx* plane. The three-point option is the most common and is the default option.

3D Array

The 3D Array command allows you to array objects along the *xy* plane (rows and columns) like the ARRAY command does but also allows you to array in the *z* direction (levels). You can create both rectangular and polar arrays with the 3D Array command just like you can with the ARRAY command. The 3D Array command does not use a nice dialog box like the ARRAY command does, so entering the correct values can be hard the first few times until you get used to inputting the values at the command line.

Chapter 5: Working with Solids

In This Chapter

↙ **Creating solid primitives**

↙ **Editing solids**

*I*n the previous chapter, we covered many of the commands that allow you to take the knowledge that you already have about 2D drafting and apply it to 3D. In this chapter, you discover many of the 3D commands that allow you to create and edit 3D objects. AutoCAD allows you to create 3D objects known as primitives. *Primitives* are very basic objects like boxes, cones, and spheres that can be used to create complex models. You also find out more about modifying commands that are used to manipulate a 3D solid.

Creating Solid Primitives

AutoCAD offers a pretty good variety of primitive 3D objects that can be used to create complex models. The primitive objects help to form the foundation of 3D modeling in AutoCAD: You can combine these primitives with other primitives or even manipulate a primitive so that it is filleted (with rounded edges), shelled (hollowed out), and more.

Polysolid

A polysolid is very similar to a 2D polyline, except it has a single uniform width and a height. Polysolid is great for creating 3D walls to create a conceptual look of a building (see Figure 5-1) or for creating rectangular duct work. To start the POLYSOLID command, choose Draw⇨Modeling⇨Polysolid. After you start the POLYSOLID command, you can draw a polyline-like object that allows you to create both straight and curved segments. If you already have lines, arcs, and polylines in your drawing, you are able to convert those to solid with the Object option of the POLYSOLID command. You are also able to specify the height, width, and justification for how the new solid object is created.

Figure 5-1:
The outline
of a 2D
floor plan
converted
to 3D walls
with the
POLYSOLID
command.

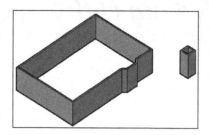

Box

A box is a six-sided object that is either a cube or rectangular. A box could be used for virtually anything from a table (see Figure 5-2) to a door or even a building in the background of a conceptual drawing. To start the BOX command, choose Draw ⇨Modeling⇨Box. After specifying the first corner or the center of the box, you can then finish defining the base of the box by selecting the opposite corner, creating a cube, or defining its length. Based on the option you select, you may need to define the box's height.

Figure 5-2:
A table
created
from boxes.

Wedge

A wedge is half of a box diagonally from an upper edge to a lower edge. A wedge might be useful for creating a ramp, a roof slope, or even a slice of chocolate cake. Figure 5-3 shows some of the different sizes of wedges that can be created with the WEDGE command. To start the WEDGE command, choose Draw⇨Modeling⇨Wedge. After specifying the first corner or the center of the wedge, you can then finish defining the base of the wedge by selecting the opposite corner, creating a cube, or defining its length. Based on the option selected, you may need to define the wedge's height.

Figure 5-3:
Some
different
shapes and
sizes of
wedges.

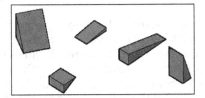

Cone

A cone is an object with a circular base that has either a point or a flat top. The base of a cone can be larger than its top and even be elliptical rather than circular. You might use a cone for a handle or pull, a cup, or a planter. Figure 5-4 shows some of the different sizes and types of cones that can be created with the CONE command. To start the CONE command, choose Draw⇨Modeling⇨Cone. After specifying the center of the cone's base, specify the radius or diameter of the base and then its height.

Figure 5-4:
Some
different
shapes and
sizes of
cones.

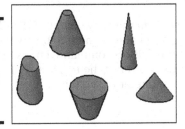

Sphere

A sphere is a full circular object that is created from the very center of the object. The sphere is one of two types of 3D solids that is created half above and half below the current XY plane (see Figure 5-5). Torus is the other type of 3D solid created above and below the current XY plane, which we discuss later in this chapter in the section called "Torus." To start the SPHERE command, choose Draw⇨Modeling⇨Sphere. After specifying the center of the sphere, you specify its radius or diameter.

Figure 5-5:
A sphere.

Cylinder

A cylinder is a circle or ellipse with height and is commonly created from the center of the object. Cylinders can be used for a variety of things, like the legs of a table or chair, glasses, or a shaft for a gear. Figure 5-6 shows some of the different sizes and types of cylinders that can be created with the CYLINDER command. To start the CYLINDER command, choose Draw⇨Modeling⇨ Cylinder. After specifying the center of the cylinder's base, specify the radius or diameter of the base and then its height.

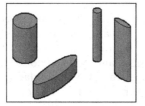

Figure 5-6:
Different shapes and sizes of cylinders.

Torus

A torus is a 3D donut that is created from the very center of the object. The torus, like the sphere, is created half above and half below the current XY plane (see Figure 5-7). To start the TORUS command, choose Draw⇨ Modeling⇨Torus. After specifying the center of the torus, specify its radius or diameter, and then the radius or diameter of the tube.

Figure 5-7:
A torus.

Pyramid

A pyramid is similar to a cone, except instead of a circular base, it has a polygon-shaped base that can have from 3 to 32 sides and either a point or a flat top. You might use a pyramid for the top of a building, base of a street sign, or even a light fixture. Figure 5-8 shows some of the different sizes and types of pyramids that can be created with the PYRAMID command. To start the PYRAMID command, choose Draw⇨Modeling⇨Pyramid. After you specify the center or the edge of the pyramid's base, specify the radius or use the inscribed option and then its height.

The PYRAMID command is new in AutoCAD 2007.

Figure 5-8:
Different
shapes and
sizes of
pyramids.

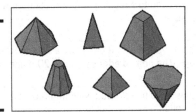

Editing Solids

You can edit a solid in many different ways, and some of these ways are not always easy to recognize. AutoCAD allows you to select a solid and access grips to modify certain characteristics of the solid, which could be its height, base size, or some other characteristic. Along with being able to edit solids directly with grips, you can also manipulate faces and edges of a solid through the SOLIDEDIT command and by using the Ctrl key when selecting objects. You can edit solid in many other ways, like using the TRIM and FILLET command, and other specialized commands used only on solids.

Solid editing

The SOLIDEDIT command allows you to modify a face, an edge, or the entire body of a 3D solid. Based on how you edit a 3D solid, you have different options available. Many of the options that are part of the SOLIDEDIT command are available on the Solid Editing toolbar or are found under the Solid Editing submenu of the Modify menu on the menu bar.

Table 5-1 lists the different options of the SOLIDEDIT command and what they are used for.

Table 5-1		SOLIDEDIT Command Options
	Command Option	**Description**
	Imprint Edges	Imprints a 2D or 3D object onto a 3D solid. The object to be imprinted must intersect one or more faces of the 3D solid that it is to be imprinted on. After the object has been imprinted onto the solid, you can then extrude the new face that is created if the imprinted object creates a closed area on the 3D solid.

(continued)

Table 5-1 *(continued)*

	Command Option	Description
	Color Edges	Allows you to specify a different color for an edge on the 3D solid.
	Copy Edges	Allows you to select edges on a 3D solid that you want to copy. The copied edges result in 2D objects such as lines and arcs.
	Extrude Faces	Allows you to extrude a selected face away or into the 3D solid that it belongs to.
	Move Faces	Allows you to move a selected face on the 3D solid. This works great for moving holes or notches in a surface.
	Offset Faces	Allows you to offset a selected face on the 3D solid.
	Delete Faces	Allows you to delete a selected face, fillet, or chamfer on the 3D solid.
	Rotate Faces	Allows you to rotate a selected face on a 3D solid.
	Taper Faces	Allows you to taper a selected face on a 3D solid. This causes the face to flare out or in based on the specified axis and angle provided.
	Color Faces	Allows you to specify a different color for a face on the 3D solid.
	Copy Faces	Allows you to select faces on a 3D solid that you want to copy. The copied edges result in 2D regions being created for each face selected.
	Clean	Performs a scrubbing of the 3D solid and cleans up any redundant edges, vertices, and unused geometry.
	Separate	Creates separate 3D solid objects based on 3D solids with disjointed volumes; this doesn't separate Boolean objects with a single volume.
	Shell	Hollows out a 3D solid based on a specified wall thickness. A positive offset distance creates the shell to the inside of the perimeter, whereas a negative value creates the shell to the outside of the perimeter.
	Check	Performs a validation on the 3D solid object to determine that it is valid with the ShapeManager.

Using grips to edit solids

Grips are a very powerful way to edit objects such as lines and arcs. You can use grips to edit some of the properties of a solid after it has been created in the drawing. To edit a solid using grips, select the solid with no command running and then select the grip you want to edit. Some grips allow you to change the overall size of the solid, whereas others allow you to change part of the solid like its base or top in the case of a cone. Figure 5-9 shows a cone selected and its grips displayed.

The grip editing of solids has been greatly improved in AutoCAD 2007. In previous releases, you could only use grips to move solids, but now you are able to modify a solid after it has been created. The Properties palette has also been updated to allow you to edit a solid after it has been created in the drawing.

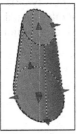

Figure 5-9:
Grips
displayed on
the selected
cone.

Booleans

3D solids can be unioned together to form a complex object using the UNION command. Along with being able to union 3D solids, you can also subtract from them with the SUBTRACT command. A 3D solid can also be created based on the intersecting of two or more 3D solids with the INTERSECT command. For more information on these commands, see Chapter 4 of this mini-book and the online Help system.

Filleting and chamfering

3D solids can be filleted and chamfered just like 2D objects. You use the FILLET and CHAMFER commands that you are already familiar with. The FILLET command allows you to fillet as many edges that you want to on a solid, whereas CHAMFER must be done face by face. Figure 5-10 shows a solid that has had its edges filleted and chamfered. To remove a fillet or a chamfer from a solid, you use the Delete Faces option of the SOLIDEDIT command.

Figure 5-10:
A 3D solid
before and
after it was
filleted and
chamfered.

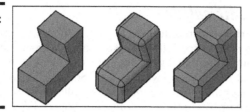

Slice

At times, you may only want a portion of the 3D solid for your model. In these cases, you can use the SLICE command. You can slice a 3D solid using a planar object like a circle, ellipse, 2D polyline, or a surface, among many others. You can keep both halves of the solid after it has been sliced, or whichever side you want to keep. Figure 5-11 shows a solid that has been sliced in half. To start the SLICE command, choose Modify⇨3D Operations⇨ Slice. After you specify the 3D solid to slice, you specify the axis or object you want to use as the cutting plane and then you decide which part of the resulting objects to keep.

Figure 5-11:
A 3D solid
sliced in
half.

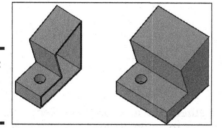

Chapter 6: Working with Surfaces

In This Chapter

✓ **Creating surfaces**

✓ **Editing surfaces**

*I*n the previous chapter, we cover creating and modifying 3D solids. This chapter takes a similar look at creating and modifying surfaces. Many commands allow you to create primitives out of surfaces instead of a 3D solid. Surfaces take a little more planning to create and modify than 3D solids do, but they do have advantages, depending on what you are trying to model.

Creating Surfaces

AutoCAD offers a variety of commands that allow you to create primitives as surfaces, which are similar to the commands that allow you to create 3D primitives. Just like the primitive 3D solids, surfaces help to form the foundation of 3D modeling in AutoCAD. Surfaces are not as easy to modify as 3D solids are, but you can deform and change their shapes much more easily than you can a 3D solid. Most of the primitives that can be created as 3D solids can be created with surfaces through the use of the 3D command or a command that is specific to the primitive.

3D face

A surface can be either three- or four-sided. Most of the commands in this chapter create meshes that are composed of multiple surfaces to create a primitive. The 3DFACE command allows you to create a single three- or four-sided surface (see Figure 6-1). As you create a surface with the 3DFACE command, you can control which sides of the surface are visible when the model is viewed as hidden, shaded, or rendered. To start the 3DFACE command, choose Draw⇨Modeling⇨Meshes⇨3D Face. After specifying the first corner, you specify two more points and then press Enter to create a three-sided surface, or specify a fourth point to create a four-sided surface. You can continue to specify additional points to create additional surfaces. As you specify points, you can toggle the visibility of the edge that is created.

Figure 6-1:
An open box created with surfaces, and a three- and four-sided surface.

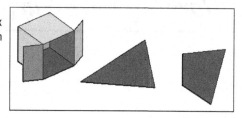

3D mesh

A mesh is a group of vertices that form a particular pattern to create a group of surfaces based on the number of vertices specified (see Figure 6-2). If a mesh is exploded, the result is individual surfaces that are created between the specified vertices. A mesh is commonly created as an open object, but can be closed through the use of the PEDIT command. To start the 3DMESH command, choose Draw⇨Modeling⇨Meshes⇨3D Mesh. After you start the 3DMESH command, you are prompted to specify the size in the M and N directions, which determines the number of vertices that you are prompted for. After the M and N directions have been specified, you specify all the vertices to create the mesh.

Figure 6-2:
A couple of meshes created with the 3DMESH command.

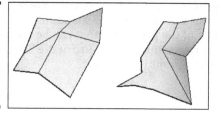

Planar surface

A planar surface is an object that can be created by specifying two corners to form a rectangular object, or selecting objects that form a closed object just like the region command does (see Figure 6-3). Unlike many of the commands that create surfaces and meshes in this chapter, exploding a planar surface results in the creation of a region. To start the PLANESURF command, choose Draw⇨Modeling⇨Planar Surface. After you start the PLANESURF command, you are prompted to specify the first corner of the planar surface and then the opposite corner, which creates the planar surface on the *xy* plane. Alternatively, you are prompted to select a closed object.

The PLANESURF command is new in AutoCAD 2007.

Figure 6-3:
Two planar surfaces: one created by picking two corners and the other created with a closed spline.

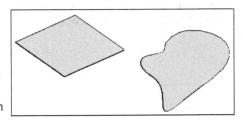

The system variables SURFU and SURFV control the number of lines that are displayed for the surface but do not affect the actual creation of the planar surface.

Box

A box is created using the AI_BOX command and looks just like one created with the BOX command. The 3D solid that is created with the BOX command can be edited using grips and retains the appearance of a box, but the surface version of a box can be easily be deformed or stretched to fit into a specific shape, which can result in the final object not being a box (see Figure 6-4). To start the AI_BOX command, type the command in at the command line or the dynamic input tooltip. After the command starts, you specify the first corner of the box, its length and width, and finally its height. After the box is created, you have the option of rotating it along the *z* axis.

Figure 6-4:
Some of the boxes that can be created with the AI_BOX command, and one (on the far right) modified with grips.

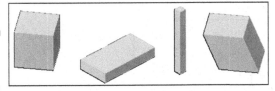

Wedge

A wedge is created using the AI_WEDGE command and looks just like one created with the WEDGE command (see Figure 6-5), but they are edited in different ways. To start the AI_WEDGE command, you type the command in at the command line or the dynamic input tooltip. After the command starts, you specify the first corner of the wedge, its length and width, and finally its height. After the wedge is created, you have the option of rotating it along the z axis.

Figure 6-5:
Some of the
wedges
that can be
created
with the
AI_WEDGE
command.

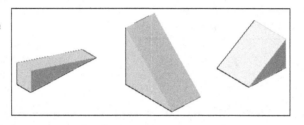

Cone

A cone is created using the AI_CONE command and can be made to look similar to one created with the CONE command (see Figure 6-6), but both are edited in different ways. To start the AI_CONE command, you type the command in at the command line or the dynamic input tooltip. When the command starts, specify the center point for the base, and then the radius or diameter of the base. After you have defined the base size, define the radius of the top of the cone. A radius of zero creates a point, whereas a radius greater than zero creates a flat top. After the base and the top of the cone have been defined, specify the height of the cone. The last bit of information is the number of segments that the cone should be created with: The higher the number, the smoother it appears. You should stay roughly around 16 segments when possible, but the number increases as the cone gets larger to give it a smooth appearance. The highest value you can use is 32,767.

Figure 6-6:
Some of
the cones
that can be
created
with the
AI_CONE
command.

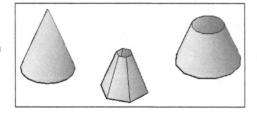

Sphere

A sphere is created using the AI_SPHERE command and can be made to look similar to one created with the SPHERE command (see Figure 6-7), but they are edited in different ways. To start the AI_SPHERE command, type the command in at the command line or the dynamic input tooltip. When the command starts, specify the center of the sphere and then its radius or diameter. After the radius or diameter has been specified, you need to specify the number of longitudinal and latitudinal segments. The greater the number of segments specified, the smoother the sphere appears.

Figure 6-7:
Some of the spheres that can be created with the AI_SPHERE command.

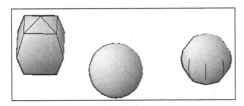

Dish and dome

A dish and a dome are created using the AI_DISH and AI_DOME commands. No command allows you to create a 3D solid as a dish or a dome, but you could create a sphere and then slice it horizontally to create both types of objects. A dish is the lower half of a sphere if it was sliced in half, whereas a dome is the upper half (see Figure 6-8). To start the AI_DISH or AI_DOME command, type the command in at the command line or the dynamic input tooltip. When the command starts, specify the center of the dish or dome and then its radius or diameter. After the radius or diameter has been specified, you need to specify the number of longitudinal and latitudinal segments. The greater the number of segments specified, the smoother the dish or dome appears. The number of latitudinal segments is half of what you would use for a sphere.

Figure 6-8:
A dish and a dome created with the AI_DISH and AI_DOME commands.

Torus

A torus that is created using the AI_TORUS command can be made to look similar to one created with the TORUS command (see Figure 6-9), but they are edited differently. To start the AI_TORUS command, type the command in at the command line or the dynamic input tooltip. When the command has been started, specify the center of the torus and then its radius or diameter. When the radius or diameter of the torus has been defined, define the radius or diameter of the torus's tube. After the overall size and tube have been specified, specify the number of segments for the torus and the tube. The greater the number of segments specified, the smoother the torus appears.

Figure 6-9:
Two of the toruses that can be created with the AI_TORUS command.

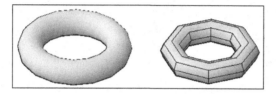

Pyramid

A pyramid that is created using the AI_PYRAMID command can be made to look similar to a three- or four-sided pyramid that is created with the PYRAMID command, but the AI_PYRAMID command offers variations that are not possible with the PYRAMID command (see Figure 6-10). The AI_PYRAMID command allows you to create a tetrahedron (three-sided pyramid) or a four-sided pyramid, which can have a point, a ridge, or a flat top. To start the AI_PYRAMID command, you type the command in at the command line or the dynamic input tooltip. When the command has been started, you specify the first corner of the pyramid's base, and then up to four other corners based on if you are creating a tetrahedron (three-sided pyramid) or a four-sided. After the base is defined, you can specify the location for the type of the pyramid's top: either a point (apex), ridge, or a top. When you define the type of top for the pyramid, you are also defining its height.

Figure 6-10:
Some of the
pyramids
that can
be created
with the AI_
PYRAMID
command.

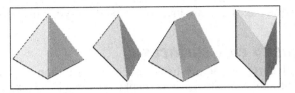

Editing Surfaces

Editing surfaces is much different than 3D solids. 3D solids are a tightly created object, whereas surfaces are looser and can be altered radically through the use of grips. Not many commands and options are available for editing surfaces, but you should know and understand a few important ones.

Controlling the visibility of edges

The most important thing to remember when creating surfaces is that you must control which edges of the surfaces should be shown as you create a patchwork of surfaces to create holes and other features (see Figure 6-11). The EDGE command allows you to control the display of an edge where two surfaces meet or, in some cases, don't meet. You usually want to hide edges where two surfaces that are parallel or nearly parallel to each other meet. You can't hide the edges of segments that are part of a mesh; the mesh must be exploded first into individual faces. To start the EDGE command, choose Draw⇨Modeling⇨Meshes⇨Edge. After the command is started, select the edge that you want to toggle the visibility for.

Figure 6-11:
A surface
before and
after the
display of its
edges has
been
toggled.

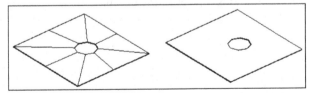

The system variables SPLFRAME controls the display of edges that have been set as invisible on a surface. Setting the variable to a value of 1 and doing a REGEN causes the edges that are invisible to be displayed on-screen.

Using grips to edit surfaces

Using grips with surfaces and meshes is much different than with solids. When you select a surface or mesh, a grip is displayed at each vertex that allows you to reposition the vertex. This causes the surface to become deformed or stretched, making it easier to blend surfaces and 3D solids together.

Working with convert to surface

AutoCAD allows you to take certain types of objects with specific property settings and convert them to surfaces: Some of these objects are 2D solids, regions, planar 3D faces, polylines that are open and have no width with thickness, and lines or arcs with thickness. To convert these objects to surfaces, you use the CONVTOSURFACE command. After the command is started and the object is created, a new Planar or Extruded surface is created. The CONVTOSOLID command allows you to take some objects with specific property settings and create extruded solids from them. For more information on these commands, refer to AutoCAD's online Help system.

The CONVTOSOLID and CONVTOSURFACE commands are new in AutoCAD 2007.

Thicken

The THICKEN command is very similar to the EXTRUDE command, except it is limited to Planar and Extruded surfaces. To start the THICKEN command, choose Modify⇨3D Operations⇨Thicken. After the command is started, select the Planar Surface that you want to thicken and specify a value for the thickness.

The THICKEN command is new in AutoCAD 2007.

Chapter 7: Rendering: Lights, Cameras, AutoCAD!

In This Chapter

✔ Adding lights into a scene

✔ Placing materials on objects

✔ Setting a background for a view

✔ Rendering a scene

A fter you understand how to navigate, visualize, create, and edit 3D solids or surfaces, you can prepare your 3D model to be rendered. *Rendering* allows you to present the concept to clients so they can visualize what the end product will look like when it is complete. Hidden line views and shaded views can help the client visualize the 3D model, but they lack the depth and realism that really sells a concept to a client. Before you generate a rendering, you add lights, materials, and a background to your 3D model. These all help bring realism to the 3D model to make it look like the final product. This chapter applies to AutoCAD only (not AutoCAD LT) and is designed to be an overview of lights, materials, backgrounds, and rendering a model. For more information on these topics, refer to AutoCAD's online Help system.

Lighting a Scene

Lighting is a key to making your drawing — also known as a scene — look realistic because it gives variation to the colors in your model. Objects closest to the lights appear brighter, whereas objects that are farther from the light source appear darker. This is what happens in real life with light coming from the sun outside, or a lamp that is indoors. AutoCAD offers three types of lights: default lights, user lights (point, spotlight, and distant), and sunlight. All of these types of lights, with the exception of the default lights, can cast shadows. To help manage the creation and editing of lights, use the Light control panel on the Dashboard, the Sun Properties palette, and the Lights in Model palette.

The lighting system has been greatly improved in AutoCAD 2007 with better control over lights and shadows.

Default lights

Previous releases of AutoCAD had a single default light, which always shined in the direction of the current view. AutoCAD 2007 now has two default lights to help bring the level of lighting up and to balance the lighting on each side of the model. Default lighting does not cast shadows, so you shouldn't use it for the final render, but it might be good enough for a conceptual drawing. You do have some control over the brightness and contrast of the default lighting with the slider controls that are available when the Light control panel of the Dashboard palette is expanded (see Figure 7-1).

Figure 7-1:
The Light control panel of the Dashboard.

User lights

User lights are lights that you add to a scene. When you place user lights in a scene, you need to disable the default lights that AutoCAD automatically creates when a drawing is opened. User lights come in three distinct types of lights:

✦ **Point light:** A point light emits light in all directions, but the light decays or falls off the farther you get from the light. The falloff defines at what point no more light is emitted; by defining the falloff value of the light, you can reduce rendering time. You can think of a point light as similar to a candle or a lamp. Figure 7-2 shows four objects illuminated by a single point light.

Figure 7-2:
Point light emitting light and casting shadows on objects in a scene.

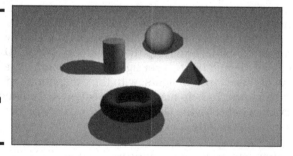

✦ **Spotlight:** A spotlight emits light in a specific direction in a cone shape and allows you to define the hotspot — the brightest part of the light — and the falloff of the light. You can think of a spotlight like track lighting, recessed lighting, or a flashlight. Figure 7-3 shows four objects illuminated by a single spotlight.

Figure 7-3:
Spotlight
emitting
light and
casting
shadows
on objects
in a scene.

✦ **Distant light:** A distant light emits light in a specific direction, but doesn't have a hotspot or a falloff like a point light or spotlight does. You can think of a distant light as being like the sun because it emits light all over every object that it is exposed to, so it is great for backdrop lighting that comes from behind a camera to fill a room with non-direct light. Figure 7-4 shows four objects illuminated by a single distant light.

Figure 7-4:
Distant light
emitting
light and
casting
shadows on
objects in a
scene.

You add lights to your scene with the LIGHT command. When you create the first light in the scene, you are prompted by a message box asking you to disable default lighting if it is not already disabled. The use of default lighting can be toggled on or off from the Light control panel of the Dashboard. The LIGHT command can be started by selecting one of the three Create Light buttons from the expanded part of the Light control panel of the Dashboard. Alternatively, choose View⇨Render⇨Light. After a light has been added to the scene, it can be modified with the Properties palette.

Point or spotlights can be selected and edited directly in a scene because a glyph is displayed to show where the light is located, unlike a distant light, which doesn't have a glyph associated with it. (A *glyph* is a non-printing object displayed in a scene that enables you to modify an object that is not part of the actual design, such as a light or camera.) If the scene is complex or you need to select a distant light in the scene, you need to use the Lights in Model palette (see Figure 7-5). The Lights in Model palette allows you to select, delete, and access the Properties palette for editing the selected light(s). To display the Lights in Model palette, use the LIGHTLIST command, which can be accessed by choosing Tools⇨Palettes⇨Lights.

The LIGHTLIST command is new in AutoCAD 2007.

Figure 7-5:
The Lights in Model palette.

Sunlight

The ability to add light that is similar to sunlight is great for outdoor scenes, or for indoor scenes with light coming in through a window. Sunlight is controlled through the Sun Properties palette (see Figure 7-6) and the Geographic Location dialog box (see Figure 7-7). Both of these interfaces allow you to designate the position of the sun based on the city that your scene would be nearest to in the physical world, or at a specific latitude and longitude. You can also designate the Northern direction of the scene to make sure that light is emitting on the scene as it would after it was built.

The SUNPROPERTIES and GEOGRAPHICLOCATION commands are new in AutoCAD 2007.

Figure 7-6:
The Sun
Properties
palette.

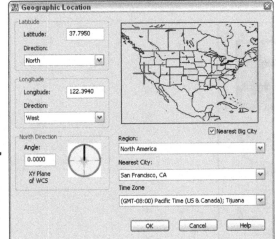

Figure 7-7:
The
Geographic
Location
dialog box.

Getting the Right Look with Materials

Materials help to give your objects that special touch of realism, whether they are made up of metal, glass, plastic, or wood. Materials allow you to make the scene much more convincing to the viewer. The MATERIALS command is used to display the Materials palette (see Figure 7-8), which allows you to create and edit materials based on a variety of properties such as transparency, shininess, a bump map, or simply a color. After the material is created, it needs to get in the scene somehow. Here are the three ways you can associate a material in a scene:

✦ **Materials by Layer:** Materials can be assigned to objects globally throughout a scene by assigning the material to a layer. Use the MATERIALATTACH command to assign a material to a layer in the scene.

✦ **Materials by Object:** Materials can be assigned to an individual object in the scene by using the MATERIALASSIGN command and selecting the object(s) you want to assign the material to.

✦ **Materials by Face:** Materials can be assigned to an individual face of a 3D solid by holding down the Ctrl while using the MATERIALASSIGN command, or using the SOLIDEDIT command and assigning a material using the Face option.

The MATERIALS, MATERIALATTACH, and MATERIALASSIGN commands are new in AutoCAD 2007.

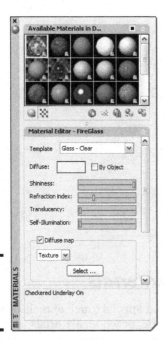

Figure 7-8: The Materials palette.

Setting Up a Backdrop

Backgrounds allow you to fill what looks like empty space beyond the 3D model in your scene. The background of the current view can be defined as a solid color, a gradient that consists of two or three colors, or an image file. To set the background of the current view, use the Background Override property of the view in the View Manager.

The BACKGROUND command has been removed from AutoCAD 2007. You now use the VIEW command and the View Manager to assign a background to a named view.

In the View Manager, select the view that you want to change the background for from the View list. You can only select views that are under the Model Views and Layout Views branches. After you have selected the view, under the General section, select the Background Override property. Then select the drop-down list next to Background Override and choose the option you want to use to open the Background dialog box (see Figure 7-9). Specify the options as desired and click OK to the exit Background dialog box. To set the view current and use the new background, select the view from the View list and click Set Current. When you exit the dialog box, the background is displayed along with the view that was selected.

Figure 7-9:
The
Background
dialog box
with
Gradient
selected.

Rendering the Final Scene

After you have created your 3D model, put lights in the scene, created and applied materials, and put a background in the current view, you are ready for the final step of putting together your image. During the rendering process, AutoCAD gathers all the materials and applies them to the objects and faces of your 3D model and calculates both light and shadows for the scene. Rendering takes place by default in the Render Window dialog box (see Figure 7-10). To start the RENDER command, you can choose View⇨ Render⇨Render, or select the Render button in the Render control panel of the Dashboard.

The RENDERCROP and RENDERWIN commands are new in AutoCAD 2007, and the RPREF and RENDER commands have been updated. The RPREF command now displays the Advanced Render Settings palette.

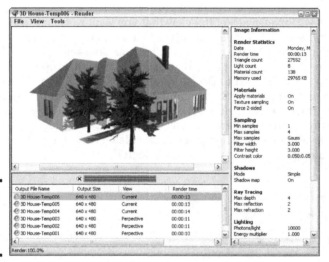

Figure 7-10: The Render Window dialog box.

Instead of rendering the entire scene to the Render Window, you can use the RENDERCROP command and specify the part of the current view that you want to render. This is a great way to test your lighting and shadows in a specific part of the scene without having to render everything in the scene. The rendering happens directly in the current viewport. AutoCAD allows you to select from five different render presets to help speed up the process. A render preset can be selected from the drop-down list in the Render control panel on the Dashboard. Render presets range from very quick renderings using the draft setting, which makes your objects appear very grainy, to a presentation-quality preset, which can significantly increase rendering times.

If the render presets don't offer the exact look you want, you can choose Manage Render Presets from the render presets drop-down list. Then you can create a copy of one of the render presets and customize it the way you want to. You can also use the Advanced Render Settings palette (see Figure 7-11) to customize and create a custom render preset. When you have the rendering settings that you want, you can then specify outputting the rendering to an image file from the Advanced Render Settings palette or the Render Window dialog box.

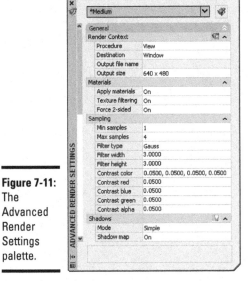

Figure 7-11:
The
Advanced
Render
Settings
palette.

Book VI

Advanced Drafting

The 5th Wave   By Rich Tennant

It started out as a wrap-around porch, and then Stuart went to a CAD workshop for retirees.

Contents at a Glance

Chapter 1: Playing with Blocks

This book of the *AutoCAD & AutoCAD LT All-in-One Desk Reference For Dummies* takes a look at creating and managing reusable content. Reusable content is content that needs to be created only once and then can be used in many different drawings. The ability of CAD to reuse content was a huge advantage for those drafters who ventured into the world of CAD early on. If you have ever had the pleasure of drafting on a board, you may have used plastic templates for things like circles, furniture in a house plan, and mechanical fasteners. These plastic templates allowed you to draw the same objects over and over again without drawing them completely from scratch each time.

Working with Reusable Content

AutoCAD allows you to create geometry templates called *blocks*. A block is an object that is made up of many different objects and given a name to reference when you want to place the block in a drawing. Blocks are great for providing a consistent look to your drawings. You may have already used a block in your drawings for a border that contains project name, date, and other information that relates to that particular drawing. Blocks can be defined with static or dynamic geometry. You also can associate different information with each instance of the block inserted into the drawing through the use of attributes. Attributes are often used to store costing, descriptions, room numbers, and other information that a user would like to extract out of a drawing based on each instance of a block. The extracted attribute information can be imported into an external application, such as Microsoft Excel, or even placed on a drawing in a table object.

Blocks are not the only form of reusable content in AutoCAD. AutoCAD can reference entire drawings and files into a drawing, called *external referencing*. When a drawing file is referenced into another drawing, it is referred to as an *xref*. Xrefs allow you to share drawings with others who may need to ensure that their drawings match up with yours. For example, you can share a floor plan with the building systems contractor and the landscaper at one time. If the floor plan is used as an xref, the next time the drawing is opened by the contractors, the updates are displayed (of course, they would need the updated drawing file). AutoCAD is also capable of referencing file raster images and DWF files.

Drawings often display schedules. Sometimes drafters create this information in a word processor or spreadsheet program. AutoCAD allows you to copy and paste content from Windows-based applications through the use of the Windows Clipboard, but doing so causes the information to become static. AutoCAD can keep some of this information dynamic through the use of Object Linking and Embedding (OLE). Being able to reuse content has advantages, but being able to access that content quickly makes it even more valuable. AutoCAD provides two interfaces that allow you to organize and access content quickly; these interfaces are called the *DesignCenter* and *Tool Palettes window*. For more information on DesignCenter and the Tool Palettes window, see Chapter 4 of Book VI.

Creating Blocks

Creating a block isn't all that difficult once you have the objects created that you want to combine into a block. Blocks contain geometry and text that you create in AutoCAD, such as rectangles, circles, arcs, and lines. All you have to do, for example, is draw a table and some chairs. When you create the block, it looks just like the original objects you used to create it.

AutoCAD allows you to create a block directly from a drawing without the need of doing much else. To create a block, you use the BLOCK command to display the Block Definition dialog box (see Figure 1-1). When you create a block, you need to know three things:

✦ **Name.** The text string that is used to specify which block to insert into the drawing.

✦ **Base point.** The point on the block that will be used to help place it into the drawing when it is being inserted. This point is usually established on an object that is selected when creating a block, but it may not be based on how the block is inserted later in a drawing.

✦ **Objects.** Which objects in the drawing should be a part of the block when it is created.

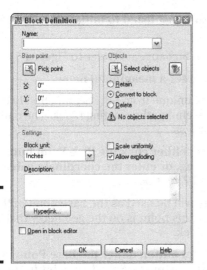

Figure 1-1:
The Block
Definition
dialog box.

AutoCAD provides other options beyond these three that can be specified in the Block Definition dialog box, but the others alter the behavior of the block when it is placed into the drawing and are not required to create a block.

Accessing the Block Definition dialog box

To start the BLOCK command and display the Block Definition dialog box, follow one of the following methods:

+ **Draw menu.** Choose Draw⇨Block⇨Make.

+ **Draw toolbar.** Click the Make Block tool on the Draw toolbar.

+ **Keyboard input.** Type **BLOCK** and press Enter.

+ **Command alias.** Type **B** and press Enter.

The following procedure starts the BLOCK command and explains how to create a block.

1. **Add the geometry to your drawing that you want to combine into a block.**

If you want to control the visibility of the objects within the block later, be sure to place the objects on specific layers so that they can be turned on and off or frozen and thawed.

2. **Use any of the four methods just listed to initiate the BLOCK command.**

   The Block Definition dialog box appears (refer to Figure 1-1).

3. **In the Name combo box, enter a meaningful name.**

   The name entered must be unique from others that already exist in the drawing, or you end up redefining the existing block. The name entered must be 255 characters or less.

4. **Under the Base Point area, either click the Pick Point button and select a point in the drawing, or enter the coordinate value for the base point in the X, Y, and Z text boxes.**

   The point that you specify will be used as the base point of the block or its insertion point. Usually this point is on the geometry that is being selected to make up the block.

5. **If you clicked the Pick Point button under the Base Point area, you are returned to the drawing window. Specify a point in the drawing to use as the base point for the block.**

   After you select the base point for the block in the drawing window, you return to the Block Definition dialog box.

6. **Under the Objects area, click the Select Objects button.**

   You are returned to the drawing window where you can select the objects that you want to add to the block.

7. **In the drawing window, select the objects you want to add to the block. Press Enter to complete selecting objects and return to the Block Definition dialog box.**

   The objects you select can be text, lines, circles, and even other blocks. Any object you can select can be added to the block. You can use the QuickSelect button to the right of the Select Objects button to filter objects by specific property values. Quick Select was covered under Chapter 5 of Book VI.

8. **In the Block Definition dialog box under the Objects area, click one of the selected object modes.**

   The different object modes affect what happens to the selected objects after the block is created.

   - **Retain.** The selected objects are left as in the drawing.

   - **Convert to block.** The selected objects are removed from the drawing, but the new block is inserted at the same location of the original objects.

   - **Delete.** The selected objects are removed from the drawing.

9. Uncheck the Open in Block Editor option at the bottom of the dialog box for now; we cover that option in a little bit.

AutoCAD 2006 introduced a block editor environment for editing blocks and adding dynamic properties. If the Open in Block Editor is checked, the block is opened in the block editor when the Block Definition dialog box is closed.

10. Click OK.

The Block Definition dialog box closes. Results vary based on the selected object mode.

Creating geometry on layer 0 (zero) is usually a "No-No" in AutoCAD, but when geometry is added to a block that is on layer 0, it takes on the properties of the layer that the block is inserted on. This is a great way to check and see if a block happens to be on the correct layer.

Exploring some advanced options

The preceding section covers the basic options in the Block Definition dialog box that you need to create a block. In this section, we cover the other options, as some of them can be used to enforce CAD standards. The following list describes some of the more advanced options and fields contained in the Block Definition dialog box:

✦ **Block unit.** Specifies the units in which the block is being created. This setting affects how the block is inserted into the drawing. If the block is created in the units of Inches and inserted into a drawing that is specified as Millimeters, AutoCAD scales the block accordingly. If Block unit is set to Unitless, scaling of the block is controlled by the Insertion Scale options in the Options dialog box under the User Preferences tab.

✦ **Scale uniformly.** When this option is checked, the block can only be scaled equally along all axes.

✦ **Allow exploding.** When this option is checked, the block can be exploded by using the EXPLODE command. For more information on the EXPLODE command, see Chapter 2 of Book II.

✦ **Description.** The description is used in different interfaces within AutoCAD that can display the block; some of these interfaces are DesignCenter and tool palettes.

✦ **Hyperlink.** Allows you to specify a hyperlink for the entire block. The hyperlink could be to a view in the drawing or a layout, or an external location such as a file, or to a website via a URL.

✦ **Open in block editor.** When this option is checked, the block opens in the Block Editor for further editing after the Block Definition dialog box closes.

Inserting Blocks

AutoCAD stores blocks in what is called the *block definition table*. The block definition table is used to hold information and settings about the block. In order to get the block to be displayed in the drawing, you need to insert a reference to the block definition from the table. An inserted block in the drawing is known as a *block reference* because it refers back to its definition in the table. To insert a block into the current drawing file, you use the INSERT command, which opens the Insert dialog box (see Figure 1-2). The INSERT command can insert a block from within the current drawing or an entire drawing file as a block. It just depends on where the information you want to insert into the drawing is located.

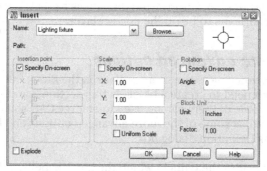

Figure 1-2: The Insert dialog box is used to create a reference to a block definition.

To start the INSERT command and display the Insert dialog box, follow one of the following methods:

✦ **Insert menu.** Choose Insert➪Block.

✦ **Insert toolbar.** Click the Insert Block tool on the Insert toolbar.

✦ **Draw toolbar.** Click the Insert Block tool from the Insert flyout on the Draw toolbar.

✦ **Keyboard input.** Type **INSERT** and press Enter.

✦ **Command alias.** Type **I** and press Enter.

The following procedure starts the INSERT command and explains how to insert a block into a drawing.

1. **Use any of the previously listed methods to initiate the INSERT command.**

The Insert dialog box appears (refer to Figure 1-2).

2. **In the Insert dialog box, either click the down arrow on the Name drop-down list and select the block that is defined in the drawing to insert, or click the Browse button to insert a drawing as a block.**

   The selected name is displayed in the text box of the Name drop-down list. If you clicked the Browse button, the Select Drawing File dialog box appears. If the block has a preview saved with it, the preview appears to the right of the Browse button.

3. **If you click the Browse button, in the Select Drawing File dialog box, browse and select the drawing file that you want to insert as a block. Click Open.**

   The name of the selected drawing file is displayed in the text box of the Name drop-down list and the path to the drawing is displayed just below the drop-down list.

4. **In the Insert dialog box under the Insertion Point area, either check or uncheck the Specify On-Screen option. If unchecked, enter the coordinate value for the insertion point of the block in the X, Y, and Z text boxes.**

   If Specify On-Screen is checked, you will be prompted for the insertion point of the block during the block insertion process after the Insert dialog box is closed.

5. **Under the Scale area, either check or uncheck the Specify On-Screen option. If unchecked, enter the scale for the *x, y,* and *z* axes in the text boxes. If Uniform Scale is checked, you can enter a scale only in the X axis text box and the value is automatically assigned to the two other axes.**

   If Specify On-Screen is checked, you will be prompted for the scale of the block during the block insertion process. If the block was created with the Scale Uniformly option checked, the Uniform Scale option is disabled and checked (forcing you to use only uniform scale).

6. **Under the Rotation area, either check or uncheck the Specify On-Screen option. If unchecked, enter the rotation angle in the Angle text box.**

   If Specify On-Screen is checked, you are prompted for the rotation angle of the block during the block insertion process.

7. **Under the Block Unit area, all you have to do is verify the current insertion units and scale that you want applied to the block.**

   The Unit value is based on the current setting of the system variable INSUNITS. This variable specifies the drawing's current units for inserted blocks. The Factor value is the result of the unit used when the block was created and the current value of INSUNITS. To change the current

INSUNITS value, close the Insert dialog box and type **INSUNITS** at the command line or the dynamic input tooltip. Then enter the corresponding integer for the insertion units you want. For more information, look up the topic "INSUNITS" in the AutoCAD online Help.

8. **At the bottom of the Insert dialog box, check or uncheck if you want the block to be exploded after it is inserted into the drawing.**

   If the Allow Exploding option was unchecked in the Block Definition dialog box when the block was created, the Explode option is disabled.

9. **Click OK.**

   The Insert dialog box closes, and you are returned to the drawing window. The INSERT command may still be running based on whether you checked any of the Specify On-Screen options for the insertion point, scale, or rotation. Specify the prompts as required. Here are the three possible prompts:

   ```
   Specify insertion point or [Basepoint/Scale/Rotate]:
   Specify scale factor <1>:
   Specify rotation angle <0>:
   ```

You can create custom toolbars or pull-down menus to help insert blocks. If you do create your own custom toolbars and menus, you need to use the –INSERT command instead of the INSERT command for the menu macro. You must run the –INSERT command from the command line or dynamic input tooltip.

Managing Blocks

Blocks are a powerful feature of AutoCAD and no doubt you will be using them as often as you can. AutoCAD offers several tools and commands for managing blocks. Some of the ways to manage blocks in a drawing are as follows:

+ Rename a block definition

+ Redefine a block definition

+ Purge a block definition

+ Export a block to its own drawing file

Renaming a block definition

You can rename blocks by using the RENAME command. Follow these steps to rename a block:

1. **At the command line or the dynamic input tooltip, type** RENAME **and press Enter.**

2. **In the Rename dialog box, select Blocks from the Named Objects list.**

3. **After selecting the Blocks named object, select the block that you want to rename from the Items list.**

   The name of the selected block from the Items list is displayed in the Old Name text box.

4. **Enter the new name in the text box directly below the Old Name text box and click Rename To.**

5. **Rename additional blocks if necessary, and then click OK to exit the Rename dialog box.**

Redefining a block definition

You can redefine (or edit) a block definition. In releases prior to AutoCAD 2006 and AutoCAD LT 2007, you insert a block and then explode it. After exploding it, you can make the necessary changes to the geometry and then reblock it using the BLOCK command once again. Or you might use the REFEDIT command.

Redefining a block in AutoCAD 2006 is so much simpler with the introduction of the Block Editor. The Block Editor allows you to edit a block in its own drawing window. You use the command BEDIT to start the Block Editor. Follow these steps to edit a block definition with the Block Editor:

1. **In the drawing window, select the block that you want to redefine.**

2. **Right-click and select Block Editor from the shortcut menu.**

3. **If a message box is displayed about seeing a demonstration in the New Features Workshop, click No.**

   The block definition is opened in the Block Editor.

4. **In the Block Editor, make your changes to the existing geometry or add geometry.**

5. **Click Close Block Editor to exit the Block Editor.**

6. **When prompted to save the changes, click Yes.**

   You are returned to the drawing window, and the references to the block that was redefined are updated.

Purging a block definition from a drawing

You can completely remove blocks from a drawing by using the PURGE command and Purge dialog box. Follow these steps to purge a block definition:

1. **Before you can purge the block, you must remove all inserted references of the block.**

2. **At the command line or the dynamic input tooltip, type** PURGE **and press Enter.**

3. **In the Purge dialog box, double-click the All Items node if it is not already expanded, and then expand the Blocks node.**

   The block definitions that can be purged appear.

4. **Select the block and click Purge.**

   By default the Confirm Purge dialog box is displayed.

5. **On the Confirm Purge dialog box, click Yes.**

   The block definition is removed from below the Blocks node and from the drawing.

6. **Click Close to exit the Purge dialog box.**

Exporting a block definition

Blocks that are created using the BLOCK command are defined in the current drawing only, but many times you will want to be able to access the block from other drawings. The Write Block dialog box, shown in Figure 1-3, is used to export a block out of the current drawing and make a new drawing file based on a selected block. The Write Block dialog box is displayed with the WBLOCK command.

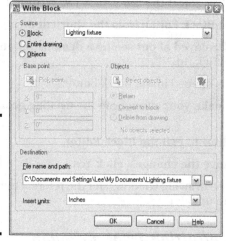

Figure 1-3:
The Write Block dialog box is used to export a block definition

Follow these steps to export a block definition to a new drawing file:

1. **At the command line or the dynamic input tooltip, type** WBLOCK **and press Enter.**

2. **Under the Source area of the Write Block dialog box, select Block.**

   All the controls under the Source area except for the drop-down list become disabled.

3. **From the drop-down list, select the block you want to export.**

   By default the Confirm Purge dialog box appears.

4. **Specify a filename and path in the text box under the Destination area, or click the ellipsis button next to the File Name and Path text box to specify a path and name using a dialog box.**

   If the ellipsis button is clicked, the Browse for Drawing File dialog box appears. Browse to the location where you want to create the new drawing file and enter a name. Click Save once you have specified the new folder location and filename, and return to the Write Block dialog box.

5. **In the Write Block dialog box, specify the Insert units for the new drawing by selecting one of the options from the drop-down list.**

   AutoCAD applies the insertion units to the drawing and uses them when the drawing is inserted into another drawing.

6. **Click OK to export the block as a new drawing and to close the Write Block dialog box.**

**Book VI
Chapter 1**

Playing with Blocks

You can create a new drawing instead of using the WBLOCK command. To define the insertion point that should be used when inserting the drawing into another drawing, use the BASE command or the INSBASE system variable. Either the BASE command or INSBASE system variable allows you to redefine the insertion point that is used for inserting a drawing as a block.

Enhancing Blocks with Attributes

Blocks can store custom information, and that information can later be extracted into an external file or a table object (AutoCAD only). To store custom information on a block, you use an attribute object. You can use attributes to hold a part number or description or even project information in a block. You will often find that title blocks contain attributes in them, which allows the user to edit all the attributes at one time instead of individually like you would have to with text or multiline text. Attributes may appear like standard text objects, but they are much more than that. You can change the text value of attributes when they are part of a block.

Adding an attribute to a block definition

Attributes are added to a block the same way as lines or arcs. First they are added to the drawing and then added to the block. When an attribute is added to a drawing, it is first known as an *attribute definition*. The attribute definition is stored in the block definition and is used to describe what the actual attribute of the block reference should be like. To create an attribute definition, you choose the ATTDEF command to display the Attribute Definition dialog box (see Figure 1-4).

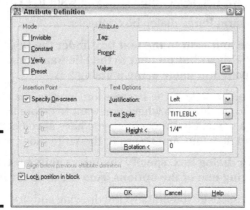

Figure 1-4: Creating an attribute definition.

To start the ATTDEF command and display the Attribute Definition dialog box, follow one of the following methods:

+ **Draw menu.** Choose Draw⇨Block⇨Define Attributes.

+ **Keyboard input.** Type **ATTDEF** and press Enter.

+ **Command alias.** Type **ATT** and press Enter.

The following procedure starts the ATTDEF command and explains how to create an attribute definition and then add it to a block.

1. **Add the geometry to your drawing that you want to combine into a block.**

2. **Use any of the methods previously listed to initiate the ATTDEF command.**

The Attribute Definition dialog box appears (refer to Figure 1-4).

3. **In the Attribute Definition dialog box, select the options under the Mode area that you want to use for the attribute definition.**

Attributes can have four different modes:

• **Invisible.** When this option is checked, the attribute is invisible. By default, the attribute is invisible, but the system variable ATTMODE set to a value of 2 displays all invisible attributes in the drawing.

- **Constant.** When this option is checked, the attribute has a fixed value and can't be changed.

- **Verify.** When this option is checked, you are prompted to verify that the value entered is correct for the block being inserted into a drawing.

- **Preset.** When this option is checked, the default value is automatically assigned to the block when it is inserted into a drawing.

4. **Under the Attributes area, specify the attribute's tag, prompt, and value.**

   The tag is the value you see on-screen before the attribute is added to a block. The prompt is what the user sees in the Edit Attributes or the Enhanced Attribute Editor (AutoCAD only). The value defines the default value that the attribute has. If you are using AutoCAD (and not AutoCAD LT), you can specify a field to define the attribute's value.

5. **Under the Insertion Point area, either check or uncheck the Specify On-Screen option. If it's unchecked, enter the coordinate value for the insertion point of the block in the X, Y, and Z text boxes.**

   If Specify On-Screen is checked, you will be prompted for the insertion point of the block after you click OK to close the Attribute Definition dialog box.

6. **Under the Text Options area, specify the attribute's justification, text style, height, and rotation.**

   The Justification of the attribute controls its insertion point. The Text Style is used to control the font and other text characteristics. Height is used to specify the height of the attribute, and Rotation controls its rotation angle after the attribute is created. Both the height and rotation properties have buttons that can be used to specify a distance or angle using points in the drawing.

7. **Initially, the Align below Previous Attribute Definition check box is disabled. Check the option if you have inserted an attribute in your drawing and want the next one placed below the previously created one.**

   When this option is checked, the attribute is positioned below the previously created attribute.

8. **Check the Lock Position in Block option if you want to disable grip editing and other ways of editing the attribute's position.**

   This option is usually used in conjunction with adding dynamic parameters to the block. Dynamic blocks are discussed in the next chapter.

9. **Click OK.**

   The Attribute Definition dialog box closes, and you are returned to the drawing window. The ATTDEF command might still be running depending on whether you checked the Specify On-Screen options for the insertion point. If you need to specify an insertion point for the attribute definition, the following prompt will be displayed:

```
Specify start point:
```

10. **Start the BLOCK command and create the block like you normally would — just don't forget to add the attribute.**

When you insert a block with attributes or edit the attribute values, you are prompted to edit the attribute values in a specific order. This order is determined by how the attributes are added to the selection set when the block is created. Select each attribute in the order you want to see it displayed when you insert or edit the block.

Inserting a block with attributes

You insert a block with attributes the same way as you insert a block without attributes, except that after the block has been inserted into the drawing, you are prompted to change the values for the attributes that are contained in the block with the Edit Attributes dialog box (see Figure 1-5) or at the command line. You are not prompted for attributes that are flagged as Constant or Preset.

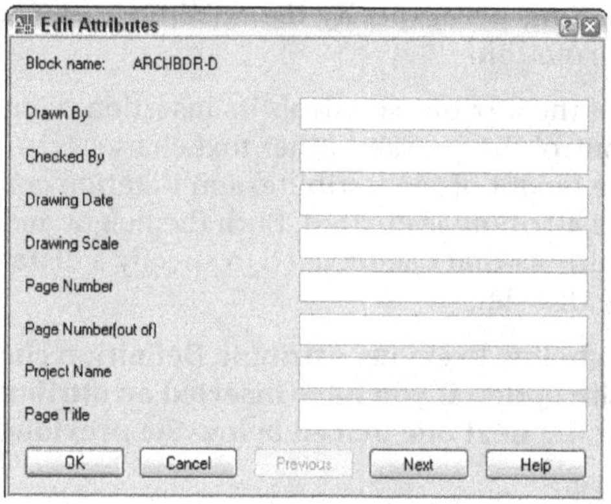

Figure 1-5:
Editing
attribute
values after
a block is
inserted.

Edit Attributes

Block name: ARCHBDR-D

Drawn By

Checked By

Drawing Date

Drawing Scale

Page Number

Page Number(out of)

Project Name

Page Title

OK   Cancel   Previous   Next   Help

The system variables ATTDIA and ATTREQ affect how you are prompted for attribute values when you insert a block. ATTDIA toggles the display of the Edit Attributes dialog box or the use of the command line for changing attribute values when a block with attributes is inserted into a drawing. ATTREQ controls whether prompts for changing attributes even appear when a block with attributes is inserted into a drawing.

Changing an attribute's value in a block

You can change attribute values that are stored in a block by using the Properties palette, ATTEDIT (Edit Attributes), EATTEDT (Enhanced Attribute Editor) — AutoCAD only, or DDEDIT (Edit Text) commands. The easiest way is to double-click the block that has attributes you want to edit, which launches the default attribute editor. Make the change to the attributes in the dialog box that is displayed.

Managing attributes in blocks

When you redefine blocks with attributes, you need to be aware of a few additional commands. Attributes are part of a block, but they are not added to a block reference until you insert the block reference into a drawing. If you redefine a block and add attributes to a block, use the ATTSYNC (Attribute Synchronize) command. Using this command ensures that all the existing blocks in the drawing are updated. The BATTMAN (Block Attribute Manager) command is used to modify the properties of the attributes on a block. You can use this command to change the order in which the attributes appear when edited.

Extracting attribute data from blocks

You can extract attributes from a drawing by using the ATTEXT (Attribute Extraction) command, which you can find in both AutoCAD and AutoCAD LT, or the EATTEXT (Enhanced Attribute Extraction), which is available only in AutoCAD and not AutoCAD LT. For information on extracting attributes out of your drawing, see the online Help topic "Extract Data from Block Attributes," which you can access from the Contents tab of the online Help system. Choose User's Guide⇨Create and Modify Objects⇨Create Use Blocks (Symbols)⇨ Attach Data to Blocks (Block Attributes).

Chapter 2: Dynamic Blocks

*I*n Chapter 1 of this minibook, we discuss how to create and manage blocks with or without attributes. The types of blocks that you created using the BLOCK command and any blocks that were created prior to AutoCAD 2006 are known as a *static block* or a *legacy block* (1.0 version of blocks). AutoCAD 2006 introduced a new type of block called a *dynamic block* (2.0 version of blocks). Static blocks can primarily be altered through placement, rotation, overall scaling, and editing attributes. Dynamic blocks take static blocks and enhance them by adding a new level of editing. Dynamic blocks can allow you to stretch geometry in the block in one direction and confine the distance by set increments. This chapter focuses on how to add dynamic behavior to a block.

Dynamic blocks are supported in AutoCAD LT 2006, but they can't be created. AutoCAD LT 2007 supports the creation of dynamic blocks, with some limitations. One of the main limitations is the ability to use Fields in attributes. (Fields are not supported by AutoCAD LT.)

What Makes a Block Dynamic?

Dynamic blocks are static blocks with some new tricks — maybe you can teach an old block new tricks. Dynamic blocks are created in the Block Editor. They contain custom properties by adding parameters and actions. Parameters and actions bring blocks to life by allowing you to rotate, move, or modify objects within each instance of a block. If you want to move objects within a static block, you simply explode the block and then reblock it with a different name; otherwise, reblocking the block with the same name changes all the instances of that block in the drawing. Dynamic blocks allow you to assign the following actions to objects within a block:

- ✦ Move
- ✦ Scale
- ✦ Stretch
- ✦ Polar Stretch

- ✦ Rotate
- ✦ Flip (or *Mirror*)
- ✦ Array
- ✦ Lookups

After parameters and actions have been assigned to a block, the block doesn't look any different until you select it when no command is running. Based on the type of parameters added to the block, you will see different types of grips appear. Some of these grips appear in the form of circles, arrows, and triangles (see Figure 2-1).

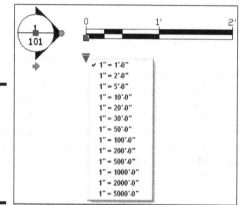

Figure 2-1:
Dynamic blocks can display different types of grips.

Block Editor Environment

The Block Editor, shown in Figure 2-2, was mentioned briefly in Chapter 1 of this minibook because it can be opened when creating a block with the Block Definition dialog box. The Block Editor is a special instance of the drawing window that allows you to work with a block definition in the same way that you would with a drawing file and is used to extend the behavior of a block through the use of parameters and actions. Unlike the main window, the Block Editor doesn't allow you to use some commands, such as BLOCK, REFEDIT (AutoCAD only), and PLOT, and it doesn't contain layout tabs because blocks cannot contain layouts.

After you open the block definition, you can add or remove geometry, add or remove parameters and actions, and work with attributes. If you are using AutoCAD and not AutoCAD LT, you can capture block and custom properties by using Fields that can be used in attributes.

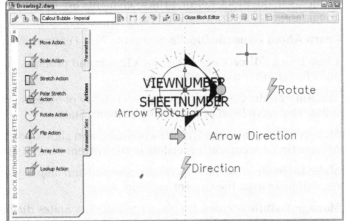

Figure 2-2:
The Block
Editor is
used to
modify block
definitions.

Components of the Block Editor

Even though the Block Editor is similar to a drawing window, it still uses
some specialized interfaces. One of these interfaces is a toolbar along the
top of the drawing window (see Figure 2-3). This toolbar contains tools that
you can use to enhance a legacy block or modify a dynamic block. Here is a
list of what you can accomplish by using the Block Editor toolbar:

✦ **Edit or Create Block Definition.** Displays the Edit Block Definition
dialog box and allows you to open a different block definition from
inside the Block Editor.

✦ **Save Block Definition.** Saves the changes made to the block definition.

✦ **Save Block As.** Displays the Save Block As dialog box and allows you to
save the block definition as a new block.

✦ **Block Definition Name.** Displays the open block definition's name.

✦ **Authoring Palettes.** Displays or hides the Block Authoring Palettes
window.

✦ **Parameter.** Starts the BPARAMTER command and allows you to add a
parameter without using the Block Authoring palettes.

✦ **Action.** Starts the BACTION command and allows you to add an action
without using the Block Authoring palettes.

✦ **Define Attribute.** Starts the ATTDEF command and displays the
Attribute Definition dialog box, allowing you to add an attribute definition to the block definition.

✦ **Update Parameter and Action Text Size.** Starts the REGEN command to
update the display of text, arrowheads, grips, and a few other display

elements in the Block Editor. (These elements are based on the current zoom factor of the drawing window.)

✦ **Learn About Dynamic Blocks.** Starts the New Features Workshop.

✦ **Close Block Editor.** Closes the Block Editor and prompts you to save any changes that were made.

✦ **Visibility Mode.** Controls the current visibility of objects in the Block Editor that have been assigned to a Visibility State.

✦ **Make Visible.** Starts the BVHIDE command and allows you to associate objects that are currently invisible in the current visibility state.

✦ **Make Invisible.** Starts the BVHIDE command and allows you to disassociate objects from the current visibility state.

✦ **Manage Visibility States.** Displays the Visibility States dialog box so you can create, edit, or delete visibility states from the block.

✦ **Block Visibility State List.** Specifies which visibility state is current.

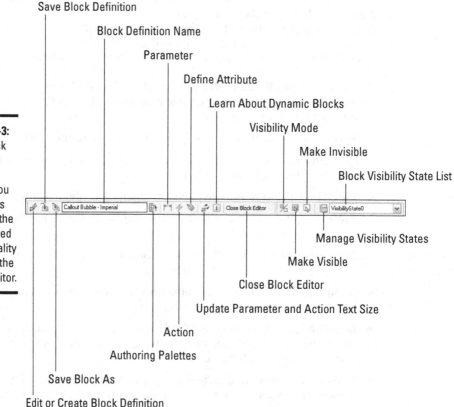

Figure 2-3:
The Block Editor toolbar allows you to access some of the specialized functionality found in the Block Editor.

Save Block Definition

Block Definition Name

Parameter

Define Attribute

Learn About Dynamic Blocks

Visibility Mode

Make Invisible

Block Visibility State List

Manage Visibility States

Make Visible

Close Block Editor

Update Parameter and Action Text Size

Action

Authoring Palettes

Save Block As

Edit or Create Block Definition

You can use the Block Authoring Palettes window (see Figure 2-4) to place parameters and actions in a block. By using the parameters, you can also define custom properties for the block. After a parameter has been added to the block, an action must be associated with that parameter. The action is used to define how the geometry that is associated with the parameter should be moved or changed in the drawing. The Block Authoring Palettes window has three tabs on it, one for the available parameters and one for the available actions. The final tab is one that contains both parameters and actions in what are called *parameter sets*. If you are new to creating dynamic blocks, the parameter sets allow you to get up the learning curve much faster by combining many of the common parameter and action combinations into easy-to-use tools.

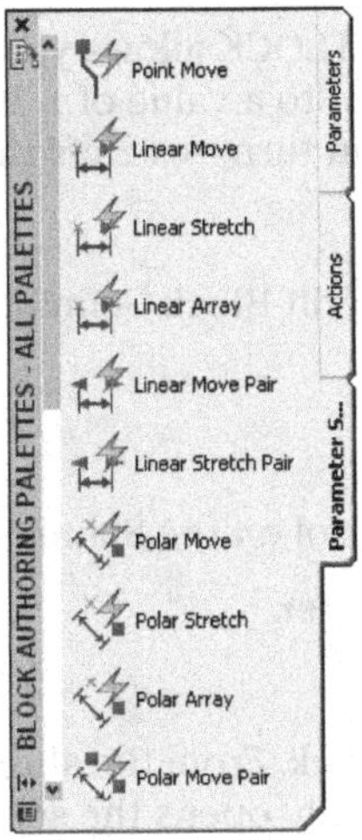

Figure 2-4:
The Block Authoring Palettes window contains parameters and actions for dynamic blocks.

Editing a block definition

To start the Block Editor, you use the BEDIT command. The BEDIT command displays the Edit Block Definition dialog box (see Figure 2-5). From the Edit Block Definition dialog box, you select a block from the list to edit or enter a name in the text box to create a new block. The Edit Block Definition dialog box displays a preview of the block that is selected from the list and its associated description. If the preview displays a small lightning bolt in the lower-right corner, the selected block is a dynamic block. This indicator is displayed in many of the different interfaces and dialog boxes where block previews are displayed.

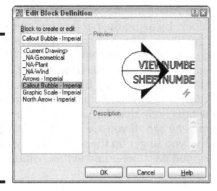

Figure 2-5:
Use the
Edit Block
Definition
dialog box
to open
a block
definition
for editing.

When set to 0, the system variable BLOCKEDITLOCK allows you to edit blocks by using the BEDIT command. When set to a value of 1, it doesn't allow the BEDIT command to be started, and in turn, restricts the modifying of dynamic properties of a block.

To start the BEDIT command and display the Edit Block Definition dialog box, use one of the following methods:

✦ **Tools menu.** Choose Tools⇨Block Editor.

✦ **Standard toolbar.** Click the Block Editor tool on the Standard toolbar.

✦ **Keyboard input.** Type **BEDIT** and press Enter.

✦ **Command alias.** Type **BE** and press Enter.

✦ **Shortcut menu.** Select a block and right-click. From the shortcut menu, select Block Editor. This option automatically opens the selected block's block definition in the Block Editor.

The following procedure uses the Tools menu to start the command and modifies a block.

1. **Start the BEDIT command by using one of the methods described in the preceding list.**

The Edit Block Definition dialog box appears.

2. **In the Edit Block Definition dialog box, select a block from the list and click OK.**

The selected block is opened in the Block Editor. If a message box is displayed about seeing how dynamic blocks are created, click No. If you want to suppress the message box so it is not shown in the future, check the Do Not Display This Alert Again option.

3. **Make the necessary changes to the block.**

4. **On the Block Editor toolbar that is displayed along the top of the Block Editor, click Close Block Editor.**

   A message box asks you to save your changes.

5. **Click Yes on the message box to save the changes.**

   Clicking Yes closes the Block Editor and saves the changes made to the block definition. If you click No, the Block Editor closes and the changes are discarded, and if you click Cancel, you remain in the Block Editor.

If you add or remove attributes from the block definition, the changes are not reflected in the block references that currently exist in the drawing until you erase and reinsert the blocks. If you are using AutoCAD and not AutoCAD LT, you can use the ATTSYNC command to update the attributes on the block references.

Going Dynamic

Once you have a block open in the Block Editor, you can add parameters and actions to your block. Most parameters require an action in order for them to be used, but there are a few that require no actions. AutoCAD offers ten parameters for you to place in the drawing, three that do not require any associated actions.

Table 2-1 lists the available parameters and the actions that can be associated with them.

Table 2-1	Parameters and Actions	
Parameter	*Description*	*Actions*
Point	Defines a point in the block so you can move or change geometry associated with the point.	Move Stretch
Linear	Modifies geometry in a block along a linear path.	Array Move Scale Stretch

(continued)

Table 2-1 *(continued)*

Parameter	Description	Actions
Polar	Modifies geometry in a block along a polar path.	Array Move Scale Stretch Polar Stretch
XY	Modifies geometry in a block across a horizontal and vertical distance.	Array Move Scale Stretch
Rotation	Rotates geometry contained in the block around a given point.	Rotate
Alignment	Aligns a block so it is perpendicular or tangent to the geometry that it is being inserted next to.	No action required
Flip	Mirrors the entire block along a reflection line.	Flip
Visibility	Controls the display of geometry contained within a block. Also can be used to have one block that might display multiple different views or styles of similar geometry.	No action required
Lookup	Creates a table with a list of values that match up with a custom property.	Lookup
Base Point	Redefines the insertion point of a block.	No action required

Adding parameters

You can add parameters to a block by using the Block Authoring Palettes or the BPARAMETER command. The following procedure uses the Block Authoring Palettes to add a point parameter to a block.

1. **Open an existing block by using the Edit Block Definition dialog box, or create a new block using the Block Definition dialog box and make sure that the Open Block in Editor option is checked.**

For information on the Edit Block Definition dialog box, see the section "Editing a block definition" earlier in this chapter. For information on the Block Definition dialog box, see Chapter 1 in this minibook.

2. **In the Block Editor, if the Block Authoring Palettes interface is not displayed, click the Authoring Palettes button on the Block Editor toolbar.**

The Block Authoring Palettes interface should be displayed.

3. **On the Block Authoring Palettes interface, click the Parameters tab and then click the Point Parameter tool.**

The Parameters tab is displayed and the BPARAMETER command starts with the Point option.

4. **At the command line or dynamic input tooltip, select a point in the drawing window for the parameter to reference, or select one of the available options by right-clicking and selecting the option from the shortcut menu.**

Here is the command line prompt:

```
Command: _BParameter Point
Specify parameter location or
    [Name/Label/Chain/Description/Palette]:
```

5. **In the Block Editor, select the location in the drawing window where you want the label to appear for the parameter.**

This prompt is displayed at the command line:

```
Specify label location:
```

The label is a visual reference to the parameter. The label is used in the Block Editor, Properties palette, and to reference the property in a Field (AutoCAD only). The parameter will be displayed with a yellow box and an exclamation point in it (because no action has been associated with the parameter).

6. **In the drawing window, select the parameter that was just placed and right-click. From the shortcut menu, select Properties.**

The Properties palette appears with the parameter's properties.

7. **In the Properties palette, change the properties under the Property Labels, Geometry, and Misc areas to change the behavior of the parameter.**

   The Properties palette allows you to control the different types of properties associated with each parameter type. The properties vary based on each parameter.

8. **In the Block Editor, click Save Block Definition on the toolbar.**

   A message box appears that allows you to save the changes to the block definition or cancel the current save.

9. **In the message box, click Yes to save the changes made.**

   The message box closes. You can stay in the Block Editor to add actions, or click Close Block Editor to exit.

Adding actions

You add actions to a block by using the Block Authoring Palettes or the BACTIONTOOL command. The following steps use the Block Authoring Palettes to add a move action to a point parameter in a block:

1. **Open an existing block using the Edit Block Definition dialog box, or create a new block using the Block Definition dialog box and make sure that the Open Block in Editor option is checked. If you create a new block, you need to first add a parameter to the block.**

   For information on the Edit Block Definition dialog box, see the section "Editing a block definition" earlier in this chapter. For information on the Block Definition dialog box, see Chapter 1 in this minibook.

2. **In the Block Editor, if the Block Authoring Palettes interface is not displayed, click the Authoring Palettes button on the Block Editor toolbar.**

   The Block Authoring Palettes interface appears.

3. **On the Block Authoring Palettes interface, click the Actions tab and then click the Move Action tool.**

   The Parameters tab is displayed and the BACTIONTOOL command starts with the Point option.

4. **At the command line or dynamic input tooltip, select the parameter that you want to associate with the action.**

   The command line prompt is as follows:

   ```
   Command: _BActionTool Move
   Select parameter:
   ```

5. In the Block Editor, select the parameter that you want to associate with the action.

The following prompt is displayed at the command line:

```
Specify selection set for action
Select objects:
```

6. Select the objects that you want to associate with the action, and press Enter when done selecting objects.

The following prompt appears at the command line:

```
Specify action location or [Multiplier/Offset]:
```

After you create the action, the yellow box with an exclamation point in it near the parameter disappears. This indicates that the parameter now has an action associated with it.

7. Specify a point in the Block Editor to place the action, or select one of the available options by right-clicking and selecting the option from the shortcut menu.

The point that you specify should be near the parameter so that you know which actions are associated with each parameter. The actual placement has no bearing on how the action works.

8. In the drawing window, select the action that was just placed and right-click. From the shortcut menu, select Properties.

The Properties palette appears, showing the action's properties.

9. In the Properties palette, change the properties under the Property Labels, Geometry, and Misc areas to change the behavior of the parameter.

The Properties palette allows you to control the types of properties associated with each action type. The properties vary based on each action.

10. In the Block Editor, click Save Block Definition on the toolbar.

A message box appears that allows you to save the changes to the block definition or cancel the current save.

11. In the message box, click Yes to save the changes made.

The message box closes. You can stay in the Block Editor to add actions, or click Close Block Editor to exit the Block Editor.

Based on the parameter you selected, you may need to associate the action with a parameter point.

Using parameter sets

Using parameter sets is no different than placing a parameter and then an action. They simplify the process of having to place each individually by combining the two into a streamlined process. To use a parameter set, display the Block Authoring Palettes interface while in the Block Editor and click the Parameter Sets tab. When the Parameter Sets tab is active, click the parameter set you want to use and follow the prompts at the command line or the dynamic input tooltip.

Visibility states

You can use visibility states to control the display of geometry within a block. This can be a great advantage when you are doing drawings and need to change out a block from one to another. For example, you may have a plumbing drawing that uses several types of valves. You can use one block to represent six types of valves. In releases prior to AutoCAD 2006, you had to erase the block and then find the other block to insert, which takes time. You can accomplish this task much more quickly by using dynamic blocks and visibility states. The Visibility States dialog box, shown in Figure 2-6, allows you to create, rename, delete, set current, or change the order of a visibility state for the block.

Figure 2-6:
Managing
and creating
visibility
states in
one place.

Follow these steps to place a visibility parameter in a block:

1. **Open an existing block using the Edit Block Definition dialog box, or create a new block using the Block Definition dialog box and make sure the Open Block in Editor option is checked.**

   For information on the Edit Block Definition dialog box, see the section "Editing a block definition" earlier in this chapter. For information on the Block Definition dialog box, see Chapter 1 in this minibook.

2. **In the Block Editor, if the Block Authoring Palettes interface is not displayed, click the Authoring Palettes button on the Block Editor toolbar.**

   The Block Authoring Palettes interface appears.

3. **On the Block Authoring Palettes interface, click the Parameters tab and then click the Visibility Parameter tool.**

   The Parameters tab is displayed, and the BPARAMETER command starts with the Visibility option.

4. **At the command line or dynamic input tooltip, select a point in the drawing window for the visibility grip to be displayed, or select one of the available options by right-clicking and selecting the option from the shortcut menu.**

   Following is the command line prompt:

   ```
   Command: _BParameter Visibility
   Specify parameter location or [Name/Label
        /Description/Palette]:
   ```

5. **In the drawing window, select the parameter that was just placed and right-click. From the shortcut menu, choose Properties.**

   The Properties palette appears, showing the parameter's properties.

6. **In the Properties palette, change the properties under the Property Labels, Geometry, and Misc areas to change the behavior of the parameter.**

Follow these steps to define a new visibility state and associate geometry in the block to the visibility state for a block:

1. **On the Block Editor toolbar, click the Manage Visibility States button.**

   The Visibility States dialog box appears.

2. **In the Visibility States dialog box, click New.**

   The New Visibility State dialog box appears (see Figure 2-7).

Figure 2-7:
Defining
a new
visibility
state.

3. **Enter a name in the Visibility State Name text box.**

   You use the name to select and manage the visibility state when the block has been inserted into the drawing.

4. **Specify one of the three options under the Visibility Options for New States.**

   These options control the display of the geometry in the drawing. You can hide or show all the objects in the block, or leave the objects as they appear based on the current visibility state.

5. **Click OK.**

   The New Visibility State dialog box is closed, and you are returned to the Visibility States dialog box. The new visibility state is listed in the list box.

6. **In the Visibility State dialog box, click OK.**

   The Visibility State dialog box is closed, and you are returned to the Block Editor.

7. **In the Block Editor, select the visibility state you want to modify by choosing it from the Visibility State drop-down list on the toolbar.**

   The visibility state is set current.

8. **Click either the Make Visible or Make Invisible.**

   If you click Make Visible, all the geometry currently marked as invisible is displayed in a light gray color so you can select them and make them visible again. If you click Make Invisible, only the visible geometry is displayed, allowing you to select which should not be displayed.

9. **Click the visibility state from the Visibility State drop-down list that you want to use as the default state.**

   The selected visibility state will be the one that is displayed when the block is initially inserted into the drawing.

10. **On the Block Editor toolbar, click the Save Block Definition button.**

    A message box appears that allows you to save the changes to the block definition or cancel the current save.

11. **Click Yes to save the changes made.**

    The message box closes. You can stay in the Block Editor to add actions or click Close Block Editor to exit the Block Editor.

Using Dynamic Blocks

Dynamic blocks can be used and modified similar to how you use a legacy block, including the methods you use for inserting blocks, editing attributes, and manipulating properties through the Properties palette. Some differences exist between the two, however, which are covered in the following sections.

Inserting a dynamic block

Dynamic blocks are inserted into the drawing just like you would insert a legacy block. You can use the Insert dialog box by starting the INSERT command and dragging and dropping blocks from the DesignCenter or Tool Palettes window. Chapter 4 of this minibook discusses DesignCenter and the Tool Palettes window. If you use the Tool Palettes window to insert a dynamic block, you can specify the value for each of its custom properties before the block is inserted into the drawing.

While the block is being dragged on-screen, you can toggle through the points at which parameters are referencing in the dynamic block. These points are called the *insertion cycling order.* You can specify the insertion cycling order while you are in the Block Editor by using the Insertion Cycling Order dialog box (see Figure 2-8), which is displayed by choosing the BCYCLEORDER command. Pressing the Ctrl key toggles through the various insertion cycling points in the block while you drag the block on-screen.

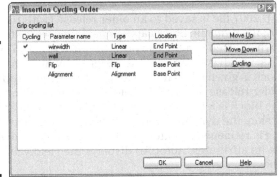

Figure 2-8: Defining insertion cycling for a block can make inserting it easier.

Modifying a dynamic block

The key benefit to dynamic blocks is that they can be manipulated without first being exploded. After you finish adding the parameters to a block and associating actions to each parameter that needs one, you can modify the block without exploding it. This allows you to take advantage of attributes in your drawing, which would not be possible if you exploded the block.

Using a dynamic block's custom grips

To modify a dynamic block, you can select the block to enable its grips and manipulate the geometry assigned to the parameter and action. You can also use the Properties palette to manipulate custom properties of a dynamic block under the Custom area. Select the custom property in the Properties palette and change its value. Some custom properties reference points, rotation angles, or a list of values.

Resetting a dynamic block

You may want to reset a dynamic block to its initial state. You can reinsert the block, but that requires unnecessary work. AutoCAD allows you to reset a dynamic block to its initial state by using the Reset Block option from the shortcut menu that appears when you select the block and right-click. Doing so resets only the custom properties of the block and none of the attribute values.

The RESETBLOCK command allows you to reset multiple block references at a single time.

Dynamic Blocks in Older Releases

When an AutoCAD 2007 file is saved to an older release (with the exception of AutoCAD 2006), the dynamic blocks appear as if they were static blocks. Dynamic blocks when listed in a release prior to AutoCAD 2006 show as anonymous blocks, which is a name that is assigned by AutoCAD and not the name that the block is given when it is created. The custom properties do not work in an older release because the release doesn't understand the information. If the block is left unaltered in an older release after it is saved to a previous version, the dynamic properties of the block will work again when the drawing is reopened in AutoCAD 2006 or later. If the dynamic block contains Fields in its attributes, AutoCAD displays the Field values with their last updated value.

Because dynamic blocks are relatively new, older applications that are used to extend AutoCAD and work with blocks may not work correctly with dynamic blocks. You must test each application that manipulates blocks with dynamic blocks, and if they don't work correctly, you need to contact the vendor of the application to see if an updated version is available.

Chapter 3: External References

In This Chapter

✓ Blocks versus External references

✓ DWG references

✓ DWF underlays

✓ Raster images

✓ Controlling object display with draw order

✓ Object linking and embedding (OLE)

✓ Managing external references outside of AutoCAD

The first two chapters of this minibook explain how to create blocks and dynamic blocks. Blocks form the cornerstone of reusable content in drawings. In this chapter, you read about external references and how you can use them to improve communication and keep file size down. External references are used to link DWG, DWF, and raster image (AutoCAD only) files into a drawing. By linking these files into the drawing, it allows you to have the most up-to-date geometry or image displayed. Some types of external references allow you to snap directly to the geometry that they reference.

Blocks versus External References

Blocks are groups of objects that have a specific name. The block is stored in the drawing file and when a change is required, it needs to be redefined in the drawing. This can be a problem if the block is contained in a number of different drawings. External references might be a group of objects but can also be an image file. External references don't have all their geometry stored in the drawing file; external references maintain in the drawing only a reference to the filename, its inserted location, and its scale and angle of rotation. When you open a drawing that references the external reference, the external reference file is reloaded. This makes external references ideal for buildings that can span multiple drawings. The floor plan could be in an external reference, which allows others to reference the floor plan without inserting all the objects into each drawing.

Working with External References

In past releases of AutoCAD, you had to use several dialog boxes to manage the various types of external references. AutoCAD 2007 introduces a single interface that allows you to manage DWG references, DWF underlays, and raster image references (AutoCAD only). This single interface is called the *External References palette* (see Figure 3-1). The External References palette allows you to attach, detach, reload, and unload the various types of references available in AutoCAD. The EXTERNALREFERENCES command is used to display the External References palette.

Along the top of the palette you are able to access tools for attaching an external reference, reloading external references, or launching Help. The File References area is the main portion of the palette that displays which files are currently referenced in the drawing. This area allows you to control how you view the referenced files in the palette, either in the default list view, which just shows which files are referenced, or the tree view, which displays the relationship between the parent (or host) drawing and all the files that are currently being referenced. The lower portion of the palette displays details about a selected reference, or a preview of the selected reference.

Figure 3-1:
The External
References
palette is
used to
manage
attached
DWG, DWF,
and raster
image files.

To start the EXTERNALREFERENCES command and display the External References palette, follow one of the following methods:

✦ **Tools menu.** Choose Tools➪Palettes➪External References.

✦ **Insert menu.** Choose Insert➪External References.

+ **Reference toolbar.** Click the External References button on the Reference toolbar.

+ **Keyboard input.** Type **EXTERNALREFERENCES** and press Enter.

+ **Command alias.** Type **ER** and press Enter.

DWG References

AutoCAD allows you to reference an entire drawing file into another drawing. The drawing that is being referenced is referred to as an *xref*, which is short for *external reference*. When a drawing is referenced into another drawing, all the styles contained in the file are maintained, so the drawing looks just like it would if you opened the file. Attaching an xref is similar to a block with the exception of needing to specify an attachment and path type. There are two different attachment types for xrefs: attachment and overlay. The attachment types control how the xref is displayed and used for certain operations. The following list explains the two attachment types:

+ **Attachment.** Attachments are used for visual reference and allow you to snap to objects contained in the xref. Attachments are plotted.

+ **Overlay.** Overlays are used for visual reference and allow you to snap to objects contained in the xref, but if the file that contains an overlay is referenced into another drawing, AutoCAD does not load or display the overlay.

When an xref is attached to a drawing, you can control how AutoCAD stores the pathing information to the source file that is associated with the xref. There are three different path types for Xrefs: Full path, Relative path, and No path. Here is a description of the three path types:

+ **Full path.** The absolute path to the file is maintained, which includes the drive letter and all folders. This option is the least flexible as it requires the drawings to be placed in specific locations in order for AutoCAD to find them.

+ **Relative path.** Only the path relative to the parent (or host) drawing is maintained with the xref. This option is more flexible than Full path if your xrefs are stored in subfolders above or below the parent drawing.

+ **No path.** No path information is maintained with the xref. AutoCAD looks in the parent (or host) drawings folder for the xrefs. This option is the easiest to maintain because it looks for the xrefs in the same folder as the parent drawing. Even though it is the easiest to use, it doesn't allow for much in the form of organization as the other two options.

When AutoCAD loads an xref, it first looks in the folder that is specified by the path type. From there, it looks in the following locations in the listed order:

✦ Current folder of the parent (or host) drawing

✦ Project search paths specified under the Project Files Search Path on the Files tab of the Options dialog box, or the PROJECTNAME system variable (AutoCAD only)

✦ Support search paths specified under Support File Search Path on the Files tab of the Options dialog box

✦ The path specified in the Start-in property of the shortcut used to start AutoCAD or AutoCAD LT

Attaching an xref

Xrefs are attached to a drawing through the External References palette or the XATTACH command. During the attachment process, you need to determine the type of attachment that should be used, where in the drawing the xref should be placed, its scale and rotation, and the path type that should be used. When the xref is attached to a file, all its named objects are suffixed with a "|<*filename*>". For example, if a drawing file named 1234 - Floor Plan contained a layer called TitleBlock, and the file was referenced into another drawing, the layer would look like `TitleBlock|1234 - Floor Plan`.

To start the XATTACH command and display the Select Reference File dialog box, follow one of these methods:

✦ **Insert menu.** Choose Insert⇨DWG Reference.

 ✦ **Reference toolbar.** Click the Attach Xref button on the Reference toolbar.

✦ **Insert toolbar.** Click the Attach Xref button on the Insert toolbar.

✦ **Keyboard input.** Type **XATTACH** and press Enter.

✦ **Command alias.** Type **XA** and press Enter.

✦ **Right-click over the File References area in the External References palette.** From the shortcut menu, select Attach DWG.

Here's how to attach a DWG reference.

1. **Initiate the XATTACH command by using one of the methods described in the preceding list.**

   The Select Reference File dialog box is displayed.

2. **In the Select Reference File dialog box, browse to and select the drawing file that you want to attach. Click Open.**

The Select Reference File dialog box closes, and the External Reference dialog box appears (see Figure 3-2). The selected filename and path are displayed under Found In and Saved Path. The drop-down list allows you to select a previously attached DWG file, and Browse allows you to specify a different DWG file to reference.

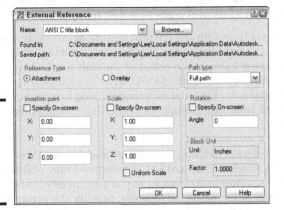

Figure 3-2:
Attaching
an xref is
similar to
inserting
a block.

3. **In the External References dialog box under the Reference Type area, specify the type of attachment you want the xref to be.**

   You can select from either Attachment or Overlay.

4. **Under the Path Type area, specify the type of pathing that the xref should maintain when attached.**

   You can select from either Full path, Relative path, or No path. If you want to use the Relative Path option, the drawing that the xref is being attached to must be saved first.

5. **Under the Insertion Point area, either check or uncheck the Specify On-Screen option. If it is unchecked, enter the coordinate value for the insertion point of the block in the X, Y, and Z text boxes.**

   If Specify On-Screen is checked, you are prompted for the insertion point of the xref after you click OK to close the External Reference dialog box.

6. **Under the Scale area, either check or uncheck the Specify On-Screen option. If it is unchecked, enter the scale for the X, Y, and Z axes in the text boxes. If Uniform Scale is checked, you can only enter a scale in the X axis text box, and the value is automatically assigned to the two other axes.**

   If Specify On-Screen is checked, AutoCAD prompts you for the scale of the xref after you click OK to close the External Reference dialog box.

7. **Under the Rotation area, either check or uncheck the Specify On-Screen option. If it is unchecked, enter the rotation angle in the Rotation text box.**

If Specify On-Screen is checked, you are prompted for the rotation angle of the xref after you click OK to close the External Reference dialog box.

8. **In the Block Unit area, there is nothing for you to do except verify the current insertion units and scale that will be applied to the block.**

The Unit value is based on the current setting of the system variable INSUNITS. This variable specifies the drawing's current units for inserted blocks. The Factor value is the result of the unit used when the xref was created, and the current value of INSUNITS. To change the current value of INSUNITS, close the External Reference dialog box and change the value under the Insertion Units area of the Units dialog box.

9. **Click OK.**

The External Reference dialog box closes, and AutoCAD returns you to the drawing window. The XATTACH command may still be running depending on whether you checked any of the Specify On-Screen options for the insertion point, scale, or rotation. Specify the prompts as required. Here are the possible prompts:

```
Specify insertion point or
     [Scale/X/Y/Z/Rotate/PScale/PX/PY/PZ/PRotate]:
Enter X scale factor, specify opposite corner, or
     [Corner/XYZ] <1>:
Enter Y scale factor <use X scale factor>:
Specify rotation angle <0>:
```

External reference notification

AutoCAD offers a notification system for various features. External references are part of this notification system. You can see when a drawing has an xref in it by the appearance of the Manage Xrefs icon in the status bar area. When a change occurs to one of the attached external references, the icon changes and a notification balloon is displayed (see Figure 3-3). Click the link in the notification balloon to reload the external references that have changed.

Figure 3-3:
Stay informed with the External Reference notification.

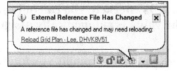

The External Reference notification can be turned on and off with the XREFNOTIFY system variable (AutoCAD only). The default value is 2, which displays the balloon and the icon changes to reflect a change to one of the xrefs. Instead of completely disabling the notification, you may want to use the TRAYSETTINGS command to control how long the notification is displayed.

Editing an xref

DWG references can be edited using many of the common editing commands that AutoCAD offers, but there are a few that are unique to xrefs. There will be times when you will want to make changes directly to the drawing file that are being referenced; in these cases, AutoCAD allows you to edit the xrefs in-place or open them in a drawing window. The commands that allow you to perform these editing operations are REFEDIT and XOPEN.

The commands REFEDIT and XOPEN are available only in AutoCAD and not AutoCAD LT.

Editing a reference in place

Initiating the REFEDIT command displays the Reference Edit dialog box (shown in Figure 3-4) and allows you to edit an xref or block in-place. AutoCAD opens the xref or block for modification right where it is inserted in the drawing. This can be great when you want to modify the xref or block based on surrounding objects in the drawing.

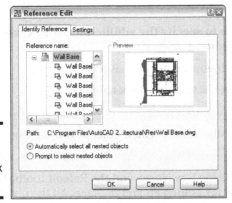

Figure 3-4:
Editing an xref or block in-place.

Book VI
Chapter 3

External References

To start the REFEDIT command and display the Reference Edit dialog box, use one of the following methods:

✦ **Tools menu.** Choose Tools⇨Xref and Block In-Place Editing⇨Edit Reference In-Place.

✦ **Refedit toolbar.** Click the Edit Reference In-Place button on the Refedit toolbar.

✦ **Keyboard input.** Type **REFEDIT** and press Enter.

✦ **Select an xref and right-click.** From the shortcut menu, select Edit Xref In-Place.

✦ **Double-click.** Double-click with the left mouse button over an xref.

Here's how to edit a DWG reference:

1. **Use any of the previously mentioned methods to initiate the REFEDIT command.**

This command prompt is displayed at the command line:

```
Select reference:
```

2. **At the command prompt, select the xref you want to edit.**

The Reference Edit dialog box is displayed.

3. **In the Reference Edit dialog box on the Identify Reference tab, select the Automatically Select All Nested Objects option.**

This selects all the objects in the xref, even any attributes that it may contain.

4. **Click the Settings tab to specify the additional settings you want to use during the in-place editing.**

It is best to have the following options selected:

• Create unique layer, style, and block names

• Lock objects not in working set

This way, you can easily identify which objects you are working with.

5. **Click OK.**

The Reference Edit dialog box closes and the Refedit toolbar appears. This toolbar is useful for editing an xref in-place. All the objects that are not part of the xref are faded, which allows you to identify which objects are in the xref.

6. **Modify the objects you want to change. You can add and remove objects from the xref by using the Add to Working Set and Remove from Working Set tools on the Refedit toolbar.**

7. **Click Save Reference Edits on the Refedit toolbar to save the changes made.**

   A message box appears asking you to confirm the changes you are making to the xref.

8. **Click OK on the message box to save the changes made.**

   The changes are committed back to the xref, and the in-place editing session is closed. The xref is automatically reloaded.

The degree to which the background objects are faded is controlled by the XFADECTL system variable. By default, the setting is 50.

Opening a reference

The XOPEN command opens an xref in its own drawing window, which enables you to use any editing commands without the limitations of the REFEDIT command. Once you save the changes to the file that is open for editing, the External Reference Notification is displayed, which allows you to reload the external reference by clicking the link.

Clipping an xref

Clipping an xref enables you to control how much of the xref is displayed. When working with large xrefs, loading the file can take a while. By clipping the xref, you can reduce the amount of time it takes to load it. The XCLIP command controls the clipping boundary of an xref. The XCLIP command has the following options:

✦ **ON.** Enables the clipping for an xref.

✦ **OFF.** Disables the clipping for an xref.

✦ **Clipdepth.** Controls the distance of front and back clipping planes from the clipping boundary. The option has the options of Front, Back, Distance, and Remove.

✦ **Delete.** Removes the clipping boundary for an xref.

✦ **Generate Polyline.** Creates a Polyline object based on the clipping boundary.

✦ **New boundary.** Adds a clipping boundary to the xref. You can create the clipping boundary by picking two points (rectangular), creating a closed polyline object by picking points (polyline), or selecting a closed polyline object.

The XCLIP command is available only in AutoCAD and not AutoCAD LT. If you open a drawing that contains a clipped xref in AutoCAD LT, it displays clipped.

To start the XCLIP command, use one of the following methods:

+ **Modify menu.** Choose Modify⇨Clip⇨Xref.

+ **Reference toolbar.** Click the Clip Xref button on the Reference toolbar.

+ **Keyboard input.** Type **XCLIP** and press Enter.

+ **Command Alias.** Type **XC** and press Enter.

+ **Select an xref and right-click.** From the shortcut menu, select Xref Clip.

Clipping a drawing reference (xref)

Here's how to clip an xref based on a rectangular boundary:

1. **Use any of the previously mentioned methods to initiate the XCLIP command.**

This command prompt is displayed at the command line:

```
Select objects:
```

2. **At the command prompt, select the xref that you want to clip and press Enter to end selecting objects.**

The following command prompt appears at the command line:

```
Enter clipping option
[ON/OFF/Clipdepth/Delete/generate Polyline/
    New boundary] <New>:
```

3. **Press Enter to accept the default option of creating a new boundary.**

The following command appears at the command line:

```
Specify clipping boundary:
[Select polyline/Polygonal/Rectangular] <Rectangular>:
```

4. **Press Enter to accept the default option of creating a rectangular clipping boundary.**

The following command prompt appears at the command line.

```
Specify first corner:
```

5. **Specify the first corner and then the opposite corner of the rectangular clipping boundary. The points should be outside the area of the xref you want left visible.**

The command ends, and the xref is clipped based on the boundary you specified.

The boundary that appears when you use the XCLIP command can be controlled by using the Modify menu, Object, External Reference, and clicking Frame. By default, the frame is hidden.

Even though the XCLIP command is intended to be used with xrefs, you can also use it to clip blocks.

Editing a clipped xref

You can modify the clipped boundary of an xref by running the XCLIP command again, or selecting the clip boundary and using grips to modify what is displayed. You can use the XCLIP command to replace the clipping boundary that is already assigned to the xref, remove the clip boundary, or turn the clip boundary on or off.

If you set the system variable XCLIPFRAME to a value of 0, you can't use grips to modify the clip boundary of an xref. If you set XCLIPFRAME to a value of 1, you can modify the clip boundary of an xref.

Increasing the performance of xrefs

When you are working with a number of xrefs or working with large xrefs, there are a few things you can do to help increase performance. If you are no longer using some of the attached xrefs, the best thing to do is unload the xref through the External References palette. To unload an xref, select the xref and right-click. From the shortcut menu, select Unload. The link to the xref still exists, but the objects in the file are not loaded into memory. You can use the Reload option from the shortcut menu to load the xref back into the drawing if you need it later.

AutoCAD allows you to control how xrefs are loaded through a process called *demand load*. Demand loading helps improve the overall performance of working with xrefs by loading only the part of the drawing that is needed. Demand loading can be changed by selecting a new option from the Demand Load Xrefs drop-down list under the External References (Xrefs) section on the Open and Save tab of the Options dialog box. AutoCAD provides three options for demand loading:

+ **Disabled.** Demand loading is turned off and the entire drawing is loaded.

+ **Enabled.** Demand loading is turned off and only the part of the drawing that is required is loaded. This option locks the file so it can't be edited by others by opening it or using the REFEDIT command.

+ **New boundary.** Demand loading is turned off and only the part of the drawing that is required is loaded. This option creates a copy of the drawing file, and the copy gets loaded into AutoCAD. The original file is not locked and allows others to edit the file by opening it or using the REFEDIT command. This is the default option that AutoCAD uses.

If you use demand loading, you can take advantage of indexing in your drawing file. Indexing allows AutoCAD to locate specific objects and layers in a drawing that is being referenced. AutoCAD offers two types of indexing, called *spatial* and *layer*. We talk more about spatial and layer indexing in Book VIII.

Binding an xref

An xref can be entirely bound to its parent (or host) drawing. You can also bind select named styles to an xref's parent drawing. To integrate all the objects and styles in an xref, right-click the xref that you want to bind in the External References palette and select Bind from the shortcut menu. The Bind Xrefs dialog box appears, which allows you to specify one of the two bind types: Bind or Insert.

If you choose Bind for the bind type, the named object in the xref is bound with the name structure of `<file name>$#$<symbol name>`. For example, if you bind an xref with the filename Grid Plan that has a layer called Grid into a drawing, it is bound with the name `Grid Plan$0$Grid`. If you choose Insert for the bind type, the same layer name as previously mentioned is just Grid. The named objects are merged cleanly into the existing named objects of the parent drawing when the Insert bind type is used.

You can also bind a named object and not any of the objects in the xref by using the XBIND command. The XBIND command displays the Xbind dialog box (see Figure 3-5). In the Xbind dialog box, expand the xref under the Xrefs area and expand each of the named object tables that you want to bind into the parent drawing. Select the named object and click the Add button. The named object is added to the Destinations to Bind area. Click OK to bind the named objects to the parent drawing.

Figure 3-5:
Xbind
allows you
to bind
selected
named
objects into
the parent
drawing.

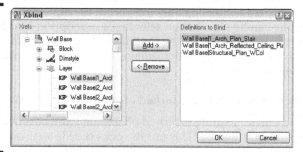

Raster Images

AutoCAD allows you to reference many different kinds of raster images into your drawing files. You may want to reference a raster image that holds a company logo or maybe it is a rendered image of a part in a drawing. Raster images are files that are made up of a series of dots, which are referred to as *pixels.* AutoCAD and AutoCAD LT are vector-based programs, which means they store objects in the form of coordinate values and properties to regenerate the objects when the file is opened, viewed, or plotted. Raster images are referenced into a drawing the same way that you reference a drawing file. Unlike xrefs, raster images cannot be bound to a drawing.

AutoCAD LT does not support the attaching of raster images in the External References palette. If you open a drawing that was created in AutoCAD, you can work with the raster image in the External References palette.

Attaching a raster image

To attach raster images to a drawing, you use the External References palette or the IMAGEATTACH command. During the attachment process, you need to determine where in the drawing the image should be placed, its scale and rotation, and the path type that you want to use. When an image is scaled, it can appear grainy on-screen; when plotted, the graininess is due to how the image was created and its DPI (dots per inch). The greater the DPI, the larger the image can be scaled before it starts to appear grainy.

To start the IMAGEATTACH command and display the Image dialog box, use one of these methods:

+ **Insert menu.** Choose Insert⇨Raster Image Reference.

+ **Reference toolbar.** Click the Attach Image button on the Reference toolbar.

+ **Insert toolbar.** Click the Attach Image button on the Insert toolbar.

+ **Keyboard input.** Type **IMAGEATTACH** and press Enter.

+ **Command alias.** Type **IAT** and press Enter.

+ **Right-click the File References area in the External References palette.** From the shortcut menu, select Attach Image.

To attach a raster image to your drawing, follow these steps. For more information on some of the options in the Image dialog box, see the section "DWG References."

1. **Use any of the previously mentioned methods to initiate the IMAGEATTACH command.**

The Select Image File dialog box appears.

2. **In the Select Image File dialog box, browse to the raster image file that you want to attach and select it. Use the Files of Type drop-down list to filter the displayed files in the dialog box. Click Open.**

The Select Image File dialog box closes, and the Image dialog box (see Figure 3-6) is displayed. The filename and path you selected appear in Found In and Saved Path. The drop-down list allows you to select a previously attached raster image file, and Browse allows you to specify a different raster image file to reference.

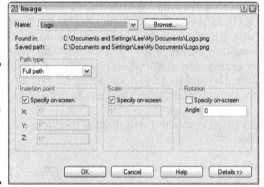

Figure 3-6:
Attaching a
raster image
reference is
similar to
attaching
an xref.

3. **In the Image dialog box, click Details to display additional information about the image.**

The Image Information area provides you feedback on how the image will be scaled upon being inserted. AutoCAD automatically calculates the number of pixels by the current units to determine the size of the image when it is inserted. The current AutoCAD units are determined by the setting under the Insertion Scale area of the Units dialog box.

4. **In the Path Type area, specify the type of pathing that the raster image should maintain when attached.**

5. **In the Insertion Point area, specify how and where the image should be inserted.**

6. **In the Scale area, specify how the image should be scaled.**

7. **In the Rotation area, specify how the image should be rotated.**

8. **Click OK.**

   The Image dialog box closes and you are returned to the drawing window. The IMAGEATTACH command may still be running depending on whether you checked any of the Specify On-Screen options for the insertion point, scale, or rotation. Specify the prompts as required. Here are the possible prompts:

   ```
   Specify insertion point <0,0>:
   Specify scale factor or [Unit] <1>:
   Specify rotation angle <0>:
   ```

Book VI
Chapter 3

External References

Clipping a raster image

Like xrefs, raster images can be clipped to show only part of the image. Only showing what is necessary in the drawing can help to save time when you need to regenerate the drawing during zooming because only the necessary section of the drawing is displayed, especially if a large image is attached. The IMAGECLIP command controls the clipping boundary of a raster image. The IMAGECLIP command has the same options as the XCLIP command, with the exceptions of Generate Polyline and Select Polyline.

To start the IMAGECLIP command, follow one of these methods:

✦ **Modify menu.** Choose Modify⇨Clip⇨Image.

✦ **Reference toolbar.** Click the Clip Image button on the Reference toolbar.

✦ **Keyboard input.** Type **IMAGECLIP** and press Enter.

✦ **Command Alias.** Type **IC** and press Enter.

✦ **Select a raster image and right-click.** From the shortcut menu, select Image and then Clip.

Clipping a raster image reference

Here's how to clip a raster image based on a rectangular boundary:

1. **Use any of the previously mentioned methods to initiate the IMAGECLIP command.**

2. **At the command prompt, select the raster image you want to clip and press Enter to end selecting objects.**

3. **Press Enter to accept the default option of creating a new boundary or select one of the other available options.**

4. **Press Enter to accept the default option of creating a rectangular clipping boundary or select the other available option.**

5. **Specify the first corner and then the opposite corner of the rectangular clipping boundary. The points should be outside the area of the image you want left visible.**

The boundary that is displayed before and after you use the IMAGECLIP command can be controlled by choosing Modify⇨Object⇨Image⇨Frame (which starts the IMAGEFRAME command). The toggle controls all image frames. By default the frame is displayed and plotted. You have three options to control how the frame should be displayed: 0 hides the frame from display and plotting, 1 displays the frame and is plotted, and 2 displays the frame and is not plotted.

You can use the IMAGEFRAME command to lock images so they can't be selected by using a value of 0.

Editing a clipped image

You can modify the clipped boundary of a raster image by running the IMAGECLIP command again or selecting the clip boundary and using grips to modify what is displayed. You can use the IMAGECLIP command to replace the clipping boundary that is already assigned to the image, remove the clip boundary, or turn the clip boundary on or off. IMAGEFRAME must be set to a value of 1 or 2 in order to select the image so the clipped boundary can be modified.

Controlling the appearance of a raster image

AutoCAD allows you to tweak an image after it is attached to a drawing. You can alter the appearance of the image by changing its level of brightness, contrast, or fade. You can use the Properties palette or the IMAGEADJUST command. The IMAGEADJUST command displays the Image Adjust dialog box (see Figure 3-7) for controlling the values, and as the values are changed, the preview in the dialog box is updated. If you use the Properties palette, the changes are dynamically displayed in the drawing window.

Figure 3-7:
Adjusting the appearance of an image.

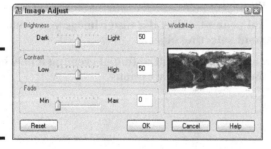

If you have an image that is fairly large in size, it can slow down the regeneration process of the drawing. You can clip the image, but this is not always an option depending on the drawing you are working on. The command IMAGEQUALITY allows you to control the quality of the image that you see on-screen. You can choose from either High or Draft; selecting Draft can help to decrease the amount of time it takes to regenerate the display of a drawing. This setting does not affect plotting because plotting is always done as High. If your attached image type supports transparency, you can control whether the image is displayed transparent so objects beneath it are displayed. The command TRANSPARENCY allows you to toggle transparency for an image on or off.

DWF Underlays

Design Web Format (DWF) files are commonly used for exchanging drawings in a secure electronic format that non-CAD users can view and print using a free viewer, such as Autodesk DWF Viewer, or view, print, and perform markups of drawings with Autodesk DWF Composer. DWF and drawing files are vector based files unlike raster images, which are made up of pixels. When a DWF file is attached to a drawing, it is known as an *underlay*. Since a DWF file is a vector-based file, AutoCAD allows you to snap to the objects that are referenced in. A DWF file cannot be bound to a drawing file, which helps to maintain the files security. We talk more about DWF files in Book VIII.

Attaching a DWF underlay

To attach DWF files to a drawing, you use the External References palette or the DWFATTACH command. When you attach a DWF file, you need to determine where in the drawing the DWF underlay should be placed, its scale and rotation, the path type that should be used, and which one of the sheets from the DWF file is being referenced. Attaching DWF files is limited to 2D DWF files only; if you select a 3D DWF file, AutoCAD informs you that the selected file doesn't contain any sheets that can be attached. Layer information is not imported into the drawing when a DWF file is attached; all the objects in the DWF underlay are placed on the current layer.

To start the DWFATTACH command and display the Attach DWF Underlay dialog box, use one of the following methods:

+ **Insert menu.** Choose Insert⇨DWF Underlay.

+ **Insert toolbar.** Click the Insert a DWF Underlay button on the Insert toolbar.

♦ **Keyboard input.** Type **DWFATTACH** and press Enter.

♦ **Right-click the File References area in the External References palette.** From the shortcut menu, select Attach DWF.

To attach a DWF file, use the following steps. For more information on some of the options in the Attach DWF Underlay dialog box, see the section "DWG References."

1. **Use any of the previously mentioned methods to initiate the DWFATTACH command.**

The Select DWF File dialog box appears.

2. **In the Select DWF File dialog box, browse to and select the DWF file that you want to attach. Click Open.**

The Select DWF File dialog box closes, and the Attach DWF Underlay dialog box (shown in Figure 3-8) is displayed. The selected filename and path are displayed under Found In and Saved Path. The drop-down list allows you to select a previously attached DWF file, and Browse allows you to specify a different DWF file to reference.

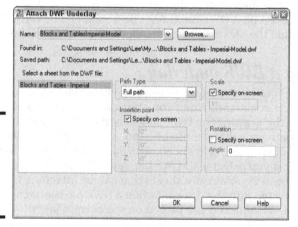

Figure 3-8:
Attaching a
DWF file is
similar to
attaching
an xref.

3. **In the Attach DWF Underlay dialog box, select a listed sheet in the Select a Sheet from the DWF File list box.**

The selected sheet is highlighted and is the one that is attached.

4. **In the Path Type area, specify the type of pathing that the raster image should maintain when attached.**

5. **In the Insertion Point area, specify how and where the image should be inserted.**

6. **In the Scale area, specify how the image should be scaled.**

7. **In the Rotation area, specify how the image should be rotated.**

8. **Click OK.**

    The DWF Attach Underlay dialog box closes, and you are returned to the drawing window. The DWFATTACH command may still be running depending on whether you checked any of the Specify On-Screen options for the insertion point, scale, or rotation. Specify the prompts as required. Here are the possible prompts:

    ```
    Specify insertion point:
    Specify scale factor or [Unit] <1.0000>:
    Specify rotation angle <0>:
    ```

Only one sheet from the DWF file can be attached at a time. If you need to attach multiple sheets from the DWF file, you need to repeat the preceding steps for each of the sheets that you want to attach.

The system variable DWFOSNAP controls whether object snaps can be used on objects that are part of the DWF underlay. By default, you can use object snaps with DWF underlays. Set the system variable DWFOSNAP to a value of 0 (zero) to disable the use of object snaps with DWF underlays, or 1 to enable the use of object snaps with DWF underlays.

Clipping a DWF underlay

DWF underlays can be clipped just like xrefs to show only part of the referenced sheet. The DWFCLIP command is used to control the clipping boundary of a DWF underlay. The DWFCLIP command has the same options as the XCLIP command, with the exceptions of Generate Polyline and Select Polyline.

To start the DWFCLIP command, use one of the following methods:

✦ **Keyboard input.** Type **DWFCLIP** and press Enter.

✦ **Select a DWF underlay and right-click.** From the shortcut menu, select DWF Clip.

Clipping a DWF reference

To start the DWFCLIP command and clip a DWF underlay based on a rectangular boundary, follow these steps:

1. **Use any of the previously mentioned methods to initiate the DWFCLIP command.**

2. **Press Enter to accept the default option of creating a new boundary or select one of the other available options.**

3. **Press Enter to accept the default option of creating a rectangular clipping boundary or select the other available option.**

4. **Specify the first corner and then the opposite corner of the rectangular clipping boundary. The points should be outside the area you want left visible of the DWF underlay.**

You can control the boundary that is displayed before and after you use the DWFCLIP command by using the DWFFRAME system variable. The DWFFRAME system variable controls the display of the frames for all DWF underlays in a drawing. By default the frame is displayed and not plotted. You have three options to control how the frame should be displayed: 0 hides the frame from display and plotting, 1 displays the frame and is plotted, and 2 displays the frame and is not plotted.

Editing a DWF reference

You can modify the clipped boundary of a DWF underlay by running the DWFCLIP command again, or by selecting the clip boundary and using grips to modify what is displayed. You can use the DWFCLIP command to replace the clipping boundary that is already assigned to the DWF underlay, remove the clip boundary, or turn the clip boundary on or off.

Controlling the appearance of DWF underlay

AutoCAD allows you to adjust the appearance of the objects of a DWF underlay by changing its level of brightness, contrast, or fade. You can use the Properties palette or the DWFADJUST command. The DWFADJUST command works from the command line only, unlike the IMAGEADJUST command. If you use the Properties palette, the changes are dynamically displayed in the drawing window.

Draw Order

Draw order determines how objects are displayed on-screen and how they are plotted. When you draw new objects, they are placed at the top of the draw order and therefore appear above other objects in the drawing. AutoCAD provides several different commands that allow you to control the draw order of objects in the drawing. You use the commands DRAWORDER and TEXTTOFRONT to help control the order in which objects are displayed. For example, you can use the DRAWORDER commands to display objects on top of a raster image or text in front of other objects when it is assigned a background mask so that it hides the objects that need to be masked out below the text.

The DRAWORDER command has four options and allows you to bring objects all the way to the front, send them all the way to the back, or bring them up in front or behind selected objects. The TEXTTOFRONT command allows you to quickly bring all text and/or dimensions to the front. If you are using fills or background masks with your text and dimensions, you want to make sure that they are all the way at the top of the display order to make sure that all objects below them are properly masked.

Object Linking and Embedding (OLE)

Object linking and embedding — or OLE as it is often referred to — allows you to place information from one Windows-based application into another while being able to keep the ability to edit the information using the original application. For example, you can link information from a spreadsheet and have it displayed in AutoCAD. Then if the spreadsheet is updated, the changes are reflected in AutoCAD the next time the drawing file is loaded. You use the INSERTOBJ command to insert and link a document into a drawing. The INSERTOBJ command displays the Insert Object dialog box (see Figure 3-9).

**Book VI
Chapter 3**

External References

Figure 3-9:
Attaching a
file to a
drawing
other than
a drawing,
DWF file,
or image.

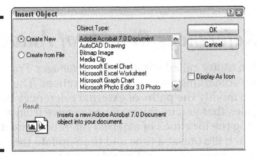

To start the INSERTOBJ command and display the Insert Object dialog box, use one of the following methods:

+ **Insert menu.** Choose Insert⇨OLE Object.

+ **Insert toolbar.** Click the OLE Object button on the Insert toolbar.

+ **Keyboard input.** Type **INSERTOBJ** and press Enter.

To start the INSERTOBJ command and link a word processor document, follow these steps:

1. **Use any of the previously mentioned methods to initiate the INSERTOBJ command.**

The Insert Object dialog box appears.

2. In the Insert Object dialog box, select the Create from File option.

Create from File allows you to link to an existing file, whereas if you use Create New, you can't link to the newly created file.

3. Select the Link check box.

This way, you keep a live link between the drawing and the selected file.

4. Click Browse and then select the word processor document or the file that you want to link to in your drawing. After you select the file, click Open to return to the Insert Object dialog box.

This way, you keep a live link between the drawing and the selected file.

5. Click OK and the document is placed into the drawing.

The document is placed in the upper-left corner of the drawing window.

Once an OLE object is placed in the drawing, you can modify it using many of the standard AutoCAD commands. If you want to edit the document, you can either double-click the object or select the object, right-click, and then choose an option from the OLE submenu. OLE objects cannot be rotated and are plotted best when using a system printer over a plotter.

Managing External References Outside of AutoCAD

AutoCAD comes with a utility called the *Reference Manager.* From the name, you can tell it must do something with external references. The Reference Manager allows you to modify the paths of external references that are attached to drawing files that you might create or receive from a contractor. This can make updating the locations of external references much easier than having to open each file one at a time and then update the external references location. The Reference Manager enables you to update the locations of xrefs, DWF underlays, raster images, plotter configurations, plot styles, shapes, and font files.

The Reference Manager is available only with AutoCAD and not with AutoCAD LT.

Follow these steps to access and edit dependency files of a drawing through the Reference Manager:

1. Click Start (Windows button)⇨[All] Programs⇨Autodesk⇨AutoCAD 2007 and Reference Manager.

The Reference Manager dialog box appears (see Figure 3-10).

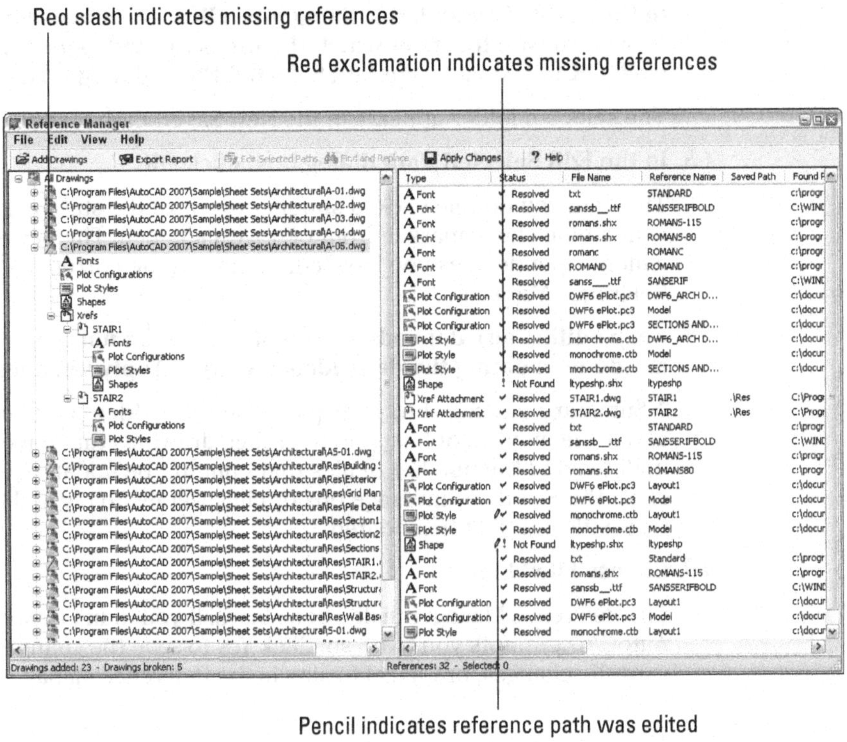

Red slash indicates missing references

Red exclamation indicates missing references

Book VI
Chapter 3

External References

Figure 3-10:
Editing the
dependen-
cies of a
drawing
with the
Reference
Manager.

Pencil indicates reference path was edited

2. **In the Reference Manager dialog box, click Add Drawings.**

   The Add Drawings dialog box appears.

3. **In the Add Drawings dialog box, browse and select the drawing files for which you want to check or edit the dependencies. Click Open.**

   The Add Xrefs dialog box is displayed.

4. **In the Add Xrefs dialog box, click Yes to load any external references that the drawing might have so that you can check those as well, or click No to not check external references.**

   The selected files are added to the tree view in the Reference Manager.

5. **If a slash appears through the drawing icon in the tree view, the file has a problem. Select the drawing, and all the dependencies for the drawing appear in the list on the right.**

6. **Double-click the item that has a status of Not Found, indicated by a red exclamation point.**

   The Edit Selected Paths dialog box is displayed.

7. In the Edit Selected Paths dialog box, click the ellipsis button to browse for the folder in which the file is located. Select the folder and click OK to return to the Edit Selected Paths dialog box.

The selected folder appears in the New Saved Path text box.

8. In the Edit Selected Path dialog box, click OK.

The item you double-clicked should now have the status of Resolved with a blue check mark in front of it with a pencil. The pencil shows which dependencies you have edited during the current session of the Reference Manager.

9. Keep editing any dependencies that need to be updated. When you are done updating the dependencies, click Apply Changes.

A Summary message box is displayed and provides some information about the number of host and reference drawings that have been updated and the number of files that couldn't be updated. Click OK to close the Summary message box or click Details to try and figure out why a file couldn't be updated.

10. Choose File⇨Exit.

The Reference Manager dialog box closes. If you didn't apply the changes, AutoCAD prompts you to do so. Click Yes to save the changes, No to discard the changes, or Cancel to stay in the Reference Manager dialog box.

Chapter 4: Organizing Your Drawings

In This Chapter

✔ Implementing standards

✔ Using the Windows Clipboard

✔ Using the DesignCenter

✔ Understanding Tool Palettes

AutoCAD enables you to create content once and then reuse it in other drawings. Being able to create reusable content is one thing, but being able to organize and manage all that reusable content is another. AutoCAD offers many ways to manage and organize usable content. You can use the Windows Clipboard to transfer content between two open drawings or another Windows-based application. It is not always efficient to open a drawing just to access its content, so AutoCAD comes with two interfaces to help you access content from drawings that might be saved locally on your computer or on a network drive. These two interfaces are called *DesignCenter* and *Tool Palettes*.

Why Bother to Organize Drawings?

It takes time to develop accurate drawings, but you can make the process go faster and faster over time. By creating good CAD standards and high-quality reusable content, you can improve your efficiency. We talk about CAD standards in detail in Book VIII, but for now, we address the importance of properly naming and managing reusable content.

It's all in the name

Many things in AutoCAD that can be reused are given a name, such as a text style, layer, or even a layout. It is a good idea to keep these names meaningful so that you or anyone else looking at the name can decipher its intended purpose. At times this can cause problems; obviously, if you are sharing drawings with other clients, you will most likely both have a title block in your drawings. It is a good idea to prefix or suffix your blocks with text that denotes scale, units, or even a company identifier to avoid problems with duplicate names. Not only will this avoid problems when exchanging drawings with other contractors, it will also help you when searching for named objects in your own drawings.

An example of creating a uniquely named block to be used for an A-sized title block by company ABC might be *TitleBlock-A-ABC.* Now this is only a recommendation that we have observed through the years of exchanging drawings with other companies. There is nothing wrong with calling your title block *TB* or *TitleBlock.* No matter how you decide to name objects such as layers, text styles, and layouts to name a few, it is a good idea to develop a naming convention and make sure everyone in your company follows it. Doing so makes managing CAD drawings much easier.

Using the Windows Clipboard

AutoCAD is a Windows-based program, and like most Windows-based programs, AutoCAD is capable of using the Windows Clipboard to exchange information between two programs. The two programs may be two instances of AutoCAD, or AutoCAD and another Windows-based program, or even two different drawing windows. You can copy or cut objects from a drawing and place them on the Windows Clipboard. From there, you can paste them into AutoCAD or another application. You can also copy information from other Windows-based programs and paste that information into an open drawing.

Copying objects from a drawing

You can copy objects to the Windows Clipboard in a couple of ways. You are able to do a basic copy of select objects in the drawing window through the use of the COPYCLIP command, the standard keyboard shortcut of CTRL+C, or by clicking the Copy button from the Standard toolbar. When you use COPYCLIP on objects in the drawing, AutoCAD copies the objects to the Windows Clipboard and calculates an insertion point to use when pasting the copied objects from the Clipboard. The insertion point is based on the lower-left corner of the extents of the selected objects, also known as the *bounding box* of the selected objects.

If you want control over choosing the insertion point of the copied objects, you can use the command COPYBASE or the keyboard shortcut Ctrl+Shift+C. If you are not concerned with accurate placement, you can copy objects within the same drawing or between two drawings by dragging them on-screen. If you select the objects without any command running and start dragging the objects, they are moved if you released the mouse button, but if you hold the Ctrl key while dragging the objects, a plus sign appears near the crosshairs, allowing you to copy the objects instead of moving them.

Cutting objects from a drawing

Copying objects in your drawing or between files using the Windows Clipboard is nice, but at times you might just want to cut (or move) objects. To cut objects from one drawing and place them onto the Windows Clipboard, use the CUTCLIP command, the standard keyboard shortcut of CTRL+X, or the Cut button from the Standard toolbar. When you use CUTCLIP on objects in a drawing, AutoCAD moves the objects to the Windows Clipboard and calculates an insertion point to use when pasting the copied objects from the Clipboard. The insertion point is based on the lower-left corner of the extents of the selected objects, also known as the bounding box.

AutoCAD does not provide a cut operation that is similar to the COPYBASE command. You can cut objects within the same drawing by dragging them on-screen. If you select the objects without any command running and start dragging the objects, they are moved when you release the mouse button.

Pasting objects into a drawing

After you place objects on the Windows Clipboard, you can paste them into a drawing or another Windows-based application. The pasted results vary based on the application into which you are pasting the objects. You can choose from three options to paste between drawings. The first is a standard paste, which doesn't give you much control over the placement of the objects you are pasting. This option of paste is started by using the PASTECLIP command, the standard keyboard shortcut Ctrl+V, or the Paste button from the Standard tool. If you used the COPYBASE command, you already know the insertion point of the objects being pasted back into AutoCAD. If you used COPYCLIP or CUTCLIP, you don't know the insertion point until you begin pasting the objects into the drawing.

The second option for pasting is to paste objects to their original coordinates where they were before they were copied or cut to the Windows Clipboard. This option of paste is started by the PASTEORIG command. This can be useful when copying and pasting title blocks between layouts or drawings. The final option of pasting content between drawings is the ability to paste the contents of the Windows Clipboard as a block. This option of paste is started by the PASTEBLOCK command or the keyboard shortcut Ctrl+Shift+V.

If you are pasting objects from other Windows-based applications, you may want to use the PASTESPEC command. Using this command, you can define how objects on the Windows Clipboard are pasted into AutoCAD. For example, if you copy cells in a spreadsheet program to the Windows Clipboard, you can paste the copied cells into AutoCAD as a table object.

AutoCAD DesignCenter

The AutoCAD DesignCenter is an interface that allows you to perform *data mining*. Data mining is a popular buzz phrase in the marketing world, but you can do it with AutoCAD drawings, as well. Data mining allows you to locate information that is of importance to you and reuse it. In marketing, data mining might determine whether a product will sell; in AutoCAD, you are mining your data for reusable content in the form of drawings, images (AutoCAD only), layers, blocks, and other named objects.

DesignCenter (see Figure 4-1) was originally introduced in AutoCAD 2000. It allows you to access content that is stored in drawing, hatch pattern, line-type pattern, and image (AutoCAD only) files, and reuse the content in any drawing that you have open. The command ADCENTER is used to display the DesignCenter.

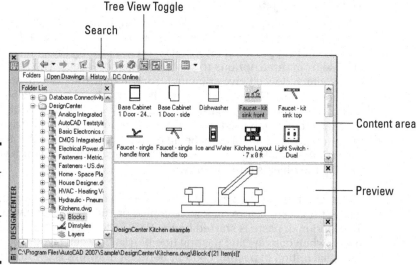

Figure 4-1: DesignCenter allows you to mine your drawings for reusable content.

To start the ADCENTER command and display the DesignCenter palette, use one of these methods:

- ✦ **Tools menu.** Choose Tools⇨Palettes⇨DesignCenter.
- ✦ **Standard toolbar.** Click the DesignCenter button on the Standard toolbar.
- ✦ **Keyboard input.** Type **ADCENTER** and press Enter.
- ✦ **Command alias.** Type **ADC** and press Enter.
- ✦ **Shortcut Key.** Press the key combination CTRL+2.

Locating resources in drawings

By using DesignCenter, you can access content in a number of ways. You can access content that has or has not been opened in AutoCAD. The content can be stored locally on your computer, on a network, or even in an online library of blocks. In order to locate information by browsing, you use one of the four tabs along the top of the DesignCenter palette. These four tabs are as follows:

✦ **Folders.** Allows you to browse your local and network drives for drawing or image (AutoCAD only) files.

✦ **Open Drawings.** Allows you to access any drawing files currently open in AutoCAD.

✦ **History.** Allows you to access any drawing files that have been recently open during the current AutoCAD session.

✦ **DC Online.** Allows you to access blocks from an online portal hosted by Autodesk. The online portal has many different 2D and 3D blocks available for use in your drawings, and they are organized into categories to make it easier to find which blocks you might be interested in.

Browsing for content is not always the most efficient way to find something, especially when you don't remember exactly which drawing file something might be located in. Well, you are in luck; DesignCenter has a search feature that allows you to look for drawings that contain specific content. Maybe there is a drawing with a block in it that you want to use in your current drawing; it is possible to search for that block based on a wild character string. Click the Search button on the DesignCenter toolbar to display the Search dialog box (see Figure 4-2).

Book VI
Chapter 4

Organizing Your Drawings

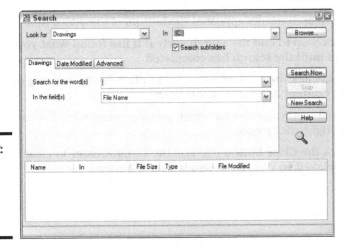

Figure 4-2:
Using the Search feature of Design Center.

To search for a block, follow these steps:

1. **Use any of the previously mentioned methods to initiate the ADCENTER command.**

   The DesignCenter palette appears.

2. **In the DesignCenter palette, click Search.**

   The Search dialog box appears.

3. **In the Search dialog box, select Blocks from the Look For drop-down list.**

   Normally, you would select the type of content that you want to search for from the Look For drop-down list. This controls many of the options in the Search dialog box.

4. **Either select a folder from the In drop-down list to scan for content, or click Browse and browse to the location where you want to start scanning for content.**

   If you click Browse, the Browse for Folder dialog box appears. Browse to the folder you want to select in the Browse for Folder dialog box, select the folder, and then click OK. You can also uncheck the Search Subfolders option to limit the scanning for the content in the folder that you select.

5. **In the Search for the Name text box, enter the block name for which you want search.**

   You can use wild characters to help broaden the search if you don't quite remember the name of the block. You can use a pound (#) symbol to replace a single character or an asterisk (*) to replace a range of characters.

6. **Click Search Now.**

   The search results appear at the bottom of the dialog box.

7. **Click Stop to end the search early if it has found what you wanted, or wait until the search has completed.**

8. **Right-click the content you want to place in the drawing or load into the Content Area of DesignCenter.**

   Based on the content for which you were searching, the options vary on the right-click menu.

9. **Click the Close button ("X") on the DesignCenter to close it, or leave it displayed so you can access it later if necessary.**

Adding resources to drawings

After you find the content you want by using one of the four tabs or the Search dialog box, you can get it into a drawing. Position the DesignCenter so that you can see the drawing window that you want to drop the content into and then select the icon that represents the content from the Content Area. Press and hold the left mouse button over the icon and drag it over the drawing window. Release the mouse button to insert or add the content to the drawing window. AutoCAD ignores duplicate named objects.

To add a block to a drawing, follow these steps:

1. **Use any of the previously mentioned methods to initiate the ADCENTER command.**

   The DesignCenter palette is displayed.

2. **In the DesignCenter palette, click the Folders tab.**

   The Folders tab and Folders List tree view appear. If they do not, click the Tree View Toggle button along the top of the DesignCenter palette.

3. **In the Folders List tree view, browse to the folder that contains the drawing with the block you want to add to your drawing.**

   The Folders List tree view is similar to Windows Explorer.

4. **When you locate the drawing that contains the block you want to place in your drawing, select the drawing under the Folder List tree view.**

   The available named objects are displayed in the content area to the right of the Folder List tree view.

5. **In the Content Area, double-click the Blocks icon.**

   Icons for the blocks in the drawing are displayed in the Content Area.

6. **Right-click over the icon for the block that you want to insert into the drawing, and select Insert Block.**

   The Insert dialog box appears.

7. **In the Insert dialog box, complete the options and click OK to place the block. Don't forget to follow the command prompts.**

   You could have also dragged and dropped the block from the Content Area into a drawing, but it doesn't give you as much control over its placement.

8. **Click the Close button ("X") on the DesignCenter to close it, or leave it displayed.**

Inserting hatches and loading linetypes

Hatch patterns can be dragged and dropped from DesignCenter. Use the Folders tab and browse to the folder that the Hatch Pattern (PAT) files are stored in. By default the hatch pattern (PAT) files that come with AutoCAD can be found in the folder *C:\Documents and Settings\<user name>\ Application Data\Autodesk\AutoCAD 2007 (or AutoCAD LT 2007)\R17.0 (or R12.0)\enu\Support.* User name varies based on what your Windows login is. Select the hatch pattern file, and then drag and drop the pattern from the Content Area into an enclosed area of your drawing. The enclosed area will be hatched. You can also load linetypes from a Linetype Pattern (LIN) file in the same way you drag and drop hatch patterns into a drawing.

Using the Tool Palettes Window

The Tool Palettes window is an interface that allows you to organize content on palettes of tools. These palettes of tools can be used to reference existing content such as blocks, xrefs, or images (AutoCAD only) and even custom commands. Tool palettes can be organized so that they can be shared across the company with other drafters, making it easy to develop and maintain CAD standards with them. The Tool Palettes window (see Figure 4-3) was originally introduced in AutoCAD 2004. The command TOOLPALETTES is used to display the Tool Palettes window.

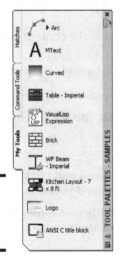

Figure 4-3:
The Tool
Palettes
window.

To start the TOOLPALETTES command and display the DesignCenter palette, use one of the following methods:

✦ **Tools menu.** Choose Tools⇨Palettes⇨Tool Palettes.

✦ **Standard toolbar.** Click the Tool Palettes Window button on the Standard toolbar.

✦ **Keyboard input.** Type **TOOLPALETTES** and press Enter.

✦ **Command alias.** Type **TP** and press Enter.

✦ **Shortcut key.** Press Ctrl+3.

Blocks, xrefs, images, tables, and hatches

Tool palettes are designed to allow you to add and organize content on the fly from drawings that you are currently working on or even drawings that have already been created. Tool palettes allow you to organize blocks, xrefs, images (AutoCAD only), tables, hatch patterns, and gradient fills (AutoCAD only). To create a tool out of these objects, you simply open a drawing and drag and drop the content directly from the drawing window onto the Tool Palettes window. Dragging and dropping from a drawing works to create many of these different tools, but you can also drag and drop content from Windows Explorer or DesignCenter.

Command and flyouts tools

Commands and flyouts can be added to a tool palette allowing you to access the commands that you use regularly. Commands can be customized so they perform a specific combination of commands and command options called a *macro.* A flyout is somewhat limited in the level of customization that can be done with them. Commands can be added to a tool palette by dragging some types of geometry such as lines, arcs, and dimensions from a drawing onto a tool palette, or by dragging commands from the Command List pane in the Customize User Interface (CUI) editor. For more information on creating tools on tool palettes, choose User's Guide⇨The User Interface and Tool Palettes⇨ Customize Tool Palettes on the Contents tab of the online Help system.

Modifying tools on a tool palette

You can modify any of the tools that are placed on a tool palette. The properties you can customize depend on the type of tool. Most tools have a set of general properties that they all have in common, such as current layer, color, and linetype. To modify a tool, set the tab that the tool is on current and right-click the tool. From the shortcut menu, select Properties to display the Tool Properties dialog box (See Figure 4-4). Change the properties as necessary and click OK to apply the changes.

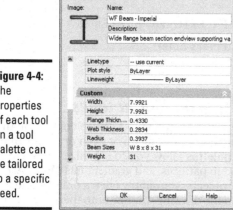

Figure 4-4:
The properties of each tool on a tool palette can be tailored to a specific need.

Chapter 5: AutoCAD Utilities

In This Chapter

✓ Filtering objects during selection

✓ AutoCAD calculator

✓ Auditing and recovering drawings

This chapter focuses on some of the utilities that AutoCAD offers to make you a more efficient drafter. Some of these utilities will help you precisely select what you want to modify or remove from a drawing. We show you how to use the AutoCAD calculator for math calculations and unit conversions, and even to calculate points in a drawing.

At times, AutoCAD may not want to open a drawing or it may crash because of a bad drawing that was received from a contractor, a defect in the program, or even a Windows crash. In these cases, you may need to call upon a few utilities that allow you to recover and audit a drawing file that might contain errors.

Filtering Objects during Selection

In Book II, we talk about how to select objects using single and multiple object selection. Those options are great when you know the exact location of the objects that you want to modify, but what if you wanted to select all the circle objects on a specific layer. You can zoom and pan around the drawing to select each one and then modify the objects, but that can take some time. AutoCAD provides two commands, FILTER and QSELECT (Quick Select), to locate and select objects with specific property values.

Quick Select

Quick Select was originally introduced with AutoCAD 2000 and has only seen minor changes. When you use QSELECT, the Quick Select dialog box appears (see Figure 5-1). From this dialog box, you can specify the objects to which you want to apply the filter, the type of object you want to find, and the property and value you want to use for the filter. You cannot run QSELECT during the execution of another command.

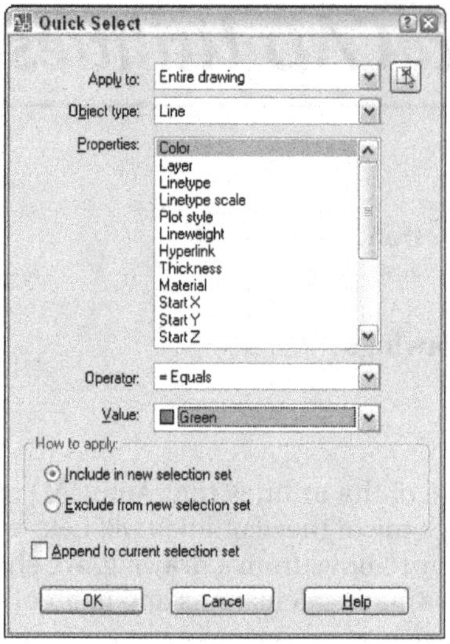

Figure 5-1:
Quick Select
allows you
to filter
objects by
a single
property.

To start the QSELECT command and display the Quick Select dialog box, use one of the following methods:

✦ **Tools menu.** Choose Tools⇨Quick Select.

✦ **Keyboard input.** Type **QSELECT** and press Enter.

✦ **Properties palette.** Click Quick Select.

To select all the blocks with a specific name, follow these steps:

1. **Initiate the Quick Select command by using one of the previously described methods.**

The Quick Select dialog box is displayed.

2. **In the Quick Select dialog box, either select Entire Drawing from the Apply To drop-down list or click the Select Objects button.**

If you click the Select Objects button, AutoCAD returns you to the drawing window where you are prompted to select the objects in the drawing to which you want to apply the filter. When you finish selecting objects, press Enter to return to the Quick Select dialog box.

3. **Select Block Reference from the Object Type drop-down list.**

Only the object types that are contained in the drawing appear in the Object Type drop-down list. To search for all objects in the drawing that are set to a color other than ByLayer, for example, select Multiple.

4. **Select Name from the Properties list.**

   All the available properties for the object type that you selected from the Object Type drop-down list are displayed in the list.

5. **Select = Equals from the Operator drop-down list.**

   The = Equals operator looks for a perfect match between the value and property of the selected object type. There are different operators available, and the ones that are available in the list are based on the type of property selected.

6. **From the Value drop-down list, select the name of the block you want to filter for.**

   The Value field changes between a drop-down list and a text box, depending on the property you select. In the case of the Name property, the values are pulled from the objects stored in the AutoCAD drawing and are presented as a list of choices to choose from. If you had selected Radius of a circle, you would have been presented with a text box in which to enter a value.

Book VI
Chapter 5

AutoCAD Utilities

7. **Select the option Include in New Selection Set or Exclude in New Selection Set.**

   Include in New Selection Set is the commonly used option because you want to work with the objects that result from the filter, but if you want everything but what you specified, select the Exclude in New Selection Set option.

8. **Select the Append to Current Selection check box to append the results of the filter to the objects that are currently selected.**

   This option allows you to use multiple filters to select objects in the drawing.

9. **Click OK.**

   The objects in the drawing or current selection that match the filter criteria are selected, and their grips should be displayed. Now you can run one of the modify commands on the objects, such as erase or move.

Filter

Filter is the original command for selecting objects in the drawing based on their property values. Filter is a little more cumbersome than Quick Select, but it is much more powerful as it allows you to create complex filters. The complex filters can select more than one object type and can include more than one property at a time. Filter one-ups Quick Select by allowing you to run the command transparently, which means you can use the FILTER command at the `Select objects:` command prompt for many of the modify commands. To use the FILTER command transparently, you add an apostrophe in front of the command name. When you use the FILTER command, the Filter dialog box appears (see Figure 5-2).

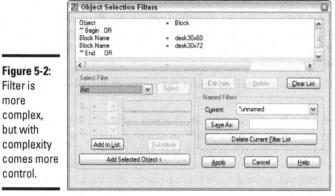

Figure 5-2:
Filter is
more
complex,
but with
complexity
comes more
control.

The following procedure starts the FILTER command from the command line or the dynamic input tooltip and creates a filter that selects two different blocks based on their name and the layer they are on.

1. **At the command prompt or the dynamic input tooltip, enter FILTER and press Enter.**

The Filter dialog box appears (refer to Figure 5-2).

2. **In the Filter dialog box, select Block from the drop-down list under the Select Filter area.**

The drop-down list contains many common object types, group codes, and properties. You can add other properties to a filter by using the Add Selected Object button and then clicking the Delete button to remove the properties you are not interested in using with the filter.

3. **Click Add to List.**

The object type of Block is added to the list box at the top of the Filter dialog box.

4. **Select ** Begin Or from the drop-down list under the Select Filter area. Click Add to List.**

The items that begin with ** are group codes that allow you to build complex conditional statements that let you look for more than one object type or property at a time.

5. **Select Block Name from the drop-down list under the Selection Filter area. Click Select.**

    The Select Block Name(s) dialog box appears.

6. **In the Select Block Name(s) dialog box, hold the Ctrl key and select the blocks that you want to filter for in the drawing. Click OK. In the Filter dialog box, click Add to List.**

    The selected block names are added to the list box at the top of the dialog box.

7. **Select Layer from the drop-down list under the Selection Filter area. Click Select.**

    The Select Layer(s) dialog box appears.

8. **In the Select Layer(s) dialog box, select the layer on which you want to isolate the blocks. Click OK. In the Filter dialog box, click Add to List.**

9. **Select ** End Or from the drop-down list under the Select Filter area. Click Add to List.**

    For each conditional ** Begin you have, you must have a ** End to balance it out.

10. **Enter a name in the text box to the right of the Save As button to save the filter for future use, and then click Save As.**

    The filter is saved to a file named Filter.nfl in the folder C:\Documents and Settings\<user name>\Application Data\Autodesk\AutoCAD 2007 (or AutoCAD LT 2007) \R17.0 (or R12.0)\enu\Support by default.

11. **Click Apply to use the filter that you created.**

    You are returned to the drawing window where you can select objects in the drawing window to search for the objects that match the criteria of the filter. If some objects are found, they are selected. To use the objects found in a modify command such as ERASE, start the command and when the Select Objects prompt is displayed, specify the option Previous to use the objects selected with the filter.

AutoCAD Calculator

AutoCAD had a calculator command for a long time, but one of the things it lacked was ease of use. The calculator that AutoCAD offered was command line-based only and forced you to remember all the functions that could be used, rather than its being a graphical interface. Many users turned to third-party applications or even the calculator that comes with Windows. The problem was that these other calculators were not integrated into AutoCAD's workflow. The command line-based calculator that comes with AutoCAD was not available in AutoCAD LT.

This all changed with the introduction of the new calculator command QUICKCALC in AutoCAD 2006. The QUICKCALC command could do everything that the legacy calculator could do but made it accessible through a graphical user interface. Along with the change to a graphical interface, the calculator was integrated into AutoCAD's workflow by incorporating it into the Properties palette. The QUICKCALC command displays as either the QuickCalc palette (see Figure 5-3) or a dialog box. When a command is running in AutoCAD, QuickCalc is displayed as a dialog box instead of as a palette. Following is an overview of the types of expressions that QuickCalc offers.

- ✦ **Basic expressions.** The Number Pad area offers most of the basic functionality for inputting basic math expressions such as adding, subtracting, and multiplying. The area contains numbers, parentheses for grouping expressions, and buttons for storing results in memory.

- ✦ **Scientific expressions.** The Scientific area offers many common expressions related to scientific and engineering applications. These functions range from being able to calculate sine (sin) and cosine (cos) to convert radians to degrees (r2d) and degrees to radians (d2r). There are a total of 15 expressions that are available to you.

- ✦ **Unit conversion expressions.** The Units Conversion area offers the ability to convert between different units of measure. QuickCalc allows you to convert units of measurement based on length, area, volume, and angular values.

- ✦ **Geometry and variable expressions.** The Variables area and some of the tools along the top of the QuickCalc interface allow you to calculate values based on existing geometry in the current drawing. You can calculate the midpoint between two endpoints (mee) or the radius of a selected circle or arc (rad). You can create custom variables to store values that you might use often.

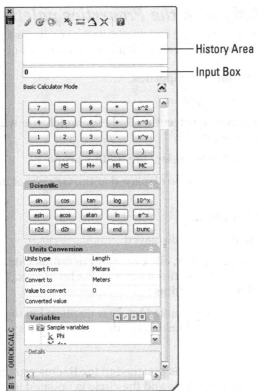

History Area

Input Box

Figure 5-3:
QuickCalc palette makes using calculations and expressions in commands easier.

The legacy calculator is available in AutoCAD only and can be started by using the CAL command. This command is still great for when you might want to use calculator expressions in a command macro.

To start the QUICKCALC command and display the QuickCalc palette or dialog box, follow one of the methods outlined below:

✦ **Tools menu.** Choose Tools⇨Palettes⇨QuickCalc.

✦ **Standard toolbar.** Click the QuickCalc tool on the Standard toolbar.

✦ **Keyboard input.** Type **QUICKCALC** and press Enter

✦ **Command alias.** Type **QC** and press Enter.

✦ **Shortcut key.** Press Ctrl+8.

✦ **Properties palette.** Select a property and click the Calculator icon.

Using QuickCalc with the Properties palette

The following procedure uses the QuickCalc dialog box through the Properties palette to reduce the radius of a circle by a factor of .75.

1. **Choose Tools⇨Palettes⇨Properties.**

The Properties palette appears.

2. **In the drawing window, select the circle for which you want to reduce the radius by a factor of .75.**

3. **On the Properties palette, select the Radius property.**

The Calculator icon should be displayed at the far right of the text box for the radius.

4. **Click the Calculator icon.**

The QuickCalc dialog box is displayed.

5. **In the QuickCalc dialog box, click behind the radius value that was added from the Properties palette in the Input Box. Type the expression *.75 after the radius value and press Enter.**

The result of the radius multiplied by .75 is displayed in the Input Box, and the full expression and result are added to the History Area.

6. **Click Apply.**

The result of the expression is assigned to the Radius property of the circle in the Properties palette and the circle is updated in the drawing window.

If the system variable CALCINPUT is set to 1, you can enter expressions directly into many of the text boxes that appear in dialog boxes and on palettes in AutoCAD. For example, if you enter =1+2.75 in the Thickness property of the Properties palette and press Alt+Enter, the expression is evaluated to the value of 3.75. If you are using AutoCAD and not AutoCAD LT, you can use AutoLISP variables in your expressions.

Using QuickCalc with a command

The following procedure uses the QuickCalc dialog box at the Specify radius of circle or [Diameter] command prompt of the Circle command.

1. **Choose Draw⇨Circle⇨Center, Radius.**

The CIRCLE command starts and displays the following command prompt at the command line:

```
Specify center point for circle or [3P/2P/Ttr (tan tan
radius)]:
```

2. **Specify the center point for the circle by selecting a point in the drawing window or by entering a coordinate value.**

    The following command prompt appears at the command line.

    ```
    Specify radius of circle or [Diameter] <5.6964>:
    ```

3. **Choose Tools⇨Palettes⇨QuickCalc.**

    The QuickCalc dialog box appears.

4. **In the QuickCalc dialog box, enter the expression 0.675+1.285 in the Input Box and press Enter.**

    The result of the two numbers added together is displayed in the Input Box, and the full expression and result are added to the History Area.

5. **Click Apply.**

    The result of the expression is placed at the command line.

6. **Press Enter to use the result at the command prompt.**

    The circle is created with a radius based on the result value.

Auditing and Recovering Drawings

Although computers crash less frequently today because operating systems and software are more stable, the occasional crash still occurs, and it usually is at the least convenient of times. There are a number of things that can cause AutoCAD to crash, such as lack of memory for the drawing file that is being opened or the drawing file being corrupted.

A corrupted drawing file is the most common reason why you may need to jump into disaster recovery mode. A corrupted drawing could be due to a file that was exported out of a CAD package that can write DWG files other than AutoCAD or AutoCAD LT. This doesn't mean that AutoCAD never writes bad DWG files; it is just very rare that AutoCAD writes bad DWG files that it can't open. In these cases, you need to use the AUDIT and RECOVER commands.

Auditing a drawing

Auditing a drawing is a manual process unless AutoCAD detects that a drawing needs to be recovered. Audit allows you to check the integrity of the current drawing for any potential errors in the objects contained in the drawing. Errors might be in the form of bad data formatting or even missing information that AutoCAD expects to be there. To audit a drawing, you use the AUDIT command (choose File⇨Drawing Utilities⇨Audit). The command prompt `Fix any errors detected? [Yes/No] <N>:` appears at the command line or the dynamic input tooltip. Specify Yes or No to automatically fix any errors that AutoCAD detects in the drawing file. Any errors that are fixed are displayed in the Text Window; press F2 to display the Text Window and review the corrections that AutoCAD made. Below is an example of the output in the Text Window.

```
Auditing Header

Auditing Tables

Auditing Entities Pass 1
Pass 1 600      objects audited

Auditing Entities Pass 2

AcDbDimStyleTableRecord: "14-ROMANS-115"
                              Not in Table
Added
Pass 2 600      objects audited

Auditing Blocks
 9          Blocks audited
Total errors found 1 fixed 1
```

Recovering a drawing

If AutoCAD can't successfully open a drawing in AutoCAD due to a problem with the file, it will suggest performing a recovery on the drawing file. The RECOVER command is used to select a drawing file that needs to be recovered; during this process AutoCAD audits a drawing file in memory for any defects and attempts to fix them. In most cases the recovery of a drawing file is successful, but there are times when all errors can't be fixed.

To recover a drawing, you use the RECOVER command (choose File⇨ Drawing Utilities⇨Recover). The Select File dialog box appears. This dialog box allows you to select the drawing you want to recover. AutoCAD audits the drawing, and if everything is successful, a message box appears informing you that the recovery and audit of the drawing file completed successfully. Any errors that are fixed are displayed in the text window. Press F2 to display the Text Window and review the corrections that AutoCAD made.

Using the Drawing Recovery Manager

If AutoCAD happens to crash, you will usually get the option to save any open files before AutoCAD completely closes. When you open AutoCAD the next time, the Drawing Recovery Manager palette appears (see Figure 5-4). The Drawing Recovery Manager palette was introduced in AutoCAD 2006 and it shows the files that are available for you to recover after a crash. The files that AutoCAD usually displays in the Drawing Recovery Manager palette are the drawing files that you saved on the way out of AutoCAD during the crash, the last saved version of the drawing files, the last autosave file associated with the drawing files, and the last back-up file of the drawing files that were open.

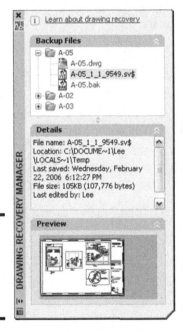

Figure 5-4:
The
Drawing
Recovery
Manager
palette.

Each drawing that was open during the crash is represented by a blue folder. Expand the folder by clicking the plus sign next to the drawing that contains the files that can be recovered. Once the folder is expanded, you can select a file to see its details and view a preview, or double-click the file to open it in a drawing window. After the file is opened, save it with the same name as the original drawing file that was open when AutoCAD crashed (to replace the corrupted file) or save the file with a different name (to create a new copy). If one of the backup or autosave files overwrites the original file that was open during the crash, all the files that are related to that drawing are removed from the Drawing Recovery Manager palette.

Book VII

Publishing Drawings

The 5th Wave   By Rich Tennant

Contents at a Glance

Chapter 1: Page Setup

In This Chapter

✓ **Preparing for output with page setups**

✓ **Organizing a drawing with layouts**

✓ **Looking at a model through viewports**

*T*his minibook walks you through the process of efficiently generating a hard copy of your drawing. After all, the design process should be the hard part and getting your drawing on paper should be rather straightforward. We wish we could say creating a hard copy of your drawing is as easy as 1-2-3 — but it does take a little more effort than that.

Printing in AutoCAD and AutoCAD LT is referred to as *plotting* or *publishing*. If you're wondering why the term *printing* isn't used, it's because plotting deals with larger sheets of paper and specialized devices called *plotters*. Printing, on the other hand, deals with smaller paper sizes for things like office documents. Plotting is done one drawing and one layout at a time, so if you have multiple drawings and layouts to plot, you will likely find yourself using the Publish feature.

Before you plot or publish your drawings, you need to do some setup work. The type and amount of setup that you need to do before you can generate a hard copy of your drawing is determined by whether you are plotting a drawing from the Model tab or layout tabs. Plotting from the Model tab is the easiest way, but it doesn't allow as much flexibility as plotting from a layout tab.

Layout tabs allow you to take advantage of floating viewports to specify different views of your drawing at different scales while keeping the geometry at full scale. When you plot a drawing from the Model tab, you need to duplicate and scale the geometry of different parts of the design. This can result in lost time while you ensure that everything is properly updated. One way to help manage drawing views and sets of drawings for plotting is to use sheet sets. Sheet sets allow you to electronically represent a drawing set in AutoCAD, which allows you to quickly navigate, manage, and distribute a set of drawing files.

Preparing for Output with Page Setups

Sending a drawing to a plotter or to an electronic file for output can be challenging at first because of the number of options that AutoCAD and AutoCAD
LT offer. AutoCAD offers a feature called the Page Setup Manager, which controls how the Model tab or layouts within a drawing are outputted.

The options that are part of a page setup are a subset of the options that are
found in the Plot dialog box, which is covered in Chapter 3 of this minibook.
Page setups help to provide consistency in the way your drawings are plotted. You can use the Page Setup Manager, shown in Figure 1-1, to create new
page setups, import page setups from other drawing files, and assign page
setups to layouts within the drawing.

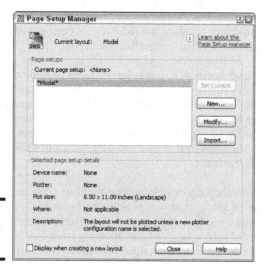

Figure 1-1:
Page Setup
Manager.

Each layout in a drawing can have its own page setup, but to get the most
flexibility out of using page setups, you should use one page setup across
multiple layouts. Page setups are most commonly created in a drawing template (DWT) file, so they are available when a new drawing is created based
on the drawing template. For more information on drawing templates, see
the section "Creating a Good Foundation" in Chapter 1 of Book VIII.

Options of a page setup

From the Page Setup Manager, you create or select an existing page setup to
modify. The steps for each process vary slightly, but in the end you end up
in the Page Setup dialog box (see Figure 1-2). The Page Setup dialog box is

where you make the actual option selections that define the characteristics of a page setup. As previously mentioned, a page setup contains a subset of the options found in the Plot dialog box.

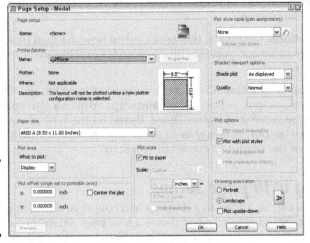

Figure 1-2:
The Page Setup dialog box.

Following is a general overview of the types of options that are part of a page setup.

+ **Printer/Plotter.** Specifies the default device that the layout should be sent to when plotted or published. This allows you to quickly create different page setups that might be used during the checking process and for final output.

+ **Paper size.** Specifies the default paper size to be used, whether it is a check plot to be printed on 11x17 paper or the final design on an ANSI E 34x44 large format paper.

+ **Plot area.** Specifies the default area of the drawing that you want to output. This can be the limits of the drawing, a named view, or a windowed area. The options that you can select depend on how your drawing was set up and whether you are outputting a Model or layout tab.

+ **Plot offset.** Specifies the offset value for the origin of the printable area, and whether or not the plot should be centered within the printable area.

+ **Plot scale.** Specifies how the objects in the plot area should be scaled in order for them to be displayed properly on the paper size specified. You can specify an exact scale such as 1/4" = 1' or a custom size that just fits the drawing on the specified paper size.

✦ **Plot style table.** Specifies which plot style should be used during the outputting of a drawing. A plot style can control the color and lineweights of objects as they are sent to a printer, plotter, or electronic file.

✦ **Shaded viewport options.** Controls how viewports defined on a layout should be plotted.

✦ **Plot options.** Options in this area control how the final plot appears. This area also controls whether plot styles and lineweights are used during output.

✦ **Drawing orientation.** Controls the direction in which the drawing should be output — portrait or landscape. You can also specify that the output be generated upside-down. Based on the type of device you are using for output, you may need to specify the upside-down option in order for the output to come out correctly.

Working with page setups

Page setups can be added to a drawing in a couple of different ways. You can use the Page Setup Manager and define a new page setup through the Page Setup dialog box, or you can import them from an existing drawing or drawing template (DWT) file. When you create a page setup or import it into a drawing, you can then assign it to a layout. If the page setup is later changed, all the layouts that were assigned the page setup are updated.

To start the PAGESETUP command and to access the Page Setup Manager, use one of the following methods:

✦ **File menu.** Choose File⇨Page Setup Manager.

 ✦ **Layouts toolbar.** Click the Page Setup Manager button on the Layouts toolbar.

✦ **Keyboard input.** Type **PAGESETUP** and press Enter.

✦ **Layout tab shortcut menu.** When the Model and layout tabs are visible, right-click the current layout tab at the bottom of the drawing window and select Page Setup Manager.

Creating a page setup

When you create a page setup, you first need to determine if you are plotting from the Model tab or a layout. If you create a page setup for the Model tab, it can be used only with the Model tab. Any page setups created with a paper space layout active are available only for paper space layouts.

To create a page setup, follow these steps:

1. **Use any of the previously mentioned methods to initiate the PAGESETUP command.**

2. **Choose File⇨Page Setup Manager.**

   The Page Setup Manager is displayed.

3. **In the Page Setup Manager, click New.**

   The New Page Setup dialog box appears (see Figure 1-3).

**Book VII
Chapter 1**

Page Setup

Figure 1-3:
Naming the
new page
setup.

4. **In the New Page Setup dialog box, enter the name of page setup in the New Page Setup Name text box.**

   The name entered is displayed in the text box.

5. **Select one of the existing page setups from the Start With list box or choose <None> to start with default settings only.**

   Selecting a page setup from the Start With list box can be helpful if a page setup already exists that is close to the one you want to create.

6. **Click OK.**

   The New Page Setup dialog box closes and the Page Setup dialog box appears.

7. **In the Page Setup dialog box, specify the different options you want to be associated with the page setup.**

   The options that you select will be used with the layout that the page setup is associated with when it is plotted or published.

8. **Click OK.**

   The Page Setup dialog box closes and you are returned to the Page Setup Manager. The page setup that was created should now be listed in the list box under the Page Setups section.

9. **In the Page Setup Manager, click Close.**

   The Page Setup Manager closes and you are returned to the drawing window.

At the bottom of the Page Setup Manager is a check box labeled *Display when creating a new layout.* If the check box is selected, the Page Setup Manager appears when a layout is initialized the first time or when a new layout is created. The option is also available from the Display tab of the Options dialog box but is called Show Page Setup Manager for new layouts.

Importing a page setup

Importing a page setup is the fastest and most efficient way of adding a page setup to a drawing. To import a page setup from an existing drawing file, follow these steps:

1. **Use any of the previously mentioned methods to initiate the PAGE-SETUP command.**

   The Page Setup Manager appears.

2. **In the Page Setup Manager, click Import.**

   The Select Page Setup From File dialog box appears.

3. **In the Select Page Setup From File dialog box, browse and select a drawing, drawing template (DWT), or DXF file that contains the page setup that you want to import. Click Open.**

   The Import Page Setups dialog box appears with the available page setups listed (see Figure 1-4).

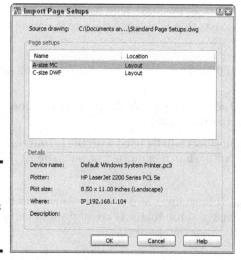

Figure 1-4:
Reusing page setups through importing.

4. **In the Import Page Setups dialog box, select the page setup you want to import from the Page Setups list box. You can select multiple page setups by holding Ctrl+Shift when you select page setups. Click OK.**

   The Import Page Setups dialog box closes and you are returned to the Page Setup Manager. The selected page setups are displayed in the Page Setups list box.

5. **In the Page Setup Manager, click Close.**

   The Page Setup Manager closes and you are returned to the drawing window.

Assigning a page setup to a layout

After you create or import a page setup into your drawing, you can put it to work. To set a page setup to the current layout, follow these steps:

1. **Use any of the previously mentioned methods to initiate the PAGE-SETUP command.**

2. **Right-click over the active tab, and choose Page Setup Manager from the shortcut menu.**

   The Page Setup Manager is displayed. The current layout's name is displayed along the top and to the right of the label *Current layout.*

3. **In the Page Setup Manger, select the page setup from the Page Setups list box.**

   Layouts are listed first in the list box and have an asterisk (*) before and after their names. Named page setups are listed after the layouts in the list box. If a layout has been assigned a named page setup, the name of the page setup is displayed after the layout's name and placed within a set of parentheses.

4. **Click Set Current.**

   The page setup is assigned to the current layout and its name is displayed to the right of the *Current page setup* label under the Page Setups section.

5. **Click Close.**

   The Page Setup Manager closes and you are returned to the drawing window.

Organizing a Drawing with Layouts

Layouts are used to help control how a drawing is plotted or published. In AutoCAD R14 and earlier, layouts were referred to as *Model Space* and *Paper Space*. This changed with the introduction of layouts with AutoCAD 2000. AutoCAD R14 and earlier supported a single Model Space and a single Paper

Space. AutoCAD 2000 made it possible to have one Model tab which represents the old Model Space and multiple paper space layouts.

AutoCAD 2007 and AutoCAD LT 2007 allow you to save all the way back to the AutoCAD R14 file format, which doesn't support multiple paper space layouts. In order to exchange a drawing that contains multiple layouts with a user on AutoCAD R14, you will need to set each layout as current, one at a time, and save the drawing out once for each layout.

Think of a layout as a piece of paper and a way to visually organize how parts of your drawing will appear on the sheet of paper. Generally, you should do all your designing and drawing on the Model tab, but there are some exceptions to this rule. At times, you may need to add annotation and dimensions that are related to part of your drawing that is being displayed through a floating viewport.

Floating viewports are small windows into the Model tab of the drawing and are covered later in this chapter in the section "Looking at a Model through Viewports." Most commonly, you will find a title block that has been inserted or referenced on a layout, in addition to one or more floating viewports.

Working with layouts

Layouts, unlike page setups, are not managed through a dialog box. Layouts are managed through the tabs that appear along the bottom of the drawing window. Everything that you might need for creating or modifying a layout is at the tip of your cursor. The LAYOUT command is used for working with paper space layouts.

To start the LAYOUT command, use one of the following methods:

✦ **Insert menu.** Choose Insert⇨Layout, and a submenu with three different options are displayed.

✦ **Layouts toolbar.** Click the New Layout or Layout from Template button on the Layouts toolbar.

✦ **Keyboard input.** Type **LAYOUT** and press Enter.

✦ **Layout tab shortcut menu.** When the Model and layout tabs are visible, right-click a layout tab at the bottom of the drawing window and select one of the different options above the top separator bar of the menu.

Creating a layout using the Create Layout Wizard

Layouts contain title blocks, viewports, and references to page setups. To make the process of creating a layout as efficient as possible, AutoCAD comes with a wizard called Create Layout and is launched by the LAYOUTWIZARD command (see Figure 1-5). The Create Layout Wizard steps you through the process of creating and setting up a layout.

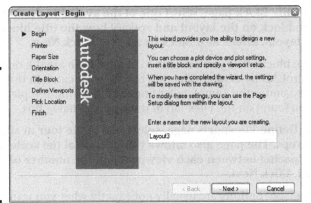

Figure 1-5:
The Create Layout Wizard gets you on the fast track to creating a layout.

To use the Create Layout Wizard, follow these steps:

1. **Launch the Create Layout Wizard by using one of the previously described methods.**

   The Create Layout Wizard appears.

2. **In the Create Layout Wizard on the Begin page, enter a name in the Enter a Name for the New Layout You Are Creating text box. Click Next.**

   The name of the layout can be a maximum of 255 characters, which is a very long layout name. The layout tab is roughly 31 characters (at the most).

3. **On the Printer page, select one of the printers that are available, including both system printers and PC3 files. Click Next.**

   The printer you specify is used as the default output device for the layout.

4. **On the Paper Size page, select one of the available paper sizes from the drop-down list and the drawing units. Click Next.**

   The paper size is assigned to the layout and used during output. The available paper sizes that you can select from are determined by the printer that you previously selected. Drawing units are typically in inches or millimeters, but if you choose a printer that generates an image file, you also have the option of pixels. The paper size is displayed under the Paper Size in Units section.

5. **On the Orientation page, select either Portrait or Landscape. Click Next.**

   The orientation controls which way the paper is turned for output.

**Book VII
Chapter 1**

Page Setup

6. **On the Title Block page, select one of the available drawings to use for the title block on the layout and specify how the title block is placed on the layout, either as a Block or an Xref. Click Next.**

   The title blocks that you are able to choose from are the ones that come with AutoCAD by default. The title blocks are located in the path that is specified under the Template Settings and Drawing Template File Location found on the Files tab of the Options dialog box.

7. **On the Define Viewports page, select one of the four available viewport setups. The page also allows you to control the scale of the viewports, spacing between each viewport and the number of viewports created. Click Next.**

   The available options are usually not exactly what you want, but they do allow for a good starting point. Remember, you can resize and adjust the scale of the viewports using grips and the Properties palette later.

8. **On the Pick Location page, click the Select Location button to specify the area of the layout you want the viewports to be created in. Click Next.**

   As mentioned in the previous step, you can modify the viewports once they are on the layout using grips and the Properties palette.

9. **On the Finish page, click Finish.**

   The Create Layout Wizard closes, and the new layout is created based on the options that you specified during the wizard.

Importing a layout

The Create Layout Wizard is nice, but there are some things you will most likely need to do after you use the wizard, such as assigning a page setup to adjust other settings of the layout to control the output that is not part of the wizard. As with page setups, AutoCAD allows you to import layouts that are in an existing drawing. Importing a layout allows you to spend less time setting up your drawing and more time on drafting.

To import a layout into a drawing, follow these steps:

1. **Choose Insert⇨Layout⇨Layout from Template.**

   The Select Template From File dialog box is displayed. This dialog box allows you to browse for a drawing, drawing template (DWT), or DXF file that contains the layout you want to import.

2. **In the Select Template From File dialog box, select the drawing, drawing template (DWT), or DXF file that contains the layout you want to import. Click Open.**

The Insert Layout(s) dialog box appears and lists the available paper space layouts that can be imported (see Figure 1-6).

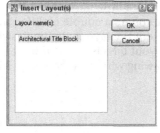

Figure 1-6:
Importing an existing layout from a drawing.

3. **In the Insert Layout(s) dialog box, select a layout or multiple layouts from the list box. Click OK.**

The layouts are imported to the drawing and are positioned to the right of the last layout tab.

Page setups are not automatically imported when importing a layout. If you want to keep the page setup with the layout, you must first import the page setup and then the layout separately.

Book VII
Chapter 1

Page Setup

Modifying a layout

Layout tabs can be modified in a variety of ways. They can be removed from a drawing or repositioned. You can use the LAYOUT command for many of these tasks, but using the shortcut menu of a layout tab is the most flexible. If you right-click a layout tab, you can access the following options for modifying a layout:

✦ **Delete.** Allows you to remove the selected layout or layouts from the drawing.

✦ **Rename.** Displays the Rename Layout dialog box so that you can change the text string that appears on the layout tab.

✦ **Move or Copy.** Displays the Move and Copy dialog box so you can control the order in which layouts are displayed and allows you to quickly create a copy of an existing layout in the drawing.

✦ **Select All Layouts.** Allows you to select all the tabs in the drawing except for the Model tab.

Navigating Layouts

A drawing contains at least one layout at all times and one Model tab but may contain many more layouts than that. Once you get past about four or five layouts, navigating layouts becomes a little more difficult as tabs start becoming hidden from view. AutoCAD offers a couple of different ways to navigate through the tabs that represent the layouts in the drawing file. The most common way to navigate the layout tabs is to use the set of four controls located at the bottom of the drawing window (see Figure 1-7).

Figure 1-7:
Layout
navigation
controls.

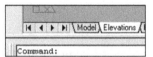

The far left control jumps to the very first layout tab, and the far right control jumps to the very last layout tab. The two controls located in the middle allow you to step one layout tab at a time backward and forward. You can also use the keyboard combinations Ctrl+Page Up and Ctrl+Page Down to step backward and forward one layout tab at a time.

In this version of AutoCAD, you can turn off the display of the layout tabs and still be able to access different layouts efficiently. If you are using an earlier release, you can turn off the display of the layout tabs, but navigating layouts is difficult. If you right-click a layout tab, you have the option to Hide Layout and Model tabs from the shortcut menu. When the layout tabs are hidden, three new controls are displayed in the status bar area to allow you to access the Model tab and the different paper space layouts in the drawing.

Appearance of layouts

The appearance of layouts and the layout tab can be controlled through the Display tab of the Options dialog box. To access the Options dialog box, select the Tools menu and then Options. The Layout Element section controls many of the visual cues that are present when a layout tab is current (see Figure 1-8). These include the printable area, the overall paper size, and a shadow to give the paper an appearance of depth.

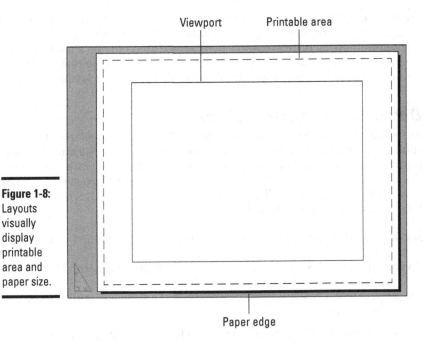

Viewport   Printable area

Paper edge

Figure 1-8:
Layouts
visually
display
printable
area and
paper size.

The background color can be modified so that it is easier to tell that you are in a layout versus the Model tab, or you can make them appear the same. The different color options are available through the Colors button under the Window Elements section of the Display tab in the Options dialog box. It is also possible to control the color of the UCS Icon when a layout tab is active through the UCS Icon dialog box. The UCS Icon dialog box can be displayed by selecting the View menu, Display, UCS Icon, and then Properties.

Looking at a Model through Viewports

Layouts by themselves do not provide all the necessary requirements for getting your drawing set up and ready for output. When you use the Create Layout Wizard, you are prompted to define viewports and provide a scale for them, so you know viewports are important on a layout. Viewports allow you to see part or all of the objects that are on the Model tab and to have these objects displayed at a specific scale.

AutoCAD offers two types of viewports, tiled and floating. *Tiled viewports* are created only on the Model tab and provide a way to work in the drawing without outputting it. *Floating viewports* are created only on a paper space layout and are used to organize a drawing for output. The following sections cover how to create and work with floating viewports on a layout.

Defining a viewport's shape

AutoCAD supports two types of floating viewports, rectangular and irregular (polygonal and closed objects, such as a circle or spline). Rectangular viewports are the most common of the two, but being able to create a viewport from a circle or polyline object can allow you to conserve space on a layout or jazz one up for plotting. The VPORTS command is used to create both rectangular and irregular viewports.

AutoCAD LT does not support the creation of irregular floating viewports.

To start the VPORTS command, use one of the following methods:

+ **View menu.** Choose View⇨Viewports, and a submenu with nine options is displayed.

+ **Viewports toolbar.** Click the Display Viewports Dialog button on the Viewports toolbar. You can also choose to use the buttons Single Viewport, Polygonal Viewport, or Convert Object to Viewport on the toolbar.

+ **Layouts toolbar.** Click the Display Viewports Dialog button on the Layouts toolbar.

+ **Keyboard input.** Type VPORTS and press Enter.

Creating a rectangular viewport

Rectangular viewports are the most common and the easiest to create. The Viewports dialog box, shown in Figure 1-9, offers some standard configurations for quickly laying out rectangular viewports. You can specify up to four viewports with a different visual style and view for each one. The Viewports dialog box offers some default views for 3D drawings, such as Top, Left, and Southwest.

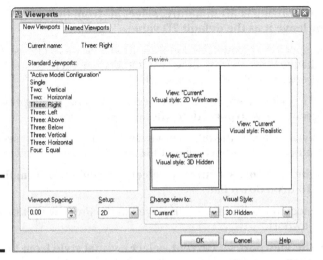

Figure 1-9:
The
Viewports
dialog box.

To add a viewport configuration to a layout, follow these steps:

1. **Select the paper space layout that you want to create floating viewports on. Make sure that no viewports already exist on the layout by erasing any that are, or be sure to have enough area to add some additional ones.**

2. **Initiate the VPORTS command by using one of the previously described methods.**

The Viewports dialog box is displayed. This dialog box allows you to create some basic viewport layout configurations.

3. **In the Viewports dialog box, make sure that you are on the New Viewports tab. Select the configuration you want to use from the Standard Viewports list box.**

The Preview area updates to reflect the viewport configuration you selected.

4. **In the Viewport Spacing text box, enter the amount of space you want between the viewports that are created. This only affects the viewports that you are currently creating.**

The size of the spacing should be a rather small number since you need to specify a scale of 1 in the Plot dialog box when plotting a paper space layout.

**Book VII
Chapter 1**

Page Setup

5. **If your drawing is 3D in nature, select 3D from the Setup drop-down list or leave it as the default 2D value.**

   If you specify 3D, you have some additional views to choose from under the Change View To drop-down list. Otherwise, there is no other difference between specifying 2D and 3D.

6. **In the Preview area, click the different sections of the preview that represent the viewports that will be created later.**

   When you select in the different viewports of the Preview section, you are setting that viewport current for adjusting its view and visual style.

7. **With the viewport set current, select a named view from the Change View To drop-down list.**

   The selected named view is displayed in the Preview section for the current viewport.

8. **With the viewport set current, select a visual style from the Visual Style drop-down list.**

   The selected visual style is displayed in the Preview section for the current viewport.

9. **Repeat Steps 5 through 7 for each of the viewports in the Preview section.**

10. **Click OK.**

    The Viewports dialog box closes, and you are returned to the drawing window where the prompt below is displayed at the command line or in a dynamic tooltip.

    ```
    Specify first corner or [Fit] <Fit>:
    ```

11. **In the drawing window, specify the first point on the layout in the printable area where you want to create the viewports.**

    You are specifying a rectangular area where the viewports will be created. The next prompt below is then displayed at the command line or in a dynamic tooltip.

    ```
    Specify opposite corner:
    ```

12. **In the drawing window, specify the opposite corner to finish defining the area where you want the viewports to be created.**

    The viewports are created in the defined area based on the options specified in the Viewports dialog box. You should notice that the objects on the Model tab are displayed in each of the viewports.

Creating an irregular viewport

Irregular viewports are created by using the command line version of the VPORTS command. The command line version of the command is accessible by placing a hyphen in front of the command. The –VPORTS command has some additional options that the dialog box version of the command doesn't have for working with viewports and creating irregular viewports.

The two options that the –VPORTS command offers for creating irregular viewports are Polygonal and Object. The –VPORTS command displays the prompt below at the command line or dynamic tooltip when it is first started.

```
Specify corner of viewport or
[ON/OFF/Fit/Shadeplot/Lock/Object/Polygonal/Restore/2/3/4]
    <Fit>:
```

To add an irregular viewport to a layout using the Polygonal option.

1. **Select the paper space layout where you want to create a floating viewport.**

2. **Choose View⇨Viewports⇨Polygonal Viewport.**

   The –VPORTS command starts and displays the following prompt at the command line or at the dynamic tooltip.

   ```
   Specify start point:
   ```

3. **In the drawing window, specify the first point of the polygonal object that will be used to define the viewport.**

   After selecting the first point of the polygonal object, the following prompt appears at the command line or at the dynamic tooltip.

   ```
   Specify next point or [Arc/Length/Undo]:
   ```

4. **Specify the next point or select one of the available options. This example assumes that you selected the next point.**

   After selecting the next point of the polygonal object, the previous prompt is displayed again except with a Close option added in. The following prompt appears at the command line or at the dynamic tooltip.

   ```
   Specify next point or [Arc/Close/Length/Undo]:
   ```

5. **Continue specifying points as necessary to define the polygonal object. Once done specifying points, right-click and select Close, or type C at the command prompt and press Enter.**

   The command ends and the objects on the Model tab appear.

Irregular viewports can be created in a drawing based on closed objects. The objects that can be created into a viewport are circles, closed polylines, ellipses, closed splines, and regions. First, draw the closed object you want to create into a viewport on a paper space layout; then select View⇨Viewports and Object. After you start the –VPORTS command, select the object. The command ends and the objects from the Model tab are displayed in the viewport.

Controlling scale

Paper space layouts are plotted at a scale of 1:1, so in order to get the objects in the viewports to be plotted and displayed correctly, you have to specify a scale for each viewport. You do this by using the scale list on the Viewports toolbar or using the Properties palette. The following procedure uses the Properties palette to change the scale for a floating viewport.

1. **Select a viewport on a paper space layout for which you want to change the scale.**

The grips for the selected viewport appear.

2. **With the viewport selected, right-click and select Properties from the shortcut menu to display the Properties palette.**

The Properties palette appears.

3. **In the Properties palette, select the scale for the viewport from the Standard Scale drop-down list.**

The viewport is updated to display the objects on the Model tab at the specified scale. You can also specify a custom scale by typing the scale value in the Custom Scale text box on the Properties palette.

You can use the SCALELISTEDIT command to display the Edit Scale List dialog box to control which scales are available for use in the program. This controls the list of scales in places like the Viewports toolbar and the Plot dialog box.

Controlling the display within a viewport

You can move in and out of viewports on a paper space layout by double-clicking inside the viewport. This places you in model space so you can interact with the objects on the Model tab. By entering the viewport this way, you can control which part of the objects on the Model tab are displayed through the viewport by panning. Once you have the objects positioned correctly, you can then lock the viewport. To lock the display of a viewport, select the viewport, and then right-click, select Display Locked, and then click Yes or No.

At times you may find that you may want to edit objects through a viewport. In this case, there is a way to open a viewport so that it fills the entire drawing area. If you double-click on a viewport object or its border, the viewport is maximized in the drawing window. This allows you to pan and zoom in a viewport even if its display has been locked to prevent any accidental changes to its scale. Figure 1-10 shows a viewport that has been maximized; you can tell when a viewport is maximized by the appearance of the red border in the drawing window. Double-clicking just outside the red border of a maximized viewport will restore the viewport back to its original size and scale. You can also click the Maximize and Minimize Viewport controls in the status bar.

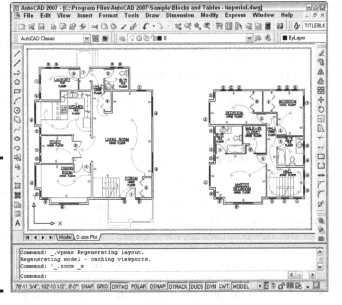

Figure 1-10:
Maximizing a viewport can make editing within it much easier.

**Book VII
Chapter 1**

Page Setup

At times, you will want to hide certain layers that might contain objects that you don't want displayed in the viewport. In this case, you can specify whether objects are frozen only in the viewport instead of globally across the entire drawing. To freeze layers for a specific viewport, double-click to enter the viewport. You will be able to tell when focus has been shifted to the viewport when its border is displayed as bold and the crosshairs are present within the viewport. On the Layers toolbar, select the Freeze or Thaw in Current Viewport icon (see Figure 1-11) next to the layer that you want to freeze for the viewport. To exit the viewport, simply double-click outside the viewport's bold border.

Figure 1-11:
Freezing a
layer in the
current
viewport
only.

Another way to control the display of objects in a viewport is by completely turning off the viewport altogether. The viewport remains in the drawing, but any objects that would normally be displayed through the viewport do not. To control the display of the objects through a viewport, select the viewport, and right-click. From the shortcut menu select Display Viewport Objects, and then click Yes or No.

Modifying a Viewport

Viewports can be modified by using the Properties palette, MOVE and COPY commands, grips, and many other methods. Grip editing to adjust the size, shape, and location of a viewport is by far one of the most efficient ways of modifying viewports. Adjusting a viewport by using grips has no effect on the scale or the viewpoint within the viewport. It will, however, affect which objects are displayed through the viewport. Grips are not the only way that you can control the shape of a viewport after it has been created. The VPCLIP command also allows you to control the shape of the viewport by re-creating its overall shape, and not affect the viewpoint or scale of the viewport.

You can use the VPCLIP command to create irregularly shaped viewports by selecting the viewport and then the closed object you want to use as the new clipping boundary.

You can use the COPYCLIP command to copy viewports between layouts. When you go to paste the copied objects viewports to a different layout, AutoCAD turns off the display of the objects within the viewport. To turn the display of the objects back on, select a viewport and right-click. From the shortcut menu, choose Display Viewport Objects, and then click Yes or No.

Chapter 2: Sheet Sets without Regret

In This Chapter

✔ Understanding a sheet set

✔ Creating a sheet set

✔ Managing drawings with a sheet set

✔ Publishing, eTransmitting, and archiving a Sheet Set

S heet sets were first introduced in AutoCAD 2005 and are still a relatively new concept in AutoCAD. They are based on an old drafting concept called a *drawing set*. Sheet sets are designed to be the digital equivalent of a drawing set that contains numerous drawings, which often include references to details, sections, and elevations within the drawing set along with a drawing or two that contain an index of all drawings in the set.

AutoCAD LT does not support Sheet Sets.

Overview of a Sheet Set

Sheet sets are designed to take advantage of the existing drawings that you have been creating over the years. A sheet set contains sheets, which are references to paper space layouts — sorry, the Model tab cannot be used as a sheet. If you are using the Model tab for plotting and publishing today, you will need to switch to the use of paper space layouts in order to take advantage of sheet sets. A sheet set and all of the references to its sheets are stored in a file with the extension of DST and are accessed through the Sheet Set Manager (see Figure 2-1). By using references to the drawing files, it is possible to use your own directory structures while being able to take advantage of the benefits that sheet sets offer. Some of the benefits that sheet sets offer are

✦ **Fast file access.** Because a sheet set knows right where a file is located, drawings can be accessed in a very short amount of time without the need to browse and open a file.

✦ **Consistent drawing creation.** Sheet sets can be set up to specify the directory structure and location in which new sheets should be created when they are added to the sheet set. Along with simplifying the specification and the location of a drawing file when a sheet is created, you can specify which drawing template (DWT) file should be used to create the sheet.

✦ **Quickly make updates.** Sheet sets allow you to create references to views on sheets (paper space layouts) and manage the names and numbers of views. This allows you to quickly renumber a view and not have to worry about exactly where that view is placed. The next time the drawing is opened, the numbering is updated. This also works very well for project information in a title block that is on a paper space layout.

✦ **Publishing drawings.** Creating a drawing set can be time-consuming when it is time to package things up and to get them ready to send off to the client. Sheet sets allow you to organize drawings and then be able to publish the entire set or the selected drawings quickly.

✦ **Packaging up drawings.** During the project cycle revisions will happen, there is no doubt about that. Sheet sets allow for eTransmitting or archiving of an entire set of drawings.

✦ **Create an index table of sheets.** One of the things that can take time to generate, but is fairly automated with sheet sets, is the creation of an index of all the sheets in the set. Since all the sheets are named and numbered in the sheet set, it is possible to create an index in a few clicks.

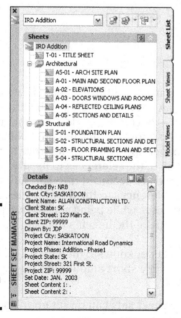

Figure 2-1:
Sheet Set
Manager
allows you
to work with
DST files.

Sheet Set Manager

The Sheet Set Manager is the tool in AutoCAD that you use to work with sheet sets. It allows you to do everything that you need to do in order to efficiently work with a sheet set. From inside the Sheet Set Manager, you can open sheets (drawings), add and remove sheets, add and remove subsets, change the order of subsets and sheets, work with model views, and much more. The Sheet Set Manager is organized into three areas by tabs. The Sheet List tab is where you access sheets and subsets in the sheet set, while any views that have been placed from the Model Views tab are displayed on the Sheet Views tab. The three tabs that are used in this chapter can be used to accomplish many tasks in the Sheet Set Manager. The Sheet Set Manager can be displayed with the command SHEETSET.

To start the SHEETSET command, use one of the following methods:

✦ **Tools menu.** Choose Tools⇨Palettes⇨Sheet Set Manager.

✦ **Standard toolbar.** Click the Sheet Set Manager button on the Standard toolbar.

✦ **Shortcut key.** Press the key combination Ctrl+4.

✦ **Keyboard input.** Type **SHEETSET** and press Enter.

✦ **Command alias.** Type **SSM** and press Enter.

Creating a Sheet Set

Sheet sets are commonly created by using the Create Sheet Set Wizard. The Create Sheet Set Wizard allows you to create a new sheet set by using an existing sheet set as a template or by creating one from scratch. You create a sheet set from scratch the first time so you can define some of the common properties that your projects have and then use that sheet set as a template for any future sheet sets that you create. After a sheet set is created, you can then import references to paper space layouts from your existing drawing files.

After you add some drawing layouts to a sheet set, you typically organize those layouts in the sheet set using subsets. Subsets enable you to organize sheets into folders that can be used to represent actual folder locations on a drive or not. Once the subsets have been created, you can designate a drawing template (DWT) file to the sheet set or subset to help manage the creation of new sheets (drawings) when they are created through the Sheet Set Manager. A drawing template (DWT) file commonly has a title block that has been updated to take advantage of sheet set and sheet properties with fields.

The last part of setting up a sheet set involves working with model views. Sheet sets take advantage of named views and allow you to place them on a sheet. Named views are covered in Book II. To access named views from other drawings, they must first be in a location that has been designated through the Sheet Set Manager as a resource location for the sheet set. To finish the setup for adding views to a sheet, you need to specify which callouts and label blocks will be used when views are placed on a sheet. You don't need to do all of these in order to start using sheet sets.

Starting from scratch

The Create Sheet Set Wizard provides an option to create a new sheet set using existing drawings — from scratch — and requires the most input. This option provides for a good understanding of what is involved with the initial setup of a sheet set. After you create a sheet set, you can use the other option of creating a sheet set from an existing one. You can use the NEW-SHEETSET to start the Create Sheet Set Wizard (see Figure 2-2).

To start the NEWSHEETSET command, follow one the following methods:

+ **File menu.** Choose File⇨New Sheet Set.

+ **Keyboard input.** Type **NEWSHEETSET** and press Enter.

+ **Drop-down list in the Sheet Set Manager.** Click the down arrow on the drop-down list along the top of the Sheet Set Manager and select New Sheet Set.

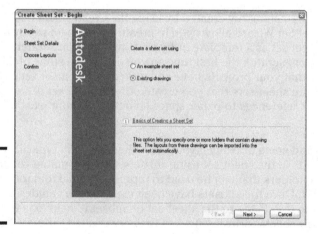

Figure 2-2:
The Create
Sheet Set
Wizard.

To create a new sheet set, follow these steps:

1. **Start the NEWSHEETSET command.**

The Create Sheet Set Wizard appears. You can also choose New Sheet Set from the drop-down list if you have the Sheet Set Manager open. If you use the Sheet Set Manager to create a new sheet set, you must have at least one drawing open.

2. **In the Create Sheet Set Wizard on the Begin page, select the Existing Drawings option. Click Next.**

The Existing Drawings option allows you to start from scratch with creating a sheet set. If you already have a sheet set created and want to create a new sheet set based on the existing one, select the An Example Sheet Set option.

3. **On the Sheet Set Details page, enter a string for the name of the sheet set in the Name of New Sheet Set text box.**

The name entered is used as the name for the DST file when the wizard is finished. This is also the name of the top level node displayed in the Sheet Set Manager when the sheet set is opened.

4. **Enter a description for the sheet set in the Description text box (optional).**

The description is displayed in the Sheet Set Manager and can be referenced in a field and placed as part of the index sheet.

5. **Specify where to create the new sheet set by entering a value in the Store Sheet Set Data File (.dst) Here text box or click the ellipsis button to browse to a folder.**

The specified location is where the DST file will be created when the Create Sheet Set Wizard is finished. If the ellipsis button is clicked, the Browse for Sheet Set Folder dialog box is displayed. Browse to a location in the dialog box and click open to select that folder. By default, the folder that is used to store sheet sets in is AutoCAD Sheet Sets under My Documents. It is best to place the sheet set on a network drive for others in the office to access.

6. **Click Sheet Set properties to specify standard and custom properties for the sheet set.**

The Sheet Set Properties dialog box appears (see Figure 2-3). The dialog box allows for specifying a variety of properties that range from the location in which callout blocks are stored to the project name and even custom properties that you can add, such as drawn by or checked by information. Custom properties are explained later under the section "Managing Drawings with a Sheet Set."

**Book VII
Chapter 2**

**Sheet Sets without
Regret**

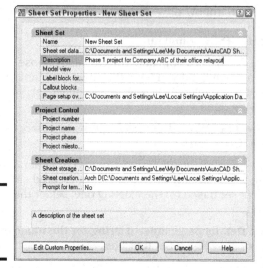

Figure 2-3:
Sheet Set
Properties
dialog box.

7. Click OK.

The Sheet Set Properties dialog box closes, and you are returned to the Create Sheet Set Wizard.

8. In the Create Sheet Set Wizard, click Next.

The wizard advances to the next page.

9. On the Choose Layouts page, click Import Options to control the behavior for importing layouts.

The Import Options dialog box appears (see Figure 2-4). This dialog box controls naming and folder structure when importing layouts.

Figure 2-4:
Specifying
import
behavior in
the Import
Options
dialog box.

10. In the Import Options dialog box, specify the options that you want and click OK.

Check or uncheck the Prefix Sheet Titles with Filename to control whether the name of the file is added to the layout name to make up the sheet title.

The Create Subsets Based on Folder Structure and Ignore Top Level Folder options are used to control how the folder structure on the drive that the layouts are being imported from affects the organization structure of the sheet set. Click OK to close the Import Options dialog box and return to the Create Sheet Set Wizard.

11. **On the Choose Layouts page, click Browse.**

The Browse for Folder dialog box is displayed. Select a folder and click OK for a list of the drawings in that folder to be displayed in a tree along with folder structure and the paper space layouts contained in each drawing (see Figure 2-5). Only drawings that are not part of a sheet set already are displayed and can be imported into a sheet set.

Figure 2-5:
Tree
displays
folder
structure
and
available
layouts in
drawings
for import.

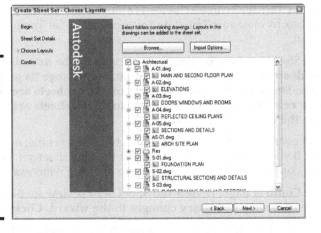

12. **In the tree view, uncheck the layouts you do not want to import as references into the sheet set. Click Next.**

The checked layouts are marked for import once the Create Sheet Set Wizard is finished. The next page of the wizard is displayed.

13. **On the Confirm page, review the Sheet Set Preview section and click Back to make any necessary changes in the wizard. Click Finish.**

The Create Sheet Set Wizard closes, and the new sheet set DST file is created with the specified name and in the designated folder. The Sheet Set Manager is displayed if it is hidden and the DST file is opened.

Starting from an existing sheet set

You can create a sheet set by using an existing sheet set as a template. Here's how:

1. **Using one of the previously described methods, initiate the NEWSHEETSET command.**

The Create Sheet Set Wizard appears.

2. **In the Create Sheet Set Wizard on the Begin page, select the An Example Sheet Set option. Click Next.**

   The An Example Sheet Set option allows you to select an existing sheet set to use as a template.

3. **On the Sheet Set Example page, select the Select a Sheet Set to Use as an Example option and then select one of the sheet set files listed, or select Browse to Another Sheet Set to Use as an Example option and then click the ellipsis button to browse to a location that contains a DST file. Click Next.**

   If you choose the Select a Sheet Set to Use as an Example option, the DST files that are used are located in the Template directory. The location of the DST files can be changed through the Files tab of the Options dialog box by choosing Template Settings⇨Sheet Set Template File Location.

4. **On the Sheet Set Details page, you can specify the new sheet set file's name, description, and save to location, and change its properties with the Sheet Set Properties dialog box. Any subsets are copied over, but any references to layouts that make up the sheets are not carried over to the new sheet set. Click Next.**

   You get everything that was in the selected sheet set file, minus any sheets. If you want to keep the sheets in the new sheet set, you must make a copy of the original sheet set file by using Windows Explorer.

5. **On the Confirm page, review the Sheet Set Preview section and click Back to make any necessary changes in the wizard. Click Finish.**

   The Create Sheet Set wizard closes and the new sheet set (DST) file is created with the specified name and in the designated folder. The Sheet Set Manager is displayed if it is hidden and the DST file is opened.

Managing Drawings with a Sheet Set

There are a number of ways to work with drawings through a sheet set, which includes navigating to existing files, creating new sheets (drawings), working with title block information, and model views. Some companies have taken the approach of first implementing sheet sets as a way to open and publish drawings much faster, and others have changed their entire drafting process to include the use of sheet sets to manage the views and title block information as well as the benefits of opening and publishing drawings much faster.

Opening a sheet set

After closing and restarting AutoCAD, the OPENSHEETSET command allows you to open a sheet set (DST) file that was previously created. Just like the

NEWSHEETSET command, the OPENSHEETSET command displays the Sheet Set Manager if it is not currently displayed.

To start the OPENSHEETSET command, use one of the following methods:

+ **File menu.** Choose File⇨Open Sheet Set.

+ **Keyboard input.** Type **OPENSHEETSET** and press Enter.

+ **Drop-down list in the Sheet Set Manager.** Click the down arrow on the drop-down list along the top of the Sheet Set Manager and select Open Sheet Set.

You can open one of the 10 most recently used sheet set (DST) files from the drop-down list in the Sheet Set Manager.

To open a sheet set file, follow these steps:

1. **Initiate the OPENSHEETSET command by using one of the methods described previously.**

   The Open Sheet Set dialog box appears. You can use this dialog box to browse and select an existing sheet set (DST) file.

2. **In the Open Sheet Set dialog box, select the sheet set (DST) file you want to open. Click Open.**

   The Open Sheet Set dialog box closes and the selected sheet set (DST) file is loaded into the Sheet Set Manager.

Importing existing drawings as sheets

If you have been using AutoCAD at your company for many years, you most likely have created hundreds, if not thousands, of drawings. This is one of the concerns that Autodesk kept in mind when adding sheet sets in AutoCAD 2005. Sheet sets are designed to work in combination with drawing files so that you do not have to completely reinvent a process. You can import paper space layouts from drawings when you create a sheet set based on existing drawings by using the Create Sheet Set Wizard. Most of the time, however, you won't know which drawings need to be imported right away, or which drawings might come from a vendor that will need to be added to the sheet set later on.

The Sheet Set Manager allows you to import paper space layouts from a drawing into a sheet set file after it has been created. This allows for a lot of flexibility in the workflow of a project. Paper space layouts can be imported at the main root of the sheet set or at the subset level; it all just depends on how the sheet set is laid out. The following procedure steps you through importing paper space layouts as sheets and assumes you already have a sheet set open in the Sheet Set Manager. To open a sheet set, refer to the section "Opening a sheet set."

1. **In the Sheet Set Manager on the Sheet List tab, right-click the top level node that displays the sheet set's name.**

The sheet set shortcut menu is displayed.

2. **On the shortcut menu, click Import Layout as Sheet.**

The Import Layouts as Sheets dialog box appears (see Figure 2-6). The dialog box allows you to browse for drawings that contain paper space layouts that you want to import as sheets.

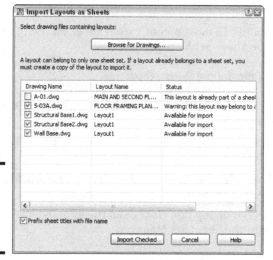

Figure 2-6: Importing layouts as sheets into a sheet set.

3. **In the Import Layouts as Sheets dialog box, click Browse for Drawings.**

The Select Drawings dialog box appears, allowing you to browse for drawing files. You can select more than one drawing by holding Ctrl+Shift while selecting files.

4. **Click Open.**

The Select Drawings dialog box closes, and you are returned to the Import Layout as Sheets dialog box. The selected files are scanned for paper space layouts. During the scanning of the drawings for paper space layouts, the layouts are added to the grid in the center of the Import Layouts as Sheets dialog box and evaluated as to whether they are referenced by a sheet set already.

5. **In the Import Layouts as Sheets dialog box, uncheck the layouts you do not want to import as sheets into the sheet set.**

By default, if a layout is already associated with a sheet set, the layout is unchecked, and all other layouts are checked. Only paper space layouts can be imported.

6. Uncheck or check the Prefix Sheet Titles with File Name option.

This option controls whether the filename that a layout comes from is added to the sheet's title. This can be helpful if you do not normally give your layout tabs a specific name in each drawing. The sheet's title can be changed later.

7. Click Import Checked.

The Import Layouts as Sheets dialog box closes and the checked layouts are added to the sheet set as sheets.

Organizing with subsets

Subsets are used to organize sheets in a sheet set. A subset may represent a folder on a local or network drive, but it doesn't have to. Subsets can be created at the root level of a sheet set or within another subset. Typically, a subset is used to group similar drawings together (such as by floor or discipline) so that you can find them quickly. The following steps show how to create a subset. They assume that you have a sheet set open in the Sheet Set Manager. To open a sheet set, refer to the section "Opening a sheet set."

1. In the Sheet Set Manager on the Sheet List tab, right-click the top level node that displays the sheet set's name or a subset.

The sheet set or subset shortcut menu is displayed.

2. On the shortcut menu, click New Subset.

The Subset Properties dialog box appears (see Figure 2-7). You can use this dialog box to specify the name of the subset, whether the folder is created relative to its parent, where new sheets that are added to the subset are created, and which drawing template (DWT) file to use to create new sheets under the subset.

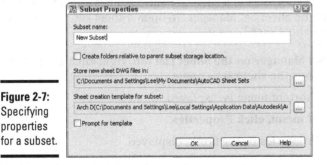

Figure 2-7:
Specifying
properties
for a subset.

3. **In the Subset Properties dialog box, specify the name of the subset in the Subset Name text box.**

   The name is used in the Sheet Set Manager and for the folder that new sheets will be created in.

4. **Specify the location where the folder that represents the subset should be created and whether it should be created relative to its parent in the tree of the Sheet List tab.**

   A new folder is created as necessary, based on the options you specify.

5. **Specify the drawing template that will be used when a new sheet is created under the subset.**

   If the Prompt for Template option is checked, the user of the sheet set will be prompted to specify a drawing template when a new sheet is created under the subset.

6. **Click OK.**

   The Subset Properties dialog box closes, and the new subset is created.

You can control the order in which sheets and subsets appear on the Sheet List tab by dragging them up and down. Sheets can also be added to a subset by dragging them onto the subset or into a specific location within the subset.

Setting up a sheet set and subset for adding new sheets

Sheets can be created at both the sheet set and the subset level. In order to make this process as streamlined as possible, you must do some minor setup for each of these areas of a sheet set. There are three properties that need to be set, and they are the same between a sheet set and subset. The only difference in the process is how you access the properties.

Setting up drawing template settings for a sheet set

The following steps show how to change the properties used when a new sheet is added to the root level of a sheet set and assumes you already have a sheet set open in the Sheet Set Manager. To open a sheet set, refer to the section, "Opening a sheet sset."

1. **In the Sheet Set Manager on the Sheet List tab, right-click the top level node that displays the sheet set's name.**

   The sheet set shortcut menu is displayed.

2. **On the shortcut menu, click Properties.**

   The Sheet Set Properties dialog box is displayed.

3. **In the Sheet Set Properties dialog box under the Sheet Creation area, click the Sheet Storage Location text box to display an ellipsis button.**

   The ellipsis button is displayed.

4. **Click the ellipsis button for the sheet storage location property to browse and select the location in which any new sheets that are added to the sheet set are added to. Click Open.**

   The Browse for Folder dialog box is displayed allowing you to browse and select the folder where any new sheets will be saved. After clicking the Open button you will be returned to the Sheet Set Properties dialog box.

5. **Click the Sheet Creation Template text box to display an ellipsis button.**

   The ellipsis button is displayed.

6. **Click the ellipsis button for the sheet creation template property to browse, and select the drawing template (DWT) file that you want to use when a new sheet is added to the sheet set.**

   The Select Layout as Sheet Template dialog box appears (see Figure 2-8).

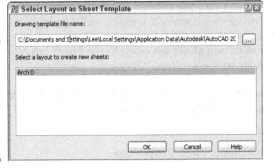

Figure 2-8:
Using a layout in a drawing as a template for new sheets.

7. **In the Select Layout as Sheet Template dialog box, enter the path and filename for a drawing template file in the Drawing Template File Name text box or click the ellipsis button to browse for and select a drawing template (DWT) file.**

   If the ellipsis button is clicked, the Select Drawing dialog box is displayed. Browse to and select the drawing, drawing template, or drawing standards file that contains the layout you want to use as the template for new sheets. Click Open to close the Select Drawing dialog box and return to the Select Layout as Sheet Template dialog box.

8. **Select the layout you want to use as the sheet template in the Select a Layout to Create New Sheets list box. Click OK.**

   The Select Layout as Drawing Template dialog box closes, and the specified drawing file and selected layout are applied to the Sheet Creation Template property in the Sheet Set Properties dialog box.

9. **In the Sheet Set Properties dialog box under the Sheet Creation area, specify Yes or No in the Prompt for Template property.**

   The Prompt for Template property controls whether the template specified in the Sheet creation template is used when a new sheet is created. You can choose to use that sheet creation template or one of your own choosing.

10. **Click OK.**

    The Sheet Set Properties dialog box closes and the changes to the properties are applied to the sheet set.

Setting up drawing template settings for a subset

Setting up a subset for when a new sheet is created under the subset is similar to setting up a sheet set. Refer to the previous topic for information on setting up the properties that are related to when a new sheet is added to a sheet set. The following steps provide a quick walk-through of how to access the properties of a subset (not a full in-depth walk-through of each property) and assume that you have a sheet set open in the Sheet Set Manager. To open a sheet set, refer to the section, "Opening a sheet set."

1. **In the Sheet Set Manager on the Sheet List tab, right-click the subset that you want to adjust the properties for.**

   The subset shortcut menu appears.

2. **On the shortcut menu, click Properties.**

   The Subset Properties dialog box appears.

3. **In the Subset Properties dialog box, specify the new location where the sheets will be created, the drawing template that will be used for the new sheets added to the subset, and whether the user will be prompted to specify a drawing template when a new sheet is added to the subset.**

   The properties in the Subset Properties dialog box, except for the Subset name field, are the same as those under the Sheet Creation area of the Sheet Set Properties dialog box. See the topic "Setting up drawing template settings for a sheet set" for more information on these properties.

4. **Click OK.**

   The Subset Properties dialog box closes and the changes to the properties are saved.

Adding a new sheet

A new sheet can be added to a sheet set or a subset. How the new sheet is defined is based on the properties that have been set up for the sheet set or the subset. When a new sheet is created, a new drawing file is created. The new drawing then has its layout referenced into the sheet set file at the location that the new sheet was created. Once the properties have been defined for the sheet set or subset, a new sheet is rather easy to create.

The following steps show how to add a new sheet to either the root of a sheet set or a subset, and assume that you already have a sheet set open in the Sheet Set Manager. To open a sheet set, refer to the section, "Opening a sheet set."

1. **In the Sheet Set Manager on the Sheet List tab, right-click the sheet set or subset to which you want to add a new sheet.**

The shortcut menu appears.

2. **On the shortcut menu, click New Sheet.**

The New Sheet dialog box appears (see Figure 2-9). The dialog box allows you to specify a number, title, and filename for the new sheet.

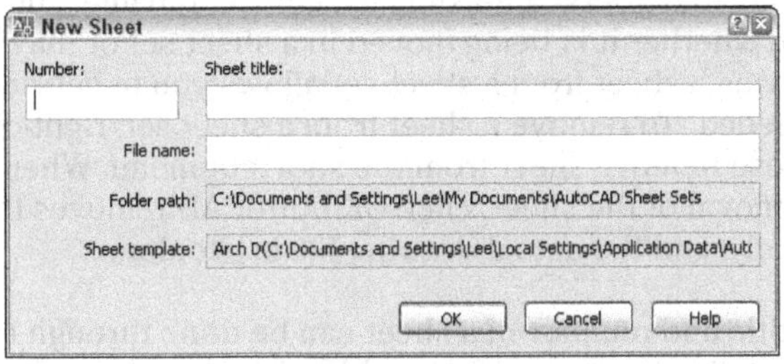

Figure 2-9:
Adding a
new sheet
to a sheet
set or
subset.

3. **In the New Sheet dialog box, enter a drawing number for the sheet in the Number text box.**

The number can be displayed in a title block through the use of a field, can be displayed as part of the index sheet table, and is shown in the tree view on the Sheet List tab.

4. **Enter a title for the sheet in the Sheet Title text box.**

The title can be displayed in a title block through the use of a field or as part of the index sheet table, and is shown in the tree view on the Sheet List tab.

5. **Enter a filename for the sheet in the File Name text box.**

AutoCAD uses the filename you enter to save the new sheet to the specified location in the Folder Path text box.

6. Click OK.

The New Sheet dialog box closes and the new sheet is added to the sheet set or the subset.

You can control the order in which sheets and subsets appear on the Sheet List tab by dragging them up and down. Sheets can also be added to a subset by dragging them onto the subset or into a specific location within the subset.

The Sheet Set Manager in AutoCAD 2007 allows you to select and move multiple sheets at once, unlike previous releases that allowed you to move only a single sheet at a time.

Opening a sheet

Opening a sheet in a sheet set is straightforward. You can just double-click on the sheet, and the drawing opens with the referencing layout displayed. If you want, you can also right-click over a sheet and select Open or Open read-only from the shortcut menu.

Removing, renaming, and renumbering a sheet

At times you may find yourself needing to remove, rename, and renumber a sheet based on whether it is being moved in a sheet set or may no longer be needed. Removing a sheet from a sheet set allows you to get rid of it when it no longer is needed. To remove a sheet from a sheet set, right-click on the sheet and choose Remove sheet from the shortcut menu. When asked to confirm the removal of the sheet, click OK. AutoCAD removes the sheet from the sheet set only, and the actual drawing file is left alone.

Changing the title and number of a sheet can be done through the Rename & Renumber Sheet dialog box (see Figure 2-10). The Rename & Renumber dialog box allows you to change the number of the sheet along with its title, and you can even change the actual filename. To rename and renumber a sheet, right-click over the sheet and select Rename & Renumber for the shortcut menu. Change the number and title in the dialog box. You can navigate to the next or previous sheet and change its title or number without leaving the dialog box.

Although you can use AutoCAD or Windows Explorer to rename drawing files, it is best to rename drawings that are linked to a sheet set file using the Sheet Set Manager to avoid missing files.

Figure 2-10:
Renaming
and
renumbering
a sheet.

The ability to move to the previous sheet in the Rename & Renumber dialog box was first added to AutoCAD 2006. AutoCAD 2006 also introduced the ability to change the file name of the drawing for a sheet using the Rename & Renumber dialog box.

Sheet set and sheet properties

Sheet sets and individual sheets use two types of properties, standard and custom. Standard properties are available for you to use without doing any additional setup. Standard properties can be accessed by right-clicking over the top level node of the sheet set or a sheet and selecting Properties. Based on which one you right-click over, different properties are available to you. Some of these properties can be referenced in a text or attribute object via fields.

Custom properties require a little more work because you need to define the property before you can use it. Custom properties allow you to incorporate the use of sheet sets into your current drafting process much more easily by allowing you to define properties that you might be accustomed to using during your project management cycle for client, drafter, or project information. Even though sheet sets and sheets come with predefined properties for you to use, they do not cover everything that you might want to store with a sheet set or sheet. Custom properties, like standard properties, can be displayed in a title block via fields.

The following steps show how to define a custom property for a sheet and then change its value, and assume that you already have a sheet set open in the Sheet Set Manager. To open a sheet set, refer to the section, "Opening a sheet set."

1. **In the Sheet Set Manager on the Sheet List tab, right-click the top level node that displays the sheet set's name.**

The shortcut menu appears.

2. **On the shortcut menu, click Properties.**

The Sheet Set Properties dialog box appears.

3. **In the Sheet Set Properties dialog box, click Edit Custom Properties.**

The Custom Properties dialog box appears (see Figure 2-11). The dialog box allows for adding and modifying custom properties that you can have at the sheet or sheet set level. These custom properties allow you to populate information down to title blocks in your sheets so that the information can be edited from a central location without opening each sheet individually.

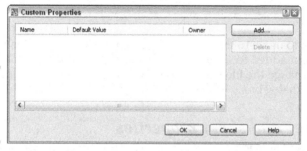

Figure 2-11:
The Custom Properties dialog box.

4. **In the Custom Properties dialog box, click Add.**

The Add Custom Property dialog box appears (see Figure 2-12). The dialog box allows for defining a new sheet set or sheet property.

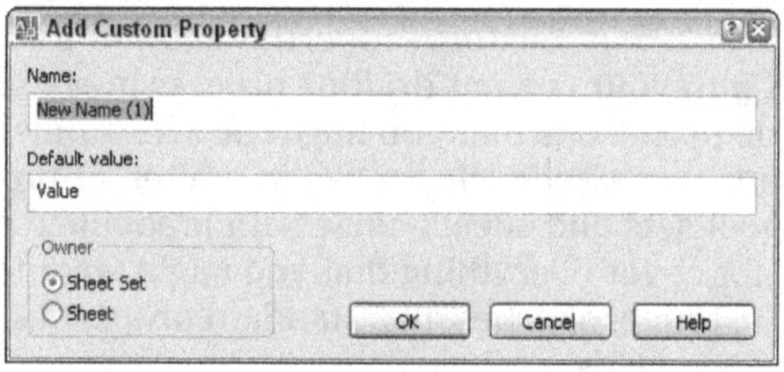

Figure 2-12:
Adding a custom property.

5. **In the Add Custom Property dialog box, enter a name for the custom property in the Name text box.**

The name of the field can be pretty much anything you want to use. The value entered appears in the Sheet Set Properties, Sheet Properties, and Field dialog boxes.

6. **Enter an initial value for the property in the Default Value text box.**

This value is the default value for the property.

7. Select either Sheet Set or Sheet from the Owner area based on the type of property you want to create. This procedure uses the Sheet as the Owner type.

The owner type controls where the property will be accessible from, even though both types of custom properties are created through the Sheet Set Properties dialog box.

8. Click OK.

The Add Custom Property dialog box closes and you are returned to the Custom Properties dialog box. The new custom property should now be listed. Once the custom property has been created, you can only change its default value. If you want to change its name or owner, you will need to delete the custom property and then re-create it. Be careful about deleting custom properties; if the custom property is used in a field, it will become unresolved because it no longer exists. Double-click the default value for the custom property to edit the value.

9. In the Custom Properties dialog box, click OK.

The Custom Properties dialog box closes, and you are returned to the Sheet Set Properties dialog box. If you added a custom property that had its owner set to Sheet Set, the properties would be displayed under the Sheet Set Custom Properties section (see Figure 2-13) of the Sheet Set Properties dialog box. Also notice that custom properties that are designated as an owner of Sheet are displayed under the Sheet Custom Properties section. This allows you to change the default value of a sheet custom property.

Book VII
Chapter 2

Sheet Sets without Regret

Figure 2-13:
Both sheet and sheet set custom properties are displayed in the Sheet Set Properties dialog box.

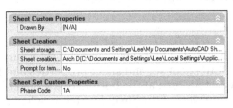

10. In the Sheet Set Properties dialog box, click OK.

The Sheet Set Properties dialog box closes and you are returned to the Sheet Set Manager.

11. **In the Sheet Set Manager, right-click over the sheet you want to change the custom properties for.**

The shortcut menu is displayed.

12. **On the shortcut menu, click Properties.**

The Sheet Properties dialog box appears (see Figure 2-14).

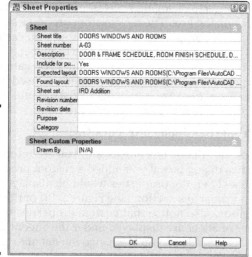

Figure 2-14: Sheet properties are changed through the Sheet Properties dialog box.

13. **In the Sheet Properties dialog box, change the custom sheet property under the Sheet Custom Properties section.**

Click in the text box next to the custom property and make the change to its value.

14. **Click OK.**

The Custom Properties dialog box closes and you are returned to the Sheet Set Manager. Both sheet set and sheet properties and their values are displayed in the Details area at the bottom of the Sheet Set Manager when a node in the tree view of the Sheet List tab is selected. If the Details area is not displayed, click the Details button just below the tree view on the Sheet List tab.

Setting up callouts and label blocks

Callout and label blocks are used with model space views that are dragged and dropped from the Model Views tab onto a sheet. Label blocks are automatically placed under the model space view when you drop them onto a sheet. They commonly hold the view number, view title, and the viewport's scale. A view is assigned a number and a title by accessing the properties of a view that has been placed on a sheet from the Sheet Views tab. Placing views on a sheet are discussed further in the section, "Adding model views to a sheet."

Callout blocks, unlike label blocks, are not automatically placed in a drawing. A callout block typically has the view number and the sheet in which the view is placed. The callout may point to a particular side of a building plan, indicating on the sheet where the elevation is located.

When a callout block is added to a sheet, AutoCAD creates a hyperlink back to the sheet the view is placed on. This allows you to move to the sheet with the view on it rather quickly by pressing and holding down the Ctrl key while double-clicking on the callout block.

Callout and label blocks use fields to reference information that is contained in the sheet set. These fields are defined through the use of the SheetSetPlaceholder field name under the category SheetSet in the Fields dialog box. To learn more about fields, refer to Book III. For information on creating blocks, refer to Book VI.

Setting up label blocks

The following steps show how to define label blocks for placing with model space views, and assume that you have a sheet set open in the Sheet Set Manager. To open a sheet set, refer to the section, "Opening a sheet set."

1. **In the Sheet Set Manager on the Sheet List tab, right-click the top level node that displays the sheet set's name.**

   The shortcut menu appears.

2. **Click Properties.**

   The Sheet Set Properties dialog box appears.

3. **In the Sheet Set area of the Sheet Set Properties dialog box, click the Label Block for Views text box to display an ellipsis button.**

   The ellipsis button appears.

4. **Click the ellipsis button for the Label Block for Views property to specify a block or drawing file.**

   The Select Block dialog box appears (see Figure 2-15). You can use this dialog box to browse for a drawing file and then use the drawing file as the label block, or select a block from the drawing as a label block.

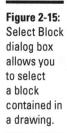

Figure 2-15:
Select Block
dialog box
allows you
to select
a block
contained in
a drawing.

5. **In the Select Block dialog box, click the ellipsis button to the right of the Enter the Drawing Name text box.**

   The Select Drawing dialog box appears, allowing you to select a drawing or drawing template (DWT) file that contains the block you want to use as a label block or is the label block saved as a file.

6. **In the Select Drawing dialog box, browse to and select the drawing or drawing template file that contains the label block you want to use when placing model space views. Click Open.**

   The Select Drawing dialog box closes and the selected file is added to the Select Block dialog box.

7. **In the Select Block dialog box, select either the Select the Drawing as a Block or Choose Blocks in the Drawing File option.**

   The selected option determines which block is used for a label block.

8. **If you select Choose Blocks in the Drawing File, select a block from the list box.**

   The selected block is used as the label block.

9. **Click OK.**

   The Select Block dialog box closes, and the block name and path are assigned to the Label Block for Views property in the Sheet Set Properties dialog box.

10. **In the Sheet Set Properties dialog box, click OK.**

    The Sheet Set Properties dialog box closes, and the changes are saved.

Setting up callout blocks

Setting up callout blocks is very similar to setting up a label block, with the exception of being able to associate multiple blocks from a drawing for use as callout blocks. The following steps show how to define which callout blocks are available for placing in a drawing to reference a model space view on a sheet, and assume that you have a sheet set open in the Sheet Set Manager. To open a sheet set, refer to the section, "Opening a sheet set."

1. **In the Sheet List tab of the Sheet Set Manager, right-click the top level node that displays the sheet set's name.**

2. **On the shortcut menu, click Properties.**

3. **In the Sheet Set Properties dialog box under the Sheet Set area, click the Callout Blocks text box to display an ellipsis button.**

4. **Click the ellipsis button for the Callout Blocks property to specify a block or drawing file.**

The List of Blocks dialog box appears, allowing you to browse for drawing files, and use a drawing file as the callout block or select a block from the drawing as a callout block (see Figure 2-16).

Figure 2-16:
The List
of Blocks
dialog box.

5. **In the List of Blocks dialog box, click Add.**

The Select Block dialog box appears, allowing you to browse for a drawing file, and use the drawing file as the callout block or select a block(s) from the drawing as a callout block.

6. **In the Select Block dialog box, click the ellipsis button to the right of the Enter the Drawing Name text box.**

7. **In the Select Drawing dialog box, select the drawing or drawing template file that contains the label block you want to use when placing model space views. Click Open.**

8. **In the Select Block dialog box, select either the Select the Drawing as a Block or Choose Blocks in the Drawing File option.**

9. **If you select Choose Blocks in the Drawing File, select a block from the list box.**

10. **Click OK.**

    The Select Block dialog box closes, and you are returned to the List of Blocks dialog box. The selected file and/or block(s) are added to the list box.

11. **In the List of Blocks dialog box, click OK.**

    The List of Blocks dialog box closes, and you are returned to the Sheet Set Properties dialog box where the callout blocks are added to the Callout Blocks property.

12. **In the Sheet Set Properties dialog box, click OK.**

    The Sheet Set Properties dialog box closes, and the changes are saved.

Adding resource drawings

Sheet sets allow you to take advantage of model space views that you have defined in drawings. The location of these drawings needs to be made available to the Sheet Set Manager in order for you to place them onto a sheet. Resource drawings are defined through the Model Views tab of the Sheet Set Manager. The locations that are added for resource drawings most commonly contain details or elevations but could also be for plans.

The following steps show how to define a drawing resource location for a sheet set, and assume that you already have a sheet set open in the Sheet Set Manager. To open a sheet set, refer to the section, "Opening a sheet set."

1. **In the Sheet Set Manager on the Model Views tab, double-click the Add New Location node under the Locations section.**

    The Browse for Folder dialog box appears.

2. **In the Browse for Folder dialog box, specify the folder that contains the drawings with the model views that you want to place on a sheet. Click Open.**

    Clicking Open after selecting the folder that contains the drawing files with the model views in them closes the Browse for Folder dialog box and returns you to the Sheet Set Manager. AutoCAD loads all the drawings into the Locations section on the Sheet Set Manager that are contained in the specified folder (see Figure 2-17).

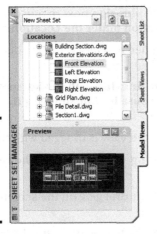

Figure 2-17:
Resource
drawings
available
to the
sheet set.

Adding model views to a sheet

After you have set up the callout and label blocks and the resource drawings for the sheet set, you are ready to place model space views on a sheet. Model space views must first be created and saved in a drawing that is in the location where your resource drawings are stored. A model view can be assigned a category and a layer state. The layer state affects how layers appear in the viewport that is created when the model view is added to a sheet. The category is used to organize views on the Sheet Views tab of the Sheet Set Manager. For information on model views, see Book II.

Model views that are placed on a sheet don't introduce any new concepts in AutoCAD, but they do use a combination of existing features. Model views use named views to define what is displayed, xrefs to get the geometry in the drawing, viewports to display the xref'd drawing, and blocks and attributes to help link the information from a sheet set into the drawing.

The following procedure explains how to place a model view on a sheet and adjust the views number and title. The procedure assumes you have already defined a resource location for drawings, specified a label block to use, set up the properties for creating a new sheet, and have a sheet set open. If you need help with any of these tasks, refer to previous sections in this chapter for some help.

> *1.* **On the Sheet tab of the Sheet Set Manager, create a new sheet for the model views that you want to add to the sheet set, or open an existing sheet. Make sure that the sheet is open before you continue.**

2. **On the Model Views tab, click the plus-sign next to one of the drawings defined by the resource location under the Location section.**

   The node for the drawing is expanded and any views are displayed below it.

3. **Select one of the views below the drawing with the left mouse button and continue to hold down the mouse button and drag the view over the drawing window.**

   As you drag the view, the name of the view is dragged with the cursor.

4. **Release the mouse over the drawing window to start the referencing process.**

   A preview of the view is displayed for dragging on the screen along with the label block below the view.

5. **Right-click over the drawing window to specify a specific scale for the view.**

   AutoCAD guesses at a scale based on the size of the drawing and the view that is being referenced. By right-clicking, you can choose a scale from a shortcut menu.

6. **Select a scale from the shortcut menu for the view.**

   The preview image that is being dragged is updated to reflect the new scale.

7. **Pick a point in the drawing window to place the model view, and create the viewport and insert the label block.**

   The viewport is created based on the specified scale, and the label block is inserted below the viewport.

8. **On the Sheet Views tab, locate the view that was just added in the tree based on the sheet name or category of the view. Right-click over the view and select Rename & Renumber.**

   The Rename & Renumber View dialog box appears (see Figure 2-18).

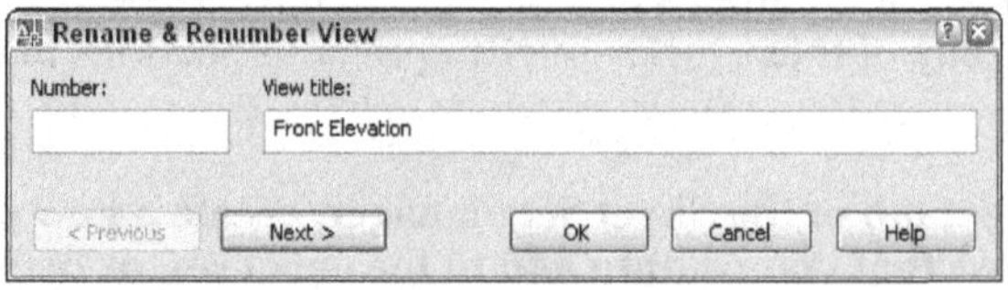

Figure 2-18:
Renaming
and renum-
bering a
view.

9. **In the Rename & Renumber View dialog box, enter a number in the Number text box for the view. A title should already exist, as it is the name of the model space view.**

The number can be any text as you want, but usually it is a number with maybe a letter at times.

10. **Click OK.**

The Rename & Renumber View dialog box closes, and you are returned to the Sheet Set Manager.

11. **Activate the drawing window and type** REGEN **at the command line or dynamic tooltip prompt.**

Fields are not updated until an action in the drawing causes a regen or a save. The field in the label block will be updated.

12. **On the Sheet List tab, open a sheet that needs to have callout blocks added to it to reference the sheet with the model view on it and zoom to the location where the callout block needs to be inserted.**

The sheet opens in its open drawing window.

13. **On the Sheet Views tab, locate the view for which you need to place callout blocks. Right-click the view and select Place Callout Block, and then the block you want to place.**

The first time you place a callout block, the option Select Blocks may appear on the shortcut menu only.

14. **If you select the Select Blocks from the shortcut menu, the View Category dialog box appears. In the Select the Callout Blocks to be Used in This Category list box, place a check mark next to each block you want to choose from. Click OK.**

The blocks selected are now available via the Place Callout Block *submenu* on the shortcut menu.

15. **If you had to select the callout blocks using the View Category dialog box, right-click over the view again and select Place Callout Block, and then the block you want to place.**

A preview of the callout block appears in the drawing window and is ready to be placed.

16. **Pick a point on-screen to place the callout block.**

The callout block is inserted into the drawing and any fields should be resolved.

Book VII
Chapter 2

Sheet Sets without Regret

Publishing, eTransmitting, and Archiving a Sheet Set

After you create all the sheets for your sheet set and add any views that you need on a sheet, you can package the set and get it off to the client. An entire sheet set or selected sheets can be published using the page setup that is assigned to each layout or a page setup override, along with the ability to publish the sheets to a multi-sheet DWF file. To work with the publish options for a sheet set, right-click the top-level node of the sheet set and choose an option from the Publish submenu. Publishing is explained in the next chapter of this book.

eTransmitting and archiving a sheet set are very similar. When you *eTransmit* a sheet set, you are packaging all the drawing and support files for that project to send to a client or customer electronically. When you *archive* a sheet set, you are essentially doing an eTransmit, but the package is not sent to a client or customer. You can eTransmit a subset within a sheet set, but you can't archive a subset. Archiving can only be done for the whole sheet set.

You can start the eTransmit process from the shortcut menu after right-clicking the sheet set or a subset node and selecting eTransmit, or by using the ETRANSMIT command outside the Sheet Set Manager when the sheet set is open. Doing so opens the Create Transmittal dialog box.

To create an archive of the sheet set, right-click the sheet set node and click Archive, or use the ARCHIVE command when the sheet set is open in the Sheet Set Manager. Doing so opens the Archive a Sheet Set dialog box.

For information on using the eTransmit and archive features of sheet sets, refer to the online Help system that comes with AutoCAD.

Chapter 3: Print, Plot, Publish

In This Chapter

✔ **Configuring printers and plotters**

✔ **Defining and using plot styles**

✔ **Plotting from the Model tab and paper space**

✔ **Publishing drawings**

*E*ven with the growth of the Internet and online project collaboration sites, many people still want or need drawings to be delivered in hard copy format — in other words, printed. Many years ago, the idea of a paperless society was born with the introduction of the Internet. Despite what some predicted, however, our dependency on paper has not dwindled that much, so you still need to hang onto those printers and plotters for the time being.

Throughout this book, we've covered many of the necessary techniques to set up your drawings and prepare them for output. Page setups and layouts play an important role in getting your drawings onto a sheet of paper, but in order to get to the finish line, you need to do a little bit more work yet. This chapter looks at configuring a printer or plotter to output your drawings and also covers plot styles, which can be used to affect output.

You Say Printing, We Say Plotting, They Say Publishing

Printing, *plotting*, and *publishing* are all terms that we cover in this chapter. For the most part, they all produce the same result: a hard copy or an electronic file. The process of getting to the end result varies based on which path you decide to take. In AutoCAD, printing usually involves small drawings that can be output to a laser or inkjet printer. Output is usually done on an 8½x11 sheet of paper, but might also include 11x17, based on your printer's capabilities. Most AutoCAD users think of printing as something that word processing and spreadsheet programs do, whereas plotting is what AutoCAD does.

Plotting is a common way of outputting a drawing from AutoCAD to a hard copy because drawing files are usually printed on very large sheets of paper. Plotting requires specialized hardware that holds rolls of paper in different widths for printing drawings that are greater in size than 8½x11 or 11x17. Some older plotters required you to manually load sheets of paper. Based on the plotter you have available, it might also be able to print 8½x11 and 11x17 sheets. When a drawing is printed or plotted, only the Model tab or a paper space layout can be sent to a device at a single time. To get around this limitation, you can use the publishing feature in AutoCAD.

Publishing is used to output more than just the Model tab or one paper space layout at a time. Publishing allows you to set up multiple drawings and layouts contained in the files for outputting to a device. This can make sending out a drawing set easier because a list of drawings and layouts can be saved for future use. You can publish all the sheets in a sheet set directly from the Sheet Set Manager. For more information on sheet sets and the Sheet Set Manager, see Chapter 2 of this book.

Working with drivers

To use printers and plotters with software, you must often install additional software called *print drivers*. Print drivers come from the hardware manufacturer and provide a way for software applications like AutoCAD to communicate with them. So when you or someone from your IT department installs a printer through Windows, you are setting up what AutoCAD calls a *system printer*. System printers are the printers that AutoCAD and other Windows-based applications have access to. For most applications, this is enough, but AutoCAD is not just any ordinary program.

AutoCAD allows manufacturers to develop a form of print drivers that can enhance the abilities of their printers or plotters in a way that can't be done through a standard print driver. AutoCAD refers to these drivers as *non-system drivers,* which means the driver can't be installed as part of the Windows operating system. Most companies that develop plotters, such as Hewlett-Packard (HP), Xerox, and Océ, develop custom drivers that AutoCAD can use. These drivers are often much more efficient and flexible in communicating with the printer or plotter the driver is designed for. Some of the improvements in non-system drivers allow you to control which paper sizes are available to choose from, as well as additional features like line merge and AutoSpool.

Setting up and using system drivers is much easier than setting up and using non-system drivers. The ease of setup and use is balanced out by the better control over plotting that non-system drivers offer. Because printing and plotting in AutoCAD is so different from other Windows-based applications, the Help system offers some great information on the topic. For additional information on print drivers, launch the online Help for AutoCAD and select Driver and Peripheral Guide; then choose Use Plotters and Printers from the Contents tab.

Configuring a printer or plotter

Configuring a device for AutoCAD usually requires a little more work than installing a system printer. At times, you might even find that configuring a system printer as a non-system printer might have some advantages. The first thing you want to do before configuring a new device is to determine whether it might have already been configured for you. (CAD managers and IT personnel often set up printers and plotters to ensure that there is consistency to the output.) After you have determined which devices you have available, you can set up a new one if you need to.

Determining which printers and plotters are available

The first step on the road to plotting is making sure that AutoCAD can access the device that you want to output to. The following procedure opens the Options dialog box and checks to see which system and non-system printers are available:

1. **Choose Tools⇨Options.**

The Options dialog box is displayed.

2. **In the Options dialog box, click the Plot and Publish tab.**

The Plot and Publish tab (see Figure 3-1) is set current.

Book VII
Chapter 3

Print, Plot, Publish

System printers

Figure 3-1: Many of the plotting and publish options in AutoCAD are in the Options dialog box.

Non-system printers

Hide system printer option

3. **Click the down arrow on the Use as Default Output Device drop-down list under the Default Plot Settings for New Drawings section.**

Both system and non-system printers are displayed in the drop-down list, unless the Hide System Printers option has been checked under the General Plot Options section.

- System printers are indicated by an icon that shows a small laser printer with a sheet of paper on top next to its configured name in Windows.

- Non-system printers are indicated by an icon that shows a plotter with a sheet of paper coming out in front next to its configured name in AutoCAD.

The non-system printers that are configured for AutoCAD are displayed in the list with a file extension .PC3. The .PC3 file extension stands for AutoCAD Plotter Configuration and is the third generation of the file format. The .PC3 files were first used with AutoCAD 2000.

4. **Click somewhere other than the Use as Default Output Device drop-down list to close the drop-down list.**

AutoCAD has access to all the system printers and some select non-system printers out of the box. The non-system printers that are available are capable of producing output to an electronic file only, such as to a .DWF or .PDF file, and some types of image files. Now that you have an idea of which printers and plotters are available to you from AutoCAD, you should know if you are missing one that your office uses on a daily basis for production drawings.

5. **Click Cancel.**

The Options dialog box closes.

Setting up a non-system printer

AutoCAD provides a wizard to help you set up non-system printers. The wizard can be accessed from within AutoCAD or through the Windows Control Panel. No matter which method you use, the Add Plotter Wizard is displayed. You can use the PLOTTERMANAGER command to display a window that allows you to access the wizard and any previously defined non-system printers.

To start the Plotter Manager, follow one of these methods:

✦ **File menu:** Select File⇨Plotter Manager.

✦ **Keyboard input:** Type **PLOTTERMANAGER** and press Enter.

✦ **Select Tools⇨Options to display the Options dialog box:** Make sure the Plot and Publish tab is selected. Click the Add or Configure Plotter button under the Default Plot Settings for New Drawings section.

The following procedure launches the Add Plotter Wizard and creates a non-system printer:

1. **Use one of the previously listed methods to open the Plotter Manager.**

A window titled Plotters is displayed. This window contains a shortcut to the Add Plotter Wizard and displays all the previously configured .PC3 files.

2. **In the Plotters window, locate the Add-A-Plotter Wizard shortcut and double-click it.**

The Add Plotter Wizard is launched.

3. **In the Add Plotter Wizard on the Introduction page, read through the information and click Next.**

The next page of the wizard is displayed and is really the starting point of configuring a new non-system printer (see Figure 3-2).

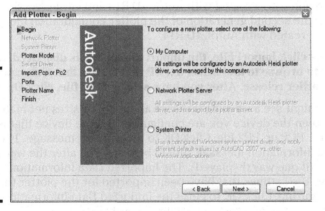

Figure 3-2:
The Add Plotter Wizard is used to configure a non-system printer.

4. **On the Begin page, select one of the three different types of plotters to set up. Click Next.**

The page allows you to choose from three different types of plotters:

- **My Computer:** The plotting is handled locally by your computer through a port, plot to file, or by using a specified AutoSpool utility (an application that controls where the plot file is sent).

- **Network Plotter Server:** The plotting is done via a folder in a network location where the plotter checks for plot files.

- **System Printer:** The plotting is done through a system printer. By configuring a non-system printer for a system printer, it allows AutoCAD to do some additional things with the plot information before sending it to the system printer.

Clicking Next advances the wizard to the next page, which is different depending on which of the three options you selected. In this example, we use the My Computer option because going through it covers the most steps in the wizard.

5. **On the Plotter Model page, select a manufacturer from the list on the left and then one of the available models from the list on the right. Click Next.**

   Based on the selected manufacturer, you might have a list of models for a physical device or a virtual device. A *physical device* would be in the form of a plotter, whereas a *virtual device* allows you to take the output from AutoCAD and convert it into a specific format of electronic file. Clicking Next advances the wizard to the next page.

6. **On the Import PCP or PC2 page, click the Import File button if you have a .PCP or .PC2 file available to you. Click Next.**

   .PCP files were the very first plotter configuration files that AutoCAD used and were created with AutoCAD R13 and earlier versions. .PC2 files were the second generation of the plotter configuration file type and were created with AutoCAD R14.

7. **If you click Import File, the Import dialog box is displayed and allows you to browse to and select a .PCP or .PC2 file that was exported out of an earlier release. After you have selected the file, click Open.**

   You might see a warning message about paper sizes not matching between the device you are configuring and the device that is contained in the .PCP or .PC2 file. Click OK to the warning message. The Imported Data Information message should be displayed after the warning message (if one was displayed). The Imported Data Information message displays the settings that have been imported for the plotter that you are configuring. Click OK to close the Imported Data Information dialog box, and you return to the Add Plotter Wizard.

8. **In the Add Plotter Wizard on the Ports page, select one of the three types of ports to be used for the plotter, and select a port from the list based on the port option selected.**

   The page allows you to choose from three different types of ports:

   - **Plot to Port:** Allows for the output to be sent to a location such as LPT1 or a UNC path. This option depends on whether you are specifying a physical or virtual device.

   - **Plot to File:** Specifies that the output will be created as an electronic file that can then be viewed or sent to a graphics/print shop for printing.

   - **AutoSpool:** Specifies that the output should be sent to an application that determines how to route the output file. The program used for AutoSpool is specified on the Files tab of the Options dialog box under Print File, Spooler, Prolog Section Names, Print Spool Executable. An

AutoSpool program can be used to log plots or even redirect output based on paper size.

Click Next to advance the wizard to the next page.

9. On the Plotter Name page, enter a name in the Plotter Name text box. Click Next.

The name entered is displayed in the lists that allow you to specify an output device in AutoCAD, and is also used for the name of the PC3 file that is created when the wizard is finished. Click Next to advance the wizard to the next page.

10. On the Finish page, click Edit Plotter Configuration or Calibrate Plotter to further configure the new device. Click Finish.

Based on the device you are configuring, the Calibrate Plotter button might be disabled. The Calibrate Plotter button allows you to verify drawing measurements that the device can handle. The Edit Plotter Configuration button launches the Plotter Configuration Editor dialog box (see Figure 3-3) and allows you to specify custom paper sizes and other device specific settings. Make any necessary changes in the Plotter Configuration Editor dialog box, and click OK to save changes and close the dialog box.

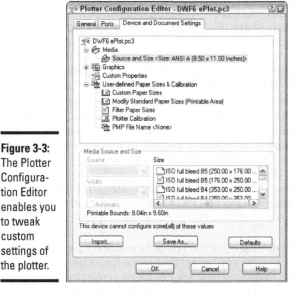

Figure 3-3:
The Plotter Configuration Editor enables you to tweak custom settings of the plotter.

In the Plotters window, the new device is added and ready for use in AutoCAD.

11. Click the X on the Plotters window to close it.

Editing a non-system printer configuration

At times, you may want to edit a non-system printer configuration in order to add or remove available paper sizes, along with options such as line merge and others. The following procedure explains how to modify a plotter configuration (.PC3) file for a non-system printer.

1. **Use one of the previously listed methods to open the Plotter Manager.**

2. **In the Plotters window, double-click the plotter configuration (PC3) file you want to edit.**

   The Plotter Configuration Editor dialog box is displayed.

3. **In the Plotter Configuration Editor dialog box, make the necessary changes and click Save & Close.**

   The changes are saved to the .PC3 file.

4. **Click the X on the Plotters window to close it.**

Putting style in your plots

AutoCAD uses *plot styles* to control the output of objects in a drawing. Plot styles can be used to control lineweight and even the color in which objects are plotted. Most printers/plotters in offices today are capable of outputting in grayscale, whereas some may even support color. Even though AutoCAD drawings are displayed and created in color, you can use plot styles to control whether that is the same with the final output. Plot styles can be used to map colors to grayscale colors or even to a different color altogether.

AutoCAD supports two different plot styles, *color-dependent* and *named*. Color-dependent plot styles are the most commonly used of the two and represent how plotting was handled before the introduction of plot styles in AutoCAD 2000. Color-dependent plot styles allow you to map specific AutoCAD colors to different lineweights and even to different colors. When you create a new drawing, the drawing template determines the type of plot style used when plotting.

You can switch between a drawing using color-dependent or named plot styles. You use the command **CONVERTPSTYLES** to toggle a drawing between the two plot styles.

Named plot styles are the newest of the two plotting methods. Named plot styles allow you to create a name and assign that name a specific lineweight and color. This allows you to display multiple colors on-screen but use one plot style for multiple layers and colors. Named plot styles do have limitations, unlike color-dependent plot styles. Named plot styles are not supported well when it comes to objects such as tables and dimensions that can display multiple colors and object levels.

For example, a table can have different colors for the grid and text but can only be assigned one plot style. In this case, the object would be plotted using one named plot style; whereas if color-dependent was used in the drawing, each color could be plotted using a different lineweight. Plot styles are saved in files outside AutoCAD with the file extensions .CTB and .STB. .CTB stands for AutoCAD Color-Dependent Plot Style Table, whereas .STB stands for AutoCAD Plot Style Table–Named plot styles.

The Add Plot Style Table Wizard is used to create new plot styles. Like the Add Plotter Wizard, the Add Plot Style Table Wizard can be launched from AutoCAD or the Windows Control Panel. The command **STYLESMANAGER** is used to display a window that allows you to access the wizard and any previously defined plot styles.

To start the **STYLESMANAGER** command, follow one of the methods outlined below:

+ **File menu:** Select File⇨Plot Style Manager.

+ **Keyboard input:** Type **STYLESMANAGER** and press Enter.

+ **Select Tools⇨Options to display the Options dialog box:** Make sure the Plot and Publish tab is selected. Click the Plot Style Table Settings button and then click Add or Edit Plot Style Tables in the Plot Style Table Settings dialog box that appears.

Book VII
Chapter 3

Print, Plot, Publish

Setting up a plot style

The following procedure launches the Add Plot Style Table Wizard and creates a color-dependent or named plot style:

1. **Use one of the previously listed methods to open the Plot Style Manager.**

A window titled Plot Styles is displayed. This window contains a shortcut to the Add Plot Style Table Wizard and displays all the previously configured .CTB and .STB files.

2. **In the Plot Styles window, locate the Add-A-Plot Style Table Wizard shortcut and double-click it.**

The Add Plot Style Table Wizard is launched.

3. **In the Add Plotter Wizard, read through the information and click Next.**

The next page of the wizard is displayed and is really the starting point of configuring a plot style table (see Figure 3-4).

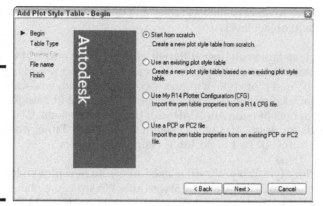

Figure 3-4:
The Add
Plot Style
Table
Wizard is
used to
create a
plot style.

4. On the Begin page, select one of the four different methods for configuring a plot style. Click Next.

The page allows you to choose from four different methods for configuring a plot style:

- **Start from Scratch.** Use this option if you are not upgrading from a release prior to AutoCAD 2000, or if you don't want to base the new plot style on an existing style.

- **Use an Existing Plot Style Table.** If you have an existing plot style that is close to the one you want to configure, use the existing one as a template for the new plot style.

- **Use My R14 Plotter Configuration (.CFG).** Pen tables, as they once were called in AutoCAD R14, were stored in a configuration (.CFG) file. If you have one of these files around, you can import the pen information into the wizard for the new plot style.

- **Use a .PCP or .PC2 File.** AutoCAD 14 and earlier versions allowed you to export your plot device configuration and pen table to a single configuration file that could be shared with other computers. The pen table contained in these files can be imported into the wizard for the new plot style.

Clicking Next advances the wizard to the next page, which is different based on which of the four options you selected. This procedure uses the Start from Scratch option.

5. On the Pick Plot Style Table page, select either Color-Dependent Plot Style Table or Named Plot Style Table option. Click Next.

6. Select either the Color-Dependent or Named Plot Style Table option, based on the type your drawings use. Clicking Next advances the wizard to the next page. In these instructions, we use the color-dependent option because it is the most commonly used plot style.

7. **On the File name page, enter a name in the File name text box. Click Next.**

The name entered is the one that is displayed in the list of plot styles within AutoCAD and is also used for the name of the .CTB or .STB file that is created when the wizard is finished. Clicking Next advances the wizard to the next page.

8. **On the Finish page, click the Plot Style Table Editor button to configure lineweights, colors, and other settings for the new plot style. Click Finish.**

9. **Based on the type of plot style created, the options in the Plot Style Table Editor dialog box (see Figure 3-5) differ. Make any necessary changes in the dialog box.**

The Plot Style Table Editor dialog box is displayed and allows you to define how the linework will look when it is plotted.

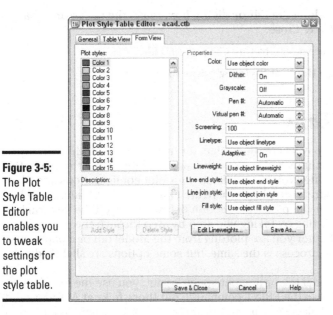

Figure 3-5:
The Plot Style Table Editor enables you to tweak settings for the plot style table.

10. **In the Plot Style Table Editor dialog box, select the color or named plot style from the Plot Styles list box on the Form View tab. Then modify the properties based on how you want the linework assigned to the plot style to appear when plotted.**

Based on the plot style you are creating, you might want to assign a lineweight or linetype property that will override the values assigned to the objects in a drawing when it is plotted.

11. **Click Save & Close.**

The changes to the plot style are saved, and the new plot style is added to the Plot Style window and is ready to use in AutoCAD.

12. **Click the X on the Plot Styles window to close it.**

Editing a plot style

As your standards change, you need to make some changes based on the colors that are used in your drawing or the lineweights used during output. The following procedure explains how to modify a plot style file.

1. **Use one of the previously listed methods to open the Plot Style Manager.**

2. **In the Plot Styles window, double-click the Plot Style (.CTB or .STB) file you want to edit.**

The Plot Style Table Editor dialog box is displayed.

3. **In the Plot Style Table Editor dialog box, make the necessary changes and click Save & Close.**

The changes are saved to the .CTB or .STB file.

4. **Click the X on the Plot Styles window to close it.**

Outputting Made Easy

Plotting is not as easy as creating a line, for instance, in AutoCAD, and this is mainly due to the number of options that are available. Over the years, the plotting process (after you have defined your plot configurations and plot styles) has been streamlined, but there are still a number of things you have to know before you can plot. This section helps get you on the fast track to understanding plotting by taking you step-by-step through the process. Depending on whether you are plotting from the Model tab or a paper space layout, the general process is the same, but some options are slightly different.

To plot out the Model tab or a paper space layout, you use the PLOT command. (You don't use the PRINT command, but those folks at Autodesk did create a command alias so you can type in PRINT at the command line or at the dynamic input tooltip.) To start the PLOT command, use one of the following methods:

✦ **File menu:** Click File➪Plot.

✦ **Standard toolbar:** Click the Plot button on the Standard toolbar.

✦ **Shortcut key:** Press the key combination CTRL+P.

✦ **Keyboard input:** Type **PLOT** and press Enter.

✦ **Right-click the Model tab or a paper space layout:** From the shortcut menu, select Plot.

Plotting the Model tab

The following procedure takes you step-by-step through the basics of plotting the Model tab of a drawing:

1. **Click the Model tab at the bottom of the drawing window.**

2. **Use one of the previously listed methods to open the Plot dialog box.**

The Plot dialog box (see Figure 3-6) is displayed.

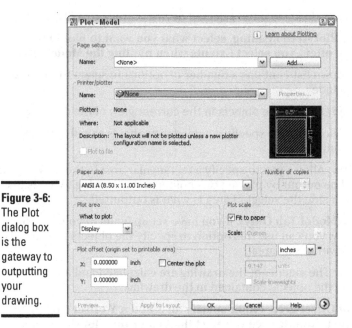

Book VII
Chapter 3

Print, Plot,
Publish

Figure 3-6:
The Plot dialog box is the gateway to outputting your drawing.

3. **In the Plot dialog box, if a named page setup is contained in your drawing, select it from the Name drop-down list under the Page Setup heading and skip to Step 10. If you don't have a named page setup, continue on with the next step.**

A page setup saves you the time of having to specify the printer/plotter, paper size, what to plot, scale, and other settings. Page setups were covered in Book VII, Chapter 1.

4. **In the Printer/Plotter area, select a printer from the Name drop-down list.**

   The drop-down list contains both the system and non-system printers, unless the Hide System Devices option is selected from the Plot and Publish tab of the Options dialog box.

5. **In the Paper Size area, select the paper size that your output will best fit on for the area that is to be plotted and the designated scale.**

   The drop-down list contains all the available paper sizes that the device can output to. If you are using a .PC3 file, you can add or remove paper sizes from the list through the Plotter Configuration Editor dialog box. For more information, see the section "Editing a non-system printer configuration" in this chapter.

6. **In the Number of Copies area, enter the number of copies you want to produce.**

   This option is disabled if the selected device outputs to a file.

7. **Under the Plot Area heading, select what you want to plot in the drawing — often, you select Extents when plotting the Model tab.**

   The drop-down list contains a number of options to select from. These options include

   - **Display:** Outputs the objects in the current view of the drawing.

   - **View:** Allows you to specify a named view that is saved in the drawing to output.

   - **Window:** Allows you to specify a rectangular area in the drawing that should be output by picking two points in the drawing. What is displayed inside the selected area is what is outputted.

   - **Limits (Model Tab Only):** If you have set up limits in your drawing properly, you can use this option to specify the objects that are displayed within this area.

   - **Extents:** The extents of the drawing are calculated and are used to print all the objects contained in the drawing.

8. **In the Plot Offset area, either specify an X and a Y offset from the edge of the printable area or select the Center the Plot check box.**

   The option that you selected in the Plot Area determines whether the Center the Plot check box is enabled.

9. **In the Plot Scale area, either specify the print area to be fit on the specified paper size by checking Fit to Paper, or uncheck Fit to Paper and specify a scale (by selecting a standard scale from the drop-down list or entering a number in the text boxes for a custom scale).**

   During production, you specify a specific scale for all your drawings. You might choose Fit to Paper if you are doing conceptual designs and are not concerned about a specific scale. For more information on scaling your drawing, see the section "Scaling your drawing" later in this chapter.

10. **Click Preview and verify that everything you want to plot will fit. After you have finished verifying your drawing, right-click and select Exit from the context menu to quit the Preview and return to the Plot dialog box.**

    A digital representation of the output is displayed on-screen. The preview is a great way to verify that the paper size is not too small for the scale that you specified. If it is, return to the Plot dialog box and make the necessary changes.

11. **Click OK.**

    The drawing is sent to the specified device using the options that you selected. If you followed these instructions, you created a basic plot in 10 steps. As we mentioned, however, other settings can also affect your plot, and those are covered in the section titled "More plotting options," later in this chapter.

You can click the Apply to Layout button at the bottom of the dialog box to save the option changes that you just made. When you return to the Plot dialog box the next time, the options are already set for you.

After the plotting process has finished, you might see a small notification balloon (see Figure 3-7) displayed in the lower-right corner of AutoCAD. This balloon informs you when plotting has been completed successfully or if an error was encountered. This notification is extremely handy if background plotting is enabled or when you are using the PUBLISH command. Both background plotting and the PUBLISH command are explained later in this chapter.

Book VII
Chapter 3

Print, Plot, Publish

Figure 3-7:
The plot
notification
balloon.

Plotting a paper space layout

Earlier in this chapter, we discussed plotting a drawing from the Model tab. Plotting a layout really is not much different, and if you have properly set up your layouts in your drawing, plotting a drawing from a layout tab is actually easier. The reason is that you don't have to worry about drawing scale because that has been defined for each of the viewports on the layout. Your device and paper sizes should already be defined as well, if you used a page setup for your layouts. So all you have to do is verify the settings in the plot dialog box to make sure that the scale is set to 1:1 and that what you are plotting is set to the Layout.

1. **Click one of the paper space layout tabs at the bottom of the drawing window.**

2. **Use one of the previously listed methods to open the Plot dialog box.**

3. **In the Plot dialog box, if necessary, specify the printer/plotter, paper size, and the number of copies.**

4. **Under the Plot Area heading, select what you want to plot in the drawing — often, you select Layout when plotting a paper space layout tab.**

The drop-down list contains a number of options that you can select. The only difference between plotting the Model tab and a paper space layout tab in this case is that there is a Layout (Paper Space Layout Only) option in place of the Limits option. With the Layout option, all the objects on the layout that fall within the specific printable area of the specified paper size are printed.

5. **In the Plot Offset area, specify an X and a Y offset from the edge of the printable area.**

6. **In the Plot Scale area, you specify a scale of 1:1 from the drop-down list in almost all cases.**

A scale of 1:1 is selected because the scale of the model geometry is handled by each of the floating viewports on the layout.

7. **Click Preview and verify that everything you want to plot will fit. After you have finished verifying your drawing, right-click and select Exit to return to the Plot dialog box.**

8. **Click OK.**

Scaling your drawing

When you output your drawings, you must specify a specific scale for your drawing. This means you don't use the Fit to Paper check box in the Plot dialog box much. If you are plotting from the Model tab, you specify a drawing scale. The drawing scale is usually always determined up-front before you begin drawing, and Chapter 5 of Book I explains how to calculate this value. If you are plotting from a paper space layout, you use a scale of 1 to 1 (1:1) because the scaling of the geometry is handled by the floating viewports on the layout.

More plotting options

The Plot dialog box has a button with an arrow on it located in the lower-right corner; by default, this button points to the right. This is a toggle that expands the Plot dialog box and reveals additional settings that are not required to output a drawing but do affect the appearance of the output. Below is a list of these additional options that are revealed when the More Options button is clicked:

✦ **Plot Style Table (Pen Assignments):** The drop-down list allows you to specify a plot style that can be used to control the color and lineweights of the drawing during output. You can use the Edit button to the right of the drop-down list to edit the selected plot style.

✦ **Shaded Viewport Options:** The options in this area are used to control how shaded and rendered views are output. The Shade Plot drop-down list allows you to specify how views that don't have a specific visual style assigned to them are displayed. The Quality drop-down list and the DPI text box control the resolution at which shaded and rendered views are output.

✦ **Plot Options:** The options in this area control a wide range of settings. Each one of the settings in this area is described in the following list:

- **Plot in Background:** Determines whether control of AutoCAD is released after a plot is sent and the actual process of the plot is done in the background so you can get back to work sooner. If the option is unchecked, you have to wait until the plot has completed processing and is sent to the device. Enabling background plotting is slower; so if you need a plot right away, don't use background plotting.

  You can control background plotting through the Plot and Publish tab of the Options dialog box under the Background Processing Options area. There is an option for Plotting and one for Publishing (by default, Publishing is the only one checked). We discuss the Publishing option later in this chapter.

- **Plot Object Lineweights:** Controls whether object lightweights assigned to layers and objects are used instead of the assigned plot style.

- **Plot with Plot Styles:** Controls whether plot styles are used when plotting.

- **Plot Paperspace Last:** Controls whether paper space geometry is plotted before model space geometry is.

- **Hide Paperspace Objects:** Controls whether AutoCAD automatically performs the HIDE command on the paper space layout.

- **Plot Stamp On:** Adds a plot stamp along the edge of the drawing when it is outputted. The plot stamp is configured using the PLOTSTAMP command.

- **Save Changes to Layout:** Specifies whether changes to the plotting settings for the layout are saved when OK is clicked. This saves the changes for you so you don't have to remember to click the Apply to Layout button before clicking OK.

✦ **Drawing Orientation:** Controls whether the drawing is plotted in the portrait or landscape direction. You can also specify whether the drawing is plotted upside down by checking the Plot Upside-Down option.

Publishing Drawings

Using the PLOT command to output your drawings is easy if you only have a few drawings that need to be outputted, but it can be a very large task if you have many drawings and layouts. Prior to AutoCAD 2004, you had to use an external batch plotting utility in order to output many drawings at one time. AutoCAD 2004 introduced a command called PUBLISH. The PUBLISH command allows you to batch a number of drawings together in order to output them all based on their defined page setups or override that page setup with one of your choice. The other feature that the PUBLISH command introduced was multisheet .DWF files. Prior to AutoCAD 2004, .DWF files were only capable of containing a single representation of a layout from either the Model tab or a paper space layout tab.

The PUBLISH command in AutoCAD LT only supports plotting to .DWF files.

To start the PUBLISH command, use one of the following methods:

✦ **File menu:** Click File⇨Publish.

✦ **Standard toolbar:** Click the Publish button on the Standard toolbar.

✦ **Keyboard input:** Type **PUBLISH** and press Enter.

✦ **Right-click over a layout tab after multiple layout tabs:** From the shortcut menu, select Publish.

The following procedure takes you step-by-step through the basics of using the Publish dialog box:

1. **Use one of the previously listed methods to open the Publish dialog box.**

The Publish dialog box (see Figure 3-8) is displayed. If no layout tabs were selected, all the open drawings and their layouts are pulled into the dialog box.

2. **In the Publish dialog box, click the Add Sheets button to add layouts from other drawings not currently open in AutoCAD.**

The Select Drawings dialog box is displayed.

3. **In the Select Drawings dialog box, browse to and select the drawings whose layouts you want to add to the Publish dialog box. Click Open.**

The Select Drawings dialog box closes and all the layouts in the selected drawings are imported into the list box.

4. **If you do not want a layout that has been imported, select the layout from the list and right-click. From the shortcut menu, select Remove, and the layout is removed.**

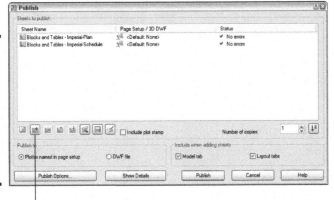

Figure 3-8:
The Publish dialog box makes printing multiple layouts and drawings a breeze.

Add Sheets button

5. **Click Publish to start the publishing process.**

6. **The Save Sheet List dialog box is displayed. Click Yes to save the list of sheets out to a Drawing Set Description (.DSD) file. This file can then later be reopened in the Publish dialog box to republish all the layouts in the sheet list again.**

   If background plotting is enabled for publishing, the Processing Background Plot dialog box is displayed.

7. **The Processing Background Plot dialog box (see Figure 3-9) is displayed when background plotting is enabled for the PLOT or PUBLISH command. By default, AutoCAD displays the same notification balloon as the PLOT command, when the PUBLISH command finishes.**

**Book VII
Chapter 3**

**Print, Plot,
Publish**

Figure 3-9:
The background plotting message.

Book VIII

Collaboration

The 5th Wave   By Rich Tennant

"Why, of course. I'd be very interested in seeing this new milestone in the project."

Contents at a Glance

Chapter 1: CAD Management: The Necessary Evil

*A*utoCAD & AutoCAD LT All-in-One Desk Reference For Dummies is designed to help both AutoCAD and AutoCAD LT users improve the quality of the designs that they publish and effectively share them with others. As you progress through this book, you discover how to manage the drafting environment and CAD standards that are defined by your company, and some of the different ways to effectively work with drawing files.

CAD standards are one of those topics that is not discussed enough in the office, and yet they play a very important role in sharing drawing files. CAD standards ensure that the drawing files you create look similar to the drawing files that everyone else in the office creates. All the drawing files should have the same look and feel when they are presented to a potential client. If your work doesn't have a uniform look, the client might get the impression that your company doesn't have enough experience to handle the project.

After the drawing files have been completed, it's usually time for them to be shared with others. During this stage of the project, you might find that printing hard copies and mailing them to the client or off-site team members takes too much time. If you need a timely response to a question or a change, you will most likely share files electronically. The type of file sharing you use depends on your target audience and the phase of the project. You might use a Web site to display files and images or use an Internet project site like Buzzsaw. In the end, you have to ensure that you are efficiently collaborating with your team and client.

Getting a Handle on the Basics of CAD Management

CAD management refers to managing the day-to-day operations involved in drafting with AutoCAD. CAD management is not necessarily the sole responsibility of one individual, but one individual often heads up the duties included in this area. If you are a mid- to large-size company, you might have a full-time CAD manager in this role; in a smaller company, the chores may be handled by a senior level drafter. The CAD manager may or may not be a supervisor at the company.

CAD management commonly covers the following areas:

✦ **Budgeting:** Estimating the amount of money needed for a specific period of time for CAD-related expenses. This might be software upgrade costs, hardware purchases, office supplies (such as paper for the plotter), training costs, and even consulting fees.

✦ **CAD standards enforcement:** Making sure that all drafters are following the company's defined CAD standards — this is one of the responsibilities that many don't like about CAD management. Ensuring that CAD standards are followed helps ensure that a high level of quality is maintained for drawings that are sent out.

✦ **Managing the drafting environment:** Maintaining and managing support files through a centralized location to make sure that all drafters are using the same set of files when working with drawing files. This helps to reduce potential errors and the extra cost of keeping the files in sync if they are all running locally on each user's own computer.

✦ **Conducting and coordinating training:** Rolling out new procedures or even providing upgrade training for a new release. Training for upgrades might be outsourced, but the coordination of this training is usually handled by the individual responsible for CAD management in your office. Training might also be related to company rules and policies, and even departmental ones, if they exist.

✦ **Resource management:** Overseeing the resource pool of CAD drafters to ensure that current and future projects are completed in a timely manner.

A project involves much more than just one drafter creating drawing files with AutoCAD; instead, a whole team with specialized skills is usually at work on a project. This team might include individuals who are responsible for overseeing the project, drafters, estimators, manufacturing and builders, and the client. This is the same approach that should be taken with CAD management and standards. One individual might have leadership responsibility, but everyone should be involved to a degree. Having everyone involved at some level helps to ensure that the standards are widely accepted and are uniform across an organization.

Due to the growing complexity of projects these days, more people from different areas of the company are getting involved, so having representation from across the company in defining CAD standards is a good idea. CAD standards shouldn't just stay in the drafting department: The output from the drawing files might be used for marketing material, in print or on the Internet, and will surely end up in front of your clients as well. Clients end up reviewing drawings during many phases of a project, and, from these drawings, they build a perception of what kind of skill level your company has. For these reasons, many people need to get involved with CAD standards.

Some of the most interesting ideas for improving CAD standards and using the information maintained in a drawing file can come from different groups in a company coming together. That doesn't mean that everyone in the company should have a direct vote in what is part of the CAD standards, but getting feedback from individuals in the company who deal with the information that is generated from a drawing file is a good idea. Often CAD standards are thought of in terms of drawings only, but they really encompass everything related to how the CAD information is used.

Here are some items that are part of the non-typical CAD standards that should be looked at as a company:

+ **Title blocks:** Information added to a title block could be used downstream to populate a project management system, if one exists.

+ **Content of a drawing:** How the drawing is created can affect how its information can be used downstream for things such as renderings and animations that might be done by an internal or external art department.

+ **Annotation, such as notes and dimensions:** Some notes on a drawing might be there for legal reasons; it is good to have a company view on these types of notes because the information might already be covered in a bid packet or specification document.

+ **AutoCAD support file locations:** Companies want to make sure that file access is optimal for all users throughout the company. This ensures an efficient working environment and also ensures that everything is properly backed up in case of a catastrophe.

+ **File exchanging practices (use of e-mail or FTP sites):** Policies in place for the use of e-mail might delay the sending of information for a project. An example of an e-mail policy that can affect the sending or receiving of files for a project can be the total allowable size of all files coming in or going out during normal business hours. It's wise to communicate with internal and external departments to see what can be sent out efficiently without conflicting with company e-mail policy.

+ **Drawing name convention and storage locations:** Naming conventions are important so that individuals in the company can find a drawing file in a timely manner. This could affect how the files might be archived and the file rights that individuals may need to access them. Storing these types of files in a centralized location on a network drive accessible to everyone is good practice.

✦ **Training, seminars, and learning material:** Sending employees to training or purchasing training materials for them is often hard to justify financially. This is because at times the true return of investment (ROI) is unclear. You must determine as a company how training is conducted when a new release comes out or a new individual is brought onboard.

Managing the Drafting Environment

AutoCAD is a complex drafting program with many different options and support files. Proper management of the AutoCAD environment is not something that just happens overnight. Given the sophisticated drafting environment in AutoCAD, a small group of appointed individuals at your company should be in charge of making updates to support files. Having a small group in charge of updates is especially critical in preventing unauthorized changes that could affect new or existing drawings in a negative way when the files are shared with a large group of drafters. So what is included in the drafting environment?

When we say *drafting environment,* we're not talking about background colors and size of the crosshairs — those things don't affect the final output of a drawing file. Instead, we're referring to template file locations and where AutoCAD looks for support files such as blocks, fonts, and customization. When you first install AutoCAD, it often looks locally for things such as menu customization, hatch patterns, blocks, fonts, drawing template files, and anything else that is ordinarily shipped with the product. Because AutoCAD doesn't force specific locations for files, it allows you the flexibility to determine how you want to manage all these support files. The default out-of-the-box locations are local on the computer, but this is not the best way to manage support files.

If a CAD standard changes, you need to update the drawing template files; but if AutoCAD looks locally for these files, updating the files can be a nightmare, depending on how many users you are supporting. Instead of letting all users have their own copies of the drawing template files, place the drawing template files on the network and redirect AutoCAD to look in that location. This way, when a change is made, all the users get the change instantaneously.

All the support paths and folder locations in which AutoCAD looks for the files it needs are defined on the Files tab of the Options dialog box. This means that you can have your drawing template files, plot style files, font files, linetype definition files, and blocks on a network location so you don't have to worry about any computer using outdated files when changes are made. This also gives you control over who can make changes to these files, as opposed to whether they are stored locally on each machine. The other advantage of having these files on the network is that they don't get lost or forgotten during an upgrade to a newer release.

Creating a Good Foundation

This book is designed to put you on the right path from the start and to help you develop good drafting habits when creating objects like layers, text styles, and blocks. One of the final pieces of the puzzle is how to pull all this information together to start building a good foundation in managing and understanding CAD standards. This isn't just applicable to CAD managers: Good CAD standards should be practiced by all drafters.

When creating drawings, you often find that you are using the same layers, linetypes, title blocks, and specific styles again and again. As you know, a layer can be added using the Layer Properties Manager, but adding layers manually to each new drawing file can be time-consuming and can introduce errors. This is where the concept of drawing template files comes into play. These files have the file extension .DWT and are located by default under *<drive>*:\Documents and Settings*<user name>*\Local Settings\Application Data\Autodesk*<product>**<release>**<language>*\Template. If the concept of templates sounds familiar, it's because applications that are part of MS Office utilize templates to store formatting and styles that can be reused when creating a new file.

A drawing template is not much different from a drawing file you are used to creating with AutoCAD. The only difference is that you can provide a description for the template that appears when you use the StartUp dialog box. And when you use it to create a new drawing, AutoCAD creates a new unnamed drawing with those styles and features and the default name *Drawing1*. The numeral at the end of the default name is incremented for each new drawing that is created while the session of AutoCAD is open.

You use a drawing template file to ensure that the styles and formatting are ready to go when you need to create a drawing, and that styles and formatting are consistent among drawings. The most common items included in a drawing template file are

+ **Blocks:** (Book VI, Chapter 2)

+ **Dimension styles:** (Book III, Chapter 2)

+ **Layers:** (Book I, Chapter 5)

+ **Layouts:** (Book VII, Chapter 1)

+ **Linetypes:** (Book I, Chapter 5)

+ **Materials:** (Book V, Chapter 7)

+ **Multiline styles:** (Book II, Chapter 1)

+ **Page setups:** (Book VII, Chapter 1)

+ **Table styles:** (Book III, Chapter 1)

+ **Text styles:** (Book III, Chapter 1)

+ **UCSs (User Coordinate System):** (Book V, Chapter 3)

+ **Viewports:** (Book VII, Chapter 1)

+ **Views:** (Book II, Chapter 3)

+ **Drawing objects in model and paper space:** (Book I, Chapter 5)

+ **Drawing limits and some drafting settings:** (Book I, Chapters 5 and 6)

AutoCAD LT does not support the creation or editing of materials used for rendering 3D objects or Multiline styles used to create Multiline objects.

Creating a drawing template file

The following procedure uses the File menu to start the SAVEAS command and creates a drawing template file.

1. **Create reusable content in the drawing that you want to have available when you use the template to create a new drawing.**

2. **From the File menu, choose Save As.**

The Save Drawing As dialog box is displayed.

3. **In the Save Drawing As dialog box, select AutoCAD Drawing Template (*.DWT) from the Files of Type drop-down list.**

By default, AutoCAD navigates to the location that is specified for drawing template files when AutoCAD Drawing Template (*.DWT) is selected from the drop-down list. This location can be changed using the OPTIONS command. We recommend changing where AutoCAD looks for drawing template files to a centralized location, such as a network, to make it easy for multiple users to access the files.

4. **Browse to a different location or use the location specified by AutoCAD for saving drawing template files.**

5. **Enter a different filename other than the one that AutoCAD provides by default.**

You might want to add some information to the filename to help identify what the template is used for. For example, you might give your template the name *E-Size Lot Plan* if you are doing architectural drawings, or *B-size Part* if you are doing mechanical drawings.

6. Click Save.

The Template Description dialog box (see Figure 1-1) is displayed and allows you to specify a description and the type of measurement the template should be set to.

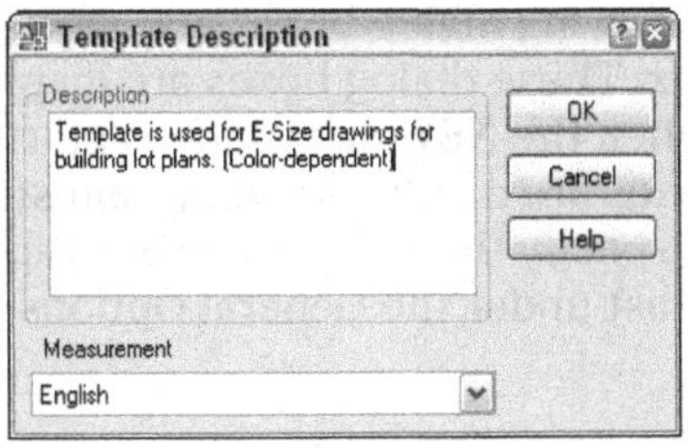

Figure 1-1:
The Template Description dialog box.

7. Enter a description of your choice in the Description text field and specify the type of measurement from the Measurement drop-down list.

The description is displayed in the Create New Drawing and Startup dialog boxes. The Measurement option controls which linetype and hatch pattern files are used, along with controlling some settings for inserting blocks into a drawing.

8. Click OK.

The Template Description dialog box closes and the drawing template is saved to the specified location.

The measurement option found in the Template Description dialog box controls a system variable called MEASUREMENT. This variable can be changed at any time by typing **MEASUREMENT** at the command prompt or dynamic input tooltip, and entering the new value. Use a value of 0 to specify English (Imperial), and 1 to specify Metric.

Using a drawing template file

After you have created a drawing template file, you must understand how to use it to create new drawings. Below are some of the common ways to use a drawing template file to create a new drawing:

+ **NEW command:** Start the NEW command and select the drawing template that you want to begin with.

+ **QNEW command:** The QNEW command is similar to the NEW command, with one key difference. You can specify a default drawing template file that will be used to create a new drawing when the command is used or each time AutoCAD starts. If no default template file is specified, the QNEW command behaves like the NEW command. To specify the default drawing template file that should be used, start the OPTIONS command and browse to the template that you want to use for the QNEW command under the Template Settings node of the Files tab.

✦ **Startup and Create New Drawing dialog boxes:** Both the Startup (see Figure 1-2) and Create New Drawing dialog boxes are controlled by a setting in the Options dialog box. These dialog boxes are displayed when AutoCAD first starts up or when the NEW command is started. To control whether these dialog boxes are displayed on system startup, start the OPTIONS command and specify the value Show Startup dialog box from the Startup drop-down list under the General Options section of the System tab.

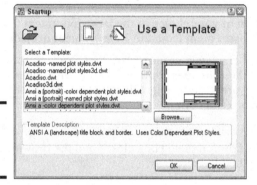

Figure 1-2:
A different
take on
startup.

✦ **Double-click drawing template file:** From Windows Explorer, you can double-click a drawing template file to create a new drawing. If AutoCAD is not running already, it starts, and the new drawing is created.

Specifying a drawing template file for use with QNEW

Often, you find yourself using a specific drawing template repeatedly. The QNEW command was created for this situation. But out of the box, QNEW works just like the NEW command. To make the QNEW command live up to its potential, you need to specify the default drawing template to use through the Options dialog box. This saves you some time because you don't have to browse and select the drawing template you commonly use for most of the new drawings you create.

The following procedure shows you how to use the Tools menu to start the OPTIONS command and specify a drawing template to use to create a new drawing when the QNEW command is used:

1. **From the Tools menu, choose Options.**

The Options dialog box is displayed.

2. **In the Options dialog box, click the Files tab along the top of the dialog box.**

The Files tab is used to specify things like support folders for AutoCAD to find hatch pattern files or plotter device information.

3. **Click the plus sign next to Template Settings to expand it.**

The settings related to this group are displayed with additional nodes (see Figure 1-3).

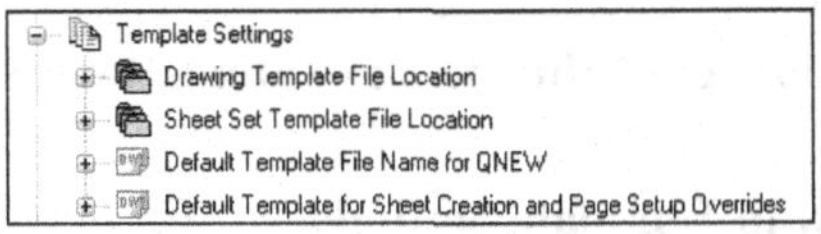

Figure 1-3:
The settings related to template settings.

Template Settings
Drawing Template File Location
Sheet Set Template File Location
Default Template File Name for QNEW
Default Template for Sheet Creation and Page Setup Overrides

AutoCAD users see a total of four nodes, whereas AutoCAD LT users see only two. The options Drawing Template File Location and Default Template File Name for QNEW apply to both AutoCAD and AutoCAD LT.

4. **Click the plus sign next to Default Template File Name for QNEW.**

If no template has been specified, you should see the value None. This designates that QNEW works just like the NEW command does.

5. **Select the value of None from under Default Template File Name for QNEW and click Browse.**

The Select a File dialog box is displayed and allows you to select a drawing template file.

6. **In the Select a File dialog box, specify the drawing template that you want to use when the QNEW command is used.**

The selected drawing template file should be highlighted and the name placed in the File Name text field.

7. **Click Open.**

The Select a File dialog box closes and the value is added under the Default Template File Name for QNEW node.

8. **In the Options dialog box, click Apply or OK.**

Clicking Apply saves the changes made and keeps the dialog box displayed, whereas clicking OK saves the changes and closes the Options dialog box.

Book VIII
Chapter 1

CAD Management:
The Necessary Evil

Specifying the location of drawing template files

If you create templates for a number of users in your office, you want to be sure they can access them. To make the most of the time you spend creating your own templates, place them in a centralized location and then have AutoCAD look there for them. To specify where AutoCAD looks for drawing template files, you need to change a setting in the Options dialog box.

The following procedure shows you how to use the Tools menu to start the OPTIONS command and specify a new location for AutoCAD to look in for drawing template files when the NEW command is started (or at AutoCAD startup if the Startup dialog box is displayed):

1. **From the Tools menu, choose Options.**

   The Options dialog box is displayed.

2. **In the Options dialog box, click the Files tab along the top of the dialog box.**

3. **Click the plus sign next to Template Settings.**

   The settings that are related to this group are displayed with additional nodes.

4. **Click the plus sign next to Drawing Template File Location.**

5. **Select the value under Drawing Template File Location and click Browse.**

   The Browse for Folder dialog box is displayed and allows you to select a new location that AutoCAD looks in for drawing template files.

6. **In the Browse for Folder dialog box, specify the location for drawing template files.**

   The location can be on a local or network drive. Most commonly, if you are maintaining drawing template files for a group of users, you specify a location on a network drive.

7. **Click OK.**

   The Browse for Folder dialog box closes and the value is added under the Drawing Template File Location node.

8. **In the Options dialog box, click Apply or OK.**

   Clicking Apply saves the changes and keeps the dialog box displayed, whereas clicking OK saves the changes and closes the Options dialog box.

Chapter 2: CAD Standards

In This Chapter

✔ Understanding CAD standards

✔ Checking drawings for CAD standards

✔ Translating layer standards

✔ Batch standards checking

AutoCAD is a very robust and complex drafting tool, so not all users discover or thoroughly understand every feature of the product; one such frequently overlooked feature is the built-in CAD standards tool. This chapter helps to shine some light on the topic of CAD standards and the built-in tools that AutoCAD offers to help make the managing of CAD standards easier. Don't get discouraged: Developing a good set of CAD standards and getting them implemented may take some time.

CAD standards can be handled in lots of different ways, as you might already know from your experiences working at different companies or working with a client's set of drawings. Many companies create their own set of CAD standards; others adopt an industry standard like those defined by an organization such as the American Institute of Architects (AIA), National CAD Standards, or the Construction Standards Institute (CSI). No matter how your CAD standards came about, they must be followed to avoid potential problems. If your company doesn't have such standards, maybe this is your time to shine by helping to establish them.

CAD Standards Overview

Book VIII, Chapter 1 is a primer of what is involved in establishing CAD standards. Drawing template files are one of the cornerstones of CAD standards because they help to promote the use of a company's standards. However, drawing templates alone won't get the job done. Creating and maintaining CAD standards is something of an art form when you consider everything you need to understand and appreciate to get drawings to look the way you want them to.

CAD standards affect both creating and editing geometry. This is because you are trying to make sure all your drawings look a certain way when they are plotted to paper. If everyone doesn't follow CAD standards, you may edit someone else's drawings only to discover that the established standards weren't followed. Then, you have to spend additional time correcting the problem. Without CAD standards, all your objects would probably look the same, with none of the necessary variations.

The variations in a drawing help to convey a design idea that you have drafted. The variations might be in the form of different lineweights, linetypes, or even text styles. CAD standards cover the range of the drafting process from creation to presentation; for this reason, a specialized individual usually takes responsibility for CAD standards. In most mid- to large-size companies, CAD standards are determined by a CAD manager; in smaller companies, a senior level drafter often takes the responsibility. No matter who defines the CAD standards, they must be defined and understood by all drafters.

Below is an overview of some of the important things you should keep in mind when establishing or modifying a set of CAD standards:

✦ **Remember plotting.** One of the key things to keep in mind when establishing CAD standards is how your drawings will look when they are plotted. This can affect such things as linetype scale, text size, dimension scale, and how you establish the use of lineweights for your objects.

✦ **Don't make constant changes.** We don't recommend making changes to your CAD standards on a daily or even weekly basis; otherwise, you're defeating the purpose of standards. And, as obvious as it sounds, remember to keep track of the changes you make. Changes might cause problems for third-party applications or even possibly your own internal customization. Tracking changes provides a good way to keep track of when changes were made and also offers a way to communicate the standards to other drafters in the office when problems arise. Having an implementation date as to when the standards were updated ensures that everyone stays on the same page.

✦ **Keep it simple.** One thing that can save you time is to create customization that incorporates your established CAD standards. If dimensions should be on a specific layer, consider customizing the menu items and toolbars so that they set a specific layer current before starting one of the dimension commands. You don't have to be a power user to set up this type of customization, and it can cut down on errors and time.

✦ **Make it straightforward.** CAD standards should not be in the form of complex manuals that require the use of a secret decoder ring to understand them. CAD standards should not only make sense to your internal drafters, but also to those with whom you share files. If you use cryptic or abbreviated names for layers and styles, a new person may have a hard time stepping in and becoming efficient right away. The length of file names and the amount of memory were limited in the old (DOS) days, but now you can be more descriptive with the names you use for named objects.

The following lists the most common items you should consider incorporating into your CAD standards:

✦ **Blocks:** (Book VI, Chapter 1)

✦ **Dimension styles:** (Book III, Chapter 2)

✦ **Drawing Template (.DWT) Files:** (Book VIII, Chapter 1)

✦ **Layers:** (Book I, Chapter 5)

✦ **Layouts:** (Book VII, Chapter 1)

✦ **Linetypes:** (Book I, Chapter 5)

✦ **Page setups:** (Book VII, Chapter 1)

✦ **Sheet Set Template (.DST) Files:** (Book VII, Chapter 2)

✦ **Table styles:** (Book III, Chapter 1)

✦ **Text styles:** (Book III, Chapter 1)

✦ **Tool Palettes:** (Book VI, Chapter 4)

✦ **Viewports:** (Book VII, Chapter 1)

✦ **Views:** (Book II, Chapter 3)

The remainder of this chapter focuses on the CAD standards tools found in AutoCAD, not AutoCAD LT.

Using AutoCAD's CAD Standards Tools

AutoCAD provides several different tools that help keep drawings in sync with defined CAD standards. These tools are

✦ **Standards Manager:** Used to configure and check for CAD standard violations.

✦ **Layer Translator:** Used to configure layer mappings and change layers in a drawing to match those defined by your CAD standards.

✦ **Batch Standards Checker:** Used to check a set of drawings against a defined set of CAD standards.

The CAD standards tools provided with AutoCAD help with only a small subset of the items that are part of a good set of CAD standards. Blocks, layouts, page setups, and table styles, for example, are not part of the standards that AutoCAD is designed to manage.

Drawing standards (.DWS) files

A drawing standards file is, for the most part, the same as a drawing or drawing template file, except for its file extension and the type of content that might be saved in it. Here are the most common items found in a drawing standards file:

✦ **Dimension styles:** (Book III, Chapter 2)

✦ **Layers:** (Book I, Chapter 5)

✦ **Linetypes:** (Book I, Chapter 5)

✦ **Text styles:** (Book III, Chapter 1)

The reason for the limited content of drawing standards files is that these types of objects are supported with the built-in CAD standards tools.

The following procedure uses the File menu to start the command and saves the current drawing as a drawing standards file:

1. **Create a new drawing based on a drawing template file or from scratch. Add to the drawing any layers, linetypes, dimension styles, or text styles that you want in the drawing standards file.**

2. **From the File menu, choose Save As.**

   The Save Drawing As dialog box is displayed.

3. **In the Save Drawing As dialog box, select AutoCAD Drawing Standards (*.DWS) from the Files of Type drop-down list.**

   By default, AutoCAD navigates to the folder of the current drawing file. Storing drawing standards files in a network location so they can be used by others in the office is best.

4. **Browse to a different location or use the location that is specified by AutoCAD to save your drawing standards file in.**

5. **Enter a filename different from the one AutoCAD provides by default.**

   You might want to name the drawing standards file based on a project name or the type of drawing that the drawing standards file will be used with. For example, you might give the standards file for your elevation drawings the name *Elevations,* or name the standards file for your plan drawings *Plans.*

6. **Click Save.**

The drawing standards file is created with the specified name and location.

Managing standards

AutoCAD provides a set of tools that allow you to associate a drawing standards file with a drawing and then check that drawing against the associated drawing standards files. This set of tools is known as the Standards Manager and is broken up into two parts: The first is used to configure and associate drawing standards files to a drawing, and the second is used to check for violations in the drawing.

When configuring a drawing to use a drawing standards file, you are specifying which file should be used to check CAD standards against and which plug-ins should be used (essentially, a plug-in is a set of rules used to determine whether there are problems in the drawing). During the checking of the drawing file, you can fix any problems the plug-in finds.

Configuring standards

A drawing standards file can be associated with a drawing using the STANDARDS command. You can start this command in a number of ways:

✦ **Tools menu:** Select Tools⇨CAD Standards⇨Configure.

✦ **CAD Standards toolbar:** Click the Configure button on the CAD Standards toolbar.

✦ **Keyboard input:** Type **STANDARDS** and press Enter.

✦ **Command alias:** Type **STA** and press Enter.

The following procedure starts the STANDARDS command, configures the drawing to use a drawing standards file, and specifies which plug-ins to use:

1. **Use any of the four methods just listed to initiate the STANDARDS command.**

The Configure Standards dialog box (see Figure 2-1) is displayed.

2. **In the Configure Standards dialog box, click the Standards tab.**

On the Standards tab, you associate the drawing standards files to be used for the current drawing. If more than one drawing standards file is specified, the order of the files is important. For example, if more than one of the associated drawing standards files has the same name for a layer, the first one encountered from the top of the list is used for validating the standard.

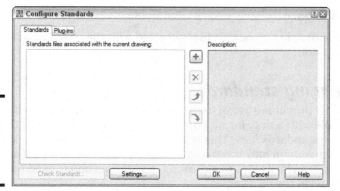

Figure 2-1:
Configuring
standards
for a
drawing.

3. **Click the + (plus sign) button located in the middle of the dialog box.**

The Select Standards File dialog box is displayed. From this dialog box, you can select which drawing standards files you want to associate with the drawing. Although more than one drawing standards file can be associated with a drawing, only one at a time can be selected from the Select Standards File dialog box.

4. **Browse to and select the drawing standards file you want to associate with the drawing.**

5. **Click Open.**

The drawing standards file is added to the list box on the left. When the drawing standards file is selected in the list box on the left, some of the file's properties are displayed in the list box on the right.

6. **Add any additional drawing standards files that you need.**

When more than one drawing standards file is associated with a drawing, the Move Up and Move Down buttons are enabled, allowing you to change the order in which the files are used to check for standards violations.

7. **Click the Plug-Ins tab.**

On the Plug-Ins tab (see Figure 2-2), you can select which plug-ins you want to use for checking the drawing for violations against the associated drawing standards files. AutoCAD comes with a total of four plug-ins — this number hasn't changed since the feature was first introduced.

8. **Select the plug-ins that you want to use when checking for standards violations in the current drawing.**

A check mark next to the plug-in means it will be used when checking standards; a plug-in with no check mark means it will not be used.

Figure 2-2:
Selecting
plug-ins for
checking
standards.

9. **Click the Settings button at the bottom of the Configure Standards dialog box.**

The CAD Standards Settings (see Figure 2-3) dialog box is displayed. From this dialog box, you can control the display of the notification icon that appears in the status bar when CAD standards are configured, and you can specify how errors are handled during the process of checking for standards violations.

Figure 2-3:
Fine-tuning
the behavior
of the CAD
standards
tools.

10. **Click OK.**

The drawing standards files are associated with the current drawing and the dialog box is closed. By default, a book icon (see Figure 2-4) appears in the status bar denoting that at least one drawing standards file is associated with the drawing.

**Book VIII
Chapter 2**

CAD Standards

Figure 2-4:
Icon in the
status bar
denotes the
use of CAD
standards.

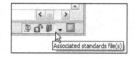

> You can right-click some of the notification icons in the status bar to access specific settings for that feature. For example, if you right-click the book icon used for CAD standards, you can access some of the options for configuring and checking standards.

Checking standards

After a drawing standards file has been associated with a drawing, you can begin to check for standards violations. CAD standards can be checked for a drawing using the CHECKSTANDARDS command. You can start this command in a number of ways:

- ✦ **Tools menu:** Select Tools⇨CAD Standards⇨Check.
- ✦ **CAD Standards toolbar:** Click the Check tool on the CAD Standards toolbar.
- ✦ **Keyboard input:** Type **CHECKSTANDARDS** and press Enter.
- ✦ **Command alias:** Type **CHK** and press Enter.

The following procedure starts the command and then checks a drawing for violations against the associated drawing standards file and selected plug-ins:

1. **Use any of the four methods just listed to initiate the CHECKSTANDARDS command.**

The Check Standards dialog box (see Figure 2-5) is displayed. If no standards file has been associated with the drawing file yet, the Associate Standards (see Figure 2-6) message box is displayed. If the message box is displayed, click OK to go to the Configure Standards dialog box.

2. **In the Check Standards dialog box, each one of the standards violations is displayed at the top in the Problem area.**

The Problem area lets you know what is wrong during the checking process.

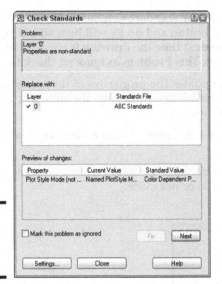

Figure 2-5:
A violation
has been
detected.

Figure 2-6:
No
standards
file has been
associated
with this
drawing yet.

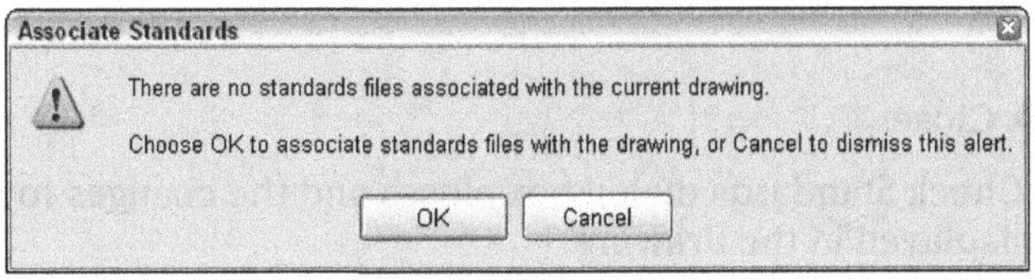

3. In the Replace With area, select one of the available fixes.

The Replace With area allows you to designate one of the named objects
in the associated standards file that should be used to fix the problem.
When the drawing is compared to the standards file, it attempts to
locate a recommended fix for you; the recommended fix is designated
with a blue check mark next to it in the Replace With area. After an item
is selected from the Replace With area, an overview of the changes that
will be made is displayed in the Preview of Changes area.

The Preview of Changes area gives you an idea of what is going to
happen when the fix is applied. In some cases, a fix can't be made; for
example, if your drawing standards file uses color-dependent plotting
whereas the current drawing is name dependent.

4. **Click the Fix button to fix the standards violation. If you want to skip a violation, click the Next button and no fix will be made. If you also want to skip the violation the next time the drawing is checked for standards violations, click the Mark This Problem as Ignored check box.**

Clicking the Fix button updates the properties of the named object in the drawing so it matches the drawing standards file after you are through checking for standards violations.

5. **After all violations have been looked at, the Checking Complete message box is displayed.**

The Checking Complete message box (see Figure 2-7) displays a summary of the changes made or not made.

Figure 2-7:
All
violations
have been
evaluated.

6. **Click Close.**

The Check Standards dialog box closes and the changes to the violations are displayed in the drawing.

Translating layers

The Configure and Check Standards tools are designed to help automate the process of keeping similarly named layers and styles in sync. But what happens if you get a set of drawings from a client or customer and need to make their drawings conform to your layers? You don't want to have to go through each drawing one by one and map each layer or group of layers to the layer used in your CAD standards.

This is where the Layer Translator comes into play. The Layer Translator allows you to map a single layer or a group of layers to a single layer based on your established CAD standards. After the translation map for layers is set up, you can save the map to a drawing, drawing standards, or drawing template file for use later on additional drawings.

The Layer Translator is accessed through the LAYTRANS command. You can start this command in several ways:

+ **Tools menu:** Select Tools⇨CAD Standards⇨Layer Translator.

+ **CAD Standards toolbar:** Click the Layer Translator tool on the CAD Standards toolbar.

+ **Keyboard input:** Type **LAYTRANS** and press Enter.

The following procedure starts the command, creates a layer translation map, and translates the layers in a drawing.

1. **Use any of the three methods just listed to initiate the LAYTRANS command.**

The Layer Translator dialog box (see Figure 2-8) is displayed.

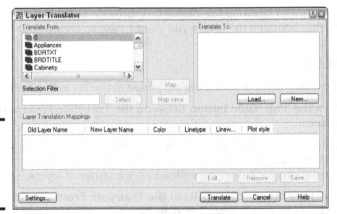

Figure 2-8:
Translating from one layer to another.

2. **In the Layer Translator dialog box, click the New button located below the Translate To area.**

The New Layer dialog box (see Figure 2-9) is displayed.

In the New Layer dialog box, you are creating a new layer to be used in the layer translation process from scratch. At minimum, you must specify a name.

3. **Modify the properties as necessary for the new layer.**

4. **Click OK.**

The new layer is added to the list under the Translate To area.

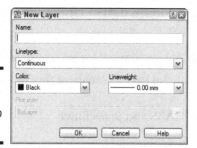

Figure 2-9:
Create a
new layer to
map to.

5. **In the Layer Translator dialog box, click the Load button located below the Translate To area.**

   The Select Drawing File dialog box is displayed and allows you to select a drawing, drawing standards, or drawing template file to load layers from for use in the Translate To list.

   In the Select Drawing File dialog box, browse and select an existing file that contains the layers you want to use to create your layer translation from.

6. **Click Open.**

   The layers in the selected file are added to the list in the Translate To area.

7. **Click the Map Same button between the Translate From and Translate To areas.**

   Any layers that have the same name between the two lists will be automatically mapped. This helps speed up the process when creating the translations for a drawing with a larger number of layers.

8. **Select the layer or layers from the Translate From area that you want to create a layer translation map for.**

   The selected layer or layers become highlighted. You can press and hold down the Ctrl key to select multiple layers or the Shift key to select a range of files.

Layers that appear with a white icon next to them in the Translate From area don't have any objects on them. These layers can be purged from the list and the drawing by right-clicking the list and selecting Purge Layers.

Use the Selection Filter field to quickly select a number of layer names that are similar in name. You can use wildcard characters to help create a complex criterion if needed. For example, you can enter TXT* and click the Select button to highlight all the layers that begin with the letters TXT.

9. **Select the layer from the Translate To area that you want the selected layer or layers in the Translate From area to be translated to.**

   Layers in both the Translate From and Translate To areas should now be highlighted.

10. **Click the Map button to create the layer translation.**

    The layer translation is added to the Layer Translation Mappings area near the bottom of the dialog box. Each layer that has a translation is removed from the Translate From list to let you know which ones haven't been mapped yet.

11. **Click Settings.**

    The Settings dialog box (see Figure 2-10) is displayed. The default settings are the best to help maintain good quality CAD standards. The last option in the Settings dialog box is nice so you can see what is on what layer in real-time when a layer or layers are selected from the Translate From list. Only the selected layers are displayed in the drawing.

Figure 2-10:
Taking full control of the translation.

12. **In the Settings dialog box, select the desired options and click OK.**

    The changes to the settings are saved and the Settings dialog box is closed.

13. **In the Layer Translator dialog box, click Save.**

    The Save Layer Mappings dialog box is displayed allowing you to save the layer translations that you have created for re-use.

    In the Save Layer Mappings dialog box, browse to the location that you want to export the layer translations to and specify a name for the file. Use the Files of Type drop-down list to create either a drawing or drawing standards file.

14. **Click Save.**

    The file is created in the specified location with the provided name.

Book VIII
Chapter 2

CAD Standards

15. **In the Layer Translator dialog box, click Translate.**

The Layer Translator dialog box closes and the layers are updated based on the specified layer translations.

Batch checking drawings

Both standards tools discussed up to this point must be set up and run drawing by drawing. This isn't a very efficient process if you have hundreds of drawings for a single project. Wouldn't it be nice if a utility could check a large number of drawings at once so you don't have to go through each drawing one by one?

You're in luck! An external utility called the Batch Standards Checker allows you to take a number of drawings and check them for standards violations. The Batch Standards Checker is very similar to the Configure Standards dialog box in how some of the tabs work. One of the downsides to the Batch Standards Checker is that it can't fix any problems it finds; it is only designed to check for violations, but it is still much faster than checking each file individually.

The following procedure uses the Batch Standards Checker to check drawing files for any standards violations:

1. **Click the Start button⇨[All] Programs⇨Autodesk⇨AutoCAD 2007⇨ Batch Standards Checker.**

The Batch Standards Checker (see Figure 2-11) application is displayed.

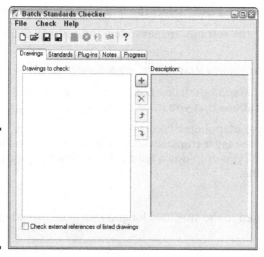

Figure 2-11:
Checking
standards
for more
than one
drawing at a
time.

2. **In the Batch Standards Checker, click the Drawings tab.**

   The Drawings tab allows you to specify which drawing and drawing template files that you want to check for standards violations in.

3. **Click the + (plus sign) button to add drawing or drawing template files to the list for processing.**

   The Batch Standards Checker – File Open dialog box is displayed and allows you to select multiple drawing and drawing template files.

4. **In the Batch Standards Checker – File Open dialog box, browse and select the files that you want to check for standards violations.**

   The name of each selected file is added to the File Name text field.

5. **Click Open.**

   The selected files are added to the Drawings to Check list. You can view some of the properties of the files in the Description area on the right side of the dialog box. You can change the order in which files are processed or remove then from the list altogether using the buttons in the middle of the dialog box.

6. **Optionally, click Check External References of Listed Drawings.**

   When the check box has a check mark, each drawing is checked for external references. If a drawing contains external references, those files are also checked to make sure they don't contain any standards violations.

7. **Click the Standards tab.**

   The Standards tab (see Figure 2-12) allows you to specify which drawing standards files should be used to check for standards violations.

8. **Select one of the top two options to control which drawing standards files are used to check the selected drawing files.**

9. **The top option, Check Each Drawing Using Its Associated Standards Files, is useful if each drawing on the Drawings tab has at least one associated drawing standards file. If not, use the Check All Drawings Using the Following Standards Files option.**

10. **If Check All Drawings Using the Following Standards Files is selected, click the + (plus sign) button to add drawing standards files to the list for processing.**

    The Batch Standards Checker – File Open dialog box is displayed and allows you to select multiple drawing standards files.

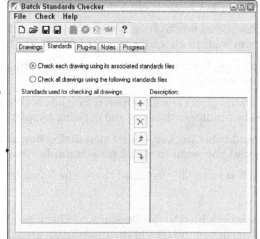

Figure 2-12: The Standards tab should look similar to the Configure Standards dialog box.

11. **In the Batch Standards Checker – File Open dialog box, browse and select the drawing standards files you want to use.**

The name of each selected file is added to the File Name text field.

12. **Click Open.**

The selected files are added to the Standards Used for Checking All Drawings list. You can view some of the properties of the files in the Description area on the right side of the dialog box. You can change the order in which files are processed or remove them from the list altogether using the buttons in the middle of the dialog box.

13. **Click the Plug-Ins tab.**

The Plug-Ins tab (see Figure 2-13) allows you to specify which plug-ins are used when checking the specified drawings against the selected drawings standards files.

14. **Check or uncheck the plug-ins that you want to use for checking standards against the specified drawing files.**

The same plug-ins are available here that are available in the Configure Standards dialog box of the STANDARDS command.

15. **Click the Notes tab.**

The Notes tab allows you to provide a description for the standards check file, just in case the file is needed at a later date to reprocess the same drawing files after they have been revised.

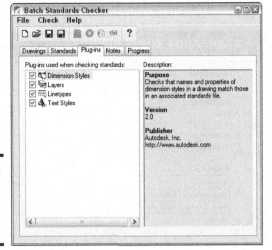

Figure 2-13:
Controlling
which plug-
ins are
used.

16. **Enter any type of textual note that you want to in the Enter Notes to Be Included in the Report text box.**

17. **From the File menu, choose Save Check File.**

The Batch Standards Checker – File Save dialog box is displayed.

18. **In the Batch Standards Checker – File Save dialog box, browse to a location and enter a name for the Standards Check (CHX) file.**

19. **Click Save.**

The Standards Check file is created in the specified location with the provided name. The Standards Check file contains information about which drawings are to be processed, the drawing standards files to use, and the other options you have specified up to this point.

20. **From the Check menu, choose Start Check.**

The Progress tab is displayed and shows the current progress of the files being checked.

21. **When the process is finished, the Standards Audit Report is displayed.**

The Standards Audit Report (see Figure 2-14) is displayed in your Internet browser. You can view the different results by clicking the controls located on the left side of the report. The information is stored in the Standards Check file that you saved earlier and can be viewed later by opening the file and choosing View Report from the Check menu.

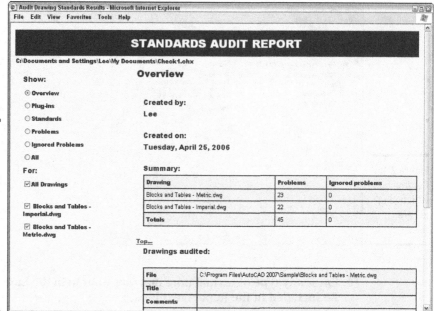

Figure 2-14:
The Standards Audit Report reveals all problems with your standards (well, okay, maybe not *all* problems).

Chapter 3: Working with Drawing Files

In This Chapter

✔ File naming standards

✔ Partially loading a drawing

✔ Controlling what happens during a save

✔ Digitally signing and password-protecting drawings

As you might have noticed, drawing files are the main by-product of using AutoCAD. They are much more important than the paper copy that is generated when the Plot button is clicked. Paper copies of drawings are designed for presenting a concept or design, but they can't be modified like the drawing file can. For this reason, you need to take care of your drawing files by storing them in safe locations. You also must ensure that they are properly backed up and must use a logical naming convention so you can later easily find the files.

Many users of AutoCAD don't fully realize the amount of control they have over their drawing files. This chapter explains some of the different concepts that you might not know about working with drawing files. The concepts we cover range from password-protecting or using digital signatures to protect your drawing files when you share them, to controlling how objects and layers are indexed to make loading a drawing as an external reference more efficient.

It's All in the Name: Creating Naming Conventions

Following proper naming conventions is critical to being able to easily find any document, whether it was created with MS Word or AutoCAD. A series of drawing files named Drawing1, Drawing2, and so on won't be very helpful to you in the future. Instead, you should come up with a meaningful naming convention that tells you at a glance what project a drawing file pertains to. The key to creating a good naming convention is to make sure it is easy to remember and understand. If it is overly complicated, many users tend to do their own thing, making it harder to find files later.

If you are in the architectural field, you might want to include such things as project number, building number, drawing type, and drawing size in your filename conventions. An example of such a filename might be A12345-01-P-D.DWG. This type of convention ensures that files related to the same part of the building and project are grouped together. Of course, good file organization helps to make your projects run more efficiently and effectively, too. Store drawing files in a centralized location so that all drafters who need access to them can get to them. In addition, if you have processes in place to regularly back up all network files, storing them on a network ensures that your drawing files are frequently backed up.

Autodesk first introduced a feature called Sheet Sets with AutoCAD 2005. Many people turned off the feature because they didn't fully understand the concept. Sheet Sets are great for helping you organize drawings not just by file, but also by directory structure. (Sheet Sets are covered more fully in Book VII, Chapter 2.) Sheet Sets not only provide a way to organize drawings, but they also provide some structure for naming drawings.

AutoCAD 2006 and later versions add support to the Windows search feature for finding text strings located in a drawing file. This can help you find drawing files that might not have been placed in the correct project folder.

Part of a Drawing Can Be a Good Thing: Working with Partial Open

Part of a drawing as a good thing? You may be thinking that we have slipped off the deep end. You could be right, but hear us out before you jump to any conclusions. We're referring to a feature called Partial Open, which has been part of the product for the past few releases. This feature allows you to open part of a drawing file into AutoCAD based on a view and selected layers.

AutoCAD LT does not support the Partial Open feature.

Partially opening a drawing file can be a great timesaver when you want to work on a floor plan that contains a lot of annotation, hatches, and dimensions. Instead of waiting for that geometry to load at the beginning of the editing process, you can choose not to load that information until you need to see it. If you happen to need any information in part of the drawing that has not been loaded, you can specify the area of the drawing that you want those objects to be displayed in. The key to being able to take full advantage of this feature is a good set of layer standards and the use of named views. Figure 3-1 shows the same drawing file two different ways: The drawing on the left was opened using Open, and the one on the right was opened using Partial Open.

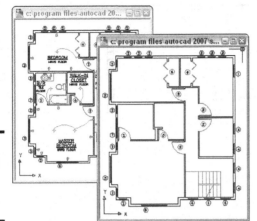

Figure 3-1:
Using Open
versus
Partial
Open.

A drawing file can be partially opened by using the OPEN or PARTIALOPEN command. You can start these commands in one of two ways:

+ **Keyboard input.** Type **PARTIALOPEN** and press Enter.

+ **Select File dialog box.** Start the OPEN command, click the drop-down arrow next to the right of the Open button, and click Partial Open or Partial Open Read-Only.

The following procedure explains how to use the Partial Open feature to load geometry based on a selected view and layers, and how to control the loading of xrefs when a drawing is being partially opened:

1. **Use either of the two methods just listed to partially load a drawing file.**

Based on the method used, you are prompted to enter the name of the drawing you want to partially open at the command line, the dynamic input tooltip, or in a dialog box. After entering the name of the drawing, the Partial Open dialog box (see Figure 3-2) is displayed. If you selected the Partial Open Read-Only option, the same dialog box is displayed. The only difference is that you won't be able to edit the drawing and save it back to the file.

2. **In the Partial Open dialog box, select a named view under the View Geometry to Load heading.**

By default, two named views are available in every drawing file. These are *Extents*, which represents the drawing's extents (the largest area required to display all objects in a drawing), and *Last*, which represents the view the drawing was saved with.

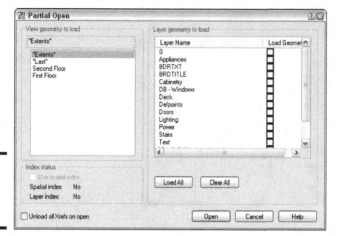

Figure 3-2:
What to
partially
open . . .

3. **Select the Use Spatial Index check box under the Index Status area if it's available.**

   Spatial indexing allows for information to be located in a drawing much faster, although it does increase the file size. See "Indexing the content of a drawing" later in this chapter for more information. This option is only available if either spatial or layer indexing was enabled when the file was last saved.

4. **In the Layer Geometry to Load area, select the layers that contain the geometry you want to display.**

   You don't need to specify any layers, but if you don't specify at least one, AutoCAD prompts you with a message box (see Figure 3-3). Click No to select some layers before continuing.

Figure 3-3:
AutoCAD's
friendly
reminder
that you
forgot to do
something.

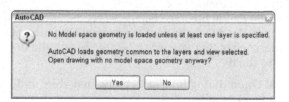

5. **If the file you are loading contains Xrefs, you can select the Unload All Xrefs on Open check box in the lower-left corner.**

Selecting this check box unloads all the Xrefs attached to the drawing. They are not displayed until they are reloaded through the External References palette. This is a great feature if you want to quickly load a drawing that contains a lot of Xrefs and then view only the ones that you are interested in.

6. **Click Open to finish the partial open process.**

   The drawing is partially opened in the drawing editor. You can tell when you are working in a partially opened drawing in two ways: The first is that the Partial Load option is available under the Files menu, and the second is that the text *(Partially Loaded)* appears after the drawing name in the title bar (see Figure 3-4).

Figure 3-4:
The signs of a partially opened drawing file.

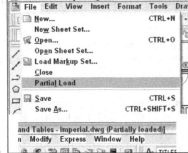

7. **If you need to load additional layers, you can use the Partial Load option from the Files menu. This displays the Partial Load dialog box (see Figure 3-5), which is very similar to the Partial Open dialog box.**

Figure 3-5:
Loading more layers in a partially opened drawing file.

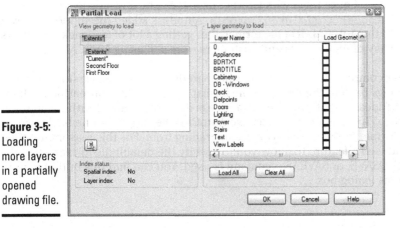

Controlling What Happens during a Save

AutoCAD is a very powerful application that contains many different features designed for specialized uses. Some of these features are not always easy to find or understand because they are not in the standard workflow. These items include being able to control the default version in which files are saved, password protection, digital signatures, and utilizing indexing for your drawings.

Getting a handle on drawing file formats

What is a drawing file format and why is it important? A *drawing format* is the structure of how AutoCAD stores information in a drawing file. A format change occurs when major changes are made to the application to support new object types and features. AutoCAD has been on a regular schedule of making a format change about every three releases. By giving you a number of older drawing file formats to save to, AutoCAD makes it easier for you to share your drawing files with customers who might be on an older release than you are. We covered the different drawing file formats and which releases they belong to earlier in Book I, Chapter I.

If you need to exchange drawings with users who still use AutoCAD R12 or R13, you can save your drawings to an R12 .DXF file format. By saving to the R12 .DXF file format, some object types are converted to much simpler types of objects. Multiline text, for example, is converted to a block that contains single line text, and dimensions will no longer be associative.

You are now, once again, able to save back to the AutoCAD R14 file format. This file format was removed a couple releases back and was only supported through an external utility called the Autodesk DWG TrueConvert (formally known as Autodesk Batch Drawing Converter). DWG TrueConvert is available for download if you need to save more than one file to a different format so you can exchange them with another user. It can be downloaded from the URL www.autodesk.com/migrationtools. Autodesk added the support of saving back to the AutoCAD R14 file format after getting a lot of feedback from users that many of their clients and customers were still using AutoCAD R14.

If your company is in the process of upgrading to a newer version, saving drawings back to the previous file format during the rollout period is often a good idea so that everyone can access drawings created with the newer release. This is important because AutoCAD files might not be backward compatible to the release you are upgrading from. For this reason, Autodesk introduced a feature to allow you to specify the default file format when the SAVE, QSAVE, or SAVEAS command is used. You can find this option in the Options dialog box.

The following procedure explains how to set the default file format for saving:

1. **Choose Tools⇨Options.**

The Options dialog box is displayed.

2. **In the Options dialog box, click the Open and Save tab along the top of the dialog box.**

The Open and Save tab is used to specify options that are related to saving and opening files.

3. **On the Open and Save tab, click the drop-down arrow for the Save as Open under the File Save area and make a selection.**

The drop-down list contains the different .DWG, .DWT, and .DXF file formats that you can specify as the default file format for saves.

4. **Click Apply or OK.**

Clicking Apply saves the changes and keeps the dialog box displayed, whereas clicking OK saves the changes and closes the Options dialog box.

In the Options dialog box under the Open and Save tab, you specify the default save format that will be used when saving a drawing file. This is great when you need to work on projects that must be saved to a specific drawing file format, and eliminates one additional step when saving the drawing.

Indexing the content of a drawing

Indexing a drawing is not quite the same as filing someone's name in a Rolodex or indexing a book, but the end results are the same. We index things to make them easier and faster to find later. AutoCAD offers two different types of indexing: layer indexing and spatial indexing.

AutoCAD LT does not support file saving with either layer or spatial indexing.

Both of these types of indexing improve the performance when the drawing is demand loaded. Demand loading is a process used with loading external references (Xrefs) and when partially opening a drawing. When demand loading is used, AutoCAD only loads the data from the drawing that is required to properly display the drawing file — objects are loaded as they are required from the drawing to improve overall performance of loading and displaying the drawing file. Layer indexing improves the loading of objects on layers that are on and thawed. Objects on a layer that is frozen or off are not read in with the drawing file. Those layers are read in only when specifically requested.

Spatial indexing is used to organize objects in 3D space and improves the loading performance of a referenced file that has been clipped. Clipping a referenced file allows you to define which part of a referenced file is

**Book VIII
Chapter 3**

**Working with
Drawing Files**

displayed in the drawing by defining the area to be displayed using a rectangular or polygonal boundary. (Clipping referenced files is covered more in Book VI, Chapter 3.) Both layer and spatial indexing are only helpful if the file is being used as an Xref or is being partially opened. Otherwise, it offers no benefit. If indexing is enabled, saving the drawing file takes slightly longer. Indexing is available in four different options:

✦ **None:** Indexing is disabled.

✦ **Layer:** Only layer indexing is enabled.

✦ **Spatial:** Only spatial indexing is enabled.

✦ **Layer & Spatial:** Layer and spatial indexing are enabled.

The following procedure explains how to set the indexing type when saving a drawing file:

1. **Choose File⇨Save As.**

The Save Drawing As dialog box is displayed.

2. **In the Save Drawing As dialog box, choose Tools⇨Options.**

The Saveas Options dialog box (see Figure 3-6) is displayed. It contains some different options for both .DWG and .DXF file formats.

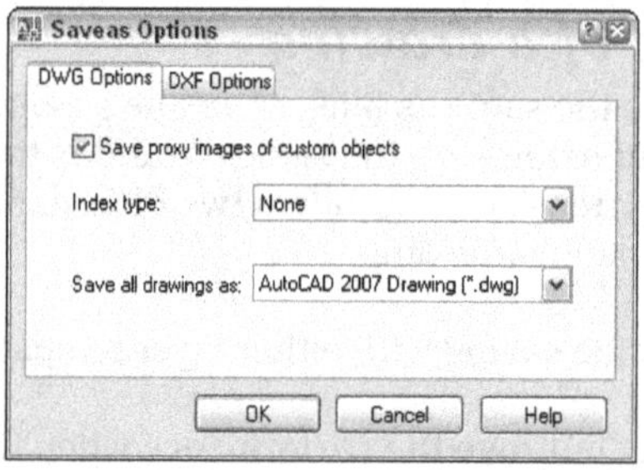

Figure 3-6:
Drawing file
options.

3. **In the Saveas Options dialog box, click the drop-down arrow for Index Type.**

The drop-down list displays the various indexing options you can save your drawing with.

4. **Select an option from the drop-down list.**

5. **Click OK.**

The Saveas Options dialog box closes and you are returned to the Save Drawing As dialog box.

6. **Specify the filename and location for the drawing you are saving and click Save.**

The Save Drawing As dialog box closes and the drawing is saved with the indexing type specified.

Protecting Your Drawings

You work hard to create the perfect design, so you have every right to make sure that it is kept safe. AutoCAD offers two different options to make sure your design doesn't get altered without your permission: password protection and digital signatures. Password protection locks the file down and doesn't allow anyone to view it without first entering the password. Digital signatures aren't as secure as password-protected files, but they do offer a level of protection by indicating whether the file was altered after it was signed. This can be critical when you need to have a client sign off on a design.

AutoCAD LT does not support the ability to password-protect your drawing files.

Password-protecting

Password-protecting a drawing file in AutoCAD is very similar to password-protecting a file in any other application: You provide a password or phrase and specify the type of encryption you want to use. Although password protection offers benefits, it also has a downside.

If you use password protection, you must record the password in a safe place so that you don't forget it; otherwise, you won't be able to open the file. No amount of magic can unlock the file after the password has been lost, so you might want to make a backup copy of the drawing file without the password before you save it with one.

We also recommend that you talk to your CAD manager or a senior-level drafter before you start using password protection on drawing files. After all, the drawing file does belong to the company.

Assigning a password to a drawing file

The following procedure explains how to password-protect a drawing file.

1. **Choose File➪Save As.**

The Save Drawing As dialog box is displayed.

Removing the security option for password-protecting a drawing file

Some companies worry that employees might abuse the capability to password-protect drawing files. This is one reason why Autodesk allows your CAD manager or IS department to remove the feature during installation. The option can be disabled when Custom is selected on the Select Installation Type screen during the installation process. If Typical was selected during installation, you can remove the password-protect feature through the Add and Remove Programs option in the Windows Control Panel. The following figure shows the Drawing Encryption option that controls whether the password protection feature is available. Disabling this feature only prevents people from password-protecting a drawing file and has no impact on their ability to receive and open one from someone else.

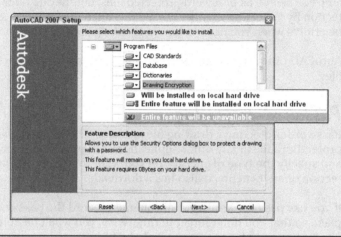

2. **In the Save Drawing As dialog box, choose Tools⇨Security Options.**

   The Security Options dialog box, which contains different options for working with passwords and digital signatures (see Figure 3-7), is displayed.

3. **In the Security Options dialog box, enter the password or phrase in the Password or Phrase to Open This Drawing text field.**

   The value that you enter is masked in the text field as it is entered.

4. **Optionally, click Encrypt Drawing Properties.**

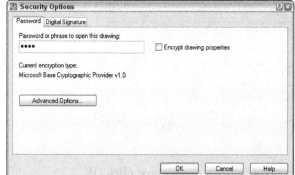

Figure 3-7:
Securing
the contents
of a drawing
with a
password.

Drawing properties are the kind of information you can view through
Windows Explorer, such as author, title, and custom properties. Figure
3-8 shows what the Properties dialog box looks like in Windows Explorer
when it is not encrypted through the use of password protection (on the
left) and when it is encrypted (on the right). The left image shows that
three additional tabs (Statistics, Custom, and Summary) are displayed
when the drawing file is not password-protected.

Figure 3-8:
Encrypting
properties
helps to
hide some
content.

5. **Optionally, click Advanced Options.**

The Advanced Options dialog box (see Figure 3-9) is displayed. Select an
encryption provider that you want to use and the key length. The key
length is used to determine the overall length of the encryption key. The
higher the value used, the greater the level of security your drawing will
have. Based on your operating system and what country you are in, your
encryption options may vary. We recommended using the greatest key
length possible for the encryption provider you select — in most cases,
the value is 128. After all, you want to be sure your data is protected.
When you are finished, click OK to accept the changes.

Figure 3-9:
Choosing an
encryption
type.

6. In the Security Options dialog box, click OK.

The Confirm Password dialog box (see Figure 3-10) is displayed. It warns you of the dangers of forgetting or losing your password, which we mentioned earlier in this chapter.

Figure 3-10:
Confirming
your
password
is a good
thing.

7. In the Confirm Password dialog box, reenter the password in the Reenter Password to Open This Drawing text field and click OK.

If the passwords match, both the Confirm Password and Security Options dialog boxes close, and you are returned to the Save Drawing As dialog box.

8. Finish specifying the filename and location for the drawing you are saving and click Save.

The Save Drawing As dialog box closes and the drawing is saved with the specified password.

Removing the password or the phrase from the Security Options dialog box removes password protection from the drawing file altogether.

Working with a password-protected drawing

Password protection goes beyond just needing to enter a password to open a drawing file. Password protection affects any operation that brings the contents of the drawing file into another drawing; this includes, but is not limited to, opening, referencing, or inserting the drawing file into another drawing.

The following procedure explains how to open a drawing that has been saved with a password.

1. **Choose File⇨Open.**

The Select File dialog box is displayed.

2. **In the Select File dialog box, browse and select the file you want to open.**

The selected file should be highlighted in the dialog box and its name displayed in the File Name text field.

3. **Click Open.**

The Select File dialog box closes and the Password dialog box is displayed (see Figure 3-11).

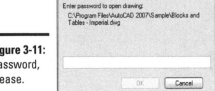

Figure 3-11:
Password, please.

4. **In the Password dialog box, enter the password and click OK.**

If you entered the correct password, the drawing file should finish loading. If not, an error message is displayed asking you to retry or cancel the operation. The password is cached in memory; so if you close the drawing and reopen it without restarting AutoCAD, you won't need to re-enter the password.

Digital signatures

Unlike password protection, digital signatures don't keep anyone from viewing the contents of a file. Instead, they notify the person viewing the file whether a change has been made after it was signed. Digital signatures require a little more work to use them the first time because you must first obtain a digital ID.

You have to obtain a digital ID from a company such as VeriSign (http://www.verisign.com) or IdenTrust (http://www.digsigtrust.com). After you obtain a digital ID, you can start signing drawing files. Digital IDs can be used with other applications besides AutoCAD; some programs such as Outlook also support digital IDs for signing e-mails. Some companies offer trial periods for testing the use of a digital ID and then require a small annual fee to keep the digital ID valid beyond the trial period.

Obtaining a digital signature from VeriSign

Autodesk has wired AutoCAD to take you to VeriSign's Web site to obtain a digital signature for signing drawing files, so we thought that we would follow Autodesk's recommendation. The following procedure is an overview of how to obtain a digital signature from VeriSign, but feel free to use a different vendor if you want to. The steps will vary from vendor to vendor. If you don't have a digital ID yet, the Valid Digital ID Not Available dialog box is displayed (see Figure 3-12).

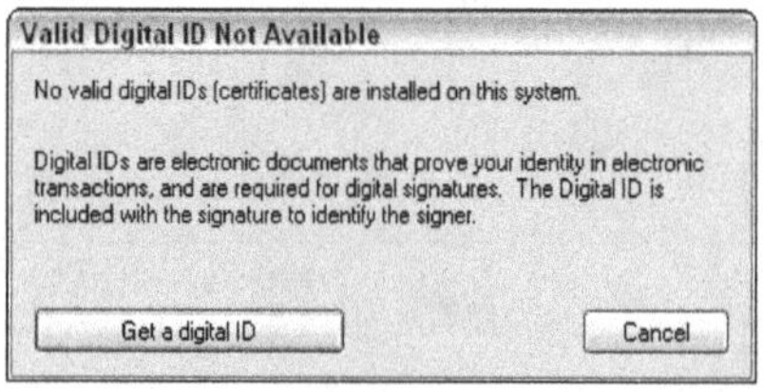

Figure 3-12: No digital ID found on the computer.

Follow these steps to obtain a digital ID from VeriSign:

1. **Choose File⇨Save As.**

The Save Drawing As dialog box is displayed.

2. **In the Save Drawing As dialog box, choose Tools⇨Security Options.**

The Security Options dialog box is displayed and contains different options for working with passwords and digital signatures.

3. **In the Security Options dialog box, click the Digital Signature tab.**

The Valid Digital ID Not Available dialog box is displayed.

4. **In the Valid Digital ID Not Available dialog box, click Get a Digital ID.**

The Products & Services page of VeriSign's Web site is displayed (see Figure 3-13). The Products & Services page can be confusing — none of the options seem to call out and say "Pick me if you are using AutoCAD!"

Figure 3-13:
Oh, so many products and services to choose from.

5. On the Products & Services page, click the Manages PKI Services link under the Security Services section.

The Managed PKI Services page is displayed with even more options.

6. On the Managed PKI Services page, click the PKI Applications link under the Managed PKI Services Include section (which we are sure you knew without our telling you).

The PKI Applications page is displayed with more options.

7. On the PKI Applications page, click the Digital IDs for Secure Email link (Confused yet? You're not the only one!).

The Digital IDs for Secure Email page is displayed.

8. On the Digital IDs for Secure Email page, click Buy Now (don't worry, you get the chance to try before you buy).

The Digital IDs for Secure Email – Digital ID Enrollment page is displayed.

9. On the Digital ID Enrollment page, click Buy Now again (this time it lets you know that you have an option for a 60-day trial).

The Choose Your Browser page is displayed.

10. On the Choose Your Browser page, click Microsoft or Netscape.

The Enrollment page is displayed.

Book VIII Chapter 3

Working with Drawing Files

11. **On the Enrollment page, enter all the required information and click Accept.**

After you submit the information, you'll receive an e-mail explaining how to obtain the new digital signature. Follow the information in the e-mail to finish the process.

Digitally signing a drawing file

The following procedure explains how to digitally sign a drawing file. It assumes that you have already obtained a digital signature from a vendor of your choice or from VeriSign, as explained in the preceding steps.

1. **Choose File⇨Save As.**

The Save Drawing As dialog box is displayed.

2. **In the Save Drawing As dialog box, choose Tools⇨Security Options.**

The Security Options dialog box is displayed and contains different options for working with passwords and digital signatures.

3. **In the Security Options dialog box, click the Digital Signature tab.**

The Digital Signature tab (see Figure 3-14) displays the different digital signatures found on the computer and some options.

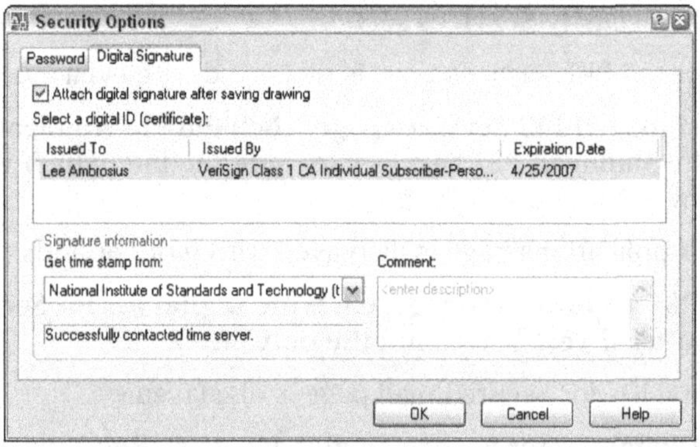

Figure 3-14: No ink is required for using digital signatures.

4. **On the Digital Signature tab, select the Attach Digital Signature After Saving Drawing check box.**

After you select this option, other controls on the tab become enabled.

5. **Select a digital ID from the Select a Digital ID (Certificate) area.**

The first digital ID in the list is selected by default; if you have more than one digital ID, you need to specify which one you want to use.

6. Optionally, you can specify a time stamp from the Get Time Stamp From drop-down list box, which we recommend doing.

The time stamp helps to validate the digital signature.

7. Optionally, you can add comments for the individual who will be opening or viewing the file later.

For example, you might want to add a comment about whether the file has been approved for manufacturing.

8. Click OK.

The Security Options dialog box closes and you are returned to the Save Drawing As dialog box.

9. Finish specifying the filename and location for the drawing you are saving and click Save.

The Save Drawing As dialog box closes and the drawing is saved with a digital signature. You know that the drawing has been signed when the Validate Digital Signatures icon (see Figure 3-15) appears in the status bar.

Figure 3-15:
Success!
The drawing
has been
digitally
signed.

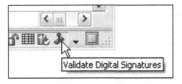

Validate Digital Signatures

Opening a digitally signed drawing file

Digitally signed drawings serve a different purpose than a drawing you might be creating or editing. This is why they are displayed in a slightly different way in Windows Explorer. The icon for a digitally signed drawing file includes two red and yellow marks (okay, we know you can only see them in black and white in this book) in the upper-right corner (see Figure 3-16).

The following procedure explains how to open a drawing that has been saved with a digital signature:

1. Choose File⇨Open.

The Select File dialog box is displayed.

2. In the Select File dialog box, browse and select the file you want to open.

**Book VIII
Chapter 3**

**Working with
Drawing Files**

Figure 3-16:
The top icon
is displayed
for a
drawing file;
the bottom
icon is
displayed
for a
digitally
signed
drawing file.

The selected file should be highlighted in the dialog box and its name displayed in the File Name text field.

3. **Click Open.**

The Select File dialog box closes and the Digital Signature Contents dialog box is displayed (see Figure 3-17).

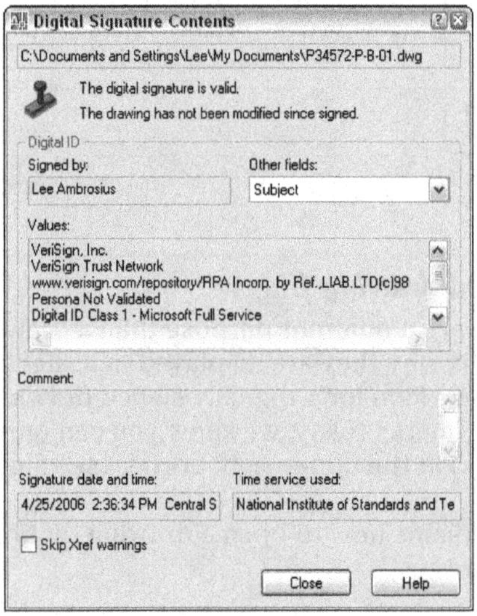

Figure 3-17:
Digital
signature
information.

4. **In the Digital Signature Contents dialog box, review the information to make sure everything is correct; then click Close.**

The Digital Signature Contents dialog box closes and the Validate Digital Signatures icon is displayed in the status bar. If the digital signature is invalid, you see a warning notification at the top of the Digital Signature Contents dialog box (see Figure 3-18).

Figure 3-18:
When digital signatures go bad.

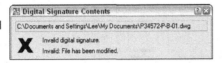

You can control the display of the Digital Signature Contents dialog box with the system variable SIGWARN. Enter SIGWARN at the command prompt to change its current value. A value of 0 suppresses the display of the dialog box unless the digital signature is invalid. A value of 1 displays the dialog box. (This is the default behavior.)

Digitally signing a batch of drawings

If you have a large set of drawing files that need to be digitally signed all at once, Autodesk offers an external utility to do so. This utility is properly named Attach Digital Signatures. It's pretty basic and easy to understand. The following procedure explains how to access and digitally sign multiple drawing files at one time:

1. **Click Start⇨[All] Programs⇨Autodesk⇨AutoCAD 2007⇨Attach Digital Signatures.**

The Attach Digital Signatures dialog box (see Figure 3-19) is displayed.

2. **In the Attach Digital Signatures dialog box, click Add Files.**

The Select File dialog box is displayed.

3. **In the Select File dialog box, browse and select the drawing files that you want to digitally sign.**

The selected files are highlighted and each name is displayed in the File Name text field.

4. **Click Open.**

The Select File dialog box closes and you are returned to the Attach Digital Signatures dialog box. The names of the selected files are added to the list box.

5. **Specify the digital ID, time stamp, and comments as desired.**

Book VIII
Chapter 3

Working with Drawing Files

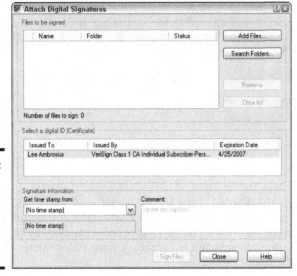

Figure 3-19:
Attaching
digital
signatures
to multiple
drawing
files.

6. Click Sign Files.

The process of signing the files begins. When it is completed, you are
given a summary of the number of files that were signed.

7. On the Signing Complete message box, click OK.

This closes the message box that tells you the number of files signed.

8. In the Attach Digital Signatures dialog box, click Close.

The Attach Digital Signatures dialog box closes.

Chapter 4: Sharing Electronic Files

In This Chapter

✔ **Sharing drawings with non-AutoCAD–based products**

✔ **Taking drawings to the Internet**

✔ **Emulating paper digitally**

✔ **Working with the Design Web Format (DWF)**

Drawing files are one of the by-products of using AutoCAD. The electronic version of a drawing is much more important than the paper copy that is produced when you use the PLOT and PUBLISH commands. To deliver a set of drawings efficiently to a client or someone else, the drawings must remain as digital data. This doesn't mean that a hard copy of the drawing file isn't important; it is just slower to deliver and changes can't be communicated in an ideal way.

This chapter focuses on delivering a representation of a drawing file in a digital format that can't be modified; well, the original drawing isn't affected. Sharing drawing files can be challenging; others want your drawing files, but they may not be able to view or use them with their software application of choice. AutoCAD offers a few solutions to help share drawing files with people who don't own a CAD program or people who do own a CAD program but use something other than AutoCAD.

AutoCAD also offers a variety of options for accessing FTP sites, project management sites developed by Autodesk to work with their products such as Buzzsaw and Streamline, and publishing drawing files to Web sites.

Sharing Drawings with Non-AutoCAD–based Products

When you work with CAD, you often need to share your drawing files with others. However, not everyone's CAD application is the same. For this reason, CAD applications must be able to communicate in other file formats. AutoCAD provides various different output file formats so that it can more easily exchange drawing files with other programs. You may be familiar with some of these file formats, and others you may not be.

You can use three commands to export to a different file type: SAVEAS, EXPORT, and PLOT. Other commands are available, such as BMPOUT, PNGOUT, JPGOUT, and TIFOUT, that you can use to export objects in a drawing to a raster image file. Here are the listed file formats that can be exported out of AutoCAD.

✦ **DXF.** Drawing Interchange Format

✦ **WMF.** Microsoft Windows Metafile

✦ **ACIS.** ACIS solid object file

✦ **STL.** Solid object stereolithography file

✦ **EPS.** Encapsulated Postscript file

✦ **DXX.** Attribute extract DXF file

✦ **BMP.** Windows Bitmap file

✦ **JPG.** JPEG graphic file

✦ **PNG.** Portable Network Graphics file

✦ **TIF.** Tag Image File Format

✦ **3D DWF.** 3D Autodesk Design Web Format

✦ **DWF.** Design Web Format

✦ **PDF.** Adobe Acrobat Portable Document File

✦ **PLT.** AutoCAD Plot file

AutoCAD LT does not support the file formats of ACIS, STL, EPS, DXX, or 3D DWF.

Taking Drawings to the Internet

AutoCAD can and does play a role in being able to connect to the Internet to access drawings that have been posted for you to reference, or to be able to push content to a Web site. All of AutoCAD's primary file access commands are capable of utilizing FTP — *File Transfer Protocol*. This allows you to access and place files on a remote server that could be just around the block or halfway around the world. For the most part, the location of the FTP site is transparent to you because it is integrated into AutoCAD.

Autodesk offers two project collaboration sites that users of their products can sign up to use for a fee. The project collaboration sites are similar to FTP sites and how they are integrated into AutoCAD and other Autodesk products, but they offer much more than just a place to park drawing files. These sites allow for history tracking when files change, embedded file viewers, permissions-based access, and a built-in notification system, to just name a few bullet points of these services.

Project collaboration sites are great, but sometimes they are overly based on the type of information you need to share across the Internet. Autodesk does offer publishing tools that can take a set of drawing files and publish them to Web-friendly formats, such as DWF, JPG, and PNG. This feature is rather basic in its abilities, but if you are not familiar with Web page design, they are great for putting together a nice little interface for your clients to access drawings and information from.

Using an FTP site

Working with an FTP site from inside AutoCAD is similar to accessing an FTP site through Internet Explorer. Both require the location, a user name, and password. The only difference is that you can open and save to the FTP site right from AutoCAD instead of downloading the files first and then later re-uploading them.

Virtually every file navigation dialog box inside AutoCAD can access an FTP site. One of the nice things is that it allows you to configure the FTP site as a reusable location. So if you happen to be working on a project over a period of time, you won't have to worry about forgetting the address, user name, or password but rather just need to set it up once and it is there until you remove it.

The following procedure uses the File menu to start the OPEN command and configure and use an FTP location from inside AutoCAD.

1. **From the File menu, choose Open.**

The Select File dialog box appears.

2. **In the Select File dialog box, choose Tools⇨Add/Modify FTP Locations.**

The Add/Modify FTP Locations dialog box appears (see Figure 4-1).

3. **In the Add/Modify FTP Location dialog box, enter the location in the Name of FTP site.**

Even though the text field is called Name of FTP site, it is actually the URL for the FTP location. A sample URL is `ftp.`*`websitename`*`.com/drawings`.

4. **Select the logon type under the Log On As area of either Anonymous or User.**

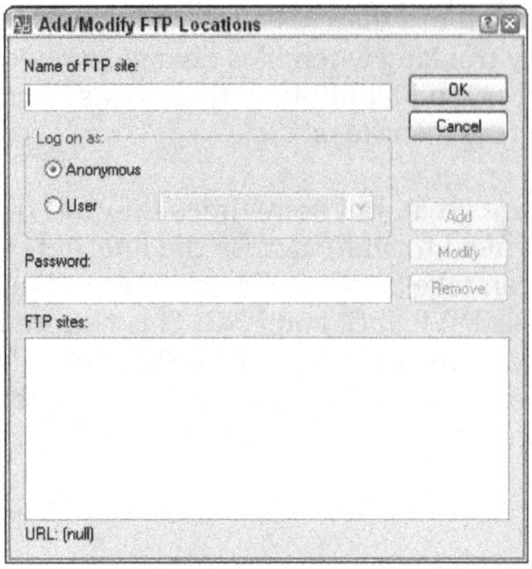

Figure 4-1:
Establishing
an FTP
location.

If you specify User, you must enter the user name that has been set up for you to access the FTP site. If no user name and password are required, you can use Anonymous.

5. Enter the password that is associated with the user name if one exists in the Password text field.

As the password is entered, it is automatically masked so that the actual values of the keys pressed do not appear on-screen.

6. Click Add.

An entry for the FTP location is added to the list box at the bottom of the dialog box. You can later select the FTP location from the list box and click Modify or Remove to make changes to it.

7. Click OK.

The Add/Modify FTP Location dialog box closes and you are returned to the Select File dialog box.

8. In the Select File dialog box, click FTP in the shortcuts pane on the left side.

The Select File dialog box updates and displays an FTP Locations item which contains the FTP locations that have been defined.

9. Finish specifying the file name and location for the drawing you are looking to open, and click Open.

The Select File dialog box closes and the drawing is opened in the drawing editor. Don't forget that you can access the FTP location from most file navigation dialog boxes from inside AutoCAD.

Publishing drawings to the Web

One of the great things about AutoCAD is its robust set of features that doesn't just focus on drafting-based features but contains tools for presenting design concepts across the Internet. One of these presentation tools helps to deliver drawing files to the Web through a wizard. This wizard allows you to specify some basic Web template designs, the visual output for the drawing files specified, and different layouts in drawing files. Autodesk calls this feature Publish to Web.

AutoCAD LT does not support the feature Publish to Web.

The Publish to Web feature is not meant to be a one-size-fits-all type of feature; it is designed for people not familiar with HTML and Web page design. If you are familiar with HTML and creating Web pages, you may find that the implementation is limiting, but if you don't know how to create Web pages, you may find it purely magical. The feature does offer some nice capabilities for dragging and dropping from the images on the Web pages with i-drop to being able to quickly modify an existing set of drawings that might have been changed by editing the Publish to Web file that it creates. See the sidebar, "Autodesk i-drop," for information on i-drop.

Drawing files can be published to Web pages by using the PUBLISHTOWEB command. You can start this command in a number of ways:

✦ **File menu.** Choose File⇨Publish to Web.

✦ **Keyboard input.** Type **PUBLISHTOWEB** and press Enter.

✦ **Command alias.** Type **PTW** and press Enter.

Use any of the three methods to initiate the PUBLISHTOWEB command. The following procedure uses the File menu to start the PUBLISHTOWEB command and creates a simple Publish to Web project.

1. **The Publish to Web feature can't be used on drawings that are not first saved, so save the current drawing before continuing on.**

2. **Use one of the previously described methods to initiate the PUBLISHTOWEB command.**

   The Publish to Web dialog box appears (see Figure 4-2).

3. **In the Publish to Web dialog box, select Create New Web Page and click Next.**

   The option is pretty self explanatory. If you select Edit Existing Web Page, you are prompted to select an existing file with the extension PTW that was created previously with the Publish to Web feature. After you specify the file, you can edit the page title and description.

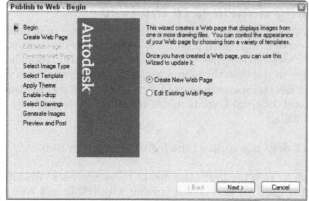

Figure 4-2:
Publishing
content with
Publish to
Web for
viewing on
the Internet.

4. **On the Create Web Page page, enter the name of the Web page you are creating, the location where you want the files created, and a description to display on the published file. Click Next.**

   You can use the Create Web Page page to capture basic configuration information (see Figure 4-3).

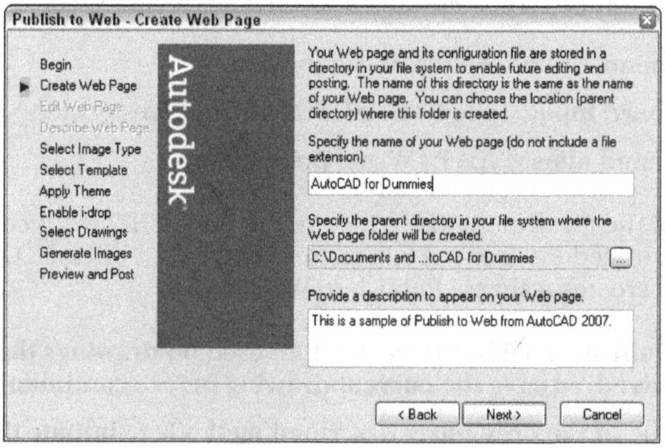

Figure 4-3:
Configuring
the Publish
to Web file.

5. **On the Select Image Type page, specify the type of image to create and its size. Click Next.**

   The Select Image Type page is used to specify the output format for the drawing layouts when they are published. There are three image type options to chose from: DWF, JPEG, and PNG. The image size is available when you specify JPEG and PNG. You can choose from four sizes: Small, Medium, Large, and Extra Large.

6. On the Select Template page, select the template for the desired layout from the Templates list box. Click Next.

The Select Template page is used to specify the basic layout of the images and text on the Web page when the final output is published (see Figure 4-4). You can choose from four templates: Array of Thumbnails, Array plus Summary, List of Drawings, and List plus Summary.

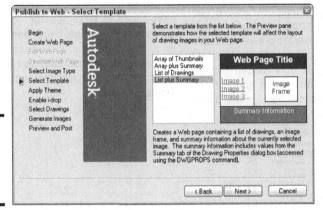

Figure 4-4:
Organizing the content of the Web page.

7. On the Apply Theme page, specify the color theme for the Web page by selecting it from the drop-down list. Click Next.

The Apply Theme page is used to add some color to the Web page. If you know HTML, you can change the colors later for the Web page beyond the total of seven themes that AutoCAD provides.

8. On the Enable i-drop page, specify whether i-drop should be enabled on the Web page. Click Next.

The Enable i-drop page is used to enable i-drop for the thumbnails that are generated during the publish process. This allows users of the Web page to drag and drop associated drawing files from the Web page into the drawing window.

9. On the Select Drawings page, specify the layouts from the current drawing file or select a different file. Each layout can have its own label and description. Click Add after a layout has been specified, along with a label and description for it.

The Select Drawings page is used to specify the layouts you want to add to the final published Web page (see Figure 4-5). You work with one drawing at a time and add each layout that you want to the drawing set to be processed. Each layout added to the Web page is displayed under the Image list.

10. Click Next when you finish adding different layouts.

**Book VIII
Chapter 4**

**Sharing
Electronic Files**

Autodesk i-drop

Autodesk i-drop is a technology that allows for content to be dragged-and-dropped from a Web page. There are two parts to i-drop. One part is used on a Web page to indicate where the content is stored and access it from the page. The second part is built into AutoCAD and picks up when content from an i-drop–enabled Web page is dropped into the drawing window. The AutoCAD side downloads the content to the local drive. The downloaded content usually contains a drawing file that is to be inserted as a block but can also contain things like company spec guides or marketing material. The following figure shows an image of the DC Online tab of DesignCenter; this tab utilizes i-drop technology.

To use an i-drop–enabled image such as the ones found in DesignCenter, you place the cursor over the image. If the image supports i-drop, an eye dropper icon appears. Click and hold down the mouse button over the image, and then drag and drop the content over the drawing window.

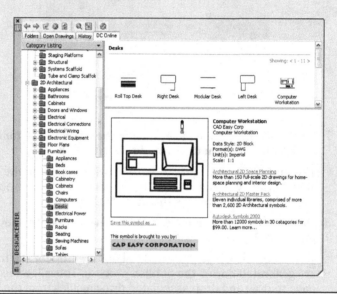

There is now a limit to the number of layouts that can be specified.

11. **On the Generate Images page, specify what files should be regenerated: only those files that have been changed or all drawing files. Click Next.**

The Generate Images page gives you some control over how long the republishing of a Web page will take. Based on the number of layouts and the size of drawing files, you may want to regenerate the output for changed drawing files only. AutoCAD starts processing the images for output.

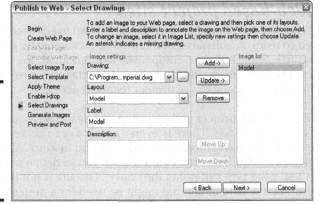

Figure 4-5:
Specifying
drawings
that should
be part of
the Web
page.

12. **On the Preview and Post page, you can preview the results that have been published to the output directory or post them directly to a specific location. Click Preview.**

The Preview and Post page lets you view what work the feature has done (see Figure 4-6) and allows you to step back and make any necessary changes.

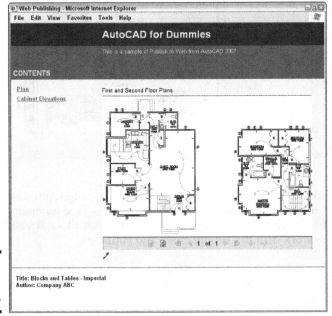

Figure 4-6:
Publish to
Web results.

Using Web-based project sites

As the Internet becomes more content-enriched and users become more accustomed to using it, software companies are expanding its possibilities for business use. Some software companies, like Autodesk, are building project-based collaboration sites that allow their customers to share and post drawing files for members of project teams to access.

Autodesk Buzzsaw is a project collaboration site designed around the AEC community (see Figure 4-7). There is even a quick way to access Autodesk Buzzsaw from the file navigation dialog boxes found in AutoCAD for opening or saving a drawing file. The project site allows you to define who is part of the project and what types of rights they have. The site is not just for placing drawing files but any kind of file that might be used for a project. The site works very similar to that of a standard file browser application with built-in revision tracking and file viewing.

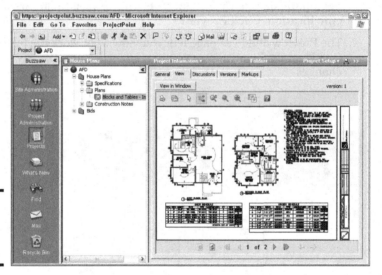

Figure 4-7:
Autodesk
Buzzsaw
project site.

Autodesk Buzzsaw has a sister (or brother) site called Autodesk Streamline that is targeted at manufacturers instead of the AEC community. You can use Autodesk Buzzsaw for any type of project, but Autodesk Streamline is optimized to work with the supply chain and suppliers.

The following steps assume that a project site has already been created on Autodesk Buzzsaw. The steps use the File menu to start the OPEN command and open a drawing.

1. **Choose File⇨Open.**

The Select File dialog box appears.

2. **In the Select File dialog box, click Buzzsaw from the list of locations located on the left side of the dialog box.**

The list box in the center of the dialog box displays a listing of the project site shortcuts that have already been created. You can use one of these shortcuts if the project site you want to access is listed.

3. **Double-click the Add a Buzzsaw location shortcut in the list.**

The Log in to Buzzsaw Site dialog box appears (see Figure 4-8).

Figure 4-8: Logging into an Autodesk Buzzsaw project site.

4. **In the Log in to Buzzsaw Site dialog box, enter the URL to the project site in the Buzzsaw Site text field. Then enter your assigned user name and password in the Buzzsaw User Name and Password text fields.**

The log-in information can be retained by selecting the Save Login Name and Password check box.

5. **Click OK.**

The Create a Buzzsaw Location Shortcut dialog box appears (see Figure 4-9).

6. **In the Create a Buzzsaw Location Shortcut dialog box, specify the path under the project site to the project folder you want to access. Also enter a name for the shortcut as you want it to appear in the list box after it is created. Click OK.**

If you are not sure of the path to the project folder, click the Browse button and a dialog box with a tree view appears so that you can select a folder (see Figure 4-10). After you click OK in the Create a Buzzsaw Location Shortcut dialog box, you are returned to the Select File dialog box.

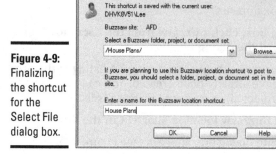

Figure 4-9:
Finalizing
the shortcut
for the
Select File
dialog box.

Figure 4-10:
Selecting a
folder on the
Buzzsaw
site.

7. **In the Select File dialog box, open the new shortcut to the Buzzsaw project and select the file you want to open. Click Open.**

The Select File dialog box closes, and the selected file opens in the drawing window.

Emulating Paper Digitally

The concept of our society using less and less paper when the Internet was born was just a great vision, and well, we are still waiting for it to happen. The design industry is starting to make the shift of relying on electronic file sharing and delivering content in this form, but having a paper copy is still nice. The downside to using lots of paper is higher costs when compared to using a combination of paper and electronic file sharing.

Paper drawing sets have the following costs behind them:

✦ **Paper.** Paper doesn't simply grow on trees; well, in a way it does, but it costs money to print drawing files out on any size of paper.

✦ **Delivery.** Someone has to deliver your printed drawing files to your client, and that usually leads to paying out money to a delivery service. This cost can quickly grow based on the number of drawing sets sent out to how much they weigh.

✦ **Time.** It can cost time and money just having to wait for the set of drawings to be delivered by a delivery service to your client's doorstep, and then you have to wait for a set of drawings to be marked up and returned.

✦ **Hardware maintenance.** The more you plot out to hard copy, the more frequently your plotters and printers will need to be serviced. This can cost downtime and money to keep the hardware going.

By no means is going completely electronic the answer either, but based on the phase and size of the project, you might find that speed of delivery and lower costs are nicely associated with using electronic files. There are two common electronic file formats that are often used for sharing drawing files. These two file formats are Design Web Format (DWF) and Portable Document Format (PDF).

AutoCAD and AutoCAD LT now come with a Plotter Configuration file that allows you to create a PDF file from a drawing without purchasing any additional software.

Design Web Format (DWF)

DWF is Autodesk's solution to a paperless representation of a drawing file or a set of drawing files in a lightweight file format. This means it doesn't include all of the object properties that are in a drawing file, but rather it contains just enough information to display the drawing accurately on-screen. DWF files, just like DWG files, are vector-based files instead of raster. This allows for them to be loaded faster and allows for you to manipulate certain aspects of the file as if you were viewing the original drawing file.

DWF files have grown in popularity over the last few years with more AutoCAD users using them with their clients. Autodesk has kept on increasing the efficiency and features that DWF supports. It all started with the support of 2D objects in a single sheet file to what it is today with support for 2D/3D objects, metadata, real-time shading and viewing, and multi-sheet support.

Most of the products that Autodesk develops for the design community are able to produce DWF files through devices that work with PLOT or PUBLISH or as a system printer such as the Autodesk DWF Writer. Autodesk DWF Writer can be used to print a Word document to a DWF file. Autodesk offers two DWF file viewers: a free viewer called *Autodesk DWF Viewer*, and one that must be purchased called *Autodesk DWF Composer*.

Portable Document File (PDF)

PDF is Adobe's solution to a paperless representation of a drawing file or any other document that can be printed. There are a number of PDF drivers on the market, so when we refer to PDF, we are referring to it as a file format. Some of the different drivers don't take advantage of all the features equally. If you want to take full advantage of the file format, use an application like Acrobat Professional from Adobe. A PDF file can be viewed by using a free view from Adobe, which is called *Adobe Acrobat Reader.*

Unlike DWF, PDF is a much more widely used file format because it has been around for a longer period of time and is more commonly used for non-engineering type file formats, such as Word documents and spreadsheets. PDF over recent years has gone through some transformations to help improve the type of data that can be stored in the files so it is much more useful to the design community. PDF files offer security options in the form of password protection and digital signatures.

The ability to produce a PDF file from inside AutoCAD out of the box has been on the wish list for many years now. AutoCAD 2007 comes with its own plotting device to output to a PDF file format. This driver is called "DWG to PDF.pc3" and is available through the PLOT or PUBLISH command.

Head-to-head comparison

Both DWF and PDF files have their places in the design community; it just depends on what your needs are and whom you are working with. It all comes down to what the client wants, but that may not always be the case. Below is an overview of a comparison between the two file formats.

✦ **Sharing.** DWF files are much smaller than PDF files, which is partly because of the optimization of the viewer engine. DWF was originally designed for design data and PDF was designed for Word documents. However, most clients most likely have Adobe Acrobat Reader on their computer versus either Autodesk DWF Viewer or Autodesk DWF Composer used to view the files.

✦ **Efficiency.** Both DWF and PDF files can be created from AutoCAD without any additional software to download and install. This once was a problem since AutoCAD only shipped with support for creating DWF files.

✦ **Viewing.** Both viewers support panning and zooming of a file, but Autodesk supports a much wider range of resolutions. This allows you to zoom in on a small area of a DWF file and have it still look crisp and clear. Both file formats support 3D objects, but due to the nature of the design of DWF, it does display 3D geometry better.

✦ **Printing.** No surprises here, since they are both document files that can be printed using both standard and large paper formats.

✦ **Markups.** The markup process is smoother between DWF and AutoCAD because of integrated tools. If you need to do markups, Autodesk DWF Composer will cost you less than Adobe Acrobat.

✦ **Speed.** The same drawing file takes less time to create a DWF file when compared to a PDF file. This is due to the way the two files are generated.

✦ **Compatibility.** Each version of AutoCAD starting with AutoCAD 2000 has shipped with the ability to create DWF files. AutoCAD 2007 is the first to support PDF, so if you have other releases of AutoCAD in your office, you need to obtain a PDF print driver from Adobe or a third-party provider. Some of the third-party utilities and even Adobe's Acrobat might not always support the latest version of AutoCAD, so it is nice to have a PDF drive ship with AutoCAD.

✦ **Security.** Both DWF and PDF file formats support password protection, but PDF goes beyond that with support for digital signatures.

Working with DWFs

Creating a DWF file is pretty straightforward through either the PLOT or PUBLISH command, but what happens once the file has been created? After you create the file, you can share it, and based on whom you are sharing it with, they will need a viewer. Autodesk offers two DWF viewers, Autodesk DWF Viewer and Autodesk DWF Composer. Autodesk DWF Viewer is a basic application that allows you to view and print DWF files to a system printer. Autodesk DWF Composer is used to do the same tasks as Autodesk DWF Viewer but also supports the ability to merge DWF files, markups, and measuring from point to point in a file.

So which DWF viewer is right for you? Table 4-1 shows some key differences between Autodesk DWF Viewer and Autodesk DWF Composer.

Table 4-1	Autodesk DWF Viewer versus Autodesk DWF Composer	
Feature	*Autodesk DWF Viewer*	*Autodesk DWF Composer*
View 2D and 3D objects	X	X
Printing and plotting	X	X
Measure from point to point accurately		X
Create and track markups for revisions		X
Create DWF files from drawing files		X
Ships with AutoCAD	X	
Cost	Free	Around $200

Creating a DWF file

Autodesk provides a number of ways for you to create a DWF file, whether you are using AutoCAD or one of the many different Autodesk products. From inside AutoCAD, you use the PLOT and PUBLISH commands to create a DWF file. The following procedure uses the File menu to start the PLOT command and create a DWF file.

1. **Choose File⇨Plot.**

   The Plot dialog box is displayed.

2. **In the Plot dialog box, choose DWF6 ePlot.pc3 from the Printer/Plotter drop-down list.**

   The DWF6 ePlot.pc3 plot device becomes active.

3. **Click the Properties button just to the right of the Printer/Plotter drop-down list.**

   The Plotter Configuration Editor – DWF6 ePlot.pc3 dialog box appears. From here, you can access various properties for the device.

4. **In the Plotter Configuration Editor – DWF6 ePlot.pc3 dialog box, select Custom Properties from the tree view and then click the Custom Properties button under the Access Custom Dialog area.**

   The DWF ePlot Properties dialog box appears (see Figure 4-11). From this dialog box, you can specify various options related to creating a DWF file. Properties range from embedding fonts to whether layer names and on/off states are maintained to the files resolution settings.

5. **In the DWF ePlot Properties dialog box, specify the options as necessary and then click OK twice to return to the Plot dialog box.**

   The changes are saved, and the DWF ePlot Properties and Plotter Configuration Editor – DWF6 ePlot.pc3 dialog boxes are closed.

6. **In the Plot dialog box, specify the necessary options for your plot and then click OK.**

   The Browse for Plot File dialog box appears, allowing you to specify the name of the DWF file that will be created and the location where you want to create it.

7. **In the Browse for Plot File dialog box, enter the name for the file and the location where you want to save it, and then click Save.**

   The DWF file is created in the specified location with the name that you entered. After the plot is created, a notification balloon appears to inform you that the Plot and Publish job has completed (see Figure 4-12). You can right-click over the Plot/Publish icon and select View DWF File to view the DWF file.

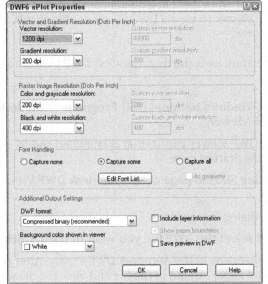

Figure 4-11:
Unlocking
the
properties
of the DWF6
ePlot
device.

Figure 4-12:
Plot
notification
balloon.

Viewing a DWF file

Using the DWF file viewer is pretty straightforward and has a very small
learning curve. The viewer is not designed for engineers who already know
AutoCAD, but someone who is familiar with browsing the Internet and creating Word documents.

DWF files can be viewed in a variety of different ways. Here are a few:

✦ **Embedded in a Document.** DWF files can be embedded in a Word document or even a PowerPoint presentation file.

✦ **Viewed from a Browser.** DWF files can be placed in-line on a Web page
to allow for direct viewing and interaction.

✦ **Stand-alone file viewing.** The Autodesk DWF viewers support the ability
to open a file directly from a local, network, or remote file location.

**Book VIII
Chapter 4**

**Sharing
Electronic Files**

These files are not embedded in a document or part of a Web page. You can launch the viewer to view a DWF file by double-clicking the file in Windows Explorer.

The following procedure uses the free Autodesk DWF Viewer to open a DWF file.

1. **Choose Start (Windows button)⇨[All] Programs⇨Autodesk and Autodesk DWF Viewer.**

The Autodesk DWF Viewer application is launched and by default displays the Getting Started page.

2. **From the Getting Started page of the Autodesk DWF Viewer, choose File⇨Open.**

The Open File dialog box appears.

3. **Browse to and select the DWF file you want to open. Click Open.**

The selected file opens in the Autodesk DWF Viewer. After the file opens, you can pan and zoom around in the file and view the drawing properties published with the file.

Electronically marking up a DWF file

You can use DWF files with Autodesk DWF Composer to communicate changes (or *revisions* as they are often called) to a drafter. Autodesk DWF Composer contains a number of mark-up and commenting tools that range from creating a simple line to much more complex tools that allow for the creation of revision clouds around areas in the file. As mark-up and commenting objects are added, Autodesk DWF Composer records by whom and when they were added to the DWF file.

Once the markups and comments have been added to the DWF file by using Autodesk DWF Composer, you can send them back to a drafter to make the necessary changes or plot them off with the viewer. If the DWF file with the markups is sent back to a drafter who has access to the original drawing files, the markups can be imported into AutoCAD by using the Markup Set Manager palette.

Even though you can attach DWF files in AutoCAD, the markups are not imported and managed this way. AutoCAD provides a feature that is specifically designed to work with markups that were created with Autodesk DWF Composer, called *Markup Set Manager*. You launch the Markup Set Manager palette by using the MARKUP command. You can start this command in a number of ways:

✦ **Tools menu.** Choose Tools⇨Palettes⇨Markup Set Manager.

 ✦ **Standard toolbar.** Click the Markup Set Manager button on the CAD Standards toolbar.

✦ **Keyboard input.** Type **MARKUP** and press Enter.

✦ **Shortcut Key.** Press the key combination **CTRL+7.**

✦ **Command alias.** Type **MSM** and press Enter.

Because Autodesk DWF Composer must be purchased separately, explaining how to create markup files and exchange them between Autodesk DWF Composer and AutoCAD is beyond the scope of this book. To find out more about using Autodesk DWF Composer to exchange DWF files and create markups, visit Autodesk's Web site at `www.autodesk.com/dwfcomposer`.

Book IX

Customizing AutoCAD

The 5th Wave   By Rich Tennant

© RICHTENNANT

"Somebody order a birthday cake in the shape
of an aluminum VTEK engine block?"

Contents at a Glance

Chapter 1: The Basics of Customizing AutoCAD

In This Chapter

✔ Understanding the benefits of customizing AutoCAD

✔ Customizing the AutoCAD startup process

✔ Changing options and using user profiles

✔ Creating and managing command aliases

*B*ook IX is designed to help both AutoCAD and AutoCAD LT users improve their workflow through customization. The majority of the customization options in Book IX are available in both AutoCAD and AutoCAD LT. Although AutoCAD LT supports a majority of the same customization options that AutoCAD does, there are exceptions. In this chapter, we mention these exceptions as they arise.

Have you ever wanted to learn how to start AutoCAD with a specific user profile already set current, or wanted to add your own custom command aliases? Maybe you already understand some of the available customization options but want to find out more about some you don't use. Whatever the reason, customization can help you to improve accuracy and efficiency during the design process. Customization isn't necessarily easy, but you don't have to be a programmer to take advantage of these features either.

Why Customize AutoCAD?

AutoCAD is one of the most popular design and drafting programs out on the market today, but if you take a good look at the program, you'll probably find that you've barely scratched the surface of what it can do. AutoCAD is designed to be very flexible and to adapt to the way you work. And if you don't like the layout of the program, you can always change the way it looks.

Not only can you customize the user interface — often referred to as the UI — but you can also make changes to help reduce repetitive tasks and ensure that CAD standards are followed. The level of customization that AutoCAD offers is much more dynamic than many of the other programs out on the market. Customizing AutoCAD is often confused with topics like AutoLISP and VBA. These languages can be used to customize AutoCAD, but they fall into the category of programming and are covered later in Book X. You can customize AutoCAD without resorting to any programming.

AutoCAD offers a large variety of customization options; so many, in fact, that you will probably not use all of them. The options range from creating new ways to start commands to defining how AutoCAD starts up. Customization can also be used to define the appearance of line work in a drawing with custom linetypes or custom patterns for hatched areas. Below is an overview of the different customization options available in AutoCAD:

✦ **Blocks:** Blocks are a form of customization because you are creating reusable content. This is one of the most natural forms of customization because you are extending the capabilities of AutoCAD without really knowing that you are customizing it. For more information on blocks, see Book VI, Chapters 2 and 3.

✦ **Drawing templates:** You might not have thought of drawing templates as a customization, but they are used to preset drafting options and the appearance of a base drawing, so they are a type of customization. For more information on drawing templates, see Book I, Chapter 3.

✦ **Command aliases:** Command aliases are used to allow faster access to commands from the command line. Many of the commonly used commands in AutoCAD have a command alias associated to them. An example of a command alias is L for the command LINE. For more information on command aliases, see "Creating and Managing Command Aliases" later in this chapter.

✦ **User profiles:** User profiles are used to control the appearance of AutoCAD, drafting settings, and where AutoCAD should look to find core and user-customized files. For more information on user profiles, see "Changing Options and Working with User Profiles" later in this chapter.

✦ **Diesel:** Diesel is a macro language that can be used to customize the status bar area of AutoCAD and to control parts of the user interface, like pull-down items. For more information on using Diesel, see Chapter 2 of this minibook.

✦ **User interface:** The user interface refers to the visual aspect of AutoCAD's controls, such as toolbars and pull-down menus, among other features. Many components of the user interface are controlled by an external file that is customized using the Customize User Interface (CUI) editor. For more information on customizing the user interface, see Chapter 3 of this minibook.

✦ **Tool Palettes:** Tool Palettes are one of the newest methods of customizing AutoCAD, and they provide ways to organize and access reusable content like blocks, hatches, and command tools. Tool Palettes allow for multiple levels of organization, so you can access the right tool or content quickly based on the task that you are trying to perform. For more information on customizing Tool Palettes, see Book VI, Chapter 4.

✦ **Scripts:** Script files are structured files that allow you to automate standard commands and options. Because these files are based on commands and options that you already use, they are fairly easy to create to reduce repetitive tasks. For more information on script files, see Chapter 4 of this minibook.

✦ **Linetypes:** Linetypes are used to control the appearance of line work in a drawing file when it is viewed and plotted. AutoCAD comes with a variety of default linetypes, but you might need to create your own for a project to represent something like a cable line or a flow direction. For more information on linetypes, see Chapter 4 of this minibook.

✦ **Shapes:** Shapes are one of the earliest forms of blocks that AutoCAD offered, but they still serve a purpose in AutoCAD even today. Shapes can be found in complex linetypes. For more information on shapes, see Chapter 4 of this minibook.

AutoCAD LT does not support the creation of custom Shape files because it does not support the COMPILE command.

✦ **Hatch patterns:** Hatch patterns are used to control the appearance of filled or hatched areas. AutoCAD ships with a number of default patterns, but you might want additional hatch patterns to represent things like wood or other patterns not available by default. For more information on hatch patterns, see Chapter 4 of this minibook.

✦ **Command line switches:** Command line switches are used to control some of the AutoCAD startup behavior. For more information on command line switches, see "Using command line switches" later in this chapter.

Customizing the AutoCAD Startup Process

AutoCAD offers a number of options to control how it starts up. Some of these options can be controlled through the desktop shortcut (or icon), whereas others are controlled through specially named files.

Startup options

Several different startup options are available to you. Some, but not all, of these use a programming language. AutoCAD LT doesn't support the programming options that AutoCAD does, so it is limited to startup options that don't involve a programming language. Below is an overview of the different startup options available in AutoCAD:

✦ **Command line switches:** Command line switches are parameters that can be defined with a shortcut file that is used to start AutoCAD. Command line switches can be used to perform a variety of tasks from starting with a specific drawing template to specifying the default Workspace to start with. For more information on command line switches, see "Using command line switches" later in this chapter.

✦ **Acad.LSP/Acaddoc.LSP/Acad2007.LSP/Acaddoc2007.LSP:** These AutoLISP files are automatically loaded at the startup of AutoCAD. Neither Acad.LSP nor Acaddoc.LSP ships with the program but instead must be created by the user. For more information on the files Acad.LSP, Acaddoc.LSP, Acad2007.LSP, and Acaddoc2007.LSP, see Book X, Chapter 2.

✦ **Acad.MNL:** Acad.MNL is an AutoLISP file that is associated with the customization file Acad.CUI and is loaded when the customization file is loaded. For more information on the Acad.MNL file, see Chapter 3 in this minibook.

✦ **Acad.RX:** Acad.RX is a plain text file that defines which ObjectARX or ObjectDBX files should be loaded at startup. For more information on the Acad.RX file, see Book X, Chapter 2.

✦ **Acad.DVB:** Acad.DVB is a VBA project that is automatically loaded at startup. For more information on the Acad.DVB file, see Book X, Chapter 2.

✦ **Appload – Startup Suite:** The Startup Suite is a feature of the Application Load dialog box to load custom programs developed with AutoLISP, VBA, and ObjectARX. For more information on using the Startup Suite, see Book X, Chapter 2.

AutoCAD LT does not support AutoLISP, VBA, or ObjectARX programming; so the files Acad.LSP, Acaddoc.LSP, Acad2007.LSP, Acaddoc2007.LSP, Acad.MNL, Acad.RX, and Acad.DVB can't be used to control its startup process. AutoCAD LT also doesn't support the use of the APPLOAD command, which is used to load the different types of custom program files.

Using command line switches

Command line switches are used to control the behavior of AutoCAD when it is started from a desktop shortcut or the Start menu. You can customize the desktop shortcut so a specific drawing template is used to create the default drawing that is displayed when AutoCAD is started. You can also use command line switches to control which user profile is used when AutoCAD is started. This enables you to have multiple profiles for AutoCAD on the computer and use different desktop shortcuts to switch between them. When using command switches, make sure that you use " " (double quote marks) around the name of a drawing or drawing template file, workspace, or path that contains a space. If you don't use " " for the name with a space, AutoCAD thinks it is another command line switch or argument.

Table 1-1 lists the different command line switches that are available for AutoCAD.

Table 1-1	Command Line Switches
Switch and Syntax	*Description*

No switches
`"...\acad.EXE" "drawing1"`
`"drawingn"`
	If a list of drawings with spaces between each one is provided, AutoCAD opens each file in the list that it can find.

`/b`
`"...\acad.EXE" ["drawing"]`
`/b "script"`
	The `/b` switch indicates to AutoCAD that it should run the specified script file after it has been started and the default or specified drawing has been opened. For more information on using script files, see Chapter 4 in this minibook.

`/c` `"...\acad.EXE" /c "path"`	Allows you to specify the location of the acad2007.CFG (acadlt2007.CFG) file.

`/ld`
`"...\acad.EXE" /ld "objectarx`
`or objectdbx file"`
	Allows you to load an ObjectARX or ObjectDBX file at startup. Note: This command line switch is not available for AutoCAD LT. For more information on ObjectARX and ObjectDBX files, see Book X, Chapter 1.

`/nologo` `"...\acad.EXE" /nologo`	Suppresses the AutoCAD splash screen at startup.
`/nossm` `"...\acad.EXE" /nossm`	Suppresses the Sheet Set Manager when AutoCAD starts up, if it was open when AutoCAD was closed. Note: This command line switch is not available for AutoCAD LT. For more information on the Sheet Set Manager, see Book VII, Chapter 2.

`/p`
`"...\acad.EXE" /p`
`"profile_name"`
	Controls which AutoCAD user profile is used at startup. You can also specify an exported profile file with the .ARG extension in place of the profile name. This loads the profile from the ARG file and makes it current. Note: This command line switch is not available for AutoCAD LT. For more information on user profiles, see "Changing Options and Working with User Profiles" later in this chapter.

(continued)

Table 1-1 *(continued)*

Switch and Syntax	Description
/r "...\acad.EXE" /r	Restores the system-pointer device settings and creates a backup of the current configuration file. Note: This command line switch is not available for AutoCAD LT.
/s "...\acad.EXE" /s "path"	Allows you to specify additional support paths that might not be defined under the Files tab of the Options dialog box. Note: This command line switch is not available for AutoCAD LT. For more information on support paths and options, see "Changing Options and Working with User Profiles" later in this chapter.
/set "...\acad.EXE" /set "sheet_set"	Allows you to specify a Sheet Set file that should be loaded at startup. Note: This command line switch is not available for AutoCAD LT. For more information on the Sheet Set Manager, see Book VII, Chapter 2.
/t "...\acad.EXE" /t "drawing_template.DWT"	Allows you to specify a drawing template that should be used to create the default drawing that is created when AutoCAD is started. For more information on drawing templates, see Book I, Chapter 3.
/v "...\acad.EXE" "drawing.DWG" /v "kitchen"	Allows you to specify a specific view in the drawing that is being opened. For more information on views, see Book II, Chapter 3.
/w "...\acad.EXE" "workspace"	Allows you to specify a Workspace that should be loaded upon startup. The Workspace must exist in one of the loaded customization (.CUI) files. For more information on Workspaces, see Chapter 3 in this minibook.

The /w command line switch is new in AutoCAD 2007 and AutoCAD LT 2007.

Creating a new desktop shortcut

Follow these steps to create a new desktop shortcut:

1. **Right-click over the Windows Start button and click Explore.**

Windows Explorer is launched.

2. **Navigate to the AutoCAD install folder. By default, AutoCAD is installed in the folder C:\Program Files\AutoCAD 2007 (AutoCAD LT 2007).**

The contents of the AutoCAD 2007 (AutoCAD LT 2007) folder should be displayed in the pane on the right side of Windows Explorer.

3. **Locate the file Acad.EXE (or Acadlt.EXE) and right-click the filename.**

   The file should highlight and a shortcut menu should appear.

4. **From the shortcut menu, click Copy.**

   The information about the executable file is copied to the Windows Clipboard.

5. **Minimize all open applications until you see the Windows desktop.**

6. **Right-click over an empty area of the desktop and click Paste Shortcut from the shortcut menu.**

   A new desktop shortcut should be created titled Shortcut to acad.EXE (or Shortcut to acadlt.EXE).

You can right-click an empty area of the Windows taskbar and click Show the Desktop instead of minimizing all application windows one at a time. If you have a keyboard with a flying Windows key on it, you can also press and hold down the key while pressing the M key on the keyboard to minimize all application windows.

Modifying a desktop shortcut

Follow this procedure below to modify the AutoCAD desktop shortcut and add a command line switch:

1. **Right-click the AutoCAD desktop shortcut and click Properties.**

   The Properties dialog box (see Figure 1-1) for the desktop shortcut is displayed.

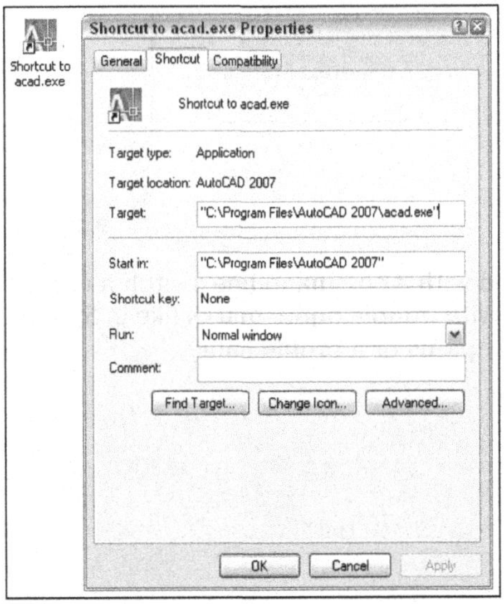

Figure 1-1:
The shortcut Properties dialog box.

2. **Click the General tab and enter a new name for the desktop shortcut in the text field next to the icon (see Figure 1-2).**

   The name is displayed on the desktop below the shortcut.

Figure 1-2:
The shortcut
name field.

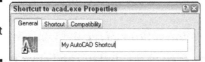

3. **Click the Shortcut tab and locate the Target text field just above the middle of the Shortcut Properties dialog box.**

   The Target text field controls the string that is executed when the short-cut is double-clicked with the pointing device.

4. **Position the cursor to the right of the text in the Target text field and click.**

   The cursor should be located to the right of the text C:\Program Files\ AutoCAD 2007\acad.EXE (or AutoCAD LT 2007\acadlt.EXE).

5. **Enter a space and then the text** /nologo /t "ANSI A -Named Plot Styles.DWT" **(see Figure 1-3).**

   The /nologo switch suppresses the splash screen and the /t switch with the specified drawing template is used to create the default Drawing1.DWG file.

Figure 1-3:
The shortcut
target field
with
command
line
switches.

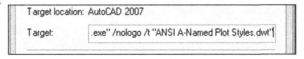

If a value that is used with a command line switch has a space, you must surround the value with double quote marks like in Step 5. This applies to values such as file paths or a profile name.

6. **Click OK to save the changes and exit the shortcut Properties dialog box.**

7. **Double-click the desktop shortcut to start AutoCAD.**

You should notice that no splash screen is displayed and Drawing1.DWG now has a title block based on the one that is defined in the ANSI A - Named Plot Styles drawing template.

Changing Options and Working with User Profiles

The Options dialog box (Figure 1-4) is used as the central hub to control many of the behavioral attributes of AutoCAD. From the Options dialog box, you can control drafting settings for grips, selection methods, and the appearance of AutoSnap markers that are displayed when using running object snaps. The Options dialog box also contains settings that control the appearance of AutoCAD and where it looks to find its support files. Figure 1-5 shows the Options dialog box in AutoCAD LT.

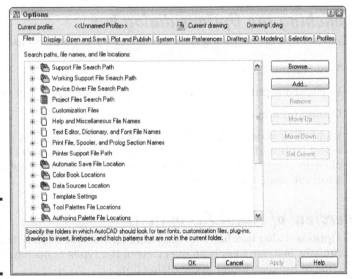

Figure 1-4:
The Options
dialog box –
AutoCAD.

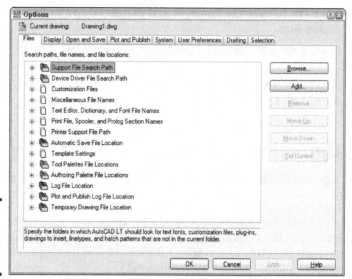

Figure 1-5:
The Options
dialog box –
AutoCAD LT.

Launching the Options dialog box

To launch the Options dialog box, use one of these methods listed:

✦ **Tools menu:** Choose Tools➪Options.

✦ **Keyboard input:** Type **OPTIONS** at the command line and press Enter.

✦ **Command alias:** Type **OP** and press Enter.

✦ **Right-click shortcut menu:** Right-click over the command line, and then select Options from the shortcut menu that appears. You can also right-click an empty area of the drawing window and choose Options from the shortcut menu that appears.

Overview of AutoCAD options

The Options dialog box has way too many options for us to list each one individually. Instead, here is an overview of the types of options found under each one of the tabs found in the dialog box:

✦ **Files:** Contains the folders that the program uses to search for support, menu, user-defined, and other files.

✦ **Display:** Contains options that control how a drawing is viewed, along with settings that control the appearance of the program's application window.

✦ **Open and Save:** Contains options that control the processes of opening and saving files.

✦ **Plot and Publish:** Contains options that are used for outputting a drawing or a set of drawings to hard copy or electronic formats.

✦ **System:** Contains options that control the pointing device and some other general options that control the behavior of the program.

✦ **User Preferences:** Contains options that are unique to users and the way they work with certain features found in the program.

✦ **Drafting:** Contains options that affect how things like points are selected in a drawing or how you are prompted for input.

✦ **Selection:** Contains options that affect how objects are selected and the behavior of grip editing.

✦ **Profiles:** Contains options to create and manage user profiles.

The Options dialog boxes for AutoCAD and AutoCAD LT have numerous differences; one of the biggest is that AutoCAD LT does not support user profiles.

Some options are stored in the drawing, whereas others are not saved at all or are stored in the Windows Registry. The options that can be set through the Options dialog box and are stored in the drawing are denoted with the small drawing file icon to the left of the option.

Working with user profiles

A user profile is used to store options that are defined in the Options dialog box by a given name. This allows you to access a specific configuration of options for task-based procedures or to share them with others in your company. User profiles are stored with the Windows profile in the Registry.

Creating a user profile

Follow this procedure to create a new user profile in AutoCAD.

1. **Launch the Options dialog box using one of the previously described methods.**

   The Options dialog box is displayed.

2. **In the Options dialog box, click the Profiles tab along the top.**

   The options for working with profiles should be displayed. In the upper-left corner of the Options dialog box, you can find out which of the profiles is current (see Figure 1-6).

Figure 1-6:
Identify the current profile.

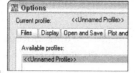

3. **Click the Add to List button.**

The Add Profile dialog box (see Figure 1-7) is displayed.

Figure 1-7:
The Add Profile dialog box.

4. **Enter a name in the Profile Name text field and a description in the Description text field.**

The name is what appears in the Available Profiles list and what can be used with the /p command line switch to load a profile at startup.

5. **Click Apply & Close to add the profile to the list.**

The Add Profile dialog box closes, the new user profile is added to the Available Profiles list, and you are returned to the Options dialog box.

6. **Click OK to exit the Options dialog box.**

Setting a user profile current

Follow this procedure to set a user profile current:

1. **Launch the Options dialog box using one of the previously described methods.**

2. **In the Options dialog box, click the Profiles tab along the top.**

3. **Select the user profile from the Available Profiles list that you want to set current and click Set Current.**

The user profile is set current and the options are applied to AutoCAD.

4. **Click OK to exit the Options dialog box.**

Exporting and importing a user profile

Profiles can be exported out of AutoCAD, which enables you to back them up in case you need to reinstall AutoCAD, or to share them with others in your company. Follow this procedure to export a user profile and then import it back into AutoCAD:

1. **Launch the Options dialog box using one of the previously described methods.**

2. **In the Options dialog box, click the Profiles tab along the top.**

3. **Select the user profile from the Available Profiles list and click Export.**

   The Export Profile dialog box is displayed. This dialog box is a standard Windows file navigation dialog box.

4. **In the Export Profile dialog box, specify a location to export the profile to and enter a name for the file in the File Name text field.**

   By default, AutoCAD uses the name of the drawing file for the name of the file that the user profile is being exported to.

5. **Click Save.**

   The user profile is exported out using the specified filename and location, and you are returned to the Options dialog box. The user profile file has the file extension of .ARG.

6. **In the Options dialog box, click Import.**

   The Import Profile dialog box is displayed. This dialog box is a Windows standard file navigation dialog box.

7. **In the Import Profile dialog box, browse to the location that you have saved the exported file to and select the user profile file that you want to import.**

8. **Click Open.**

   The Import Profile dialog box (see Figure 1-8) is displayed; this box is different from the previous Import Profile dialog box.

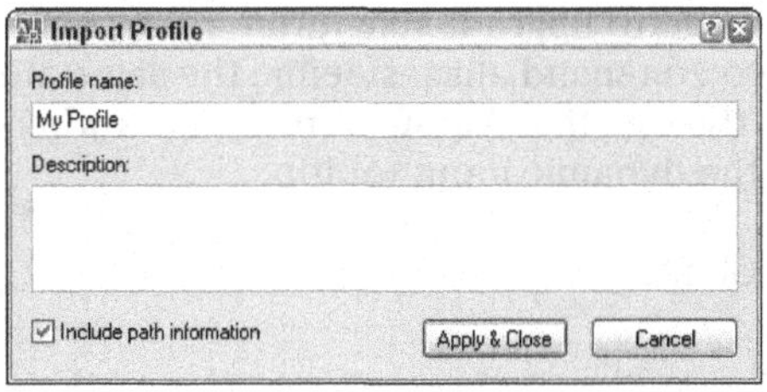

Figure 1-8:
The Import
Profile
dialog box.

9. **In the Import Profile dialog box, you can use the default name and description or make changes as necessary to these two values.**

   You also have the option of including the paths that are stored in the user profile file or using the ones from the current profile.

10. **Click Apply & Close to complete the importing of the user profile.**

    A new user profile based on the imported user profile file is added to the Available Profiles list, or the options for a profile are updated if the user profile with the specified name already exists.

11. **Click OK to exit the Options dialog box.**

Creating and Managing Command Aliases

Command aliases provide a quick way for you to access a command from the command line without being forced to type the entire command name. Command aliases are stored in the Acad.PGP (or Aclt.PGP) file, which is a plain text file stored by default under C:\Documents and Settings*<user name>*\Application Data\Autodesk\AutoCAD 2007\R17.0\enu\Support (or C:\Documents and Settings*<user name>*\Application Data\Autodesk\ AutoCAD LT 2007\R12\enu\Support). You often hear these files referred to as the program's PGP (Program Parameters) files. An example of a command alias is L, which is used to start the LINE command.

Editing the PGP file

Because a PGP file is a plain text file, it can be edited using a text editor like Notepad. Two different formats of aliases can be created: external commands and command aliases. External commands allow you to start applications outside AutoCAD such as Notepad, and command aliases allow you to start commands that are found inside AutoCAD such as the LINE command. Typically, you use command aliases more often than external commands.

The PGP file allows you to define your own command aliases or modify the ones that come with AutoCAD. Adding new command aliases to the bottom of the PGP file is a best practice: If you do, AutoCAD can identify which ones you have added when you go to upgrade to a future release of AutoCAD. One thing to note is that if two command aliases define the same alias, the latter one defined in the file is the one that AutoCAD recognizes when it's entered at the command line or the dynamic input tooltip.

Here's a sample of the PGP file:

```
J,         *JOIN
L,         *LINE
LA,        *LAYER
```

The syntax for a command alias is as follows:

```
Alias, *AutoCAD Command Name
```

You should keep the alias to as few characters as possible because the whole idea of an alias is to save you keystrokes. Between the alias and command name, you must use a comma to separate the two arguments, and the command name must be prefixed with an * (asterisk).

AutoCAD LT doesn't support external commands in the PGP file.

Opening the PGP file

To open the PGP file for the program, use one of the methods listed below:

✦ **Tools menu:** Choose Tools⇨Customize⇨Edit Program Parameters (acad.PGP) or (aclt.PGP).

✦ **External:** Start Notepad, browse to the location of the PGP file, and open it.

Adding a new command alias

Follow these procedures to create a new command alias:

1. **Open the PGP file using one of the previously described methods.**

2. **Scroll to the bottom of the file to the section -- User Defined Command Aliases -.**

   The section – User Defined Command Aliases – is where you should add your own command aliases. Command aliases placed below this section are automatically migrated forward when you upgrade to a new release of AutoCAD.

3. **Don't make changes to any of the command aliases that come with AutoCAD; instead, create a new command alias with the same command name and add it to the User Defined Command Aliases section. AutoCAD uses the last one it finds in the file; this way, your custom command alias is migrated to a new release automatically.**

4. **A command alias uses the syntax Alias, *Command. On a new line, enter the alias you want and the AutoCAD command it should execute when typed at the command line, separated by a comma.**

   Don't forget to precede the AutoCAD command name with an asterisk (*).

5. **The new command alias should be added to the PGP file using the syntax Alias, *Command.**

6. **From the menu bar in Notepad, choose File⇨Save.**

   The changes to the PGP file are saved to the file.

7. **Switch back to AutoCAD and type** REINIT **at the command line.**

   The Re-initialization dialog box (see Figure 1-9) is displayed.

Figure 1-9:
The Re-
initialization
dialog box.

8. **Select the check box next to PGP File and click OK.**

   The changes to the PGP file are available for use right away; you don't
   need to close and restart AutoCAD.

Working with the AutoCAD Alias Editor

If you are a user of AutoCAD, you might have heard of a collection of tools
called Express Tools. Express Tools is a collection of tools that extends the
base functionality of AutoCAD in a variety of useful ways. One of the tools
in the collection is called the AutoCAD Alias Editor (see Figure 1-10).

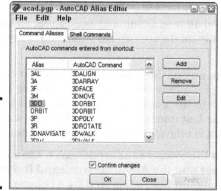

Figure 1-10:
The
AutoCAD
Alias Editor
dialog box.

This utility allows you to create both external commands and command
aliases using a dialog box interface instead of using a text editor like

Notepad. It also provides you with a list of all the available commands and system variables that are found in the program. For more information on Express Tools, see Chapter 4 in this minibook.

To launch the AutoCAD Alias Editor dialog box, do one of the following:

✦ **Express menu:** Choose Express➪Tools➪Command Alias Editor.

✦ **Keyboard input:** Type **ALIASEDIT** at the command line and press Enter.

Express Tools are not supported for AutoCAD LT because they are a collection of custom programs written with AutoLISP, VBA, and ObjectARX, which AutoCAD LT does not support.

Chapter 2: Customizing the Interface

AutoCAD allows you to personalize the overall appearance of the application window and display settings that can affect performance. Many users personalize their AutoCAD session to reflect the way they like to work or the way they want things displayed on-screen. AutoCAD gives you a lot of control over the appearance of colors and font sizes throughout the application window. The appearance settings include changing the background color of the drawing window and the crosshair color.

Not only does AutoCAD offer a variety of options to control colors of specific elements found in the application, but it also provides options to control whether certain user interface elements are displayed. Some of the features that you can control are the buttons located on the status bar and the icons that appear in the AutoCAD tray. This chapter explains how to control the appearance of AutoCAD and how to control user interface items such as toolbars and pull-down menus.

Getting Familiar with the Status Bar

AutoCAD takes full advantage of every space on its application window, and the status bar is no different. The status bar located at the bottom of the application window offers a variety of tools that allow for quick access to drafting settings and even notifications about changes that are taking place in the software and open drawings.

A number of different tools can be found on the status bar. These tools include the ability to toggle the dynamic input feature on and off and to change Object Snap settings to how lineweights are displayed in the drawing.

Table 2-1 lists the different buttons found on the status bar.

Table 2-1   **Status Bar Buttons**

Button	Name	Description
`30.4630, 14.8486, 0.0000`	Coordinates	Toggles between the different coordinate display settings.
`SNAP`	Snap Mode	Toggles grid or polar snapping on and off.
`GRID`	Grid Display	Toggles the display of the grid on and off.
`ORTHO`	Ortho Mode	Toggles orthomode on and off.
`POLAR`	Polar Tracking	Toggles polar tracking on and off.
`OSNAP`	Object Snap	Toggles running object snaps on and off.
`OTRACK`	Object Snap Tracking	Toggles object snap tracking on and off.
`DUCS`	Allow/Disallow Dynamic UCS	Toggles dynamic UCS on and off.
`DYN`	Dynamic Input	Toggles dynamic input on and off.
`LWT`	Show/Hide Lineweight	Toggles the display of lineweights on and off.
`MODEL`	Model or Paper Space	Toggles between model and paper space, and switches paper space layouts. If the layout tabs are not displayed three buttons are displayed and allow you to switch between model and paper space, along with switch between different paper space layout tabs.
	Minimize/Maximize and Viewport Navigation	Toggles between maximized and minimized viewport states and allows you to switch between different viewports.
	Icon Tray	Displays the current notification icons for the features that are in use in the current session and drawing. It also allows you to access the Tray Settings.

Many of the tools located on the status bar are not just toggles that turn a setting on or off, but they also allow for accessing the settings for the drafting tool. To change the settings of a drafting tool, right-click the status bar button and select Settings from the menu that appears. This displays a dialog box so you can change the behavior of the drafting tool.

AutoCAD allows you to control many of the features that are displayed in the user interface. The status bar is no different; AutoCAD allows you to control which of the different buttons are displayed at the bottom of the application window in the status bar. So if you don't use the Grid or Snap toggles, you can choose to turn them off. To control the display of the different buttons on the status bar, click the small black arrow that points downward in the lower-right corner of the application window (see Figure 2-1). A shortcut menu (see Figure 2-2) with options to control the different buttons on the status bar is displayed. Select the item from the shortcut menu that you want to toggle the display of. A check mark next to an item signifies that that item is currently displayed on the status bar.

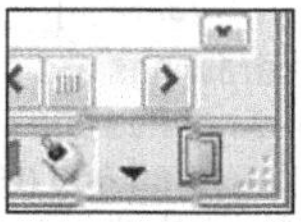

Figure 2-1:
The status
bar menu.

Figure 2-2:
The shortcut
menu to
toggle the
display of
buttons on
the status
bar.

✔ Cursor coordinate values
✔ Snap (F9)
✔ Grid (F7)
✔ Ortho (F8)
✔ Polar (F10)
✔ OSnap (F3)
✔ OTrack (F11)
✔ Dynamic UCS (F6)
✔ Dynamic Input (F12)
✔ Lineweight
✔ Layout/Model
✔ Clean Screen (Ctrl+0)
Tray Settings...

Getting to know the Icon Tray

Tray icons, located in the lower-right corner of the status bar, allow you to quickly access certain features. A number of different icons are displayed in the tray and each one serves a specific purpose.

Table 2-2 lists the different tray icons in AutoCAD.

Table 2-2		Tray Icons
Button	*Name*	*Description*
	Communication Center	Allows you to access the Communication Center and receive information about available updates, tips and tricks, and much more.

(continued)

Table 2-2 *(continued)*

Button	Name	Description
	Toolbar/Window Lock	Allows you to control whether toolbars and dockable windows (palettes) can be moved (floated) around the screen, or whether they are stationary (docked).
	CAD Standards Notification	Allows you to identify that a drawing has CAD Standards associated with it, access the CAD Standards tools, and receive notifications when the drawing becomes out of sync with the associated CAD Standards files.
	External Reference Notification	Allows you to identify that External Reference drawings are contained in the drawing and notifies you when the files have been updated and need to be reloaded. The notification balloon allows you to reload the file that has changed without needing to open the External Reference dialog box.
	Plot Notification	Allows you to access information about recent plotted files and to receive information about a job that is being processed in the background.
	Attribute Extraction Notification	Allows you to identify that a Table object in the drawing is linked to blocks in the drawing. If the original information that the Table points to is changed, you will be notified that the Table has become out of sync.
	Trusted Autodesk DWG	Allows you to identify whether the current drawing was created with an application developed by Autodesk or a non-Autodesk product.
	Validate Digital Signatures	Allows you to identify whether the current drawing has been digitally signed, and if the digital signature is valid.
	Clean Screen	Allows you to enable or disable Clean Screen.

The Clean Screen tray icon is new in AutoCAD 2007.

AutoCAD LT does not support CAD Standards, so the CAD Standards Notification is not present in the software. AutoCAD LT does not support the Attribute Extraction Notification either because it doesn't support the Enhanced Attribute Extract (or EATTEXT) command. Although AutoCAD LT does support external references, the External Reference Notification is not part of AutoCAD LT.

The Icon Tray allows you to customize some options that apply to all the icons that are contained in this area of the status bar. Here is an overview of the available tray settings:

✦ **Display icons for services:** Controls whether icons for services that are running in AutoCAD are displayed on the status bar.

✦ **Display notifications from services:** Controls whether the services display a notification balloon when something they are monitoring changes.

✦ **Display time:** Controls the maximum length of time in seconds that a notification balloon should be displayed if the user doesn't close it before the time period expires. The time range is from 1 to 10 seconds.

✦ **Display until closed:** Controls whether the notification for the service is displayed until the user dismisses it.

Follow these procedures to change the available tray settings:

1. **Click the small black arrow that points downward in the lower-right corner of the application window.**

A shortcut menu with options to control the different tools on the status bar is displayed.

2. **On the shortcut menu, click Tray Settings.**

The Tray Settings dialog box (see Figure 2-3) is displayed.

Figure 2-3:
The Tray
Settings
dialog box.

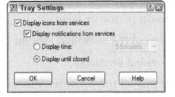

3. **Change the options to the desired combination of settings and click OK.**

The Tray Settings dialog box closes and the status bar is updated based on the selected options.

Powering the status bar with DIESEL

DIESEL — Direct Interpretively Evaluated String Expression Language — is a macro language that allows you to control the behavior of menu macros and display text on the status bar. This can be a great way to display information about drafting settings that is not normally displayed on the status bar, like Linetype Scale or the current elevation for new objects to be drawn at. The system variable MODEMACRO is used to display a DIESEL macro on the status bar. The result of the macro is displayed on the far left side of the status bar (see Figure 2-4).

Figure 2-4:
Running a
DIESEL
macro on
the status
bar.

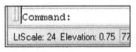

The DIESEL expression used to generate the results shown in Figure 2-4 is

```
$(eval, "LtScale: " $(getvar, "ltscale") " Elevation: "
    $(getvar, "elevation"))
```

Because DIESEL is a macro language, you can use a number of functions with it. DIESEL offers functions for manipulating strings, performing mathematics, and getting system variable values. Some of the more common functions that are available in DIESEL are

- ✦ Eval: Passes the DIESEL expression to the evaluator and returns a value.
- ✦ Upper: Converts the string to all uppercase letters.
- ✦ If: A conditional statement that returns one of two values based on whether the conditional expression is true or false.
- ✦ Getvar: Returns the current value of the specified system variable.
- ✦ +: Returns the sum of all the provided numbers.
- ✦ –: Returns the results of subtracting all the provided numbers from each other.

For more information on other DIESEL functions, refer to the topic "Catalog of DIESEL Functions" in the AutoCAD Help system.

Follow these steps to display the results of a DIESEL expression on the status bar:

1. **At the command line, type** MODEMACRO.

AutoCAD displays the command prompt:

```
Enter new value for MODEMACRO, or . for none <"">:
```

Enter the DIESEL expression that you want evaluated and displayed on the status bar, or enter just a period (.) at the command prompt to end the evaluation of the current DIESEL expression and to reset the value back to no DIESEL expression (""). Then press Enter to start evaluation.

2. **AutoCAD updates the status bar with the results of the DIESEL expression or returns an error message (see Figure 2-5) in its place.**

The figure shows that the + function can't be evaluated by displaying $(+, ??) on the status bar. This is because a string (A) can't be added to a number (2).

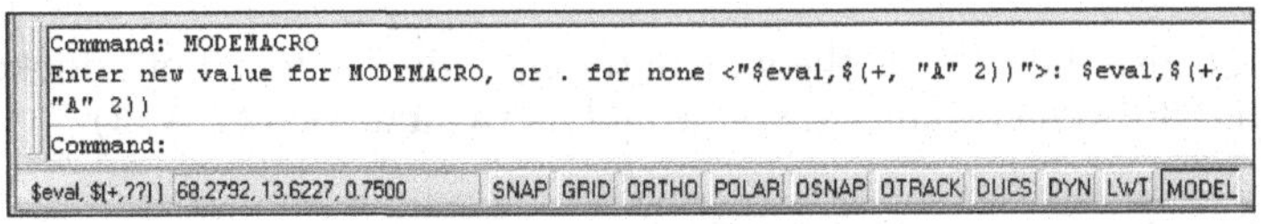

Figure 2-5:
Oops, the +
function
isn't
evaluating
correctly.

```
Command: MODEMACRO
Enter new value for MODEMACRO, or . for none <"$eval,$(+, "A" 2)]">: $eval,$(+,
"A" 2))
Command:
```
```
$eval, $(+,??) | 68.2792, 13.6227, 0.7500      SNAP GRID ORTHO POLAR OSNAP OTRACK DUCS DYN LWT |MODEL|
```

Training Your Toolbars and Dockable Windows to Stay

Have you ever tried to click a toolbar or dockable window (palette) only to accidentally move it? This can cause all sorts of cascading effects to happen: The toolbars can be rearranged or the toolbar or dockable window can even disappear off the screen. Most of us like everything to stay as it is after we come up with the perfect layout of toolbars and windows.

This is where the user interface (UI) lock option comes into play. With the UI lock option, you can make toolbars and dockable windows that are floating or docked stay put on-screen. When the option is turned on, you can't accidentally move them from their current position. This is especially useful if you are using a dual monitor setup, where you might have the toolbars and dockable windows on a separate monitor.

Locking UI toolbars and dockable windows

To lock toolbars and dockable windows, use one of these methods:

✦ **Window menu:** Choose Window⇨Lock Location and select one of the available options.

✦ **Icon Tray:** Click the Toolbar/Window Position icon on the status bar and click one of the available options from the shortcut menu.

✦ **Keyboard input:** Type **LOCKUI** at the command line and specify a value based on the sum of the allowed bitcodes for the system variable.

Table 2-3 lists the bitcodes for the LOCKUI system variable.

Table 2-3	LOCKUI Bitcodes
Value	*Description*
0	Toolbars and dockable windows are not locked.
1	Docked toolbars are locked.
2	Docked dockable windows are locked.
4	Floating toolbars are locked.
8	Floating dockable windows are locked.

Because the value is the sum of the bitcodes, to lock both docked toolbars and dockable windows, you would use a value of 3 (1 + 2).

Locking and unlocking toolbars and dockable windows

Follow these steps to lock and unlock toolbars and dockable windows in the AutoCAD user interface:

1. **From the menu bar, choose Window⇨Lock Location⇨ Docked Toolbars.**

The grip handles on the left side of the toolbar (see Figure 2-6) are removed and the toolbar can't be undocked or relocated. A check mark should be next to Docked Toolbars.

Figure 2-6:
The toolbar grip handles have been removed.

2. **From the menu bar, choose Window⇨Lock Location and click Docked Toolbars again.**

The grip handles on the left side of the toolbar should be visible again. The toolbar can be undocked and relocated once again. The check mark next to Docked Toolbars should disappear.

Controlling the Appearance and Displays of AutoCAD

AutoCAD allows you to not only customize the display of tools and icons on the status bar, but it also allows you to customize the color scheme that is used. The color scheme can range from the background color of the drawing window to the crosshair color. The latest release offers many additional options to control the color for 3D-related elements.

3D drafting has been largely enhanced in the latest version. To make it easier to use, a new set of options has been introduced to identify whether you are working in 2D or 3D drafting mode.

AutoCAD LT does not support 3D drafting, so some of the color options aren't available.

To change the display settings for AutoCAD in the Options dialog box, choose Tools⇨Options. In the Options dialog box that appears, click the Display tab. Specify the desired changes to the display options and click OK to save the changes and close the Options dialog box. In the next several sections, we cover many of the options found on the Display tab.

Window elements

The options for AutoCAD's window elements (see Figure 2-7) can be found in the Options dialog box under the Display tab. The Window Elements section holds settings for controlling the color scheme of AutoCAD, the display of the screen menu, and whether toolbar buttons are displayed as normal or large buttons, among other settings.

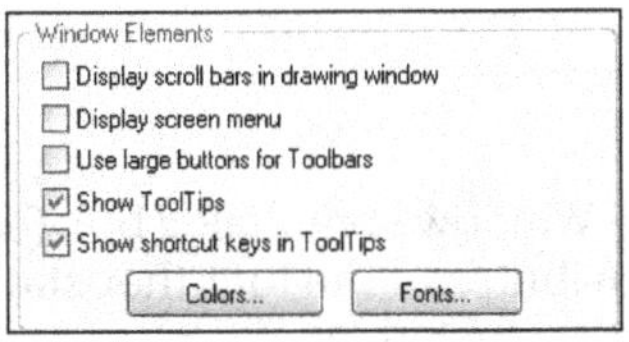

Figure 2-7:
The Window Elements section of the Options dialog box.

Window Elements
☐ Display scroll bars in drawing window
☐ Display screen menu
☐ Use large buttons for Toolbars
☑ Show ToolTips
☑ Show shortcut keys in ToolTips
[Colors...]   [Fonts...]

Here is an overview of the options found under the Window Elements section:

✦ **Display Scroll Bars in Drawing Window:** Toggles the display of the vertical and horizontal scroll bars in the drawing window.

✦ **Display Screen Menu:** Toggles the display of the legacy screen menu (side bar menu).

✦ **Use Large Buttons for Toolbars:** Toggles the display setting of whether toolbars should be displayed with icons that are 16×16 or 32×32 pixels.

✦ **Show ToolTips:** Toggles the display of tooltips when the cursor is hovering over a toolbar button.

✦ **Show Shortcut Keys in ToolTips:** Toggles the display of shortcut keys that are associated with a command as part of the tooltip when the cursor is hovering over a toolbar button.

✦ **Colors:** Opens the Drawing Window Color dialog box (see Figure 2-8) and allows you to change the color for the defined interface elements of the different application contexts.

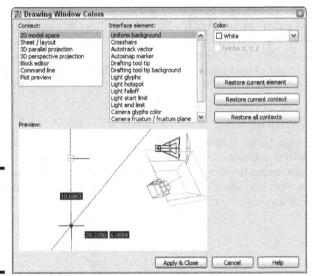

Figure 2-8:
The Drawing Window Colors dialog box.

✦ **Fonts:** Opens the Command Line Window Font dialog box (see Figure 2-9) and allows you to specify the attributes of the font that should be used for text in the command line and text window.

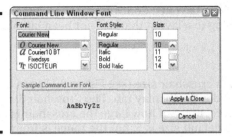

Figure 2-9:
The
Command
Line
Window
Font dialog
box.

Layout elements

The options for AutoCAD's layout elements (see Figure 2-10) can be found in the Options dialog box under the Display tab. The Layout Elements section holds settings for controlling the appearance of layout tabs other than model space, and the visibility of both model and layout tabs at the bottom of the drawing window, among other settings.

Figure 2-10:
The Layout
Elements
section in
the Options
dialog box.

Here is an overview of the options found under the Layout Elements section:

✦ **Display Layout and Model tabs:** Controls the display of the model and layout tabs at the bottom of the drawing window.

✦ **Display Printable Area:** Controls the display of the printable area. The printable area when enabled is represented by the area within the dashed line on a layout tab.

✦ **Display Paper Background:** Controls the display of the area that represents the size of the paper. The paper background is determined by the selected paper size and the specified plot scale.

✦ **Display Paper Shadow:** Controls the display of a shadow around the bottom and right edges of the paper background to give the appearance that it is floating.

✦ **Show Page Setup Manager for New Layouts:** Controls the display of the Paper Setup Manager when a new layout is added to a drawing. The dialog box is only displayed if the layout has not been initialized yet.

✦ **Create Viewport in New Layouts:** Controls whether a single viewport is created when switching to a layout that has not been initialized yet.

Crosshair size

The options for AutoCAD's crosshair size (see Figure 2-11) can be found in the Options dialog box under the Display tab. The Crosshair Size section allows you to specify a percentage of how large the crosshair is compared to the total screen size. The default size is 5, but the range is from 1 to 100.

Figure 2-11:
The Cross-
hair Size
section in
the Options
dialog box.

Display resolution

The options for AutoCAD's display resolution (see Figure 2-12) can be found in the Options dialog box under the Display tab. The Display Resolution section holds settings for how arcs and circles should appear on-screen and settings that control the appearance of renderings, among other things.

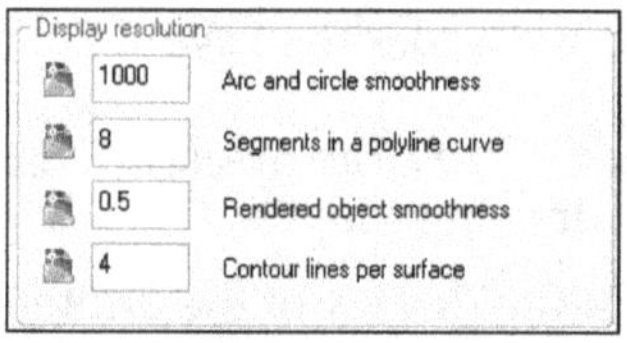

Figure 2-12:
The Display
Resolution
settings in
the Options
dialog box.

Display resolution	
1000	Arc and circle smoothness
8	Segments in a polyline curve
0.5	Rendered object smoothness
4	Contour lines per surface

Here is an overview of the options found under the Display Resolution section:

✦ **Arc and Circle Smoothness:** Controls the display of arcs, circles, and ellipses. The higher the number, the smoother the objects display on-screen, but a high number negatively affects performance.

✦ **Segments in a Polyline Curve:** Controls the number of line segments to display a curve on a polyline. The higher the number, the smoother the objects appear, but it impacts performance negatively.

♦ **Rendered Object Smoothness:** Controls the display of rendered and shaded curved surfaces. The value is multiplied by the value specified for arc and circle smoothness to come up with the factor used for rendering and shading.

♦ **Contour Lines per Surface:** Controls the number of contour lines for a single surface.

Display performance

The options for AutoCAD's display performance (see Figure 2-13) can be found in the Options dialog box under the Display tab. The Display Performance section holds settings for whether raster images are displayed during real-time pan and zoom operations, whether text is represented by rectangular boxes to improve regeneration time, and whether hatch objects are displayed in the drawing, among other settings.

Figure 2-13:
The Display Performance section in the Options dialog box.

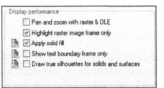

Here is an overview of the options found under the Display Performance section:

♦ **Pan and Zoom with Raster & OLE:** Controls whether raster images and OLE objects remain on-screen while either real-time pan or zoom are active.

♦ **Highlight Raster Image Frame Only:** Controls whether just the raster image frame is highlighted when the raster image is selected, or the entire raster image.

♦ **Apply Solid Fill:** Controls whether hatch, polylines with width, or 2D solids are displayed as filled, or simply their outlines are displayed.

♦ **Show Text Boundary Frame Only:** Controls whether text is represented as a rectangular box to show just position and rotation, or as normal text.

♦ **Draw True Silhouettes for Solids and Surfaces:** Controls whether mesh drawn on a 3D solid object is hidden and whether silhouette curves of 3D solids are displayed as wireframes.

Reference Edit fading intensity

The options for AutoCAD's Reference Edit fading intensity (see Figure 2-14) can be found in the Options dialog box under the Display tab. The Reference Editing Fading Intensity setting allows you to specify the percentage that the geometry that is not being edited with the REFEDIT command is faded into the background. The default fade value is 50, but the value can range from 0 to 90.

Figure 2-14:
The Reference Edit Fading Intensity section in the Options dialog box.

Organizing Your Space

AutoCAD uses a feature called Workspaces to allow you to control the layout of user interface elements. Workspaces control user interface elements such as toolbars, pull-down menus, and dockable windows, among some other user interface items. Workspaces are saved with a user-specified name in a customization (CUI) file. A majority of Workspace customization is handled through the Customize User Interface (CUI) editor, but it can also be managed through the user interface from the Window pull-down menu and the Workspaces toolbar. For more information on how to use the CUI editor, see the section, "Using the Customize User Interface editor," later in this chapter.

Using the Workspaces toolbar

The Workspaces toolbar (see Figure 2-15) offers some level of control over Workspaces but not the full control that the Customize User Interface (CUI) editor does.

Figure 2-15:
The Workspaces toolbar.

From the Workspaces toolbar, you can do the following:

✦ **Set a Workspace Current:** From the drop-down list, you can select one of the defined Workspaces and set it current.

✦ **Save a Workspace:** From the drop-down list, you can select the Save Current As option to store as a Workspace the current display settings for toolbars and dockable windows. The Save Workspace dialog box (see Figure 2-16) is displayed, allowing you to save the changes to an existing Workspace or create a new one.

Figure 2-16:
The Save
Workspace
dialog box.

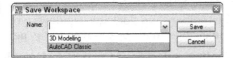

✦ **Workspace Settings:** The button to the right of the Workspaces drop-down list on the Workspaces toolbar displays the Workspace Settings dialog box (see Figure 2-17). The Workspace Settings dialog box allows you to specify which Workspace is set current when the My Workspace button is clicked on the Workspaces toolbar. The dialog box also allows you to change the order of how the Workspaces appear in the drop-down list of the Workspaces toolbar and controls whether changes to the current Workspace are saved automatically before switching Workspaces.

Figure 2-17:
The
Workspace
Settings
dialog box.

✦ **My Workspace:** Sets the Workspace specified in the Workspace Settings dialog box as current.

All of the tools that are on the Workspaces toolbar, except for the My Workspace tool, can be found under Window⊅Workspaces.

Creating a new Workspace

Follow this procedure to create a new Workspace using the Workspaces toolbar.

1. **If the Workspaces toolbar is not displayed, right-click on one of the toolbars that is displayed and select Workspaces.**

   The Workspaces toolbar is displayed.

2. **Move some of the toolbars and dockable windows around on-screen.**

   By moving some of the toolbars and dockable windows, you should be able to tell whether the changes have been saved to the new Workspace.

3. **On the Workspaces toolbar, select Save Current As from the drop-down list.**

   The Save Workspace dialog box is displayed.

4. **In the Save Workspace dialog box, enter a name for the new Workspace in the Name text field and click Save.**

   The new Workspace is saved to the main customization file and added to the drop-down list on the Workspaces toolbar. An entry for that Workspace is also added under Window⊅Workspaces.

5. **Switch between different Workspaces from the drop-down list to see how they are different.**

Saving changes to an existing Workspace

To update an existing Workspace, follow the same steps that were in the previous section, "Creating a new Workspace." Instead of entering a name in the Name text field in Step 4, select an existing Workspace name from the drop-down list. Then click the Save button to update the Workspace.

Using the Customize User Interface editor

The Customize User Interface (CUI) editor offers a full range of control over Workspaces, unlike the Workspaces toolbar. The one thing that you can't define using the CUI editor is which Workspace is displayed when the My Workspace button on the Workspaces toolbar is clicked.

From the CUI editor, you can do the following:

✦ **Create a Workspace.** The Customizations In pane allows you to create a new Workspace.

✦ **Manage Workspaces.** The Customizations In pane allows you to rename, delete, and set a Workspace current, among other options.

✦ **Transfer Workspaces.** The Transfer tab allows you to transfer Workspaces between two different CUI files.

✦ **Display and Order Pull-Down Menus.** The Workspace Contents pane allows you to specify which pull-down menus from the loaded CUI files are displayed on the menu bar area of AutoCAD and the order they appear in.

✦ **Display and Position Toolbars.** The Workspace Contents pane allows you to specify the location of a toolbar and which ones should be visible when the Workspace is set current.

✦ **Display and Position Dockable Windows.** The Workspace Contents pane allows you to specify the location of a dockable window and which ones should be visible when the Workspace is set current, along with some other properties specific to a dockable window.

✦ **Other User Interface Options.** The Properties pane allows you to specify additional user interface settings to control the display of scroll bars and model and layout tabs, among other settings.

Creating a new Workspace

Follow these steps to create a new Workspace using the CUI editor:

1. **From the menu bar, choose Tools⇨Customize⇨Interface.**

The Customize User Interface (CUI) editor is displayed.

2. **In the Customize User Interface editor, click the Customize tab along the top.**

The Customize tab is set current.

3. **In the Customizations In pane, right-click the Workspaces node and choose New⇨Workspace.**

The Workspaces node expands and a new Workspace is added named *Workspace1*.

4. **Enter a new name for the Workspace in the text field or change the default name under the Properties pane.**

The Workspace is renamed.

5. **Click Customize Workspace under the Workspace Contents pane.**

The Workspace is now opened for editing.

6. **Under the Customizations In pane, expand the Toolbars and Menus nodes. After the nodes are expanded, select the toolbars and pull-down menus you want displayed when the Workspace is set current.**

As you select toolbars and pull-down menus from the Customizations In pane, they are added to the Workspace under the Workspace Contents pane.

7. Click Done under the Workspace Contents pane after you have added the desired toolbars and pull-down menus to the Workspace.

The changes are saved to the Workspace.

8. Click OK.

The changes are saved to the main CUI file.

Changing the order of pull-down menus

Follow these procedures to reorder the pull-downs that are part of a Workspace:

1. **From the menu bar, choose Tools⇨Customize⇨Interface.**

The Customize User Interface (CUI) editor is displayed.

2. **In the Customize User Interface editor, click the Customize tab along the top.**

The Customize tab is set current.

3. **In the Customizations In pane, click the plus sign next to the Workspaces node to expand it.**

The Workspaces node should expand, revealing the Workspaces that exist in the main CUI file.

4. **Select the Workspace in which you want to change the pull-down menu order.**

The Workspace Contents pane is displayed, allowing you to make changes to the properties of the associated toolbars and pull-down menus.

5. **In the Workspace Contents pane, click the plus sign next to the Menus node.**

The associated pull-down menus are displayed under the Menu node.

6. **Select the pull-down menu you want to reposition. Keep holding down the mouse button and drag it to its new position.**

A horizontal indicator is displayed between the pull-down menus to show where the pull-down menu being dragged will be placed when the mouse button is released.

If you move the CUI editor so that you can see the menu bar along the top of AutoCAD, you can click Apply to see the pull-down menus change positions without needing to exit the CUI editor first.

7. Click OK.

The changes are saved to the main CUI file.

Other Workspace settings

Follow these procedures to adjust some of the other properties for the Workspace.

1. **From the menu bar, choose Tools➪Customize➪Interface.**

The Customize User Interface (CUI) editor is displayed.

2. **In the Customize User Interface editor, click the Customize tab along the top.**

The Customize tab is set current.

3. **In the Customizations In pane, click the plus sign next to the Workspaces node to expand it.**

The Workspaces node should expand, revealing the Workspaces that exist in the main CUI file.

4. **Select the Workspace you want to change properties for.**

The Properties pane is displayed, allowing you to access the properties for a Workspace.

5. **Change the properties for the Workspace as desired.**

The Properties pane contains many different properties that control some of the different user interface elements.

If you select one of the rows in the Properties pane for the Workspace, a brief description appears in the lower portion of the pane for the selected row. This gives you an idea of what the property is used for, if you are unsure about it.

6. **Click OK.**

The changes are saved out to the main CUI file.

Maximizing the drawing space

AutoCAD displays tools such as toolbars, pull-down menus, and the status bar throughout the user interface so you can quickly access different drafting tools as they are needed. At times, you might not need these tools and might instead want more space to work with. AutoCAD offers a tool to suppress the display of some of the user interface elements so you have more drawing real estate; this tool is called Clean Screen.

Clean Screen does exactly what the name suggests: gives you a clean screen to work with. It maximizes AutoCAD and turns off all the toolbars and dockable windows and even hides the caption bar along the top of AutoCAD. The pull-down menus are still available along with the command line.

To use the Clean Screen tool, use one of the methods listed below:

✦ **View menu:** Click View on the menu bar, and then move your mouse pointer down to Clean Screen and click.

✦ **Icon Tray:** Click the Clean Screen icon on the status bar.

✦ **Shortcut key:** Press Ctrl+0 (zero).

✦ **Keyboard input:** Type **CLEANSCREENON** on the command line and press Enter. Typing **CLEANSCREENOFF** returns AutoCAD to its previous state.

Chapter 3: Customizing the Tools

In This Chapter

✔ Getting to know the Customize User Interface editor

✔ Customizing toolbars, menus, and shortcut keys

✔ Customizing double-click actions

✔ Migrating and transferring customization

✔ Working with partial and enterprise customization files

AutoCAD customization goes beyond just being able to change the appearance of the application window or controlling the regeneration process of a drawing. AutoCAD allows you to create your own toolbars, pull-down menus, and shortcut keys, among other user interface elements. This flexibility allows you to further integrate AutoCAD into your workflow and to manage CAD standards.

To customize the user interface, you use the Customize User Interface (CUI) editor. The CUI editor is a graphical editor that reads and writes to customization files, which have a file extension of .CUI. The CUI editor and .CUI file format were first introduced with AutoCAD 2006.

How Customizing the User Interface Has Changed

Users have been able to customize the user interface dating all the way back to AutoCAD R13 and even earlier versions. Since then, many additions, including toolbars and shortcut keys, have been made to the user interface, but one thing has always remained consistent: Customization was done via editing a plain text file with a text editor. That all changed with the introduction of AutoCAD 2006 and the .CUI file format.

If you are relatively new to AutoCAD, you might not know much about previous releases of the software. Those of you who have done some menu customization with AutoCAD 2005 and earlier versions are familiar with the file types .MNU, .MNS, .MNC, and .MNR. The .CUI file format replaced the .MNU, .MNS, and .MNC file formats.

Getting to Know the Customize User Interface Editor

The Customize User Interface (CUI) editor (see Figure 3-1) is a graphically based editor that allows you to customize many of the user interface elements, such as toolbars and pull-down menus. It is also designed to allow you to migrate and transfer existing menu customization into the latest release of AutoCAD. In the next few sections, we cover the different panes of the CUI editor, launching the CUI editor, and some of the basics involved with customizing the AutoCAD user interface. The CUI editor has three main panes: Customizations In pane, Command List pane, and Dynamic pane. The Dynamic pane covers the entire right side of the Customize tab of CUI editor and is the most active pane — it displays information and properties for the selected item in the Customizations In or Command List pane.

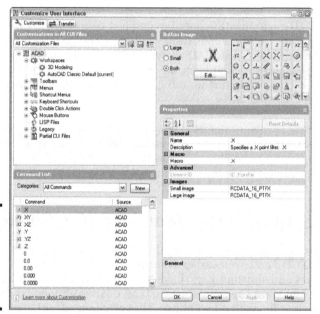

Figure 3-1:
The
Customize
User
Interface
(CUI) editor.

The Customizations In pane

In Customizations In pane (see Figure 3-2), you can access the user interface elements of any of the loaded customization files in the CUI editor. Two different base customization files can be loaded: *main* and *enterprise customization* files. The main and enterprise customization files can load additional menus known as *partial customization* files. Enterprise and partial customization files are designed to make managing and sharing customization files with multiple users easier. Each of the loaded customization files can contain any number and type of user interface elements, such as toolbars, pull-down menus, shortcut keys, and so on. The main and enterprise customization files can be specified under the Customization Files node of the Files tab in the Options dialog box. For more information on partial and enterprise customization files, see the section "Working with Partial and Enterprise Customization Files" later in this chapter.

Book IX
Chapter 3

Customizing
the Tools

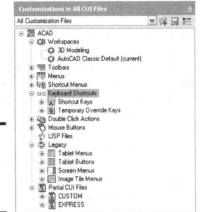

Figure 3-2:
The
Custom-
izations
In pane.

The top of the pane contains tools that allow you to open a customization file, load a partial customization file, save changes to all the current customization files, and control which user interface elements are displayed in the tree view for all the loaded customization files. The tree view under the Customizations In pane is where you create new user interface elements such as toolbars and pull-down menus. The tree view allows you to add commands to a user interface element and control the order in which they appear after the CUI editor is closed.

The Command List pane

The Command List pane (see Figure 3-3) is where you find all the commands that are used in the CUI file. This is one of the changes over previous releases of AutoCAD, and it is a good change. In previous releases, if you wanted to use the same command for a toolbar button, a pull-down menu item, and a shortcut key, you would duplicate that command macro three times. If you needed to make a change to the macro, you had to change it three separate times. In the .CUI file format, the command is maintained in a central location and is referenced by the toolbar, pull-down menu, and shortcut key. You only have to make the change once.

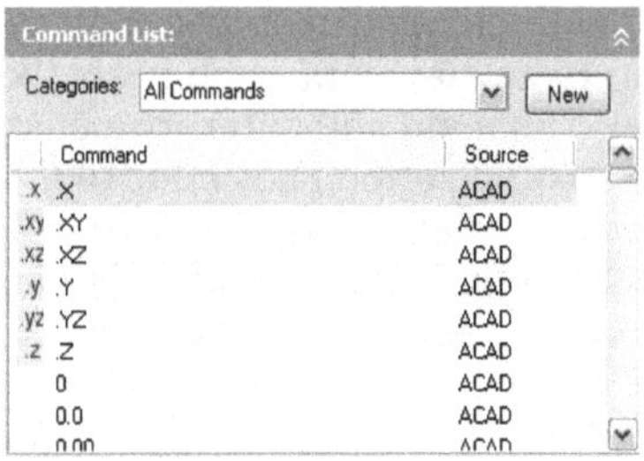

Figure 3-3:
The Command List pane.

The Command List pane is also where you go when you want to add a command onto a toolbar. To add the command to a toolbar, you drag it from the Command List pane and drop it onto the correct node under the Toolbars node. Along the top of the Command List pane is a drop-down list of categories that filter the commands displayed in the Command List pane.

The Dynamic pane

The Dynamic pane runs the entire right side of the CUI editor and reacts to what you select under the Customizations In and Command List panes. The Dynamic pane can display a number of different panes based on what is selected on the left side of the CUI editor. Here is an overview of each of the different panes that can be found under the Dynamic pane:

✦ **Information:** The Information pane provides an overview of what each top-level node does in the Customizations In pane. The Information pane is available only when a top-level node in the Customizations In pane is selected, or when one of the nodes under Keyboard Shortcuts or Legacy is selected.

✦ **Button Image:** The Button Image pane (see Figure 3-4) allows you to access and select one of the preloaded images for a button or create a new image. The Button Image pane is active when a command is selected below one of the nodes in the Customizations In pane or in the Command List pane.

Figure 3-4:
The Button Image pane.

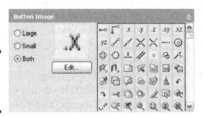

✦ **Preview:** The Preview pane allows you to get an idea of what a toolbar will look like before you close the CUI editor. The Preview pane is only available when a toolbar is selected under the Toolbars node of the Customizations In pane.

✦ **Properties:** The Properties pane (see Figure 3-5) allows you to adjust the properties of a selected item in the CUI editor. The properties that can be edited change based on the item selected in the Customizations In pane.

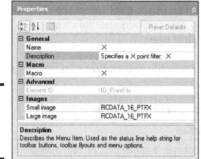

Figure 3-5:
The
Properties
pane.

✦ **Shortcuts:** The Shortcuts pane provides you with an overview of all the shortcut and temporary override keys that have been set up and also allows you to produce a hard copy of the keys or to copy the list to the Windows Clipboard.

✦ **Workspace Contents:** The Workspace Contents pane allows you to customize which toolbars, pull-down menus, and dockable windows should be displayed when the workspace is set current. The pane is also used to control the order of how the pull-down menus should appear on the menu bar.

Launching the Customize User Interface (CUI) editor

To launch the CUI editor, use one of these methods:

✦ **Tools menu:** Choose Tools⇨Customize⇨Interface.

✦ **Keyboard input:** Type **CUI** at the command line and press Enter.

✦ **Right-click the shortcut menu:** Right-click a toolbar and click Customize from the shortcut menu that appears.

Commands in the CUI editor

Commands in the CUI editor are not the same as an AutoCAD command like LINE. A command in the CUI editor can be made up of AutoCAD commands and options and AutoLISP expressions. After a command is created, it can be used in most of the user interface elements supported in the CUI editor.

Understanding a command macro

The core of a command in the CUI editor is its macro property. The macro is what is carried out when the command is selected from a toolbar button, pull-down menu item, or one of the other user interface elements that is referencing the command. Macros can contain special characters that are normally not allowed at the command line.

Table 3-1 lists the common special characters that can be part of a macro.

Table 3-1	Special Characters for a Macro
Special Character	*Description*
; or [blank space]	A semicolon or a space acts like the user pressed the Enter key.
\	A backslash pauses for user input.
_	An underscore translates the command or option so it can be used in an international version.
*	An asterisk repeats the command until Escape is pressed.
^C	Acts like the Escape key was pressed a single time.
\ \	Double backslashes allow for the use of the backslash in a macro.
.	A period forces AutoCAD to use the standard AutoCAD command even if the command was undefined or redefined as something else.

An example of a macro is

```
^C^C._line;\\\_c
```

The above macro starts the LINE command and allows the user to select a total of three points and then closes the object.

✦ `^c^c`: Issues two different cancels to exit any running command.

✦ `._line`: Starts the LINE command.

✦ `;`: Issues an Enter to start the LINE command.

+ \ \ \: Requests the user for three different pieces of input. In this case, the input is in the form of points in the drawing.

+ _c: Uses the Close option for the LINE command to draw a line between the first and last points.

Creating a new command

Follow these steps to create a new command in the CUI editor:

1. **From the menu bar, choose Tools⇨Customize⇨Interface.**

The CUI editor is displayed.

2. **Click the New button in the Command List pane.**

A new command named *Command1* is added to the list box by default, and the Button Image and Properties panes are displayed. If the name already exists, the next number in the sequence is used in the name.

3. **In the Properties pane, change the command's Name, Macro, and Element ID.**

The Name is used to locate the command in the list under the Command List pane; the Macro defines what happens when the command is selected from the user interface; and the Element ID is used to uniquely identify the command through automation or when migrating the command between releases. For information on these and other properties, take a look at the description provided at the bottom of the Properties pane.

4. **Click Apply to stay in the CUI editor and save the changes, or click OK to exit the CUI editor and save the changes.**

The changes are saved to the file.

Assigning an image to a command

Assigning a small and large image to a command is optional. However, if you plan on using the command on a toolbar or pull-down menu, you might want to add images to it so that it matches many of the commands that come with AutoCAD. Follow these procedures to assign an image to a command:

1. **From the menu bar, choose Tools⇨Customize⇨Interface.**

The CUI editor is displayed.

2. **Select a command from the list under the Command List pane.**

The command is highlighted and its properties are displayed in the Properties pane.

3. **In the Button Image pane, select either the Large, Small, or Both option. Then, click one of the images from the list.**

Based on the size option that you select, the value is populated in the Small and/or Large Image properties for the command. Optionally, you can also edit an existing image to create a new image for your command using the Edit button. If you have an image that you created in a separate program or one that already exists from a previous release, you can select the Small or Large Image fields under the Properties pane and then click the ellipsis button that is displayed (see Figure 3-6).

Figure 3-6: Browsing for a custom image.

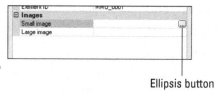

Ellipsis button

4. **Click Apply to stay in the CUI editor and save the changes, or click OK to exit the CUI editor and save the changes.**

   The changes are saved to the file.

Assigning a help string to a command

Assigning a help string to a command is optional. However, a help string can give the users of the custom command a brief description of the command before they select it. Help strings appear in the status bar when the cursor is hovering over a command on a toolbar, pull-down menu, or shortcut menu.

Even though user interface elements like toolbars and pull-down menus have a description property that is never displayed to the user, so you can use it to track changes or revision information. Follow these procedures to assign a help string to a command:

1. **From the menu bar, choose Tools⇨Customize⇨Interface.**

   The CUI editor is displayed.

2. **Select a command from the list under the Command List pane.**

   The command should be highlighted and its properties are displayed in the Properties pane.

3. **In the Properties pane, enter the help string value in the Description field.**

4. **Click Apply to stay in the CUI editor and save the changes, or click OK to exit the CUI editor and save the changes.**

   The changes are saved to the file.

Customizing Toolbars and Pull-Down and Shortcut Menus

Because AutoCAD is a Windows-based application, it utilizes toolbars, pull-downs, and shortcut menus as part of its user interface. These are by far the most widely used UI elements in AutoCAD: They provide access to a majority of the drafting and editing commands.

Toolbars

Toolbars are small windows that can be docked along the edges of the application window or undocked *(floating)*. They allow you to quickly access commands and options through buttons, drop-down lists, and flyouts. A *flyout* is a way to access the commands that are contained on another toolbar through a single button. They help keep the user interface looking cleaner than if the whole toolbar was visible.

Creating a new toolbar

Follow these steps to create a new toolbar:

1. **From the menu bar, choose Tools⇨Customize⇨Interface.**

   The CUI editor is displayed.

2. **In the Customizations In pane, right-click the Toolbars node and choose New⇨Toolbar.**

   A new toolbar with the default name *Toolbar1* is created under the Toolbars node.

3. **In the Properties pane, change the toolbar's Name and Alias.**

   The Name is used to locate the toolbar and is the value that is displayed in its caption toolbar; Alias is used to uniquely identify the toolbar through automation or when migrating the toolbar between releases. You can also change the properties under the Appearance section to control how the toolbar is initially displayed.

4. **In the Command List pane, select the command that you want to add to the toolbar. Hold down the mouse button after selecting the command and drag it up to the new toolbar under the Toolbars node of the Customizations In pane. Release the mouse button when the cursor is over the toolbar to add the command (see Figure 3-7).**

   A reference to the command is added under the toolbar.

   To select more than one command at a time to assign to a toolbar, hold down the Shift or Ctrl key while selecting commands.

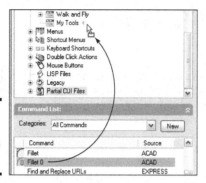

Figure 3-7:
Adding a
command to
a toolbar.

5. **Click Apply to stay in the CUI editor and save the changes, or click OK to exit the CUI editor and save the changes.**

   The changes are saved to a file.

   When adding a new user interface element such as a toolbar or pull-down menu, make sure to add a command to it before clicking Apply. Otherwise, the user interface element will not be saved to file.

Creating a new flyout

Follow these steps to create a flyout on a toolbar:

1. **From the menu bar, choose Tools⇨Customize⇨Interface.**

   The CUI editor is displayed.

2. **Create a new toolbar and change its Name and Alias in the Properties pane.**

   A new toolbar is created under the Toolbars node, and the Name and Alias properties are updated based on the provided values.

3. **Click and drag the new toolbar above or below one of the commands on the toolbar that you want to create the flyout on.**

   A new reference to the toolbar is created on the toolbar (see Figure 3-8).

Figure 3-8:
Adding a
flyout to a
toolbar.

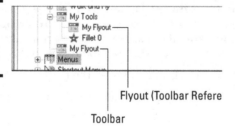

4. **Add commands to the new toolbar or flyout.**

The new commands are displayed under the toolbar and flyout.

5. **Click Apply to stay in the CUI editor and save the changes, or click OK to exit the CUI editor and save the changes.**

The changes are saved out to file.

You can also right-click a toolbar and choose New➪Flyout to create a new toolbar and add the flyout reference to a toolbar. This method does introduce at least one additional step: When you rename the toolbar, the name of the flyout does not change automatically to match the toolbar name, so you will have to rename the flyout manually.

Commands and flyouts can be rearranged by dragging then up and down under their associated toolbar node.

Pull-down menus

Pull-down menus take up much less space than toolbars and contain a much wider selection of commands when compared to toolbars. Pull-down menus might not be as efficient as toolbars are, but they do offer a much greater set of organization. Similar to flyouts on a toolbar, pull-down menus support submenus. Submenus are different than flyouts because they are part of the pull-down menu and do not rely on another pull-down menu for their content.

Creating a new pull-down menu

Follow this procedure to create a new pull-down menu:

1. **From the menu bar, choose Tools➪Customize➪Interface.**

The CUI editor is displayed.

2. **In the Customizations In pane, right-click the Menus node and choose New➪Menu.**

A new pull-down menu with the default name *Menu1* is created under the Menus node.

3. **In the Properties pane, change the pull-down menu's Name and Alias.**

The Name is used to locate the pull-down menu and is the value that is displayed as the caption in the menu bar; and Alias is used to uniquely identify the pull-down menu through automation or when migrating the pull-down menu between releases.

4. **Add any of the commands from the Command List pane that you want to be displayed under the pull-down menu.**

5. **Click Apply to stay in the CUI editor and save the new command, or click OK to exit the CUI editor and save the new command.**

   The changes are saved to file.

Creating a new submenu

Follow these steps to create a submenu on a pull-down menu:

1. **From the menu bar, choose Tools⇨Customize⇨Interface.**

   The CUI editor is displayed.

2. **In the Customizations In pane, click the plus sign next to the Menus node.**

   The pull-down menus are displayed under the Menus node.

3. **Right-click over the pull-down menu that you want to add a submenu to and choose New⇨Sub-Menu.**

   A new submenu is added under the pull-down menu.

4. **In the Properties pane, change the submenu's Name.**

   The name of the submenu is displayed under the pull-down menu.

5. **Add any of the commands from the Command List pane that you want to be displayed under the submenu.**

6. **Click Apply to stay in the CUI editor and save the changes, or click OK to exit the CUI editor and save the changes.**

   The changes are saved out to file.

Commands and submenus can be rearranged by dragging them up and down under their associated pull-down menu or submenu node.

Using special characters in a pull-down item name

Pull-down menu item names can contain special characters to control some of the behavior of the item. Table 3-2 lists some of the special characters that can be used in combination with a pull-down menu item name.

Table 3-2	Special Characters for a Pull-Down Item Name
Special Character	*Description*
&	An ampersand displays an underscore under the character that follows the ampersand. This allows users to access the pull-down menus by pressing the ALT modifier key plus the character that is underlined.

Special Character	Description
&&	Two ampersands together display an ampersand.
~	A tilde disables the menu item, making it not selectable.
!c or !.	The character combination !c and !. puts a check mark in front of the pull-down menu item.
\t (or tab character)	Forces the text to the right side of the pull-down menu. This is often used to display the command alias for a command in the pull-down menu.

Here's an example of using a special character in the pull-down menu:

```
Save &As...
```

The A is the access key from the keyboard. To access the Save As command, press Alt+F to open the Files pull-down menu, and then press Alt+A.

Shortcut menus

Shortcut menus are used to display additional options specific to the selected object(s) or the active command or the current state of AutoCAD. Shortcut menus are displayed by pressing the right mouse button over the drawing window and based on the current value of the system variable SHORTCUTMENU. By default, the system variable SHORTCUTMENU is set to a value of 11, which indicates to AutoCAD that it should display shortcut menus when options are available for the active command, when no command is active and objects are selected, or when no command is active and no objects are selected.

Shortcut menus are created much like pull-down menus with one main exception: their aliases. Most shortcut menus are set up to work specifically with a specific command or object(s). To designate a shortcut menu to be used with a command, you use the alias syntax of COMMAND_*commandname*. An example of an Alias used to assign additional options to the LINE command's right-click menu is COMMAND_LINE. The alias is assigned to the Aliases property of the shortcut menu under the Properties pane of the Dynamic pane.

Shortcut menus can be associated to a specific object type, and when a single object of the designated object type is selected in the drawing window and the right mouse button is pressed, additional options are displayed on the right-click menu. To designate a shortcut menu to be used when an object of a certain type is selected, you use the alias syntax of OBJECT_ *objectname*. Just like the alias for a command based shortcut menu, the alias is assigned to the Aliases property of the shortcut menu. AutoCAD comes with many different shortcut menus. One example is the Hatch Object

Menu, which uses the alias OBJECT_HATCH to display the Hatch Edit option on the right-click menu when a hatch object is selected in the drawing before you press the right mouse button.

To identify the object name for an object, you can use the LIST command on the object. The LIST command displays the object name in the AutoCAD Text Window. This sample shows the results of the LIST command in the AutoCAD Text Window after a line was selected:

```
      LINE        Layer: "0"
                  Space: Model space
           Handle = 93
    from point, X=  14.5169  Y=   7.9505  Z=   0.0000
      to point, X=  27.3742  Y=  15.9583  Z=   0.0000
Length =  15.1471,   Angle in XY Plane =       32
  Delta X =  12.8573, Delta Y =    8.0077, Delta Z =   0.0000
```

The object name is listed in the top-left of the returned values; in this case, LINE. An example of an Alias used to assign additional options to the Edit shortcut menu when a line object is selected is OBJECT_LINE. If you want to display a shortcut menu when more than one object of a specific object type is selected, you use the alias syntax of OBJECTS_*objectname*.

In some instances, the object name is not used, and that is because the LIST command returns the same object name for the different insert objects.

Table 3-3 lists the names to be used for blocks and external reference (Xref) objects.

Table 3-3	Special Object Names Used for Blocks and Xrefs
Object Name	*Description*
BLOCKREF	Block without attributes
ATTBLOCKREF	Block with attributes
DYNBLOCKREF	Dynamic block without attributes
ATTDYNBLOCKREF	Dynamic block with attributes
XREF	External reference

Follow these procedures to create a shortcut menu.

1. **From the menu bar, choose Tools⇨Customize⇨Interface.**

   The CUI editor is displayed.

2. **In the Customizations In pane, right-click the Shortcut Menus node and choose New⇨Shortcut Menu.**

A new shortcut menu with the default name *ShortcutMenu1* is created under the Shortcut Menus node.

3. **In the Properties pane, change the shortcut menu's Name.**

   The Name is used to locate the shortcut menu.

4. **In the Properties pane, change the shortcut menu's Aliases. To do this, click in the Aliases field and then click the button on the right side of the field.**

   The Aliases dialog box is displayed (see Figure 3-9).

Figure 3-9:
The Aliases
dialog box.

5. **In the Aliases dialog box, position the cursor behind the last alias in the list box and click. Press Enter to start a new line.**

   A new line is started for the new alias.

6. **Enter the new alias to display additional options during an edit operation or a command.**

   Aliases are used to uniquely identify the shortcut menu through automation or when migrating the shortcut menu between releases. Aliases are used to determine the associated operation: edit or command.

7. **Click OK to exit the Aliases dialog box.**

   The aliases that were in the Aliases dialog box are added to the Aliases property.

8. **Add any of the commands from the Command List pane that you want to be displayed under the shortcut menu.**

9. **Click Apply to stay in the CUI editor and save the changes, or click OK to exit the CUI editor and save the changes.**

   The changes are saved out to file.

Separator bars

Separator bars are used to organize and group commands together on a tool-bar, pull-down menu, or shortcut menu. Separator bars can be inserted by right-clicking over a toolbar, pull-down menu, or shortcut menu and selecting Insert Separator. A separator bar is displayed as a horizontal or vertical line in the user interface, and as a short dash in the CUI editor.

Creating a New Shortcut Key

Shortcut keys allow you to access commands by using a keyboard combination that includes at least one modifier key and another key on the keyboard. Shortcut keys must use the Ctrl modifier key, but the Ctrl key can also be combined with the Shift or Alt key.

Follow these procedures to create a shortcut key:

1. **From the menu bar, choose Tools⇨Customize⇨Interface.**

The CUI editor is displayed.

2. **In the Customizations In pane, click the plus sign next to the Keyboard Shortcuts node.**

The Keyboard Shortcuts node is expanded and displays two additional categories: Shortcut Keys and Temporary Overrides.

3. **In the Command List pane, select the command that you want to add to create a shortcut key for. Hold down the mouse button after selecting the command and drag it up to the Shortcut Keys node of the Customizations In pane. Release the mouse button when the cursor is over the node to add the command.**

A new shortcut key is created based on the command dropped onto the node.

4. **In the Properties pane, select the Key(s) field and click the button that appears on the right side of the field.**

The Shortcut Keys dialog box is displayed (see Figure 3-10).

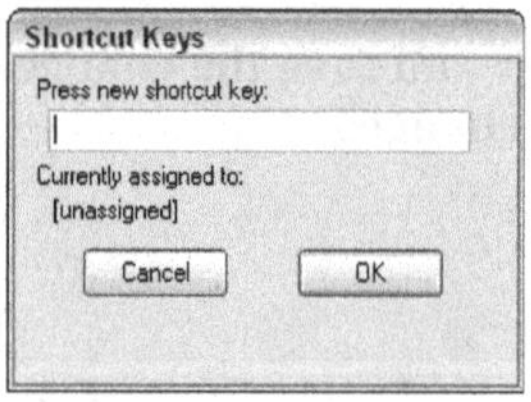

Figure 3-10: The Shortcut Keys dialog box.

5. **In the Shortcut Keys dialog box, click in the Press New Shortcut Key text field.**

   The focus is set to the Press New Shortcut Key text field.

6. **Press and hold down the CTRL key while pressing the other modifier key or the other key from the keyboard.**

   The key combination appears in the field. If the combination is already assigned to a different command, the other assignment is listed below the Press New Shortcut Key text field.

7. **Click Assign to assign the key combination and click OK to exit the Shortcut Keys dialog box.**

   The Shortcut Keys dialog box is closed and the key combination is placed in the Key(s) property field.

8. **Click Apply to stay in the CUI editor and save the changes, or click OK to exit the CUI editor and save the changes.**

   The changes are saved out to file.

Customizing Double-Click Actions

Double-click actions control what happens when you double-click an object in the drawing window. Double-clicking objects in the drawing allows you to quickly access a default edit command that is set up by object name like shortcut menus are. Double-click actions require the use of an object name to identify which command should be run when a user double-clicks an object in the drawing window.

The object name is the value listed by the LIST command or for special object names used for blocks and Xref objects. For information on the special object names used for blocks and Xrefs, see the section "Shortcut menus" and Table 3-3 earlier in this chapter.

AutoCAD has supported double-click editing since AutoCAD 2000i, but with the new release, you can customize which command is executed when an object is double-clicked in the drawing window.

Follow the procedures below to create a double-click action.

1. **From the menu bar, choose Tools⇨Customize⇨Interface.**

   The CUI editor is displayed.

2. **In the Customizations In pane, right-click the Double-Click Actions node and choose New⇨Double-Click Action.**

A new double-click action with the default name *DoubleClick1* is created under the Double-Click Actions node.

3. **In the Properties pane, change the double-click action's Name.**

The Name is used to locate the double-click action.

4. **Enter the object name that the double-click action should be associated with in the Object Name property field.**

The Object Name is used to identify which double-click action should be fired off when a user double-clicks an object in the drawing window.

5. **In the Command List pane, select the command that you want to associate with the double-click action. Hold down the mouse button after selecting the command and drag it up to the new double-click action in the Customizations In pane. Release the mouse button when the cursor is over the node to add the command.**

The command is now associated with the double-click action and the specified object name.

6. **Click Apply to stay in the CUI editor and save the changes, or click OK to exit the CUI editor and save the changes.**

The changes are saved out to file.

Migrating and Transferring Customization

Upgrading to a new version of AutoCAD has always been a somewhat time-consuming problem with all of the customization and settings that need to be updated for a new release. Since AutoCAD 2005, AutoCAD has offered a utility called Migrate Custom Settings, which allows you to easily migrate a majority of your custom settings to a new release.

The utility migrates only settings, profiles, and customization located in specific support files but doesn't do anything with menu customization. To resolve part of this problem, the CUI editor was designed with a Transfer tab. The Transfer tab allows you to migrate custom toolbars, pull-down menus, and other user interface elements to the new release.

Transferring customizations has always been a manual process: opening two customization files with a text editor, and then copying and pasting sections between the two files. The problem is that the approach of copying and pasting between two files can result in missing information or a file structure problem. The CUI editor resolves this problem by migrating your menu customization files forward to the .CUI file format and allowing you to move user elements by dragging and dropping right in the editor.

Follow this procedure below to transfer customization from one customization file to another and to migrate customization from a legacy .MNU or .MNS file format:

1. **From the menu bar, choose Tools➪Customize➪Interface.**

The CUI editor is displayed.

2. **Click the Transfer tab along the top of the CUI editor.**

A second Customizations In pane is displayed on the right side of the CUI editor (see Figure 3-11).

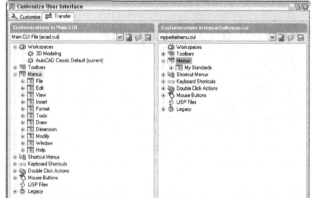

Figure 3-11:
The Transfer tab of the CUI editor.

3. **In the Customizations In pane on the right side, click the Open Customization File button.**

The Open dialog box is displayed, allowing to you select a customization file (.CUI) or a menu file (.MNU/.MNS).

4. **Select the type of file you want to open by choosing one of the options from the Files of Type drop-down list and browsing for the file you want to open.**

The selected file's name appears in the File Name text field.

5. **Click Open.**

The selected file is opened and displayed in the Customizations In pane. If a .MNU/.MNS file is selected, a .CUI file is automatically generated.

6. **Expand the nodes of the two files and then drag and drop the user interface elements from the pane on the right to the one on the left.**

The user interface elements are added in the file, along with any commands that are associated with the elements.

The Legacy node contains tablets, image tile menus, and screen menu customization. If you have customized any of these sections in previous releases, don't forget to transfer these elements too.

7. **Switch back to the Customize tab and make any necessary changes to the transferred user interface elements.**

   You may need to add additional commands or even update workspaces to include or exclude toolbars and pull-down menus.

8. **Click Apply to stay in the CUI editor and save the changes, or click OK to exit the CUI editor and save the changes.**

   The changes are saved out to file.

Working with Partial and Enterprise Customization Files

Partial and enterprise customization files are ways of organizing and sharing customization between users. Whether you work in a large or small company, you can use an enterprise customization file to share standard company tools with all the members of your drafting teams. You might use tools in an enterprise customization file to ensure layer and annotation standards, along with accessing company title blocks.

A partial customization file can contain a subset of customization when compared to the main customization file. The customization in the partial customization file is usually personal or task-based customization. You might use different partial customization files for different disciplines like Civil or Architectural.

Loading an enterprise customization file

Follow the procedures below to load an enterprise customization file.

1. **From the menu bar, choose Tools⇨Options.**

   The Options dialog box is displayed.

2. **Click the Files tab, and click the plus sign next to the Customization Files node.**

   The Customization Files node expands and shows some additional nodes: Main Customization Files, Enterprise Customization File, and Custom Icon Location.

3. **Click the plus sign next to the Enterprise Customization File node.**

The Enterprise Customization File node expands and shows the current value; by default, the value is a period (.).

4. **Select the current value and click Browse.**

The Select a File dialog box is displayed.

5. **Browse to the location of the customization (.CUI) file that you want to use for the enterprise customization file. Select the file and click Open.**

The location of the selected file is added under the Enterprise Customization File node.

6. **Click Apply to stay in the Options dialog box and save the change, or click OK to exit the Options dialog box and save the change.**

The change is saved to the Windows Registry.

Loading a partial customization file

Follow the procedures below to load a partial customization file.

1. **From the menu bar, choose Tools⇨Customize⇨Interface.**

The CUI editor is displayed.

2. **Click the Customize tab to make it current, and click Load Partial Customization File under the Customizations In pane.**

The Open dialog box is displayed.

3. **Browse to the location of the customization (CUI) file that you want to load as a partial customization file. Select the file and click Open.**

The selected file is loaded as a partial customization file and is added to the Partial CUI Files node.

4. **In the Warning box that appears, click OK.**

The Warning box notifies you that any workspaces contained in the partial customization file won't be available for use. The partial customization file is displayed in the Customizations In pane.

5. **Select All Customization Files from the drop-down list at the top of the Customizations In pane to show all the loaded customization files.**

The tree view in the Customizations In pane returns to its default display state.

6. **Click Apply to stay in the CUI editor and save the changes, or click OK to exit the CUI editor and save the changes.**

The changes are saved out to file.

Chapter 4: Delving Deeper into Customization

In This Chapter

✔ **Working from a script**

✔ **It's all in the linetype**

✔ **Getting familiar with shapes**

✔ **Creating custom patterns**

✔ **Getting to know the Express Tools**

Many aspects of customizing AutoCAD are left untapped by most users. Much of this is due to the many ways AutoCAD can be customized beyond just the user interface and appearance of the application window. Special file types and formats are used to automate tasks in AutoCAD and also to define custom linetypes and hatch patterns.

AutoCAD allows you to create script files that can be used to automate repetitive tasks through standard AutoCAD commands and options. Although AutoCAD comes with a variety of linetypes and hatch patterns, they don't always cover everything that you might want to represent in your drawing. AutoCAD allows you to define your own custom linetypes and hatch patterns. All three of these customization options can be done with a text editor because they are plain text files. Unlike with customization files, you don't need to use a special editor for these options.

Working from a Script

Have you ever received a set of drawings from a client that didn't use the same drafting settings or conform to the CAD standards that you use? Or maybe you have had to manually update older drawings to match your company's new CAD standards? Script files can be used for these tasks and much more.

What is a script file?

A script file is used to automate functionality in AutoCAD using standard AutoCAD commands, options, and AutoLISP expressions. (AutoLISP expressions are not supported by AutoCAD LT, however.) A *script file* is a plain text file that contains commands and options in a specific format and has the file extension of .SCR. The structure of a script is very similar to the way AutoCAD commands and options are entered at the command line. Here is an example of a script file that does some basic drawing setup and demonstrates how to use comments in a script file:

```
; Created 11/13/05 by Lee Ambrosius
LTSCALE 24
BLIPMODE 0
LIMITS 0,0 24,17
ZOOM EXTENTS
```

The opening line of the example is a comment that is ignored during the execution of the script. Comments don't execute, but they can contain very important information that comes in handy when updates are made to the script file, for example. Comment lines begin with a semicolon, so AutoCAD ignores everything to the right of a semicolon.

The second line, LTSCALE 24, sets the linetype scale system variable to a value of 24. The space between LTSCALE and the value 24 is just like pressing the Enter key while entering values at the command line or dynamic input tooltip. AutoCAD automatically issues an Enter for each new line as the script is being evaluated.

The next line, BLIPMODE 0, turns blip markers off. The next line, LIMITS 0,0 24,17, is used to set the lower-left and upper-right drawing limits. The last line, ZOOM EXTENTS, is used to make sure the drawing is zoomed to its limits. At the end of the script file, make sure that there is a single blank line to let AutoCAD know when the script file ends.

Alternatively, commands and options can be on separate lines or on the same line; neither method is right nor wrong, but rather a preference. The following example shows the same script as previously shown with commands and options on separate lines.

```
;; Created 11/13/05 by Lee Ambrosius
LTSCALE
24
BLIPMODE
0
LIMITS
0,0
24,17
ZOOM
EXTENTS
```

Using script files can offer both disadvantages and advantages. Here are some of the disadvantages:

✦ There is no way to pause for user input during a command.

✦ Dialog boxes can't be called during the execution of the script.

✦ Only a single script can be running in AutoCAD at a single time. You can't call another script while a script is running.

✦ AutoCAD does not ship with any sample scripts, which can make it difficult to get started creating your own scripts.

Here are some of the advantages:

✦ The syntax is very basic and can be created by anyone who can use commands in AutoCAD.

✦ Scripting is great for automating very basic and repetitive tasks.

✦ Scripts require very minimal maintenance from release to release.

✦ Scripts can be used transparently with AutoCAD commands.

✦ Some commands bypass the use of dialog boxes. These commands are typically prefixed with a hyphen. For example, the –LAYER is the command line version of the LAYER.

✦ AutoLISP expressions can be used in a script (if you're not using AutoCAD LT and know how to use AutoLISP). Using AutoLISP with your scripts allows you to build much more complex and robust scripts.

Here are some commands specifically used for working with script files:

✦ **RSCRIPT:** Repeats the last run script file.

✦ **RESUME:** Continues a script that has been paused by the user pressing the Backspace key during the execution of the script.

✦ **DELAY:** Pauses a script for the specified duration. The time duration is specified in milliseconds. One thousand milliseconds is equal to 1 second, and the maximum delay is a value of 32,767, which is equal to just a little longer than 32 seconds.

✦ **SCRIPT:** Loads and runs a script file through a standard file select dialog box.

✦ **-SCRIPT:** Loads and runs a script file from the command line.

Creating a script file

Because script files are plain text files, they can be created and edited with an application such as Notepad. Follow these procedures to create a new script file using Notepad:

1. **Choose Start⇨[All] Programs⇨Accessories⇨Notepad.**

   Notepad is launched and a blank document is created.

2. **From the menu bar in Notepad, choose File⇨Save As.**

   The Save As dialog box is displayed.

3. **In the Save As dialog box, enter a name for the script file and make sure that .SCR is added to the filename in the File Name text field.**

4. **Browse to the location where you want to save the script file and click Save.**

   The script file is created in the specified location.

5. **Enter the AutoCAD commands and options in Notepad that you want to execute when the script file is run.**

   Don't forget that each command and option must be followed by a space, unless it is the last command or option on the line.

   The text area of Notepad should contain the commands and options that you want to use in the script file.

6. **From the menu bar in Notepad, choose File⇨Save.**

   The contents of the Notepad document are saved to the script file.

Loading and running a script file

Use one of these methods to load and run a script file:

✦ **Tools menu:** Choose Tools⇨Run Script.

✦ **Keyboard input:** Type SCRIPT at the command line and press Enter.

✦ **Command alias:** Type SCR at the command line and press Enter.

These steps describe how to load and run a script file.

1. **Use any of the three methods just listed to initiate the DIMLINEAR command.**

   The Select Script File dialog box is displayed.

2. **In the Select Script File dialog box, browse to the location where the
script file is stored and select it. After the script file has been selected,
click Open.**

The selected script file is executed in AutoCAD.

You can also drag and drop a script file from Windows Explorer onto a
drawing window to load and run the script in that drawing file.

Running a script file at startup

You can load and run a script file using one of the command line switches
with a desktop shortcut. The /b switch is the command line switch that allows
you to load and run a script at startup. This can be a great way to make sure
that session-specific drafting settings are configured when AutoCAD is first
launched. Below is an example target path using the /b switch with a script file:

```
"C:\Program Files\AutoCAD 200X\acad.exe" /b Startup
```

The preceding example starts AutoCAD with a script file named Startup. The
script file in this example must exist in the support search paths of AutoCAD.
You can also specify the absolute path for the script file. See Chapter 1 in this
minibook for more information about command line switches.

It's All in the Linetype

Linetypes are repeating patterns used to help convey design ideas. Whether
the drawings you create are architectural or mechanical, you most likely use
more than one linetype in a drawing. Linetypes come in two different classifi-
cations: simple and complex. Complex linetypes are the same as simple linetypes with additional support for shapes and text strings.

Linetype files are plain text files that can be edited with a text editor and
have the file extension .LIN. AutoCAD ships with two different linetype
files, Acad.LIN (Acadlt.LIN) and Acadiso.LIN (Acadltiso.LIN). The Acad.LIN
(Acadlt.LIN) file is used for imperial unit drawings, whereas Acadiso.LIN
(Acadltiso.LIN) is used for metric-based drawings. A linetype pattern is
defined using two different lines in the .LIN files.

The first line of a linetype file contains the Name and Description line; the
second is the descriptor line that tells AutoCAD how to create the pattern.
Linetype files also support the use of comments to help keep track of when
changes were last made. Comments are defined with a semicolon, so
AutoCAD ignores everything to the right of the semicolon. A section of the
Acad.LIN file that ships with AutoCAD appears next:

```
;;   Note: in order to ease migration of this file when
     upgrading
;;   to a future version of AutoCAD, it is recommended that
     you add
;;   your customizations to the User Defined Linetypes section
     at the
;;   end of this file.
;;
*BORDER,Border __ __ . __ __ . __ __ . __ __ . __ __ .
A,.5,-.25,.5,-.25,0,-.25
```

The system variable PSLTSCALE determines how linetype patterns appear when objects are displayed through a viewport. If the system variable PSLTSCALE is set to a value of 0, the linetype scale is determined by the system variable LTSCALE. However, if the system variable is set to a value of 1, linetype scaling is controlled by the scale factor of the viewport. See Book I, Chapter 5 for more information about linetype scale.

A utility that allows you to make a linetype out of geometry in a drawing is a part of Express Tools (which comes with AutoCAD, but not AutoCAD LT). This utility is great for getting started with creating your own linetypes. The utility can be found on the menu bar under Express⇨Tools⇨Make Linetype.

Simple linetypes

Simple linetypes are made up of only dashes, dots, and spaces and are the most commonly used linetypes. Examples of simple linetypes are CENTER (___ _ ___ _ ___) and HIDDENX2 (___ ___ ___).

Simple linetype structure

The best way to understand how a simple linetype is created is to take a look at one of the linetypes that comes with AutoCAD. One of the most commonly used linetypes is CENTER:

```
*CENTER,Center ____ _ ____ _ ____ _ ____ _ ____ _ ___
A,1.25,-.25,.25,-.25
```

Line 1 of the CENTER linetype's definition:

+ ***:** Designates the start of the linetype.

+ **CENTER,:** The name of the linetype pattern. This name must be unique in the file; otherwise, AutoCAD uses only the first linetype with the name in the file and ignores all other instances. A comma is used to separate the name of the linetype from its description.

✦ ____ _ ____: The description of the linetype pattern. The description is displayed in the Linetype Manager, Layer Properties Manager, Properties Palette, Properties toolbar, and other places in the application. The description is optional and can only be a maximum of 47 characters in length.

Line 2 of the CENTER linetype's definition:

✦ **A,:** The alignment flag is used to force AutoCAD to start and end the linetype with a dash instead of a space or dot. A comma is used to separate each data element.

✦ **1.25,:** The length of a dash when LTSCALE is equal to 1. Dashes are represented by a positive value.

✦ **-.25,:** The length of a space when LTSCALE is equal to 1. Spaces are represented by a negative value.

✦ **.25,:** The length of a dash.

✦ **-.25,:** The length of a space.

One of the other elements that is part of a simple linetype is a dot, which is presented by a value of 0 in a linetype pattern. You should place a gap on the left and right side of a dot so it stands out in the linetype pattern.

Creating a simple linetype

Because linetype files are plain text files, they can be created and edited with an application such as Notepad. Follow these steps to create a new simple linetype:

1. **Choose Start⇨[All] Programs⇨Accessories⇨Notepad.**

Notepad is launched and a blank document is created.

2. **From the menu bar in Notepad, choose File⇨Open.**

The Open dialog box is displayed.

3. **In the Open dialog box, select All Files from the Save As Type drop-down list.**

You should be able to see all file types and not just those with the extension .TXT.

4. **Browse to the location of Acad.LIN (Acadlt.LIN) and select the file, and then click Open.**

Acad.LIN (or Acadlt.LIN) should open into Notepad. By default, Acad.LIN can be found in the folder C:\Documents and Settings*<user name>*\ Application Data\Autodesk\AutoCAD 2007\R17.0\enu\Support.

If you are using AutoCAD LT, Acadlt.LIN can be found in the folder C:\ Documents and Settings*<user name>*\Application Data\Autodesk\ AutoCAD LT 2007\R12\enu\Support.

5. **Scroll all the way to the bottom of the linetype file and position the cursor on the very last blank line in the file.**

   Above the last couple of blank lines, you should see a set of comments that begins with the comment `;; User Defined Linetypes.`

6. **Enter the new linetype pattern.**

   The linetype pattern file should now include the name and description for the linetype on one line and a descriptor on the next line.

7. **From the menu bar in Notepad, choose File⇨Save.**

   The updated contents of the linetype file are saved to file.

8. **Load and use the linetype just as you would any other linetype that comes with AutoCAD.**

   The linetype works just like any of the linetypes that come with AutoCAD.

Using a custom linetype file

Adding custom linetypes to one of the linetype files that comes with AutoCAD is the easiest way to go, but at times, you might want to keep your custom linetypes in a separate file. Follow these procedures to load a linetype from a custom linetype file:

1. **From the menu bar, choose Format⇨Linetype.**

   The Linetype Manager dialog box is displayed.

2. **In the Linetype Manager dialog box, click Load.**

   The Load or Reload Linetypes dialog box is displayed.

3. **In the Load or Reload Linetypes dialog box, click File.**

   The Select Linetype File dialog box is displayed.

4. **In the Select Linetype File dialog box, browse to the location of the custom linetype file and select it. Click Open.**

   The Select Linetype File dialog box closes and the linetypes are displayed in the list box.

5. **In the Load or Reload Linetypes dialog box, select the linetypes that you want to use in the drawing and click OK.**

The selected linetypes are loaded into the current drawing and are ready for use. You are returned to the Linetype Manager dialog box.

6. **In the Linetype Manager dialog box, click OK.**

The Linetype Manager dialog box is closed.

Complex linetypes

Complex linetypes are made up of dashes, dots, and spaces, along with text strings or shapes. Examples of complex linetypes are TRACKS (Tracks -|-|-|-) and HOT_WATER_SUPPLY (Hot water supply - - HW - -).

The best way to understand how a complex linetype is created is to take a look at one of the linetypes that comes with AutoCAD. Complex linetypes are not as common as simple linetypes, but one that is commonly used is HOT_WATER_SUPPLY, which is a linetype with a text string in it:

```
*HOT_WATER_SUPPLY,Hot water supply ---- HW ---- HW ---- HW ----
A,.5,-.2,["HW",STANDARD,S=.1,R=0.0,X=-0.1,Y=-.05],-.2
```

Line 1 of the HOT_WATER_SUPPLY linetype's definition:

✦ ***** : Designates the start of the linetype.

✦ **HOT_WATER_SUPPLY,:** The name of the linetype pattern.

✦ **Hot water supply - - HW - -:** The description of the linetype pattern.

Line 2 of the HOT_WATER_SUPPLY linetype's definition:

✦ **A,:** The alignment flag.

✦ **.5,:** The length of a dash.

✦ **-.2,:** The length of a space.

✦ **[ ],:** Designates the beginning and end of complex data in the linetype.

✦ **"HW",:** Text string that is displayed in the linetype.

✦ **STANDARD,:** Text style that should be used to format the text string. If the text style is missing when the linetype is used, the current text style that is in the system variable TEXTSTYLE is used as a substitute.

✦ **S=.1,:** Scale multiplier used to calculate the height of the text.

✦ **R=0.0,:** Rotation angle relative to the line.

✦ **X=-0.1,:** X-offset value, the amount the text is shifted in the X-direction.

✦ **Y=.-05,:** Y-offset value, the amount the text is shifted in the Y-direction.

✦ **-.2:** The length of a space.

Displaying a shape isn't much different from displaying a text string in a complex linetype. To display a shape in a linetype, you use the name of the shape in the same location as the text string, and the shape file that contains the shape in place of the text style name. Shapes are stored in compiled files with a file extension of .SHX. Here is an example of a complex linetype using a shape file:

```
*FENCELINE2,Fenceline square ----[]-----[]----[]-----[]----[]---
A,.25,-.1,[BOX,ltypeshp.shx,x=-.1,s=.1],-.1,1
```

Getting Familiar with Shapes

Shape files were the only way to create a block-like object in early releases of AutoCAD. Shapes are not as commonly used now that AutoCAD has a true block object, but they still are used with complex linetypes and are very efficient. A shape is defined through a series of lines, arcs, and circles, but these elements are defined through a series of codes.

A shape is comprised of three components: a shape number, definition bytes, and the shape name. The syntax of a shape as it appears in a shape file is

```
*shapenumber, definitionbytes, shapename
```

An example of a shape that looks like an equilateral triangle is

```
*139,5,TRIGEQ
1,013,01D,018,0
```

To find out more about creating shape files, refer to the topic "Create Shape Definition Files" in the AutoCAD online Help files.

AutoCAD LT does not support the creation of shape files because it lacks the COMPILE command. The COMPILE command is used to generate a compiled shape file (.SHX) from a shape file (.SHP).

A utility that allows you to make a shape out of geometry in a drawing is part of Express Tools, which comes with AutoCAD, but not AutoCAD LT. The Make Shape utility is great for getting started with creating your own shapes. The utility can be found on the menu bar under Express➪Tools➪Make Shape.

Creating Custom Patterns

Hatch patterns are repeating patterns used to help convey design ideas. Whether you create drawings that are used to construct a building or used to manufacture a gear, you have most likely used the HATCH command. The HATCH command uses pattern files to define how the geometry is arranged when a specified area is filled.

Hatch pattern files are plain text files that can be edited with a text editor and have the file extension .PAT. AutoCAD ships with two different hatch pattern files: Acad.PAT (Acadlt.PAT) and Acadiso.PAT (Acadltiso.PAT). The Acad. PAT (Acadlt.PAT) file is used for Imperial unit drawings, whereas Acadiso.PAT (Acadltiso.PAT) is used for metric-based drawings.

A hatch pattern is defined by the first line containing the name and description for the pattern followed by single or multiple descriptor lines used to tell AutoCAD how to generate the pattern. Hatch pattern files also support the use of comments to help keep track of when changes were last made. Comments are defined with the use of a semicolon, so AutoCAD ignores everything to the right of the semicolon. Here is a section of the Acad.PAT file that ships with AutoCAD:

```
;;  Note: in order to ease migration of this file when
    upgrading
;;  to a future version of AutoCAD, it is recommended that
    you add
;;  your customizations to the User Defined Hatch Patterns
    section at the
;;  end of this file.
;;
*SOLID, Solid fill
45, 0,0, 0,.125
```

The structure of a hatch pattern

The best way to understand how a hatch pattern is created is to take a look at one of the patterns that comes with AutoCAD. One of the most basic hatch patterns is ANGLE. In this example, you can see some similarities between linetypes and hatch patterns:

```
*ANGLE, Angle steel
0, 0,0, 0,.275, .2,-.075
90, 0,0, 0,.275, .2,-.075
```

Line 1 of the ANGLE hatch pattern's definition:

✦ ***:** Designates the start of the hatch pattern.

✦ **ANGLE,:** The name of the hatch pattern. This name must be unique in the file; otherwise, AutoCAD only uses the first hatch pattern with the name in the file and ignores all other instances. A comma is used to separate the name of the hatch pattern from its description.

✦ **Angle steel:** The description of the hatch pattern. The description is displayed as part of a tooltip for a Hatch tool on a Tool Palette and also appears in the Description field when the hatch pattern is selected in the DesignCenter. The name and description line must not exceed 80 characters in length.

Line 2 of the ANGLE hatch pattern's definition:

✦ **0,:** The angle to be used for the hatch pattern data to follow on the same line. The specified value is added together with the SNAPANG system variable's value to calculate the angle to be used when the geometry is created from the descriptor line.

✦ **0,:** The X-origin for the starting point of the hatch pattern. The specified value is affected by the system variable SNAPBASE.

✦ **0,:** The Y-origin for the starting point of the hatch pattern. The specified value is affected by the system variable SNAPBASE.

✦ **0,:** The X-offset used to determine the distance between line segments.

✦ **.275,:** The Y-offset used to determine the distance between line segments.

✦ **.2,:** The length of a dash.

✦ **-.075:** The length of a space.

The second line draws all the horizontal dash segments of the hatch pattern. The dashes are drawn at a length of 0.2 and then followed by a space of 0.075 in length (see Figure 4-1). You can get an idea of how the hatch pattern looks if you draw a line that is 0.2 units going in the zero direction, and then copy that line over 0.275 in the zero direction. A descriptor line must not exceed 80 characters in length.

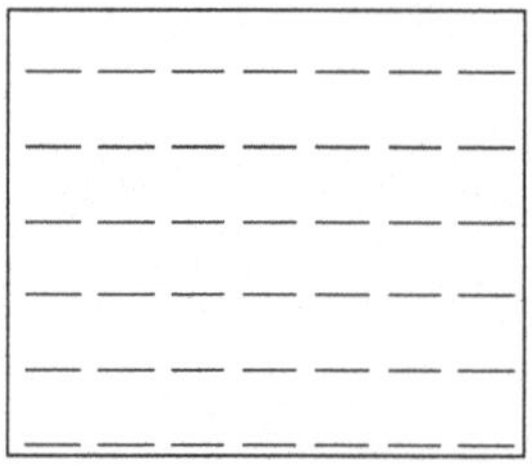

Figure 4-1:
The first part of the ANGLE hatch pattern.

Line 3 of the ANGLE hatch pattern's definition:

✦ **90,:** The angle to be used for the hatch pattern data to follow on the same line

✦ **0,:** The X-origin for the starting point of the hatch pattern

✦ **0,:** The Y-origin for the starting point of the hatch pattern

✦ **0,:** The X-offset used to determine the distance between line segments

✦ **.275,:** The Y-offset used to determine the distance between line segments

✦ **.2,:** The length of a dash

✦ **-.075:** The length of a space

The third line draws all the vertical dash segments of the hatch pattern. The dashes are drawn at a length of 0.2 and then followed by a space of 0.075 in length (see Figure 4-2). You can get an idea of how the hatch pattern looks if you draw a line that is 0.2 units going in the zero direction and then copy that line over 0.275 in the zero direction. Do the same starting in the left corner of each of the new horizontal lines and draw the same size line at an angle of 90 degrees. Figure 4-3 shows what the completed ANGLE hatch pattern looks like when it is used to hatch a filled area.

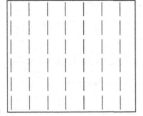

Figure 4-2:
The second part of the ANGLE hatch pattern.

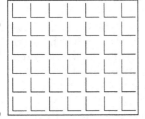

Figure 4-3:
Both lines of the ANGLE hatch pattern.

Creating a hatch pattern

Follow the procedures below to create a new hatch pattern.

1. **Choose Start⇨[All] Programs⇨Accessories⇨Notepad.**

Notepad is launched and a blank document is created.

2. **From the menu bar in Notepad, choose File⇨Open.**

The Open dialog box is displayed.

3. **In the Open dialog box, select All Files from the Save As Type drop-down list.**

You should be able to see all file types, not just those with the extension .TXT.

4. **Browse to the location of Acad.PAT (Acadlt.PAT) and select the file, and then click Open.**

Acad.PAT (or Acadlt.PAT) should be selected and opened into Notepad. By default, Acad.PAT can be found in the folder C:\Documents and Settings*<user name>*\Application Data\Autodesk\AutoCAD 2007\ R17.0\enu\Support. If you are using AutoCAD LT, Acadlt.PAT can be found in the folder C:\Documents and Settings*<user name>*\Application Data\Autodesk\AutoCAD LT 2007\R12\enu\Support.

5. **Scroll all the way to the bottom of the hatch pattern file and position the cursor on the very last blank line in the file.**

You should see a set of comments right above the last blank line that starts off with the comment `; ; User Defined Hatch Patterns`.

6. **Enter the new hatch pattern header and descriptor lines.**

The hatch pattern file should now include a header line for the hatch pattern and at least one descriptor line.

7. **From the menu bar in Notepad, choose File⇨Save.**

The updated contents of the hatch pattern file are saved out to file.

A utility that is part of Express Tools allows you to use an image, block, external reference (Xref), or a wipeout object as a hatch pattern. This can be a great timesaver because you are using techniques that you already understand to create a hatch pattern. This utility is called Super Hatch and can be found on the menu bar under Express⇨Draw⇨Super Hatch.

If you don't add your custom hatch patterns to one of the hatch pattern files that comes with AutoCAD, a hatch pattern file can only contain a single hatch pattern. The pattern name and the file name must be the same. If you create a file named glass.PAT, the pattern in the file must be named GLASS.

Adding your custom hatch patterns to one of the standard hatch pattern files that comes with AutoCAD makes the hatch pattern much easier to use.

Using a custom hatch pattern file

Follow this procedure to use a custom hatch pattern that is saved in its own file:

1. **From the menu bar, choose Draw⇨Hatch.**

The Hatch and Gradient dialog box is displayed.

2. **In the Hatch and Gradient dialog box, select Custom from the Type drop-down list.**

The Custom Pattern drop-down list and Browse button become enabled.

3. **Click the Ellipse button to the left of the Custom Pattern drop-down list.**

The Hatch Pattern Palette dialog box should be displayed. AutoCAD displays all custom hatch pattern files that it can find in its support search paths in the list box.

4. **In the Hatch Pattern Palette dialog box, select one of the custom hatch pattern files from the list.**

A preview of the pattern is displayed on the right side of the dialog box.

5. **Click OK to select the custom hatch pattern and return to the Hatch and Gradient dialog box.**

You are returned to the Hatch and Gradient dialog box. Continue creating the hatch object as you would if you were using a predefined pattern.

Working with Express Tools

Express Tools is a collection of tools that are not part of the core AutoCAD program. These tasks are provided as-is without any type of support from Autodesk. Many of these tools provide enhanced versions of functionality beyond what is in the core program, or provide unique functionality to assist in certain types of tasks.

Slowly, over the past several releases, many of the commonly used Express Tools have been making their way into the core program, which is great for users of AutoCAD LT. This section only provides a brief overview of many of the commonly used tools.

Express Tools are not available for use with AutoCAD LT. However, the Layer tools have been integrated into AutoCAD and are now available to AutoCAD LT users.

Installing Express Tools

Express Tools can be installed during the installation process of AutoCAD. To install Express Tools, click the check box on the Install Optional Tools page (see Figure 4-4). If you installed AutoCAD without installing Express Tools, you can use the Control Panel in Windows to make changes to the installation using Add or Remove Programs. To access Add or Remove Programs, choose Start ⇨Control Panel⇨Add or Remove Programs.

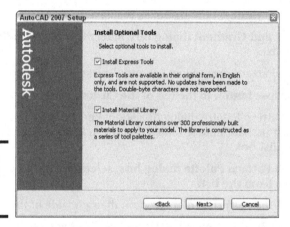

Figure 4-4:
Installing
Express
Tools.

After Express Tools has been installed, the Express menu should appear on the AutoCAD menu bar. If the Express menu is not displayed, type the command EXPRESSMENU or EXPRESSTOOLS at the command line.

Layer tools

The Layer tools give you capabilities ranging from selecting an object and displaying only the objects on that layer to being able to freeze a layer just by selecting it.

All of the Layer tools that were previously part of Express Tools have been integrated into AutoCAD 2007 and AutoCAD LT 2007 and can be located under the Layer Tools submenu of the Format menu.

✦ **Layer Manager:** Layer Manager allows you to save and restore layer states. This functionality is very similar to the layer states in the Layer Properties Manager.

✦ **Layer Walk:** Layer Walk allows you to dynamically step through all the layers in a drawing to see the objects placed on those layers, without forcing you to freeze or thaw or turn layers off and on.

✦ **Layer Match:** Layer Match allows you to select objects in the drawing that should be moved to a different layer based on the layer a selected object is already on.

✦ **Change to Current Layer:** Change to Current Layer allows you to select an object in a drawing and set the layer current that the object is on.

✦ **Copy Objects to New Layer:** Copy Objects to New Layer allows you to move selected objects to another layer or new layer altogether.

✦ **Layer Isolate:** Layer Isolate allows you to turn off all layers except the ones selected.

✦ **Isolate Layer to Current Viewport:** Isolate Layer to Current Viewport freezes the layer in all viewports except the active viewport.

✦ **Turn Off:** Turn Off allows you to turn off a layer by selecting an object that is on that layer.

✦ **Turn All Layers On:** Turn All Layers On turns on all layers that are currently marked as off.

✦ **Freeze Layer:** Freeze Layer allows you to freeze a layer by selecting an object that is on that layer.

✦ **Thaw All Layers:** Thaw All Layers thaws layers that are currently marked as frozen.

✦ **Layer Lock:** Layer Lock allows you to lock a layer by selecting an object that is on that layer.

✦ **Layer Unlock:** Layer Unlock allows you to unlock a layer by selecting an object on that layer.

✦ **Layer Merge:** Layer Merge allows you to move all the objects on one layer to another layer.

✦ **Layer Delete:** Layer Delete allows you to delete all the objects on a layer and then purge it from a drawing.

Block tools

The Block tools give you capabilities ranging from being able to explode a block and have the attributes converted to text objects to converting a block to an external reference (Xref).

✦ **List Xref/Block Properties:** List Xref/Block Properties allows you to get information about a nested object in a block or Xref.

✦ **Copy Nested Objects:** Copy Nested Objects allows you to make a copy of objects in a block without exploding the block first.

✦ **Explode Attributes to Text:** Explode Attributes to Text allows you to explode a block, but instead of attribute definitions being created after the explosion, you are left with text objects in their place with the value that was in the attribute before the block was exploded.

✦ **Convert Shape to Block:** Convert Shape to Block allows you to generate a block based on a shape definition.

✦ **Export Attribute Information:** Export Attribute Information allows you to export attribute and block name information to a tab-delimited text file. This allows you to work with the information in a spreadsheet program.

✦ **Import Attribute Information:** Import Attribute Information allows you to import previously exported attribute and block name information back into AutoCAD to sync up the values.

✦ **Convert Block to Xref:** Convert Block to Xref allows you to replace a block with a specified Xref.

✦ **Replace Block with Another Block:** Replace Block with Another Block allows you to replace a block with a specified block.

Text tools

The Text tools give you capabilities ranging from being able to create text along an arc to being able to change the case of several selected text objects at one time:

✦ **Text Fit:** Text Fit allows you to stretch or shrink a text object by selecting a new or end point.

✦ **Text Mask:** Text Mask allows you to place a mask object behind a text or mtext object with an offset value.

✦ **Unmask Text:** Unmask Text allows you to remove a mask object from behind a text or mtext object.

✦ **Explode Text:** Explode Text allows you to explode a text or mtext object into geometry that can be assigned thickness or an elevation.

✦ **Convert Text to Mtext:** Convert Text to Mtext allows you to select text objects and create a single mtext object with the values from the selected text objects.

✦ **Arc-Aligned Text:** Arc-Aligned Text allows you to create a text object that follows along an arc's curve.

✦ **Rotate Text:** Rotate Text allows you to change the orientation of a text, mtext, or attribute.

+ **Enclose Text with Object:** Enclose Text with Object allows you to place a circle, slot, or rectangle around a text or mtext object.

+ **Rotate Text:** Rotate Text allows you to change the orientation of a text, mtext, or attribute.

+ **Automatic Text Numbering:** Automatic Text Numbering allows you to create a numbered list.

+ **Change Text Case:** Change Text Case allows you to change the case of selected text and mtext objects.

Layout tools

The Layout tools offer capabilities ranging from listing a viewports scale to synchronizing viewports:

+ **Align Space:** Align Space allows you to adjust a viewport based on points selected in model space and paper space.

+ **Synchronize Viewports:** Synchronize Viewports allows you to update a viewport's zoom factor based on a specified viewport.

+ **List Viewport Scale:** List Viewport Scale allows you to obtain a viewport's current scale factor.

+ **Merge Layout:** Merge Layout allows you to merge the objects in a layout into another layout or create a new layout based on the layouts being merged.

Dimension tools

The Dimension tools range from leader tools to tools that enable you to import and export dimension styles out of a drawing:

+ **Leader Tools:** The Leader Tools submenu contains commands that allow you to attach and detach leader lines to multiline text, tolerance, or block reference objects.

+ **Dimstyle Export:** Dimstyle Export allows you to export a specified dimension style out of a drawing to a text file.

+ **Dimstyle Import:** Dimstyle Import allows you to import a previously exported dimension style into a drawing.

Modify tools

The Modify tools give you capabilities ranging from being able to perform multiple editing operations in a row to controlling display order by color:

+ **Multiple Object Stretch:** Multiple Object Stretch allows you to perform more than one crossing polygon before doing a stretch.

+ **Move/Copy/Rotate:** Move/Copy/Rotate allows you to perform move, copy, and rotate operations in a row on objects created during the command.

+ **DrawOrder by Color:** DrawOrder by Color allows you to control the draworder of objects in a drawing by the color they are assigned or by the color of the layer they are on.

+ **Flatten Objects:** Flatten Objects allows you to convert 3D objects into 2D objects.

Draw tools

The Draw tools range from inserting a breakline to a feature known as Super Hatch. Super Hatch allows you to use an image, block, external reference (Xref), or a wipeout object as a hatch pattern.

File tools

The File tools are used to help with the management of drawing and backup files. The utilities perform functions ranging from moving backups to a specified location to being able to save all open drawings in AutoCAD:

+ **Move Backup Files:** Move Backup Files allows you to specify where .BAK files should be placed after each save.

+ **Save All Drawings:** Save All Drawings allows you to save all open drawings without needing to switch to each one and saving each individually.

+ **Quick Exit:** Quick Exit allows you to exit all open drawings; you are prompted only for the ones that need to be saved. AutoCAD closes automatically after the command is done.

+ **Revert to Original:** Revert to Original allows you to close and reopen the current drawing.

Tools

The tools are a variety of different types of routines, ranging from editing the PGP file to creating custom linetypes:

+ **Command Alias Editor:** Command Alias Editor allows you to create new and modify existing command aliases in a PGP file.

+ **System Variable Editor:** System Variable Editor allows you to view and modify the values of system variables through a dialog box instead of at the command line.

✦ **Make Linetype:** Make Linetype allows you to generate a linetype based on the geometry in a drawing.

✦ **Make Shape:** Make Shape allows you to generate a shape based on the geometry in a drawing.

Command line only tools

Some Express Tools are not found in the Express Tools pull-down menu. These commands are available only from the command line. Some of those commands are mentioned in the following list. In parentheses after the name of the command is the command name that has to be typed at the command line in order to run it:

✦ **Block Count (BCOUNT):** Block Count allows you to get a quick count of the number of times a block is inserted into a drawing.

✦ **Edit Time (EDITTIME):** Edit Time allows you to keep track of the amount of time that you are spending in a drawing file. You can specify a timeout period so if nothing happens in AutoCAD, the timer tracking is suspended after a specified interval.

✦ **List AutoLISP Commands (LSP):** List AutoLISP Commands allows you to get information about loaded AutoLISP routines.

✦ **Create Selection Set (SSX):** Create Selection Set allows you to create a selection set based on some filtering options that you can select by using the "previous" selection option.

✦ **Toggle Frames (TFRAMES):** Toggle Frames toggles the frames used for images and wipeouts on or off.

Book X

Programming AutoCAD

The 5th Wave   By Rich Tennant

AutoCAD Expertise .50¢ - Min.

Contents at a Glance

Chapter 1: The AutoCAD Programming Interfaces

In This Chapter

✓ Finding out what programming AutoCAD can do for you

✓ Covering the available programming interfaces

✓ Mastering the ins and outs of the programming interfaces

✓ Figuring out which programming interface is best for you

*H*ave you ever wanted to create a command alias that represented a specific option of a command? Or maybe you have established CAD standards, but some of the settings can't be set up through a drawing template alone. So you want to make sure the settings are finished before any work on a design begins? If so, you have come to the right place. AutoCAD is more than just a drafting tool. Although customizing AutoCAD can help increase productivity by itself, the programming interfaces allow you to tap into much more powerful resources that are contained in the depths of AutoCAD. (Okay, saying the resources are in the depths of AutoCAD might be a bit of an exaggeration since they are used every time you run a command in the AutoCAD interface.)

This minibook is aimed at AutoCAD users only. Sorry, AutoCAD LT users — the programming interfaces are limited to AutoCAD.

The supported application programming interfaces (APIs) for AutoCAD are available after you install AutoCAD or after you've downloaded them from the Autodesk Web site. APIs are used to communicate with the AutoCAD application, any open drawing files, and objects in a drawing. With some of the APIs, you can create your own custom commands that users can execute from the command line. The power behind some of these programming interfaces is that you don't need to be a programmer to take advantage of them.

Discovering What You Can Do by Programming AutoCAD

You might be thinking to yourself, "I'm not a programmer, so why do I want to know about programming interfaces?" The best reason to discover the programming interfaces is to simplify repetitive tasks in your workflow. If you can create very basic custom programs that save 15 minutes a day, the effort is worth your time — especially if you can share these programs with your coworkers.

Over time, your 15-minute savings can grow into much more as you become more efficient with the programming interface. Custom programs don't need to be complex to increase efficiency. They can be simple, like creating new commands that can be used to perform a Zoom Previous from the command line, or complicated, taking on issues such as CAD standards.

Managing CAD standards can be a nightmare, but the process can be improved by using programming interfaces. Tasks such as making sure dimensions are placed on the correct layer can be accomplished if you understand the programming interfaces and how AutoCAD works. You don't need to understand how the information is actually written to the file, but you do need to know how it is logically organized. By logically organized, we mean you should understand that objects such as layers aren't just floating around inside a drawing; instead, they are stored in a table that contains all the layers in a drawing.

The advantages of using APIs

The advantages of APIs differ based on whether you are already using third-party applications or add-ons for AutoCAD. Even if you are, you may still discover advantages to in-house programming. Here are some of the benefits for creating custom programs for AutoCAD:

+ **Accuracy:** By creating a custom program that runs consistently every time, you can increase the accuracy of your drawings. If a process has a large number of steps in it, some steps might be overlooked. This can cause errors to creep into your design.

+ **Appearance:** Programming can aid in making drawings look uniform by allowing you to set up drawing options that can't be defined in a drawing template or by allowing you to automate the updating of objects in a drawing.

+ **Efficiency:** Repetitive tasks can be speeded up, enabling drafters to spend more time on the design process.

✦ **Training efficiency:** Training a new employee is always a challenge. If a complex or large set of processes must be followed, new employees take even longer to be productive. Wrapping custom programs around processes can help get them up and productive in a shorter period of time.

✦ **The downstream effect:** Being able to get things done faster and more efficiently during the drafting process is great, but don't forget about those people who use the data after the design has been completed. Custom programming can be used to extract information out of a drawing or set of drawings that can be useful downstream in manufacturing, sales and marketing, and many other areas.

The other side of the story

There are always two sides to every story. We've covered some of the benefits of using the programming interfaces in AutoCAD, but there has to be a downside, right? There is, and here are some of the disadvantages to programming in AutoCAD:

✦ **Cost:** Programming in AutoCAD costs money — how much depends on which programming interface you go with. These costs might be in the form of software, time, or consulting fees. In the case of a couple of the programming interfaces, no additional software packages need to be purchased, but, regardless, time is always a cost in these types of projects.

✦ **Maintenance:** AutoCAD changes from release to release. When you upgrade to a new version, you often have to spend time updating your custom programs. Some feature your custom program was using may get broken, or you may want to take advantage of a new feature that is introduced to improve a process even further.

✦ **Learning curve:** Even though a number of the programming interfaces are easy for non-programmers to pick up and understand, they still require you to put in some time if you want to become proficient. So before you promise your boss that you can deliver improved productivity, make sure you are comfortable with the programming language you chose first.

Getting to Know the Available Programming Interfaces

As AutoCAD has evolved over the years, so have the different programming interfaces that are available. When AutoCAD was first introduced to the world, no programming interfaces were built into the application. Only about three years after the product was released was the first programming interface added to the software. This programming interface was AutoLISP, which was based on the LISP programming language. The introduction of AutoLISP allowed users of AutoCAD to tailor the program for how they wanted to work to improve productivity.

After AutoLISP came the introduction of ADS (AutoCAD Development System), which introduced C-style coding as a programming option. ADS had a rather short life span because the C language was already being overshadowed by the next generation of the C programming language, C++. ADS, which was only around for about three years, evolved into ObjectARX, which is still the premier programming option in AutoCAD 2007. If you look at the install directory of AutoCAD, you can see that this is the tool of choice by Autodesk itself to extend the core functionality of AutoCAD.

In 1997, Autodesk extended the programming interfaces it was offering to include ActiveX, which allowed VB programmers to extend the core functionality of AutoCAD. ActiveX is not just for VB programmers; many other mainstream languages such as Java and C++ support ActiveX so they can interface with AutoCAD. Autodesk didn't stop with ActiveX support. It kept up with the ever-changing landscape of technology and introduced a programming interface for .NET that could be used with the new .NET languages by Microsoft and other development language vendors.

AutoLISP

AutoLISP is a programming language based on the LISP language. LISP stands for *list processing*. It was first introduced back in 1958 and was popular during the '70s and '80s. Programmers often joke that the LISP acronym really stands for *Lost In Stupid Parentheses*. Take one look at the code, and you might agree. LISP uses start and end parentheses for a statement, as the following example shows:

```
(command "line" "0,0" "5,5" "")
```

In the example, you can see the use of the parentheses to start and end the expression. The example uses the LINE command to draw a line starting at the coordinate 0,0 and ending at 5,5. As you can see, it's not much different from what you are use to typing in at the command line. Although not a very powerful statement, it is rather easy to understand.

AutoLISP can be used to organize multiple statements into a custom command that a user can enter at the command line or use in a command macro for a toolbar button. To create a new command or a function that can be used to extend the built-in AutoLISP functions, use the function DEFUN — DEfine FUNction.

Although AutoLISP is no longer used as the primary development tool by Autodesk as it once was, it is still the primary tool that many users work with because it is easy to learn after you get past all the parentheses. As a whole, the programming interface is by far one of the most cost-effective and forgiving of the four different programming interfaces we discuss in this book.

The last major update to the AutoLISP programming language was back in 1998 when Autodesk purchased a package called Vital LISP. Vital LISP was then renamed to Visual LISP and sold as an add-on originally for AutoCAD 14. Visual LISP was then included as part of the AutoCAD 2000 release in 1999. The Visual LISP environment extended the functionality of the AutoLISP language by adding hundreds of functions and allowing AutoLISP to access the AutoCAD Object Model similar to VBA and ActiveX.

**Book X
Chapter 1**

**The AutoCAD
Programming
Interfaces**

The AutoCAD Object Model is the documented structure of the relationships between AutoCAD and other objects like lines and blocks that are contained in an AutoCAD Drawing file. The object model is used as a road map to locate and access the various different objects in the ActiveX programming interface for AutoCAD.

ActiveX automation

ActiveX automation is also known as Component Object Model (COM) automation. COM automation is a form of component-based software architecture that allows an application to expose its internal functionality in the form of objects. COM allows applications to cross-communicate with each other to exchange information or interact. Many of the modern programming languages like VB/VBA, C++, and Java are capable of using COM automation.

So why is ActiveX automation important in AutoCAD? ActiveX automation allows you to use a rich and modern programming language like VB or VBA. When you can use a programming language like VB or VBA when communicating with AutoCAD, you can exchange information with data sources like an MS Access database or even an MS Excel spreadsheet. This can allow you to improve downstream processes by providing CAD information in different systems to non-CAD users who might use the information for billing or manufacturing.

One of the advantages to using ActiveX automation is that you are not limited to just building applications in AutoCAD. If you want to develop a stand-alone application with VB and communicate with AutoCAD, you can. If you create a VBA project in MS Word and want to communicate with AutoCAD, you can do that too. In the remainder of this minibook, we discuss ActiveX and VBA as one and the same because VBA uses ActiveX automation.

VBA

VBA — Visual Basic for Applications — has been around for some time and is an extension of the very popular programming language Visual Basic (VB). VBA is defined as an object-oriented programming (OOP) language. The concept behind OOP is that a computer program is developed using a collection of individual units, or *objects,* as opposed to a listing of instructions. Each one of the objects has the ability to receive messages, process data, and transmit messages to other objects.

VBA is part of the programming and development tools that are developed by Microsoft. Its roots date back to MS-DOS and programming languages like QBasic and MS-Basic. VB has been around longer than VBA and, unlike VBA, VB can be used to build standalone applications that are not dependent on a host application.

A *host application* is a program that allows the VBA environment to run inside it; an example of this is AutoCAD. Many popular Windows-based programs have VBA technology built into them. Some of the other applications are Autodesk Inventor, AutoCAD-based vertical products such as Architectural Desktop (ADT), and Microsoft Word and Excel.

VBA in AutoCAD has been a welcomed feature from both the development and non-development communities. This programming option allows for the integration of business applications directly into the AutoCAD environment and allows companies to tap into an existing development community that knows VB/VBA already.

ObjectARX and ObjectDBX

ObjectARX and ObjectDBX are not programming languages like VBA, but instead are programming interfaces that allow developers to create and extend AutoCAD using the object-oriented C++ programming language. ObjectARX is a collection of library and include files that provides you with the versatility of tools that Autodesk uses to extend the core functionality of AutoCAD and other AutoCAD-based products such as Autodesk Architectural Desktop (ADT) and AutoCAD Mechanical Desktop (MDT).

The vertical products are a collection of ObjectARX programs that are focused on a specific target audience and the type of work they perform. ObjectDBX files are used to define custom drawing objects like the ones found in ADT, instead of user interface elements and commands like in ObjectARX files. If your programs are calculation-intensive, you might want to take a look at using ObjectARX for these types of tasks.

ObjectARX allows for smaller or more compact files, faster execution, and tighter integration into AutoCAD and Windows. Unlike the other programming options, with ObjectARX, you need to purchase additional development tools and download the software development kit from the Autodesk Web site. When purchasing the development tools, you are limited to the version that was used to build the AutoCAD release for which you are creating ObjectARX and ObjectDBX programs.

.NET

.NET is Microsoft's alternative to portable programming languages like Java and J2EE. .NET represents Microsoft's latest generation of the programming languages that offer flexibility for both application development and usability. To make .NET appealing to the development community, the development environment Visual Studio .NET incorporates more than 20 different languages, such as RPG, COBOL, and C#.

The .NET programming interface is very similar to the basic concept of ActiveX automation, but with much greater flexibility through the use of newer programming languages and technologies. Like ObjectARX, a separate development environment must be obtained; it isn't supplied with AutoCAD. However, like ActiveX automation, the .NET API is available upon installing AutoCAD. .NET help and samples are available as part of the ObjectARX development kit and must be downloaded from the Autodesk Web site.

Book X
Chapter 1

The AutoCAD Programming Interfaces

Comparing Strengths and Weaknesses of the Programming Interfaces

Now that you have an idea of the programming interfaces that are available to use with AutoCAD, you'll want to see how they stack up. Here, we break down some key areas to help you understand how the different programming interfaces measure up against each other:

✦ **Learning curve:** If you are not experienced with programming and don't have much time to dedicate to mastering a programming language, AutoLISP is the best option for you. It is very powerful but doesn't require you to learn a lot of different concepts to get a basic program together. If you do have a background in programming, you may want to look at using VBA in AutoCAD because it is based on a universal programming language.

If you have a considerable amount of programming experience, you might consider using ObjectARX or .NET, which take longer to learn but are very powerful. (.NET has far fewer pain points compared to ObjectARX.)

✦ **Execution speed:** Both AutoLISP and VBA use interpreters to talk to AutoCAD, which can cause a lag in execution time and overall execution speed. ObjectARX is by far the fastest and most efficient of all the different programming interfaces. .NET, although flexible, uses Just In Time (JIT) compiling, which can cause an initial performance lag the first time the program is run.

✦ **Cost:** AutoLISP and VBA are both built in to AutoCAD, so no additional development tools must be purchased. ObjectARX and .NET require the purchasing of additional tools that can range in price from hundreds to thousands of dollars. This might affect which programming interface you use first.

✦ **User input:** All of the different programming interfaces allow you to get information from a user, but how a user's input is collected varies slightly. AutoLISP has better command line support over VBA because AutoLISP allows you to create custom commands and VBA doesn't. If you are looking to offer dialog boxes in your programs, you might want to look at VBA over AutoLISP.

AutoLISP uses a language called DCL (Dialog Control Language) that defines how a dialog box should look. This is different from the other programming languages, which use a graphical editor to design the look of dialog boxes.

ObjectARX has the best support in this area; but it also has a number of additional things you have to contend with, such as Microsoft Foundation Classes (MFC), which are tools that help you create robust dialog boxes and user interfaces. .NET is very flexible in gathering user input, but, unlike ObjectARX, it lacks some control over UI elements that are specific to AutoCAD.

✦ **Maintenance:** AutoLISP and VBA are the easiest to maintain as they typically work on future releases with few changes required. ObjectARX programs typically need to be rebuilt about every third release of AutoCAD due to binary compatibility issues with the library files. .NET is a young programming interface for AutoCAD. Until it matures, you can almost guarantee that any custom programs will need to be rebuilt to some degree between releases. In the long term, we hope that .NET API follows suit with AutoLISP and VBA to reduce the amount of maintenance between releases.

✦ **Longevity:** AutoLISP has been around the longest and is the easiest of the four programming interfaces to learn. VBA is newer to AutoCAD than AutoLISP, but it is nearing the end of its life cycle according to Microsoft. (This is due to the fact that ActiveX is being replaced by .NET, which is much newer and more flexible.) Keep in mind that just because VBA is getting close to the end of its life cycle doesn't mean that support will suddenly stop; it will just be slowed down.

ObjectARX and .NET are probably the APIs most likely to be around for a while because they are the ones used by Autodesk. ObjectARX seems to have a very bright future, but no one ever knows for sure where technology will go.

Deciding Which Programming Interface Is Best for You

So which of the four programming interfaces is best for you? The two that most users find easiest to use and learn are AutoLISP and VBA, which is why we cover them in this book. But just because AutoLISP and VBA are covered in this book doesn't necessarily make them the right choices for you. To determine which option is best for you, read the following descriptions of each programming interface and make a decision based on which description most closely matches your scenario.

**Book X
Chapter 1**

The AutoCAD
Programming
Interfaces

AutoLISP is a good fit if you know AutoCAD and the commands that are available to you pretty well, or if you don't have much or any experience in programming. Most first-time AutoLISP programmers feel that it is a much more natural transition into programming because they can use the commands that they are already familiar with to automate tasks. It also allows for plenty of growth because it can communicate with other applications using the Visual LISP functions via ActiveX automation. AutoLISP is the easiest for beginners to learn and work with.

Typically, VBA is a good fit if you don't really know much about AutoCAD but have a background in VBA or VB programming. VBA enables companies with IS departments to get involved with extending AutoCAD because a large number of programmers know VB. VBA is a good starting point for beginners, but because you are not using AutoCAD commands, the learning curve is higher. VBA is a programming interface that both beginners and intermediate users can work with.

.NET is the middle-of-the-road option between VBA and ObjectARX. Although it requires you to understand one of the newer programming languages, such as VB.NET or C#, it isn't as complex as mastering ObjectARX or C++. Although the .NET programming interface does have some limitations in its current implementation, it is improving with each new release. .NET provides some of the simplicity of application development that comes with VBA but has the power of C++ with a smaller learning curve. Although .NET is different from VBA, the syntaxes look and feel very similar to each other. One of the important things that the two share is the capability to use ActiveX automation. You could start with VBA and, over time, transition to .NET.

ObjectARX should typically be left up to those who have experience with C++ because a lot of things can go wrong in a hurry if you don't understand the C++ programming language. In C++, you are responsible for managing your own memory, so if you make a mistake, you can develop programs that bring AutoCAD to its knees quickly. If you can tame the C++ programming language beast, you will have just about everything you can imagine at your fingertips for creating custom programs in AutoCAD.

Chapter 2: Using Custom Programs

*B*efore doing any custom programming, you first need to understand a little more about how custom programs that you might create or even download from the Internet can be used in AutoCAD. AutoCAD also ships with a variety of custom programs that extend the core functionality of the application. Although the majority of custom programs are written with ObjectARX, some are written in AutoLISP or VBA. AutoCAD 2007 ships with an add-on called Express Tools, which is a collection of different custom programs that are not part of the core application. See Book IX, Chapter 4 for more information on Express Tools.

So how do these custom programs that you've created or downloaded get loaded into AutoCAD? As you discover in this chapter, there are many ways of loading custom programs into AutoCAD, and the approach varies based on what type of custom program it is. So before you even get the program loaded, you need to understand how different custom programs are represented on disk through Windows Explorer.

Identifying Application Files

Custom programs are stored in application files, which can be identified by their file extensions or their designated icons in Windows Explorer. The programming interface in which you choose to write your custom programs determines which file extension the application file has. At some point, you'll most likely download programs from the Internet or perhaps a coworker will share his or her custom program with you. So you'll find yourself working with a different type of application file than what you normally create.

Table 2-1 lists the various application files you may encounter in AutoCAD.

Table 2-1		**Application Files**
Icon	*File Extension*	*Description*
	.LSP	AutoLISP application source file
	.MNL	AutoLISP menu source file
	.FAS	Fast-load AutoLISP file
	.VLX	Visual LISP executable file
	.DVB	AutoCAD VBA source file
	.ARX	ObjectARX file
	.DBX	ObjectDBX file
	.DLL	.NET/application extension file

Loading and Unloading Applications

Most of the custom programs that can be used in AutoCAD can be loaded or unloaded through a single dialog box. But, like everything else in AutoCAD, you can load or unload programs in any number of ways. The Load/Unload Applications dialog box provides the basics for loading and unloading applications; but if you are sharing custom programs with other users, there are much more efficient ways to load the application files.

The Load/Unload Applications dialog box

The Load/Unload Applications dialog box (see Figure 2-1) allows you to perform a variety of tasks that deal with loading and unloading application files. Through the Load/Unload Applications dialog box, you can load application files that are created with AutoLISP (.LSP, .FAS, and .VLX), VBA (.DVB), ObjectARX (.ARX), or ObjectDBX (.DBX). .NET application files can't be loaded using the Load/Unload Applications dialog box. Instead, they must be loaded with the NETLOAD command, which we cover in the section "Loading a .NET file" later in this chapter. The APPLOAD command is used to launch the Load/Unload Applications dialog box.

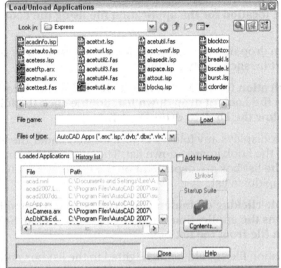

Figure 2-1:
The Load/
Unload
Applications
dialog box.

Launching the Load/Unload Application dialog box

To launch the Load/Unload Applications dialog box, use one of the following methods:

✦ **Tools menu:** Choose Tools⇨Load Application.

✦ **Keyboard input:** Type **APPLOAD** at the command line and press Enter.

✦ **Command alias:** Type **AP** and press Enter.

Loading an application file

The following procedure initiates the APPLOAD command and explains how to load an existing application file:

1. **Use any of the three methods just mentioned to launch the Load/Unload Applications dialog box.**

2. **In the dialog box, click the Files of Type drop-down list and specify the type of application file you want to use to filter the list box.**

The selected option controls the type of application files that are displayed in the list box. The default selection is AutoCAD Apps. The drop-down list box also allows you to filter on AutoLISP, VBA, ObjectARX, and ObjectDBX files.

3. **Specify the location for the application file using the Look In drop-down list.**

   The Look In drop-down list allows you to select a folder or named location to start in, such as My Documents.

4. **If the application file is located in a folder below the location you selected in the Look In drop-down list, double-click the folder in the list box below the Look In drop-down list.**

   The list box displays any folders or files located under the folder selected in the Look In drop-down list. The types of files that are displayed in the list box are dependent on the file filter selected in the Files of Type drop-down list.

5. **Keep double-clicking on folders until you have navigated to the folder that contains the application file that you want to load. Select the application file from the list box.**

   The application file should be highlighted in the list box and its name added to the File Name text box.

6. **Click Load.**

   The application file should be loaded into AutoCAD. You can tell by checking the lower-left corner (see Figure 2-2) of the Load/Unload Applications dialog box whether the application file was loaded successfully.

Figure 2-2:
The load
status of the
application
file.

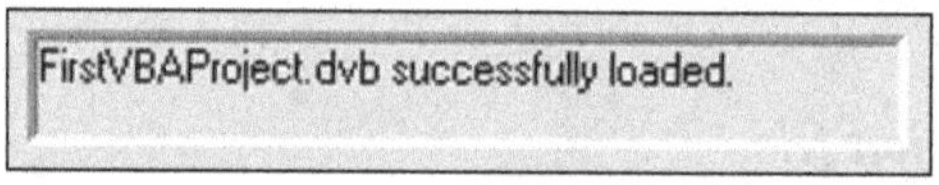

FirstVBAProject.dvb successfully loaded.

7. **Click Close.**

   Clicking the Close button exits the Load/Unload Applications dialog box.

If you are going to use the custom program fairly often, you can select the Add to History check box below the Load button. This adds the application file to the History List tab. The next time that you want to load the application file, just select it from the History List tab and click the Load button instead of browsing to it again. To get the application file off the History List tab, select it and click Remove.

AutoLISP files, when they are loaded into AutoCAD, are different from VBA, ObjectARX, ObjectDBX, and .NET application files because they are accessible only in the drawing that they were loaded into. So if you use the Load/Unload Applications dialog box to load an AutoLISP file, it is available only in the current drawing. The exceptions to this are AutoLISP menu source (.MNL) files and any AutoLISP files that get loaded by other application files or that use a special naming convention that AutoCAD looks for. These specially named files are covered later under the section "Automatically loading AutoLISP files" later in this chapter.

Because AutoCAD is a Windows-based program, it supports many standard Windows features. One of the supported features is the capability to use drag-and-drop. You can drag and drop application files like AutoLISP (.LSP), VBA (.DVB), and ObjectARX (.ARX) files directly into a drawing to load them. This is a fast and easy alternative to the APPLOAD command when you are testing custom programs.

Determining which application files are loaded

You can tell which application files have already been loaded into AutoCAD by checking the items listed in the Loaded Applications tab (see Figure 2-3) at the bottom of the Load/Unload Applications dialog box. The list displays all application files that are loaded into AutoCAD, which include AutoLISP, VBA, ObjectARX, ObjectDBX, and .NET files.

Figure 2-3:
Loaded
application
files.

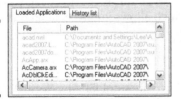

Unloading an application file

Unloading an application file is the reverse of loading an application file. It seems obvious, but AutoCAD doesn't allow you to unload everything that can be loaded because after certain files are loaded, AutoCAD becomes dependent on them while a drawing is open. If you take a look at the Loaded Applications tab, you can see that some items are in black text, whereas a majority of them are in gray text.

The items shown in black text can be unloaded without any impact to a drawing or AutoCAD in general. Unloading a file is very rarely required; from time to time, however, you might need to unload an application file. Follow these procedures to unload an application from AutoCAD:

1. **From the Tools menu, choose Load Applications.**

   AutoCAD launches the Load/Unload Applications dialog box.

2. **Click the Loaded Applications tab in the lower half of the Load/Unload Applications dialog box.**

   The applications that are currently loaded in AutoCAD should be displayed.

3. **Select one of the application files from the list to unload.**

   Although you can select any of the application files in the list, only the application files that are displayed in black text can be unloaded.

4. **Click the Unload button located above the Startup Suite section.**

   Clicking Unload removes the application file from AutoCAD's memory and disables any command references that might have been created when the file was loaded.

5. **Click Close.**

   Clicking the Close button exits the Load/Unload Applications dialog box.

Loading an AutoLISP file

Other than the Load/Unload Applications dialog box, AutoCAD has no built-in command that you can use to load an AutoLISP. However, you can use an AutoLISP function called Load, which allows you to load an AutoLISP file. The syntax for the Load function is

```
(load AutoLISP_filename [Error_message])
```

✦ **AutoLISP_filename:** The path to the AutoLISP file. Normally you would use a backslash (\) between folders in Windows Explorer, but with AutoLISP, that is interpreted as something else, so you need to use double backslashes (\\) or a single forward slash (/). For example, C:\ Program Files\AutoCAD 2007\Support\3d.lsp would be C:/Program Files/ AutoCAD 2007/Support/3d.lsp.

+ **Error_message:** This parameter is optional, and the value that is entered in this parameter is echoed at the command line if the AutoLISP file is not loaded.

An example of the Load function is

```
(load "C:/Program Files/AutoCAD 2007/Support/3d.lsp" "3d.lsp
  missing")
```

If you installed Express Tools when you installed AutoCAD, a command called LSP is available. The LSP command allows you to load an AutoLISP file as well as see which commands and variables have been defined through AutoLISP. To find out more about Express Tools, go to Book IX, Chapter 4.

**Book X
Chapter 2**

**Using Custom
Programs**

Loading and unloading a VBA file

VBA application files can be loaded in any number of ways: by using the command line, a dialog box, or even an AutoLISP function. Only a few of the different methods for loading and unloading a VBA application file are being explained in this chapter; the others are covered later in Chapter 4 of this minibook.

Using VBALOAD and VBAUNLOAD with a VBA file

Working with VBA application files in AutoCAD is pretty straightforward. To load a VBA application file, you use the command VBALOAD; to unload it, you use the command VBAUNLOAD. It really can't get much more simple than that.

To load a VBA application file, use one of the following methods:

+ **Tools menu:** Choose Tools⇨Macros⇨Load Project.
+ **Keyboard input:** Type **VBALOAD** at the command line and press Enter.

Loading a VBA file

The following procedure initiates the VBALOAD command and explains how to load an existing VBA application file:

1. **Use either of the two methods just listed to display the Open VBA Project dialog box.**

AutoCAD launches the Open VBA Project dialog box, which allows you to browse for an existing VBA application file.

2. **Specify the location for the VBA application file using the Look In drop-down list.**

The Look In drop-down list allows you to select a folder or a named location like My Documents to start in.

3. **If the VBA application file is located in a folder below the location that you selected in the Look In drop-down list, double-click the folder in the list box below the Look In drop-down list.**

   The list box displays any folders or files located under the folder selected in the Look In drop-down list. The types of files that are displayed in the list box are dependent on the file filter selected in the Files of Type drop-down list.

4. **Keep double-clicking on folders until you have navigated to the folder that contains the application file you want to load. Select the application file from the list box.**

   The VBA application file should be highlighted in the list box and its name added to the File Name text box.

5. **Click Open.**

   The Open VBA Project dialog box closes and AutoCAD starts loading the VBA application file.

6. **In the AutoCAD message box, click Enable Macros to finish loading the VBA application file.**

   The AutoCAD message box (see Figure 2-4) is displayed when macro virus protection is enabled. This option protects you and your drawings from macro viruses that can become embedded in a drawing file. This option and others for VBA are explained in Chapter 4 of this minibook. After you click Enable Macros, the VBA application file is added to the Projects list box of the VBA Manager dialog box.

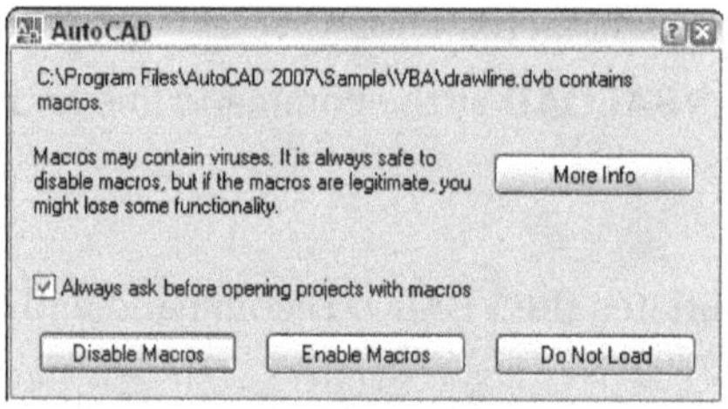

Figure 2-4:
The virus protection warning.

7. **Click Close.**

   Clicking the Close button exits the VBA Manager dialog box.

The VBAMAN command can be used to display a dialog box that allows you to access a majority of the VBA environment options. The VBAMAN command is explained in Chapter 4 of this minibook.

Loading a VBA file using AutoLISP

You can load a VBA application file using the AutoLISP function `Vl-vbaload`. The `Vl-vbaload` function works just like the AutoLISP function `Load` discussed in the section "Loading an AutoLISP file" earlier in this chapter. The syntax of the `Vl-vbaload` function is as follows:

```
(vl-vbaload VBA_filename)
```

The `VBA_filename` should be the full path to the VBA file. Normally you would use a backslash (\) between folders in Windows Explorer. But with AutoLISP, the backslash is interpreted as something else, so you need to use double backslashes (\\) or a single forward slash (/).

An example of the `Vl-vbaload` function is

```
(vl-vbaload "C:/Program Files/AutoCAD 2007/Sample/VBA/
    drawline.dvb")
```

If the application file is loaded, the value returned by the function is the path of the filename, and if the application file is not loaded, the value `nil` is returned.

Unloading a VBA file

The VBAUNLOAD command is used to unload VBA application files and is accessible only from the command line. The following procedure explains how to unload a VBA application file.

1. **Type** VBAUNLOAD **at the command line or the dynamic input tooltip.**

AutoCAD displays the command prompt:

```
Unload VBA Project:
```

2. **At the command prompt, enter the full name of the VBA application file.**

If you loaded a VBA application file called Drawline.DVB and it was located in the directory C:\Program Files\AutoCAD 2007\Sample\VBA, you would enter **C:\Program Files\AutoCAD 2007\Sample\VBA\ Drawline.DVB** to unload the file.

Loading and unloading an ObjectARX file

Unlike with AutoLISP files, AutoCAD offers a built-in command that allows you to load an ObjectARX or ObjectDBX file. This command is called ARX, which makes sense, considering the type of application files that it can load or unload. There are also two AutoLISP functions that can be used to load and unload an ObjectARX or ObjectDBX file.

Using the ARX command

The ARX command offers a number of different options, but the two most important are Load and Unload. The command prompt for the ARX command looks like this:

```
Enter an option [?/Load/Unload/Commands/Options]:
```

The command options for the ARX command are described as follows:

✦ **?:** Lists all the ObjectARX and ObjectDBX application files that are currently loaded in AutoCAD.

✦ **Load:** Displays the Select ARX/DBX File dialog box to specify an ObjectARX or ObjectDBX application file to load.

It is possible to load an ObjectARX or ObjectDBX application file through a command macro or a script file by setting the system variable FILEDIA to a value of 0. When FILEDIA is set to 0, the following command prompt is displayed for the ARX command:

```
Enter ARX/DBX file name to load:
```

✦ **Unload:** Allows for unloading an ObjectARX or ObjectDBX application file that is currently loaded and displays the command prompt:

```
Enter ARX/DBX file name to unload:
```

✦ **Commands:** Lists all the commands that are exposed in the loaded ObjectARX application file. ObjectDBX application files usually do not contain user interface elements and commands.

✦ **Options:** Contains three different sub-options that are used mainly for developing an ObjectARX application. The three options are Group, Classes, and Services. If you want to know more about these options, look up the ARX command in the AutoCAD Online Help system under the Command Reference Guide.

Loading an ObjectARX file using AutoLISP

You can load an ObjectARX or ObjectDBX application file using the AutoLISP function `Arxload`. `Arxload` works just like the AutoLISP function Load, which we discussed in the section "Loading an AutoLISP file" earlier in this chapter. The syntax of the `Arxload` function is explained below:

```
(arxload ObjectARX/ObjectDBX_filename [Error_message])
```

✦ **ObjectARX/ObjectDBX_filename:** The path to the ObjectARX or ObjectDBX file. Normally you would use a backslash (\) between folders in Windows Explorer, but AutoLISP interprets the backslash as something else. So you need to use double backslashes (\\) or a single forward slash (/).

✦ **Error_message:** This parameter is optional, and the value that is entered in this parameter is echoed at the command line if the ObjectARX or ObjectDBX file is not loaded.

An example of the `Arxload` function is

```
(arxload "C:/Program Files/AutoCAD 2007/geom3d.arx" "geom3d.
   arx missing")
```

If the application file is loaded, the return value of the function is the filename, and, if the application file is not loaded, the error message is returned.

Unloading an ObjectARX file using AutoLISP

You can unload an ObjectARX or ObjectDBX file using the AutoLISP function `Arxunload`. The syntax of the `Arxunload` function is this:

```
(arxunload ObjectARX/ObjectDBX_filename [Error_message])
```

✦ **ObjectARX/ObjectDBX_filename.** Enter the filename of the ObjectARX or ObjectDBX file to unload.

✦ **Error_message.** This parameter is optional, and the value that is entered in this parameter is echoed at the command line if the ObjectARX/ObjectDBX file is not unloaded.

An example of the `Arxunload` function is

```
(arxunload "geom3d.arx" "geom3d.arx unable to be unloaded")
```

If the application file is unloaded, the return value of the function is the filename, and, if the application file is not unloaded, the error message is returned.

Loading a .NET file

.NET is the new kid on the block, and the files created using the .NET API can't be loaded into AutoCAD using the APPLOAD command. It might seem like .NET files were left out of the loop, but you can still load them through the NETLOAD command. By default, this command displays the Choose .NET Assembly dialog box, which allows you to browse for a .NET application file and load it. After it is loaded, the .NET application file can't be unloaded from AutoCAD unless AutoCAD is restarted.

You can load a .NET application through a command macro or a script file by setting the system variable FILEDIA to a value of 0 before using the NETLOAD command. When FILEDIA is set to 0 and the NETLOAD command is used, the following command prompt is displayed:

```
Assembly file name:
```

As a workaround to not being able to load .NET application files using the Startup Suite, you could create an AutoLISP file that uses the NETLOAD command. An example of loading a .NET application file with AutoLISP is as follows:

```
(setvar "FILEDIA" 0)
(command ".NETLOAD" "C:/DotNet/Samples/DockingPalette.dll")
(setvar "FILEDIA" 1)
```

Automatically Loading Application Files

Just being able to load custom programs is a huge step toward increasing your productivity; but having to load application files again and again can be counterproductive. You can have AutoCAD do the work of loading custom programs for you in a couple of different ways. One is by using the Load/ Unload Applications dialog box, and the other is through specially named application files that AutoCAD loads automatically.

Using the Startup Suite

The Startup Suite (see Figure 2-5) area is located in the lower-right corner of the Load/Unload Applications dialog box. The Startup Suite controls which application files are loaded at the startup of AutoCAD and with each drawing that is opened. The Startup Suite has the same limitations as loading application files through the Load/Unload Applications dialog box. The Startup Suite is limited to AutoLISP (.LSP, .VLX, and .FAS), VBA (.DVB) ObjectARX (.ARX), and ObjectDBX (.DBX) application files, so you can't directly load a .NET application file using the Startup Suite.

Figure 2-5:
The Startup
Suite helps
to automat-
ically load
application
files.

To add an application file to the Startup Suite, follow these steps:

1. **From the Tools menu, choose Load Applications.**

AutoCAD launches the Load/Unload Applications dialog box.

2. **Click the Contents button in the Startup Suite area located in the lower-right corner of the Load/Unload Applications dialog box.**

The Startup Suite dialog box (see Figure 2-6) should now be displayed.

Figure 2-6:
The Startup
Suite dialog
box.

3. **Click the Add button in the Startup Suite dialog box.**

The Add File to Startup Suite dialog box should now be displayed.

4. **Click the Files of Type drop-down list and specify the type of applica-tion file to filter the list box by.**

The selected option controls the type of application files that are dis-played in the list box. The default selection is AutoCAD Apps. The drop-down list box allows you to filter on AutoLISP, VBA, ObjectARX, and ObjectDBX files.

5. **Specify the location for the application file using the Look In drop-down list.**

The Look In drop-down list allows you to select a folder or a named location like My Documents to start in.

6. **If the application file is located in a folder below the location that you selected in the Look In drop-down list, double-click the folder in the list box below the Look In drop-down list.**

   The list box displays any folders or files located under the folder selected in the Look In drop-down list. The types of files that are displayed in the list box are dependent on the file filter selected in the Files of Type drop-down list.

7. **Keep double-clicking on folders until you have navigated to the folder that contains the application file you want to load. Select the application file from the list box.**

   The application file should be highlighted in the list box and its name added to the File Name text box.

8. **Click Add.**

   The application file is added to the Startup Suite dialog box and is loaded into AutoCAD. You are also returned to the Startup Suite dialog box.

9. **Click Close.**

   Click Close to exit the Startup Suite dialog box and return to the Load/Unload Applications dialog box.

10. **Click Close to exit the Load/Unload Applications dialog box.**

Getting AutoCAD to do some of the work

The Startup Suite is great to automatically load application files for a small group of AutoCAD users but isn't very efficient for large groups. This is why AutoCAD is designed to look for certain named files when it is first started and when a drawing is created or opened. These files are specific to several of the different application types.

Automatically loading AutoLISP files

AutoCAD looks for several different AutoLISP application files when it first starts, when a new drawing is created or opened, and when a CUI file is loaded. These specially named files are loaded in a specific order to allow you the option of overriding standard AutoCAD commands and defining your own custom commands. These specially named files can be great for loading AutoLISP, VBA, ObjectARX, and ObjectDBX application files. As explained under the previous sections, you can use the different AutoLISP functions to load the different types of application files.

Table 2-2 lists the specially named AutoLISP files that AutoCAD looks for when it is started and when a new drawing is created or opened. The table is arranged in the order that the files are loaded in, from first to last.

Table 2-2	Load Order for Specially Named AutoLISP Files
Filename	*Description*
ACAD2007.LSP	The file is installed with AutoCAD and is loaded only once per AutoCAD session.
ACAD.LSP	The file is not installed with AutoCAD but rather needs to be created manually with a text editor such as Notepad. Like ACAD2007.LSP, this file is loaded only once per AutoCAD session, unless the system variable ACADLSPASDOC is set to a value of 1.
ACADDOC2007.LSP	The file is installed with AutoCAD and is loaded with each drawing that is created or opened.
ACADDOC.LSP	The file is not installed with AutoCAD, but rather needs to be created manually with a text editor like Notepad. Like ACADDOC2007.LSP, this file is loaded with each drawing that is created or opened.
ACAD.MNL	The file is installed with AutoCAD and is loaded when the customization file ACAD.CUI is loaded. ACAD.CUI is the default customization file that is loaded with AutoCAD.
<cui_filename>.MNL	When a partial or enterprise customization file is being loaded, AutoCAD looks for an .MNL file that has the same name as the CUI file and loads it.

Book X
Chapter 2

Using Custom Programs

If you don't know a lot about AutoLISP, but you happen to have been given some AutoLISP files to use, you can use the Customize User Interface editor to associate AutoLISP files to a .CUI file under the LISP Files node. After a .CUI file is loaded into AutoCAD, any associated AutoLISP files are loaded automatically. You can use this as an alternative to using the Startup Suite found in the Load/Unload Applications dialog box or using the AutoLISP Load function to load an AutoLISP file in combination with the <cui_filename>. MNL file. To find out more about customization files, see Book IX, Chapter 3.

Automatically loading VBA files

When AutoCAD first starts up, it looks for a VBA application file named ACAD.DVB and loads it automatically. If a public procedure named AcadStartup exists in one of the standard code modules, it is run automatically after the file has been loaded.

If you are using VBA for your custom programs, this can be a great way to initialize some variables and do anything else you need to do when AutoCAD first starts up. The AcadStartup procedure is run only when AutoCAD is first started, so if you need to perform a task every time a new drawing is created or opened, you need to handle this through events. We explain more about this process and the use of events later in Chapter 4 of this minibook.

Automatically loading ObjectARX files

Similar to how AutoCAD looks for specially named AutoLISP or VBA files, AutoCAD looks for a file to load ObjectARX application files from. The file is named ACAD.RX. If AutoCAD finds an ACAD.RX file, it steps through the file and loads each of the ObjectARX files listed in it. The ACAD.RX is a file that must be created manually with a text editor like Notepad. Below is an example of what an ACAD.RX file might look like:

```
C:\ObjectARX\Utilities\customInsert16.arx
    geom3d.arx
```

It is possible to use the full file path to the ObjectARX file or just the file name only. If you use only the filename to load the ObjectARX file, the file must be loaded in one of the support paths listed under Support File Search Path of the Files tab in the Options dialog box.

Running a Program in an Application File

You usually load an application file because you want to run one of the custom programs defined in the file. Custom programs are usually accessible in two different ways, as a command or as a function. Custom commands are run by typing the command name at the command line and pressing Enter to execute it. A custom command can be created using AutoLISP, ObjectARX, or .NET, but not VBA.

A custom function, if it is exposed through AutoLISP or ObjectARX, must be enclosed in parentheses to be executed. If the function is defined with VBA, it is known as a procedure and can be executed using a command like VBAMAN. The VBAMAN command, along with other additional methods of executing a procedure defined in a VBA application file, are covered in greater depth in Chapter 4 of this minibook.

To execute a procedure in a VBA application file, follow these steps:

1. **From the Tools menu, choose Macros⇨VBA Manager.**

   AutoCAD launches the VBA Manager dialog box.

2. **Click the Macros button located on the right side of the VBA Manager.**

   The Macros dialog box (see Figure 2-7) is displayed and shows all the available procedures to run in the loaded VBA application files.

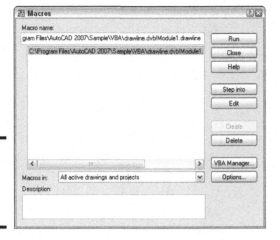

Figure 2-7:
Putting a
procedure
(or macro)
to work.

3. **Select the procedure that you want to run from the list box in the
middle of the dialog box.**

The selected procedure is highlighted in the list box. You can resize the
Macros dialog box by clicking one of the corners of the dialog box and
dragging outward. This allows you to see more of the names of the procedures in the list box.

4. **Click Run.**

The procedure starts executing. Follow any onscreen prompts for input
that might be displayed while the procedure is being executed.

You can use the -VBARUN command to execute a procedure in a VBA application file from a command macro or a script file. We explain the -VBARUN command later in Chapter 4 of this minibook.

Chapter 3: Introducing AutoLISP

In This Chapter

✔ Accessing the AutoLISP Development Environment

✔ Using the VLIDE

✔ Creating a basic program

✔ Getting information to and from the user

✔ Using the debug tools in the Visual LISP IDE

✔ Using ActiveX Automation with AutoLISP

The AutoLISP functionality of AutoCAD has always been one of those features that many users don't know about and don't take advantage of. This is partly because many users who are new to AutoCAD just don't have the time to master all the features that are offered. The program is much more robust than it was during its earlier days, so not as many people are forced to resort to programming in AutoLISP. The numbers of users who know AutoLISP is on the decline today because it is now a niche feature that helps to improve workflow, rather than a necessary tool to create features that aren't part of the product.

Utilities like Revision Cloud and Justify Text were once originally AutoLISP programs found in AutoCAD; a majority of the Express Tools that ship with AutoCAD were also developed with AutoLISP. For more information on Express Tools, see Book IX, Chapter 4. As we discuss in this chapter, AutoLISP is a very powerful language that is easy to master. After you start creating your own custom programs, you might wonder why you didn't start working with AutoLISP sooner.

Accessing the AutoLISP Development Environment

Over the years, the main development environment for creating AutoLISP programs has been Notepad. Notepad was the tool of choice simply because Autodesk didn't offer a development tool for working with AutoLISP files. This all changed when Autodesk purchased a program called Vital LISP. Vital LISP was developed by a third-party software company and extended the capabilities of AutoLISP. Shortly after Autodesk purchased Vital LISP, they renamed the product to Visual LISP.

Visual LISP includes a complete AutoLISP development environment (see Figure 3-1). The development environment includes the capability to see color-coded syntax, use debugging tools, and much more. The development environment is know as the VLIDE — Visual LISP Integrated Development Environment. The VLIDE is accessible directly from AutoCAD.

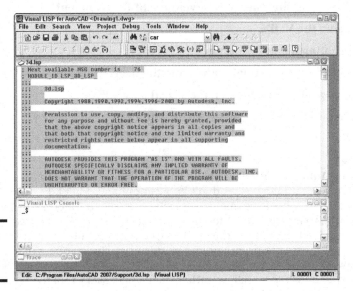

Figure 3-1:
The Visual
LISP IDE.

Launching the Visual LISP IDE

To launch the Visual LISP IDE, use one of these methods:

✦ **Tools menu:** Choose Tools⇨AutoLISP⇨Visual LISP Editor.

✦ **Keyboard input:** Type **VLIDE or VLISP** at the command line and press Enter.

Loading an existing AutoLISP application file

Use either of the two methods to initiate the VLIDE or VLISP command. The following procedure uses the Tools menu to launch the integrated development environment and explains how to load an existing AutoLISP application file.

1. **Choose Tools⇨AutoLISP⇨Visual LISP Editor.**

AutoCAD launches the Visual LISP Editor.

2. **From the Files menu in the Visual LISP Editor, choose Open File.**

   The Open File to Edit/View dialog box is displayed, allowing you to open AutoLISP, DCL, SQL, or C/C++ source files. The two that you are going to be working with are AutoLISP and DCL files.

3. **Click the Files of Type drop-down list and specify the type of application file to filter the list box by.**

   The selected option controls the type of application files that are displayed in the list box. The default selection is All Files. The drop-down list box allows you to filter on LSP, DCL, SQL, and C/C++ source files.

4. **Specify the location for the application file using the Look In drop-down list.**

   The Look In drop-down list allows you to select a folder or a named location like My Documents to start in.

5. **If the application file is located in a folder below the location that you selected in the Look In drop-down list, double-click the folder in the list box below the Look In drop-down list.**

   The list box displays any folders or files located under the folder selected in the Look In drop-down list. The types of files that are displayed in the list box are dependent on the file filter selected in the Files of Type drop-down list.

6. **Keep double-clicking on folders until you have navigated to the folder that contains the application file you want to load. Select the application file from the list box.**

   The application file should be highlighted in the list box and its name added to the File Name text box.

7. **Click Open.**

   The application file should be opened in its own text window within the Visual LISP Editor.

If you are opening an AutoLISP file for view only, you can select the Open As Read-Only check box at the bottom of the Open File to Edit/View dialog box to avoid accidentally making changes to the file.

Using the VLIDE

Although AutoLISP is not a mainstream programming language, it's nice to have a development environment dedicated to AutoLISP. In order to take full advantage of the development environment, you should understand some of its basic functionality and behavior.

The Text window is where you edit and view source code that makes up an AutoLISP application file. This window allows you not only to edit your source code but also to run validation tools on it to test it for things like missing parentheses. Like most development environments, the main window controls how code is represented on-screen. Color coding (see Figure 3-2) is one of the biggest advantages that the Visual LISP editor has over an application like Notepad. (Although this is a black and white book, the different colors are represented by grayscale in the figure.)

Figure 3-2: AutoLISP said, "Let there be color!" and there was.

```
;;;------------------------------------------------------------------
;;; Draw a sphere, dome, or dish

(defun spheres (typ / cen r numseg ax ax1 e1 e2)
  (setq numseg 0)
  (initget 17)                         ;3D point can't be null
  (setq cen (getpoint (strcat "\nSpecify center point of " typ": ")))
  (initget 7 "Diameter")               ;Radius can't be 0, neg, or null
  (cond
    ((= typ "sphere") (princ "\nSpecify radius of sphere or [Diameter]: "))
    ((= typ "dome"  ) (princ "\nSpecify radius of dome or [Diameter]: "))
    ((= typ "dish"  ) (princ "\nSpecify radius of dish or [Diameter]: "))
  )
  (setq r (getdist cen ))
  (if (= r "Diameter")
    (progn
      (initget 7)                      ;Diameter can't be 0, neg, or null
      (setq r (/ (getdist cen (strcat "\nSpecify diameter of "typ": ")) 2.0))
    )
  )
)
```

Table 3-1 lists some of the default colors for many of the common elements as they appear in the Text window.

Table 3-1	Color Coding the Text Window
Window Element	**Description (Default Color Scheme)**
:WINDOW-TEXT	Variables and function names that are not protected. (Black text with a white background.)
:LEX-SPACE	Empty space in the file that is represented by a space or tab. (Black text with a white background.)
:LEX-STR	A string value that is surrounded with double quote marks. (Magenta text with a white background.)
:LEX-SYM	Variables and function names that are protected. (Blue text with a white background.)
:LEX-NUM :LEX-INT	Whole number. (Dark green text with a white background.)
:LEX-REAL	Real or float number. (Teal text with a white background.)
:LEX-PAREN	Parentheses. (Red text with a white background.)
:LEX-COMM	Comment. (Purple text with a gray background.)

Controlling color coding in the Text window

You can change the default colors that are displayed in the Text window for color coding to a certain degree, but the changes are limited to a predetermined color palette. Follow these steps to change the color-coding scheme:

1. **From the Tools menu in the Visual LISP editor, choose**
   Window Attributes⇨Configure Current.

   The Window Attributes dialog box (see Figure 3-3) is displayed.

Figure 3-3:
Adjusting
the Text
window
colors.

2. **Click on the drop-down list under the Text Colors section.**

   The drop-down list controls the window element that is currently being edited when the color swatches are clicked.

3. **Click a color swatch in the top row to adjust the color of text for the selected element.**

   The top row of color swatches controls the foreground color or the color of the text. The changes in the dialog box appear in both the dialog box along the top of the Text Colors section and in real-time in the editor window, giving you a good understanding of how the changes affect the Text window.

4. **Click a color swatch in the bottom row to adjust the color of background for the selected element.**

   The bottom row of color swatches controls the background color, which in most cases is the color white, except for highlighting, debugging, and comments.

5. **In order to use color coding, make sure that the Lexical Colors check box is checked under the Text Colors section.**

6. **Click OK to save the changes made in the Window Attributes dialog box.**

7. **Click Yes to save the color scheme as the default editor colors; click No to use the color scheme only while the Text window is open.**

You can control the number of spaces that appear in the Text window when the tab key is pressed on the keyboard by adjusting the value in the Tab Width text box of the Window Attributes dialog box.

You can control the left margin of the Text window through the Left Margin text box in the Window Attributes dialog box. The value controls the amount of white space from the left edge of the application window to where text first appears. The value is expressed in pixels.

Controlling text size and font style in the Text window

Changing the text size and font style for the Text Window adds a level of personalization to the Visual LISP Editor. Based on the screen resolution that you are running, you may need to change the size of the text for legibility. Follow these steps to change the size and font style used in the Text window:

1. **From the Tools menu in the Visual LISP Editor, choose Window Attributes⇨Font.**

The Font dialog box (see Figure 3-4) is displayed.

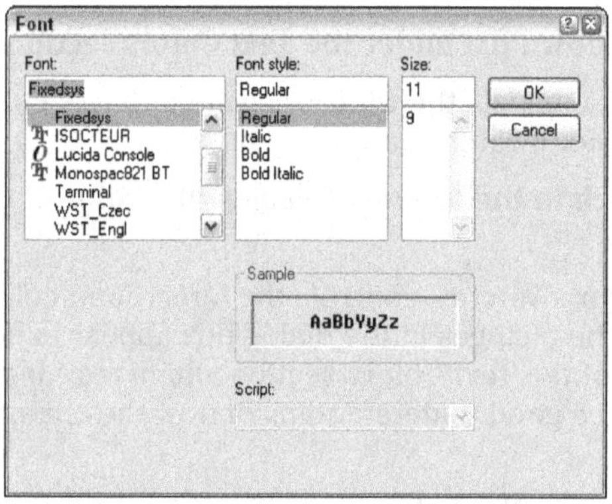

Figure 3-4:
Adjusting
text size and
font style.

2. **Select one of the available fonts from the Font list box.**

After you've selected a font, the Sample section updates with a preview of the current font settings.

3. **Select one of the available font styles from the Font Style list box.**

After you've selected a font style, the Sample section updates with a preview of the current font settings.

4. **Select one of the available sizes from the Size list box.**

After you've selected a size, the Sample section updates with a preview of the current font settings.

5. **Click OK to save the changes made in the Font dialog box and update the Text window.**

Navigating the Text window

Navigating the Text window doesn't require much of an explanation: It uses a lot of common Windows functionality that can be found in basic text editors like Notepad. The Text window can be maximized and minimized and contains both horizontal and vertical scroll bars, but it also contains some other nice options that you won't find in Notepad.

The Visual LISP Editor offers a few ways to improve navigation of both small and large source files. These navigation tools can be found under the Search menu. One option is called Bookmarks and another is called Go to Line:

✦ **Bookmarks:** Bookmarks allow quick navigation between different sections of a source file. These markers only remain active while the file is open in the Visual LISP Editor. To create a bookmark, click the Search menu, and choose Bookmarks⇨Toggle Bookmark. A dark green oval (see Figure 3-5) appears in the left margin of the Text window.

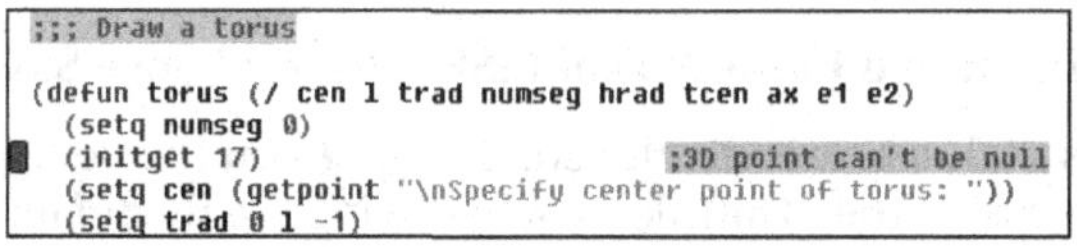

Book X
Chapter 3

Introducing
AutoLISP

Figure 3-5:
Bookmark in
left margin.

```
;;; Draw a torus

(defun torus (/ cen l trad numseg hrad tcen ax e1 e2)
  (setq numseg 0)
  (initget 17)                          ;3D point can't be null
  (setq cen (getpoint "\nSpecify center point of torus: "))
  (setq trad 0 l -1)
```

To navigate between the different bookmarks, select Next Bookmark or Previous Bookmark from Search⇨Bookmarks. Choose Search⇨ Bookmarks⇨Clear All Bookmarks to remove all the active bookmarks in the Text window.

✦ **Go to Line:** Go to Line isn't as useful as it once was in releases of AutoCAD prior to 2006. This is because in those earlier versions, menu files needed to be edited outside AutoCAD using a text editor. The Go to Line option was perfect for quickly jumping to a line in a menu file when an error was encountered during the compiling process in AutoCAD.

The Go to Line option is still helpful to find a problem in a .DXF file when there is an error during loading. To use the Go to Line option, click the Search menu and choose Go to Line. The Go to Line dialog box (see Figure 3-6) is displayed. In the text field, enter the line in the file you want to jump to and click OK.

Figure 3-6:
Go here,
go there.

Creating a Basic Program

Now that you have a taste for the Visual LISP editor, we are sure you're just itching to get started. In the rest of this chapter, as you become familiar with the AutoLISP language, we show you some of the other features of the Visual LISP editor when it makes sense to introduce them.

Creating a new AutoLISP file

To start off creating a basic program, make sure that a blank Text window is available. The following steps explain how to create an empty Text window and to save the contents of the window to a new empty application file.

1. **From the Files menu in the Visual LISP Editor, choose New File.**

A new Text window is created and is titled *<Untitled-0>*. The name appears in the caption bar of the Visual LISP Editor if the Text window is maximized or in the caption bar of the Text window. The name of each new Text window is incremented by a value of 1, so the next new Text window would be titled *<Untitled-1>*, and so on.

2. **From the Files menu in the Visual LISP Editor, choose Save As.**

The Save As dialog box is displayed, allowing you to specify a new name for the contents of the <Untitled-0> Text window. By default, Visual LISP offers up the name tmp.LSP for the new filename.

3. **Click the Save As Type drop-down list and specify the type of Lisp Source File, if it is not already selected.**

The default file type is Lisp Source File.

4. **Specify the location the application file should be saved to using the Save In drop-down list.**

The Save In drop-down list allows you to select a folder or a named location like My Documents to save the new file to.

If the desired save to location is in a folder below the location that you selected in the Save In drop-down list, double-click the folder in the list box below the Save In drop-down list.

The list box displays any folders or files located under the folder selected in the Save In drop-down list. The types of files that are displayed in the list box depend on the file filter selected in the Save As Type drop-down list.

5. **Keep double-clicking on folders until you have navigated to the folder that you want to save the new file to and type a new name in the File Name text box for the file.**

You should make the name as descriptive as you can without making it too long, just in case you need to find the file at a later date through Windows Explorer.

6. **Click Save to write all the contents of the Text window to the file name and location that you specified. You should also notice that the Text window now displays the updated filename.**

Anatomy of an AutoLISP expression

To use the AutoLISP programming language, you must understand how it is structured and what makes up an AutoLISP expression. An AutoLISP expression must begin with either a left (open) parenthesis [(] or an exclamation point (!):

✦ **(:** An open parenthesis is used to denote the start of an AutoLISP expression and must be balanced with a closing parenthesis to denote the end of the expression.

✦ **!:** An exclamation point is used to instruct the AutoLISP interpreter to return the value for the symbol that follows the exclamation point.

If you enter either an opening parenthesis or exclamation point at the command line in AutoCAD, it informs AutoCAD that the following information should be sent to the AutoLISP interpreter. The AutoLISP interpreter then evaluates and analyzes the expression(s) accordingly. If a return value is generated, it is displayed in the command line.

Table 3-2 shows some different AutoLISP samples that can be typed directly at the command line in AutoCAD and what the expected results are.

Table 3-2	Sample AutoLISP Expressions
AutoLISP Expression	*Expected Result*
`!XY`	Returns the value of the variable XY, which by default is `nil`.
`(command "._circle" "5,5" "10")`	Draws a circle at the coordinate 5,5 on the current layer with a radius of 10 units.

(continued)

Table 3-2 *(continued)*

AutoLISP Expression	Expected Result
(setq X 4 Y 5 XY 9)	Sets the variable X to a value of 4; sets Y to a value of 5; and sets XY to a value of 9. The value 9 is returned to the command line because XY is the last variable that is set, and the function setq returns the value that it sets to a variable.
(+ 15 (* 2 12))	Returns a value of 39. The innermost functions are evaluated first in AutoLISP. The 2 multiplied by 12 is evaluated first for a value of 24. The value of 24 is then added to 15 to get an end result of 39.
(setq str (strcat "Welcome to " "AutoLISP"))	The return value is "Welcome to AutoLISP". The strcat function is used to concatenate string variables together.

Now that you know how to identify an AutoLISP expression, the next step is to understand how an AutoLISP expression is structured when it starts with an open parenthesis. At minimum, an AutoLISP expression must have an open (left) parenthesis, a function name, and a closing (right) parenthesis but can contain arguments as well (see Figure 3-7). Usually AutoLISP expressions include arguments like many of the samples in Table 3-2.

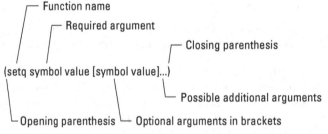

Figure 3-7:
The anatomy of an AutoLISP expression.

AutoLISP function and variable names are not case-sensitive like function and variable names in other programming languages such as C++, or even VB. In other languages, a variable with the name A might represent something different than a variable with the name a, but not in AutoLISP.

Adding comments

A *comment* is a string of information that is used to describe a line or series of lines in an application file that do not get evaluated. A comment can identify what is taking place in a function or command, or can be a general note at the top of the file that includes general revision or author information. A semicolon (;) is placed at the front of a text string to designate it as a comment. By default, a comment appears in purple text with a gray background within the Visual LISP Editor. A sample comment is

```
; New Custom command to create a dimension style
```

To command or just to function

When you are creating custom programs in AutoLISP, you have to make a decision whether the custom program will be used to define a new command or a function. Typically, a command is used by entering its name at the AutoCAD command line or executing it from one of the user interface elements. Functions are not usually entered at the command line or with a user interface element, but used in an AutoLISP application file.

AutoLISP commands, on the surface, seem just like normal commands to users unless they try to use the commands in another AutoLISP program. AutoLISP commands are different core commands from those defined in ObjectARX because they can't be used with the AutoLISP function Command. To create your command or function in AutoLISP, use the function Defun, which stands for Define Function. The syntax for the Defun function is as follows:

```
(defun function_name ([arguments . . .] [/ variables . . .])
    expressions
    . . .
)
```

Here's a breakdown of the syntax:

✦ **Function_filename:** The function or command name that can be typed in at the command line or used in a command macro for a toolbar button.

✦ **Arguments:** Arguments are used to receive values from the calling function. Arguments are not used when creating a command.

✦ **Variables:** The variables that are defined with the Defun function are declared locally to the function or command. This is a way to manage variables that should exist only while the function or command is running. After the function or command ends, the variables are reset to the previous values they held.

✦ **Expressions:** A Defun function is a way to group other AutoLISP expressions with a specified name that can be used to reference those lines. Expressions represent AutoLISP expressions that should be executed when the function or command is run from the command line or a command macro.

An example of creating a custom function with the Defun function is

```
(defun RTD (rad)
  (* (/ rad PI) 180)
)
```

The preceding example shows a custom function named RTD with a single argument named rad. (RTD is short for Radians to Degrees.) If you take a look at the expressions, you can see that there is a single expression using nested expressions. To convert a radians value, the value of rad is divided by the value of PI and then multiplied by 180.

So if you typed in **RTD** at the command line, you would get a warning about the command not being found. This is because it is a function, so it must be typed in at the command line using opening and closing parentheses like this: **(RTD 1.57079633)**. After the RTD function is evaluated, a value of 90 is returned to the command line.

 There are three predefined variables in AutoLISP: PI, T, and PAUSE. PI holds the value 3.14159, T holds a non-nil value and evaluates to T, and PAUSE is used in conjunction with the Command function to wait for the user to supply some input via the mouse or keyboard.

An example of creating a custom command with the Defun function is

```
(defun c:HL2 ()
  (command ".line" "0,0" "2,0" "")
)
```

The preceding example shows a custom command named HL2 with no arguments. HL2 is short for Horizontal Line of 2 units. If you take a look at the expressions, you can see that there is a single expression with no nesting, but it is using multiple arguments. The function Command is used, which allows you to automate tasks using the built-in AutoCAD commands.

In this case, the command that is being used is LINE. A line is being generated from the coordinates 0,0 to 2,0. Because only a single line with a start and end point is required, " " (two double quote marks with no text between) is used as the last argument to end the LINE command. " " is like pressing Enter on the keyboard. To run the custom command, all you need to do is type **HL2** at the command line. You do not need to add opening and closing parentheses as you did to use the function.

Creating your first AutoLISP program

It's time to put everything together and create your first custom command. This example has you create a new AutoLISP file, add a new command, and then load it into AutoCAD:

1. **From the Tools menu in AutoCAD, choose AutoLISP⇨ Visual LISP Editor.**

   AutoCAD launches the Visual LISP Editor.

2. **From the Files menu in the Visual LISP Editor, choose New File.**

   An empty Text Window titled *<Untitiled-0>* is created.

3. **From the Files menu in the Visual LISP Editor, choose Save As.**

   The Save As dialog box is displayed, allowing you to save the contents of the current Text window.

4. **In the Save As dialog box, make sure the Save As Type drop-down list is set to Lisp Source File and enter MyStuff.LSP in the File Name text box. Then specify the save to location by selecting My Documents from the Save In drop-down list.**

5. **Click Save.**

   The contents of the Text window are written to a file named MyStuff.LSP located in the My Documents folder.

6. **In the Text Window titled MyStuff.LSP, enter the following code:**

   ```
   ;; Defines a two letter command to start a Zoom Window
   (defun c:ZW ( )
       (command ".Zoom" "Window")
   )
   ```

7. **From the Files menu in the Visual LISP Editor, choose Save.**

   The new command is saved out to the MyStuff.LSP file.

8. **Switch back to AutoCAD by clicking the icon in the Windows taskbar area or select the Windows menu in the Visual LISP Editor and choose Activate AutoCAD.**

   Focus should now be shifted to the AutoCAD application window.

9. **At the command line, type ZW.**

   This error message should be displayed in the command line window because the AutoLISP file hasn't been loaded yet:

   ```
   Unknown command "ZW". Press F1 for help.
   ```

10. **Switch back to the Visual LISP Editor by clicking on its icon in the Windows taskbar area, or select the Tools menu in AutoCAD and choose AutoLISP⇨Visual LISP Editor.**

    Focus should now be shifted to the Visual LISP Editor.

11. **From the Tools menu in the Visual LISP editor, choose Load Text in Editor.**

    The custom command should now be ready to use in AutoCAD.

12. **Switch back to AutoCAD and type ZW again.**

This time, no error message is displayed and the ZOOM command starts with the Window option automatically. The first prompt that is displayed is `Specify first corner`.

13. **Select two points on-screen to complete the Window option of the ZOOM command.**

More Than Just the Essentials of AutoLISP

After you have a good foundation of what it takes to create an AutoLISP file and create a custom command, it's time to introduce you to some more functions. AutoLISP can perform math calculations, string manipulation, and much more. All these are important in adding functionality to your custom programs.

Supported data types

AutoLISP is a programming language, so it uses data types to represent certain types of information. Data types play a role in how your application exchanges information with functions, and even with AutoCAD and the user. Table 3-3 shows the different data types that are available in AutoLISP.

Table 3-3	Data Types in AutoLISP	
Data Type	*Brief Description*	*Examples*
Integer	A whole number with no decimal place, and values fall in the range of –32,768 and 32,767.	`10`
Real	Any number with a decimal place and 14 significant places of precision.	`1.0, 0.23451, .5`
String	Any number of alphanumeric characters enclosed in double quotes.	`"Hello"`
List	An expression enclosed in parentheses.	`(0.5 0.5 0),` `("Hello" "World"),` `(1 "Hello")`
Symbol	Variables used to hold data.	`PI, abc, retVal`
Selection set	A valid selection set to hold references to entities.	`<Selection set: 1>`
Entity name	A valid entity name used to reference an individual entity in the drawing.	`<Entity name:` `0cf0121>`
VLA-object	A valid COM object used with ActiveX Automation.	`#<VLA-OBJECT` `IAcadApplication` `00c2db8c>`
File descriptor	A reference point to an open file in memory.	`#<file "acad.pgp">`

Math functions

Because AutoCAD is a drafting program, you most likely find yourself needing to work with numbers from time to time. AutoLISP math functions come in a variety of different forms, from standard math functions like + (addition) and – (subtraction) to much more complex functions, such as `sin` (sine) and `atan` (arctangent).

Table 3-4 shows some of the different math functions that are available in AutoLISP.

Table 3-4	Some of the Basic Math Functions	
Function Syntax	*Description*	*Result*
`(+ [number number ...])`	Sums all numbers together and returns the value. Example: `(+ 1 2.5)`	3.5
`(- [number number ...])`	Subtracts all the numbers from the first one and returns the value. Example: `(- 1 0.25)`	0.75
`(* [number number ...])`	Multiplies all the numbers together and returns the value. Example: `(* 1 3 5)`	15
`(/ [number number ...])`	Divides the first number by the product of all the remaining numbers and returns the value. Example: `(/ 2 5)`	0
`(abs number)`	Returns the absolute value. Example: `(abs -1.34)`	1.34
`(sqrt number)`	Returns the square root of the number. Example: `(sqrt 3)`	1.73205

String functions

Strings provide feedback to the user in the form of error messages or give feedback on the current status of a command if it takes a while to run. Another thing that strings are useful for is command prompts. Because AutoCAD is still primarily command-prompt based, you will surely be asking the user of your custom programs to provide information at the command line.

Table 3-5 shows some of the different string manipulation functions that are available in AutoLISP.

Table 3-5	Some of the Basic String Manipulation Functions	
Function Syntax	*Description*	*Result*
(strcase *string* [flag])	Returns the string in either uppercase or lowercase. If the optional flag value is set to T, the string is returned in lowercase. Example: (strcase "Hello")	"HELLO"
(strcat [*string* . . .])	Concatenates all the supplied strings together and returns a single string. Example: (strcat "Hello"" " "World")	"Hello World"
(substr *string* *start* [*length*])	Returns a portion of the string based on the start position and the length supplied. Example: (substr "Hello World" 7)	"World"
(vl-string-subst *replace_string* *pattern string* [*start*])	Looks for the pattern in the string and replaces it with the replace_string value, and returns the result of the replace. Example: (vl-string-subst "Planet" "World" "Hello World")	"Hello Planet"

List functions

Lists are everywhere in AutoLISP: You've been working with lists and weren't even aware of it. Lists are used to represent groups of things. Up until this point, every line you have added to the MyStuff.LSP file has been a list with a function and arguments. Lists are used to represent things like coordinates or even how you work with entity properties.

Table 3-6 shows some of the different list functions that are available in AutoLISP.

Table 3-6	Some of the Basic List Functions	
Function Syntax	*Description*	*Result*
(list [expression . . .])	Returns a list of all the provided expressions. Example: (list 1.3 12.75 0)	(1.3 12.75 0)
(car list)	Returns the first item in a list. There are combinations of car and cdr to get items in other places of the list, such as cadr. Example: (car (list 1.3 12.75 0))	1.3
(cdr list)	Returns all items in a list except the first one. There are combinations of car and cdr to get items in other places of the list, such as cadr. Example: (cdr (list 1.3 12.75 0))	(12.75 0)
(nth index list)	Returns the item in the location of the list specified by the value of index. The first item in the list is index 0. Example: (nth 2 (list 1.3 12.75 0))	0
(reverse list)	Reverses the item order of the list and returns the new list. Example: (reverse (list 1.3 12.75 0))	(0 12.75 1.3)

Book X
Chapter 3

Introducing AutoLISP

Data conversion functions

As you start using more AutoLISP functions, you will want to use the results of one AutoLISP function with another, but each AutoLISP function requires you to use specific data types for its parameters. In these situations, you need to convert data from one data type to another. AutoLISP contains some functions specifically for this purpose.

Table 3-7 shows some of the different conversion functions that are available in AutoLISP.

Table 3-7   **Some of the Basic Conversion Functions**

Function Syntax	Description	Result
(atof *string*)	Returns the string as a real number. Example: (atof "12.5")	12.5
(atoi *string*)	Returns the string as an integer. Example: (atoi "1.75")	1.75
(itoa *int*)	Returns the integer as a string. Example: (itoa 12)	"12"
(rtos *number* [*mode* [*precision*]])	Returns the real number into a formatted string. Mode is a value of 1 – 5 and precision is 0 through 8, the same as LUPREC. Mode: 1 – Scientific 2 – Decimal 3 – Engineering 4 – Architectural 5 – Fraction Example: (rtos 2.5 2 8)	"2.50000000"

Saving and accessing values for later

Now that you have all these different values being returned by math, string, list, and conversion functions, it sure would be nice to save the values for use later in your custom programs. AutoLISP offers some different ways to store and retrieve values. Some of the ways affect how AutoCAD features behave or can be used to temporarily store information that can be recalled later in your program, such as a calculation or user input that might be needed for another function.

Table 3-8 shows some of the different data storage and retrieval functions that are available in AutoLISP.

Table 3-8   **Data Storage and Retrieval Functions**

Function Syntax	Description	Result
(setq *variable value* [*variable value*] ...)	Sets the value to a variable. The variables only exist while the drawing is open. Example: (setq msg "Error occurred")	"Error occurred"

Function Syntax	Description	Result
`(setvar variable_ name value)`	Sets the value to a system variable. Example: `(setvar "clayer" "0")`	`"0"`
`(gertvar variable_name)`	Returns the current value of a system variable. Example: `(getvar "clayer")`	`"0"`

Exchanging information with AutoCAD

One of the pain points of drafting is initially setting up CAD standards and then trying to manage them. In this procedure, you create a custom command that draws a circle on a specific layer and sets it to a specified diameter:

Book X Chapter 3

Introducing AutoLISP

1. **From the Tools menu in AutoCAD, choose AutoLISP➪Visual LISP Editor.**

   AutoCAD launches the Visual LISP Editor.

2. **From the Files menu in the Visual LISP Editor, choose Open File.**

   The Open File to Edit/View dialog box is displayed, allowing you to open an existing file.

3. **In the Open File to Edit/View dialog box, browse to the My Documents folder and select the file MyStuff.LSP.**

4. **Click Open.**

   The contents of the MyStuff.LSP are loaded into a Text window.

5. **In the Text window, place the cursor behind the last parenthesis and press Enter twice so there is a blank line below the ZW command.**

6. **In the Text window, enter the following expressions and command:**

```
;; Custom command to create a new layer and draw a
;; 0.5 diameter circle.
(defun c:BCIRC ( / cur-layer)
    ;; Store the current layer
    (setq cur-layer (getvar "clayer"))

    ;; Create a new layer called Hole and set it current
    (command ".layer" "m" "Hole" "c" "5" "" "")

    ;; Draw a 0.5 diameter circle and ask the user for
    ;; the center point
    (command ".circle" PAUSE "d" 0.5)

    ;; Restore the original layer
```

```
(setvar "clayer" cur-layer)

;; Stop an return values from being echoed
(princ)
)
```

7. **From the Files menu in the Visual LISP Editor, choose Save.**

The new command is saved out of the MyStuff.LSP file.

8. **From the Tools menu in the Visual LISP Editor, choose Load Text in Editor.**

The custom command is loaded into AutoCAD and should now be ready to use.

9. **Switch back to AutoCAD.**

Focus should now be shifted to the AutoCAD application window.

10. **At the command line, type** BCIRC.

You should be prompted for the center point of the circle. A new circle object should be generated on the layer Hole, which is blue. The circle that is created should have a diameter of 0.5. The program should restore the previous layer before the CIRCLE command was started. If the user presses the Escape key, the previous layer won't be restored. To resolve this, modify the command to look like the following code:

```
;; Custom command to create a new layer and draw a
;; 0.5 diameter circle.
(defun c:BCIRC ( / cur-layer)
;; Store the current layer
    (setq cur-layer (getvar "clayer"))

    ;; Create a new layer called Hole and set it
    current
    (command ".layer" "m" "Hole" "c" "5" "" "s" cur-
layer "")

    ;; Draw a 0.5 diameter circle and ask the user for
    ;; the center point
    (command ".circle" PAUSE "d" 0.5)

    ;; Change the layer of the new circle
    (command ".change" "l" "" "p" "la" "Hole" "")

    ;; Stop an return values from being echoed
    (princ)
)
```

With the revised code, the layer is never changed; instead, the object's properties are modified with the CHANGE command. Although the second solution requires more code, it is much better because the drawing properties are never changed. If the user presses the Escape key, it won't affect the current layer.

Getting Information to and from the User

User input comes in a variety of different ways in AutoCAD. Typical user input in AutoCAD is done through the command line and with the pointing device. AutoLISP is full of different functions for collecting user input.

Table 3-9 shows some of the different user input functions that are available in AutoLISP.

Table 3-9	Some of the Basic User Input Functions	
Function Syntax	*Description*	*Result*
(getpoint [*point*] [*message*])	Requests the user to enter a point or select one in a drawing.	(21.9975 13.1977 0.0)
	Example: (getpoint "\nPick first point: ")	
(getcorner *point* [*message*])	Requests the user to enter a point or select one in a drawing for the opposite corner of a rectangle.	(24.4237 14.9183 0.0)
	Example: (getpoint '(0 0) "\nPick opposite corner: ")	
(getdist [*point*] [*message*])	Requests the user to pick up to two points to calculate the overall distance between the two points.	7.93347
	Example: (getdist "\nPick two points: ")	
(getint [*message*])	Requests the user to enter a whole number.	29
	Example: (getint "\nEnter your age: ")	
(getreal [message])	Requests the user to enter any number with or without decimal places.	32.6
	Example: (getreal "\nEnter a number: ")	

Giving feedback to the user

Programming is all about giving and taking, so you should make sure that you are not just taking input from your users and not giving them feedback.

Feedback can be in the form of text at the command line or even an alert message box when a problem happens.

Table 3-10 shows some of the different user feedback functions that are available in AutoLISP.

Table 3-10	Some of the Basic User Feedback Functions	
Function Syntax	*Description*	*Result*
`(alert message)`	Displays a message box with an OK button on it. Example: `(alert "Hello World")`	
`(prompt message)`	Displays a text string in the command line. Example: `(prompt "\nHello World")`	`Hello` `Worldnil`

`(princ [expression [filedescripter]])`	Prompt returns the value of `nil`, along with many other AutoLISP functions. You can keep AutoCAD from echoing `nil` and the last return value by using a function called `Princ`. Optionally, `Princ` can also be used to display a text string or write a text string to a file. When `Princ` is used to display a text string, it may display the text string twice because it displays and echoes the message. It is best not to use `Princ` to display a text string at the command line.
	
	Examples:
	`(prompt "\nHello World")`
	`(princ)` or `(princ "\nSelect object::")`
		`Hello`
		`World`
		
		`Select`
		`object:`
		`"\nSelect`
		`object:"`

`(textscr)`	Displays the AutoCAD Text window. Example: `(textscr)`	
`(graphscr)`	Displays the AutoCAD graphics screen. Example: `(graphscr)`	

Other functions to note

As you might have already noticed, a lot of functionality is packed into the AutoLISP programming language. The functions we cover in this section help to make your custom programs much more robust.

Table 3-11 shows some of the different other functions that are available in AutoLISP.

Table 3-11	Some of the Other Functions	
Function Syntax	*Description*	*Results*

`(while`
`testcondition`
`[expression ...])`
	Evaluates the test condition. If it is true, the expressions are evaluated repeatedly until the test condition is false.	`Count down: T-10`
		`Count down: T-9`
		`Count down: T-8`
		`Count down: T-7`

	Example:
	`(setq cnt 10)`
	`(while (> cnt 0)`
	` (prompt`
	`  (strcat "\nCount`
	`down: T-"`
	`   (itoa cnt)`
	`   )`
	`  )`
	`  (setq cnt (1- cnt))`
	` )`
	`(prompt "\nBlast off")`
		`Count down: T-6`
		`Count down: T-5`
		`Count down: T-4`
		`Count down: T-3`
		`Count down: T-2`
		`Count down: T-1`
		`Blast off`

`(if testcondition`
`then expression`
`[else expression])`
	Evaluates the test conditional expression and evaluates one of the two expressions. If the test conditional expression is true, the `then` expression is evaluated, and, if not, the `else` expression is evaluated.	`Number greater`
		`than 3.`

	The function `progn` is used to group more than one AutoLISP expression together as `IF` can only handle one expression for the `then` and `else` expressions.	

	Example:
	`(setq XY 3.1)`
	`(if (> XY 3)`
	` (progn`
	`  (prompt "\nNumber`
	`greater than 3.")`
	`  (prompt "\nanother`
	`line...")`
	`  )`
	`  (prompt "\nNumber`
	`less than 3.")`
	` )`	

(continued)

Book X
Chapter 3

Introducing
AutoLISP

Table 3-11 *(continued)*

Function Syntax	Description	Results
`(ssget [selection-method] [point1 [ point2]] [point-list] [filter-list])`	Allows the user to select objects on-screen similar to commands like copy and move, but `ssget` has special selection methods and filtering built into it to give your custom commands and programs some additional control. There are also functions like `sslength` and `ssname`, which are specific to working with the returned selection set value.	You selected 7 objects.

	Example:
	`(setq SS (ssget))`
	`(if (/= SS nil)`
	  `(prompt`
	   `(strcat "\nYou selected "`
	    `(itoa (sslength SS))`
	    `" objects."`
	   `)`
	  `)`
	  `(prompt "\nNo objects selected.")`
	`)`	

`(entsel [message])`	Allows the user to select only an individual object. The return value is a list of the points selected on-screen and the entity name of the object selected.	A circle was not selected.

	Example:
	`(setq ENT (entsel "\`
	`nSelect a Circle: "))`
	`(if (/= ENT nil)`
	  `(progn`
	   `(if (= (cdr (assoc 0`
	`(entget (car ENT))))`
	     `"CIRCLE"`
	   `)`
	   `(prompt "\nA Circle`
	`was selected.")`
	   `(prompt "\nA Circle`
	`was not selected.")`
	  `)`
	  `)`
	 `(prompt "\nNo object`
	`was selected.")`
	 `(princ)`
	`)`	

Using the Debug Tools in the Visual LISP IDE

One of the most challenging aspects of programming is the process of debugging a custom program. *Debugging* is the process of looking for errors in a program and correcting them. These problems in the program are referred to as defects or *bugs*. A *defect* is simply when the program isn't doing something that the creator intended it to do. The debugging process can be short and very simple in the beginning, but over time, as your programs evolve, the process becomes much longer and more difficult. The Visual LISP editor provides several different tools that can help to make the debugging process go more smoothly.

Breakpoints

Breakpoints are used to identify locations in your custom programs where you would like to stop and evaluate what is happening. This allows you to locate and fix defects in the routine much faster than having to step through the entire program again and again. A breakpoint is represented by a parenthesis with a red background (see Figure 3-8) and is available between AutoCAD sessions — if you close and reopen AutoCAD, the breakpoints are still available the next time you open the LISP file in the Visual LISP editor.

```
(setq ENT (entsel "\nSelect a Circle: "))
(if (/= ENT nil)
  (progn
    (if (= (cdr (assoc 0 (entget (car ENT))))
           "CIRCLE"
      )
      (prompt "\nA Circle was selected.")
      (prompt "\nA Circle was not selected.")
    )
  )
  (prompt "\nNo object was selected.")
  (princ)
)
```

Figure 3-8:
A break-
point.

Watch what is happening

Watch is a nice process to use when you are getting an unexpected result during the execution of your custom program. Watch is used to evaluate the current value of a variable or the return value of an expression so you can validate when an incorrect value is being returned. Using watch is a two-step process: First you set up a watch through the Add Watch dialog box (see Figure 3-9), and then you monitor the changes in the Watch dialog box (see Figure 3-10).

Figure 3-9:
Setting up
a watch.

Figure 3-10:
Keeping a
watch out
for strange
activity.

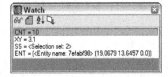

Setting up breakpoints and using watch

In this procedure, you use breakpoints and watch to monitor what current value that a variable holds during execution of the custom command BCIRC. If you didn't create the MyStuff.LSP file with the BCIRC command back under the section titled "Exchanging information with AutoCAD," you should go back to that section and perform the steps there first before continuing on.

1. **Launch the Visual LISP Editor and open the MyStuff.LSP file from the My Documents folder.**

The MyStuff.LSP file should be open in the Visual LISP Editor.

2. **Position the cursor over the variable `cur-layer` in the custom command BCIRC and double-click.**

The variable `cur-layer` should now be highlighted.

3. **Right-click over the variable and select Add Watch.**

The variable `cur-layer` should be added to the Watch dialog box and its current value should be `nil` (see Figure 3-11). As the custom command is being executed, you are able to see the value of the variable change as it is being set to a different value.

Figure 3-11:
A variable
added to the
Watch
dialog box.

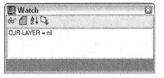

4. **Position the cursor over the left parenthesis of the first line that starts with the Command function and right-click.**

The right-click menu for the Text window should be displayed.

5. **From the right-click menu, select Toggle Breakpoint.**

The left parenthesis is highlighted with a red background, denoting the breakpoint has been set.

6. **From the Tools menu in the Visual LISP Editor, choose Load Text in Editor.**

   The custom command is loaded into AutoCAD and should now be ready to use.

7. **Switch to AutoCAD and type** BCIRC **at the command line to run the custom command.**

   Focus switches back to the Visual LISP Editor and highlights the line the breakpoint is set on (see Figure 3-12). Notice that the variable cur-layer in the Watch dialog box is no longer nil, as it currently holds the value of the system variable CLAYER.

Book X
Chapter 3

Introducing
AutoLISP

Figure 3-12:
Evaluation
of the
custom
command
paused due
to the
placement
of break-
point.

8. **Press F8 on the keyboard to resume stepping through the next expression after the breakpoint.**

   The next line or expression is highlighted, allowing you to evaluate what is happening line by line in the Watch window and in AutoCAD.

9. **Press F8 a few more times.**

   The next line or expression is highlighted and evaluated.

10. **Press CTRL+F8 to resume normal execution of the custom program.**

    The routine finishes executing.

One thing that can be very helpful when you are first getting started is to add expressions in your custom program that use the Prompt or Alert function so you know which expression is executing. This can be much less distracting than stepping through expressions using the Visual LISP Editor when testing your custom programs.

AutoLISP error messages

As you first start to create your own custom programs with AutoLISP, you will certainly encounter some problems. AutoCAD lets you know that there is a problem but really doesn't clearly explain how to fix or identify the problem. This can be frustrating, but remember that you have breakpoints and the Watch window at your disposal to help you identify what is going wrong.

Table 3-12 shows some of the more common errors that AutoCAD displays when it can't evaluate an AutoLISP expression.

Table 3-12	Some Common AutoLISP Error Messages
Error Message	*Description*
AutoCAD rejected function	One of the functions that you are using in your custom program can't be used in the current context. This could be related to functions like Setvar, with a read-only variable, Tblnext using an invalid table entry, or if one of the Getxxx functions for getting input is used in the Command function.

	Example:
	`(setvar "ACAD" "c:\\")`
	`; error: AutoCAD variable setting rejected:`
	`"ACAD" "c:\\"`

Bad argument \type	An incorrect data type was passed into an argument.

	Example:
	`(setq strName nil)`
	`(strcat "Hello" strName)`
	`; error: bad argument type: stringp nil`

(_>	Extra opening parenthesis or an unbalanced one. This can be one of the hardest errors to find if your program is large.

	Example:
	`((strcat "Hello" " World!")`
	`(_>`

extra right paren	Extra closing parenthesis or an unbalanced one. Like the extra opening parenthesis, this can be hard to find if your program is large.

	Example:
	`(strcat "Hello" " World!"))`
	`; error: extra right paren on input`

("_>	A double quote mark that represents a string is missing.

	Example:
	`(strcat "Hello" " World!)`
	`("_>`

Error Message	Description

too few arguments	Required arguments for a function are missing.
	
	Example:
	`(alert)`
	`; error: too few arguments`

too many arguments	There are too many arguments for the function that is being used.
	
	Example:
	`(prompt "Hello" " World!")`
	`; error: too many arguments`

If you are having problems with unbalanced parentheses in your custom programs, the Visual LISP Editor offers a Parentheses Matching tool under the Edit menu. This can help you identify where the problem with the parentheses exists.

Going GUI with DCL

AutoLISP was designed to be used as a way to automate repetitive tasks and to create custom commands to complete a task that couldn't normally be completed easily in AutoCAD. As technology moved forward, AutoLISP needed to evolve from a command line utility to having the ability to utilize a dialog box for managing settings and collecting information from the user. To do this, AutoLISP utilizes a language called DCL — Dialog Control Language. This language is used to lay out the structure of the dialog box controls and overall size.

Basics of DCL

DCL files are plain text files but must follow a specific structure and definition system. Two definition systems, the dialog box and tiles, make up the controls that should be displayed. Each of the different tiles and the dialog box have different attributes that can be set to control appearance and functionality. An example of a dialog box structure looks like this:

```
MYDLG : dialog { label = "My Dialog";
                <Tiles go here>
}
```

The structure that a tile (or control) follows is similar to that of the dialog box. An example of the structure of a Toggle tile is

```
: toggle { label = "Use second edit box, too.";
        value = "0";
}
```

Table 3-13 shows some of the common tiles used in DCL.

Table 3-13	Some Common DCL Tiles
DCL Tile	*Description*

Dialog	Defines a dialog box object and is used as a container to hold different tiles.
	
	Example:
	`MYDLG : dialog { label = "My Dialog";`
	`}`

Button	Creates a push button or command button with a caption.
	
	Example:
	`: button { label = "Import...";`
	`        action = "(btn_import)";`
	`        key = "btn_import";`
	`        mnemonic = "I";`
	`}`

List_box	Creates a vertical list of strings that can be selected individually or as multiples.
	
	Example:
	`: list_box { action = "(list_clicked)";`
	`        list = "Yes\nNo\nUnknown";`
	`        key = "list";`
	`        value = "Unknown";`
	`}`

Ok_only	Creates an OK button only. Example: `ok_only;`
Ok_cancel	Creates an OK and Cancel button combination. Example: `ok_cancel;`

Popup_list	Creates a drop-down list.
	
	Example:
	`: popup_list { action = "(pop_clicked)"`
	`        list = "Yes\nNo\nUnknown";`
	`        key = "pop";`
	`        value = "Unknown";`
	`}`

Radio_button	Creates a radio or option button.
	
	Example:
	`: radio_button { label = "On";`
	`        action = "(radio_clicked)";`
	`        key = "radio_on";`
	`}`

DCL Tile	Description
Toggle	Creates a check box.
	Example:

	``
	: toggle { label = "Use second edit box, too.";
	        action = "(toggle_ed2)";
	        value = "0";
	}
	``

Adding comments

A *comment* is a line or series of lines in the DCL structure that do not get interpreted. A comment can be used to identify what is taking place at a location in a dialog box or can be a general note at the top of the file that includes general revision or author information. Double forward slashes are placed in front of a text string to designate it as a comment. By default, a comment appears in the purple text with a gray background within the Visual LISP Editor. A sample comment is

```
// Created on October 16, 2005 by LA
```

Using AutoLISP to add interaction to DCL

DCL needs AutoLISP in order to do anything: A DCL file itself doesn't do anything other than take up space on a disk as a file. In these steps, we show you how to display a dialog box with AutoLISP and add an action to a tile to make it interactive:

1. **Launch the Visual LISP Editor and open the file MyStuff.LSP from the My Documents folder.**

The MyStuff.LSP file should be open in the Visual LISP Editor.

2. **Create a new file with the name MyStuff.DCL and make sure it is saved as the type DCL Source File instead of LSP Source File.**

A new Text window should be created and titled MyStuff.DCL.

3. **In the MyStuff.DCL Text window, enter the following dialog box and tile definitions:**

```
// Dialog box is a support file of MyStuff.lsp
MYSTUFF :dialog { label = "MyStuff Example";
    : toggle {    label = "Use second edit box, too?";
                  value = "0";
                  key = "tgl1";
    }
    :boxed_column { label = "Edit Box group";
          : edit_box {  label = "1st Edit Box";
                        key = "edBox1";
```

**Book X
Chapter 3**

Introducing
AutoLISP

```
                                  }
                                  : edit_box {  label = "2st Edit Box";
                                                key = "edBox2";
                                                is_enabled = "False";
                                  }
                        }
                        ok_cancel;
            }
```

4. **From the Files menu in the Visual LISP Editor, choose Save.**

The new dialog box and tile definitions are saved out to the MyStuff.DCL file.

5. **From the Tools menu in the Visual LISP Editor, choose Interface Tools⇨Preview DCL in Editor.**

The Enter the Dialog Name dialog box (see Figure 3-13) is displayed. This dialog box allows you to control which dialog box defined in the file should be previewed.

Figure 3-13: Which dialog box should be previewed?

6. **Select MYSTUFF from the down-down list in the Enter the Dialog Name dialog box and click OK to preview the MyStuff Example dialog box.**

The MyStuff Example dialog box (see Figure 3-14) should now be displayed, but if you click on anything, nothing is going to happen because there is no AutoLISP code to interact with the action that is defined for the Toggle tile.

Figure 3-14: Previewing the MyStuff Example dialog box.

7. **Click any control to return to the Visual LISP Editor.**

The preview of the MyStuff Example dialog box should close and the Visual LISP Editor should now have focus.

8. From the Window menu in the Visual LISP Editor, choose MyStuff.LSP or reopen the file if it isn't open.

A Text window with MyStuff.LSP should now be displayed.

9. In the MyStuff.lsp Text window, enter the following custom command:

The preview of the MyStuff Example dialog box should be closed and the Visual LISP Editor should now have focus.

**Book X
Chapter 3**

Introducing
AutoLISP

```
;; Custom command to display the MyStuff Example
;; dialog box.
(defun c:MS_DCL ()
   ;; Function executed when the OK button is clicked
   (defun do_exit ()
     (done_dialog 1)
   )

   ;; Function executed when the Cancel button is
   clicked
   (defun do_cancel ()
      (done_dialog 0)
   )

   ;; Function executed when the Toggle is clicked
   (defun edit_tgl ()
      ;; Get the current value of the Toggle
      (setq EDTGL (get_tile "tgl1"))

      ;; If the Toggle is checked then enabled the
      ;; second text box.
      (if (= EDTGL "1")
         (mode_tile "edBox2" 0)
         (mode_tile "edBox2" 1)
      )
   )

   ;; Load the MyStuff Example dialog box into memory
   (setq dld (load_dialog "MYSTUFF.DCL"))

   ;; Check to see if the dialog box was loaded
   (if (> dld 0)
      (prong
         ;; Create a reference to the dialog box
         (new_dialog "MYSTUFF" dld)

         ;; Set the actions for the OK and Cancel
buttons
         (action_tile "accept" "(do_exit)")
```

```
(action_tile "cancel" "(do_cancel)")

;; Enable the dialog box
(start_dialog)

;; Unload the dialog box
(unload_dialog dld)
      )
    )
  )
```

10. **From the Tools menu in the Visual LISP Editor, choose Load Text in Editor.**

The new custom command MS_DCL should now be loaded into AutoCAD and ready to use.

11. **Switch to AutoCAD and type MS_DCL at the command line.**

One of two things happens: The dialog box either will or won't be displayed. If the dialog box doesn't display, check the expressions that are part of the MS_DCL command. If they seem fine, make sure that the MyStuff.DCL file is in one of the AutoCAD support paths.

If you are sure that a file is in one of the AutoCAD Support Search Paths, you can use the AutoLISP `FindFile` function to find the file. Below is an example of this function:

```
(findfile "acad.pgp")

"C:\\Documents and Settings\\<user name>\\Application
    Data\\Autodesk\\AutoCAD
2007\\R17.0\\enu\\support\\acad.pgp"
```

Usually by default, AutoCAD does find files in My Documents; however, that can vary from install to install. You can either add the My Documents folder to the Support File Search Path under the Files tab of the Options dialog box or move it to one of the folders listed there.

12. **Click the toggle (check box) and note that nothing happens.**

There is a function defined as `edit_tgl`, but it is not assigned to the toggle.

13. **Below the AutoLISP expression (`action_tile "cancel"` "(do_cancel)"), add this expression:**

```
(action_tile "cancel" "(do_cancel)")
(action_tile "tgl1" "(edit_tgl)")
(start_dialog)
```

The key from the DCL file is how you associate a function with a tile. You could also use the action attribute for the tile in the DCL file.

14. **Reload the AutoLISP file using Load Text in Editor and type** MS_DCL
in the command line of AutoCAD. Click the toggle again to see what
happens.

This time, the toggle should enable the second edit box through the
edit_tgl function that was defined in the MS_DCL command.

Using ActiveX Automation with AutoLISP

Using ActiveX Automation with AutoLISP allows you to do things more efficiently and access things that you just can't do normally with AutoCAD commands and AutoLISP functions alone. One thing that you normally can't do
with AutoLISP is to manipulate the AutoCAD application or other open documents. With ActiveX Automation, you can even create objects and change
their properties without the need to issue additional commands, like CHANGE.
To enable the ActiveX Automation features of AutoLISP, use the function
Vl-Load-Com. The Vl-Load-Com function doesn't take any arguments.

Referencing the AutoCAD Application

The AutoCAD application object is the gatekeeper for accessing the objects
that represent all open drawings. The AutoCAD application object is
retrieved by the function Vlax-Get-Acad-Object. This function doesn't
require any arguments, but it does return a reference to an AcadApplication
object, which is the object that represents the AutoCAD application. With
this object, you can access other properties specific to the application
object such as its visibility and position on-screen.

When you have a reference to an object, you can use the function Vlax-Dump-
Object. This function requires one argument: a reference to an object like
AcadApplication. The function also has an optional argument that allows you
to see just the properties of the object or both the properties and methods.
An example of how the Vlax-Dump-Object is used is (vlax-dump-object
(vlax-get-acad-object) T). If the example is entered at the command line
in AutoCAD, it displays all the properties and methods associated with the
AutoCAD application.

Using methods of an object

Methods in ActiveX Automation are, for the most part, the same as an
AutoLISP function. They can either return a value or not based on how the
method is set up. Methods are called in a different way in ActiveX than for an
AutoLISP function because AutoLISP is not able to communicate directly
with ActiveX Automation.

Where to go from here

You might be wondering where to go from here. You can find a lot of information in the AutoCAD Online Help system under the topics AutoLISP, Visual LISP, and DXF. Another great resource is the Internet. You can even find Web sites that are dedicated to tutorials on AutoLISP that you can work through.

To use a method, you use the function `Vlax-Invoke-Method`. This function requires at least two arguments. The first argument is an object that you are calling the method on, and the second is the method that you want to call on an object. The method might require additional parameters.

An example of calling a method for an object is

```
(vlax-invoke-method (vlax-get-acad-object) 'ZoomAll)
```

Setting and retrieving a property of an object

Properties in the ActiveX Automation are attributes of an object that define the characteristics of that object — these properties can be updated or retrieved. The processes closest in AutoLISP to working with properties are the functions `Entget/Entupd` and `Setvar/Getvar`, which allow you to interact with an object and settings. The use of modifying properties on an object is very powerful because after you understand the process, you can do things that you just can't normally do with AutoLISP alone.

To retrieve the value of a property, you use the function `Vlax-Get-Property`; to set the value of a property, you use the function `Vlax-Put-Property`. The `Get` function requires two arguments, whereas the `Put` function requires three arguments. The first argument for both `Get` and `Put` is the object that you are interested in working with, and the second is the property name. In the case of the `Put` function, the third argument is the value you want to assign to the property.

An example of retrieving a property for an object is

```
(vlax-get-property (vlax-get-acad-object) 'FullName)
```

An example of setting a property for an object is

```
(vlax-put-property (vlax-get-acad-object) 'WindowState 2)
```

Revising the BCIRC command

Using ActiveX Automation with AutoLISP adds a whole new level of complexity to your program, but the ability to use ActiveX Automation with AutoLISP is great when you realize that you can enhance your existing custom programs without the need to rewrite them in a different language like VBA. Earlier in the chapter, you created the custom command BCIRC, which added a new layer to the drawing and asked the user to pick a point to draw a 0.5 diameter circle at. The following steps do the same thing with ActiveX Automation:

1. **Launch the Visual LISP Editor and open the file MyStuff.LSP from the My Documents folder.**

   The MyStuff.LSP file should be open in the Visual LISP Editor.

2. **In the Text window, place the cursor behind the last parenthesis on the very last function/command in the file and press Enter twice so there is a blank line at the beginning.**

3. **In the Text window, enter the following expressions and command:**

```
;; Initiate ActiveX Automation
(vl-load-com)

;; Custom command to create a new layer and draw a
;; 0.5 diameter circle.
(defun c:BCIRC-AX ( / acadObj docObj mspaceObj curlayer
    layersObj newLayer colorObj circObj)

    ;; Get a reference to the AutoCAD object
    (setq acadObj (vlax-get-acad-object))

    ;; Get a reference to the active drawing
    (setq docObj (vlax-get-property acadObj
'ActiveDocument))

    ;; Get a reference to Model Space
    (setq mspaceObj (vlax-get-property docObj
'ModelSpace))

    ;; Get a reference to the active layer
    (setq curlayer (vlax-get-property docObj
'ActiveLayer))

    ;; Get a reference to the Layers table of the
    ;; current drawing
    (setq layersObj (vlax-get-property docObj 'Layers))

    ;; Create the new layer named Hole
```

```
(setq newLayer (vlax-invoke-method layersObj 'Add
"Hole"))

;; Assign the ACI Color Blue to the new layer
(setq colorObj (vlax-get-property curlayer
'TrueColor))
(vlax-put-property colorObj 'ColorMethod
acColorMethodByACI)
(vlax-put-property colorObj 'ColorIndex acBlue)
    (vlax-put-property newLayer 'TrueColor
colorObj)

;; Get the center point for the circle
(setq utilityObj (vlax-get-property docObj
'Utility))
(setq centerPoint (vlax-invoke-method utilityObj
'GetPoint nil "\nSelect the Center Point: "))

;; Create the new circle in the drawing
(setq circObj (vlax-invoke-method mspaceObj
'AddCircle centerPoint 0.25))
    (vlax-put-property circObj 'Layer "Hole")

;; Stop an return values from being echoed
(princ)
)
```

4. **From the Files menu in the Visual LISP Editor, choose Save.**

The new command is saved out to the MyStuff.LSP file.

5. **From the Tools menu in the Visual LISP Editor, choose Load Text in Editor.**

The custom command is loaded into AutoCAD and should now be ready for use.

6. **Switch back to AutoCAD.**

Focus should be shifted to the AutoCAD application window.

7. **At the command line, type** BCIRC-AX.

The new command should work just like the old one did, except this one isn't dependent on any of the AutoCAD commands, which is why the code is much longer. This code handled passing the point into the AddCircle command. Also, notice how much more complex the layer creation process was compared to before.

Chapter 4: Visual Basic for AutoCAD

In This Chapter

✔ Accessing the VBA environment with commands in AutoCAD

✔ Using the Integrated Development Environment (IDE)

✔ Introducing the AutoCAD Object Model

✔ Creating a basic project

*V*isual Basic for Applications (VBA), an extension of the very popular programming language Visual Basic (VB), has been around for some time. VBA is defined as an object-orientated programming (OOP) language. The concept behind OOP is that a computer program is developed using a collection of individual units, or "objects," as opposed to a listing of instructions. Each one of the objects has the capability to receive messages, process data, and transmit messages to other objects. The objects are self-contained units that can easily be reused and modified for many different purposes, thus saving time and effort.

VBA is part of the programming and development tools provided by Microsoft. Its origins date back to QBasic and MS-Basic, which were both introduced during and prior to the MS-DOS era. VB has been around much longer than VBA and, unlike VBA, VB can be used to build standalone applications that are not dependent on a host application.

A *host application* is a program that allows the VBA environment to run inside it; AutoCAD is one example. Many other popular Windows-based programs have VBA technology built into them. Some of these other applications are Autodesk Inventor, AutoCAD-based vertical products such as Architectural Desktop (ADT), and Microsoft Word and Excel.

VBA in AutoCAD has been a feature welcomed by both the non-development and development communities. This programming option allows for the integration of business applications directly into the AutoCAD environment, enabling companies to tap into an existing development community that already knows VB/VBA.

This chapter only scratches the surface of what is possible with VBA for AutoCAD. VBA for AutoCAD goes beyond just drawing simple objects, such as lines and circles. You can use VBA to do all sorts of things, from importing data from a corporate system to doing drawing setups when starting a new design. The power that VBA has is marvelous, especially when you consider how easy it is to use and the depth of capabilities it has compared to other languages.

The benefits of using VBA range from reducing repetitive tasks in AutoCAD to linking to external databases and files to help improve downstream information sharing. The sky is truly the limit, so keep on pushing the boundaries of VBA and AutoCAD.

AutoCAD Commands for VBA

Just like you use commands to draw a line in AutoCAD, you need to know and understand the different commands that are used to access the VBA environment from inside AutoCAD. There are five core commands that you should know to work with VBA projects. These five commands are

✦ VBAIDE

✦ VBALOAD

✦ VBAUNLOAD

✦ VBARUN

✦ VBAMAN

Some other commands are used to interact with the VBA environment, but the functionality that these commands provide can be found in the five commands listed above.

VBAIDE

VBAIDE is used to load the Visual Basic for Applications Integrated Development Environment (VBAIDE). This is where UserForms and code modules are added and organized into a project. The IDE provides tools that help during the coding process and to debug the procedures in a project. We discuss the IDE in greater depth in the section "Working with the IDE."

VBALOAD

VBALOAD is used to load an existing project from disk into AutoCAD. When you load the project into AutoCAD, it becomes available for both execution and editing.

VBALOAD can be used two different ways, which are controlled by whether the command's name is prefixed with a hyphen. Using VBALOAD with no hyphen launches the Open VBA project dialog box. If -VBALOAD is used, the prompt Open VBA Project is displayed at the dynamic input tooltip or command line. This can be useful when loading VBA projects with the AutoLISP programming language or a script file.

If you are working with an existing project or want to view a sample project, you must first load it into AutoCAD. Here's how:

1. **At the command line or dynamic input tooltip, type** VBALOAD **or from the Tools menu, choose Macro⇨Load Project.**

The Open VBA Project dialog box (see Figure 4-1) appears.

Book X
Chapter 4

Visual Basic for AutoCAD

Figure 4-1:
The Open
VBA Project
dialog box.

2. **Use the Look In drop-down list to specify the location for the VBA project.**

AutoCAD comes with some sample project files that can be found in the folder C:\Program Files\AutoCAD 2006\Samples\VBA by default.

3. **Select the project from the list box below the Look In drop-down list.**

All the available project files in the specified folder are displayed in the list box. VBA project files have a unique file extension of .DVB.

4. **Optionally, select the Open Visual Basic Editor check box in the lower-left corner.**

If the check box is selected, the Visual Basic Editor is launched if it isn't already. If the Visual Basic editor is minimized in the taskbar, it is restored to a normal display state.

5. Click the Open button to load the project.

6. In the AutoCAD message box, click Enable Macros.

By default, an AutoCAD message box (see Figure 4-2) is displayed when you load a VBA project. This message box informs you that the project could contain viruses or unsafe code. Clicking More Info loads the AutoCAD Online Help system.

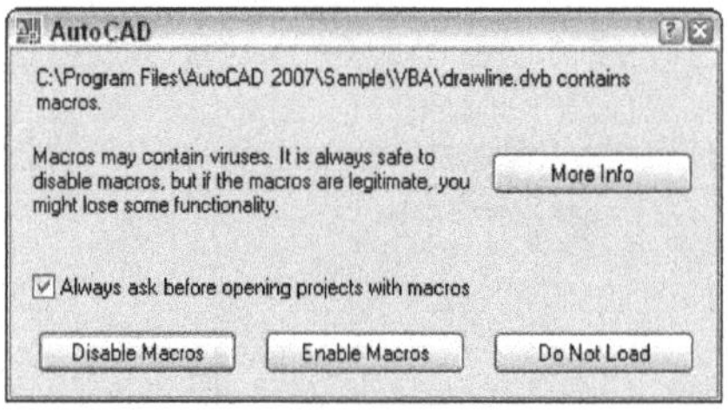

Figure 4-2:
Warning
message
about
potentially
unsafe
macros.

The other two options at the bottom of the message box — Disable Macros and Do Not Load — can be helpful if you are not sure who created the macros contained in the project. Disable Macros allows you to view the project in the editor, but code that would normally be run automatically is disabled. Do Not Load keeps the project from being loaded into the editor altogether.

If Open Visual Basic Editor was checked in the Open VBA Project dialog box, the Visual Basic Editor (see Figure 4-3) is displayed.

VBAUNLOAD

VBAUNLOAD is used to unload a VBA project from AutoCAD that was previously loaded and is no longer needed. This can help to free up system resources for other tasks. Unlike VBALOAD, which displays a dialog box or can be run from the command line, VBAUNLOAD can be run only from the command line.

After you are done working with or using a project, you can unload it without exiting AutoCAD. The following procedure describes how:

1. At the command line or dynamic input tooltip, type VBAUNLOAD.

2. At the Unload VBA Project prompt, type the full path to the project (the path from where it was loaded, plus the file name).

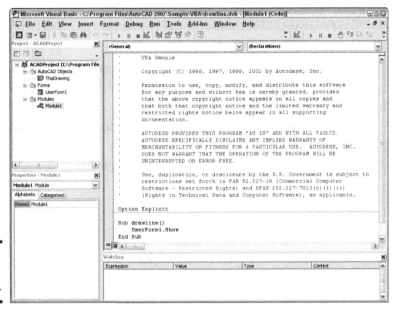

Figure 4-3:
The Visual
Basic Editor.

As an example, if the project Drawline.DVB was loaded from the
folder C:\Program Files\AutoCAD 2006\Sample\VBA, you would enter
C:\Program Files\AutoCAD 2006\Sample\VBA\Drawline.DVB at the
prompt.

VBARUN

VBARUN is used to execute a publicly defined procedure that is contained in
a code module found in a VBA project. The command launches the Macro
dialog box, which allows you to do a variety of tasks from running a macro
to changing some of the VBA environment options and even access to the
Visual Basic Editor. After the procedure has been executed, you follow any
prompts or respond to any dialog boxes that are displayed.

VBARUN can be used two different ways. The two different ways are controlled
by whether the command's name is prefixed with a hyphen. Using VBARUN
with no hyphen launches the Macros dialog box. If -VBARUN is used, the
prompt Macro Name is displayed at the command line or dynamic input
tooltip.

Using -VBARUN can be great for calling a macro from a custom button on a
toolbar or pull-down menu item. The following format shows how to use
-VBARUN from the command line or dynamic input tooltip, or as part of a
menu macro:

```
Macro name: <ACADProjectName>!<ModuleName>.<ProcedureName>
"C:/Program Files/AutoCAD 2006/Sample/VBA/drawline.
    dvb!Module1.drawline"
```

After a project has been loaded, you can execute one of the publicly defined procedures in a loaded project from AutoCAD, but not one that is defined as a private procedure. Here's how:

1. **At the command line or dynamic input tooltip, type** VBARUN **or from the Tools menu, choose Macro⇨Macros.**

The Macros dialog box (see Figure 4-4) appears.

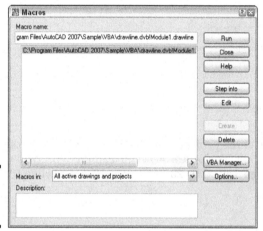

Figure 4-4:
The Macros
dialog box.

2. **Select the macro (or procedure) name from the list box in the middle of the dialog box.**

The list box displays all the macros of the loaded projects. This list may be very large because it is based on the number of projects that are loaded into AutoCAD at a given time. You can use the Macros In drop-down list to control which macros by project are listed in the list box.

3. **Click the Run button on the right side of the dialog box.**

VBAMAN

VBAMAN is used to launch the VBA Manager dialog box (see Figure 4-5). The VBA Manager dialog box offers a lot of functionality in a single dialog box. From this dialog box, you can load a project, unload a project, run a macro, and much more. Much of this functionality has been touched on with the VBAIDE, VBALOAD, VBAUNLOAD, and VBARUN commands.

Book X
Chapter 4

Visual Basic for
AutoCAD

Figure 4-5:
The VBA
Manager
dialog box.

The VBA Manager does offer some unique features, such as being able to save a loaded VBA project to a different filename, create a new project, and embed a project into a drawing file. Embedding a project into a drawing file has a couple of effects. One is that the drawing file now contains macros, so the individual receiving the file might not feel comfortable opening the file due to the Macros warning message box being displayed. The recipient of the message might not be sure what will happen if the macros are enabled.

Also, having the code embedded in the drawing file means that the code is much harder to update because it won't be in one centralized location. On the other hand, one of the benefits of having the macros embedded in the drawing file is that they are available to your clients if they open the drawing. You can provide utilities to help view your drawings or control layer display settings.

Other commands

Some less commonly used commands are available in AutoCAD for use with the VBA environment. The functionality of these commands is a subset of the functionality that can be found in the VBA Manager. These three commands are

✦ VBAPREF: Can be used to access some of the VBA environment settings. This is the same as clicking the Options button located in the Macros dialog box of the VBARUN command.

✦ VBANEW: Can be used to create an empty VBA project. This is the same as clicking the New button located in the VBA Manager dialog box of the VBAMAN command.

✦ VBASTMT: Allows for executing a single line of VBA code at the dynamic tooltip or command line. It can integrate some simple VBA code into AutoLISP. This can be great for adding message boxes and some light functionality that isn't part of AutoLISP.

Working with the IDE

The tool that is used to develop VBA projects is referred to as the Integrated Development Environment (IDE). The IDE is loaded by running VBAIDE command, by selecting the Open Visual Basic Editor option in the Open VBA Project dialog box, by clicking the Visual Basic Editor button in the VBA Manager dialog box, or by clicking the Edit button in the Macros dialog box.

The IDE is where you find yourself spending the majority of time coding, testing, and debugging any procedures and UserForms that are added to a project. A VBA project is a group of modules that is organized into a specific file structure. These modules include UserForms, class, and standard modules. The projects created in the IDE work only in AutoCAD and many of the AutoCAD-based verticals such as Autodesk Architectural Desktop. So a project created for AutoCAD can't be used in an application such as MS Word or MS Excel, although they are also host applications for VBA projects.

To load the Visual Basic Editor, choose Tools⇨Macro⇨Visual Basic Editor.

Exploring the IDE

The Visual Basic Editor is broken up into many different panes and areas; each of the panes and areas provides a set of functions that makes many of the programming tasks much easier. By default, three different panes and areas are visible at once. The four that you will most often use and should get comfortable with are

✦ Project Explorer

✦ Properties Window

✦ Code and UserForm Windows

✦ Object Browser

Project Explorer

The Project Explorer (see Figure 4-6) is used to access the properties and different modules that make up a VBA project. It provides an organizational view of the project to allow for opening and viewing the contents of a module in its proper editing window within the Visual Basic Editor.

Figure 4-6:
Project
Explorer
from the
Visual Basic
Editor.

Properties window

The Properties window (see Figure 4-7) is used to access the properties of a selected item in either the UserForm editor or the Project Explorer. The properties that can be set here range from controlling the visibility of a control on a UserForm to the name of the project or module. The Properties window helps to speed up the creation of UserForms by enabling you to change properties at design-time and not just at run-time.

Figure 4-7:
The
Properties
window
from the
Visual Basic
Editor.

Design-time is when properties of a UserForm, control, or object are changed from inside the Visual Basic Editor with one of the provided utilities, such as the Properties window.

Run-time is when properties of a UserForm, control, or object are changed during the execution of a procedure.

The Project Explorer and Properties window are usually displayed by default in the Visual Basic Editor, but if they aren't displayed, you can display them by using the View menu. The following procedure describes how:

1. **From the View menu in the Visual Basic Editor, choose Project Explorer.**

Choosing the option from the menu bar displays the corresponding pane.

2. **Click the small button with an X located in the upper-right corner of the pane to close it.**

Code and UserForm windows

Code and UserForm windows (see Figure 4-8) are the main editing areas found in the Visual Basic Editor. These windows are used for editing and designing UserForms and are where code is entered. Usually these windows take up the largest amount of room in the editor because they are where most of the work takes place. The Visual Basic Editor is a context-sensitive environment and controls the visibility of some utilities based on whether a Code or UserForm window is active. One example of this is the Toolbox, which is visible only when a UserForm window is active.

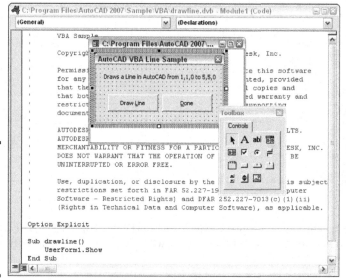

Figure 4-8: Code and UserForm windows in the Visual Basic Editor, along with the Toolbox.

Object Browser

The Object Browser (see Figure 4-9) is a window into the world of VBA programming. It allows you to perform a search on the available objects that you have access to. These objects then can be viewed in the browser to see the different properties, methods, events, classes, and constants that they might contain.

The Object Browser links you to the corresponding Help file and topics for the objects contained in the loaded libraries. This feature makes learning new objects easier because you can see their different attributes right in the browser. You can also access Help for the selected attribute by pressing F1 to open the related online help file. Many of the AutoCAD Help topics for VBA have example code associated with them. This allows you to be able to copy and paste code from the Help topic directly into the Visual Basic Editor and run it to see how it behaves.

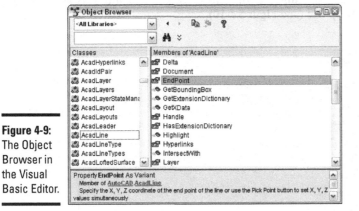

Figure 4-9:
The Object
Browser in
the Visual
Basic Editor.

The Object Browser is one of your best friends when you're getting started using VBA for AutoCAD. It helps you get in touch with information quickly to reduce the learning curve. The following procedures describe how to navigate the Object Browser:

1. **From the View menu in the Visual Basic Editor, choose Object Browser.**

2. **Click the drop-down arrow in the top list to specify which of the loaded libraries you want to look in.**

By default, <All Libraries> is selected. This allows you to view all the objects and attributes in all the loaded libraries. The objects that are associated with AutoCAD are in the library named AutoCAD. The objects associated with the Visual Basic for Applications programming language are in the library named VBA.

3. **Select an object from the Classes list box.**

The Classes list box displays the top level of the objects contained in the specified library or libraries. The types of items that are listed are Classes, Collections, Enumerators, Types, and Modules. Notice that a description of the selected item is provided at the bottom of the Object Browser.

4. Select an attribute from the Members Of list box.

The Members Of list box displays the specific constant, properties, methods, events, and objects that are related to the class selected from the Classes list box. Notice that information is displayed at the bottom of the Object Browser about the selected item. This information might be the syntax for a method or an indicator that a property is read-only.

5. If you want additional information on the selected item from the Members Of list box or the Classes list box, you can press F1 on the keyboard. This launches the AutoCAD ActiveX and VBA Reference Online Help file (see Figure 4-10).

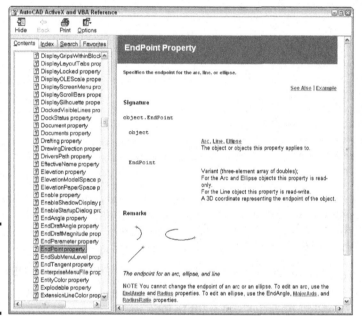

Figure 4-10: AutoCAD ActiveX and VBA Reference.

Parts of a VBA Project

A VBA project can be as simple as one class module called ThisDrawing and three lines of code, or as complex as a project that might include UserForms and both standard and class modules. The solution that is being developed determines the type of modules that will be a part of the final project. The following sections outline what the different modules in a project are and what is contained in each module.

Standard code module

Standard code modules are used to store procedures, data types, variables, and functions that are accessed by other modules in the project. Code modules should be used to hold reusable code that can be used in future projects or called from multiple places in a project. This concept is called *modular programming*. It helps to avoid redundant code and also gives you the ability to reuse the code in other, similar projects.

Class code module

Class code modules are used to store procedures and properties that define a user-defined class. A user-defined class allows you to create your own object for storing information or manipulating other objects, similar to the way AutoCAD uses objects. All AutoCAD VBA projects contain a special class module called ThisDrawing. The ThisDrawing class represents the object that defines the current drawing in the AutoCAD session. Although you can create your own classes with VBA, you don't often need to do it.

Book X
Chapter 4

Visual Basic for
AutoCAD

Procedures (subroutine or function)

A procedure is a block, or group, of code that is given a name so it can be referenced easily in a project. The two different types of procedures are sub and function. A sub, or subroutine, is a type of procedure that does not return a result; a function returns a single result after the procedure has completed all tasks and computations. Procedures to manipulate objects or return information about an object can be found throughout the AutoCAD Object Library. Some examples of procedures are

```
Function Add2WholeNumbers (Num1 as Integer, Num2 as Integer)
    As Integer
      Add2WholeNumbers = Num1 + Num2
End Function

Sub EchoValue (Value as Variant)
  MsgBox Cstr(Value)
End Function
```

Here's another example of using the previous two custom procedures Add2WholeNumbers and EchoValue:

```
EchoValue Add2WholeNumbers(1, 3)
```

This snippet displays a message box with the number 4 in it.

Declaring Variables

A variable is a way to store data in memory for use later, to hold the value of an argument that is passed into a procedure, or to capture the returning value of a function. To use a variable, you should first use the `Dim` statement to dimension (or declare) the variable as a specific data type. Declaring the variable as a specific type helps the editor to check the data integrity of the code when it is being executed and debugged.

Variables can be defined locally within a given procedure or module and globally at a module level. For most data types, you only need to dimension the variable and assign the value that you want stored with it. Some examples of variables are

```
Dim strValue as String
Dim vVar
```

Data Types

Data types are used to describe what type of data a variable holds; only a single data type can be assigned to a variable at one time. By default, when a variable is not declared with the `Dim` statement, or when it is defined with the statement but no data type, it is declared as a variant. *Variants* are often used to capture return values and as arguments for a procedure, in some cases based on the type of information that is being passed in.

Table 4-1 shows some of the commonly used data types in VBA.

Table 4-1	Common Data Types	
Data Type	*Brief Description*	*Examples*
Boolean	A true or false value.	True
Integer	Any whole number without decimal places. −32,768 to 32,767	10
Double	Any large number with decimal places and is accurate up to 16 digits. 1.80×10308 to $-4.94 \times 10\text{-}324$ for neg.; $4.94 \times 10\text{–}324$ to 1.80×10308 for positive values	1.0, 0.23451, .5
String	Any number of alphanumeric characters enclosed in double quotes. Range is from 0 to approximately 2 billion characters.	"Hello"
Object	A valid COM object.	objLine
Variant	Any numeric range up to a double, a text string, or COM object.	183.59

Assigning a value to a variable

The equal sign (=) is used for value assignment to a variable. The value on the right is assigned to the variable on the left. If an object is being returned to be stored in a variable, the Set statement must be used in conjunction with the equal (=) sign. Some examples of value assignment are

```
' String value assignment
Dim strValue as String
strValue = "Hello out there"

' Object value assignment
Dim acObjLine as AcadLine
Dim dPT1(0 to 2) as Double, dPT2(0 to 2) as Double

dPT1(0) = 0: dPT1(1) = 0: dPT1(2) = 0
dPT2(0) = 5: dPT2(1) = 5: dPT2(2) = 0

Set acObjLine = ThisDrawing.ModelSpace.AddLine(dPT1, dPT2)
```

**Book X
Chapter 4**

**Visual Basic for
AutoCAD**

The basics of working with objects

You may encounter objects throughout the use of the AutoCAD Object Library and when working with UserForms and controls. Objects come in two different distinct types: objects and collections.

Objects exist as individuals and as part of a group containing many objects of the same kind. The group of objects is referred to as a *collection*. The first object that you encountered when you opened the Visual Basic Editor is ThisDrawing, which is an example of an individual object. ThisDrawing represents an object of the data type AcadDocument. ThisDrawing is an object that represents the current drawing and is part of a collection that contains all open drawings in the application called AcadDocuments, which is part of the AcadApplication object.

Now that you are familiar with one type of object, you must know how to interact with it. After you have a reference to an object, you use a dot to access its properties or methods. At times, you are accessing an object below the current object that you are referencing. The following syntax represents how to access the properties and methods of an individual object and not one that is part of a collection. The syntax shows a space before and after the dot for readability, but there are no spaces on either side of the dot when writing the line in a code window:

```
Object . <Object or Property or Method>

ThisDrawing.FullName
ThisDrawing.ModelSpace.AddLine dPT1, dPT2
```

If you need to access an object that is part of a collection, you need to do a little more work. Objects contained in a collection have to be accessed in a slightly different way. Objects contained in a collection are indexed and are accessible by using their unique names or a number in most cases. The index is the order in which the items are added to the collection and is similar to a street address for a house. All houses have unique street numbers, so they can get their mail; indexes for collections work the same way. Most collections begin with an index of 0; however, some start with an index of 1. The collection works the same whether the first item of the collection starts at 0 or 1. (Really it's what the programmer felt like using that day for the first item's index.) Here are a few examples of how to access a layer from the Layers collection in a drawing.

```
ThisDrawing.ActiveLayer = ThisDrawing.Layers("0")

ThisDrawing.ActiveLayer = ThisDrawing.Layers(1)
```

As mentioned earlier, the Set statement must be used to store a reference to the object in a variable:

```
Dim objLayer As AcadLayer
Set objLayer = ThisDrawing.Layers("0")
```

Adding comments

A *comment* is a line or series of lines in a code module that do not get executed. A comment can be used to identify what is taking place in a procedure or may consist of a general note at the top of the module that includes general revision and author information. An apostrophe (') or single quote mark is placed at the front of a text string to designate it as a comment. By default, a comment appears in the color green within the Visual Basic Editor. An example comment is

```
' Close out application
```

Introducing the AutoCAD Object Model

The AutoCAD Object Model is the organizational structure that is used to navigate the Object Library. The AutoCAD Object Model (see Figure 4-11) is very large; only a small portion is shown here.

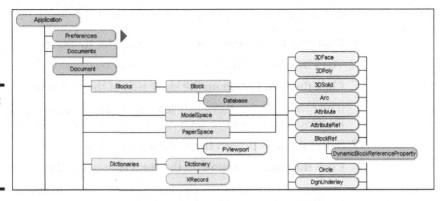

Figure 4-11:
A view of the AutoCAD Object Model.

At the top of the AutoCAD Object Model is the Application; below that are the Preferences and Documents collections. You can identify that they are collections because their names end with *s*. Just below the Documents collection are the Document objects; this is the level that ThisDrawing represents in the object model. To give you an idea of what each Document is made up of, the following properties and methods, and many others, are part of the Document object:

- ✦ **ActiveLayer:** Property to set and return the current layer.
- ✦ **FullName:** Property to return the drawing's name with path.
- ✦ **Blocks:** Method returns a reference to the AcadBlocks collection.
- ✦ **SaveAs:** Method used to save the drawing with a different name or location.

These steps show you how to open the AutoCAD Object Model Map in the AutoCAD Online Help system:

1. **From the Help menu in the AutoCAD, choose Additional Resources⇨ Developer.**

2. **Click the Contents tab and expand ActiveX and VBA Reference.**

3. **Select Object Model just below ActiveX and VBA Reference on the Contents tab.**

Create a basic VBA project

If you've come this far, you should be ready to build a small VBA project to add a line in the current drawing.

The following procedures describe how to create a new empty VBA project:

1. **From the Tools menu, choose Macro⇨VBA Manager.**

The VBA Manager dialog box should now be displayed.

2. **Click the New button on the right side of the dialog box.**

If no projects were previously loaded, a new project named ACADProject is added to the Projects list box with the location of Global1.

3. **Select the new project in the Projects list box.**

4. **Click the Save As button on the right side of the dialog box.**

The Save As dialog box is displayed, allowing you to specify a filename and location for the new VBA project.

5. **Browse to the My Documents folder using the Save In drop-down list.**

6. **Enter FirstVBAProject in the File Name field of the Save As dialog box.**

7. **Click the Save button in the Save As dialog box.**

The empty VBA project is saved to the My Documents folder. The location and filename that the project is saved to are reflected in the VBA Manager dialog box under the Location column.

Working with the new VBA project in the editor

Here is how to launch the Visual Basic Editor and work in the new project:

1. **Select the new project in the Projects list box.**

2. **Click the Visual Basic Editor button on the bottom of the VBA Manager dialog box.**

The Visual Basic Editor should be launched and be displayed on-screen. If it is not brought up on-screen, check the Windows taskbar to see whether it is minimized.

3. **In the Project Explorer, select the top node ACADProject, which represents the project.**

In the Properties window (see Figure 4-12), the properties for the project should be listed. A project has one property that can be modified from the Properties window, and that is Name.

4. **Highlight the current value of ACADProject in the Name field in the Properties Window and enter** FirstVBAProject.

This changes the name that appears in the VBA Manager dialog box and the Macros dialog box. Using a unique name lets you distinguish the project from other loaded projects.

Figure 4-12:
Name that
property.

5. **Right-click in the Project Explorer and choose Insert⇨Module.**

A new standard code module named *Module1* is added to the project.
You should also notice that a new folder named Modules is automatically created under the project. All standard code modules that are
imported or created in the project are added to this folder.

6. **Select Module1 from the Project Explorer and change the Name property for Module1 to basDraw through the Properties window.**

A project can have more than one module, so it is a good idea to give
each module a unique name. If you wanted to use the module in a different project, you would want to make sure it was imported with a unique
name; otherwise, it can't be imported into a project if that name is
already in use. The project and standard code module should both be
renamed now (see Figure 4-13).

Figure 4-13:
Visual Basic
Editor with
new project
and code
module.

Going further with AutoCAD and VBA

In addition to the information we cover in this chapter, you should explore the AutoCAD Object Model and take a look at the different objects and collections that are in the AutoCAD Object Library through the Object Browser in the Visual Basic Editor. AutoCAD also ships with a variety of samples that can be found in the folder C:\Program Files\AutoCAD 2006\Sample\VBA by default. Don't forget about the invaluable tool the Internet can be; it is a great tool for finding tutorials that demonstrate how to use VBA for AutoCAD as well as many other host applications.

Adding a new procedure to a code module

These steps describe how to create a new procedure in a code module:

1. **Click in the Code window for the new code module.**

A code window should have opened up automatically when the new code module was added. If not, double-click on basDraw in the Project Explorer for the project. Clicking in the code window sets the focus to the code window or at the desired location within the code window.

2. **From the Insert menu in the Visual Basic Editor, choose Procedure.**

This launches the Add Procedure dialog box (see Figure 4-14).

Figure 4-14: The Add Procedure dialog box.

3. **Enter** DrawLine **in the Name field.**

The name entered is what will be used by the Macros dialog box and the -VBARUN command or will be used to call the subroutine from another location in the code.

4. **Click Sub under the Type section.**

The new procedure should be a subroutine because no return value is required.

5. **Click Public under the Scope section.**

The new procedure needs to be public so it can be accessed from the Macros dialog box and outside the code module it is defined in.

6. **Click OK in the Add Procedures dialog box.**

The new procedure is added to the code window and should look like this one:

```
Public Sub DrawLine()

End Sub
```

Book X
Chapter 4

7. **Add this code between the two lines of code that were added by the Add Procedures dialog box.**

```
' Create two variables to hold the points to draw the
' line object
Dim dStartPt(0 To 2) As Double, dEndPt(0 To 2) As
    Double

' Create a Start Point of 0,0,0
dStartPt(0) = 0 ' X coordinate value
dStartPt(1) = 0 ' Y coordinate value
dStartPt(2) = 0 ' Z coordinate value

' Create an End Point of 5,5,0
dEndPt(0) = 5: dEndPt(1) = 5: dEndPt(2) = 0

' Add the line to Model Space
ThisDrawing.ModelSpace.AddLine dStartPt, dEndPt
```

8. **Click Save on the Standard toolbar in the Visual Basic Editor.**

This saves the changes that have been made to the VBA project up to this point. The DrawLine procedure has now been defined (see Figure 4-15) and is ready for use in AutoCAD.

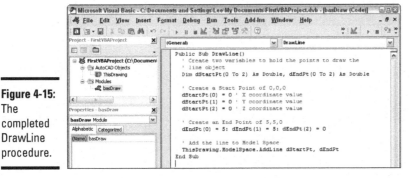

Figure 4-15:
The completed DrawLine procedure.

Visual Basic for AutoCAD (side tab)

Running the new procedure

These steps describe how to run the DrawLine procedure:

1. **From the View menu in the Visual Basic Editor, choose AutoCAD or switch to AutoCAD by clicking the icon in the Windows taskbar.**

2. **From the Tools menu in AutoCAD, choose Macro⇨Macros.**

   The Macros dialog box is launched; it should list only one macro, DrawLine.

3. **Select the macro from the list box (if it is not already selected) and click the Run button located on the right side of the Macros dialog box.**

4. **From the View menu in AutoCAD, choose Zoom⇨Extents.**

   The new line should be displayed in the center of the drawing window. If you listed the line by using the LIST command or the Properties Palette in AutoCAD, you should notice that the new line starts at 0,0,0 and ends at 5,5,0, which are the values that were defined in the DrawLine procedure.

Index

Numbers and Symbols

T

NESS, CAREERS & PERSONAL FINANCE

0-7645-5307-0

Home Buying FOR DUMMIES
0-7645-5331-3 *†

Also available:
- Accounting For Dummies †
  0-7645-5314-3
- Business Plans Kit For Dummies †
  0-7645-5365-8
- Cover Letters For Dummies
  0-7645-5224-4
- Frugal Living For Dummies
  0-7645-5403-4
- Leadership For Dummies
  0-7645-5176-0
- Managing For Dummies
  0-7645-1771-6

- Marketing For Dummi
  0-7645-5600-2
- Personal Finance For Dun
  0-7645-2590-5
- Project Management For Du
  0-7645-5283-X
- Resumes For Dummies †
  0-7645-5471-9
- Selling For Dummies
  0-7645-5363-1
- Small Business Kit For Dummies *†
  0-7645-5093-4

ME & BUSINESS COMPUTER BASICS

0-7645-4074-2

0-7645-3758-X

Also available:
- ACT! 6 For Dummies
  0-7645-2645-6
- iLife '04 All-in-One Desk Reference
  For Dummies
  0-7645-7347-0
- iPAQ For Dummies
  0-7645-6769-1
- Mac OS X Panther Timesaving
  Techniques For Dummies
  0-7645-5812-9
- Macs For Dummies
  0-7645-5656-8

- Microsoft Money 2004 For Dummies
  0-7645-4195-1
- Office 2003 All-in-One Desk Reference
  For Dummies
  0-7645-3883-7
- Outlook 2003 For Dummies
  0-7645-3759-8
- PCs For Dummies
  0-7645-4074-2
- TiVo For Dummies
  0-7645-6923-6
- Upgrading and Fixing PCs For Dummies
  0-7645-1665-5
- Windows XP Timesaving Techniques
  For Dummies
  0-7645-3748-2

OD, HOME, GARDEN, HOBBIES, MUSIC & PETS

0-7645-5295-3

0-7645-5232-5

Also available:
- Bass Guitar For Dummies
  0-7645-2487-9
- Diabetes Cookbook For Dummies
  0-7645-5230-9
- Gardening For Dummies *
  0-7645-5130-2
- Guitar For Dummies
  0-7645-5106-X
- Holiday Decorating For Dummies
  0-7645-2570-0
- Home Improvement All-in-One
  For Dummies
  0-7645-5680-0

- Knitting For Dummies
  0-7645-5395-X
- Piano For Dummies
  0-7645-5105-1
- Puppies For Dummies
  0-7645-5255-4
- Scrapbooking For Dummies
  0-7645-7208-3
- Senior Dogs For Dummies
  0-7645-5818-8
- Singing For Dummies
  0-7645-2475-5
- 30-Minute Meals For Dummies
  0-7645-2589-1

TERNET & DIGITAL MEDIA

0-7645-1664-7

0-7645-6924-4

Also available:
- 2005 Online Shopping Directory
  For Dummies
  0-7645-7495-7
- CD & DVD Recording For Dummies
  0-7645-5956-7
- eBay For Dummies
  0-7645-5654-1
- Fighting Spam For Dummies
  0-7645-5965-6
- Genealogy Online For Dummies
  0-7645-5964-8
- Google For Dummies
  0-7645-4420-9

- Home Recording For Musicians
  For Dummies
  0-7645-1634-5
- The Internet For Dummies
  0-7645-4173-0
- iPod & iTunes For Dummies
  0-7645-7772-7
- Preventing Identity Theft For Dummies
  0-7645-7336-5
- Pro Tools All-in-One Desk Reference
  For Dummies
  0-7645-5714-9
- Roxio Easy Media Creator For Dummies
  0-7645-7131-1

parate Canadian edition also available
parate U.K. edition also available

able wherever books are sold. For more information or to order direct: U.S. customers visit www.dummies.com or call 1-877-762-2974.
customers visit www.wileyeurope.com or call 0800 243407. Canadian customers visit www.wiley.ca or call 1-800-567-4797.

0-7645-5146-9

0-7645-5418-2

Also available:

- Adoption For Dummies
  0-7645-5488-3
- Basketball For Dummies
  0-7645-5248-1
- The Bible For Dummies
  0-7645-5296-1
- Buddhism For Dummies
  0-7645-5359-3
- Catholicism For Dummies
  0-7645-5391-7
- Hockey For Dummies
  0-7645-5228-7

- Judaism For Dummies
  0-7645-5299-6
- Martial Arts For Dummies
  0-7645-5358-5
- Pilates For Dummies
  0-7645-5397-6
- Religion For Dummies
  0-7645-5264-3
- Teaching Kids to Read For Dumm
  0-7645-4043-2
- Weight Training For Dummies
  0-7645-5168-X
- Yoga For Dummies
  0-7645-5117-5

TRAVEL

0-7645-5438-7

0-7645-5453-0

Also available:

- Alaska For Dummies
  0-7645-1761-9
- Arizona For Dummies
  0-7645-6938-4
- Cancún and the Yucatán For Dummies
  0-7645-2437-2
- Cruise Vacations For Dummies
  0-7645-6941-4
- Europe For Dummies
  0-7645-5456-5
- Ireland For Dummies
  0-7645-5455-7

- Las Vegas For Dummies
  0-7645-5448-4
- London For Dummies
  0-7645-4277-X
- New York City For Dummies
  0-7645-6945-7
- Paris For Dummies
  0-7645-5494-8
- RV Vacations For Dummies
  0-7645-5443-3
- Walt Disney World & Orlando For Dum
  0-7645-6943-0

GRAPHICS, DESIGN & WEB DEVELOPMENT

0-7645-4345-8

0-7645-5589-8

Also available:

- Adobe Acrobat 6 PDF For Dummies
  0-7645-3760-1
- Building a Web Site For Dummies
  0-7645-7144-3
- Dreamweaver MX 2004 For Dummies
  0-7645-4342-3
- FrontPage 2003 For Dummies
  0-7645-3882-9
- HTML 4 For Dummies
  0-7645-1995-6
- Illustrator CS For Dummies
  0-7645-4084-X

- Macromedia Flash MX 2004 For Dum
  0-7645-4358-X
- Photoshop 7 All-in-One Desk
  Reference For Dummies
  0-7645-1667-1
- Photoshop CS Timesaving Techniqu
  For Dummies
  0-7645-6782-9
- PHP 5 For Dummies
  0-7645-4166-8
- PowerPoint 2003 For Dummies
  0-7645-3908-6
- QuarkXPress 6 For Dummies
  0-7645-2593-X

NETWORKING, SECURITY, PROGRAMMING & DATABASES

0-7645-6852-3

0-7645-5784-X

Also available:

- A+ Certification For Dummies
  0-7645-4187-0
- Access 2003 All-in-one Desk
  Reference For Dummies
  0-7645-3988-4
- Beginning Programming For Dummies
  0-7645-4997-9
- C For Dummies
  0-7645-7068-4
- Firewalls For Dummies
  0-7645-4048-3
- Home Networking For Dummies
  0-7645-42796

- Network Security For Dummies
  0-7645-1679-5
- Networking For Dummies
  0-7645-1677-9
- TCP/IP For Dummies
  0-7645-1760-0
- VBA For Dummies
  0-7645-3989-2
- Wireless All In-One Desk Reference
  For Dummies
  0-7645-7496-5
- Wireless Home Networking For Dumm
  0-7645-3910-8

LTH & SELF-HELP

0-7645-6820-5 *†   0-7645-2566-2

Also available:

Alzheimer's For Dummies
0-7645-3899-3

Asthma For Dummies
0-7645-4233-8

Controlling Cholesterol For Dummies
0-7645-5440-9

Depression For Dummies
0-7645-3900-0

Dieting For Dummies
0-7645-4149-8

Fertility For Dummies
0-7645-2549-2

Fibromyalgia For Dummies
0-7645-5441-7

Improving Your Memory For Dummies
0-7645-5435-2

Pregnancy For Dummies †
0-7645-4483-7

Quitting Smoking For Dummies
0-7645-2629-4

Relationships For Dummies
0-7645-5384-4

Thyroid For Dummies
0-7645-5385-2

CATION, HISTORY, REFERENCE & TEST PREPARATION

0-7645-5194-9   0-7645-4186-2

Also available:

Algebra For Dummies
0-7645-5325-9

British History For Dummies
0-7645-7021-8

Calculus For Dummies
0-7645-2498-4

English Grammar For Dummies
0-7645-5322-4

Forensics For Dummies
0-7645-5580-4

The GMAT For Dummies
0-7645-5251-1

Inglés Para Dummies
0-7645-5427-1

Italian For Dummies
0-7645-5196-5

Latin For Dummies
0-7645-5431-X

Lewis & Clark For Dummies
0-7645-2545-X

Research Papers For Dummies
0-7645-5426-3

The SAT I For Dummies
0-7645-7193-1

Science Fair Projects For Dummies
0-7645-5460-3

U.S. History For Dummies
0-7645-5249-X

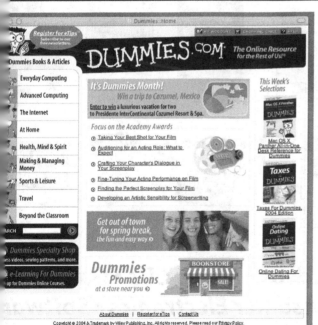

Get smart @ dummies.com®

- **Find a full list of Dummies titles**
- **Look into loads of FREE on-site articles**
- **Sign up for FREE eTips e-mailed to you weekly**
- **See what other products carry the Dummies name**
- **Shop directly from the Dummies bookstore**
- **Enter to win new prizes every month!**

parate Canadian edition also available
parate U.K. edition also available

able wherever books are sold. For more information or to order direct: U.S. customers visit www.dummies.com or call 1-877-762-2974.
customers visit www.wileyeurope.com or call 0800 243407. Canadian customers visit www.wiley.ca or call 1-800-567-4797.

More with Dummies

Products for the Rest of Us!

From hobbies to health, discover a wide variety of fun products

DVDs/Videos • Music CDs • Games
Consumer Electronics • Software
Craft Kits • Culinary Kits • and More!

Check out the Dummies Specialty Shop at www.dummies.com for more information!

9 780471 752608